Praise for *Through the Perilous Fight*

"Steve Vogel's *Through the Perilous Fight* is probably the best piece of military history that I have read or reviewed in the past five years. . . . This well-researched and superbly written history has all the trappings of a good novel. There is great heroism, treacherous self-interest, cowardice and intrigue. . . . No one who hears the national anthem at a ballgame will ever think of it the same way after reading this book."

—*The Washington Times*

"Complementing Donald R. Hickey's *War of 1812* and Alan Taylor's *The Civil War of 1812*, this title will contribute to making this war no longer one of our 'forgotten' conflicts."

—*Library Journal*

"Compelling . . . Vogel captures this desperate moment in the new nation's short history by tracing the movements of his many American and British protagonists. . . . Vogel's superb study enables us to grab both the immediate danger and its broader implication for America's future."

—*American History*

"*Through the Perilous Fight* is a wonderful and most welcome addition to the books commemorating the bicentennial of the War of 1812. Steve Vogel [tells] the story of the sack of Washington and the defense of Baltimore with verve. He humanizes the narrative skillfully."

—*Naval Historical Foundation*

"Vogel does a superb job. . . . He leavens his fast-paced narrative with lively vignettes of the principal participants in this folly, beginning with Cockburn and Francis Scott Key, the one person most Americans remember from this forgettable war as the author of those daunting soprano lines: 'And the rockets' red glare, the bombs bursting in air.' . . . Dramatic."

—*The Washington Post*

"Vogel selects the British invasion of the Chesapeake Bay in the summer of 1814 for this tight-focus treatment. Few details escape his attention, from the appearances and characters of commanders to specifications of weaponry, ships, and forts."

—*Booklist*

"The battle and strategy scenes have a clarity that surpasses what even the several maps provide. . . . A swift, vibrant account of the accidents, intricacies and insanities of war."

—*Kirkus Reviews*

"Before 9/11 was 1814—the year the enemy burned the nation's capital. Steve Vogel gives a splendid account, fast-paced and detailed, of the uncertainty, the peril, and the valor of those days."

—RICHARD BROOKHISER, author of *James Madison*

"The War of 1812 remains one of the most important and least appreciated events in American history. In these engaging pages, Steve Vogel does much to rectify that, telling the story of a critical episode of the conflict with eloquence and insight."

—JON MEACHAM, Pulitzer Prize–winning author
of *Thomas Jefferson: The Art of Power*

ALSO BY STEVE VOGEL

The Pentagon: A History

THROUGH
THE PERILOUS
FIGHT

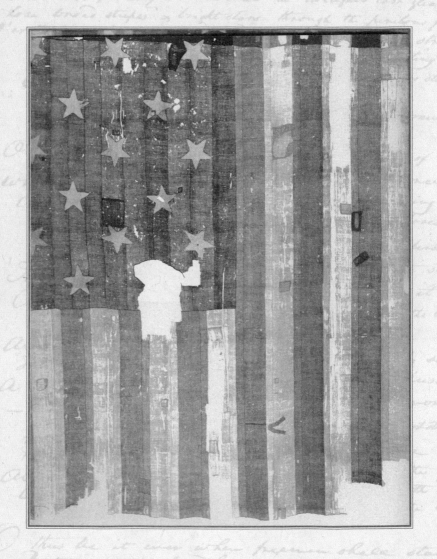

Two hundred years after the battle, tattered and frail, the Star-Spangled
Banner seemed more powerful than ever.

THROUGH THE PERILOUS FIGHT

———————— ✦ ————————

From the Burning of Washington to the Star-Spangled Banner:

The Six Weeks That Saved the Nation

STEVE VOGEL

RANDOM HOUSE TRADE PAPERBACKS

NEW YORK

2014 Random House Trade Paperback Edition

Copyright © 2013 by Steve Vogel

Published in the United States by Random House Trade Paperbacks,
an imprint of Random House, a division of Random House LLC,
a Penguin Random House Company, New York.

RANDOM HOUSE and the HOUSE colophon are
registered trademarks of Random House LLC.

Originally published in hardcover in the United States by Random House,
an imprint and division of Random House LLC, in 2013.

LIBRARY OF CONGRESS CATALOGING-IN-PUBLICATION DATA
Vogel, Steve.
The perilous fight : from the burning of Washington to the star-spangled banner:
the six weeks that saved the nation / Steve Vogel.
p. cm.
Includes bibliographical references and index.
ISBN 978-0-8129-8139-1
eBook ISBN 978-0-679-60347-4
1. Baltimore, Battle of, Baltimore, Md., 1814. 2. Cockburn, George, Sir, 1772–
1853. 3. Key, Francis Scott, 1779–1843. 4. Washington (D.C.)—History—Capture
by the British, 1814. 5. Maryland—History—War of 1812—Campaigns.
6. United States—History—War of 1812—Campaigns. I. Title
E356.B2V64 2013
973.5'2—dc23
2012039797

Printed in the United States of America on acid-free paper

www.atrandom.com

2 4 6 8 9 7 5 3 1

Book design by Caroline Cunningham

To my wife, Tiffany,

and our children, Donald, Charlotte, and Thomas

Nations will seldom obtain good national anthems by offering prizes for them. The man and the occasion must meet.

—*John Philip Sousa*

CONTENTS

———— ★ ————

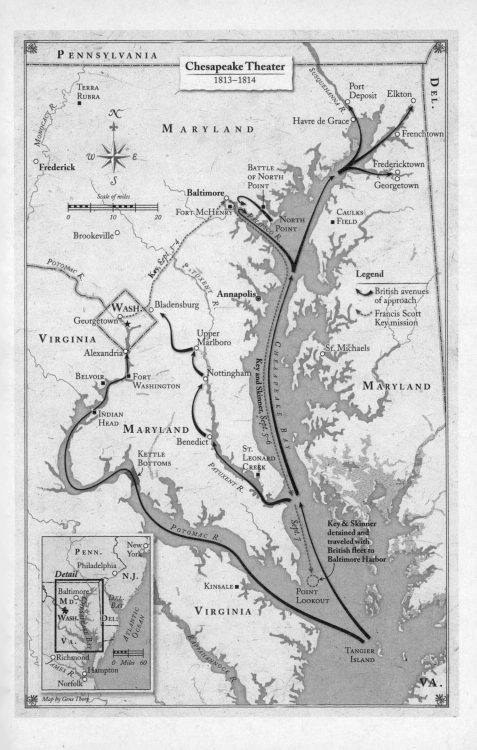

LIST OF ILLUSTRATIONS

———————— ✦ ————————

THROUGH
THE PERILOUS
FIGHT

"The most hated man in the United States,
and the most feared."

Sir George Cockburn, GCB

PRELUDE

━━━━ ★ ━━━━

I See Nothing Else Left

SAILING UNDER A white flag of truce, American agent John Stuart Skinner rounded Point Lookout and entered the broad mouth of the Potomac River, searching for the enemy fleet. The river was at its widest here, three miles from shore to shore where its water flowed lazily into the Chesapeake Bay. The sultry August weather had turned cool overnight, and the day was refreshingly crisp. Even from a distance it was easy to spot HMS *Albion*, anchored along the far Virginia shore. The 74–gun frigate, weighing nearly 1,700 tons and manned by a crew of 620, was one of the largest and most powerful British warships ever seen in these waters, and it was accompanied by nearly two dozen brigs, sloops, and tenders.

More daunting than the ships and weaponry was the man the agent had come to see: Rear Admiral George Cockburn. The "Great Bandit," as the papers called him, was the most hated man in the United States, and the most feared. Americans compared him to notorious barbarians of ancient times, among them Attila the Hun.

For more than a year, the British squadron commander had waged a campaign of terror along the Chesapeake Bay, sacking Havre de

Grace, Maryland, at the mouth of the Susquehanna, ravaging Hampton, plundering the Virginia shoreline, and torching farms in Maryland, acts that had infuriated Americans. Ruthless, witty, and swashbuckling, the lowlands Scot was determined to make Americans pay a hard price for their ill-considered war with Great Britain.

"[T]here breathes not in any quarter of the globe a more savage monster than this same British Admiral," the Boston *Gazette* declared. "He is a disgrace to England and to human nature." A Fourth of July celebration in Talbot County, Maryland, included a toast to Cockburn, "a man in person but a brute in principle; may the Chesapeake be his watery grave." One irate Virginian had offered a thousand dollars for the admiral's head or "five hundred dollars for each of his ears, on delivery."

Skinner had sailed from Baltimore on August 7, 1814, bearing official dispatches for the British. As the government's designated prisoner of war agent, Skinner was a veteran of many such missions, routinely carrying communications from Washington or negotiating prisoner exchanges. He was as familiar as anyone in America with Cockburn and his depredations. Just three weeks previously, the British had burned the Maryland plantation in Prince Frederick where Skinner had been born, and earlier in the summer, they had torched his barn and property at nearby St. Leonard. But if he held a grudge, Skinner was too savvy to make it known to Cockburn.

As usual, Skinner was courteously welcomed aboard *Albion*. For all of Cockburn's haughty bombast and undisputed ruthlessness, Skinner had found him to be a gracious host, always seating Skinner for a meal at the admiral's table and ready "to mitigate the rigors of war" with hospitality. Skinner had a rough-and-tumble personality to match his pugilistic face, as well as an innate candor, all of which Cockburn appreciated.

The admiral, his Scottish complexion reddened by the relentless Chesapeake sun, was in a good mood, having just completed a series of successful raids that had terrified residents along the Potomac shores of Virginia's Northern Neck. At 2 a.m. on August 3, Cockburn had headed up the Yeocomico River, probing the inlet off the Potomac with a force of 500 sailors and Royal Marines in twenty barges. Among them, dressed in red coats, were a special company of 120 Colonial

Marines—slaves who had escaped to the British from plantations in Virginia and Maryland, and trained to fight their former masters. Their use was a particularly brilliant and insidious stroke, unleashing deep-seated fears among the locals of a slave revolt.

A Virginia militia artillery company waiting at Mundy's Point fired on the British with six-pounder cannons, and the first shot beheaded a Royal Marine in the lead boat. But the Virginians soon ran low on ammunition, and the British swarmed ashore. Major Pemberton Claughton, a Virginia militia commander, was shocked to see a slave who had escaped from his plantation among the invaders. The admiral and his "gallant band" chased the retreating Americans ten miles almost at a run, burning every house they passed, including Major Claughton's home. Finally, the raiding party collapsed on the ground, exhausted in the 90-degree heat. But there was no time for rest—Cockburn learned that the Virginia militia was regrouping at the nearby village of Kinsale.

"What! Englishmen tired with a fine morning's walk like this," cried Cockburn. "Here, give me your musket; here, yours, my man. Your admiral will carry them for you." He placed a musket on each shoulder and began marching, rousing the men.

Returning to their boats, the British sailed to Kinsale, opened fire on the town, and scattered the militia. The village was burned and some thirty homes destroyed. A dead Virginia militiaman was dragged out, his pockets turned inside out and rifled. The British carried off five captured schooners brimming with hogsheads of tobacco, five prisoners, a field gun, and two horses belonging to a militia commander and his son.

Spreading fear was Cockburn's mission, and the sack of Kinsale had served this goal quite well. Back on the ships, Cockburn was even more pleased by the news brought to him August 7 by two British frigates, freshly arrived in the Potomac from Bermuda: Troopships carrying 4,000 battle-hardened British army soldiers would soon sail into the Chesapeake.

Captain Robert Rowley, commander of one of the squadron's ships, mused about the news in a letter home to England. "I suppose some grand attack will be meditated," he wrote.

A grand attack was precisely what Cockburn had in mind.

*

Three weeks earlier, on July 17, Cockburn had submitted a secret plan to capture the capital of the United States. All he needed were army troops that he could bring up the Patuxent River, a Maryland tributary of the Chesapeake providing a back route to Washington. "Within forty-eight hours after arrival in the Patuxent of such a force, the city of Washington might be possessed without difficulty or opposition of any kind," Cockburn had written to Vice Admiral Sir Alexander Cochrane, the fleet commander, then in Bermuda assembling reinforcements.

The British invasion of the Chesapeake was meant to force the United States to divert troops it had sent to attack British colonies in Canada. But Cockburn saw the possibility for more. The fall of the American capital could be the strategic blow that brought Britain victory. The government of James Madison, or "Jemmy," as Cockburn contemptuously called the five-foot, four-inch president, would be scattered and disgraced, and perhaps even fall. "It is quite impossible for any country to be in a more unfit state for war than this now is," he told Cochrane. Even if the Americans learned every detail of the British plan of attack, Cockburn added, they were too weak to "avert the blow."

Now in its third year, America's war with Great Britain was about to take a dangerous turn for the United States.

The War of 1812 was an outgrowth of the titanic struggle that had raged between England and France almost continuously since 1793, when the French Revolutionary government declared war on Great Britain. That conflict had only grown more desperate with the rise of Napoleon Bonaparte as emperor of France and his dominance over much of Europe by 1811. Fighting in their mind for England's survival—and even the survival of civilization—the British never hesitated to trample on American sovereignty to support the war's ends. They seized American sailors of suspected British origin to man Royal Navy ships, and they severely restricted U.S. trade with Europe.

One generation removed from the Revolutionary War, the United States seethed with resentment against her former colonial master. For many Americans in 1812, the belief was strong that the revolution was not complete, that the United States had won its freedom, but not its independence. Bowing to the arrogant British behavior would leave Americans "not an independent people, but colonists and vassals," President Madison believed. In Congress, the war hawks—an aptly named band of representatives from the South and West—were eager to see North America cleared of the British, allowing unimpeded expansion to the west, and, some hoped, to the north. In June 1812, a bitterly divided Congress, split on both party and geographic lines, had narrowly agreed to declare war.

Already fighting a war in Europe, Britain had not sought the conflict with America. But it had no interest in allowing the United States unfettered sovereignty, nor did it wish to cede any measure of control in North America. The Americans and the Loyalists who had moved across the border into Canadian territory after the American Revolution had competing visions for the future of the North American continent, neither involving the other.

The American war against one of the world's great powers had gone badly from the start for the United States and its small, unprepared military forces. Multiple invasions of the British colonies of Upper and Lower Canada had ended in humiliating failure in 1812 and 1813.

Now, driven by events across the ocean, 1814 was shaping up to be the darkest year in the young nation's history. Napoleon's abdication of power in April appeared to have ended two decades of hostilities in Europe. The British had been left in a commanding position to end the festering war in North America. Troops from the Duke of Wellington's victorious army were being sent across the ocean to punish America for its treachery, and to force a humiliating peace on the country. The United States, its military forces spread thin, its economy in ruins, and its people bitterly divided by the war, was ripe for defeat. The American experiment was in danger of dying in its infancy.

Walking the deck of *Albion*, Cockburn chatted amiably with Skinner. Cockburn handed the American agent a dispatch for Secretary of State James Monroe and a message for the Russian minister in Washington. As a courtesy, he also passed along a bundle of the latest English newspapers, though the most recent was already more than two months old. Skinner brought Cockburn news of "severe" fighting in July on the Niagara frontier between the United States and Canada, where American and British armies at Chippewa and Lundy's Lane had clashed in the bloodiest battles the war had yet seen.

They spoke about peace negotiations in the Flemish city of Ghent, where ministers from the United States and Britain had just convened. Few held much hope for peace. Cockburn knew all the British commissioners and complained to Skinner that they were a decidedly mediocre lot. The admiral posed a question: What did the American ministers think of the prospects for peace? Skinner replied that there had been no recent word from them.

Cockburn could not resist smiling as he replied. The admiral was well aware that his words would soon make their way back to Washington, and almost certainly to the president himself.

"I believe, Mr. Skinner, that Mr. Madison will have to put on his armor and fight it out," Cockburn said. "I see nothing else left."

O say can you see by the dawn's early
what so proudly we hail'd at the twilight's last gleam
whose broad stripes & bright stars through the perilous fi
O'er the ramparts we watch'd were so gallantly stre
      And the rocket's red glare, the bomb bursting
      Gave proof through the night that our flag was still
O say does that star spangled banner yet wave
      O'er the land of the free & the home of the brave

On the shore dimly seen through the mists of t.
      where the foe's haughty host in dread silence
What is that which the breeze, o'er the towering
tis it fitfully blows, half conceals half discloses
            Now it catches the gleam of the morning's first
            In full glory reflected now shines in the str.
tis the star-spangled banner — O long may it
      O'er the land of the free & the home of the br

And where is that band who so vauntingly sw
      That the havoc of war & the battle's confusi
A home & a Country should leave us no more
            Their blood has wash'd out their foul footstep
no refuge could save the hireling & slave
From the terror of flight or the gloom of the g
And the star-spangled banner in triumph doth w
      O'er the land of the free & the home of the br

O thus be it ever when freemen shall stand
      Between their lov'd home & the war's desolation
Blest with vict'ry & peace may the heav'n rescued
Praise the power that hath made & preserv'd us a
      Then conquer we must when our cause it is
And this be our motto — "In god is our trust"
And the star-spangled banner in triumph shall wave
      O'er the land of the free & the home of the brave

The townspeople now understood "what they were liable to bring
upon themselves by . . . acting towards us with so
much useless rancor," Cockburn wrote.

Admiral Cockburn Burning and Plundering Havre de Grace *on the
1st of June 1813*, etching ca. 1813 by William Charles.

CHAPTER 1

★

How Do You Like the War Now?

THE COMPLACENCY IN Washington bothered Francis Scott Key as much as anything. On August 10, the thirty-four-year-old attorney took up his pen to write his closest friend, John Randolph of Roanoke. The brilliant but eccentric congressman had retreated in self-imposed exile to his cabin in south-central Virginia after his efforts to avert war with England had failed and voters had tossed him out of office for his troubles. Key often wrote his brooding friend, keeping him abreast of developments in Washington.

Though the administration of President James Madison had mobilized over the summer to protect Washington against the British threat, Key was painfully aware that little, in fact, had been done. "The government seem to be under little or no expectation of an attack upon the city," Key wrote to Randolph. "With the present force of the enemy there is no danger; but if they are considerably reinforced, and we not better prepared, the approaching Congress may have more to do than to talk."

Key was at his parents' farm at Terra Rubra, in the rolling hills of central Maryland, where he always retreated with his wife and children to escape the suffocating heat of Washington in summer. After a half-dozen years practicing law from his Georgetown office, Key had established himself as one of the foremost attorneys in the capital. But business always grew slow in summer, more so than ever this year, with the threat of Cockburn and the British on the horizon.

Slender and of medium height, with a wiry frame and a slight stoop, Key had a mop of dark brown curly hair atop his handsome face, with an aquiline nose and deep-set blue eyes. His face often bore a pensive expression "almost bordering on sadness," according to a contemporary, "but which, in moments of special excitement . . . gave place to a bright ethereality of aspect and a noble audacity of tone and gesture which pleased while it dazzled the beholder."

Key's court oratory was attracting attention, as much for his style and charisma as for any legal brilliance. His language was beautiful, his voice sonorous, and his enunciation impeccable. But what people noticed most was the passion—"like lightning charging his sentences with electrical power," a courtroom observer would say.

Randolph's last letter to Key had expressed hope that peace might be in the offing, but the latter did not share his optimism. "I do not think (as you seem to do) that our labours are nearly over—I do not believe we shall have peace," Key wrote. "England will not treat with us but on high & haughty terms."

Before posting his letter, Key added a postscript with disturbing news about the British: "I have just read intelligence of the arrival of this formidable reinforcement & am preparing to set out for Geo Town in the morning—I fear we are little prepared for it."

Key was a child of the American Revolution, born at Terra Rubra in 1779. His father, John Ross Key, had returned home after leading a company of men from the mountains of Maryland to fight in New England with the Continental Army, and Frank was born before the elder Key departed to rejoin George Washington for the Yorktown campaign. Back at Terra Rubra with his wife, Anne Phoebe Charlton Key, and son, after the British surrender, John Key settled into a comfortable life as a country squire and attorney.

Terra Rubra, named for the red soil of the surrounding land, had been in the family for generations. Key's great-grandfather, Philip Key—a descendant of John Key, poet laureate to King Edward IV in the fifteenth century—arrived from England in 1726 and a quarter century later took a patent on 2,800 acres in the foothills of Maryland's Blue Ridge, between the Monocacy River and its tributary, Big Pipe Creek. Though the land was only ten miles from the Mason-Dixon Line—close enough to spot Big Round Top at Gettysburg on a clear day—the Keys lived the life of southern planters. The family owned scores of slaves, and they grew corn, wheat, flax, buckwheat, and tobacco. The big, white-plastered mansion, fronted with two-story columns, was the finest in the area, with two long brick wings running back on each side and a courtyard paved with brick imported from England.

Frank—as family and close friends knew him his whole life—inherited a wistful and dreamy character from his mother. He and his younger sister, Anne, with whom he was very close, spent countless hours wandering the land, alongside winding, rippling creeks and through meadows framed by blue-tinged mountains. Sometimes they sat by the springhouse, scribbling poetry.

Most unforgettable was the July morning in 1791 when President George Washington, en route to Pennsylvania, stopped at Terra Rubra, visiting the company commander who had brought him troops from Maryland. Many of John Ross Key's former riflemen flocked from miles around to hear Washington speak from the portico of the Key home and give heartfelt thanks for the aid he had received "in the darkest hours of the Revolution."

At age ten, Frank was sent to grammar school in Annapolis, and he spent much of the next decade studying in the elegant state capital. There he fell under the spell of Philip Barton Key, his dazzling uncle. Philip Key had split with his brother during the revolution, joining the British and serving as an officer in a Maryland Loyalist regiment. At war's end, Philip Key's property in Maryland was confiscated, and he moved to England to study law. But in 1785 Philip returned to Maryland and was welcomed back by his brother, who shared with him their father's inheritance. When Frank Key was accepted at St. John's College in 1794, his uncle was a leader in the Maryland bar, and upon graduation, it was agreed that young Key would stay in Annapolis to study law.

Key lived with his uncle, who supervised his study and made sure his nephew met everyone of importance in town. Among those Frank befriended was another young law student, named Roger Brooke

His face often bore a pensive expression "almost bordering on sadness," according to a contemporary, "but which, in moments of special excitement . . . gave place to a bright ethereality of aspect."

Francis Scott Key

Taney. Taney was meticulous and serious, while Key was light-hearted and impulsive, but they soon developed a bond that proved to be lifelong.

In his second year of study, Key met the beautiful and charming Mary Tayloe Lloyd, or Polly, as she was known, the youngest daughter of an old and wealthy Annapolis society family. When Polly agreed, after three years of courting, to marry the young man from the hinterlands, her friends thought he was marrying up. "I must tell you the great event of Annapolis society," Rosalie Stier Calvert wrote to her sister in December 1801. "Polly Lloyd is to be married next month to Frank Key who has nothing and who has only practiced for two years as an [attorney]."

Key established a law practice in Frederick, a thriving city of German immigrants twenty miles southwest of Terra Rubra. With Key's encouragement, Taney set up practice there as well, and he courted Key's sister. When the tall and gaunt Taney married cheerful and bright Anne at Terra Rubra in 1806, it was likened to "the union of a hawk with a skylark."

After two years in Frederick, the twenty-six-year-old Key moved to Georgetown to join Uncle Philip, who had outgrown Annapolis and established a lucrative practice in the nation's capital. Once again Philip shepherded his nephew about town, introducing him to the elite and setting him up with important cases.

Francis Scott Key soon made a name for himself in the capital's nascent legal community. His involvement in the spectacular Aaron Burr treason case in 1807, representing two adventurers who had aided the former vice president in his bizarre plot to create an indepen-

dent republic and invade Mexico, helped establish him. He made his
Supreme Court debut during the case, arguing before Chief Justice
John Marshall in the high court's chamber on the ground floor of the
Capitol.

The Keys made their home in Georgetown, the old tobacco port
just up the river from Washington that was included in the District of
Columbia's boundaries. They lived in a modest but attractive brick
Georgian home on Bridge Street—today M Street—on a slope overlooking the Potomac. Two large parlors downstairs served for enter-
taining, while the basement, which opened up to the river, included a
large kitchen, dining room, and conservatory. Outside was a beautiful
terraced garden with lofty walnut trees and Lombardy poplars, and a
lawn and orchard sloping to the Potomac's edge.

When his uncle was elected to Congress and gave up law, Key took
over the practice and moved the office into a one-story wing of his
Georgetown house. With six children by 1814—the youngest, Edward,

Theirs was a merry household.

*The Key house in Georgetown, shown in an oil painting by Key's
grandson, John Ross Key.*

was born in September 1813—the home was as much a nursery as a law office. Key supervised the children's instruction, teaching them letters and tutoring them in the classics. He was an indulgent father, lavishing the children with toys, books, and music lessons, but strictly insisting they attend services every Sunday at nearby St. John's Episcopal Church. Theirs was a merry household, with Key given to leaving notes in rhyme around the home for his wife.

The home served as a salon for Washington's social society, attracting a mix of judges, preachers, relatives, and congressmen. Uncle Philip was a regular visitor, as was William Thornton, Key's eclectic friend who had designed the Capitol Building. The most frequent guest was Randolph, for whom the home was a refuge from the bitter and rancorous Capitol invective. The Virginian had become something of an eccentric uncle to the ever-growing brood of Key children.

Randolph's small head, raised shoulders, tiny waist, and long, thin legs gave him the look of a crane, an appearance made all the more pronounced by his clothing, usually a swallowtail coat adorned with a white cravat in which he would bury his neck. Randolph was a bitter misanthrope, known in Congress as rude, merciless, and venomous. But Key delighted in Randolph's wicked wit and brilliant wordplay. The Virginian's views stimulated his own intellect and served as fodder for endless debates.

Key, a devout Episcopalian, preferred nights of quiet conversation and tended to exclude from his circle the more boisterous and hard-drinking young congressmen populating Washington. He would scurry past the taverns catering to such hellions, but once home with friends, he was not above opening a bottle of Madeira to relieve the piety, sipping on a glass or two himself.

Guests would hold forth on the issues and literature of the day. Slavery and its ills were a common topic, though Key and his circle considered abolition far too radical a solution. The poems of Byron and Scott were dissected. Philip Key, a Federalist, would denounce the Madison administration's foreign policy. But most of all in recent years, conversation had been dominated by the topic that had split both the city and the nation: the war with England.

★

Reflecting angry divisions in America, a new Congress convened in Washington in November 1811, almost half of the members having replaced incumbents. Many of the newcomers were young Republican firebrands from the South and the western frontier, areas where support for a war with Great Britain was strongest. The war hawks, as Randolph mockingly dubbed them, were a formidable lot, among them John C. Calhoun of South Carolina, and the man who quickly emerged as their leader, Henry Clay of Kentucky.

The war hawks argued that the United States must put an end to the British harassment, which had only increased in recent years. Desperate for manpower to sail its huge fleet, and faced with continuous desertions, the Royal Navy had seized thousands of American sailors from U.S. ships and impressed them into use aboard its own. Some seven thousand American citizens had been taken from 1803 to 1812. Through a series of decrees known as Orders in Council, Britain had sharply limited U.S. trade with the European continent, further enraging Americans. Along the frontier with Canada, American settlers accused the British of arming Indians and inciting attacks by them.

A war would be a golden opportunity to eject Britain from North America entirely, opening the West—and while they were at it, Canadian territory—to American settlement. Clay and others promised an easy victory over an enemy consumed with the fight on the European continent. Kentucky's militia alone would be enough to capture Canada, Clay boasted.

Randolph led the opposition, attracting crowds to the gallery with his diatribes, eviscerating opponents with his deadly debating skills, and slowing the rush to war with disruptive tactics. His high-pitched voice would rise to a shriek, and his gaunt, bony fingers would point at the targets of his recriminations. War was foolhardy, given the tiny size of the U.S. military, and the wrath it would provoke in Great Britain. It would be folly to leave the eastern seacoast unprotected while the army attacked Canada. How was it possible, he asked, for the nation to "go to war without money, without men, without a navy, . . . when we have not the courage to lay war taxes?"

But the war hawks controlled the halls of Congress. Elected speaker, Clay consolidated his power in extraordinary fashion, packing key committees with war supporters. Clay even ordered the House door-keeper to evict Randolph's dog from the floor of the House, something no previous speaker had dared do.

With a measure of regret, President James Madison had come to view a declaration of war as nearly inevitable, and necessary. Madison's political views had been colored by a near lifetime of enmity with Great Britain, dating back to 1774, when the British blockade of Boston Harbor prompted the young Virginian to join the patriots' cause. Madison's antipathy toward England only grew in the years after the birth of the American nation. During Washington's presidency, he and Thomas Jefferson helped foster the birth of political parties by creating the Democratic-Republicans in part to counter the pro-British sympathies of Alexander Hamilton and the Federalists, which grew more pronounced after France declared war on England in 1793.

Hostility toward Great Britain dominated much of Madison's eight years as secretary of state during the Jefferson administration. War was narrowly averted after the *Chesapeake-Leopard* affair in 1807, when a British ship searching for deserters attacked an American warship sailing from Norfolk, Virginia. Jefferson and Madison imposed an embargo to punish Great Britain for the inflammatory attack, but the restrictions did far more damage to the American economy than England's.

War with England loomed from the beginning of Madison's first term as president, in 1809. The administration struggled vainly for three years against the British trade restrictions and impressment of American sailors, and by 1812 Madison no longer seemed to think peace possible. "[T]housands of American citizens, under the safeguard of public law, and of their national flag, have been torn from their country and from everything dear to them," Madison charged in a war message to Congress on June 1, 1812. Madison made no recommendation for or against a declaration of hostilities, instead observing that Britain was already in "a state of war against the United States."

Consumed physically and spiritually with its struggle against Napoleon, Britain had little interest in launching a new conflict on an enormous continent across the ocean. The British paid scant attention to America and could not take the war talk seriously, considering how unprepared the United States was. Nonetheless, on June 16, Britain announced it would lift trade restrictions. That decision would have likely derailed the buildup to war, but the news arrived too late in Washington.

Congress's vote for war was the closest in American history—79 to 49 in the House, and 19 to 13 in the Senate. The vote was split along regional lines, with the South and West strongly supporting war, and the North and East, except Pennsylvania, stoutly opposed. Even more pronounced was the split along party lines, as more than 80 percent of Republicans supported the war, while Federalists, without exception, opposed it. On June 18, 1812, Madison signed a proclamation declaring war on Great Britain.

A few hours after the vote, Randolph approached a group of war hawks with a warning. "Gentlemen, you have made war—you have finished the ruin of our country—and before you conquer Canada, your idol [Napoleon] will cease to distract the world, and the capitol will be a ruin."

Like many across the country, Francis Scott Key was fervently opposed to the war. In part, this reflected his devout Christianity, and in part, his cultural affinity with England. Most of all, Key could not abide the idea that the United States would attack Canada—an innocent third party, in his view—to settle its grievances with England.

No less than Randolph, Key felt a foreboding of disaster, a sentiment heightened several days after the declaration, when a pro-war mob in Baltimore attacked the offices of the *Federal Republican* newspaper, which had published an editorial opposing the war. A second attack several weeks later was even more violent. One of the defenders of the newspaper, sixty-year-old James Lingan, a veteran of the revolution and friend of the Key family, was stomped and beaten to death. Henry "Light-Horse Harry" Lee, the Revolutionary War hero and father of Robert E. Lee, was severely beaten and crippled for life by the mob, which poured hot wax in his eyes. Key was horrified by the violence and was left with a feeling that the country—and Baltimore in particular—would face divine retribution.

Randolph considered not standing for reelection. At Key's urging, he ran again, but was defeated, and immediately left town for Roanoke, his cabin in Virginia. Randolph sent a letter asking that Key care for his rifle, flask, and papers, which he had left in his Georgetown lodgings in his haste to leave. Key, the dutiful good friend, had already taken charge of the belongings. Their friendship only grew as the nation settled into war during the subsequent months and then years, and the letters they exchanged became a chief joy for Key. Their correspondence reflected Key's profound disgust and growing depression about the bitter divisions in America over the war and the ugly recriminations exchanged by Republicans and Federalists.

"The state of society is radically vicious," Key lamented in 1813, suggesting to Randolph that the solution was to end party politics: "Put down party spirit; stop the corruption of party elections; legislate not for the next election, but for the next century."

The war changed Key's outlook on life and his view of himself. It shook his faith in man, though his belief in God was steadfast. He became dissatisfied trying court cases while the fate of the nation was at stake. Moreover, the war had brought business almost to a standstill. "I begin to fancy change of some sort," he wrote Randolph in May 1813. He sometimes thought of jumping into the fray headfirst and other times wanted to escape it altogether.

That summer, he briefly considered running for political office, hoping he might be able to turn the poisonous atmosphere in Washington. "I did feel something like it—but the fit is over," he wrote Randolph in August. "I have troubled myself enough with thinking what I should do—so I shall try to prepare myself for whatever may appear plainly to be my duty."

He was given to introspective moods and periods of silence. Polly would sometimes find him in his study, on his knees in prayer. In the spring of 1814, he gave deep thought to abandoning his law practice and entering the ministry. The rector of St. Paul's Parish in Baltimore proposed that Key join him as his assistant. For nearly a month he meditated on it, finally concluding that he was too far in debt and his family too large to make do on a minister's salary.

Throughout these dismaying times, his primary outlet was literary: reading poems, discussing them with friends, devouring literary criticism journals, and writing his own verses. "[D]oes it not appear that to produce one transcendentally fine epic poem is as much as has ever fallen to the life of one man?" he asked Randolph in September 1813. "There seems to be a law of the Muses for it."

Key was appalled in the fall of 1813 by an American military campaign targeting Montreal, and when British victories at Crysler's Farm in Ontario and Chateauguay in Quebec forced the United States to abandon its plans, he shared his delight with Randolph. "The people of Montreal will enjoy their firesides for this, and I trust many a winter," Key wrote. "This I suppose is treason, but as your Patrick Henry said, 'If it be treason, I glory in the name of traitor.' I have never thought of those poor creatures without being reconciled to any disgrace or defeat of our arms."

Yet Key felt quite differently about the United States being invaded. When the British threatened Washington in the summer of 1813 and again when they returned in 1814, Key volunteered with the local militia. Most of the U.S. Army was staged on the Canadian front, leaving the defense of Washington to ill-trained, poorly equipped local militia units. Amateur soldiers such as Key were the rule in the militia, and he had seen enough to be alarmed at the dire state of local defenses.

As the war entered its third year, Key's sense of foreboding grew. "We see what other nations have suffered—shall we escape so much more lightly?" Key wrote in his August 10, 1814, letter to Randolph. "I shall be most happy to find myself mistaken in these fears."

HMS *ALBION*, THE POTOMAC RIVER, WEDNESDAY, AUGUST 10, 1814

Key and other like-minded Americans would not be mistaken, as far as Rear Admiral George Cockburn was concerned. The admiral's raiders had taken so much loot from Kinsale and other Potomac towns that on the same day Key wrote his letter, Cockburn dispatched a ship packed with booty to the British base in Halifax, Nova Scotia.

It was time to prepare for bigger and better targets, however. Cockburn was expecting the arrival any day of the fleet commander, Vice Admiral Cochrane, with reinforcements. The 4,000 troops on the way were a far cry from the 15,000 or more Cockburn had expected, but that was certainly no reason to call off the campaign for Washington.

Cockburn's belief in himself was unmatched. "Cockburn's confidence in his luck is the very thing most to be feared," complained British army Lieutenant Colonel Charles Napier, who served with the admiral in the Chesapeake. "It is worse than 1000 Yankees."

Cockburn's hooked nose, hooded eyes, arching eyebrows, and imperial bearing gave him a haughty look, one he put to good use. He enjoyed the fear he inspired, particularly with stupid or duplicitous men, whom he despised. Cockburn—he pronounced it "Coe-burn," though to his annoyance the Americans pronounced it "Cock-burn"— professed to have "total indifference" to the virulent attacks against him in the American press, but he avidly read the newspapers and kept careful score of who said what.

The Cockburn family came from the rocky glens and high moorlands of the border country between Scotland and England, a land of feuds and bloodshed. Cockburn legend held that the family had been given land by King Malcolm as thanks for their help in defeating his enemy, Macbeth, around the year 1057. The admiral could trace his ancestry to Sir William de Veteri-Ponte, a knight who died fighting for Robert the Bruce in 1314 at Bannockburn, where the Scottish army won a stunning victory over the English.

Born into an upper-middle-class family in 1772 in Middlesex, outside London, George Cockburn was raised by a mother, Lady Augusta Ann Cockburn, who placed high value on learning and shining manners. His father, Sir James Cockburn, a dynamic and wealthy Scottish merchant, began a steady decline into debt the year George was born. By 1781 he was declared bankrupt and a few years later the family was forced to move out of their fashionable home. George was groomed from an early age for a life in the Royal Navy, attending navigational school in London, and sent to sea at age fourteen as a servant on an 18–gun navy sloop. Despite the hard times, Sir James still had influential friends in the navy, and George was placed under the wing of a powerful patron, Lord Samuel Hood, who arranged the right appointments for his apprentice. In 1793, at age twenty, Cockburn was chosen for promotion to lieutenant, launching his career as a naval officer just as revolutionary France declared war on Great Britain, an event that would shape his life. Cockburn soon had command of his first ship, *Speedy*, and proved to be a bold, meticulous, and energetic officer.

Assigned to patrol in the Gulf of Genoa, Cockburn to his great fortune joined a squadron commanded by a dashing young captain named Horatio Nelson. Inspirational, warm, and brave, Nelson took a quick liking to Cockburn, finding in him "zeal, ability and courage, which are conspicuous." Nelson gave him command of *Minerve,* a captured French frigate. At age twenty-four, Cockburn had charge of a crew of 286 and served as the senior captain in Nelson's squadron. Nelson came to think of Cockburn almost as an alter ego, trusting him with command in his absence and telling him, "we so exactly think alike on points of service that if your mind tells you it is right, there can hardly be a doubt but I must approve."

Nelson and Hood set Cockburn on his way, and he continued rising on assignments around the globe. In 1803, he was sent on a diplomatic mission to America, sailing to Norfolk, where he first laid eyes on the Chesapeake Bay, and then to New York City, where he caused an uproar when he successfully demanded the city surrender eight British sailors who deserted his ship. Following an extended mission in the Indian Ocean, Cockburn fought the French in the West Indies while commanding the 80-gun *Pompee,* one of the Royal Navy's finest ships-of-the-line—as the largest warships were called. By 1809, Britain had been at war for sixteen years, and Cockburn at sea for most of that time. On a visit home that year, at age thirty-seven, he proposed marriage to Mary Cockburn, a third cousin with whom he had kept an affectionate relationship over the years. Though the wedding was delayed so Cockburn could participate in the invasion of Holland, the couple's first and only child, Augusta, was born in the summer of 1810.

In 1812, at the relatively young age of forty, Cockburn reached flag rank and commanded a squadron off Cadiz, Spain, where by the end of the year, quiet prevailed in the war between England and France. The Admiralty, looking for a more important job for Cockburn, cast its gaze across the Atlantic.

The first seven months of the war with America had been embarrassing for the Royal Navy. Consumed by the great struggle with Napoleon, the most powerful naval force in the world had devoted scant resources to the American war. In 1812, the frigate USS *Constitution*— Old Ironsides, as she was known forever after—defeated HMS *Guerriere* and HMS *Java* in separate battles at sea, while the USS *United States* captured HMS *Macedonian,* all humiliating defeats for the British. The aging Vice Admiral Sir John Borlase Warren was conducting a lackluster campaign on the Atlantic seaboard and needed the boost of an aggressive subordinate. Cockburn would be a perfect choice.

The British naval historian William James, who was in America when the war broke out, later wrote that until Cockburn's arrival, the inhabitants of the Chesapeake Bay region "would scarcely have known, except by hearsay, that war existed." That was about to change.

On the evening of March 3, 1813, Rear Admiral George Cockburn sailed aboard HMS *Marlborough* through the Virginia capes and into the Chesapeake Bay, accompanied by a small squadron. Ten days later, after a quick survey of his new domain, Cockburn made a bold prediction. Given reinforcements, he wrote Warren, "I have no hesitation in pronouncing that the whole of the shores and towns within this vast bay, not excepting the Capital itself will be wholly at your mercy, and subject if not to be permanently occupied, certainly to be successively insulted [i.e., attacked without warning] or destroyed at your pleasure."

It would really be at Cockburn's pleasure. Though he was the subordinate officer, Cockburn believed Warren too passive and that it had been a mistake to leave the bay unmolested. He was determined to end "this supineness."

The two-hundred-mile length of the Chesapeake Bay was ideal for an expeditionary force. Its waters teemed with crabs, oysters, bluefish, and bass, providing ample food. The bay was a water highway to America's interior. The rivers flowing into the bay—among them the Elizabeth, James, York, Rappahannock, Potomac, Patuxent, Patapsco, and Susquehanna—provided ready access to some of the richest land in the country, as well as the cities of Norfolk, Richmond, Washington, and Baltimore. Along the bay's eastern shore, another series of rivers put the British within easy reach of many fishing ports and bountiful farmland. The one problem was that much of the bay was shallow—its average depth only twenty-six feet—and the rivers were filled with shoals and mud banks that made navigation hazardous for a deepwater navy.

Cockburn's instructions were to close the mouth of the Chesapeake, blockade the ports and harbors, capture and destroy trade and shipping, and gather intelligence. Wasting no time, Cockburn moved up the bay in force on March 31. The war was going to be fought on new terms, the admiral made clear to his men. "I am sorry to say violence and brutality are without control," Royal Marines Captain Thomas Marmaduke Wybourn wrote his brother-in-law from the mouth of the Rappahannock on April 4. "[E]very town, village and hamlet throughout these rivers are to be annihilated and plundered."

Throughout April, the British established their dominance of the bay, attacking ships, raiding the shores, and setting up temporary bases. They menaced Annapolis and Baltimore, raided islands in the bay, skirmished with militia, and burned plantations. The village of Frenchtown, near the head of the bay, was plundered and burned on April 29.

The real shock came a week later at Havre de Grace, Maryland, a busy little port on the west bank of the Susquehanna just above its confluence with the Chesapeake. Sailing away from Frenchtown with his loot, Cockburn's attention had been piqued when militia manning a battery at Havre de Grace made the mistake of firing at his distant ships and raising their colors in cocky defiance. "This of course immediately gave to the place an importance which I had not before attached to it, and I therefore determined on attacking it," Cockburn reported to Warren.

On Saturday afternoon, May 1, a British deserter warned townspeople that an attack was imminent. The town jumped into action; women and children were sent away, and 250 militiamen manned positions all night. But no attack came. "Exhausted with fatigue, and believing themselves to have been deceived, the inhabitants retired quietly to rest the next night," wrote Rev. Jared Sparks, who tutored children in the town.

It was a mistake. At midnight May 2, Cockburn loaded Royal Marines onto barges and snuck up on the town. At daybreak, the British fired rockets from the boats, striking one unlucky militiaman and "leaving not a single vestige of him," Wybourn reported. The militia scattered, and terrified residents poured out of homes. The British raiders landed and proceeded to methodically destroy Havre de Grace. They separated into bands of thirty or forty men and worked their way through every house in town, knocking down doors and splintering wardrobes and bureaus with their hatchets. After the raiders took what they pleased, they torched the house and moved to the next. Soon little could be heard but the roaring of flames, the crash of falling timbers, and the occasional sobs of residents.

As the rampage continued, Cockburn came ashore and was accosted by several women, who pleaded for him to stop. "He was unmoved at first," Sparks wrote, "but when they represented to him the misery he was causing, and pointed to the smoking ruins . . . he relented and countermanded his original orders."

By then, about two-thirds of the sixty-two homes in the town were ablaze. Cockburn was satisfied. The townspeople now understood "what they were liable to bring upon themselves by building batteries and acting towards us with so much useless rancor," he reported to Warren.

To further make his point, Cockburn chose as his next targets the towns of Georgetown and Fredericktown, pretty fishing villages on opposite sides of the Sassafras River, which fed into the upper bay from Maryland's Eastern Shore. Learning from informants that the towns were safe havens for trading vessels, Cockburn headed up the river on the night of May 5. Early the next morning, the British intercepted a boat with two Americans. Halting his boats about two miles below the towns, the admiral sent the Americans back with a message for the residents, reminding them about "what had happened at Havre de Grace, and to invite them to pursue a different line of conduct," Cockburn reported.

The flotilla had moved another mile upriver when the Maryland militia answered Cockburn's invitation with heavy fire from both banks. An undeterred Cockburn—"a droll character & witty in the midst of any danger," Captain Wybourn wrote—led an assault that scattered the militia.

Captain John Allen, an American militia commander who stayed in town to watch his property, soon encountered Cockburn, who turned on Allen in a fury. "Had you not fired, and I had taken any thing away, I would have paid for the same; but now, damn you, I will pay you in your own coin," the admiral told him. With that, Cockburn set loose his raiders: "Go on, my boys, knock down, burn, and destroy."

Allen's house, stable, and carriage house were soon aflame, along with his fish house, barrels of salted fish, and other provisions. His granary, packed with barrels of sugar, casks of nails and tobacco, bolts of linen, and other goods, was torched. Liquor casks were knocked open and molasses mixed in, and raiders made off with the family Bible. The home of Allen's brother was next; when his sister-in-law and her baby were found inside, Cockburn ordered his men to remove the woman and child, and get on with the destruction. The home and all adjoining buildings were set afire, and the sailors and Royal Marines helped themselves to clothes and food. The destruction continued all around town. Any valuables that could not be carried off were smashed to pieces—desks, bureaus, clocks, and mirrors among them. Beds were cut open and feathers scattered in the wind.

Before departing to impose the same fate on Georgetown across the river, Cockburn surveyed the damage. The hillsides and harbor were in flames, the town's tavern, storehouse, three granaries, and most of its seventeen houses destroyed, and smoke from burning farmhouses, ships, warehouses, and shops curled through the sky. "This will do," Cockburn told his officers.

Then the admiral turned to Allen. "How do you like the war now?" he asked.

They did not like it much, neither Allen nor many other Americans. Congressman Charles J. Ingersoll of Pennsylvania, traveling to the capital soon after the attacks, encountered universal rage wherever he passed. "On my way from Philadelphia to Washington, I found the whole country excited by these depredations," Ingersoll wrote. "Cockburn's name was on every tongue, with various particulars of his incredibly coarse and blackguard misconduct."

Writing to her cousin Edward Coles on May 13, First Lady Dolley Madison described the uproar over Cockburn's attacks and the "terror and reproach" that he would visit Washington next. The first lady told her cousin that the government had discovered a British plot to sneak a raiding party to burn the president's house. "I do not tremble at this, but feel *affronted* that the Admiral (of Havre de Grace memory) should send me notis that he would make his bow at my Drawing room *soon*," she wrote.

As far as Cockburn was concerned, the sacks of Frenchtown, Havre de Grace, Fredericktown, and Georgetown had quite salutary benefits. "These examples had their intended effect, and during the future operations in this country, the American Inhabitants did not again offer irritating or useless resistance," he wrote.

Cockburn was ruthless, but not vicious. He was cruel, but not for cruelty's sake. Cockburn was practicing a form of total warfare a half century before William Tecumseh Sherman's march to the sea. His goal was simple: Destroy the country's will to fight. He wanted to inflict so much damage to the rich country around the seat of government that the Madison administration would find it impossible, politically or militarily, to continue the war, much less send troops to attack Canada.

It would not be hard, Cockburn believed—it was already obvious the charm of war had vanished for the Americans. "How anxious they are to have an end of this foolish mad war which they rushed so headlong into," he wrote.

Under Cockburn's rules, a house that was abandoned meant the owner had joined the militia, and so it was fair game to be torched. If the home owner stayed and showed any resistance, his house could be torched. Those who chose to defend their homes were "guilty of the unnatural sin of protecting their own country," Frederick Chamier, a midshipman on the expedition, later wrote. Cockburn's men became "consummately skilled in the art of house-burning," Chamier added.

Americans in Cockburn's path were expected to turn over their livestock, tobacco, and any other goods needed by the British; Cockburn considered it "the price of his forbearance to them." Those who resisted were likely to have food and supplies confiscated; those who agreed would be paid, though sometimes only a nominal amount. The choice was often to sell to the British at the price offered—and risk being labeled a collaborator—or lose the goods, and suffer the home or plantation to be burned.

Cockburn viewed Americans as naughty children who needed to be taught a lesson. The attitude was reflected in the derisive British nickname for the Americans: Jonathan, the simple-minded, wayward brother of John Bull. "My ideas of managing Jonathan, is by never giving way to him," Cockburn told Cochrane.

Cockburn had a firm sense of moral rectitude, operating under a particular code of conduct. He considered it "dastardly" when Americans in hiding took potshots at his troops. Any farm, house, or town allowing it was to be stormed and its occupants taken prisoner, likely to be shipped to Halifax and perhaps never to return home.

Cockburn respected bravery. Personal pleas from women—especially if they were good-looking or showed any spunk—appealed to his sense of gallantry. At Georgetown, on the Eastern Shore, when Catherine "Kitty" Knight—a tall beauty who in younger days had turned George Washington's head—pleaded for the destruction to stop, a charmed Cockburn relented. "Apparently affected by my appeal, he called his men off, but left the fire burning, saying, 'Come on boys,' " she later said.

A disappointed sailor struck his boarding axe through the door panel of one of the spared homes, but dutifully followed the admiral back to the ship. Kitty Knight stamped out the fire.

Bad as it had been in the spring of 1813, the war in the Chesapeake soon grew much uglier. In mid-June, Vice Admiral Warren sailed into the bay with an army regiment and two companies of French prisoners who had been pressed into service with the British. Rendezvousing with Cockburn, Warren planned to attack Norfolk and capture the USS *Constellation*, which was bottled up at the port by the British blockade. But the attack was poorly planned and badly executed, and the invasion force was repelled at Craney Island, which guarded Norfolk at the mouth of the Elizabeth River. Exultant American defenders poured fire on invasion barges stranded in the mud, capsizing a boat filled with French troops, and, according to British witnesses, shooting down the hapless men as they struggled in the water.

Three days later, the British exacted a brutal revenge at Hampton, a village across the water from Norfolk but not as strongly defended. A landing force of Royal Marines and army troops routed the militia and captured the town. The French troops—thuggish desperadoes who had either deserted from the French army or been captured by the British during brutal fighting on the Iberian Peninsula—ran wild, raping, robbing, and murdering innocent residents, including the elderly and infirm.

British officers did little or nothing to stop the rampage, and at least some of them thought it justified. "When our boats were struck, the

Americans came down and shot the men swimming in the water; but the brutes got punished for it at Hampton," a navy officer wrote to a colleague. Though at first they downplayed the incident, more senior British officers were privately mortified. Crimes were committed "for which England ought to blush," Napier wrote. "Every horror was committed with impunity, rape, murder, pillage: and not a man was punished!" he added. The French troops were shipped to Halifax, never to fight again for England.

The French troops were under the army's command, not Cockburn's, and there is no evidence that he sanctioned the atrocities. Yet Cockburn, like the other British commanders at the scene, bore a measure of responsibility. The admiral did not want a repeat of Hampton, and for his next operation, an attack on American shipping at the fishing village of Ocracoke, on North Carolina's Outer Banks, he ordered officers to ensure that "no mischief shall be done to the unoffending inhabitants."

Around the country, in any event, Cockburn was held responsible for the rape of Hampton. Washington feared it might be next. "The affair of Hampton, which I disbelieved until the publication in the Intelligencer, inspires us with a terror we should not otherwise have felt," wrote Margaret Bayard Smith, a friend of the Madisons.

The panic grew in mid-July 1813, when Warren took ships on a foray up the Potomac River, hoping to so alarm Washington that it would abandon plans for further invasion of Canada.

American lookouts spotted the British movement, and on the morning of July 15, a messenger arrived in Washington reporting the fleet was in the Potomac. "Alarm guns were fired, and the bells set in motion, and very soon every person in the city was moving," Elbridge Gerry, Jr., the son of the vice president, wrote in his diary. Francis Scott Key enlisted as a private with the Georgetown Field Artillery, organized by his neighbor, Major George Peter, an accomplished artilleryman who had received his commission from George Washington. But most of the men were, like Key, well-to-do Georgetown gentlemen with little or no military experience. Key was assigned the job of matross, a gunner's mate responsible for loading and sponging a cannon barrel.

By evening, the militia had assembled, many in spanking new uniforms, ready to march. Major Peter's sister-in-law, Martha Peter of Georgetown, who as step-granddaughter of George Washington knew a real soldier when she saw one, was not impressed. "Each new-made officer vied with the other who should put on most finery; expecting, no doubt, by their dazzling appearance, to strike the enemy with dismay," she wrote.

The militia marched ten miles to Fort Washington, which commanded the Potomac River from atop a bluff on the Maryland shore. Detachments blocked roads leading from the Potomac. Patrols went out around the clock, scouting for any sign of a British landing. Madison's cabinet rode down in a sulky to review the troops, who were reported to be "full of ardour and enthusiasm." Madison, seriously ill with a bilious fever, remained at the president's house under Dolley's care. In Washington, men too old to march with the militia formed volunteer companies to patrol the streets each evening.

Aboard his flagship HMS *San Domingo* in the Potomac, Warren was pleased to hear the British approach had caused "much confusion" in Washington. But upon reaching the Kettle Bottom Shoals, about halfway from the bay to the capital, the ever-cautious admiral concluded that his heavy, gun-laden ships could not pass through the dangerous shallow waters. On July 21, the fleet turned around.

The threat had passed. The militia proudly marched back to Washington, where they were greeted with cheers and dinner parties. Madison and his cabinet were pleased the militia had shown they could protect the capital from the British threat. After some final flourishes, Cockburn and most of the British fleet sailed in September 1813 for Bermuda, where they would refit and rest for the winter. Washington settled into complacency.

His eyes "were windows to a mind that Thomas Jefferson, his
closest friend, considered unrivalled in the land."

James Madison in 1817.

CHAPTER 2

★

Laid in Ashes

R EAR ADMIRAL GEORGE Cockburn returned to the Chesapeake Bay in February 1814 with one overriding conviction: Washington must be taken.

A new commander-in-chief was en route who would likely be very interested in Cockburn's ideas. The Admiralty in London had recalled the lethargic Vice Admiral Warren as commander of the North American Station in November and replaced him with Vice Admiral Alexander Cochrane, an expert on amphibious warfare and an inveterate hater of America.

After arriving in Bermuda and taking command on April 1, Cochrane issued his subordinate a carte blanche. "You are at perfect liberty as soon as you can muster a sufficient force, to act with the utmost hostility against the shores of the United States," Cochrane wrote. "Their sea port towns laid in ashes & the country wasted will be some sort of a retaliation for their savage conduct in Canada; where they have destroyed our towns, in the most inclement seasons of the year; it is therefore but just, that retaliation shall be made near to the seat of their government from whence those orders emanated."

Cochrane was referring to an infamous incident on the Niagara frontier in December 1813, when American troops had burned the town of Newark (modern Niagara-on-the-Lake, Ontario), leaving some four hundred civilians homeless in the dead of winter. Moreover, eight months before that, on April 27, 1813, rampaging American troops acting without orders had looted York, the capital of Upper

Canada, and were blamed by the British for burning the provincial parliament.

Cockburn had, of course, been laying seaports in ashes and wasting the country for some time now. Havre de Grace, Frenchtown, Fredericktown, and Georgetown had been destroyed almost exactly a year earlier, well before the British in the Chesapeake had heard anything about the nearly concurrent sack of York, and eight months before Newark was burned. Now, however, Cockburn had official sanction, and henceforth the British would claim that their actions in the Chesapeake were in retaliation for American actions in Canada.

Cochrane was eager to make a "considerable" attack in the Chesapeake to force the Americans to divert troops from Canada. He was expecting reinforcements from Europe but was unsure of how many or when they would arrive. He remained in Bermuda for months anxiously awaiting more information, unsure where to attack.

Cockburn suffered no doubts as to his course of action. He had learned a great deal from the 1813 campaign, all pointing to the conclusion that the American capital could be captured with ease. He laid the groundwork, confident he could persuade the new chief when the time came. "The Rear-admiral had, from the commencement of his operations, always fixed an eye of peculiar interest upon Washington," Lieutenant James Scott, Cockburn's aide, later wrote. "It had been the concentrated object of his thoughts and actions; every measure he adopted was more or less remotely connected, conceived, and carried into execution, as affording preliminary steps to the final accomplishment of the grand ultimatum of his exertions."

Cockburn selected Tangier Island, an isolated fishing village with a deepwater harbor in the middle of the Chesapeake, to build a major British base. From its central location, the British could monitor the enemy and launch operations on either shore of the Chesapeake. Not incidentally, Tangier was within easy sail of both the Potomac and Patuxent rivers, ideal for an attack on Washington.

Sailors and Royal Marines began building a fort at the southern end of the island, clearing beautiful stands of wild cherry trees, pines, and cedars. Parson Joshua Thomas, an evangelical Methodist who preached on the island, approached the imperial Cockburn and stammered out a plea to save a grove of tall pines used for prayer meetings. "And who are you?" Cockburn asked sharply.

"I told him, with my hat in my hand, that I was a 'sinner saved by grace,'" Thomas later recalled. Cockburn's face took on "an air of solemnity," and he issued orders to spare the grove.

By late spring, the base was largely constructed. Fort Albion, as it was named, was a little piece of England, with a church and twenty houses laid out in streets, a hospital large enough to treat a hundred patients, barracks for a thousand men, storehouses, parade grounds, vegetable gardens, meadows for cattle, and a burial ground. The spared pine grove in the midst of the fort became a favored spot, catching breezes off the water and "giving life and pleasure to the languid." The romance of the place was lost on the sailors and Royal Marines, many of whom—Cockburn included—became ill with flux when well water turned brackish. The men also complained of "myriads of mosquitoes," but Cockburn insisted they were no worse at Tangier than anywhere else in the bay.

Fort Albion witnessed the birth of a new fighting force of escaped slaves, the Corps of Colonial Marines. Cockburn distributed a thousand copies of a proclamation Cochrane had issued from Bermuda inviting slaves in the Chesapeake region to join with the British, either to fight against their former masters or to settle in Canada or the West Indies.

The Union Jack flew high over Fort Albion, establishing British dominion over the bay and serving as a beacon for escaping slaves, who flooded in as word of the British proclamation spread. At night, British barges went to prearranged meeting spots to pick up slaves willing to join. In one night, more than 140 slaves escaped. It was a perilous venture for the slaves—if caught, they risked execution or being sold out of state. Others likely perished when their canoes or rafts drifted to sea.

Ezekiel Loney, a twenty-seven-year-old slave on Virginia's Northern Neck, saw his chance when four British barges came up the Rappahannock River and appeared off the Corotoman plantation just after sunrise on April 20. The panicked overseer of the plantation grabbed his belongings, gathered the livestock, and fled, directing the slaves to hide in the woods. Returning an hour later, the chagrined overseer discovered that Loney and two other slaves "had gone off to the British." The three men were soon on their way to Tangier.

About two hundred enlisted to fight their former masters, among them Loney. Sergeant William Hammond, a tough and veteran Royal Marine, taught the former slaves the basics of marching and weaponry. By the time the fine April weather had turned into a hot and sultry May, the men had been issued Royal Marine red jackets and were ready to fight. Loney had shown enough promise to be promoted to corporal.

Cockburn, who had been skeptical of how useful the Colonial Marines would be, found their skill as soldiers "astonishing" and soon was their staunchest advocate. They "are really very fine fellows," he wrote Cochrane May 10. "[T]hey have induced me to alter the bad opinion I had of the whole of their race & I now really believe these we are training, will neither shew want of zeal or courage when employed by us in attacking their old masters."

At their first test, the Colonial Marines proved Cockburn correct, landing in a shower of grapeshot—cast-iron balls the size of golf balls, packed in a bag, which spread like shotgun pellets—while assaulting a militia battery May 29 at Pungoteague, on Virginia's Eastern Shore. "[T]hough one of them was shot & died instantly in the front of the others . . . it did not daunt or check the others in the least but on the contrary animated them to seek revenge," Cockburn reported. To mark their bravery, Cockburn presented the proud Colonials with a six-pound field piece captured at the battle.

By June, Cockburn had decided he preferred the Colonials to his own Royal Marines, finding them stronger and less likely to desert. The only time he was disappointed was when several Colonials were found asleep at their posts in July. Cockburn ordered the offenders to wear their jackets inside out and cut off their grog.

While freeing the slaves was in the self-interest of the British, they relished their role as liberators exposing the hypocrisies of American liberty. Most of the escaped slaves—including many women, children, aged, and infirm—were unfit for service, and were a burden for the

British, who had to feed, clothe, and shelter them. But the escapees provided invaluable intelligence, guiding the British through the backwoods and waters, often with more intimate knowledge than their former masters. What Cockburn appreciated the most was the unalloyed fear they inspired in the Americans.

All summer, as he awaited the arrival of Cochrane with the reinforcements, Cockburn continued preparations for an invasion. He and his captains took soundings of the Potomac and Patuxent, looking for the best route to Washington. He gathered intelligence from newspapers, which helpfully reported troop strengths and movements, and from informants, of which there was no shortage. He trained his seamen as soldiers, ready to join an invasion force. In his letters to Cochrane, Cockburn pressed for an attack on the capital. "[T]he country is in general in a horrible state it only requires a little firm and steady conduct to have it completely at our mercy," he wrote June 25.

Accompanying raiding parties along the shores, Cockburn was almost disappointed at the lack of resistance: "Not a militia man or soldier to be seen except we hunt for them in the woods & then they only play at Hide & Seek with us."

One man was ready to challenge Cockburn: Joshua Barney, commander of the U.S. Chesapeake Flotilla. Red-nosed and ruddy-cheeked, with sparkling black eyes, the fifty-five-year-old Barney had a gentle face that belied his long and adventurous life at sea. The Maryland native had fought as many, if not more, naval battles against the British as any living American, and he was eager for another fight.

Raised on a farm outside Baltimore, Barney had resisted his parents' efforts to steer him toward a respectable life in a mercantile firm, and instead gone to sea at age twelve. When the American Revolution broke out he was already an experienced sailor, and at age seventeen he became the youngest captain of a Continental Navy frigate. He captured the British warship *General Monk* on Delaware Bay in 1782, an action "justly deemed one of the most brilliant that ever occurred under the American flag," in the view of James Fenimore Cooper. Barney was taken prisoner three times by the British, dramatically escaping once, and the experiences left him with a lifelong dislike of England.

"To content himself with following the plough, watching the growth of his corn, or shearing his merinos, while the blast of war was blowing in his ears, would have been an effort beyond his philosophy," his niece wrote.

Joshua Barney, while serving in the French Navy.

Near the end of the Revolutionary War, Barney sailed to Paris to deliver dispatches to Benjamin Franklin, who took a liking to the young naval hero and presented him to the royal court. A charmed Marie Antoinette allowed the handsome American the honor of kissing her cheek. Back home, Americans celebrated the dashing Barney in verse and prose, including the popular song "Barney, Leave the Girls Alone."

Brave, steady, and intrepid, Barney was dogged all his life by a prickly pride that was quick to find insult. A perceived slight prompted him to turn down a commission with the U.S. Navy after the war and instead serve with the French navy in the West Indies. Some considered him a traitor, given the tense relations that then prevailed between the United States and France. After resigning from the French navy in 1802, Barney returned to Maryland, where he dabbled in business and politics. Twice he had offered his services to the U.S. Navy, but both Jefferson and Madison turned him down.

Barney had just retired with his wife in May 1812 to a farm in Elkridge, outside Baltimore, when word came that the United States had declared war. "To content himself with following the plough, watching the growth of his corn, or shearing his merinos, while the blast of war was blowing in his ears, would have been an effort beyond his philosophy," his niece later wrote.

Barney packed his clothes, rushed to Baltimore, and within three weeks was roaming the Atlantic in command of the privateer *Rossie*, an armed cruiser. Over the next four months he captured eighteen British merchant vessels valued in total at $1.5 million, completing one of the most spectacular privateering runs of the war. Returning in November 1812, he tried again to retire to his farm, but it was too much to ask with Cockburn marauding unfettered up and down the shores of his beloved Maryland.

On Independence Day in 1813, Barney took up his pen and wrote a memorandum to Secretary of the Navy William Jones analyzing the British threat to the Chesapeake. To fight back, Barney advised building a mosquito fleet of armed barges to ply the shallow waters of the Chesapeake, powered by oars and light sails. "[F]orm them into a flying squadron . . . continually watching and annoying the enemy in our waters," Barney recommended. It would be effective, Barney promised, and cheap—they could build fifty barges for half the price of one frigate.

Jones, under intense pressure because of the navy's inability to defend the Chesapeake, leapt at the offer. Barney would report directly to Jones and outside the regular navy establishment, thus skirting ticklish issues of seniority. In Baltimore, Barney worked for months building his flotilla, battling contractors with "thick skulls," and recruiting crews. As the flotilla neared readiness in early 1814, Jones offered a benediction from Washington: "[Y]our force is our principal shield, and all eyes will be upon you."

Barney sailed from Baltimore with eighteen barges in late May, intending to attack the British base at Tangier. Getting wind, Cockburn ordered Captain Robert Barrie, commander of the 74–gun HMS *Dragon*, to hunt down Barney. After Barrie chased the American flotilla into the Patuxent, Barney staged a clever counterattack on June 10 at the mouth of St. Leonard Creek, a Patuxent tributary, running a British frigate aground before retreating up the creek and out of enemy reach.

Seeking to draw Barney out of the creek, Barrie marauded up the Patuxent, burning towns and plantations, carrying off slaves and livestock, and torching whatever tobacco that could not be fit onto ships.

On June 16, Barrie pillaged the town of Lower Marlboro. "[H]ere we passed the night without molestation *though only eighteen miles from Washington*," the astonished captain reported to Cockburn.

But Barney remained out of reach.

E arly on June 18, 1814, alarms sounded in Washington, warning that the British were coming up the Patuxent and again threatening the capital. The court where Francis Scott Key was trying a case abruptly adjourned. Key signed up again with Major Peter's Georgetown militia, this time at the rank of lieutenant and with the title of quartermaster, responsible for procuring supplies.

Peter marched with a light force of 280 militia and horse-drawn artillery from Washington on the morning of June 19, the cannons rattling through the streets. The roads into southern Maryland were jammed with terrified residents fleeing their homes along the Patuxent. Near the port of Benedict on the afternoon of June 20, an advance party of cavalry skirmished with an enemy raiding party, killing one and capturing five. The prisoners were unrepentant; one boasted that a large army was on the way and that a bloody war with America was the universal talk of the fleet.

By the time Key arrived that evening with the main American force, the action was over. "We got there just in time to see the British vessels move off, so that we had nothing to suffer but the fatigue of the march & the inconvenience of such an excursion," he wrote Randolph. The militia camped at Benedict for two weeks in case the British returned. Key's adventures as quartermaster for the Georgetown Artillery were more comic than dangerous. "I have only to tell of being knocked down by a bone of bacon and pitched by my horse over head & ears into the river and this is quite as much as I wish to know of the wars," he told Randolph.

Key wrote a reassuring note to his mother from the camp on June 23, telling her the British "have now gone down the river—and nobody seems to think there is any chance of their coming back again, at least, while the troops are in the neighborhood."

But Key was less sanguine in his note to Randolph, written July 3, two days after his return to Georgetown. Though there was much bravado in Washington about how the militia had once again stood up to the British, and the defenders were once more feted with a banquet, Key was under no illusions. "I fear that our situation here will be a very unpleasant one as long as the war lasts," he wrote. "I know of no nation in the world whose situation is so critical as ours and fear that the storm which has desolated many others is just about to pass over us."

Key confessed to his friend that he was tempted to flee ahead of that storm. "I have had a great many uneasy thoughts (which I ought to be ashamed of) of what I should do with myself & where I should go to get out the reach of the visitation," he wrote.

His faith, Key hoped, would provide the answer. "Where a man finds that he may be usefully employed, where he seems to be placed by a Master whose work he is to do, there, whatever may be the difficulties of such a situation, he ought to stand & fall—certainly he ought not to leave it without evident necessity."

Cockburn was certainly not done with the Patuxent, whatever Washington thought. On July 3, as Key fretted about the British to Randolph, the rear admiral ordered *Albion* to weigh anchor from Tangier and sail toward the Patuxent.

Joshua Barney's flotilla was on the loose again, lurking in the upper reaches of the river. Cockburn, though annoyed, could not disguise a trace of admiration for Barney's exploits. "How sharply and unexpectedly Jonathan has exerted himself," he wrote to Cochrane. The British had thought Barney was trapped in St. Leonard Creek, where he had retreated following the flotilla's first clash with the enemy on June 10. But after U.S. Army troops and U.S. Marines set up batteries on bluffs overlooking the mouth of the creek, Barney prepared a bold breakout attempt. On the night of June 25, the flotilla moved silently down the creek. In the predawn darkness, the American shore guns opened up earlier than Barney expected, catching both the British and the flotilla by surprise. Barney rushed into the fray with the cannons on every flotilla boat blazing. But after furious exchanges of fire, the poorly coordinated attack appeared to have failed. Barney was retreating back up the creek when he noticed the British had left a gap at the mouth while they repaired a damaged ship.

Barney seized the moment, ordering the flotilla to reverse course and make full speed for the Patuxent, successfully breaking the blockade. "I had the mortification to observe them rowing down the creek, and up the river," Captain Thomas Brown, the chagrined British commander, reported to Cockburn.

Despite his anxiety over Barney's escape, Cockburn sensed an opportunity. True, the flotilla threat had to be eliminated before the capital was attacked. But by fleeing up the Patuxent, Barney had presented Cockburn with an opportunity to kill two birds with one stone.

Cockburn believed the Patuxent held the key to capturing Washington. The river was not the most direct or obvious route to the capital, and that was part of the attraction. A British advance up the Potomac would leave little doubt Washington was the target. But a move up the Patuxent would be more ambiguous. It might mean an overland attack on Baltimore or Annapolis—or perhaps just a move to trap Barney.

For two weeks the admiral scouted the area, noting the lack of defenses, foraging for supplies, and teaching locals the Cockburn rules of

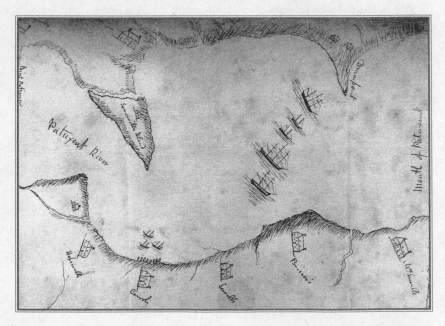

Cockburn believed the Patuxent held the key to capturing Washington. The river was not the most direct or obvious route to the capital, and that was part of the attraction.

Sketch by Commodore Joshua Barney in August 1814 showing the British blockade at the mouth of the Patuxent River.

fighting. Near Drum Point in St. Mary's County on July 8, when two brothers from the Holton family took a potshot at one of Cockburn's lieutenants and rode off at a gallop, Cockburn exacted methodical revenge against the "two heroes on horseback," as he sarcastically called them. "I ascertained who they were & where they lived, & that night I sent to their house [and] destroyed everything belonging to it." The two sons, pulled from their beds, were made to watch the destruction in their bedclothes, alongside their mother. Only a mirror was spared, at the pleading of the youngest child in the family. The elder sons were taken to *Albion*, where Cockburn ordered them sent to Halifax. "I trust this example . . . will induce Jonathan . . . to treat us in future with due respect," he told Barrie.

Cockburn did not want to linger in the Patuxent, worried that if he stayed too long the American government might finally build defenses on the roads leading to the capital. In mid-July, Cockburn embarked on an elaborate deception to keep Washington guessing at his intentions. He left Captain Joseph Nourse with a squadron in the Patuxent to continue the usual raids and keep Barney bottled up. Cockburn departed the river with the rest of his ships and headed for the Potomac, hoping to take the enemy's attention with him. "After making a flourish or two there, sacking Leonards Town [on the Potomac's Maryland shore] . . . I shall again move elsewhere, so as to distract Jonathan, do him all the mischief I can and yet not allow him to suspect that a serious and permanent landing is intended anywhere," he wrote July 16.

Nourse assured Cockburn the Americans were quite confused: "Jonathan I believe is so confounded that he does not know when or where to look for us and I do believe that he is at this moment so undecided and unprepared that it would require but little force to burn Washington, and I hope soon to put the first torch to it myself."

Cockburn was of the same opinion: "Mr. Maddison must certainly be either in confident expectation of immediate peace, or preparing to abdicate the chair."

BERMUDA, AUGUST 1, 1814

At the North American Station headquarters, Sir Alexander Cochrane had been delighted by reports that London was sending him 20,000 or more reinforcements. He envisioned joining them up with an army of free slaves Cockburn was training in the Chesapeake. "[W]ith them properly armed & backed with 20,000 British troops, Mr. Maddison will be hurled from his Throne," he exulted in a note to Cockburn July 1.

Certainly Washington and Baltimore could be captured and either destroyed or held for ransom, he informed London on July 14. But later that same day, Cochrane received word that London had sent only 4,000 troops.

Cochrane was discouraged. Not only were there fewer troops than expected, Cochrane concluded by July 23 that it was too close to the "sickly season" to launch operations in the Chesapeake region. He considered the hot August and September weather "the worst enemy we have to contend with"; he feared the fevers and dysenteries that had ravaged the British the previous summer. Cochrane was leaning toward an attack in the safer climes of Rhode Island or New Hampshire.

Then, on July 25, HMS *St. Lawrence* arrived in Bermuda from the Chesapeake, bearing letters from Cockburn outlining his secret plan for the capture of Washington. Cockburn's confident assurances restored Cochrane's willingness to at least visit the Chesapeake.

At the end of July, the army reinforcements from Europe under the command of Major General Robert Ross arrived in Bermuda. Cochrane and Ross agreed to set sail for the Chesapeake to rendezvous with Cockburn and briefly inspect the theater.

At noon on August 1, aided by a fresh breeze, Cochrane and Ross departed Bermuda aboard *Tonnant,* with the troopships to follow two days later.

BALTIMORE, THURSDAY, AUGUST 11

On the morning of August 11, American agent John Skinner sailed into Baltimore harbor, returning from his visit to the British fleet in the Potomac, where he had heard Rear Admiral Cockburn's suggestion that President Madison don his armor and prepare to fight.

It was not the first time Skinner had heard Cockburn talk about capturing Washington. That was part of Cockburn's regular repartee—

boasts and threats, "delivered under the guise of badinage," and meant to keep Skinner and the Americans guessing. Whenever they reached a point of contention in their discussions, Cockburn would jovially brush the matter aside. "Ah, well, we'll waive it for the present, I'll settle that affair at Washington." Skinner would smile politely at the jests.

This time, though, Skinner was not so sure that the admiral was joking. Cockburn was the sort, he knew, who might jest about capturing Washington and still do it.

Skinner wrote the president reporting the admiral's boast.

WASHINGTON, SATURDAY, AUGUST 13

The war had kept James Madison in Washington all summer. Instead of retreating to the comforts of his Montpelier plantation at the foot of the lovely Blue Ridge during the hot months, as was his custom, the sixty-two-year-old president remained in the capital, both to stay on top of developments as well as to assuage fears about the city's vulnerability. On Tuesday, Madison and his cabinet had traveled by Navy barge ten miles down the Potomac to Fort Washington to inspect newly repaired gun mounts, hoping the visit would calm concerns that the fortress was woefully unprepared to defend the capital.

Madison and his wife, Dolley, were staying at the President's House on Pennsylvania Avenue, despite worries that remaining in Washington would expose him again to the bilious fever that nearly killed him the previous summer. Still, conditions were better at the President's House for the Madisons than they had been for their predecessors. When John Adams moved into the mansion in November 1800, it was still a work site, smelling of horsehair plaster and wallpaper paste, and with a yawning abyss where the grand staircase was supposed to go. The mansion remained under construction during Jefferson's eight-year tenure, with constant upheaval from the Virginian's attempts to redesign the mansion to his own liking.

Jefferson, a widower, had often relied on Dolley as his unofficial hostess for parties at the President's House. Upon moving in as first lady, Dolley supervised the decoration of the still-unfinished home in a style of classical décor based on excavations at Pompeii. The large oval drawing room was one of the most elaborate and elegant interior spaces in the entire country. Striking crimson red velvet curtains hung from windows that ran from just above the floor to the ceiling, looking south to the Potomac. The state dining room, featuring a large-as-life Gilbert Stuart portrait of George Washington on the wall above the dining room table, could seat forty in comfort.

Though the roof leaked, the mansion already had taken on an air of grandeur. The tan-colored sandstone exterior was whitewashed, making it stand out from the brick or wood frame of most Washington homes, and some residents had taken to calling it the "white house."

But it was not Montpelier. A few days earlier, the president had wistfully picked up paper and pen to write to his mother, eighty-two-year-old Nelly Conway Madison, who lived at Montpelier. He assured Mother Madison that he and Dolley were in good health, but he had fading hopes of making it home. "I can not yet say how soon I shall be able to make you the visit usual at this season," he wrote August 8. "You well know that it will afford me too much gratification to be delayed a moment longer than may be necessary."

It was becoming increasingly apparent that it would be necessary to delay a visit for some time. Skinner's note confirmed what James Madison had come to recognize in recent days: The United States was fighting for its survival.

Skinner's warning was not the only one. Madison had just received an anonymous letter, dated "At Sea, July 27, 1814," and postmarked in New York on August 1. Labeled as being from "a friend," it likely was written by a sailor in the British fleet impressed into service against his will.

"Your enemy have in agitation an attack on the Capital of the United States," the anonymous correspondent warned. "The manner which they intend doing it is, to take the advantage of a fair wind in ascending the Patuxent, and after having ascended it a certain distance, to land their men, at once, and to make all possible dispatch to the Capital, batter it down, and then return to their vessels immediately." Madison turned the letter over to the commander of Washington defenses, who dutifully filed it.

At least as worrisome to Madison was the latest dispatch from Albert Gallatin, his trusted confidant and former Treasury secretary, now on diplomatic duty in Europe. The message, which arrived August 5, warned that the large British force bound for the United States was intent on inflicting "very serious injury" to America. Gallatin grimly noted that the United States could expect no help from either France or Russia. Several days after reading Gallatin's message, Madison called for Congress to meet in special session in September to consider the gloomy situation.

Even with the British threat looming, Madison was forced to take time on August 13 to bring order to his dysfunctional cabinet, where tensions had reached new heights. He penned a letter rebuking his disruptive secretary of war, John Armstrong, for failing to consult with him on important decisions, including some, Madison icily complained, that he first learned "from the newspapers." Armstrong was ordered to check with the president before making almost any decision of significance.

The president's tiny frame, wan looks, and mild-mannered personality made him easy to underestimate. Dressed head to toe in black, from his coat to his breeches and silk stockings, Madison had "the air of a country schoolmaster in mourning for one of his pupils whom he had whipped to death," a visitor to the President's House wrote in 1813. Another visitor, Frances Few, thought Madison's skin looked like parchment, and she was put off by his habit of staring at the ground. But, she added, "a few moments in his company and you lose sight of these defects. . . . [H]is eyes are penetrating and expressive—his smile charming—his manners affable—his conversation lively and interesting."

They were windows to a mind that Thomas Jefferson, his closest friend, considered unrivaled in the land. Madison's selection in 1776 as a delegate to the Virginia Convention drafting the state's constitution marked the start of his lifelong collaboration with Jefferson. Madison's brilliant and incisive mind left an indelible stamp on democratic thought at the Constitutional Convention in Philadelphia in 1787, and later in Congress, as author of the Bill of Rights.

For all his genius, the job of commander-in-chief was proving more challenging for Madison. During the buildup to war, he had made a few halfhearted proposals to increase military spending, and Congress had responded with halfhearted measures. Madison's conviction, shared with Jefferson, was that a large standing army and the heavy debts and taxes that would be required to pay for it represented a threat to democracy.

When war had been declared in June 1812, the total strength of the U.S. Army was 11,744 men, almost half of them green recruits. Worse than the numbers was the quality of the officer corps, consisting of "swaggerers, dependents, decayed gentlemen, and others fit for nothing else," in the view of one officer who was an exception to that rule, Winfield Scott, an ambitious young lieutenant colonel in 1812. The U.S. Navy had only fifteen vessels capable of going to sea, and was "so Lilliputian," a despairing John Adams wrote his son, "that Gulliver might bury it in the deep by making water on it." Congress, opposed to a large standing navy, had refused to build any new ships.

With this feeble force, the United States had challenged one of the most powerful nations on earth. The British army, nearly a quarter of a million men strong, was a veteran, disciplined, and much-feared fighting force. The Royal Navy, with a thousand warships, was at the height of its glory, famously ruling the waves. Yet most of Great Britain's armed forces had been tied up fighting France, and the British and Americans were fairly evenly matched on the ground in North America, with about 7,000 British and Canadian regulars and a small number of Canadian militia available. The Royal Navy, with about forty-five warships and an equal number of smaller vessels operating in American waters, held a stronger advantage against the U.S. Navy, though the vast majority of the British naval might lay across the ocean.

Madison knew that the United States had little military capability. A war under these conditions was reckless, without a doubt. Madison's hope was that the United States could get away without fighting the war—or at least not much of one. Declaring war, in Madison's mind, was partly a bluff, to draw Britain's attention to American grievances. Soon after the vote for war, Madison put out peace feelers, but the British were too baffled by the machinations to respond.

From the start, the fundamental American strategy was to conquer Canada. The United States intended to capture two of the Canadian colonies that made up British North America, Upper Canada and Lower Canada, or respectively modern-day Ontario and Quebec. What to do with them could be determined later. Westerners would be happy to keep the vast territory, or at least permanently remove the British from the North American continent. For Madison, conquering Canada was a means to an end, a bargaining chip to force Britain to cease its trampling of American sovereignty.

The warnings of John Randolph and other naysayers were dismissed. "[T]he acquisition of Canada this year, as far as the neighborhood of Quebec, will be a mere matter of marching," Jefferson wrote soon after war was declared. Canada's population of 500,000 was only a fraction of the 7.5 million living in the United States. Quebec was filled with native French who hated the English, while Upper Canada included many settlers who had migrated from the United States. Surely, the thinking went, the Americans would be greeted as liberators.

Canada would be invaded on three fronts. In the Northwest, which included Ohio and the territories of Indiana, Michigan, and Illinois, an army assembled in the summer of 1812 to attack across the Detroit River into Upper Canada. Farther east, in New York, troops would invade across the Niagara River, while a third force, from upstate New York and New England, would attack Montreal.

After war was declared and before the invasions were launched, Madison made the rounds in Washington, visiting the War and Navy departments to bestow words of encouragement "in a manner worthy of a commander in chief, with his little round hat and huge cockade," wrote Attorney General Richard Rush. But from the start, the war did not go as the commander-in-chief planned.

In the northwest, the aging and corpulent Brigadier General William Hull led an army of volunteers and militia across the Detroit River into Ontario, only to lose his nerve and scamper back to Detroit, where he soon capitulated to a lesser force of British and Indians. On the Niagara front, a second American army surrendered after a brutal fight at Queenston Heights on the Canadian side of the river. The attack on Montreal ended in disgrace after the U.S. commander, General Henry "Granny" Dearborn, withdrew in panic. Other than a few shining single-ship victories at sea—including those of the USS

Constitution—the war in 1812 had been a debacle for the United States. Madison was elected to a second term that fall with barely more than 50 percent of the popular vote in the divided country.

The second year of war, 1813, saw more American success, but the victories were tempered by costly defeats. Captain Oliver Hazard Perry won control of Lake Erie in September, enabling an American army under Major General William Henry Harrison to reestablish control of Detroit and much of the Northwest. But on the Niagara front, bloody back-and-forth fighting through the year ended with the British torching American settlements along the Niagara River. To the east, another attempt to capture Montreal ended again in futility. To top it off, Cockburn and his marauders had descended on the Chesapeake Bay, spreading terror on a new front much closer to Washington and bringing a torrent of criticism on Madison.

The outlook for 1814 could not have been more alarming. Almost every ship from Europe brought disquieting news of continued British success in the war with France. The defeat of Napoleon by allied armies at Leipzig in October 1813 forced the emperor to retreat to France. With the allies closing in on Paris, Napoleon abdicated unconditionally on April 6, 1814. Word of the fall of Paris arrived in Washington on May 9, followed by discomforting reports that the British were sending a punitive expedition to the Chesapeake.

Wellington was ordered in April to assemble an expeditionary force on the coast of Bordeaux and load them onto ships bound for North America, with the goal of ending the festering American war, punishing the United States, and perhaps even forcing the dissolution of the union. Some 6,000 men were being sent to Canada for an offensive into New York along the Hudson River and Lake Champlain, intended to cut New England off from the rest of the country. A smaller force of 4,000 sailed to join Admiral Cochrane's force on the east coast, with the goal of diverting American forces from the Canadian front.

The Madison administration finally stirred to action after a dispatch arrived from Gallatin on June 26 warning of a British attack that might dismember the union. A sobered cabinet agreed the next day that U.S. diplomats preparing to negotiate with the British in Ghent could abandon the American demand to end impressment, if necessary, to reach a peace agreement.

Madison decided the government should do more to protect Washington. At his order, the cabinet convened again at noon, July 1, 1814, at the President's House. The dramatic developments in Europe had utterly transformed the situation. Madison warned "unequivocally" that Washington presented "the most inviting object of a speedy attack."

Yet no one else in the cabinet shared his concern. "I was not equally impressed with the apprehension of immediate danger," Secretary of the Navy William Jones candidly admitted. Secretary of State Monroe was skeptical the British had the logistical wherewithal to mount such an operation, while Secretary of War Armstrong thought the whole idea that the British would attack Washington was ludicrous.

Still, the cabinet unanimously went along with Madison's proposal that the War Department establish a new military command responsible for the defense of the capital: the Tenth Military District, made up of the District of Columbia, Northern Virginia, and all of Maryland, including Baltimore and Annapolis. Madison wanted two or three thousand U.S. Army troops immediately deployed between the Patuxent River and Washington, and another ten to twelve thousand militia and volunteers from Washington and the neighboring states held in readiness.

"The administration are beginning (I understand) to think that the war on our coast may be almost as serious a one as that they are waging in Canada," Francis Scott Key observed in his letter to Randolph on July 3. "They have ordered 2000 men here. But if the British receive the reinforcement they expect, this force will be quite inadequate."

M adison, however, was satisfied that the measures taken would safeguard Washington and the region, and he turned his attention to other matters. In that, he failed to calculate the stubborn recalcitrance of John Armstrong, his secretary of war. Armstrong never denied that he was insulting to many in Washington, including most of the cabinet. In his view, they richly deserved it. "In the discharge of my duty, I have never hesitated . . . giving offence to bad or incompetent men, hence it is, that all my signal enemies are of one or the other of these two descriptions," Armstrong would later say.

Madison had chosen Armstrong almost by default after the inept

William Eustis resigned under pressure as secretary of war in December 1812. The president wanted Monroe to take the position, but Monroe instead wanted a military command to lead the next invasion of Canada, and in any event, northern senators did not want a Virginian in the job. Armstrong, a former senator and diplomat who had served as a staff officer with the Continental Army at Trenton and Saratoga, had a reputation for military expertise, which was needed at the moment. Just as important to Madison, Armstrong was from New York, and his appointment allowed the president to quell political complaints about his cabinet's geographic balance. Several cabinet members had deep misgivings about Armstrong, knowing firsthand his corrosive personality. Even Jefferson, who had appointed Armstrong minister to France during his presidency, considered him "presumptuous, obstinate, & injudicious."

In one area, Armstrong did a great service as secretary, invigorating the army with younger and bolder field commanders, among them Andrew Jackson and Winfield Scott. But in most respects he was a disaster. He meddled with commanders in the field and had stormy relations with his generals. He feuded with the rest of the cabinet, especially Monroe, who was furious when Armstrong blocked his appointment to command the northern army. He was disloyal to the president, keeping him in the dark, misleading him, and maneuvering to look good at Madison's expense. An air of political intrigue continually surrounded Armstrong, and many suspected, not incorrectly, that he was preparing to run for president.

In December 1813, Monroe urged Madison to fire Armstrong, accusing the secretary of botching the northern invasion and stabbing the president in the back. "[T]his man if continued in office will ruin not you and the administration only, but the whole republican party and cause," Monroe warned the president. But Madison, as usual, preferred to paper over differences rather than endure the political embarrassment in firing Armstrong. By 1814, Madison was left with an acrimonious cabinet that verged at times on paralysis.

Most disastrous was Armstrong's refusal to defend the nation's capital, which he steadfastly insisted would not be a target. He ignored pleas that the army build earthworks to defend Washington, insisting the focus be kept on Canada. In some respects, his hands were tied.

The administration had chosen to continue its offensive against Canada in 1814, despite repeated dismal failures and limited resources and troops. Diverting troops from the Canadian frontier to defend Washington was exactly what Cockburn and the British wanted, and Armstrong refused to do it.

Armstrong considered Madison a rank amateur in military matters and thought the president's orders to create a new command for Washington's defense silly. He was further miffed by Madison's selection of Brigadier General William Henry Winder to command the new military district. Monroe opposed Armstrong's choice, the far more experienced Brigadier General Moses Porter, apparently on no other grounds than that he was Armstrong's choice.

Armstrong reacted by washing his hands of the whole matter and drifted into sullen uncooperativeness. Despite Madison's orders, Armstrong told Winder he could only have 1,200 regular soldiers and that the balance of his command would have to come from militia. When Winder suggested calling up some militia immediately, Armstrong balked. It was best to wait until "the spur of the occasion" demanded their presence in battle, he insisted.

Winder feared that if called at the last moment, the militia would be of no more use than a "disorderly crowd," and asked Armstrong July 9 to immediately call out 4,000 militia. The secretary waited a week before begrudgingly authorizing Winder to call 3,000 militia into service.

Preoccupied by events in Europe and Canada, Madison did little to monitor the situation. Though evidence of Armstrong's failure to prepare for Washington's defense accumulated, the president was not willing to intervene. This reflected his habitual caution, but it was also a matter of principle. Unlike Abraham Lincoln a half century later, Madison was unwilling to seize strong executive power, determined not to undermine the foundations of republican government he and Jefferson had created.

But people in Washington could see nothing was being done, and they were growing angry. Dr. James H. Blake, mayor of Washington, complaining of "the defenseless state of this city," led a delegation of prominent citizens to meet with the president in mid-July and urge that more be done.

"For some weeks, the citizens have expected a visit from the British, and repeatedly called upon the Secretary of the War Department and the President for protection," Martha Peter wrote to a friend. "The first laughed at what he called their idle fears. The President said he was called on from all quarters for protection; that he could not protect everyone; and the District must take care of itself."

Even Dolley Madison was mystified by the lack of progress. "[O]ur preparations for defence by some means or other, is constantly retarded," she wrote on July 28, but the thought that her husband might bear some responsibility apparently did not cross her mind.

When an angry crowd gathered outside the President's House, Dolley was defiant. "[A]mong other exclamations & threats they say if Mr. M attempts to move from *this house*, in case of an attack, they will *stop him* & that he shall *fall with it*—I am not the least alarmed at these things, but entirely disgusted, & determined to stay with him."

O say can you see by the dawn's early
light so proudly we hail'd at the twilight's last gleaming
whose broad stripes & bright stars through the perilous fight
O'er the ramparts we watch'd were so gallantly streaming
And the rocket's red glare, the bomb bursting in air
Gave proof through the night that our flag was still there
O say does that star spangled banner yet wave
O'er the land of the free & the home of the brave

On the shore dimly seen through the mists of the deep
Where the foe's haughty host in dread silence reposes
What is that which the breeze, o'er the towering steep
As it fitfully blows, half conceals, half discloses
Now it catches the gleam of the morning's first beam
In full glory reflected now shines on the stream
Tis the star-spangled banner — O long may it wave
O'er the land of the free & the home of the brave

And where is that band who so vauntingly swore
That the havoc of war & the battle's confusion
A home & a Country should leave us no more
Their blood has wash'd out their foul footstep's pollution
No refuge could save the hireling & slave
From the terror of flight or the gloom of the grave
And the star-spangled banner in triumph doth wave
O'er the land of the free & the home of the brave

O thus be it ever when freemen shall stand
Between their lov'd home & the war's desolation
Blest with vict'ry & peace may the heav'n rescued land
Praise the power that hath made & preserv'd us a nation
Then conquer we must when our cause it is just
And this be our motto — "In God is our trust,"
And the star-spangled banner in triumph shall wave
O'er the land of the free & the home of the brave

Major General Robert Ross, a blue-eyed, forty-seven-year-old
Irishman with a handsome nose and cleft chin, had been personally
chosen by the Duke of Wellington to lead the expedition
to America's east coast.

*Portrait of Major General Robert Ross that hangs in the home
of his descendants in Rostrevor, Northern Ireland.*

CHAPTER 3

★

The British Invasion

THE BRITISH SQUADRON anchored near the mouth of the Potomac River was roused from a heat-induced Sunday lethargy when lookouts spotted sails coming up the Chesapeake Bay at 2 p.m. on August 14. No admiral's red ensign was flying, but the lead ship was soon recognized as the 80-gun HMS *Tonnant*, flagship of Vice Admiral Sir Alexander Cochrane, commander of the North American Station. Cochrane had lowered his admiral's flag, seeking to conceal his presence from the Americans. But it would be known soon enough.

Cochrane's hatred of America bordered on malevolence. "They are a whining, canting race, much like the spaniel and require the same treatment—[they] must be drubbed into good manners," he declared. It was a level of venom not seen in George Cockburn, who disdained the Americans but did not particularly despise them.

Cochrane's grudge dated back to the last war with the Americans, when his older brother, Major Charles Cochrane, with Cornwallis at the siege of Yorktown, peered over a parapet and was beheaded by an enemy cannonball.

Heavyset, with an oversize nose and curly hair, Cochrane was part of a Scottish clan with a long and noble line of military service, and carried himself with the dignified bearing of a man used to the privileges of his rank. He was accused of being greedy and callous, and some in England considered the entire family untrustworthy—"all

Cochrane's hatred of America bordered on malevolence. "They are a whining, canting race, much like the spaniel and require the same treatment—[they] must be drubbed into good manners," he declared.

Vice Admiral Sir Alexander Cochrane, commander of the British North American Station.

mad, money-getting and not truth-telling," as the naval hero Lord St. Vincent put it.

But Cochrane's biggest fault as a commander may have been an inability to make up his mind. "[H]is first resolves are generally correct but like his family his head is so full of schemes—that one destroys the other," Rear Admiral Pulteney Malcolm, commanding the expedition's troopships, complained to his wife.

While in Bermuda awaiting the arrival of reinforcements, Cochrane had spent many hours reviewing maps, concocting schemes, and pondering a long list of targets— New York, Philadelphia, Washington, Baltimore, Annapolis, Richmond, Norfolk, New England, Charlestown, Savannah, and New Orleans among them. Cochrane was sure about one thing: He was eager to lash out at the Americans. "I have it much at heart to give them a complete drubbing before Peace is made," he wrote.

Before departing Bermuda, Cochrane had received a report from Sir George Prevost, the British commander-in-chief in Canada, detailing how the Americans had waged war against civilians by burning mills and homes at Dover, on the north shore of Lake Erie, and asking Cochrane to retaliate. Cochrane was happy to have this justification for his already existing plans to devastate coastal cities, adding the attacks to his list of grievances against America. On July 18, Cochrane issued an order to the senior officers of the North American Station that would soon become infamous: "You are hereby required and directed to destroy & lay waste such Towns and Districts upon the Coast as you may find assailable."

But despite four months in Bermuda plotting destruction in America, Cochrane still had made no decision on where, when, or even if to attack. "I cannot at present acquaint their Lordships of what may be my future operations," Cochrane wrote to the Admiralty in London as *Tonnant* sailed into the Chesapeake. "[T]hey will depend much on the information I may receive in this quarter." That would depend on Cockburn.

Tonnant, a magnificent French ship-of-the-line captured at the Battle of the Nile by Lord Nelson, dropped anchor at 8:30. Cockburn wasted no time taking his gig to pay his respects to Vice Admiral Cochrane and General Ross.

The news was not good for Cockburn. Cochrane and Ross thought their force quite inadequate to launch any kind of a strike on the American capital and "appeared rather inclined to leave the Bay without even attempting a landing," according to Cockburn's later memoir. He went to work persuading them otherwise. Cockburn had served under Cochrane in the West Indies during the capture of Guadeloupe and Martinique in 1808 and 1809, and he knew how to handle the senior admiral.

Cockburn emphasized the paltry American defenses and pointedly reminded the new arrivals how much he had been able to accomplish with just 500 men. Reviewing his secret plan to capture the American capital, Cockburn proposed sailing the invasion force up the Patuxent River to the town of Benedict, which was the farthest that frigates or schooners could proceed before the river became too narrow and shallow. From Benedict, troops could be landed to attack Baltimore or Washington, the latter his preferred target.

Cockburn offered a new and tantalizing suggestion: Instead of marching straight to Washington, the army should move by land farther up the river, accompanied by navy barges, and hunt for Commodore Joshua Barney's flotilla, still lurking in the upper Patuxent. This would confuse the Americans and leave them unsure how to respond. Were the British targeting Washington, Baltimore, or Barney? After destroying the flotilla, the British commanders could decide whether to continue to Washington, based on the resistance they had met. At the very least, they would take care of Barney.

Retaliation for Canada was a good reason to use for motivating the troops, but the real purpose for an attack on Washington, as urged by Cockburn, was strategic: An invasion in the geographic heart of America should draw troops away from Canada. Capturing the capital would be a psychological blow to the country and might force the collapse of the government. Beyond the strategic goals, the city was home to a target that by itself was worthy of attack: the Washington Navy Yard, the oldest military installation in the country. The frigate *Columbia* and sloop-of-war *Argus* were under construction at the yard, which was also an important repair and supply center for the U.S. Navy.

Ross was dubious about sending his small force so far into American territory. The reports of disease in the Chesapeake were also frightening. While afloat, Ross was under the command of Cochrane, who would determine where the expedition would sail and what it would target. But once the target was chosen, Ross had the authority to veto landing his troops, in particular any operation he thought likely to fail or result in heavy casualties.

Ross's instructions from London were vague; he was to create a diversion somewhere "on the Coast of the United States of America" to relieve pressure on British troops operating in Canada. Lord Bathurst, the secretary of state for war and the colonies, had pointedly reminded Ross that the force was too small to take risks. Its size "will sufficiently point out to you that you are not to engage in any extended operations at a distance from the coast," Bathurst wrote. The minister wanted the troops kept healthy.

Based on his instructions, Ross had every reason to be skeptical about Cockburn's plan. Ross's staff officers, more so than the easygoing general, were jealously guarding the army commander's prerogatives. If the troops were landed, Ross would have sole command, not Cockburn, the "seageneral," as the sailors called him. British army Lieutenant George De Lacy Evans, the expedition quartermaster, was privately dismissive of the navy's intelligence about the Americans, and considered the available maps and knowledge of local roads woefully deficient.

That said, Evans, the most aggressive of Ross's subordinates, admitted that the army officers' own ideas "zealously coincided" with Cockburn's plan. In particular, they favored targeting Washington "on account of the greater political effect likely to result," he later wrote.

Cockburn proposed a raid the following morning on the shores of the Potomac, and he invited Ross along to see the state of American defenses. Cochrane approved, and Ross accepted the invitation.

Cockburn would personally show Ross how easy it would be.

Major General Robert Ross, a blue-eyed, forty-seven-year-old Irishman with a handsome nose and cleft chin, had been personally chosen by the Duke of Wellington to lead the expedition to America's east coast. He had been major general for only one year but had proven to be a brave and daring officer, with an even temperament that Wellington believed made him well suited for independent command. Ross had made an indelible name for himself in 1807 at Maida, in Calabria in southern Italy, when he rushed forward with the famed 20th Regiment on a flank attack that routed the French and almost single-handedly turned the tide of the battle.

Ross shone in one battle after another during the Peninsular War— the struggle with Napoleon for control of Portugal and Spain—from Vitoria, where he was awarded the gold medal for bravery, to Pamplona, where two horses were shot from underneath him. Though he was a strict disciplinarian, Ross's straightforward manner and fair-mindedness had won him the undying loyalty of his troops.

Wellington was fond of Ross, Anglo-Irish like himself; they had played together as boys in Dublin. But Wellington did not play favorites, and it was Ross's superb performance in the Peninsula that earned his selection to lead the expedition to America.

It was an honor Ross likely could have done without. He was still recovering from a serious wound suffered at Orthez, in southern France, in late February 1814, when he was hit in the neck attacking a French position during one of Wellington's final victories in the Peninsular War. Ross blithely described "the hit I got in the chops" as a mere inconvenience, but it nearly killed him.

His wife, Elizabeth Catherine Glascock Ross—or Ly, as he called her—was at Bilbao on the north coast of Spain when she learned he had been wounded. She left their infant son with a nurse and set out on a mule across the snowy Pyrenees to reach her husband, lying in grave condition at the army headquarters in St.-Jean-de-Luz, France. "Her anxiety and spirit carried her through, enabling her to bear the fatigue without suffering from cold or bad weather," Ross proudly wrote his brother-in-law when she arrived. Elizabeth had expected to return to Ireland with her recovering husband and their baby to rejoin their two older children following Napoleon's abdication in April. But Ross had been unable to turn down the command, and on June 3, he sailed unhappily from Bordeaux.

During the nearly eight-week journey across the ocean to Bermuda, Ross wrote letters assuring his wife that America would quickly seek peace. "Be therefore my Ly more cheerful," he wrote in June; "do not look upon the black side of the picture but be *convinced* of our speedily meeting again then our happiness will be heightened my Ly by our temporary separation."

POTOMAC RIVER, MONDAY, AUGUST 15

At 2 a.m., the Royal Marines aboard HMS *Menelaus* and other ships across the squadron were roused from their slumber. Another raid was imminent. By 3:30, they were alongside Rear Admiral Cockburn's flagship, *Albion*, loading the landing boats. When a large and cheerful army officer hopped into one of the boats, joining Cockburn and his Royal Marines, it was clear that this raid would be different.

The sun had just risen when Robert Ross stepped for the first time onto American soil on the banks of the St. Mary's River, which flowed into the lower Potomac from southern Maryland. Moving ashore, Cockburn's raiding party encountered plenty of bullocks, geese, sheep, and turkeys, but "nothing of the enemy," an officer reported. That was not surprising. Cockburn had gone ashore in the same place just three nights earlier, scaring off the local militia and burning a warehouse near Leonardtown. Residents were in no mood for more.

Cockburn took Ross well inland, displaying the complete British command of the territory, and he showed off the Royal Marines' skills maneuvering through thick woods. Ross felt at home, giving Cockburn tips on how to handle infantry. He and Cockburn established a quick rapport. They shared a certain élan, each insisting upon leading from the front. The admiral used the time ashore to press Ross for an attack on Washington.

That evening, Cockburn reported to Cochrane that he had only encountered "the same quiet and submissive conduct on the part of the inhabitants." The new arrivals were impressed, not least because the raiding party showed no sign of fever. The raid had served its purpose. Ross and Cochrane would set Cockburn's plan in motion, as soon as the fleet arrived with the troops.

CHESAPEAKE BAY, TUESDAY, AUGUST 16

Early Tuesday morning, a U.S. Navy lookout at Cape Henry, at the mouth of the Chesapeake Bay, peered through a spyglass and saw a mighty enemy force sailing in from the Atlantic Ocean—3 ships-of-the-line, 7 transports, 7 frigates, as well as assorted brigs, razes, and schooners—at least 22 ships in all.

Rear Admiral Pulteney Malcolm, commanding the fleet from the 74-gun ship-of-the-line HMS *Royal Oak*, received signaled instructions to press up the bay. The fleet swept past Norfolk, to the relief of residents and surprise of the troops on board, who had supposed the city would be their first target. The ships, moving much faster than messengers could travel on horseback, continued north on a steady breeze. "The sight is glorious, an English fleet standing up the enemy's Bay with all sail set, filled with troops panting to meet the enemy," Army Lieutenant George Gleig, aboard HMS *Diadem*, wrote in his diary.

Aboard the ships was a small but potent force from four experienced and disciplined regiments. About half the men were veterans of the Peninsular War who had earned the proud name of Wellington's Invincibles. After six long and bloody years of fighting through Portugal and Spain, the duke's magnificent army had crossed the Pyrenees and marched into France in the spring of 1814. "I could have done anything with that army," Wellington later said.

The 4th Regiment of Foot—the King's Own Royal Regiment—was a centuries-old unit that had shed blood in America at Concord and Bunker Hill. Under Wellington, they had burnished their record with legendary charges at Badajoz, Vitoria, and Salamanca. The 44th Regiment of Foot had a history in America dating to the French and Indian War, when it marched west with General Edward Braddock and was nearly massacred near present-day Pittsburgh, before retreating to safety under the leadership of a young George Washington. The 44th had fought Napoleon's forces in Egypt, Holland, and Spain, though not under Wellington's command. The 85th (Bucks Volunteers) Light Infantry Regiment, raised for service against France, had fought in the Netherlands and West Indies before joining Wellington in the Pyrenees. Sailing separately from the Mediterranean was a battalion from the 21st (Royal North British Fusilier) Regiment of Foot with a wealth of combat experience in Italy. The troops from the four regiments were tough and formidable fighters; but numbering less than 4,000, with no cavalry and a single artillery detachment, they were a mere wisp of Wellington's army.

Crammed aboard dirty transports, living below the waterline in nearly airless compartments, enduring squalls, dreadful heat, and an alarming outbreak of typhus fever, the troops had plenty of time to build a deep dislike of America for this war that was keeping them from home. The wind carrying the expeditionary force up the Chesapeake on August 16 held steady all day, and by 7 p.m. the men saw Cochrane and Cockburn's waiting ships, anchored near the mouth of the Potomac. The thunderous boom of naval guns echoed over the water, saluting the arriving forces. The largest enemy fleet ever seen in the upper Chesapeake was now complete.

POINT LOOKOUT, MARYLAND, DAWN, WEDNESDAY, AUGUST 17

The morning light brought an astonishing sight for Thomas Swann, an American military observer stationed at the aptly named Point Lookout, on the north shore of the Potomac. The British fleet anchored off the point had grown dramatically overnight. Ships-of-the-line, transports, bomb ships, frigates, schooners, sloops-of-war, and other vessels were spread over two miles. He counted at least 46 ships.

Swann wrote a brief message to Secretary of War John Armstrong and gave it to a courier to race seventy miles to Washington on horseback. The size of the fleet and the proportion of transports pointed clearly in one direction: an invasion was coming.

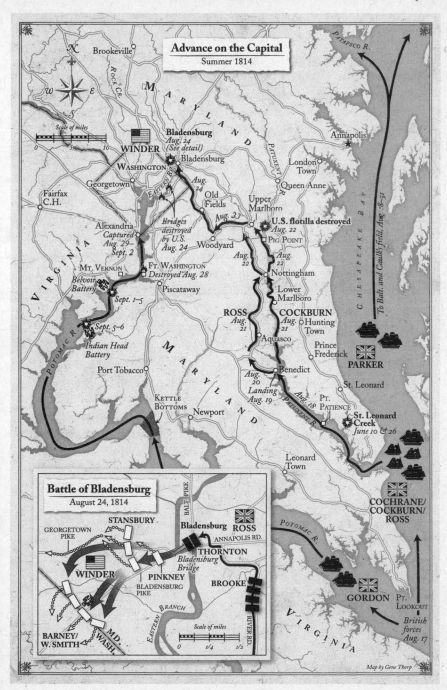

Advance on the Capital
Summer 1814

Brookeville

MARYLAND

Rock Cr.

Patapsco R.

N
W   E
S

Scale of miles
0   5   10

Bladensburg
Aug. 24
(See detail)

WINDER

Bladensburg

WASHINGTON

Fairfax
C.H.

Georgetown

Eastern Br.

*Aug.
24*

Old
Fields

Aug. 23

Upper
Marlboro

Annapolis

London
Town

Queen Anne

Patuxent R.

Alexandria
Captured
Aug. 29–
Sept. 2

VIRGINIA

Bridges
destroyed
by U.S.
Aug. 24

Woodyard

U.S. flotilla destroyed
Aug. 22

Pig Point

*Aug.
22*

*Aug.
22*

C H E S A P E A K E   B A Y

To Balt. and Gault's field, Aug. 8–31

Mt. Vernon
Belvoir
Battery
Sept. 1–5

Ft. Washington
Destroyed Aug. 28

Piscataway

Nottingham

Lower
Marlboro

ROSS
*Aug.
21*

COCKBURN
*Aug.
21*

Hunting
Town

Potomac R.

Sept. 5–6

Indian Head
Battery

Port Tobacco

MARYLAND

Aquasco

Prince
Frederick

PARKER

*Aug.
20*

Landing
Aug. 19

Benedict

Aug. 18

Patuxent R.

St. Leonard

Pt.
Patience

**St. Leonard
Creek**
June 10 & 26

KETTLE
BOTTOMS

Newport

Leonard
Town

COCHRANE/
COCKBURN/
ROSS

Battle of Bladensburg
August 24, 1814

BALT. PIKE

GEORGETOWN
PIKE

STANSBURY

Bladensburg

ROSS

ANNAPOLIS RD.

THORNTON

Bladensburg
Bridge

Potomac R.

WINDER

PINKNEY

BLADENSBURG
PIKE

BROOKE

Eastern Branch

RIVER RD.

Scale of miles
0   1/4   1/2

BARNEY/
W. SMITH

MD.
WASH.

VIRGINIA

GORDON

Pt.
Lookout

*British
forces
Aug. 17*

Map by Gene Thorp

Chesapeake Bay, 8 a.m., Wednesday, August 17

The paneled great cabin of *Tonnant* was awash with blue-coated senior Royal Navy officers Wednesday morning. Four admirals were present—Cochrane, Cockburn, Malcolm, and Rear Admiral Edward Codrington, captain of the fleet—joined by some twenty captains of the battle fleet who had been rowed in from their respective ships. Ross and his small army staff were outnumbered, but a comity of spirit prevailed between the services as they examined "bad maps" and reviewed the plan for invasion.

The troopships, along with much of the fleet, would sail up the Patuxent to Benedict, with Ross taking charge of the expedition once the soldiers landed. Accompanied by a naval force in boats and barges under Cockburn, the British would first target Barney's flotilla. The next target, if all went well, was much bolder: the capital of the United States. Ross had refused to commit to an attempt on Washington, but he had not ruled it out.

As proposed by Cockburn, a squadron led by Captain James Gordon would create a diversion up the Potomac, attacking any fortifications along the river and threatening Alexandria, Virginia, and Washington from the south. If needed, the ships of the Potomac squadron could evacuate the invading land forces. But Cochrane added his own twist: a second feint up the Chesapeake Bay. Captain Peter Parker would take several ships up the bay, hoping to draw troops away from Washington. Parker would also disrupt communications between Baltimore and Philadelphia, furthering the confusion.

The briefing was over by 9 a.m., and the officers quickly dispersed to their respective vessels. Signals were sent to weigh anchor and raise sails. Within fifteen minutes, Gordon set sail into the Potomac aboard the 38–gun frigate *Sea-Horse*, accompanied by seven ships packed with firepower. Parker, aboard *Menelaus,* prepared to move up the bay with two schooners. The rest of the fleet was preparing to sail north toward the mouth of the Patuxent when the horizon darkened and the water whipped up, as if before a tempest. Then, as quickly as it had arisen, the storm threat dissipated, and the fleet was under way.

The city of Washington slumbered on the morning of August 18, 1814, as was usually the case any time Congress was out of session. Even James Madison, not the most social of men, described Washington as "a solitude" in the summer. The capital, now fourteen years old, had grown a bit since the days of John Adams's administration, when the Abbé José Correia da Serra, the minister from Portugal, called Washington "the city of magnificent distances," and another observer described Pennsylvania Avenue as "a mud-hole almost equal to the great Serbonian bog."

Washington's population had reached 8,208 by the 1810 census, not including the 4,900 residents of Georgetown, which was within the District boundary, or the 7,200 people across the Potomac in Alex-

The President's House and the Capitol stood in the open like ancient Greek temples, with only scattered dwellings and buildings nearby, surrounded mostly by fields of wheat, corn, and tobacco.

The U.S. Capitol in 1814.

andria, also then part of the capital. But Washington itself remained a city of villages.

The capital's elite, which included high-ranking government officials, foreign diplomats, military officers, and a native gentry of plantation families, were a "detestably proud" group, in the words of one visitor. The city's good-size middle class included tradesmen, shopkeepers, and government clerks, some from families long settled in the area, others from more recent English and German immigrant stock. Lower-class whites, many of them laborers and indentured servants of Irish or northern European descent who worked laying out the streets and constructing buildings, lived in shacks and shanties scattered around town. A quarter of the city's population was African American, including about 1,400 slaves and 800 free blacks, living in shacks, some in small clusters, and others in the shadows of fine homes.

Washington was a curious mixture of hovels and mansions, about nine hundred scattered buildings, ranging from the elegant Octagon on New York Avenue to rude shacks that housed slaves. The President's House and the Capitol stood in the open like ancient Greek temples, with only scattered dwellings and buildings nearby, surrounded mostly by fields of wheat, corn, and tobacco. Sheep and cattle grazed in pastures, bordered by woods of oak trees and tulip poplars. "It was no trophy of war for a great nation," Richard Rush, Madison's attorney general, later wrote. "Our infant metropolis at that time had the aspect of merely a straggling village but for the size and beauty of its public buildings."

The village awoke with a start at 8 a.m. Thursday, when a rider kicking up dust rushed to the plain brick building housing the State, War, and Navy departments, just west of the President's House on Pennsylvania Avenue. He was carrying the message sent the previous morning from Point Lookout, warning of the growing enemy fleet.

Secretary of State Monroe hurried to the President's House to confer. "This city is their object," Monroe told Madison, who agreed. The secretary offered to lead a troop of cavalry to scout the size of the enemy force, try to gauge their target, and send back reports on their movements. It was a most unusual role for a secretary of state to undertake, but Madison, desperate for intelligence, approved, and Monroe began assembling a scouting force to depart the next day.

Working from his makeshift headquarters on the first floor of the McKeown Hotel, at the corner of Sixth Street and Pennsylvania Avenue, Brigadier General William Winder, the commander of the Tenth Military District, sent out a flurry of orders. The District militia was called en masse, and thousands more militia troops were requisitioned from Maryland, Virginia, and Pennsylvania.

Winder had been a whirlwind of activity in the seven weeks since his appointment to lead Washington's defenses, but he had accomplished virtually nothing. Few troops had been raised, no defenses erected, and no plan of defense developed.

Nothing close to the 15,000 men Madison had ordered to the field or held in immediate readiness was available. Winder had been given authority on July 17 to call out 3,000 militia, but thus far he had managed to round up a grand total of 250 men. Moreover, Secretary of War Armstrong had provided Winder with barely 600 army regulars, not even a third of what Madison had ordered. At best, if 1,400 militiamen stationed in Baltimore were counted, Winder had about 2,100 men immediately available for Washington's defense.

Winder, a thin man whose sharp features and wispy brown hair gave him an elfin look, was showing every sign of being overwhelmed by the responsibility. It was no simple matter to pick a good general, Jefferson lamented after the war's disastrous first year. "The Creator has not thought proper to mark those on the forehead who are of the stuff to make good generals," he wrote. "We are first, therefore, to seek them, blindfolded, and then let them learn the trade at the expense of great losses."

Any marks of greatness the thirty-nine-year-old Winder had displayed thus far were as a Baltimore attorney, not a general. In a state that had many brilliant lawyers, the urbane and amiable Winder was considered at the top of the profession. Though a Federalist, he supported going to war and volunteered his services; Madison, eager to broaden political support for the war, tendered Winder a commission in March 1812 as a lieutenant colonel in the regular army, though the lawyer had only limited militia experience.

"The Creator has not thought proper to mark those on the forehead who are of the stuff to make good generals," Jefferson lamented.

Brigadier General William Winder, commander of the Tenth Military District.

After war was declared, Winder marched an infantry regiment from Maryland to the Niagara front, where his relative competence and unquestioned bravery won him promotion to brigadier. But in June 1813, after American forces invaded Canada across the Niagara frontier, Winder blundered into enemy lines during a British night counterattack at Stoney Creek, on the shore of Lake Ontario, and was captured.

The British considered him a particularly valuable prisoner. "Be careful of exchanging *Genl. Winder*," a British officer warned. "He possesses more talent than all the rest of the Yankee Generals put together." This said more about the other American commanders than it did about Winder. Lieutenant Colonel Winfield Scott, who served with him on the Niagara front, had a more sour view of Winder's abilities. "It is a misfortune to begin a new career with too much rank, or rather, too late in life," Scott later said.

Winder was held as a prisoner for nearly a year in Quebec, where he put his skills as a lawyer to work, negotiating a prisoner reparation agreement that defused a tense stand-off between the U.S. and British governments. Released in the spring of 1814, Winder arrived in Washington in late June, just as the president was looking for someone to command the new military district overseeing Washington's defenses.

Madison and Monroe were reasonably satisfied with Winder's negotiations with the British. More relevant was the fact that the general's uncle, Levin Winder, happened to be governor of Maryland, a state bitterly divided over the war. It would be up to Maryland to supply a large part of the militia needed to defend the capital. Despite Armstrong's objections, Madison and Monroe calculated that the appointment of William Winder as commander was the best way to ensure that the governor, a Federalist lukewarm at best in his support for the war, sent the needed troops.

Winder's inexperience quickly showed. He embarked on a lengthy tour of his new command, intently studying the terrain, examining defenses, and issuing batches of memos. In one eighteen-day span, he traveled about Maryland, visiting Baltimore, Annapolis, Upper Marlboro, Nottingham, Piscataway, Warburton, and Port Tobacco, some of them two or three times. Instead of raising troops or developing a coherent strategy, he immersed himself in details. In the meantime, no defenses were built in or around Washington. The city "had no fortresses or sign of any; not a cannon was mounted," Attorney General Rush later said.

Moreover, no states supplied anywhere near the number of militia requested. Even Winder's uncle held back, unwilling to send militia needed to defend Maryland's towns and shores from Cockburn's raids. Virginia was in a similar position. Pennsylvania temporarily lacked the authority to call out its militia because the state was in the midst of changing its laws.

As for the District of Columbia militia, none of its 2,000 militia troops were on duty as the British sailed up the Patuxent. Major General John Van Ness, the commander of the District militia, had suggested his brigades be rotated on to duty to keep troops available, but Armstrong had refused, insisting the men were close enough to summon in an emergency.

That emergency was clearly at hand.

PATUXENT RIVER, THURSDAY, AUGUST 18

The mighty British fleet—ships-of-the-line, frigates, schooners, and brigs, all flying the red and white flag of Britain and festooned with long and tapering pendants—sailed into the mouth of the Patuxent River at 5 a.m. Thursday. No American force challenged them, but the river did its best to hold the invaders at bay. After hours of sailing, the British had made little progress against a flood tide, strong current, and shifting winds. The ships laboriously worked their way back and forth across the river, passing one another on opposite tacks.

No one appreciated the spectacle more than the soldiers. "[T]he decks of all the vessels thronged with troops arrayed for landing," wrote Captain George Laval Chesterton, an army artillery officer aboard one of the transports. Many were getting their first good look at America, and they were astonished at the beauty of the Patuxent landscape, admiring the fields of Indian corn, the luxuriant pastures, and the neat plantations, all surrounded by boundless forests.

By mid-morning, the wind had died completely, forcing the fleet to anchor below Point Patience, where the channel narrowed and the tidal stream strengthened. Commanders fretted they were losing the element of surprise. Cochrane sent signals for troops to be ready to land at a moment's notice. Troops were to pack lightly, carrying a blanket, an extra shirt, a pair of shoes, and stockings. Three pounds of pork and two and a half pounds of biscuit were issued to each man. Cartouche boxes were filled with fresh ammunition and arms and accoutrements handed out.

The big ships would not be able to sail much farther up the river, and Cochrane used the delay to move troops to the frigates and lighter vessels. He transferred his command from *Tonnant* to join Ross aboard the lighter-draft frigate *Iphigenia*.

Finally, in late afternoon, a breeze kicked in from the southwest, and the fleet moved upriver, aided by the tide. The course grew more tortuous as the Patuxent narrowed and grew shallower. It was an intricate ballet calling for extraordinary seamanship and coordination. Occasionally a ship would run aground, but the crews would quickly free it. "The air literally resounded with the shrill pipe of the boatswain; and the loud, but measured, cadences of the men in the chains, who hove the lead and shouted forth the soundings," wrote Chesterton.

Eventually the ships-of-the-line could go no farther and anchored, and the frigates soon followed suit. The smaller ships continued upriver until darkness set, anchoring a few miles below Benedict. Word spread that they would land in the morning.

Those who had not been part of Cockburn's force for the previous year expected the Americans to attack. Codrington, captain of the fleet, considered it "comparatively extraordinary" that the Americans had not taken advantage of the terrain to do so. At several points, the high, wooded banks offered spots where artillery could do tremendous damage to the crowded, slow-moving ships below.

But there was nothing, no sign of the Americans.

Moving by land and water up the Patuxent, the combined army and navy
forces appeared to spell doom for Barney and his flotilla.

*Map showing the route of the British from the Patuxent River
to Washington, published in 1818.*

CHAPTER 4

─── ★ ───

What the Devil Will They Do Here?

THE FIRST LANDING boats were lowered well before dawn into the dark waters of the Patuxent River, and by first light, there was movement throughout the fleet. Soldiers clambered down to the boats, carrying their weapons and haversacks stuffed with three days' provisions and spare clothes. The British invasion was under way.

In no time, the Patuxent was covered with a flotilla of barges and launches, all heading up the river. The current and tide ran strongly against them, and those disembarking from the bigger ships anchored downriver faced a stiff row of up to fifteen miles. Cockburn was in the first wave, leaving *Albion* at 4 a.m. to travel by barge a dozen miles to Benedict.

At Benedict, the gun brig *Anaconda* lay 150 yards off the beach, moored with spring cables. Her broadside faced the shore, her guns loaded with grape and round shot to pepper the beach with deadly fire should the British face any resistance. But when the first boats landed at noon, not a whisper of opposition was to be found. Light infantry scouts checked some three dozen houses in the town as well as farmhouses in the countryside for several miles around, and found them empty, with signs of being hastily abandoned. The town of tidy wood-frame houses and neat gardens was the biggest tobacco port on the Patuxent and one of the oldest in Maryland, though its golden era as a prosperous trade and shipping center dated to colonial days. Benedict had been sacked and burned by Loyalist troops at the end of the Revolutionary War and no one wanted a second episode.

As waves of troops landed, Ross established pickets and sent infantry to secure the heights around town. After many weeks confined to the ships, the men rolled on the sand, basked in the sun, and prepared camps. Given how long it would take to land his entire force from the distant ships, Ross did not intend to march that day. He used the time to organize his jumbled force into three brigades. The Light Brigade, which included the 85th Light Infantry bolstered by light companies from the other regiments as well as the Colonial Marines, would lead the way, under the command of Colonel William Thornton. The 2nd Brigade, under Colonel Arthur Brooke, included troops from the 4th and 44th regiments. The 3rd Brigade, commanded by Lieutenant Colonel William Patterson, included a battalion of Fusiliers and a battalion of Royal Marines. Rounding out the force were assorted artillerymen, engineers, and teamsters, along with a contingent of 100 sailors from *Tonnant* to haul guns and supplies. A half-dozen nervous horses for the senior officers, including Ross's favorite Arabian from the Peninsula campaign, were off-loaded by canvas sling. All told, the British force numbered about 4,500 men.

"Such is the little army with which we invade America," Lieutenant Gleig recorded in his diary.

NOTTINGHAM, MIDDAY FRIDAY, AUGUST 19

Ten miles upriver from Benedict, Commodore Joshua Barney was holed up at his headquarters in Nottingham, another Patuxent tobacco town. He had received no word that the British were just landing at Benedict; an officer who arrived at 9 a.m. with a scouting report knew nothing about it. But the officer did have detailed information about the size of the enemy fleet sailing up the river, and he reported that the British had "a determination to go to the city of Washington." Furthermore, the officer reported a teasing threat from Cockburn: "The admiral said he would dine in Washington on Sunday, after having destroyed the Flotilla. . . ."

That was typical of Cockburn, but also very worrisome, as far as Barney was concerned. He immediately dashed off a note to Secretary

Jones reporting Cockburn's unsettling words and sent it by courier to Washington.

Barney knew well how eager Cockburn was to even the score with the commodore after the American breakout from St. Leonard Creek two months earlier. Barney had been jubilant at the time. "[W]e have again beat them," he proudly told Jones. But it was not seen as a great victory in southern Maryland, particularly when the British launched more terrifying, punitive raids to draw the flotilla out of hiding. Throughout the region, civilians blamed Barney for bringing the wrath of Cockburn upon their heads. In Calvert County along the Patuxent, it was a close call who was more unpopular, Barney or James Madison. "[W]hen I tell you the mischief the British have done," Thomas King wrote his brother, "it will be enough to make you and every man abuse Jim Madison and old Barney in Hell if you could."

WASHINGTON, 2 P.M., FRIDAY, AUGUST 19

Navy Secretary Jones was unsure what to make of Barney's report or Cockburn's boast. Washington remained ignorant Friday afternoon that the British had begun landing troops that day at Benedict, forty miles from the capital. Jones, like others, suspected that the British move up the Patuxent was a ruse. "Appearances indicate a design on this place, but it may be a feint, to mask a real design on Baltimore," the secretary wrote to Barney upon receiving the commodore's report at 2 p.m.

Nevertheless, Jones ordered three of the navy's top officers—Captains John Rodgers, David Porter, and Oliver Perry—to hurry to Washington from points along the east coast with "all the disposable force within reach as soon as possible."

Another report arrived in Washington with news that the British were sailing up the Potomac. To General Winder, that suggested that Washington, and not Baltimore, was the British target. Winder ordered militia commanders in Baltimore to bring a rifle battalion and two companies of artillery to Washington "without the loss of a moment." He also ordered the District militia to report that evening for inspection.

Winder hurried to confer with Secretary of War Armstrong, offering a string of suggestions to address "the destitute condition" of Washington's defenses: Bring the Marine Corps into service and add them to his command. Sink vessels in the Potomac to hinder the enemy advance up that river. Make a patriotic appeal for volunteers. Get the flotilla men off the useless barges and put them in a position to defend Washington.

But Armstrong insisted Washington was safe and that Baltimore must be the target. "By God, they would not come with such a fleet without meaning to strike somewhere, but they certainly will not come here," Armstrong told Major General Van Ness, the District of Columbia militia commander. "[W]hat the devil will they do here?"

Secretary of State Monroe—or Colonel Monroe, as he now preferred to be called—had assembled two dozen dragoons from the Alexandria militia for his scouting mission, and decided to search for the British at Annapolis, where the enemy had been spotted moving up the bay. Early in the afternoon, Monroe and his dragoons took off. But they had not gone far when a courier caught up with them carrying the report from Barney. The secretary of state and his riders changed course, heading south toward Benedict, on the Patuxent River, to look for the British.

Tall and slim, with a full head of hair, the red-faced and rawboned Virginian remained full of vigor at age fifty-five. More than thirty-five years had passed since Monroe, a student from a second-tier planter family in Westmoreland County, Virginia, left the College of William and Mary in 1776 to join the Continental Army. He was nearly killed charging Hessian lines during Washington's surprise attack

Tall and slim, with a full head of hair, the red-faced and rawboned Virginian remained full of vigor.

James Monroe, circa 1819.

at Trenton that Christmas, and after recovering from his wound, served at Brandywine, Germantown, and through the bitter winter at Valley Forge.

Monroe had gone on to an impressive political and diplomatic career, including stints as U.S. senator, minister to France, England, and Spain, secretary of state, secretary of war, and governor of Virginia. His success came not least because of his knack of making good friends, chief among them Jefferson and Madison. Jefferson had taken Monroe under his wing to study law, fostered his political career, and even urged the younger man to purchase land for a home within view of Monticello, where they could create "a society to our taste."

But Monroe's three-decade-old friendship with Madison had been deeply strained during the latter years of Jefferson's presidency, when Monroe, serving as an envoy, was insulted by roughshod treatment from then–Secretary of State Madison. Monroe's own presidential ambitions led him to flirt with a challenge to Madison in the 1808 election to succeed Jefferson. "I have ever viewed Mr. Madison and yourself as two principal pillars of my happiness," a distraught Jefferson wrote to Monroe. "Were either to be withdrawn, I should consider it as among the greatest calamities which could assail my future peace of mind." In the end, Monroe backed off, and his reconciliation with Madison, engineered by Jefferson, led to Monroe's appointment as secretary of state in 1811.

But from the day war was declared, Monroe was not happy in the job, feeling removed from the action. He was desperate for military glory, eager to burnish his presidential credentials as next in line in the Virginia dynasty, following in the footsteps of Washington, Jefferson, and Madison. Moreover, Armstrong's abysmal performance as secretary of war had left a vacuum in the country's military leadership, and Monroe was confident he could fill it.

Monroe had grasped at the arrival of the British as a chance to serve as a scout. "I had a horror, at remaining here, to be involved indiscriminately in the censure, which would attach to others, and which so eminently belonged to the Secry. of War," he wrote to his son-in-law, George W. Hay, a few weeks later. Sensing disaster, he wanted to do anything—go anywhere—except stay in Washington.

GHENT, FRIDAY, AUGUST 19

At 3 p.m., the American delegates entered within the thick, dank walls of the Chartreux Convent for a meeting hastily called by the British commissioners at their quarters in the old Flemish capital.

The very makeup of the American delegation in the city of bustling canals and splendid medieval architecture underscored the eagerness with which the United States was seeking peace. Its head was the brilliant but humorless John Quincy Adams, son of the former president, whose experience as a diplomat went back to the revolutionary days, when he had served as his father's secretary in Paris. Henry Clay, the war hawk who had overpowered John Randolph's opposition to win a declaration of war, had resigned as House speaker to join the delegation, hoping he could salvage an honorable peace. The presence of Albert Gallatin, Madison's close confidant, spoke of the president's devout hope for a negotiated settlement to the war. The two other commissioners, Senator James Bayard of Delaware and diplomat Jonathan Russell, completed a most formidable group.

They faced a British delegation, led by Under Secretary for War and the Colonies Henry Goulburn, eager to impose humiliating terms on America. The British had kept the Americans stewing in steamy Ghent for weeks over the summer before even showing up. With an expeditionary force on its way to punish the United States, the British had no reason to rush. The longer they waited, and the more crushing the American defeats, the more bargaining power they would have.

As soon as the Americans took their seats, they realized no peace was in the offing. The cordial British manner of previous meetings over the last eleven days had disappeared. Goulburn had received a dispatch from London elaborating on British terms for peace. An independent Indian state be must be "permanently established" from an enormous swath of American territory. This 250,000-square-mile buffer state between the United States and Canada would encompass most of present-day Indiana, Illinois, Wisconsin, and Michigan, plus much of Ohio and Minnesota. While the British were willing to negotiate the exact borders, the creation of the state was sine qua non: not negotiable.

The U.S. delegation was stunned. At least one hundred thousand American settlers lived in that territory, some with roots dating back a century. What would happen to them? Gallatin asked. Those Americans "would have to make their own arrangements and provide for themselves," the British replied. Furthermore, the United States would be prohibited from keeping an armed naval force on the Great Lakes, and it must abandon all forts on those shores. Great Britain, on the other hand, would retain such rights. The British also insisted on free navigation of the Mississippi River, even though it ran entirely within American territory.

Agreement along the British terms would permanently stunt American growth to the west and leave the nation's military forces on the frontier impotent in the face of British power. Bayard viewed them as conqueror's demands. Clay suspected the British had no interest in a treaty. The terms were unmistakable evidence of the confidence the British had in the expeditionary force they had sent to United States, as well as their disdain for the Americans.

The meeting ended in an hour. The discouraged Americans gathered at their residence on the Rue des Champs to compose a note to Washington. "We need hardly say that the demands of Great Britain will receive from us an unanimous and decided negative," Gallatin wrote on behalf of the delegation. "And we have felt it our duty immediately to apprize you, by this hasty, but correct sketch of our last conference, that there is not at present, any hope of peace."

WASHINGTON, 9 A.M., SATURDAY, AUGUST 20

The ragtag troops of the District of Columbia militia gathered on the Capitol grounds Saturday morning, but it was not at all evident that they were prepared to march for war. The troops of the 1st Columbian Brigade, disorganized and in disgraceful shape, had failed inspection the previous evening. Some lacked guns, others shoes, and some both. Winder had sent them home with orders to report back the next morning equipped and ready to march. After a long night with "every exertion" by officers, the troops reported back Saturday morning in only marginally better condition.

Captain John J. Stull's rifle company had been issued old squirrel guns two years earlier, which the captain complained were useless. Stull had personally appealed to Armstrong for rifles from a large stockpile sitting unused in the Washington arsenal, but Armstrong replied that the rifles were needed on the Canadian front. The secretary suggested the men instead fix the squirrel guns. "I left him with indignation," Stull recalled.

In all, about 1,070 District men mustered on Saturday, ranging from the well-heeled, blue-uniformed volunteers of Major Peter's Georgetown light artillery to common militia conscripts, many of them poorly trained farmers and tradesmen lacking uniforms.

Adding to the chaos, Major General Van Ness chose this late moment to resign as commander of the District militia, refusing to serve under Winder—who as a brigadier general had lower rank, but had overall command as a regular army officer. Van Ness was replaced by one of the District militia's brigade commanders, Brigadier General Walter Smith.

As the forces mustered, Winder conferred with his staff at his headquarters in McKeown's Hotel. The three directions of British attack—up the Chesapeake, up the Potomac, and up the Patuxent—had paralyzed the American commander.

At 11:30 a.m. Saturday, a courier handed Navy Secretary Jones a message from Commodore Barney reporting that a large British force had begun landing at Benedict at noon Friday and had continued building up through the day. "No doubt their object is Washington, and perhaps the flotilla," Barney wrote.

It was the first anyone in Washington had heard that British troops had landed on American soil. Jones immediately sent orders to Barney: Should the British move on the flotilla, he should destroy the boats and bring his men to Washington. Then the navy secretary rushed to Winder's headquarters to share the news with the general.

A landing at Benedict pointed to Washington as a more likely target than Baltimore or Annapolis. But Winder remained uncertain, and decided to lead the District militia into Maryland to the Woodyard plantation, located at a key junction about fifteen miles east of the Capitol and one-third of the way to Benedict. From this central location, within two hours' march to both the Potomac and Patuxent rivers, Winder would await further intelligence on the British movements.

While the men milled about Capitol Hill awaiting orders, uplifting news arrived from the Niagara front, where British forces trying to capture Fort Erie had met disastrous defeat. Major Peter's artillery fired its guns in salute, and the infantry troops contributed their own noisy *feu de joi*. The men enthusiastically listened to a proclamation from Winder promising to "teach our haughty foe that freemen are never unprepared to expel from their soil the insolent foot of the invader."

At 2 p.m., the army moved out, the men's courage bolstered by the gun salutes and bold rhetoric. They marched east on Pennsylvania Avenue from Capitol Hill, crossed the Eastern Branch Bridge, and continued into the Maryland countryside. Stull's riflemen, still lacking guns, were promised muskets once they reached the Woodyard. They fell into the ranks, armed only with tomahawks.

Aquasco, Maryland, midday Saturday, August 20

From his hilltop position near an old gristmill at Aquasco, three miles northwest of Benedict, James Monroe could make out little about the British invaders, who remained camped outside the village Saturday morning. Monroe dared not move too close to enemy picket lines. It would hardly do for the secretary of state to be captured by the British, a consideration he and the president seemed to have ignored when he left on his scouting mission.

Nor did it help that Colonel Monroe had failed to bring along a spyglass and was unable to count the enemy ships. After five hours, with the British showing no sign of leaving Benedict, Monroe grew restless. He hastily scribbled a note to Madison at 1 p.m., reporting he was unable to gauge the size of the enemy force. "The general idea . . . is that Washington is their object, but of this I can form no opinion at this time," Monroe wrote vaguely, handing the message to a dragoon for delivery to the president. Then he dashed off to search for the British squadron coming up the Potomac.

Had he stayed a bit longer, Monroe would have seen much more to report.

BENEDICT, LATE AFTERNOON, SATURDAY, AUGUST 20

With the sounding of bugles shortly before 4 p.m., the British camp at Benedict erupted into activity. Though the last British troops finished landing Saturday morning, it had taken hours more to assemble provisions and equipment, but finally all was ready.

General Ross rode up, accompanied by several aides. Loud cheers erupted spontaneously from the men, and Ross, delighted, pulled off his hat and bowed. With a crisp order from the general, the army moved up the road leading from Benedict.

On the river below, Rear Admiral George Cockburn gave orders for a fleet of 50 small boats loaded with 350 marines to weigh anchor and continue up the river. Moving by land and water up the Patuxent, the combined army and navy forces appeared to spell doom for Barney and his flotilla. First, however, the British would have to find the commodore and his boats, now rumored to be in Nottingham, ten miles upriver.

Ross was obliged to move carefully. The British had hoped to capture horses at Benedict, but farmers had fled with their livestock. Lacking horses to pull artillery wagons, the British left most of their guns behind to secure the beachhead, and took along only two small threepounders and a six-pounder. With no cavalry, Ross was marching blind, save for some scouts sent ahead to reconnoiter the country, and two American turncoats who agreed to guide them through the countryside.

A party of twenty skirmishers moved at the front of the British column, followed by an advance guard of three infantry companies, on the lookout for any signs of ambush. Patrols of 40 to 50 men covered the flanks, sweeping the woods and fields for a half mile on either side of the column. The Light Brigade was a hundred yards behind, followed by the artillery teams dragging guns, and then the two remaining brigades with a rear guard.

Even by late afternoon, the heat remained brutal. Ross rested the men every ninety minutes, but it hardly helped. The troops, after months of cramped, shipboard life, were in abysmal shape. Their heavy wool uniforms and the tall black caps on their heads, known as shakos, only added to their misery. Soldiers struggled beneath the weight of their haversacks, blankets, canteens, weapons, and sixty rounds of ball cartridge. Men dropped from heat prostration, battalions lost their formation, and the road was soon covered with stragglers.

Cockburn's fleet kept pace with the army, communicating by signal. Above Benedict, the Patuxent became a winding, tidal river, its shores lined with dense marshes of broad-leafed cattail, white water lilies, and wild rice. The river was so narrow in places that the Royal Marines waded through water up to their necks, and then scoured the shoreline in case the Americans were waiting in ambush. But they found nothing.

After six miles, Ross halted his ragged column at a hilltop crossroads overlooking rolling farmland. They had scarcely stationed pickets and set up camp when a terrific thunderstorm hit. The flashes of lightning gave an eerie cast to the thousands of "men stretched like so many corpses" on the ground, Gleig wrote.

Four miles outside of Washington, the American column under General Winder halted, also exhausted and soon drenched by the rain. When the baggage wagons caught up, commanders found that almost no tents or camping equipment had been packed. Thirty miles apart, the men from two opposing armies lay down in open fields for a wet and miserable Saturday night.

BALTIMORE, SUNDAY MORNING, AUGUST 21

The 5th Maryland Regiment believed themselves to be the cream of the crop, and the message was clearly conveyed in their dashing blue uniforms, with white cross-belts over their chests and leather shakos on their heads, all topped by a feathery plume. The all-volunteer force from Baltimore's most prominent families was the finest militia unit in the state, and 800 men had mustered to rescue Washington. Their destination was Bladensburg, a village at a key junction along the road the British would likely take to reach the capital.

Spectators crowded the sidewalks and women waved handkerchiefs from windows Sunday morning, some crying as they bid farewell to husbands and brothers. For eighteen-year-old Private John Pendleton Kennedy, the spectacle was inspiring beyond comparison. "[T]he populace were cheering and huzzaing at every corner, as we hurried along in brisk step to familiar music, with banners fluttering in the wind and bayonets flashing in the sun," he later wrote. "What a scene it was, and what a proud actor I was in it! . . . This was a real army marching to real war." In his knapsack, Kennedy carried several shirts and stockings, as well as a pair of dancing pumps "with the idea, that, after we had beaten the British army and saved Washington, Mr. Madison would very likely invite us to a ball at the White House, and I wanted to be ready for it."

The column left town and continued in good cheer for several hours on the road to Washington. As evening approached, they made camp at Elkridge Landing, about four miles southwest of Baltimore. The 5th Maryland still faced about a thirty-mile march to Bladensburg, but as the men slept, an order arrived from Winder to slow down. Plagued by doubts of the British destination, the general directed the Maryland militia to hold at a midway point so as not to leave Baltimore exposed. In Washington, an officer asked Winder whether the Baltimore troops would arrive at Bladensburg in time. On the contrary, Winder replied: His fear was "they would be here too soon."

THE ROAD TO NOTTINGHAM, SUNDAY, AUGUST 21

At daylight, the British began their second day of march. Soldiers sang as the army's drummers and fifers played the chorus from Handel's *Judas Maccabaeus:*

> *See the conquering hero comes*
> *Sound the trumpet, beat the drums*

The open fields and countryside of the first day's march gave way to thick woods, sheltering the men from the rapidly warming sun. The Light Brigade again led the way, on the lookout for American militia that the turncoat guides warned were in the woods ahead. Spotting a glitter of arms, Gleig and his men crept up on two men sitting under a tree dressed in black coats and armed with muskets and bayonets. With great innocence the men insisted they were merely squirrel hunters. "When I desired to know whether they carried bayonets to charge the squirrels, . . . they were rather at a loss for a reply; but they grumbled exceedingly when they found themselves prisoners," Gleig wrote.

Cockburn's naval force continued apace upriver, and at midday, he and Ross met at a ferry house opposite Lower Marlboro to confer on plans while the exhausted troops rested for several hours. The movement resumed at 2 p.m., and by late afternoon the two-pronged assault approached the town of Nottingham.

NOTTINGHAM, EARLY EVENING, SUNDAY, AUGUST 21

Colonel Monroe and his dragoons rode into Nottingham shortly before 5 p.m., just ahead of the British. The old Patuxent tobacco port was empty, save for a handful of militiamen who had stayed to defend the town. Monroe had abandoned his plans to scout the Potomac, upon learning that morning that the British were advancing up the Patuxent. He hoped to find Barney's flotilla in Nottingham, but the commodore was long gone. Barney, one step ahead of the enemy, had moved the previous day seven miles to Pig Point, the farthest upriver he could possibly take his boats. The flotilla's retreat prompted most residents who had not already left to abandon Nottingham, some departing so quickly they left their chairs pushed back from tables and bread in their ovens.

Monroe was at first unsure if he had arrived ahead or behind the enemy, but the answer quickly came from around a river bend, where he saw three British barges approaching town. Encouraged by the apparent small size of the invading force, Monroe scribbled a dispatch for General Winder: "The enemy are now within four hundred yards of the shore. There are but three barges at hand, and the force in view is not considerable." Monroe breezily suggested Winder rush up some militia to cut off the enemy rear.

But before Monroe could send the dispatch, he was compelled to add a postscript, striking a less confident tone: "P.S. Ten or twelve more barges in view. There are but two muskets in town, and a few scattering militia." At 5 p.m., Monroe resignedly added another note: "Thirty or forty barges are in view."

Monroe's dragoons fired a few futile shots at the lead boats, sparking a barrage of return fire. General Ross, reconnoitering on horseback at the head of his column, rushed forward with several officers almost into the arms of Monroe's cavalry. The secretary's escape was just as narrow. The army's advance guard moved up quickly on the heels of Ross, forcing the Americans to flee out the north end of town as the British—who had not the faintest notion that the secretary of state was one of the American horsemen—entered from the south.

Ross and Cockburn were no less disappointed than Monroe to find Barney's flotilla gone. With darkness approaching, the British halted for the night. Ross remained in Nottingham with his army camped in protective positions outside the town, while Cockburn's boats anchored nearby in the Patuxent. Informants reported the flotilla had relocated to Pig Point. The hunt for Barney would resume in the morning.

The Woodyard, Sunday night, August 21

Colonel Monroe raced with his dragoons through the night to the Woodyard, the American mustering site. The District militia, after a hot and fatiguing march on Sunday, had arrived after dusk and was camped nearby, joined by a cavalry squadron and 300 regulars from the U.S. 36th and 38th regiments.

Around 11 p.m., Monroe flew into camp and rushed to meet General Winder, who called his top commanders together to hear the secretary's report. The enemy, Monroe said, was only twelve miles away at Nottingham "in considerable force, both by land and water." He guessed they numbered 6,000.

Winder ordered his troops ready to march to meet the enemy. At 2 a.m., the exhausted men were roused with reveille, tents were struck, and baggage wagons loaded. All 1,800 men were put under arms and awaited sunrise.

WASHINGTON, PREDAWN, MONDAY, AUGUST 22

At the President's House, Madison was awoken at 4:40 a.m. to receive the latest report from Monroe. The secretary warned that the enemy's goal "almost certainly" was the capital. Writing immediately in reply, Madison said it seemed "extraordinary" that such a small and ill-equipped British army would try to take Washington, particularly without cavalry. Reflecting further, the president added this thought: "He may however count on the effect of boldness & celerity on his side, and the want of precaution on ours. He may be bound also to do something, & therefore to risk everything."

NOTTINGHAM, DAWN, MONDAY, AUGUST 22

Admiral Cockburn's barges were in motion at first light Monday morning, resuming their course upriver in pursuit of Barney. Ross's army was soon moving as well, toward Upper Marlboro, a village ten miles up the road. The road would take the troops inland away from the protection of the British main fleet, now twenty miles distant.

The little army marched up a sunken road, with a luxuriant canopy of trees providing blissful relief from the heat. By 8:30 a.m. they approached St. Thomas's Church, an old brick colonial chapel. Still without cavalry, Ross was utterly unaware that the vanguard of the American army lay just ahead.

ODEN'S FARM, 8:30 A.M., MONDAY, AUGUST 22

Peering out the second-floor bedroom window of Benjamin Oden's brick farmhouse, General Winder and Colonel Monroe saw the lead elements of the British army approaching. The enemy had reached a key road junction. One road led north to Upper Marlboro, and another, the most direct route to Washington, led to the American positions at the Woodyard. The advancing British skirmished with Winder's cavalry and followed the retreating dragoons along the Woodyard fork, toward the Oden farmhouse.

Winder and Monroe watched with mounting excitement as the

British cautiously probed down the road, coming to within a mile and a quarter. This could be Winder's chance. He had positioned 300 of his best men—including Major Peter's Georgetown Artillery, Captain John Davidson's light infantry company, and Stull's riflemen, now armed with muskets—about two miles down the road in a defensive position. The rest of the American army was marching from the Wood-yard and would soon be in a position to support an attack. "I entertained a hope to [give] the enemy a serious check," Winder said. He rushed back to make sure his forces were ready.

PIG POINT, MARYLAND, 11 A.M., MONDAY, AUGUST 22

Cockburn pushed upriver for Pig Point, confident Barney was trapped. But the hamlet, named for the high-quality pig iron shipped from the site, was proving difficult to reach. With the wind blowing downriver and the channel narrowing, Cockburn continued with the small boats, leaving the larger tenders to follow as they could. At 10 a.m., one mile below Pig Point, Cockburn landed the Royal Marines under Captain John Robyns on the river's east bank, looking for any troops that might be protecting the flotilla.

Approaching Pig Point, Cockburn spotted the broad pendant of *Scorpion*, Barney's flagship, and behind it a long line of ensigns and pendants flying on the masts of the American fleet. The sight at long last of Barney's flotilla exhilarated the sailors, and the admiral ordered his boats forward at full speed. "Here, then, was the boasted flotilla; we had brought them to bay, and in a few minutes we should see what they were made of," recalled Lieutenant Scott, Cockburn's aide. The admiral raced ahead in his gig, leading the attack.

The first sign that something was amiss came as Cockburn closed on *Scorpion* and saw that it was on fire. Moments later, the sloop exploded. Cockburn instantly realized the whole flotilla had been rigged for destruction. The boats were lined up bow to stern stretching more than a quarter mile up the narrow river, with a train of gunpowder running from vessel to vessel. They exploded in a succession of blasts until the last boat, holding the flotilla's magazine, blew up with a tremendous concussion. "It was a grand sight; one vast column of flame appeared to ascend and lose itself in the clouds," recalled Scott.

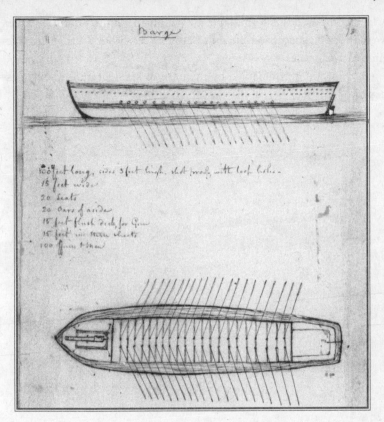

"Here, then, was the boasted flotilla."

*Joshua Barney's sketch showing a barge for his
Chesapeake flotilla.*

The British sailors, who had rushed the flotilla with visions of glory, were crestfallen. "[A] look of blank dismay pervaded the hardy tars . . . and all was disappointment and despair," wrote Midshipman Robert Barrett. Beyond the lost glory, they had hoped to capture the boats to use in future attacks along American coast. Only one of Barney's gunboats failed to explode, and the British sailors hurried to secure it, along with thirteen abandoned merchant vessels that had been hiding above the flotilla.

Cockburn professed satisfaction. "[O]ut of the seventeen vessels which composed this formidable and so much vaunted flotilla, sixteen were in quick succession blown to atoms," Cockburn wrote that evening to Cochrane.

But Barney, accompanied by the bulk of his fighting force, had escaped.

O say can you see, ~~through~~ by the dawn's early
light so proudly we hail'd at the twilight's last gleam
whose broad stripes & bright stars through the perilous fi
O'er the ramparts we watch'd were so gallantly strea
 And the rocket's red glare the bomb bursting i
 Gave proof through the night that our flag was stil
O say does that star spangled banner yet wave
 O'er the land of the free & the home of the brave

On the shore dimly ~~seen~~ through the mists of the
 deep Where the foe's haughty host in dread silence
What is that which the breeze, o'er the towering
 As it fitfully blows, half conceals, half discloses
 Now it catches the gleam of the morning's first
 In full glory reflected ~~now~~ shines on the stre
Tis the star spangled banner — O long may it
 O'er the land of the free & the home of the bra

And where is that band who so vauntingly swo
 That the havoc of war & the battle's confusion
A home & a Country should leave us no more
 ~~Their blood~~
 Their blood has wash'd out their foul footstep
No refuge could save the hireling & slave
 From the terror of flight or the gloom of the gra
And the star spangled banner in triumph doth wa
 O'er the land of the free & the home of the bra

O thus be it ever when freemen shall stand
 Between their lov'd home & the war's desolation
Blest with vict'ry & peace may the heav'n rescued
Praise the power that hath made & preserv'd us a
 Then conquer we must when our cause it is
 And this be our motto — "In God is our trust"
And the star spangled banner in triumph shall wave
 O'er the land of the free & the home of the brave

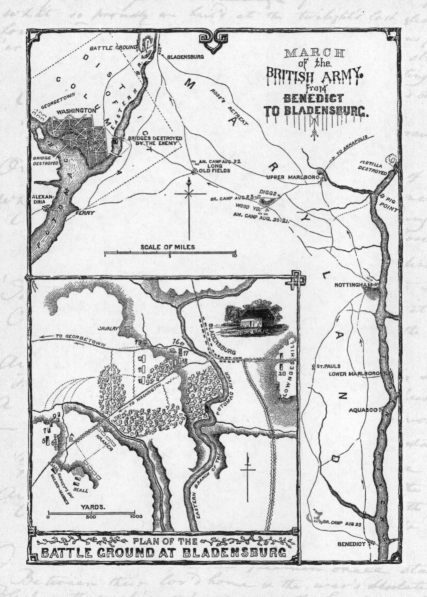

"The capture of Washington was now the avowed object of our invasion."

March of the British Army from Benedict to Washington.

CHAPTER 5

⋆

Be It So, We Will Proceed

B Y NOON MONDAY, Joshua Barney and his band of flotillamen had been on the move for much of the previous twenty-four hours, racing cross-country through thick woods and dense cedar thickets. After resting Sunday night near the village of Upper Marlboro, they took the road to the Woodyard Monday morning, hoping to join Winder's army.

To speed their escape, the men had abandoned almost everything on the boats, including the flotilla guns, personal belongings, and bedding. Some had even lost their shoes. The skeleton crew of 120 men left behind under Lieutenant Solomon Frazier had instructions to destroy the flotilla once the British attacked and then try to escape to rejoin Barney, but "by no means" to let the American boats fall into enemy hands.

Barney had reached the Woodyard when a succession of explosions rocked the Patuxent valley at noon, and black smoke rose in the sky. Frazier had carried out his instructions well, but for Barney it was a bittersweet moment.

At the American camp, the commodore was delighted to find that Navy Secretary Jones had sent him a contingent of 110 U.S. Marines and five large artillery pieces under the command of Captain Samuel Miller. With the arrival of Barney and the marines, the American force now numbered more than 2,500 men, including cavalry and twenty pieces of artillery.

But Barney was astonished to discover that the army, which had been advancing toward the enemy, was preparing to retreat. General Winder had abandoned his plans to give the enemy a check, fearing his force was too small.

Some of Winder's senior commanders, including Major Peter, were aghast. "Our officers said it was a precipitate retreat, and I thought so too," wrote a soldier with Davidson's light infantry.

The unnerving sound of Barney's flotilla being blown to bits did nothing to change Winder's mind. The flotillamen and marines fell in with the rest of the force, marching to the strategic road junction at Old Fields, five miles to the rear, where Winder would position the troops between the British and the capital and wait for reinforcements.

UPPER MARLBORO, MARYLAND, 2 P.M., MONDAY, AUGUST 22

Ross, too, had turned away from battle. His scouts could see the American column, which they underestimated at 1,500 men, retreating toward Washington. The British commander wanted to avoid piecemeal fights in favor of a decisive battle where he could destroy the entire American force.

Ross used the opportunity to execute a perfect feint, turning west toward the Oden farmhouse and advancing on the road to Washington. But after pausing for an hour, he doubled back and took the north road toward Upper Marlboro. This route would keep him close to the Patuxent and the protection of Cockburn's fleet, while still allowing an attack on Washington. It also kept open the possibility that the British were targeting Annapolis, or even Baltimore. That would keep the Americans guessing.

Hearing tremendous explosions from the Patuxent valley, Ross dispatched a party on horseback carrying rockets toward the river to assist Cockburn if needed. But word of the flotilla's destruction quickly arrived, and the British confidently continued their march, reaching Upper Marlboro around 2 p.m.

The homesick soldiers found themselves transported back to Old

England by the idyllic village of eighty elegant and neat houses nestled between green hills. Graceful swells of land were laid out with fields of corn, hay, and tobacco, broken up by patches of old forest. It all looked like home, down to the flocks of sheep grazing in the meadows.

The favorable impression of Upper Marlboro was furthered by the hospitality of Dr. William Beanes, who was among a group of citizens who greeted the British under a flag of truce. The sixty-five-year-old physician, a major landowner and owner of a gristmill, was the leading citizen of Upper Marlboro. His home, Academy Hill, built with proceeds from his flourishing medical practice, was the nicest in town, and Ross selected it as his headquarters.

Beanes was a staunch Federalist, heartily opposed to Madison and the war, and, according to the British, made little effort to conceal his feelings. His Scottish brogue gave his visitors the impression that he was an emigrant to the United States, though he was a third-generation American and patriot who as a young surgeon during the revolution had treated wounded Continental Army troops in Philadelphia.

Beanes by nature was a generous host, and as such, bottles emerged from the doctor's famous wine cellar. "There was nothing about his house or farm to which he made us not heartily welcome," wrote Gleig, who received a bottle of milk from the doctor. Beanes was willing to sell the British goods, too, including horses and provisions.

While the army camped comfortably in a large green field outside town, Ross settled in at Academy Hill to ruminate on what to do next.

WASHINGTON, MONDAY AFTERNOON, AUGUST 22

Ross's feint toward Washington had fooled Colonel Monroe, among others. Leaving the Oden farm, the secretary of state dashed off a note to Madison at 9 a.m. and went to scout elsewhere, not realizing that the British would veer toward Upper Marlboro. "The enemy are in full march for Washington," Monroe wrote. "Have the materials prepared to destroy the bridges." He signed his name, and then added a postscript: "You had better remove the records."

Monroe's message, which arrived in Washington Monday afternoon, tipped the nervous city into full-fledged alarm. "The tone of this dispatch was certainly well calculated to create a panic . . . as much so as if it had been briefly conveyed in the four words, 'Run for your lives!' " Major John Williams later wrote.

The horrors of Hampton and Havre de Grace a year earlier had not been forgotten. Women and children filled the streets of Washington, carrying bedding, clothes, and furniture from their homes. Most were on foot, as the military had seized nearly every wagon in town. A visiting New York businessman helped carry refugees. "I was compelled to purchase a horse and gig as stages, hacks, carts or wagons cannot be procured for love or money," he wrote Monday evening. "I have just returned from taking a load of children eight miles out of town, and the whole distance the road was filled with women and children. Indeed I never saw so much distress in my life as today."

At the President's House, Madison was fatalistic. "I fear not much can be done more than has been done to strengthen the hands of Genl. W[inder]," he replied to Monroe. The president gave orders to remove government papers, as Monroe suggested, though many public officials had already begun packing.

Secretary of Navy Jones, anticipating that wagons would be in short supply, lined up boats to carry off the navy's valuables. Three clerks spent Sunday at the Navy Department headquarters packing trunks with records, books, charts, instruments, and paintings, which were loaded onto two riverboats to be taken up the Potomac. Mordecai Booth, the senior clerk at the Navy Yard, searched frantically all over town Monday for wagons to carry off barrels of gunpowder, with little luck. The clerk tried to seize three wagons that had been hired to carry off private property, but the men angrily refused to give up their paying job. "[T]hey made us of such language, as was degrading to gentlemen," Booth complained. The men rode off, ignoring the clerk's commands to stop. Booth finally returned to the Navy Yard at sunset with five wagons, which were loaded the next morning with 125 barrels of powder and taken to Virginia.

At the Senate, Lewis Machen, a twenty-four-year-old clerk, anxiously awaited instruction on safeguarding the body's papers. Congress was out of session, and the principal clerk was out of town, leaving only Machen and another young clerk manning the office. By noon Sunday, Machen could wait no longer and told his colleague he would "take the responsibility on myself." He obtained a horse-drawn wagon only by threatening government seizure, and with the help of the driver, loaded it with the most valuable books and papers. They took off at sunset for Machen's farm, eight miles away in Prince George's County, Maryland. Under the groaning load, a wagon wheel broke before they made it out of town. Machen stole a wheel from an empty blacksmith's shop and continued, but two miles short of the farm, the wagon overturned and the records spilled onto the road. It was several hours more before they were able to reload the wagon and reach Machen's farm.

The House of Representatives was equally untended, and it fell to another resourceful clerk, Sam Burch, who had marched out of town with the District militia but finally convinced superiors to let him return and safeguard the papers. On Monday, Burch hunted fruitlessly for anything with wheels before finally hiring an ox-drawn cart from a farm six miles from the city. That night, Burch and another clerk hurriedly tossed the most valuable papers into the cart and spirited them out of the city.

One man in Washington was not moving with any particular urgency on Monday. At the War Department offices, Secretary of War John Armstrong spent the day working on assignments for regiments in New York. He was annoyed by the bustle across the hallway in the offices of the State Department, which were on the same floor as the War Department. Stephen Pleasonton, the upright and methodical senior State Department clerk, had received instructions from Monroe to secure the papers, and he and the other clerks filled coarse linen bags with valuable documents.

The secretary of war stopped Pleasonton in the hallway. Armstrong "observed to me that he thought we were under unnecessary alarm, as he did not think the British were serious in their intentions of coming to Washington," Pleasonton later wrote. The clerk did not back down. "I replied that we were under a different belief," Pleasonton said, "and let their intentions be what they might, it was the part of prudence to preserve the valuable papers of the Revolutionary Government."

Armstrong returned to his office, and Pleasonton continued with his work, loading the precious linen bags into carts and taking them by wagon train to Virginia, first to an abandoned gristmill near Chain Bridge and then to a safer location inside the brick-arched storage chamber of a mansion near Leesburg. Among the documents secured were the secret journals of Congress, correspondence of George Washington, the Bill of Rights, and the Declaration of Independence.

MIDDLEBROOK MILLS, MARYLAND, EVENING, MONDAY, AUGUST 22

Terra Rubra had always been Francis Scott Key's refuge, but the war had made it impossible to stay longer. Accompanied by his wife, he had departed for Georgetown, first to pack up his papers and valuables, and then to volunteer his services to the District militia. On Monday evening, they reached Middlebrook Mills, a hamlet about midway on the road from Frederick to Washington, and stopped for the night at Peck's Tavern. Key would have preferred Polly stay at Terra Rubra, but as he later told John Randolph, she "insisted on getting as near Georgetown as she could."

"Polly will stay here [at the tavern] for a few days till she hears what is likely to take place," Key wrote that night to his mother, who was looking after the children at Terra Rubra. "I go in the morning."

Key sorted through the rumors flying through the tavern. "We hear a great many different accounts of the operations and force of the enemy," he wrote his mother. "I beg you will mind nothing that you hear, till you hear it two or three times and from known authority. There is some reason to think that their object is perhaps Barney's flotilla—others suppose Fort [Washington], and that the city will not be their first object. If this is the case and they allow us time, they will I trust be too late. It is said that Genl. Winder will have a large force in a day or so—he says he expects to have 15,000 by tomorrow—his present force is stated at 8 or 9000, but it is probably not so great. The British are said to have landed 6,000 but it is mere conjecture.

"I hope we shall be preserved through these anxious times to meet again in peace and happiness," he concluded. "For this our united prayers will I trust be heard."

POTOMAC RIVER, EVENING, MONDAY, AUGUST 22

No ships with heavy guns on board had ever sailed up the Potomac River past the Kettle Bottoms. The notorious shoals, a series of intricate and constantly shifting shallows and oyster bars, stretched for miles between Nomini Cliffs in Virginia to Lower Cedar Point in Maryland, some running just a few feet in length, others continuing for acres. Washington, as well as the ports of Alexandria and Georgetown, depended on the Kettle Bottoms to defend against an attack up the Potomac. Vice Admiral Warren, Cochrane's predecessor as commander of the North American Station, had not even attempted to cross them during his foray up the Potomac the previous summer.

But in July, just before destroying Kinsale, Cockburn had scouted the Potomac and reported finding a passage the British warships could take through the shoals.

Now it would be up to thirty-one-year-old Captain James Gordon, commander of the British squadron sailing up the Potomac, to prove it could be done. Gordon was not the type to be daunted by shoals. He had joined the Royal Navy from his hometown of Aberdeen, Scotland, as a semiliterate boy and risen to become one of Nelson's captains. Gordon's left leg had been shot off below the knee by a French cannonball in the Adriatic in 1811, and he walked with a wooden leg. His life of derring-do inspired later claims that he was a model for the fictional naval hero Horatio Hornblower.

Gordon's Potomac squadron—small but loaded with firepower, including one thousand men aboard two frigates, three bomb ships, one rocket ship, and a dispatch schooner—entered the river on August 17. When they reached the Kettle Bottoms, Gordon led the way aboard his 36–gun frigate *Seahorse,* with the second frigate, *Euryalus,* and the other ships following her exact course. The British confidence grew as depth soundings showed plenty of water. Then the *Euryalus* stopped moving. "No one could tell where she hung; there was abundance of water astern, ahead, all around, and yet the ship was immovable," Charles Napier, captain of *Euryalus,* recorded. "A diver went down, and found, to the astonishment of all on board, that an oyster bank, not bigger than a boat, was under her bilge."

The crew managed to heave *Euryalus* off the shoal, but it was only the start of a lengthy ordeal up the Potomac. Lack of rain had left the river lower than normal, and each ship went aground at least twenty times. Battling contrary winds, the ships had to be painstakingly warped—hauled by an anchor that was dropped ahead by a boat, again and again—for five days and fifty miles.

But by Monday evening, August 22, "by the severest labour," as Gordon said, the Potomac squadron was clear of the Kettle Bottoms and had done what the Americans thought impossible.

The British now had two formidable forces within striking distance of Washington, one on land and one on water. All that stood between Gordon and the major Potomac ports at the nation's capital was Fort Washington, the fortress on the river eight miles south of the city.

OLD FIELDS, EVENING, MONDAY, AUGUST 22

Late Monday afternoon, President Madison decided it would be appropriate for the commander-in-chief to visit the troops and confer with General Winder at the new American camp at Old Fields, about seven miles east of Washington. He would be gone at least one night, and was worried about leaving Dolley at the President's House. "[O]n my assurance that I had no fear but for him, and the success of our army, he left, beseeching me to take care of myself, and the Cabinet papers, public and private," Dolley later related.

Some in Washington found the idea of the little president riding out to see the troops ludicrous. "Our chief, thinking his presence might occasion them great confidence, buckled on his sword, put his holsters on his saddle (pistols in, of course) and set out at five in the evening to visit the camp," Martha Peter wrote a friend. Nonetheless, Madison, accompanied by Attorney General Rush, Navy Secretary Jones, and three aides, crossed the bridge over the Eastern Branch of the Potomac and continued into Maryland.

Old Fields, a hamlet named for its worked-out tobacco fields, was located midway between Washington and Upper Marlboro. It was a good spot for the forces to muster, as it blocked a British advance on the main road to Washington, but would also allow the Americans to quickly move on Bladensburg should the British attack in that direction.

Around 8 p.m., the presidential party stopped at the Williams farm-house, about a mile from the Old Fields camp. Rush rode forward to inform Winder of the president's arrival. The general sent troops to guard the farmhouse, but exhausted by the "infinite" stream of offi-cious, self-appointed advisers, he declined to call on the president and went to bed.

The scene at Old Fields was chaotic. By now, Winder's force had grown to about 3,200 men, including cavalry. Colonel Allen McLane, an aide to Winder who arrived that evening, found the camp "very much exposed and as open as a race ground." Boisterous groups of militiamen laughed and quarreled, their tents illuminated by camp-fires. Troops approaching the sentinels shouted the countersign so loudly it could be heard from fifty yards away. "My conclusion was, if General Ross does not rout us this night it will not be our fault," said McLane.

The whole camp was roused around 2 a.m. when a sentinel fired his musket at a herd of cattle he mistook for the British army. Winder, not knowing the cause, ordered the whole force kept under arms until day-light. It was the second straight night the men were deprived of sleep.

Shortly after sunrise on Tuesday, August 23, Winder rode to Madi-son's quarters at the Williams farm for a conference with the presi-dential party, which now included Secretary of War Armstrong, who had arrived from Washington. Commodore Barney joined the group, along with senior militia officers. Winder was flummoxed trying to figure the British intentions, as he admitted to Major Peter. "[H]e in-formed me that there were such various accounts of the position and movements of the enemy that it was impossible for him to decide how to act," Peter later wrote.

Winder offered a variety of guesses about the intentions of the enemy army sitting at Upper Marlboro. He discounted the likelihood that the British would attack Washington anytime soon. Annapolis, just fifteen miles from Upper Marlboro by good road, was a better pos-sibility. But based on reports that the British squadron on the Potomac had passed the Kettle Bottoms, Winder now believed the objective was Fort Washington, the bastion on the river. Winder predicted the British army would sit at Upper Marlboro until the Potomac squadron approached the fort; then it would join forces with the ships for a combined land and water assault on the fortress. Rumors of the enemy army's size were wide-ranging, stretching from four to twelve thousand, with the best estimates putting it at five to seven thousand.

Armstrong, for his part, insisted that the British army had "no object" other than the destruction of the now-defunct flotilla. In the unlikely event the army moved on Washington, he declared, the force was so weak it would accomplish nothing more than "a mere Cossack hurrah."

Madison and his entourage rode to camp, where the American troops were drawing up in lines for a presidential review at 9 a.m. The day had already turned hot and sticky. The men did not appear to be crack soldiers, half in civilian clothes, and others wearing only bits of uniforms. But though they had been up all night, they were in good cheer.

Most impressive were Barney's flotillamen and Captain Miller's marines, who brought a bit of swagger to the review. Jones proudly noted their "appearance and preparation for battle, promised all that could be expected from cool intrepidity, and a high state of discipline." Many of the flotillamen were black, as the navy had no restrictions barring their service, unlike the army and militia. Among them was Charles Ball, who, after escaping from slavery in Georgia and returning to his native Maryland, had joined the flotilla in the Patuxent, working as a seaman and cook. Madison asked Barney if the blacks "would not run on the approach of the British?" After four months on the river and in the woods with his men, Barney gave a sure reply. "No sir," the commodore said. "They don't know how to run; they will die by their guns first."

Madison spoke briefly, exhorting the officers to be firm and faithful in their duty. He was encouraged by the enthusiasm and growing numbers of American troops. In addition to the main force at Old Fields, the Maryland militia was gathering at Bladensburg, about ten miles northwest. The assurances of Winder and Armstrong persuaded him that Washington was safe.

After the review, Madison sent Dolley a message brimming with confidence. "I have passed the forenoon among the troops, who are in high spirits and make a good appearance," he wrote. "The reports as to the enemy have varied every hour. The last and probably truest information is that they are not very strong, and are without cavalry and artillery, and of course that they are not in a condition to strike at Washington."

As the president conferred further with Armstrong and Winder, Major Thomas McKenney, a Georgetown dry goods dealer serving as an aide to General Smith, rode in with a patrol that had scouted the British position at Upper Marlboro and captured two British deserters. Briefing the presidential party, McKenney described the size and position of the British force at Upper Marlboro and predicted the enemy would reach the American position before daylight the next morning.

Armstrong scoffed. "They can have no such intention," he said. "They are foraging, I suppose; and if an attack is meditated by them upon any place, it is Annapolis."

But Madison wanted to hear more. The president interrogated the two deserters, but the men claimed to know next to nothing. Then McKenney directed the prisoners to gauge the size of the American force gathered at Old Fields, and asked them whether the British force was equal to it. Recalled McKenney, "They did so, and with a smile, said—'We think it is.'"

ACADEMY HILL, UPPER MARLBORO, MORNING, TUESDAY, AUGUST 23

General Ross was no more certain than the Americans about the next step. At his headquarters at the home of Dr. Beanes, the British commander convened a council of war to decide whether to attack Washington or retreat to the ships.

In many respects, the British found themselves in a strong position. The troops were in better shape than when they landed at Benedict four days earlier, and they were now in striking distance of the American capital. Locals were more than happy to sell the British all the cattle they needed, nor had it been a problem buying enough horses to pull the small train of artillery. Slaves were a font of useful information, and for that matter, "the white inhabitants by no means incorruptible," Evans observed.

But Ross was disturbed by the intelligence learned from informants: The American forces collecting to his front were more numerous than anticipated, and strongly placed. Moreover, though the flotilla's destruction gave the British unquestioned control of the Patuxent, the American boats no longer served as an excuse to explain the British incursion.

The small expeditionary force was now twenty-five miles from the ships at Benedict, with little artillery and no cavalry. Until now, the army had been moving alongside or at least close to the river. From here on, an attack on Washington would take the army inland, away from communication with the ships.

It was clear the American troops were saddled with "leaders devoid of talent," one of Ross's aides observed. Still, their failure to put up any resistance or even to chop a single tree across a road to slow the British progress was so odd that Ross wondered if he was being lured into an ambush. Surely the Americans could not be this incompetent. But what bothered Ross the most was that an attack on Washington "completely overstepped" his instructions from the government. The general's staff was split on whether to proceed.

The most passionate voice arguing for Washington was that of Lieutenant George De Lacy Evans. The hard-knit and sinewy Irishman was from an old Norman family that had arrived in the British Isles in the footsteps of William the Conqueror.

Photograph of Gen. George De Lacy Evans circa 1855, when Evans commanded a British division during the Crimean War.

The most passionate voice arguing for Washington was that of Lieutenant George De Lacy Evans. The hard-knit and sinewy Irishman was from an old Norman family that had arrived in the British Isles in the footsteps of William the Conqueror. Evans, though only twenty-three, had already served eight eventful years in the army, distinguishing himself by dash and daring in India and in the Peninsula. From the beginning of the expedition, the ambitious Evans had glued himself to Ross's side, making himself indispensable to the general.

As the council of war continued, Evans realized that Ross was wavering. What they needed, Evans decided, was Cockburn. "[H]is presence might have the effect of inclining the scale in favour of the forward movement," Evans later wrote.

Evans and an ally raced on horseback five miles to Mount Calvert, a brick plantation house overlooking the Patuxent where Cockburn had set up headquarters after the flotilla's destruction. The officers explained the dilemma and suggested the rear admiral accompany them to Upper Marlboro. Cockburn was happy to oblige; jumping on a spare mount the officers had brought.

Arriving at the Beanes home, Cockburn went to work. The Americans truly were as weak as they seemed, Cockburn insisted. "Let us now push on, so far as to feel their strength," he told Ross, assuring him that the British could retreat to the ships if need be. Cockburn scoffed at Ross's concerns about his troop numbers. Nothing was impossible for the soldiers who had fought their way through France and Spain. Cockburn offered to bolster Ross's force with Royal Marine artillery and seamen to carry provisions. The admiral declared he "would go himself & either conquer or die," a sailor recollected.

Ross was soon persuaded. But before the deliberations were complete, a message for Cockburn arrived from Vice Admiral Cochrane. After four days anchored off Benedict, the commander-in-chief made it clear in a curt note that he believed the British excursion had gone on long enough. "I congratulate you most cordially on the destruction of Barney's Fleet and think as this matter is ended, the sooner the army get back the better," Cochrane wrote.

Cockburn simply ignored the note. After all, Cochrane's message was not a direct order. He was not about to turn back now, notwithstanding "the halter which this note placed about his neck." Cockburn immediately issued orders for a force of 350 men, including sailors, the Colonial Marines, and a Royal Marine rocket brigade, to march from Mount Calvert and join the army.

Cockburn sent a note back to Cochrane informing him of the decision to push on to the capital, painting it as Ross's idea all along. "I find he is determined . . . to push on towards Washington, which I have confident hopes he will give a good account of," Cockburn wrote. "I shall accompany him & of course afford him every assistance in my power." He made no mention at all of Cochrane's message.

Cockburn helped steer the ship, but the decision, ultimately, was Ross's. The failure of the Americans to mount any challenge as he marched to within sixteen miles of the capital persuaded the general to continue.

To reach the capital from Upper Marlboro, the British would have to cross the Eastern Branch of the Potomac—today known as the Anacostia River—at one of three points. The southernmost route led to the main crossing, the Eastern Branch Bridge. A fork in the road led to the lesser-used upper bridge, about two miles north. But the British could expect both bridges would be destroyed if they approached the city, leaving them unable to cross the wide river.

Ross chose to cross at the third and northernmost bridge, at the village of Bladensburg, located at a critical road juncture on the northeast side of Washington. There the Eastern Branch narrowed considerably and split into two smaller, easily fordable branches. The British would be slowed if the bridge was blown, but they might not be stopped.

One road from Upper Marlboro led directly to Bladensburg, about fifteen miles away. But Ross chose a more southerly, circuitous route. It would take the British through the American camp at Old Fields, providing the British an opportunity to attack before they reached Bladensburg. More important, the southern route disguised whether the British intended to assault Fort Washington on the Potomac, or attack Washington.

At 2 p.m., bugles and drums sounded and officers ordered the troops to form up. The men gave three cheers and began marching with the light infantry in the lead. Wrote Gleig, "The capture of Washington was now the avowed object of our invasion."

OLD FIELDS, MORNING, TUESDAY, AUGUST 23

General Winder believed the pieces were falling into place to deliver a crushing defeat to the British army. Prisoners had confirmed that the enemy would not move anytime soon from Upper Marlboro, giving him time to prepare an attack. The Maryland militia had arrived in Bladensburg, with about 1,350 troops under the command of Brigadier General Tobias E. Stansbury. The crack 5th Maryland Regiment, Private Kennedy's unit, was expected anytime with 800 more men. Another 800 men with 80 horses under Colonel William Beall were marching from Annapolis. Altogether, Winder would have more than 6,000 men.

Winder wanted to unite his force near Upper Marlboro and assail the enemy the following morning from the heights around town. Winder described his intentions to Madison and his cabinet, who appeared satisfied, and he put the plan in motion. Winder sent out an advance force of 300 troops under Major Peter with instructions to move toward Upper Marlboro to reconnoiter the enemy. The American commander also sent orders to Brigadier General Stansbury in Bladensburg to move his Maryland militia troops toward Upper Marlboro and take a position outside the town. At noon, Winder left his army with General Walter Smith, the District militia commander, and rode toward Bladensburg with several troops of cavalry, intending to intercept Stansbury on the road to Upper Marlboro and hurry on the forces.

After a quick meal at the Williams farm, the president, accompanied by Armstrong and Jones, departed Old Fields at 2 p.m. to ride back to Washington.

GEORGETOWN, TUESDAY, AUGUST 23

Arriving at his home on Bridge Street, Francis Scott Key prepared to volunteer his services to the District militia. He oversaw the loading of his valuables into wagons to be sent out of town, and arranged for a friend to care for his and Randolph's papers, as well as Randolph's gun. Catching up on the latest reports from the field, Key was relieved to hear that the British were holding at Upper Marlboro. He dashed off a quick note to Randolph, reporting that the crisis might be over.

"There has been a great alarm here but I believe we are safe now," Key wrote. "If the enemy had come it might have been otherwise. The last certain [reports] state them to be at Upper Marlboro & I presume they will not come this way now."

ROAD TO UPPER MARLBORO, EARLY AFTERNOON, TUESDAY, AUGUST 23

But the British were not holding at Upper Marlboro. Major Peter had scarcely approached the outskirts of the village with the American advance force of 300 men when his scouts reported that the enemy was advancing toward the Americans.

A group of British officers suddenly appeared on the summit of a nearby hill, within range of Stull's rifle company. Peter ordered Stull to "give those red-coat gentlemen a shot." The entire company leveled its weapons and fired, but missed. The British party, which included General Ross, quickly retreated down the hill. Peter blamed the poor shooting on inaccurate muskets issued to Stull's rifle company. "Had this company been armed with rifles, those officers must have fallen, and with it the defeat of their project," he later said.

But there was no time for regrets. The British moved forward in large numbers, firing on the smaller American force. Peter narrowly escaped capture and organized a fighting retreat.

At the American camp, Brigadier General Smith was alerted of the enemy's approach. He and Commodore Barney swiftly formed the troops in a line extending a quarter mile on each side of the road. Barney set up on the right with his heavy artillery, along with the marines and regulars, while the District militia set up on the left. It was a strong position, with the big guns well situated.

Winder was still en route to Bladensburg to orchestrate his planned attack when he was overtaken by Major McKenney. The news of the enemy advance shattered Winder's grand plan to destroy the British at Upper Marlboro. "[P]utting spurs to his horse, we galloped back to camp together," McKenney wrote.

At Old Fields, the troops awaited the British in surprisingly good spirits and ready to fight. By late afternoon, the British were reported to be only three miles away.

But Winder arrived before the British. As daylight faded, he inspected the troop lines. He complimented Smith on the arrangement and then ordered the men to stand down. The British, he feared, would attack that night, when the American artillery superiority would be lost, and the inexperienced militia might disintegrate. Winder was skittish about fighting in the dark after his own experience being taken prisoner in a night fight on the Niagara frontier. To the dismay of many of his men, Winder ordered a retreat—his second in two days.

The decision was defensible; indeed, a night attack was exactly what Ross contemplated at that moment. What was inexplicable was Winder's decision on where to retreat. One road from Old Fields led up to Bladensburg and from there back down to Washington, while a second road led directly to Washington across the lower bridges. Assuming the two lower bridges were destroyed, the British would have to go through Bladensburg to get to Washington. But Winder fretted about blowing the bridges unnecessarily. If he retreated to Bladensburg, he worried, the British might attack Fort Washington or Annapolis.

The frazzled Winder was not thinking clearly. Five days and nights of crisis had left him in a "wearied and exhausted state," he acknowledged. Winder's decision reflected this. He would march his army back into Washington to defend a bridge that could be blown up by a handful of men, and leave the road to Bladensburg wide open.

A half hour before sunset, the troops marched for Washington, abandoning their strong position at Old Fields, and leaving behind nothing but hastily destroyed casks of flour and whisky.

PRESIDENT'S HOUSE, LATE AFTERNOON, TUESDAY, AUGUST 23

At the President's House, Dolley Madison was packing. A new note had arrived from the president, much more "alarming" than the one he had sent earlier in the day. Learning of the British advance, Madison reported that the enemy seemed stronger than first thought and might attack Washington "with the intention of destroying it." He warned Dolley to be "ready at a moment's warning" to flee the city.

A flood of residents was already leaving. Eleanor Jones, wife of the secretary of the navy, sent Dolley a polite note canceling plans to attend a social engagement at the President's House Tuesday evening with her husband and niece. "In the present state of alarm and bustle of preparation for the worst that may happen, I imagine it will be more convenient to dispense with the enjoyment of your hospitality today," wrote Jones, who was herself packing.

Canceling a party was a rare concession to the war, but unavoidable this time. Social events were the trademark of Dolley Madison's President's House, and she had insisted they continue after war had been declared. Her weekly open house, known as the "Wednesday drawing room," had given a democratic tone to the Madison presidency, attracting guests of all political persuasions and livelihoods: congressmen, businessmen, federal officials, diplomats, or anyone with a reputable connection. Madison usually sat unobtrusively in a corner, waiting "like a spider in his web," quietly discussing the topics of the day with a small circle of men, while Dolley was the center of attention. Some found her beautiful; others not so. Before the war, British diplomat Francis James Jackson labeled her "fat and forty but not fair." All were in agreement that her Paris-accented fashion—including an ermine-trimmed robe of pink satin and a white velvet turban with nodding ostrich plumes—was unique to Washington.

Dolley, from an old Virginia family of Quakers, was a young widow living in Philadelphia with her two-year-old son in 1794 when Madison, then serving in Congress, spotted her. Dolley was bemused by the interests of the "great little Madison," as she called him, a man seventeen years older and several inches shorter than her. But they wed after a quick courtship, and their marriage developed into a great love and partnership.

Dolley proved to be a perfect political wife. Warm-hearted and genial, she could remember anyone's name and story, and was always able to make a visitor feel special. Much as she had redecorated the President's House, she had remade the role of the first lady from being the wife of the president into a semi-official office. She was dubbed "the Presidentress" by the *Intelligencer*, and more regally, "our Queen Dolla lolla" by Rosalie Stier Calvert, a Federalist. Dolley served as Madison's ambassador of goodwill, making calls around the city in her carriage and making friends of every stripe.

That goodwill seemed to have vanished as the British approached, Dolley would write. "Disaffection stalks around us."

WASHINGTON, EVENING, TUESDAY, AUGUST 23

James Madison arrived in Washington from Old Fields early Tuesday evening, surprised and chagrined to learn that Winder's army was not far behind him. At the President's House, there was little time—and even less good news—to reassure Dolley about Washington's safety.

A stream of visitors stopped by the mansion. Colonel George Minor, who had just arrived with a regiment of 700 militia from Northern Virginia, told the president that his men lacked arms and ammunition. Madison told him to report to Secretary of War Armstrong, who "would have everything promptly arranged to my satisfaction." The colonel went straight to Armstrong's quarters a few blocks from the President's House on Pennsylvania Avenue, but when he requested weapons, the secretary cut him short. "He said that was out of the question; that it would be time enough in the morning," Minor wrote.

As far as Armstrong was concerned, the presidential rebuke he had received ten days earlier had relieved him of any responsibility for the crisis. The war secretary told Treasury Secretary George Campbell, who lived in the same boardinghouse, that Madison had chosen General Winder as his commander, and Armstrong had no intention of offering advice unless the president specifically asked for it.

Winder, riding ahead of his troops, crossed the Eastern Branch Bridge and went straight to the President's House, where he met with Madison around 9 p.m. and "informed him of the then state of things." The president's response is unrecorded, but Winder did not stay long.

News of the retreat shattered what little confidence remained in town. "I cannot find language to express the situation of the women and children, who are running the streets in a state bordering on distraction; their husbands, fathers and brothers all under arms, scarce a man to be seen in the city," a witness wrote at 1 a.m.

Margaret Bayard Smith was awoken by a friend pounding on her door. "The enemy are advancing, our own troops are giving way on all sides and are retreating to the city," he yelled. "Go, for Gods sake go." The family immediately rose, loaded a wagon, and fled north into Maryland.

That night, James and Dolley Madison slept in the President's House for the last time.

BLADENSBURG, NIGHT, TUESDAY, AUGUST 23

Six miles northeast of the capital, the scene was no less chaotic. The men of the 5th Maryland Regiment stumbled into Bladensburg at sunset Tuesday, covered in dust and sweat. Their glorious parade from Baltimore on Sunday seemed a distant memory. After several stops and starts owing to Winder's indecisiveness, they had rushed to Bladensburg through scorching heat and clouds of dust.

They joined Stansbury's brigade on Lowndes Hill, which commanded the roads leading into town on the likely British avenue of approach. Stansbury had stopped his move to Upper Marlboro that afternoon and rushed back to Bladensburg after getting word of the British advance. The 5th Maryland was a welcome addition to Stansbury's brigade, bringing his strength to around 2,100 men, but even so, the Maryland militia now in Bladensburg was by no means a formidable fighting force. Stansbury's two regiments were largely untrained, inexperienced militia from Baltimore County. The 5th Maryland, for all its élan, was dead tired and rather green itself.

Private John Pendleton Kennedy and his well-to-do companions from the 5th Maryland set up camp and sent a hired black servant to forage. He returned with two chickens and some candles stolen from Stansbury's camp. Kennedy's feet were swollen from the march, so he took off his boots and put on his dancing pumps. After smoking cigars around the campfire, the men turned in.

Around midnight, Colonel Monroe, the peripatetic secretary of state, showed up in camp with alarming news. Once again, much of it was exaggerated or just flat wrong. Monroe passed along an unconfirmed rumor that Winder was missing and that "it was feared he was taken" prisoner.

The secretary advised Stansbury "to fall forthwith" on the enemy rear guard at Upper Marlboro. It may have been Monroe's best advice of the campaign—an attack on the British rear might have prompted Ross to break off his advance for fear of being cut off from his ships. But Stansbury, believing his ill-trained and exhausted men were in no condition to launch a night attack, turned down the colonel's suggestion.

Monroe dashed off again, this time back to Washington. He had barely disappeared when nervous pickets stationed on the road to Upper Marlboro fired several muskets in quick succession. In Private Kennedy's tent, the men heard the rapid beating and long roll from the drums summoning the whole camp to arms. Someone absconded with their light, and the men struggled to dress in the dark. Kennedy sallied out of the tent in his dancing pumps. Cavalry patrols found no sign of the enemy, and at 2 a.m. Stansbury ordered the men to return to their tents.

A half hour later, Stansbury was shocked to receive a message from Winder informing him that he had retreated from Old Fields into Washington, and instructing him to "resist the enemy as long as possible" should they move toward Bladensburg. Winder had abandoned the Maryland militia, leaving its right flank and rear uncovered.

Stansbury, a prominent Baltimore politician and longtime militia commander with no combat experience, called an immediate emergency council of war in his tent with his senior commanders. Among them were William Pinkney, Madison's former attorney general and the man who had drafted the declaration of war against Britain. Pinkney, one of the finest attorneys in the land, had raised a volunteer rifle battalion from Baltimore. But he had not signed up for a suicide mission. Along with the other commanders he was incredulous that Winder expected their raw and tired militia, deprived of any support, to fight a veteran British force they estimated at three times their size.

The officers unanimously agreed that Stansbury should ignore Winder's order and instead withdraw from Bladensburg and retreat closer to Washington. It meant abandoning the good defensive position on Lowndes Hill, where volunteers from Washington and Bladensburg had dug extensive earthworks in recent days. But Stansbury and his commanders did not want to be caught by the British on the east side of the river.

Stansbury issued orders to strike tents. The men, who had barely settled back into their tents after the false alarm, marched into the night again. At 3:30 a.m., they crossed the bridge and moved out of Bladensburg.

The soldiers deemed too fatigued to fight were deprived again of rest. Every time the column stopped for a moment, whole platoons lay down in the dusty road and dozed till the officers gave word to move on. "Nothing could keep us awake," recalled Kennedy, still in his pumps. "I slept as I walked."

WASHINGTON, EARLY MORNING, WEDNESDAY, AUGUST 24

The march of General Winder's army back to Washington had dissolved into a panicked run. Crossing the Eastern Branch Bridge late in the night, the troops set up camp in the city on heights overlooking the crossing. The air was raw, and men huddled around fires, seeking what rest they could. They had been marched back and forth for four days in burning, sultry heat, sleeping at night without cover. Many had not eaten in forty-eight hours.

Leaving the President's House after his conference with Madison, Winder found his horse too exhausted to continue. He stopped at the McKeown Hotel to exchange it, but no fresh horses were to be found. The commanding general continued on foot two more miles to the American camp.

When he finally found his troops, Winder sent a party to immediately burn the rickety upper bridge and dispatched the Washington Artillery to guard the lower Eastern Branch Bridge until it was necessary to blow it up.

Continuing through the dark night on foot to the Navy Yard, the exhausted general fell hard into a ditch, badly hurting his right arm and ankle. He limped on to the yard and roused Captain Thomas Tingey around 1 a.m. The yard commandant assured Winder that several casks of powder had been loaded onto boats and would be sent to blow the lower bridge when necessary, but in response to Winder's pleas to "put beyond doubt" the bridge's destruction, Tingey agreed to send more explosives.

Winder arrived at camp around 3 a.m. and located Major Peter's tent. The Georgetown Artillery commander was trying to sleep, but Winder came in, lay down on Peter's straw mattress, and poured out his frustration about "the inefficiency of the troops he had to command." Peter dozed off as Winder went on. "When I awoke," Peter recalled, "the general was gone."

British headquarters, Melwood plantation, predawn,
   Wednesday, August 24

Lieutenant James Scott, Admiral Cockburn's aide-de-camp, rushed through the night, first aboard a small boat that carried him from a British frigate anchored in the Patuxent to the shoreline, and then atop a waiting horse, which he rode on a dark, wooded trail. At Upper Marlboro, he linked up with Royal Marine Captain Robyns, commander of the rear guard, who escorted him to the headquarters of the British expeditionary force, another five miles to the west. General Ross, after advancing from Upper Marlboro, had stopped his army that evening three miles short of Old Fields, in the vicinity of the Melwood plantation, located on what is now Andrews Air Force Base. Ross's contemplated night attack had become moot when the American force abandoned Old Fields and retreated to Washington. Instead, the British camped for the night.

Scott carried an urgent message from Vice Admiral Cochrane, commander of the fleet. Cochrane had not been happy to read the note from Cockburn that Scott delivered Tuesday afternoon reporting that the expeditionary force was marching on Washington. Cochrane thought the decision rash, believing it vital to preserve the force for continued operations, in particular an eventual assault on New Orleans. The British force had already accomplished enough and was too small to capture the American capital.

It was close to daybreak Wednesday morning when the lieutenant reached the camp with Cochrane's reply. The navy officer was taken to a shepherd's hut where Cockburn and Ross were staying. They were asleep on their cloaks when Scott entered, but arose at the commotion. Scott handed the packet to the admiral. Cockburn silently read the note and handed it to Ross without comment. Ross digested the contents. There was nothing ambivalent about the message—it recommended "in strenuous terms, an immediate retreat," according to Lieutenant Evans.

Cockburn argued forcefully against it. "No," he said, "we cannot do that. We are too far advanced to think of a retreat." Cockburn urged Ross to talk it over outside, and the two commanders paced under the stars. Scott and Evans heard smatterings of the conversation as the two commanders walked to and fro.

"If we proceed, I'll pledge everything that is dear to me as an officer that we shall succeed," Cockburn declared. "If we return without striking a blow, it will be worse than a defeat—it will bring stain upon our arms."

In contradicting Cochrane, Cockburn was risking his career. He would be held accountable for any failure, and even if they succeeded, Cochrane was not likely to be pleased by Cockburn's insolence. But in Cockburn's view, the die had been cast.

Whatever the views of the admiral, the decision belonged to Ross. His orders from London not to take any unnecessary risks weighed heavily on the Irishman. "I felt an apprehension of the consequences of failure, originating from my instructions, which bound me not to attempt anything that *might be attended* with the want of success," he would write Ly, his wife.

Yet Ross did not hesitate now. To the west, the pickets on the perimeter of the British encampment could see a glow toward Washington, where the upper bridge was burning, while the eastern sky was tinged with the blush of day.

With the dawn, Ross slapped himself in the forehead. "Well, be it so, we will proceed," the general declared.

O say can you see ~~the~~ by the dawn's early
light so proudly we hail'd at the twilight's last gleaming
whose broad stripes & bright stars through the perilous fight
O'er the ramparts we watch'd were so gallantly streaming
    And the rocket's red glare, the bomb bursting
    Gave proof through the night that our flag was still
O say does that star spangled banner yet wave
O'er the land of the free & the home of the brave

On the shore dimly seen through the mists of the deep
    Where the foe's haughty host in dread silence
What is that which the breeze, o'er the towering
As it fitfully blows, half conceals, half discloses
    Now it catches the gleam of the morning's first
    In full glory reflected now shines on the stream
'Tis the star-spangled banner — O long may it
O'er the land of the free & the home of the brave

And where is that ~~band~~ who so vauntingly swore
    That the havoc of war & the battle's confusion
A home & a Country should leave us no more
~~Their blood has~~
    Their blood has wash'd out their foul footsteps
    No refuge could save the hireling & slave
From the terror of flight or the gloom of the grave
And the star-spangled banner in triumph doth wave
O'er the land of the free & the home of the brave

O thus be it ever when freemen shall stand
    Between their loved home & the war's desolation
Blest with vict'ry & peace may the heav'n rescued
Praise the power that hath made & preserv'd us a
    Then conquer we must when our cause it is
And this be our motto - "In God is our trust"
And the star spangled banner in triumph shall wave
O'er the land of the free & the home of the brave

"[W]e took our position on the rising ground . . .
and waited the approach of the enemy."

*Commodore Joshua Barney as he appeared
around the time of the War of 1812.*

CHAPTER 6

———— ★ ————

The Enemy in Bladensburg!

EARLY WEDNESDAY MORNING, a message arrived at the President's House from General Winder. Though it was addressed to Secretary of War Armstrong, President Madison did not hesitate to open it. Winder, warning of "very threatening" news, asked to meet with Secretary of War Armstrong and other government officials as soon as possible. Madison dispatched the note to Armstrong at his boardinghouse and then rushed to Winder's headquarters near the Eastern Branch Bridge, arriving around 7 a.m. The entire cabinet was soon at hand, save Armstrong, to the astonishment of Madison, who grew increasingly furious at the secretary of war's conspicuous absence.

The war council was oddly unfocused, given the urgency of the moment. Even at this late hour, Winder was not convinced that the British intended to come to Washington—Annapolis or Fort Washington might be the targets, he suggested. An officer in attendance described the discussion as "rather desultory; first one suggestion was made and commented on, and then another; no idea seemed to be entertained that it was necessary to come instantly to a decision how we should act."

Dragoons burst in every few minutes with scouting reports and messages. Winder learned—"with considerable mortification"—that Stansbury's Maryland militia had failed to hold its position at Bladensburg and was instead retreating toward the capital. He immediately sent Stansbury an order to resume his position at Bladensburg, promising to support him should the enemy move in that direction. A rumor arrived that the enemy were indeed marching toward Bladensburg. Winder gave the report little credence, but Monroe, just back from Bladensburg and already chafing at the inaction, offered to return to assist Stansbury. Madison and Winder approved.

With Monroe gone, Bladensburg was forgotten. Winder was preoccupied with the British squadron working its way up the Potomac and proposed sending troops to man batteries on the river. "The preponderance of opinion," according to Attorney General Rush, held that the British army would move southeast and unite with the squadron for a joint attack on Fort Washington, or even—it was suggested with unfettered optimism—to embark on the ships and retreat down the Potomac.

Then a messenger reported that the British had passed through Old Fields and were heading straight to the city on a route that would take them to the Eastern Branch Bridge. Winder ordered Major Peter's artillery to reinforce the position and requested Barney and his flotillamen, quartered at the U.S. Marine Barracks near the Navy Yard, to bring up the big guns and prepare to defend the capital.

Old Fields, early morning, Wednesday, August 24

The British army had been moving rapidly since daylight—to Bladensburg, not Washington. Given a respite from the heat under a welcoming canopy of trees sheltering the road, the British made good time. They soon reached Old Fields, passing smoking ashes, bundles of straw, and scattered supplies, plain evidence of the large American force that had hurriedly left the previous evening. Just beyond the camp, they came to a fork in the road, one route leading to Washington, the other to Bladensburg.

General Ross took the road leading to Washington, moving forward until the last column had passed the fork. Spotting American cavalry scouts, Ross sent thirty mounted artillery drivers in pursuit. The makeshift British cavalry chased the Americans two miles, sounding their trumpets and causing so much racket that "the enemy supposed the whole army about to force the bridges," said Lieutenant Evans. The frantic scouts reported exactly that to Winder's war council. But in the meantime the British doubled back and took the route leading north to Bladensburg. It was the same ruse Ross had used two days earlier on the way to Upper Marlboro, and it worked again. The British had been marching for five hours, but the Americans had done nothing to reinforce Bladensburg.

AMERICAN HEADQUARTERS, WASHINGTON, MID-MORNING,
   WEDNESDAY, AUGUST 24

At 10 a.m. a messenger arrived with news that brought the war council in Washington to an abrupt end. Contrary to the last information, the enemy was in "full march" to Bladensburg. "[T]here was still as much consternation and perplexity as if Ross had that morning dropped suddenly with his army from the clouds," wrote militia aide Major Williams. Winder issued a flurry of orders directing the District militia under General Smith to break camp and race to Bladensburg.

As Winder prepared to depart, a sullen Armstrong wandered in, having stopped along the way to chat with passersby. Madison icily informed that the British were moving on Bladensburg and asked the secretary of war if "he had any advice or plan to offer upon the occasion." Armstrong did not, but he did predict, rather unhelpfully, that as the coming battle would be fought "between regulars and militia, the latter would be beaten."

Winder rushed out of the house, followed by the president and his cabinet. The general "seemed to be in a high state of excitement" and tugged "violently" at his hair, recalled Major George Biscoe, an aide. "Major Biscoe I am but a nominal commander," Winder told him. "[T]he president and secretary of war have interfered with my intended operations, and I greatly fear for the success of the day."

With that, Winder dashed off for Bladensburg. The general, who lacked formal command over Barney's flotillamen and Captain Miller's marines, left the most potent American fighting force available guarding a bridge that was not on the route the British were taking to Washington. Barney, livid, confronted the president and his cabinet as they milled

Jones, conferring with the president, recommended that the Navy Yard be destroyed if the British entered the city, rather than be allowed to fall into enemy hands.

Secretary of the Navy William Jones.

about near the bridge. Some 500 flotillamen and 120 marines were being left to do a job that "any damned corporal can better do with five," Barney heatedly declared. The president, seconded by Navy Secretary Jones and other cabinet members, judiciously agreed to send Barney's force to Bladensburg. A small detail of marines was left to guard the bridge and blow it if necessary.

Madison and the cabinet members mounted their horses, hurriedly making last-minute arrangements. Should Washington be lost, the president said, the cabinet would reassemble in Frederick, Maryland, forty-five miles to the northwest. Jones, conferring with the president, recommended that the Navy Yard be destroyed if the British entered the city, rather than be allowed to fall into enemy hands. Madison agreed, and Jones rushed to make the arrangements.

Treasury Secretary George Campbell drew the president aside. Madison could not afford to be without the aid of his secretary of war, "considering the extraordinary and menacing" situation, he told the president. Campbell did not need to mention that confidence in Winder had plummeted. Recounting his conversation with Armstrong the previous evening, Campbell told Madison that the war secretary was not going to help defend the capital unless expressly ordered by the president.

Madison was shocked. "I could scarcely conceive it possible that Genl. Armstrong could have so misconstrued his functions and duty as

Secretary of War," he wrote several days later. Madison turned his horse to Armstrong and "expressed to him my concern and surprise at the reserve he shewed in the present crisis." He instructed Armstrong to go to Bladensburg and assist Winder. Armstrong agreed and rode off.

Madison prepared to ride to Bladensburg to resolve any disputes over authority. Campbell, too ill to ride, handed Madison his pair of dueling pistols, which the president dutifully accepted. The sight of the diminutive president strapping on guns was at once comical and sobering.

After a quick stop at the Marine barracks, Madison's horse went lame, and he exchanged mounts with his friend, Charles Carroll. Accompanied by Rush and Madison's servant, a free black man named James Smith, the president of the United States set off at "full gallop" to Bladensburg.

BLADENSBURG, MORNING, WEDNESDAY, AUGUST 24

The town of Bladensburg lay almost entirely empty on the morning of August 24. Most of the 1,500 inhabitants had fled, and the pleasant brick homes scattered on the L-shaped main street were abandoned. Bladensburg sat six miles northeast of the Capitol, at the point where the turnpike from Washington to Baltimore crossed the Eastern Branch. The town's days as a thriving port had come and gone before Washington even existed. After its founding in 1742, oceangoing sloops with goods from around the world docked at Bladensburg's deepwater wharf to trade for tobacco grown in the rich surrounding soil. But from the start, Bladensburg was plagued by erosion. Silt from farming filled the channel, and the port became dormant.

The town survived as a center of commerce by virtue of good roads converging from Washington, Georgetown, Baltimore, southern Maryland, and Annapolis, a central location that also gave Bladensburg new life as a weekend destination. "People come from all directions to drink the waters on Sunday—all Georgetown in particular comes," Rosalie Stier Calvert, who lived at the nearby Riversdale plantation, wrote her sister.

Bladensburg had also gained favor as a dueling ground. Its location across the District line offered the advantage of being outside Washington's jurisdiction yet convenient to the capital. A deep, tree-lined ravine nearby provided a sheltered ground for the still common but illegal practice. Just the previous year, Joshua Barney had chosen Bladensburg for a duel against a Baltimore businessman who had called him "a most abandoned rascal." The local marshal, tipped off to the plan, chased the duelists out of Bladensburg, forcing Barney to cross the river into Virginia for the satisfaction of shooting and wounding the offender.

But Bladensburg's greatest fame was still to come.

After abandoning Bladensburg during the night, Stansbury's Maryland militia had stopped around sunrise on a hill a mile and a half east of the town. A message arrived from Winder, reiterating that the Maryland militia should defend Bladensburg if the enemy attacked. Once again, Stansbury summoned his senior commanders, and once again they agreed to ignore Winder's instructions, deciding "no good could result" from them.

Soon afterward, around 9 a.m., a third message arrived from Winder, once more ordering them back to Bladensburg. Stansbury's subordinates again urged retreat, but Winder's order was so emphatic that Stansbury reluctantly concluded he had no choice but to obey. He could not quite bring himself to cross the bridge back into town and stopped short of the Eastern Branch.

The roads from Washington and Georgetown met at a 45–degree angle before crossing into Bladensburg, creating a triangular field where Stansbury set up his troops. Up front, toward the eastern point of the triangle about 350 yards from the bridge, two companies of volunteer artillery from Baltimore took position behind a small breastwork.

Pinkney's 150-man Baltimore Rifle Battalion protected the artillery's right flank, using bushes, a fence, and the slope of the ground for cover. Two companies of Stansbury's militia, armed with muskets, took position behind the battery, guarding the Georgetown Road. The 5th Maryland was placed in a large apple orchard about fifty yards behind Pinkney's troops. Two more Maryland militia regiments, the 1st, under Lieutenant Colonel John Ragan, and the 2nd, under Lieutenant Colonel Jonathan Schutz, were farther back in the orchard, supporting the forward troops.

Considering the hurried placement, the position was relatively strong, taking advantage of the terrain and leaving the units in close support of each other. Pinkney's men up front were cheered by the sight of the 5th Maryland in their blue uniforms immediately to their rear. For their part, the men of the supporting regiments, many of whom had not eaten since breakfast the day before, were delighted to be in the shade of an orchard.

Word spread that the British were advancing rapidly, and the men rushed to prepare their positions. The earthworks—a bank of dirt with a ditch in front—had been constructed for heavy guns, but the Baltimore Artillery's six-pounders were far too small to fire over the high embankment. Stripping off their tunics, the men hastily dug openings in the parapet to allow their smaller guns to fire at the bridge and roads.

As the dirt flew around the earthworks, an alarm was raised, and the men formed into a line of battle. A cloud of dust had arisen across the river, announcing the rapid approach of a large body of troops.

En route to Bladensburg, morning, Wednesday, August 24

Maryland militia Captain Jenifer Sprigg was saying grace when the order came to forget about breakfast and start marching. The 800 men of Colonel William Beall's Annapolis militia had departed the state capital for Bladensburg two days earlier, but progress had been slow. They had spent a jittery night retreating in the dark, fearing the British were following. At daylight the regiment resumed the march to Bladensburg. They had stopped briefly to cook breakfast when Beall received word that if they did not hurry, the enemy would get there first. "One half of the poor devils hadn't taken a mouthful," Sprigg, adjutant for the regiment, wrote several days later. "I never left anything so much against my will." The men took off in a gallop.

Around 11 a.m. the Annapolis militia crested Lowndes Hill and hurried toward the village. As they approached the bridge, the men noted an array of American cannons, rifles, and muskets trained on them from across the river. Every man on the American front line was convinced the approaching troops were British. "They had their matches lighted ready to fire on us, but soon found out their mistake, not seeing any red-coats," Sprigg wrote. The defenders were ordered to stand down, and the Annapolis men, exhausted after their sixteen-mile march, passed through the American lines.

Forces were converging on Bladensburg from all points on the map. Militia and regular army troops, cavalry regiments, and artillery wagons clogged the turnpike from Washington. The poorly conditioned citizen soldiers of the District militia were falling out of formation and lagging behind in the stifling heat, terrible even by the wretched standards of August in the Chesapeake.

Behind the District militia, Commodore Barney led a procession of flotillamen and marines up the road. Horses and mules hauled big guns and wagons loaded with powder and ammunition. "The day was hot, and my men very much crippled from the severe marches we had experienced the preceding days," Barney reported. The commodore had managed to procure shoes that morning to replace those lost when the flotilla was abandoned, but the new footwear was torturous on the men's feet.

Last of all came Colonel Minor's Virginia militia regiment, delayed by their hunt for guns and ammunition. After being brushed off by Armstrong the previous evening, Minor searched all morning in vain for the officer in charge of the armory. Finally, Winder gave orders for their arms, but at the armory, the men endured an excruciating wait while a young clerk painstakingly double-counted the flints needed to fire the guns. When his men finally marched off with their weapons, Minor had to wait to sign receipts.

ADDISON CHAPEL, LATE MORNING, WEDNESDAY, AUGUST 24

Ross wanted to get to Bladensburg before the Americans did. The Light Brigade led the way, scouring fields, thickets, and ravines. The men marched in quickstep, three paces at a trot, followed by three walking. By 9 a.m. the invading army emerged from the woods and marched through open country. "The sun . . . now beat upon us in full force; and the dust rising in thick masses from under our feet, without a breath of air to disperse it," wrote Lieutenant Gleig. Many men fell behind and some collapsed altogether. Captain Thomas Falls, Ross's aide, slumped off his horse, a victim of sunstroke.

But they kept marching. By 10 a.m., after nine debilitating miles, Ross halted at Addison Chapel, a gable-roofed brick sanctuary, allowing the men to rest and stragglers to catch up. Soldiers threw themselves on the shady grass by a nearby stream and instantly fell asleep. Ross let them recover for more than an hour before resuming the march to Bladensburg, just four miles away.

BLADENSBURG, LATE MORNING, WEDNESDAY, AUGUST 24

Francis Scott Key, riding on horseback and dressed in civilian clothes, arrived at Bladensburg ahead of the troops from Washington, accompanying his neighbor, Brigadier General Walter Smith, commander of the District militia. Key was acting as a civilian aide to Smith, a lay leader at their Georgetown church. Key helped Smith scout for positions to place his troops. Key had no skills as a military tactician, but he at least knew the terrain around Bladensburg well from many visits over the years.

They selected high ground overlooking a gentle ravine about a half mile to the rear of Stansbury's Maryland militia. Smith rode off to iron out command details with Stansbury, leaving Key to direct the arriving District troops into position. The troops were not yet in sight, but shortly before noon, Key intercepted Winder as he arrived from Washington.

Key "informed me that he had thought that the troops coming from the city could be most advantageously posted on the right and left of the road near that point," Winder wrote. Key was acting at the behest of Smith, but Winder, well acquainted with Key from Maryland legal circles, was annoyed by the presumption of his fellow attorney in telling him how to array his army. As Key dashed about on his horse to show Winder the positions, Smith rode up. Winder, impatient with the delay, quickly approved the plan and left Smith and Key to oversee the positioning of the District militia.

Up front, another cloud of dust could be seen rising across the river. The Maryland troops manning the line spotted bayonets glittering in the midday sun, and distant glimpses of troops in red tunics approaching Bladensburg from the south. This time, there was no doubt it was the British.

Major Pinkney moved among the companies at the front, giving last-minute instructions. But he was distressed to see the blue-uniformed 5th Maryland Regiment troops in the orchard behind the men were gone. The regiment "had now, to the great discouragement of my companies and of the artillery, been made to retire to a hill several hundred yards in our rear . . . where it could do little more than display its gallantry," he wrote.

Likewise, Brigadier General Stansbury, giving direction to the artillery, watched in astonishment as his 1st and 2nd regiments marched out of the orchard and up the hill, and formed a battle line about 250 yards above the orchard, more than five hundred yards behind the front line. The displaced troops were no longer covered by orchard, and worse, were too far back now to support the front line. "Whose plan this was, I know not; it was not mine; nor did it meet with my approbation," Stansbury reported.

The plan belonged to Colonel Monroe, who had arrived at the scene and did not like Stansbury's arrangement. The secretary of state concluded that the left side of the American line was exposed and could be easily flanked by the enemy. Though he had no authority, Monroe decided to rearrange the troops. The regimental commanders did not question the order from the secretary of state. Even as he did it, Monroe disavowed responsibility. "Although you see that I am active, you will please . . . bear in mind that this is not my plan," he told Lieutenant Colonel Joseph Sterett, the 5th Maryland commander. Monroe also sent the Annapolis militia to a hill in the rear and directed Lieutenant Colonel Jacint Laval's cavalry squadron to a ravine so deep that the commander was unable to see anything.

Monroe would later say he acted "with reluctance and in haste." To a friend, he defended his actions, saying he had filled a vacuum. "I advanced myself on the lines . . . because I not only thought I might be useful, but that there appeared to me to be a necessity for it," Monroe wrote.

Stansbury rode back in a fury to find out who had moved his men and found the secretary of state. Before Stansbury could learn what had happened, Winder joined them, and Stansbury promptly dropped the matter. Monroe adroitly informed Winder that he had been "aiding" Stansbury in posting his troops and suggested Winder take a moment to examine the positions.

Winder appeared to recognize that the troops were not in support of one another, but he did nothing to correct it, perhaps unwilling to countermand the orders of Monroe. In any event, with the appearance of the British across the river, there was little time left.

Winder made a few adjustments, moving more firepower up front. Two guns from the Washington Artillery were rushed up and placed in the road within range of the bridge. But the general would go to battle with his troops in positions that he had almost nothing to do with selecting.

BLADENSBURG, NOON, WEDNESDAY, AUGUST 24

A cheer rose from the American troops as President Madison arrived on the scene. The president, accompanied by Attorney General Rush and James Smith, his servant, rode doggedly ahead, searching for General Winder, who he assumed was in Bladensburg. In his haste Madison failed to notice that he had ridden past the American lines into a no-man's-land between two opposing armies.

Madison's party was about to cross the bridge into Bladensburg when they encountered an American scout riding in the opposite direction. It was William Simmons, a former War Department accountant well known to Madison. The president had fired him in July for "rudeness to his superiors." Hard feelings notwithstanding, Simmons had volunteered his services to scout Bladensburg. From atop Lowndes Hill, he had watched the British advance until they reached the town. Simmons dashed back across the bridge toward American lines, where he ran almost headfirst into the president. "Mr. Madison, the enemy are now in Bladensburg," Simmons called.

Madison was shocked. "The enemy in Bladensburg!" the president repeated. The president and his companions reined back their horses and dashed back toward American lines—so fast, by Simmons account, that Rush's hat blew off. Not only was Madison the first American president to arrive on a battlefield—and the only one, save Abraham Lincoln during the Civil War—he had nearly become the first American president to be captured or killed in battle.

Madison found Winder conferring behind the lines with Armstrong and Monroe. The president asked Armstrong if he had consulted with Winder about troop positions. When the secretary said he had not, Madison told him that it "might not be too late." Armstrong dutifully complied. The president wanted to join the conversation, but his borrowed horse began bucking, and he was unable to hear a word. Madison did not miss much. Armstrong gave no suggestions, telling the president afterward that the troop disposition "appeared to be as good as circumstances admitted."

Winder's troops, many of them still huffing their way from Washington, totaled about 5,500 men. Most were militia, including about 3,000 from Maryland and 1,100 from the District of Columbia. The remainder included 500 flotillamen, 120 marines, and several hundred U.S. Army regulars from several infantry and cavalry units.

Winder rode forward a few yards, exhorting the troops on the front line to be firm. A messenger arrived with word of a great American victory in Canada, and Winder ordered the news given to the men. The report was not true, but that hardly mattered at the moment, and the troops broke out in hearty cheers.

Rush, the son of Benjamin Rush, the famed Philadelphia physician and signer of the Declaration of Independence, thought it appropriate to say a few words. A staunch Madison loyalist, the thirty-three-year-old Rush was an early and enthusiastic supporter of war with Britain, and had replaced Pinkney as attorney general when the latter resigned in January 1814 to resume private practice. Though he lacked Pinkney's stature, Rush was considered a rising star in the Republican party. But Rush had barely begun exhorting the Baltimore troops when he was cut off by an angry militia officer, who told the attorney general that his men did not need to be told their duty.

BLADENSBURG, 12:30 P.M., WEDNESDAY, AUGUST 24

The final push to Bladensburg was the hardest march yet for the British invaders. Laboring under heavy loads and miserable in their wool uniforms, their mouths open and gasping for breath, the troops were goaded on by officers. "Our poor fellows being so tired, from the long march of the morning and the excessive heat of the day, that many of them striving to keep up, fell down from actual fatigue, and breathed their last," wrote Colonel Brooke, commander of the 2nd Brigade. The Light Brigade, with lesser loads, reached the town outskirts around 12:30, but the remaining two brigades lagged several miles behind and rushed to catch up. A dozen soldiers, apparent victims of heatstroke, were left dead along the way.

The road, which had run parallel to the Eastern Branch, veered left to the town. The Americans abruptly came into view, arrayed on the rising ground across the river. Ross paused outside of town. It seemed unlikely that the Americans would have completely abandoned Bladensburg. At the least, they might have positioned sharpshooters in the brick buildings. Ross directed Major Francis Brown, commander of the advance party, to probe and clear the town.

Word came back that Bladensburg was indeed empty. Ross, accompanied by Cockburn and other officers, climbed a hill to look over the American lines. From the second floor of a house on the slope, they had a good view of the terrain across the river and into the city limits beyond. Ross examined the enemy positions with his spyglass.

The American forces were arrayed in a triangle; the first line had guns trained on the bridge and town, and a second line of troops was positioned about a quarter mile to its rear. Farther back, Ross could see a third line being formed—the arriving troops of the District militia. To Ross, the Americans appeared "strongly posted on very commanding heights," with a large cavalry force and worrisome artillery positions. He put their overall strength at eight or nine thousand; like the Americans, the British tended to overestimate the size of the enemy.

The terrain favored the Americans. First the British would have to fight their way across the river under heavy fire. Then they would find themselves in low, marshy ground, facing an uphill assault for several hundred yards against American positions.

The American troops were not terribly impressive-looking, it was true, with their motley collection of uniforms. Some were in black coats, others green; some in shooting jackets, others round frocks. Some looked like they had come straight from the farm; others ap-

peared to be on their way to church. A few units looked more professional, including the 5th Maryland in the handsome blue uniforms,
which reminded the Wellington veterans of the French army.

As Ross scanned the American lines, he was joined by Colonel William Thornton, commander of the Light Brigade. The Irish-born
Thornton was a brave and impetuous Peninsular War veteran awarded
the gold medal for bravery in France, and he urged Ross to seize the
initiative with an immediate attack. Cockburn supported the idea,
considering it a "dashing measure."

But some of Ross's staff were taken aback by Thornton's proposal,
believing it rash in the face of artillery. Most of the British force had
not even arrived, and those who had were exhausted. Captain Harry
Smith recommended Ross probe the defenses, look for a crossing point
above the bridge, and make a feint to draw off the enemy. Smith was
pointing out American gun positions when Thornton cut off the
younger officer and again pressed for an immediate attack. "I positively laughed at him," Smith recalled. "He got furiously angry with
me." Smith protested that an attack would be "mad" without the support of the remaining two British brigades, more than a mile behind.
Barely a third of his 4,200-man army was available to attack a defending American force clearly larger than the British.

From the start of the invasion, Ross had moved cautiously, and
some of those present wondered if he might yet call off the attack.
"What will be said of us in England if we stop now," one officer, possibly Cockburn, mused aloud for Ross to hear. Yet Ross was hardly a
timid soldier. At Vitoria, Pamplona, Maida, and many other battlefields in Spain and Italy, he had proven he could carry forward an attack against a strong enemy. Surely the American militia would not be
so formidable, as Cockburn had told him many times.

Bypassing Bladensburg by heading north was not a particularly
good option. The lack of roads and dense woods would make it difficult, if not impossible, to swing around to Washington, and Ross
would be exposing his rear to American attack.

It was obvious the American lines across the river were not in supporting distance of one another—potentially a fatal flaw. Ross could
see something else. Much of the American force was still arriving. He
would wait no longer. Ross ordered an immediate attack.

O say can you see by the dawn's early
[w]hat so proudly we hail'd at the twilight's last gleaming
[w]hose broad stripes & bright stars through the perilous fight
O'er the ramparts we watch'd were so gallantly streaming

And the rocket's red glare, the bombs bursting in air
Gave proof through the night that our flag was still there
O say does that star-spangled banner yet wave
O'er the land of the free & the home of the brave?

On the shore dimly seen through the mists of the deep
Where the foe's haughty host in dread silence reposes
What is that which the breeze, o'er the towering steep
As it fitfully blows, half conceals half discloses?

Now it catches the gleam of the morning's first beam
In full glory reflected now shines in the stream
'Tis the star-spangled banner — O long may it wave
O'er the land of the free & the home of the brave.

And where is that band who so vauntingly swore
That the havoc of war & the battle's confusion
A home & a Country should leave us no more
Their blood has wash'd out their foul footstep's pollution

No refuge could save the hireling & slave
From the terror of flight or the gloom of the grave
And the star-spangled banner in triumph doth wave
O'er the land of the free & the home of the brave.

O thus be it ever when freemen shall stand
Between their lov'd home & the war's desolation
Blest with vict'ry & peace may the heav'n rescued land
Praise the power that hath made & preserv'd us a nation

Then conquer we must, when our cause it is just
And this be our motto — "In God is our trust"
And the star-spangled banner in triumph shall wave
O'er the land of the free & the home of the brave.

The British were caught in a murderous crossfire.

Final Stand at Bladensburg, showing U.S. Marines, part of Commodore Joshua Barney's force, firing 12-pound cannon and muskets at the advancing British.

CHAPTER 7

———— ★ ————

The Battle for Washington

TWO COLUMNS OF British troops trotted down Lowndes Hill "in a very fine style," noted Major William Pinkney, watching from the American front line across the river. Drums beat and bugles sounded as the enemy soldiers moved down the main street of Bladensburg toward the bridge, showing little fear, to the discomfort of the Americans.

No one could explain why the bridge was still standing. Brigadier General Stansbury had ordered a party of cavalry to destroy the narrow wooden span with axes when the enemy drew near. "Why this order was not executed I never could learn," Stansbury later said. Possibly, the plan had been delayed to allow the Annapolis regiment to cross, and then was overlooked in the confusion. The Eastern Branch was fordable just above Bladensburg, but the bridge would allow the British a much quicker crossing, even though exposed to deadly fire.

When the British reached the foot of the bridge, Winder opened fire with the six-pound guns of the Baltimore Artillery. After so long without any American resistance, the British seemed surprised by the barrage, and several fell. The rest quickly dispersed, taking cover behind buildings and trees. The guns kept a sharp fire, but the British stayed out of sight; the Americans could get only occasional glimpses of redcoats as they dashed between houses.

The Americans whooped and hollered, to the irritation of the British troops. "[T]hey set up three cheers, thinking, I dare say, that we were panic-struck with their appearance," said Lieutenant Charles Furlong, an officer with the 21st Fusiliers. A Scottish soldier, his arm shattered by shot, took shelter on a house doorstep and called back with a warning: "Dinna hallo, my fine lads, you're no' yet out of the wood. Wait a wee bit, wait a wee, with your skirling."

The sounds of the guns ahead spurred the troops from Washington, who were nearing the end of their five-mile race to Bladensburg. The temperature had reached 98 degrees—blood heat—and was still rising. Coated with dust and stricken with thirst, the men clutched their muskets to their chests as they hurried forward.

The District troops rushed to form a third line on high ground overlooking a ravine, about a mile from the Bladensburg bridge. The new American line was so far back that Stansbury and Pinkney—as well as the vast majority of Maryland militia manning the first and second lines—had no idea it existed. The orchard blocked their view to the rear. Nor did Winder bother to inform them. "In a word, I was ignorant of any reinforcements," Pinkney later said.

Francis Scott Key rode up and down the dusty turnpike and across fields, directing the arriving troops to the positions chosen with General Smith, the District militia commander. Major Peter arrived ahead of his Georgetown Artillery battery, and Key escorted him to a site commanding the ravine and road. Peter, however, considered it too isolated and "no position for light artillery." To Smith's displeasure, Peter chose a spot farther back that retained a commanding field of fire.

The 1st District Regiment, under Colonel George Magruder, took position immediately left of the turnpike, while Colonel William Brent's 2nd District Regiment set up behind Peter's artillery. The 300 regulars of the 36th and 38th U.S. regiments, under Lieutenant Colonel William Scott, manned Peter's left flank. Farther out on the left flank, Davidson and Stull posted their companies on high ground at the head of the ravine.

Barney arrived ahead of the flotillamen and marines to scout his position. He would anchor the line, atop the turnpike, filling a gap between Beall's Annapolis militia, posted on a hill to his right, and the

District militia, to the left of the road. Hearing the guns up front firing, Barney sent an officer to hurry his men.

Barney planted his heaviest artillery, two enormous eighteen-pounders, in the road, and three twelve-pounders to the right. Most of Captain Samuel Miller's marines, bolstered by a contingent of flotilla-men, were posted on Barney's right to protect the guns. The battery was positioned directly on the border between Maryland and the District of Columbia, a last bastion guarding the capital of the United States. Said Barney, "[W]e took our position on the rising ground . . . and waited the approach of the enemy."

President Madison, accompanied by Monroe, Armstrong, and Rush, watched the battle on horseback from a position directly behind the front line, to the rear of the Washington Artillery. The early results had been encouraging. Then Armstrong pointed out some activity across the river in the village, where an enemy detachment was setting up equipment behind a warehouse. In a moment, the secretary announced, the president would personally see the infamous Congreve rockets in action.

The rockets were a portable and versatile substitute for regular artillery. Sir William Congreve, the son of a British army officer, had adapted them from rockets used for centuries by the Chinese. Resembling skyrockets, they could be launched from a simple tripod and were notoriously inaccurate, but this added an element of fear. They flew at up to 200 miles per hour, hissing and roaring, trailing flame and

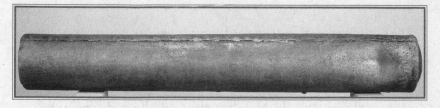

Congreve rockets photo. Resembling skyrockets, they could be launched from a simple tripod and were notoriously inaccurate, but this added an element of fear.

British Congreve rocket used in the Chesapeake campaign.

smoke, sometimes changing direction in midflight, and exploded with a thunderous clap, showering shards of metal or case shot. British rockets had ignited a conflagration at Copenhagen in 1807 and terrified a column of French troops at Leipzig in 1813. Cockburn's men had been using them in the Chesapeake for more than a year, from Havre de Grace to the battles with Barney's flotilla at St. Leonard Creek. For most of raw American militia troops at Bladensburg, who had scarcely seen a cannon fire, they were weapons of terror.

The first rockets flew high over the heads of the American frontline troops and sailed toward the rear. Several rockets whistled over the heads of the presidential party. "The enemy had saluted us with their rockets," Monroe later noted wryly.

Winder rode up to Madison and urged him to take "a more respectful distance." Madison complied, though his concern was less about personal safety than for not interfering with military command now that the battle was under way. "After some pause, the President remarked to the Secretary of War and myself that it would now be proper for us to retire in the rear, leaving the military movement to military men, which we did," Monroe recalled.

The cabinet rode back to watch from a safer position behind the third American line, anchored by Barney. Armstrong fumed, believing that Madison had reneged on his earlier instructions that the secretary take a more active role. To the conspiracy-minded Armstrong, it was a deliberate slap. "I now became, of course, a mere spectator of the combat," he said.

BLADENSBURG BRIDGE, EARLY AFTERNOON, WEDNESDAY, AUGUST 24

The British in the village remained pinned down by American artillery. When a cannonball clipped the leg off a young British soldier, he looked quizzically at his comrades, as if wondering how to react.

Colonel Thornton rode up on a gray horse, drawing his sword to rally the men. "Now my lads, forward!" Thornton called. "You see the enemy; you know how to serve them." Galloping ahead, Thornton threw himself full length atop his horse and charged across the 120-foot-long bridge. The men followed, tossing their haversacks onto the street to lighten their loads. Even before they reached the crossing, the troops came under a hailstorm of musket fire as sharp as any encountered in France. Some troops balked at continuing, but officers prodded them forward and prevented their retreat.

The Washington Artillery gun crews, with two six-pounders planted on the road ahead, waited until the enemy filled the bridge and then opened up, firing solid shot at 900 miles per hour. The opening barrage hit the British with deadly power, sweeping down seven men. But troops filled the gap and moved forward, stepping over the bodies of dead and dying comrades. Nervous American gunners rushed their subsequent fire. "[T]heir shots went generally clean over our heads," said Lieutenant Furlong, of the 21st Fusiliers.

Thornton emerged unharmed on the opposite bank, with the lead elements of the Light Brigade close behind. Watching from the village, Ross and Cockburn cheered. Ross instructed Captain Harry Smith to bring up the two remaining brigades as quickly as possible. Then he and Cockburn galloped to join Thornton's men. "Come on my boys," Ross called.

A stream of troops crossed the bridge. More light troops emerged from hiding places in the village and dashed to the riverside. As they pressed across the shallow water, Pinkney's riflemen poured fire on the British. But most made it across, taking temporary cover in the willow trees and bushes that lined the banks.

Private Henry Fulford, a Baltimore militiaman positioned behind the artillery, was disconcerted to see the British advancing through the onslaught. "The fire I think, must have been dreadfully galling, but they took no notice of it," he wrote in a letter two days later. "[T]heir men moved like clock-work: the instant a part of a platoon was cut down it was filled up by the men in the rear without the least noise and confusion whatever." These were Wellington's Invincibles, incomparable soldiers, driven by discipline and duty. It was a frightening sight for the American militia.

The numbers of British crossing the river by the bridge or through the water grew by the minute. The soldiers expertly wheeled to the right or left as they crossed, forming lines. Light troops dashed into thickets along the riverbank, quickly clearing out American skirmishers.

Thornton attacked the two Washington Artillery guns in the road, which were still laying heavy fire. Just short of the battery, the colonel's horse was hit by a cannonball and sank to the ground, but Thornton alighted on the road and continued forward, saber aloft. The gun crews hastily abandoned their position.

To Major Pinkney's right, a company of militiamen fired one volley and promptly fled at the sight of the British bayonets. Nor could the Baltimore Artillery help. Though the British were in easy range, crews could not swing the guns in their oversize parapet to reach the enemy on their flank. Pinkney's rifle battalion now faced the brunt of the British attack. They kept up their fire, but getting anxious, they hurried their shots as the British line pressed closer.

The American front line disintegrated. Pinkney had given his men no order to retreat, but, he later said, they would have been "taken prisoner or cut to pieces" if they had stayed longer. Pinkney moved back with the last of his men. But as he did, a musket ball splintered the former attorney general's arm. Several men moved him to a safer position, preventing the British from capturing the man who had drafted the declaration of war against their country.

Winder, on the hill immediately behind the 5th Maryland, was unaware that his entire front line had collapsed until he saw Pinkney's men running in his direction. His view from the second defensive line—the one chosen by Monroe—was blocked by the orchard. Nevertheless, he recognized the precariousness of the situation, particularly looking across the river, where a fresh column of British troops approached the bridge. Meanwhile, the lead brigade under Thornton had swept past the abandoned American positions and continued forward, infiltrating the orchard and firing on the militia's flank.

Winder took quick action, ordering the 5th Maryland forward in the hope of restoring his front line before more British troops crossed. Joined by Pinkney's battalion, the 600 men moved steadily down the hill in three ranks of blue. Once within range of the enemy, Sterett, the regimental commander, ordered a volley. The thunderous eruption of hundreds of muskets brought the British to a halt.

But a new barrage of Congreve rockets restored the British momentum. The rocket teams shrewdly aimed at the ranks of raw militia rather than the more professional 5th Maryland troops. This time the rockets took horizontal flight, passing closely over the heads of Schutz's and Ragan's regiments. "[T]hey began to throw them very exact about middle high right through the ranks; and as we were near the center they came hot about us," Ensign George Hoffman, in Ragan's regiment, wrote his father.

To Winder's dismay, the rockets sparked a panic. "Here they come, here they come!" yelled the men, dropping their guns and fleeing. "A universal flight of these two regiments was the consequence," reported the general. He galloped toward the men, screaming for them to halt.

Hoffman's company held long enough to fire a volley at the advancing British infantry. When the smoke cleared, Hoffman's men had vanished. "I looked round and see them tumbling over the fence which was about 20 yards from us," he wrote. Hoffman ran after them. "Form, form, for God's sake halt," he cried. The men ignored the young ensign, but they listened when Lieutenant Colonel Ragan, a cool-headed former regular, rode up. "Men, stand by me, the enemy are flying before us," the colonel called. Somehow, Winder and his regimental commanders stopped the retreat. The general rode back to rejoin the 5th Maryland and resume the attack.

By now, though, more British were on the way. Colonel Brooke's 2nd Brigade, with 1,460 infantrymen, had crossed the bridge with orders from Ross to press the American flanks. One battalion, the 4th Foot, veered left to support the Light Brigade, while the other, the 44th Foot, went right to envelop the American left flank.

For the militiamen, already jittery from the rockets and the fire from the orchard, the sight of approaching bayonets proved too much. Hoffman's company had barely re-formed into ranks when the enemy appeared on rising ground in front of them and fired down at the militia. The men again broke, ignoring pleas to halt. Ragan once more tried to stop the collapse, but his horse was hit by fire. The colonel was thrown roughly to the ground and captured by the advancing British. Brigadier General Stansbury rode along the line, raging and cursing, and ordered his officers to "cut down those who attempted to fly." Almost no one listened. Out of 1,300 men in the two militia regiments, only 80 remained. Winder had scarcely resumed his position when he looked back and saw the men "flying in the utmost precipitation and disorder."

The 5th Maryland's right flank was completely exposed by the two fleeing regiments. Worried they would be enveloped, Winder ordered the 5th Maryland and the Washington Artillery on the left flank to retreat up the hill, intending to resume the fight from a safer position. The artillery officers ignored Winder and kept firing. Winder sharply repeated his order, and the artillerists reluctantly limbered their guns and moved back.

Almost immediately, Winder second-guessed himself. Fearing the retreat might "produce some confusion" among the raw troops, he countermanded his order. Winder was right: His commands to advance, retreat, and advance again produced the utmost confusion. The artillery wagons had only moved back a short distance when Winder instructed the captain to unlimber one piece and "give them another fire."

But it was too late. The enemy was swarming near the American's right flank, and Winder again ordered retreat. Steady until now, the 5th Maryland collapsed, its confidence shot by the confounding orders. The British fired at the backs of the retreating rear rank, setting off a panic.

Private Henry Fulford ran for his life. "I shaped my course for a woods in the rear, where I intended to lay down and rest, being almost fatigued to death, but the bullets and grape shot flew like hailstones about me and I was compelled to make headway for a swamp," he wrote two days later. The Washington Artillery likewise fled in disarray.

Laval's 1st U.S. Dragoons waited in the ravine where Monroe had set him, 1,500 yards back. The cavalry commander had little idea what was happening until he peeked over the edge. "All of a sudden our army seemed routed," he reported. "They poured in torrents past us." A panicked artillery company drove its wagons through the dragoons, knocking down horses and men alike and nearly crushing Laval's leg. The commander waited in vain for orders from Winder, and then joined the retreat, under a shower of fire from an advancing enemy column.

Said John Pendleton Kennedy, running in his dancing pumps, "We made a fine scamper of it."

The collapse of the first two American lines was disastrous, but its consequences grew graver still because the men retreated in the wrong direction. The British forces sweeping through the orchard pushed the Maryland militia northwest, toward the Georgetown Road, and away from the third and final American line, anchored on the Washington turnpike. The roads veered apart like the two arms of a Y.

Though well versed by now in the art of retreat, Winder had failed to set a rallying point. Most of the retreating troops were unaware that a third line even existed, much less that they should head in its direction. Winder threw himself into the tide of troops and tried to redirect the men off the Georgetown Road toward the third American line, but he was too late. Pursued by the British, the Maryland militia raced up the Georgetown Road several miles to a point where it split in three directions. "Each individual, on the retreat, took the road that suited his inclination," said Lieutenant John Law. The third line would have to fight on its own.

Madison sent his servant, James Smith, to rush to the President's House with a message: Dolley should leave immediately. The president moved back with Rush, grimly watching developments from hilltop to hilltop as they slowly rode toward Washington.

THIRD AMERICAN LINE, MID-AFTERNOON, WEDNESDAY, AUGUST 24

Barney saw the American militia flee in chaos and knew the British would not be far behind. Soon he spotted a red-coated column of British troops cresting a rise on the turnpike. Major Peter's Georgetown Artillery, positioned to Barney's left on a bluff overlooking the road, bombarded the advancing force. The British continued forward, crossing a small bridge at the bottom of the ravine and moving up the hill.

But the British halted when they saw Barney's big guns positioned on the road, and then gingerly approached. Barney held his fire until the enemy advanced to within several hundred yards, then ordered one eighteen-pounder to fire. A mass of deadly grapeshot cleared the road.

Colonel Thornton led a second British charge, and the men ran again headlong at Barney's guns. Grape and canister shot mowed down almost every man on the road. The British were caught in a murderous crossfire between Peter's rapid-firing six-pounders and Barney's big guns, the heaviest artillery fire that Thornton had ever experienced. A third charge was equally ghastly. "[A]ll were destroyed," Barney said succinctly. "Whole companies were cut down to a man as they approached our lines," recalled Bacon, the marine quartermaster.

Thornton had no taste for another direct onslaught at the guns, and instead attacked Barney's right flank. The British colonel rode along the bottom of the ravine, protected from American fire. After a short distance, Thornton dismounted and led a charge across an open field toward Barney's guns, five hundred yards up the hill.

Barney saw his opening. He ordered his infantry—Captain Miller's marines and the spare flotillamen—to charge the British line. At the same time, the commodore poured destructive grape and canister shot on the British flank. Thornton was still running, sword in the air, and was within fifty yards of Barney's position when a musket ball tore into his upper thigh, splintering the bone. He tumbled to the ground, where he was further peppered by grapeshot. Without the fearless Thornton at its head, the British charge lost all momentum.

Cutlasses raised, the charging marines and seamen took the British utterly by surprise. "Board them!" the sailors cried. The Americans drove the British back two hundred yards into the woods. Thornton lay on the ground grievously wounded as Barney's men passed close by, then he rolled unnoticed down the ravine, hoping to escape.

The British tried to rally. An army lieutenant sprang to his feet to lead a charge but had hardly taken a step when a musket ball hit him in the neck and he fell, instantly dead. Major Francis Brown, commander of the British advance party, led a small detachment up the ravine to attack Peter's Georgetown Artillery, but they encountered stiff resistance from infantry guarding the guns. Brown had just called to his men to take cover when he was struck by canister shot and fell unconscious. The ravine had turned into a killing field.

Major Peter thought the moment right for a counterattack that would devastate the British and carry the day for the Americans. The 300 untested regulars from the 36th and 38th U.S. Infantry regiments stood at the ready. "There was a sufficient number of troops in the rear of my guns . . . to have repulsed the enemy," Peter later wrote, "killed and crippled as they were at that moment."

But General Winder had already decided to retreat. The collapse of the front lines had shaken the American commander. Riding to the third American line after his failed attempt to redirect the Maryland militia, he knew nothing of the devastating crossfire laid on the British by the guns of Barney and Peter, or the shocking repulse of the Invincibles by the marines and flotillamen. Nor did he know that the District militia were standing firm on the third line, as were the U.S. regulars and Beall's Annapolis militia.

As soon as the 5th Maryland began its retreat, Winder sent a messenger to President Madison reporting that his army had been driven back, but that he intended to form a new line of defense somewhere between Bladensburg and the Capitol. Then Winder dispatched an aide with an order for General Smith, the District militia commander: Retreat.

The day hung in the balance. Ross and Cockburn, who earlier thought the battle won, rushed forward to the line. Ross brought up the 4th Foot, its troops utterly exhausted by their race to catch up to the battle. The scorching day had reached 100 degrees; three men collapsed and died from heatstroke while climbing the one hundred feet of elevation from the river to Barney's position. But the arrival of the reinforcements lent critical support to the British assault.

The tall Irish general cut an imposing figure on the handsome Arabian steed he had brought from France. Ross took personal command of Thornton's brigade, renewing the advance and blunting the U.S. Marines' charge. The shock of the American assault had worn off, and there were not enough marines and flotillamen to sustain it. The Americans pulled back under heavy fire from British sharpshooters. Captain Miller, the Marine commander, found himself in an impromptu duel with an enemy assailant. Each man leveled his musket, fired, and missed, but the British soldier was able to reload and fire again while Miller fixed his flint, shattering the captain's arm. Another U.S. Marine officer was shot through the neck, and nearly a quarter of the Marine detachment was dead or wounded.

As Ross directed his troops forward, a burst of Barney's grapeshot killed his horse, throwing the general to the ground. Ross was uninjured, though a later inspection found four musket ball holes in different parts of his clothing.

Cockburn directed rocket fire, mounted on a white charger and conspicuous in his gold-braided hat and blue uniform with epaulets. His alarmed aide, Lieutenant Scott, urged the admiral to take cover. "Poh! Nonsense," Cockburn replied. He supervised as Royal Marine Lieutenant John Lawrence and *Tonnant* Masters Mate Jeremiah McDaniel fired several rockets directly into the American ranks.

"Capital!" Cockburn cried. "Excellent." But almost immediately, McDaniel was shot in the face. As Cockburn called for medical assistance, a musket ball tore the stirrups off the admiral's saddle. Cockburn dismounted, and while Scott and a Royal Marine tried to repair his saddle with twine, a round shot flew in, killing the marine. But Cockburn, like Ross, was untouched.

Ross had no interest in directly attacking Barney's guns. Riding a new mount, the British general moved to Barney's far right flank, directing an attack up the hill where Colonel Beall was positioned with 700 men, most of them Annapolis militia.

Beall was a Revolutionary War veteran who had served bravely with the Continental Army at Long Island, but his men were untested militia, still exhausted from their sixteen-mile run that morning to Bladensburg. From their hilltop vantage point, the men had nervously watched the British advance inexorably through American lines, and now it appeared they were next. "A good many of our men stared as if they were looking at ghosts," wrote Captain Sprigg.

As the British drew near, an aide to Winder arrived with instructions to withdraw immediately. Beall was incredulous. "Does General Winder order me to retreat before we have fired a shot?" he asked. Beall did not order a retreat—he later said he did not remember receiving the order—and in any event it was too late. As the aide repeated Winder's order, the British opened fire from the woods on the right.

Lieutenant Colonel William Wood, Thornton's second in command, led the charge from the ravine but was badly wounded by a shower of musket balls. Nonetheless, under Ross's command, the British continued up the hill. After firing several ineffectual rounds, most of the unnerved militia fled, ignoring every effort at rally. The British surged to the top of the hill.

From Barney's position below, Charles Ball, the slave turned flotillaman, watched with disgust as the American right flank dissolved. "[T]he militia ran like sheep chased by dogs," he said.

On Barney's left, the District militia troops came under attack by the 44th Foot, which had broken off its chase of the Maryland militia to join the assault on the final American line. With his left flank dangerously threatened, General Smith ordered the District militia's 2nd Regiment, positioned in the rear, to rush forward and bolster the line. Just then, Smith received orders from Winder to retreat. Angry protests erupted from the men, many of whom had yet to fire a shot. "Victory was doubtful, but we did not cease to expect it, until we were ordered to retreat, nobody near us could tell why," said a soldier in Captain Davidson's infantry company.

The U.S. regulars under Lieutenant Colonel Scott had impatiently awaited orders to advance even as the British moved within pistol-shot range and opened fire, hitting a half-dozen U.S. troops. The regulars were returning fire when Winder rode up and ordered them to retreat. When an officer protested, Winder angrily repeated his order.

With the British closing on both flanks, Winder likewise aborted an attempt by the District militia to hold, directing Smith to instead make a stand on the heights of Washington, about a mile and a half before the Capitol. Peter and the Georgetown Artillery skillfully covered the retreat, and the District militia pulled back in relatively good order. Winder did not bother sending word to Barney that he was retreating.

The commodore was infuriated, if not particularly surprised, to see he had been abandoned. "[N]ot a vestige of the American Army remained," Barney later reported to Navy Secretary Jones.

The flight of Beall's regiment was particularly aggravating, as it gave Ross a commanding height to pour fire on Barney's gun crews. The British pushed forward sharpshooters, one of whom felled Barney's horse from under him. Another shot killed Sailing Master John Warner at the commodore's side. "[T]o the honour of my officers &

men, as fast as their companions & mess mates fell at the guns they were instantly replaced from the infantry," Barney reported.

As Barney stood by the guns, a musket ball slammed into his thigh. The commodore stayed on his feet and told no one, not wanting to alarm the men. But his situation was desperate. The gun batteries were out of ammunition and could not be replenished. The ammunition wagon drivers—civilian hires—had fled. Dozens of his men were dead or wounded, and he was nearly surrounded. Barney ordered the guns spiked and his men to retreat.

Loss of blood soon made it impossible for Barney to disguise the severity of his wound. He was faint and could scarcely hold up his head. Three officers tried to carry the commodore, but he was so weak they put him down. Barney ordered them away, but Sailing Master Jesse Huffington stayed, tending Barney's wound.

The British swarmed around the battery, shooting or bayoneting those who refused to surrender. Royal Navy Midshipman Samuel Davies, the son of an English parson, squared off with "a dam rascal" who had killed one of the British sailors. "[H]e made the first blow at me with his sword at my head I parried it off like a sailor with my cutlass and then it was my turn so I run him through the guts and killed him," Davies wrote in a letter to his mother.

Bullets flew after the escaping flotillamen. "I had my horse shot through the head and my hat shot through the crown," reported Sailing Master John Webster. "I did not take time to pick up my hat."

A British corporal from the 85th Light Infantry found Barney lying in his blood by a gun battery, still tended by Huffington. The commodore was not going to surrender to an enlisted man, and he directed the soldier to find an officer to handle the matter with proper decorum. The soldier promptly returned with Captain Jonathan Wainwright, commander of *Albion*. Learning the infamous Joshua Barney was finally in British hands, Wainwright went to find the admiral.

Cockburn, accompanied by Ross, quickly appeared. Wainwright introduced the admiral using the English pronunciation, "Coe-burn."

"Oh," replied Barney. " 'Cock-burn' is what you are called hereabouts."

The commodore's impertinence aside, the two British commanders had been much impressed by Barney's fearless fight and summoned an army surgeon to treat his wound. "Those officers behaved to me with the most marked attention, respect and politeness," Barney later said.

"Well, Admiral, you have got hold of me at last," Barney told Cockburn.

Cockburn was magnanimous in victory. "Do not let us speak on that subject, Commodore," Cockburn replied. "I regret to see you in this state. I hope you are not seriously hurt."

"Quite enough to prevent my giving you any trouble for some time," said Barney.

Ross turned to Cockburn. "I told you it was the flotilla men," he said.

"Yes!" the admiral declared. "You were right, though I could not believe you. They have given us the only fighting we have had."

As the surgeon dressed Barney's wound, Ross and Cockburn conferred in low tones. Then the general turned to Barney. "Commodore Barney, you are paroled, where do you wish to be conveyed?" It was a generous gesture of respect, sparing Barney the indignity of being held prisoner. Ross offered to take Barney to Washington, but the commodore declined, having no interest in seeing the capital in British hands. Barney asked to be taken instead to Bladensburg. Ross ordered a sergeants guard to carry Barney on a litter, and Cockburn directed Wainwright to accompany the commodore and attend to his needs.

Barney winced as the soldiers jostled him along the road, and Wainwright ordered them to put the commodore down, complaining that the soldiers did not know how to carry a man. A gang of sailors gingerly carried Barney the rest of the way, although one could not resist calling mockingly to a group of American prisoners: "Come over here, Yankees, to see your countryman Barney, he looks like a spread eagle, Yankees."

A captured flotillaman, his arm dangling from a severe wound, was overcome by emotion at the sight. Kneeling, he kissed Barney's hand and burst into tears. The British sailors were moved by the devotion shown to Barney, dabbing their eyes and blowing their noses. "Well, damn my eyes!" said one. "If he wasn't a kind commander, that chap wouldn't ha done that."

PRESIDENT'S HOUSE, 3 P.M., WEDNESDAY, AUGUST 24

Dolley Madison had ordered dinner to be ready at 3 p.m. as usual, despite the cannon fire audible from Bladensburg. It was not planned to be a victory banquet, as later claimed. Hospitality was always the order of the day in Dolley Madison's home, and she was determined to convey business as usual. Every day since the invasion, with Washington bustling with officers and transients, the table had been set in preparation for unexpected guests.

Dolley had been peering through her spyglass in every direction all day, hoping to see the president returning. "She was so confident of victory that she was calmly listening to the roar of cannon, and watching the rockets in the air," according to her friend, Margaret Bayard Smith. Nonetheless, Dolley made sensible preparations for hasty departure if warranted. A wagon had been procured to carry off valuables, and the horses harnessed to the carriage.

In the dining room, Paul Jennings busied himself with preparations for the meal. The fifteen-year-old slave, born at Montpelier, had accompanied the Madisons to Washington in 1809 at the start of the president's first term to help with household chores. "I set the table myself, and brought up the ale, cider, and wine, and placed them in the coolers, as all the cabinet and several military gentlemen and strangers were expected," he later wrote.

In the kitchen below, Jean-Pierre Sioussat, chief of the household staff, supervised the cooking. French John, as he was known, had arrived in

Hospitality was always the order of the day in Dolley Madison's home, and she was determined to convey business as usual.

Dolley Madison

America as a seaman aboard a French frigate in 1804 and decided to stay. The polished Parisian quickly rose through the ranks of domestics and landed a job at the President's House, where he had made himself an indispensable part of Dolley's social offensive. Always resourceful, French John offered to lay a train of powder to blow up should the British enter the President's House. "To the last proposition I positively object," Dolley told her sister. Instead of sabotage, Sioussat prepared for dinner, ensuring that plates were placed in tin warmers on the hearth and wines decanted into cut-glass bottles on the sideboard.

Shortly before 3 p.m., a lone rider galloped down Pennsylvania Avenue, covered with dust. James Smith, Madison's manservant, rode up to the President's House, waving his hat, and crying, "Clear out, clear out!" The British had crossed the river at Bladensburg and were rapidly marching on to the city, Smith announced. The American troops "had broken and run," he reported. The president wanted "his lady to quit the city immediately."

"All then was confusion," Jennings recalled.

The wagon was hastily loaded with a hodgepodge of valuables: silver plates, china, cabinet papers, a few books, and a small bronze clock that had been in the President's House since the Adams administration. At the last minute, Dolley ordered the long, crimson red velvet drapes from the drawing room placed on the wagon. The bulky fabric took up valuable space, but the first lady apparently wanted to save some part of the most elegant room in America. The wagon was dispatched to Maryland for safekeeping.

A small crowd gathered at the President's House as news spread. Her friend Charles Carroll of Bellevue urged Dolley to come with him to his Georgetown mansion, where others were gathering. Jacob Barker, a thirty-four-year-old New York financier who had secured funding for the war and become friendly with the Madisons, hurried to the President's House with his friend and fellow Quaker Robert G. L. De Peyster to help. Dolley's sister, Anna Payne Cutts, frantic over the "horrible" news, rushed from their nearby home with her husband, Richard, to join Dolley in flight.

Dolley's first instinct was to wait for Madison, but Carroll and the others persuaded her there was no time. Dolley ordered her carriage brought to the door. Passing through the dining room, she shoved into her purse all the silver that could fit.

Barker and others were ushering Dolley to the waiting carriage when her eye fell on the portrait of George Washington hanging on the wall behind the dining room table. It must not be left behind, she decided. Fifteen years after Washington's death, the Gilbert Stuart portrait had taken on great symbolic importance to the young nation, and its capture would be a huge coup for the British.

Dolley ordered the servants to take the portrait down. It would not budge. The canvas was stretched on a light wooden frame within a heavier gilt frame, which was screwed firmly to the wall. French John and Tom Magraw, the president's Irish gardener, struggled fruitlessly to pull it off. Minutes passed. Dolley's sister begged her to get in the carriage and leave, and Carroll scolded her for risking capture to save a painting. Dolley could see the lead elements of the routed army passing by outside. The road would soon be too jammed with troops to escape.

Finally, Dolley ordered the frame broken. French John and Magraw smashed the gilt frame with a hatchet. The portrait, still in its stretcher, was gingerly lowered to the hands of Barker and others below, and placed on the floor. "I directed my servants in what manner to remove it from the wall, remaining with them until it was done," Dolley later wrote. Sioussat and Jennings, however, recalled that she left before the portrait was down.

"It has often been stated in print, that when Mrs. Madison escaped from the White House, she cut out

"[A] rabble, taking advantage of the confusion, ran all over the White House, and stole lots of silver and whatever they could lay their hands on," Paul Jennings complained.

Paul Jennings, the young Madison family slave who helped save the portrait of George Washington and accompanied the president on his flight from Washington. (Photograph taken in the 1850s.)

from the frame the large portrait of Washington . . . and carried it off," Jennings wrote in his memoir. "This is totally false. She had no time for doing it. . . . All she carried off was the silver in her reticule, as the British were thought to be but a few squares off, and were expected every moment."

In any event, at nearly eight feet tall and five feet wide, the portrait was too large to fit in the waiting carriage. Dolley agreed to depart without it, but under one condition: The painting must not be left at the President's House. "Save the portrait of General Washington, if possible," she told Barker. "[I]f you cannot save it, destroy it—under no circumstances allow it to fall into the hands of the British." Barker promised Dolley that they would see to it.

By 3:30, Dolley jumped into the carriage with several others, including her sister Anna Cutts, and Dolley's servant girl, a slave named Sukey. "I lived a lifetime in those last moments waiting for Madison's return, and in an agony of fear lest he might have been taken prisoner!" she told a friend. Madison's coachman, Joe Bolen, took off for Carroll's Bellevue mansion on Q Street in Georgetown, and Richard Cutts followed in his carriage. John Freeman, the butler, drove off with his wife and children in the coachee, carrying a feather bed lashed to the back. Most everything else—including much of the public property collected over the terms of four presidents, and the Madisons' personal valuables—was left behind.

Dolley fought a last impulse to stay. "I confess that I was so unfeminine as to be free from fear, and willing to remain in the castle," she wrote several months later to a friend. "If I could have had a cannon through every window, but alas! Those who should have placed them there, fled before me, and my whole heart mourned for my country."

U.S. CAPITOL, LATE AFTERNOON, WEDNESDAY AUGUST 24

Retreating to the District militia's rendezvous point at the heights overlooking Washington, General Winder was not encouraged by what he saw. "[L]ooking round him, [he] saw his army scattered over the face of the whole country," an officer on General Smith's staff recalled. Winder ordered a further retreat to the Capitol, hoping to find the

Maryland militia waiting, though he had given no such instructions to Stansbury. "I supposed, from the rapidity of their flight, [they] might have reached that point," Winder noted sardonically.

But apart from the District militia, which arrived soon after the general, the only other organized unit forming near the Capitol was a group of 250 flotillamen who were not under Winder's command. With Barney and many of his officers wounded or dead, the flotillamen were without a leader.

Winder was conferring with Major Peter on the north side of the Capitol when Secretary of War Armstrong and Secretary of State Monroe rode up. Armstrong asked Winder his intentions. The general replied that "his force was broken down by fatigue and dispersion" and in no shape to fight, and that he intended to retreat again, this time to the heights above Georgetown. That meant surrendering the city to the British.

Monroe and Armstrong, in agreement for once, approved Winder's decision. "[W]e united in opinion that he should proceed to occupy the heights of Georgetown," Armstrong wrote soon afterward. Monroe agreed that taking a stand at the Capitol was too risky, and that a retreat to the Georgetown heights would leave the Americans in position to launch a counterattack. With that, Monroe and Armstrong wheeled their horses and rode off. Winder gave orders for the District militia to retreat through the city, into Georgetown, and continue to Tenleytown, a hamlet within the city limits about three miles northwest of Georgetown.

For the District militia, the order ended any illusions that they could save the city. "It is impossible to do justice to the anguish evinced by the troops of Washington and Georgetown on the receiving of this order," reported Smith. "The idea of leaving their families, their houses, and their homes at the mercy of an enraged enemy was insupportable." Smith and his officers found it impossible to maintain order. Angry troops broke off to protect homes and families. Others went "in pursuit of refreshments," as a congressional report put it. "Some shed tears, others uttered imprecations, and all evinced the utmost astonishment and indignation," Major Williams wrote.

From the third floor of his home on Capitol Hill, James Ewell, a Washington physician, saw thick clouds of dust rising over the trees and soon realized the militia was retreating into the city. "Presently I beheld the unfortunate Secretary of War and suite in full flight, followed by crowds of gentlemen on horseback, some of whom loudly bawled out as they came on, 'Fly, fly! The ruffians are at hand!' "

Among those riding into the city was Francis Scott Key, accompanying the District militia. His face was streaked with dust and sweat, and his horse was steaming as he rode along roads crowded with angry militiamen and civilians abandoning their homes. Stunned at the scale of the disaster, Key hurried past the Capitol and down tree-lined Pennsylvania Avenue, continuing to the President's House, and then on to his Georgetown home. The "memorable flight from Bladensburg," as he termed it, had been humiliating. Now the retribution he long feared was at hand.

PRESIDENT'S HOUSE, WASHINGTON, 4 P.M., WEDNESDAY, AUGUST 24

Weary after sixteen miles in the saddle in the dreadful heat, James Madison reached the President's House around 4 p.m., not long after Dolley had departed. He was accompanied by Attorney General Rush and several other men, including his friend General John Mason, the commissary general of prisoners, and Tench Ringgold, a local rope manufacturer. Madison took off the pistols George Campbell had loaned him and left them on the front hall table. He needed rest.

Barker and De Peyster were still at the President's House, seeing to the first lady's requests. After much difficulty, the two men had found a horse and cart, along with a driver and a young helper. The cart had been loaded with various items that Dolley had asked to be saved, including four cases of papers from Madison's private office, several large silver urns, and two ornamental eagles from the drawing room. The Washington portrait, which they were saving for last, still lay on the dining room floor.

Madison took a seat in the dining room and poured himself a glass of wine. French John had dinner to serve but Madison was not hungry. The president, in a reflective mood, described the battle to Barker and De Peyster. Steeped as he was in the Jeffersonian distrust of a standing regular army and in the belief in the citizen soldier, the day had been quite disillusioning. "I could never have believed that so great a difference existed between regular troops and a militia force, if I had not witnessed the scenes of this day," Madison told them.

Barney and the flotillamen, on the other hand, had deeply impressed Madison with their "good conduct." But in the end, the president said, the discipline of the British troops had proven too much. "He said the fire from Barney's guns made perfect lanes through the ranks of the enemy, but that the troops filled the voids thus created, without turning to the right or to the left to see whether their companions had lost a head, a leg or an arm," Barker recalled.

Outside, exhausted troops retreating along Pennsylvania Avenue stopped in front of the President's House. French John thoughtfully set out buckets of water and bottles of wine for their refreshment. Groups of soldiers wandered into the house, and at some point, George Campbell's pistols disappeared from the front hall and were never seen again.

Madison lingered for an hour, receiving reports and planning his next step. Though the president had told his cabinet to rendezvous in Frederick, Maryland, should the capital fall, he had dropped the plan, apparently for fear the road would be jammed. (No one informed Armstrong or Campbell, who dutifully rode to Frederick.) The next plan was to meet Dolley at Bellevue, the Carroll mansion in Georgetown, and then escape together to Virginia. But with time running short, Madison sent a messenger to Secretary of the Navy Jones, who had joined Dolley's group at Bellevue, with word that everyone should meet at the Foxall Foundry, an armaments manufacturer northwest of Georgetown on the Potomac River. From there they could escape into Virginia across the Little Falls Bridge.

Before leaving, Madison, joined by General Mason, took a quick look around the President's House. While Madison left no record of his thoughts on the occasion, it must have been a despondent and anxious moment. The survival of the nation he had helped create had never seemed so tenuous, a catastrophe brought on by the decision he supported for war with Great Britain. Now he must abandon the President's House and leave the capital to face the consequences. Madison mounted his horse and slowly rode toward the river.

After the president's departure, Barker and De Peyster went back to work. With their hired help, they picked the portrait off the floor, carried it out the front door, and loaded it into the cart. They fell into the trail of the retreating army into Georgetown, the life-size image of President Washington one more refugee riding in a cart.

Much of value remained in the President's House, to the delight of some local unsavory characters. "[A] rabble, taking advantage of the confusion, ran all over the White House, and stole lots of silver and whatever they could lay their hands on," Paul Jennings complained.

After everyone else cleared out, French John closed up. He carried Dolley's brightly colored, screech-voiced macaw—a favorite pet of the first lady—a few blocks away to the home of the French minister, leaving it with the chef for safekeeping. Back at the President's House, he banked the kitchen fires, closed the doors, and left.

WASHINGTON NAVY YARD, WEDNESDAY, AUGUST 24

Around 4 p.m., smoke rose from the Eastern Branch Bridge, and minutes later a tremendous explosion rocked the area, throwing fragments of wood into the air. Navy Captain John Creighton, hearing word of the British victory at Bladensburg, had ordered the Marine guard detail to ignite the powder kegs stowed on scows beneath the bridge.

Captain Thomas Tingey, commandant of the Washington Navy Yard, had just received word that the army could not defend the installation. Secretary of the Navy Jones had left Tingey with clear orders: Should the enemy enter the city, Tingey must destroy the Navy Yard, including the ships and the stores of supplies.

Short, stout, and temperamental, Tingey had been at the yard from its creation. The London-born officer had served in the Royal Navy, but after marrying the daughter of a Philadelphia merchant, he was commissioned a captain in the U.S. Navy. His familiarity with the great shipyards of England led to his selection in 1800 to oversee the building of the nation's first navy yard in the new capital. Within a few years, Tingey had transformed a piece of undeveloped tidal front into a bustling shipyard, which served as the homeport for the fledgling American fleet and remained one of the navy's most important shipbuilding and repair facilities.

Now he had to destroy it. With a heavy heart, Tingey ordered word spread in the neighborhood, home to hundreds of Navy Yard workers, and one of the most densely populated areas in town. A strong wind was blowing, and firing the yard could create a conflagration in the surrounding homes. Horrified residents appeared at Tingey's door, imploring him not to do it. Tingey sent them away, warning "any farther importunities would cause the matches to be instantly applied." If they left him alone, Tingey promised, "I would delay the execution of the orders, as long as I could feel the least shadow of justification."

Mordecai Booth, Tingey's clerk, could not fathom the idea. Captain Creighton was also strenuously opposed, not least because *Argus*, the sloop-of-war he was slated to take command, lay nearly ready at the Navy Yard wharf. Tingey was willing to hold off, but he needed accurate intelligence about the whereabouts of the British. Creighton and Booth offered to scout. Tingey agreed to wait for their report, but with great trepidation.

BLADENSBURG, 5 P.M., WEDNESDAY, AUGUST 24

The fear was universal in Washington that the enemy was on the tail of the retreating militia. But the victorious British army had pursued the fleeing Americans for only a mile before Ross called a halt. The British captured few prisoners, "owing to the swiftness with which the enemy went off," a jocular Cockburn reported. Without cavalry, the British had been unable to fully exploit their victory. Several officers from the 85th thought they spotted Madison riding off and lamented that they would have caught the president if only they had horses.

Ross decided rest was imperative. The wounded, many with terrible injuries, were carried to makeshift hospitals in Bladensburg. Details buried some of the dead and collected stragglers, and Barney's captured artillery was destroyed. The British had suffered greater casualties than the Americans, a measure of their costly charges in the face of artillery fire. Officially, the British reported 64 dead, 138 wounded, and another 107 captured or missing, but the numbers were likely higher. The brunt of the battle had fallen on Thornton's Light Brigade, which suffered about 25 percent casualties, including 86 dead or wounded in the 85th Light Infantry alone.

The Americans, by and large, had retreated too quickly to die, suffering at most 40 dead, up to 60 wounded, and 120 captured, by

Winder's estimate. The marines accounted for roughly a quarter of the American total, a grim reflection of their brave stand with the flotillamen, who also suffered heavily.

As the British rested, Ross and Cockburn conferred. Despite the exhaustion, there was little sense in giving the Americans time to regroup. Ross chose the 3rd Brigade, which had seen little combat, to lead the way into Washington; the brigade included the bulk of the Fusilier battalion, the seamen, and the Royal Marines. Also included were the Colonial Marines; the escaped slaves would have the honor of entering the capital as conquerors.

After a two-hour rest and a hasty meal, the 3rd Brigade fell in, and around 6 p.m. began its march on Washington, with Ross and Cockburn at the head.

GHENT, MIDNIGHT (6 P.M., WASHINGTON), WEDNESDAY, AUGUST 24

For five days, the American delegation in Ghent had squabbled on the proper response to the August 19 British ultimatum. All agreed that the outrageous British demands—in particular, the creation of a permanent Indian buffer state carved from American territory—must be rejected, even though it meant the peace talks would likely collapse. But exactly how to frame the language of the American response was at issue. John Quincy Adams drafted an initial reply. "I found, as usual, that the draft was not satisfactory to my colleagues," Adams wrote pithily in his diary. Albert Gallatin wanted to strike out every expression that might offend the British; Henry Clay thought Adams's old-fashioned figurative language was improper for a state paper; Jonathan Russell wanted to tinker with the construction of each sentence; James Bayard wanted it all recast in his own language. All of Adams's colleagues agreed about one other matter: The reply was much too long.

On Wednesday evening, the delegation met after dinner to hash out a final draft. "[W]e then sat until eleven at night, sifting, erasing, patching and amending, until we were all wearied," Adams wrote. None of the delegates was happy with the end result, but they gave in to exhaustion.

The American reply would be signed and delivered to the British in the morning. It would, predicted Adams, "bring the negotiation very shortly to a close." As the clocks in Ghent tolled midnight, Adams went to bed, fearing for his country's future.

WASHINGTON, EVENING, WEDNESDAY, AUGUST 24

The sun was setting at Mason's Ferry on the Georgetown waterfront as President Madison waited for a boat to carry him across the Potomac. Yet again, events had not unfolded as planned. Retreating militia jammed the roads, forcing Madison to drop his plan to rendezvous at the Foxall Foundry with Dolley, Jones, and the rest of their party. The president had sent Tench Ringgold to the foundry with word that he would instead cross by ferry to Virginia and meet the others at Salona, the estate of the Madisons' friends the Maffitt family.

Along with Rush, General Mason, and Paul Jennings, Madison rode the ferry across the Potomac to Mason's Island, today known as Theodore Roosevelt Island, a seventy-five-acre island by the Virginia shoreline. From there, the party crossed into Virginia via a causeway, mounted their horses, and rode up the Georgetown Road away from the river.

Meanwhile, Dolley Madison and the Cutts, Jones, and Carroll families struggled in their carriages through the clogged streets of Georgetown, arriving at Foxall only to learn from Ringgold that the president had crossed downriver. The group continued upriver toward the Little Falls Bridge to cross into Virginia.

Those left in the city watched in shock as Winder's broken army retreated through the streets. "[T]he poor creatures were marched to death on a dreadfully hot day before the engagement began & then retreated 12 or 13 miles without halting," Anna Maria Thornton, wife of Key's friend William Thornton, recorded in her diary. "[T]hey were obliged to lay down in the fence corners & anywhere on the road they were so completely exhausted with hunger and fatigue."

Lieutenant Colonel Laval and his cavalry squadron retreated past the Capitol and continued to the President's House, hearing a rumor that Winder planned to make a stand there, but upon arrival "saw no army or symptoms of any," he reported.

Navy clerk Mordecai Booth, reconnoitering the city, rode to the

President's House, expecting someone there would know the whereabouts of the American army. Instead, in front of the mansion, he encountered a lone cavalry officer who started to draw his weapon until Booth identified himself. The officer dismounted, walked up the steps, pulled the bell violently, knocked on the door, and called for French John. "But all was silent as a church," Booth reported. "Then, and not until then, was my mind fully impressed that, the metropolis of our country was abandoned to its horrid fate."

BRITISH BURN THE CAPITOL · 1814

As the inferno blazed, troops stood outside watching the Capitol
"wrapped in its winding sheet of fire."

*Mural on the ceiling in the House wing of the Capitol,
depicting its burning by the British.*

CHAPTER 8

A Spectacle Terrible and Magnificent

MOVING AT A fast clip as daylight waned, the British victors soon reached the outskirts of the capital. No resistance was met, save from a party of American cavalry that fired a futile volley and fled. General Ross halted on a field two miles from the Capitol. The bulk of the 3rd Brigade, about 1,200 men, would remain here. Ross wanted no looting and would enter Washington with only 200 Fusiliers, along with Cockburn and a naval party.

A pale moon rose as the troops moved down Maryland Avenue toward the Capitol. Ross and Cockburn rode together up front, accompanied by Lieutenant George De Lacy Evans. Close behind them rode Cockburn's aide, Lieutenant Scott and two of Ross's aides, Captain Harry Smith and Captain Duncan MacDougall, flanked by the troops.

On Capitol Hill, Michael Shiner, a nine-year-old slave, spotted the British column as soon as they crested a rise. "[T]hey looked like flames of fire, all red coats and the stocks of their guns painted with red vermillion, and the iron work shined like a Spanish dollar," he later wrote. That one glimpse was enough for Shiner; he and a companion began running. An old lady named Mrs. Reid collared Shiner before he got away. "Where are you running to, you nigger, you?" she asked. "What do you reckon the British wants with such a nigger as you?"

His friend slipped away and hid in a baking oven, but Shiner, his courage bolstered by Mrs. Reid's impolite question, stuck around to watch what happened next.

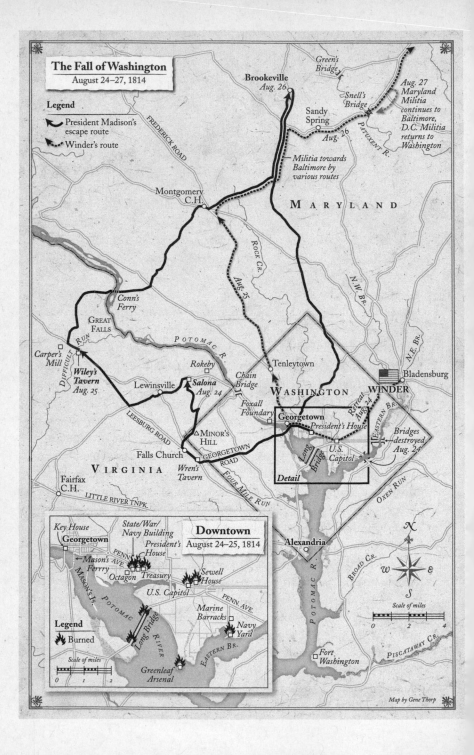

The Fall of Washington
August 24–27, 1814

Legend
— President Madison's escape route
--- Winder's route

Green's Bridge

Brookeville
Aug. 26

Snell's Bridge

Sandy Spring

Aug. 27 Maryland Militia continues to Baltimore, D.C. Militia returns to Washington

FREDERICK ROAD

Aug. 26

Patuxent R.

Montgomery C.H.

Militia towards Baltimore by various routes

M A R Y L A N D

ROCK CR.

Aug. 25

Conn's Ferry

GREAT FALLS

N.W. BR.

Potomac R.

Tenleytown

N.E. BR.

Carper's Mill

DIFFICULT RUN

Wiley's Tavern *Aug. 25*

Rokeby

Chain Bridge

W A S H I N G T O N

WINDER

Bladensburg

Lewinsville

Salona *Aug. 24*

Foxall Foundary

Retreat Aug. 24

EASTERN BR.

LEESBURG ROAD

MINOR'S HILL

Georgetown

President's House

Bridges destroyed Aug. 24

Falls Church

Wren's Tavern

GEORGETOWN ROAD

Long Bridge

U.S. Capitol

Oxen Run

V I R G I N I A

Fairfax C.H.

LITTLE RIVER TNPK.

FOUR MILE RUN

Detail

Alexandria

POTOMAC R.

BROAD CR.

N

W ⊕ **E**

S

Scale of miles

0   2   4

Fort Washington

PISCATAWAY CR.

Downtown
August 24–25, 1814

Key House

Georgetown

State/War/ Navy Building

President's House

Mason's Ferrry

PENN. AVE.

Octagon

Treasury

Sewell House

MASON'S IS.

POTOMAC

U.S. Capitol

PENN. AVE.

Marine Barracks

Legend

🔥 Burned

Scale of miles

0   1   2

Long Bridge

EASTERN BR.

RIVER

Navy Yard

Greenleaf Arsenal

Map by Gene Thorp

✳

Approaching the Capitol, Ross and Cockburn halted to confer. An officer sent forward under a flag of truce reported finding no one in arms and no opposition. Ross may have sounded a request on drums for a parley, but the only response was dead silence. The general's instructions from Lord Bathurst, the war secretary, authorized him to demand ransom in exchange for sparing a captured city, a common practice.

But Ross was not interested in negotiating a deal; instead, he wanted to deliver a message: The public buildings of Washington would burn, but private property would be left alone. "Such of the inhabitants as remain quiet in their houses, their property should be respected, and nothing but the public buildings, and stores touched," recalled Colonel Brooke, Ross's second in command. Neither Cockburn nor Ross mentioned any attempts at negotiation in their official reports to superiors or in later accounts. In any event, had a proposition to spare the capital in exchange for ransom been received, President Madison later said, it would have been summarily rejected.

Any call to parley made was either ignored or not heard by the Americans. Ross ordered a bugle to be sounded, indicating, he said, his "intention to enter the city."

The general rode forward at the head of a small party, the Capitol looming ahead. At the corner of Maryland Avenue and Second Street stood one of the finer homes in the neighborhood, the three-story redbrick Sewall house, home to Albert Gallatin for twelve years until he left for Europe on diplomatic duty. As the British rode past, a volley of musket fire rang out from the windows. "Here comes the English buggers," someone inside hollered. Two British corporals fell dead, several other soldiers were wounded, and Ross's horse was killed—the second of the day for the general.

Ross ordered the house stormed while Cockburn rode back to bring up reinforcements from the light companies camped on the outskirts. The house was surrounded "in a twinkle of the eye," according to Michael Shiner, but not quickly enough. Most of the assailants escaped, but after a struggle, the British captured three men inside.

Over the years, the shots would be variously attributed to a drunk hiding in the garden, a female sniper, or one of two local barbers: a "worthless" French hairdresser in one version and a club-footed Irishman in another. Yet the evidence is clear that the assailants were Barney's men. The three prisoners taken from the house were flotillamen, one of them an officer, according to an affidavit made in 1816 by Lawson Clarke, an American citizen who witnessed the attack.

Roaming about Capitol Hill after the battle, unwilling to quit the fight, a party of flotillamen had slipped into the empty house and laid an ambush. The angry British might have killed the men, but Ross, seeing they were flotillamen, directed they be taken prisoner, declaring them to be "the only brave Yankees he had met with that day."

The captured flotillamen were unrepentant, boasting they would do it again if they had a chance. At least one British officer did not feel as charitable as Ross; he told the prisoners they "would be hung for what they had done as soon as they got them to their ships," according to Clarke's affidavit.

"Hang and be damned," a flotillaman replied defiantly.

The citizens of Washington were at least as lucky as the British that the shots missed Ross. "I was informed by some of the British officers that it was a most fortunate thing that Maj. Gen. Ross was not killed, for in that event it would have been impossible to restrain the soldiery, who idolized him, from committing the most horrid outrages, both on our city and its inhabitants," wrote Dr. James Ewell, watching the incident from Capitol Hill.

Ross ordered the Sewall house burned, but was apologetic about it, later telling the owner, Robert Sewall, that "he felt it to be his duty to set fire to and burn the house, for the purpose of making a impression; which he did with reluctance, as it was his intention to respect private property while in Washington."

The troops expertly lit fires inside the beautifully furnished house, and fired several Congreve rockets into the burning house for good measure; when they exploded, Shiner said, "they made the rafters fly east and west."

But the British did not admire their handiwork for long. To the south, the sky was glowing with a much larger fire.

"It was a magnificent sight—but truly awful and disgraceful to America."

*Watercolor by William Thornton circa 1815, believed to depict
the burning of the Washington Navy Yard.*

WASHINGTON NAVY YARD, 8:20 P.M., WEDNESDAY, AUGUST 24

Captain Tingey was beside himself as he waited at the Navy Yard for
Captain Creighton and Mordecai Booth to return from their scouting
mission. It was well past 8 p.m., and he had heard unconfirmed reports
that the British had entered the city. Tingey resolved to wait no longer
than half past the hour before burning the yard.

At Tingey's side was Sailing Master William V. Taylor, a cool-
headed New England mariner who had fought alongside Oliver Perry
at Lake Erie. While they waited, Taylor readied the stores and vessels
for firing.

Finally, Creighton and Booth galloped into the yard. Not only were
the British in town, Creighton reported, but he had narrowly escaped
with his life after riding through the fire of a company of enemy troops
on Capitol Hill.

Tingey considered the news "incontestable proof" that it was time
to burn the yard. The commandant pulled out his watch. It was twenty

minutes after eight. He and Taylor went to work. They used torches to ignite powder trails leading to a line of storehouses. "[I]n a few moments the whole was in a state of irretrievable conflagration," Tingey reported. They moved toward the wharf. At the shipwright's department, the hull of the brand-new frigate *Essex* was nearly complete, her bottom ready for coppering, her masts almost finished, her gun carriages nearly done, and her sails ready. *Argus* was at the wharf, with all her armament and equipment on board.

Secretary Jones had been insistent that the ships, so close to completion, not fall into British hands. Tingey and Taylor touched torches to the rigged vessels, which were immediately enveloped in flame. Sickened by the sight, Tingey acted on a sudden impulse and ordered another new vessel at the wharf, the schooner *Lynx*, not to be fired.

Almost everything else was in flames: stacks of timber, the boatbuilder shops, the medical store, the plumber and smith shops, the sawmill with its tools and machinery, the rigging loft, the gun carriage shop, and much more. The nearby ordnance store detonated, adding to the conflagration.

The skeleton American crew—Tingey, Creighton, Taylor, two lieutenants, several marines, and a few African American workers—mustered in two boats. "[I]t was warm indeed before we could pull off from the flames," Taylor wrote to his wife, Abby. "We then lay on our oars to witness this destructive scene. . . . It was a magnificent sight—but truly awful and disgraceful to America."

U.S. CAPITOL, 9 P.M., WEDNESDAY, AUGUST 24

That sight lit the night as British troops with rockets took position in a field on the east side of the Capitol. Mary Hunter, who had stayed at her home at Capitol Hill while her husband took their children to safety, watched the proceedings with dismay. "I will leave you to conjecture what our feelings must have been when we saw the British flag flying on Capitol Hill," she wrote to her sister. A grim-faced British officer rode up to her door and asked suspiciously about the absence of her husband—Rev. Andrew Hunter, a scholar who served as chaplain and mathematician for the U.S. Navy. "I . . . looked at him fully in the face and very deliberately told him that my husband was gone to take a family of young children from witnessing such a horrid scene," Hunter wrote.

The Capitol—or the "palace in the wilderness," as some called it—stood almost alone atop Capitol Hill. The dome familiar to later generations was not yet built; instead, a two-story wooden gangway, which crossed a vacant yard intended one day to hold a rotunda, joined the two rectangular sandstone wings. The Capitol had been under construction for two decades, and from the moment President Washington laid the cornerstone in 1793, the project had proven to be contentious and expensive.

When Washington became the capital in 1800, the House, Senate, Supreme Court, and Library of Congress were crammed into the still-unfinished north wing. In 1807, construction of the south wing had moved far enough along for the House to move into a magnificent chamber designed by Benjamin Latrobe. If Dolley Madison's oval drawing room at the President's House was the most elegant room in America, the hall of the House of Representatives, with its ornate carvings and statues, was the most beautiful. William Allen, architectural historian for the Capitol, later wrote, "It was being built for the ages, a permanent ornament for the republic's future."

The evidence suggests that, even before setting foot in Washington, Ross and Cockburn had agreed to burn the government and military buildings in Washington, despite claims otherwise. Lieutenant Gleig, who remained with the main force outside of the capital, later blamed the shots fired from the Sewall house for prompting the British to immediately "burn and destroy everything in the most distant degree connected with government." Lieutenant Scott, Cockburn's aide, likewise wrote that "the conduct adopted by the Americans, in disregarding the various parleys sounded by the General before our entrance, and the fire of concealed enemies, were the causes of the destruction of their Capitol and public buildings."

But in the report he would soon send to London, Ross called the destruction of Washington's public buildings "the object of the expedition." He described beginning the work immediately upon entering Washington, "judging it of consequence to complete the destruction of the public buildings with the least possible delay so that the army might retire without loss of time."

Captain Harry Smith was blunt about the British intentions. "We entered Washington for the barbarous purpose of destroying the city," he wrote in his autobiography. "Admiral Cockburn would have burnt the whole, but Ross would only consent to the burning of the public buildings." The young officer had served with Wellington and had no objection to burning arsenals, dockyards, frigates, barracks, and the like, but this was something entirely different. "[W]ell do I recollect that, fresh from the Duke's humane warfare in the South of France, we were horrified at the order," he later wrote.

Lieutenant Evans shared no such compunctions and led the assault on the Capitol. Wary of another ambush, the British troops formed a line, raised their muskets, and fired a volley into the building. Evans and his men entered through a large door on the northeast side, and Cockburn followed with a party of sailors.

The British were startled by the grandeur of the building, particularly in comparison to its surroundings. Scott chortled about America's "unseemly bias for monarchal splendor." Impressive as the building was from the outside, the sights inside were even grander. "It was an unfinished but beautifully arranged building; the interior accommodations were upon a scale of grandeur and magnificence little suited to pure Republican simplicity," Scott said.

Cockburn poked into a room on the ground floor of the south wing, where Madison had a small office that he used for signing bills. The gilt lettering on the green leather label of a book caught Cockburn's eye: "President of the U. States." The bound volume with marbled sides was rather mundane, an account of the receipts and expenditures of the U.S. government for the year 1810, with entries ranging from the payment of bounties on pickled fish to pension payments made to Pierre L'Enfant for his work in designing the city of Washington. But a book belonging to "Jemmy" Madison was worth keeping as a souvenir. Later Cockburn would write on the inside cover, "Taken in President's room in the Capitol at the destruction of that building by the British on the capture of Washington 24th August 1814."

The tour complete, it was time to destroy the Capitol. The British considered blowing it up with gunpowder captured at Bladensburg, but decided against it, as the debris might damage homes in the area. It would have to be burned.

The British started in the south wing. Cockburn's sailors, well versed in arson, took the lead under the command of Lieutenant George Pratt, an expert on pyrotechnics. Sailors rubbed gunpowder paste on the woodwork around doors and windows and set them afire. A mass of papers from the clerk's office, among them the secret journals of Congress, proved a handy source of combustible material. They fired rockets through the roof of the House chamber, but to their surprise it did not ignite. Men sent to investigate discovered that the roof was covered with sheet iron. Undaunted, they tossed the representatives' mahogany desks, tables, and chairs into a pile in the middle of the room, sprinkled it with rocket powder, and ignited it. The red silk drapes, trimmed in gold, were torched. "[T]here was no want of materials for the conflagration," Benjamin Latrobe later wrote in a sad letter to Jefferson detailing the destruction. Dry loose lumber used for stages and seats in the galleries fueled the fire. The great chamber was soon ablaze with heat so intense that the glass of two hundred skylights in the ceiling melted. Behind the Speaker's desk, a marble statue of Liberty was consumed by fire. The sandstone columns were "unable to resist the force of flame, and I believe no known material would have

A book belonging to "Jemmy" Madison was worth keeping as a souvenir. Later Cockburn would write on the inside cover, "Taken in President's room in the Capitol at the destruction of that building by the British on the capture of Washington 24th August 1814."

The President's account book, later returned to the Library of Congress.

been able to resist so sudden and intense a heat," Latrobe wrote. "The exterior of the columns and entablature scaled off, and not a vestige of sculpture or fluting remained."

Driven from the south wing by the heat, the British rushed across the wooden gangway to the north wing of the Capitol, housing the Senate, Supreme Court, and Library of Congress. The last was home to some three thousand books, meant to provide Congress with reference to history, law, and the classics, many of them hard-to-find volumes from Europe. Now, together with the library's manuscripts, maps, and furniture, the books fueled a furious inferno throughout the north wing. The fire was so hot that the marble columns in the neighboring Senate chamber turned to lime and collapsed, and the exterior walls nearly collapsed.

The vaultlike basement chamber below, where John Marshall presided over the Supreme Court, was damaged but survived the fire with

"I shall never forget the destructive majesty of the flames as the torches were applied to beds, curtains, etc.," wrote Harry Smith. "Our sailors were artists at the work."

Capture of the City of Washington, *engraving published in London in 1815.*

its Doric columns still standing. A vestibule outside the chamber featuring unique corncob columns was spared, as were hallways and staircases providing an escape route for the British.

The fire burst through the windows of the Capitol. "The flames floated away in masses, which alighted upon the houses to leeward, setting them ablaze likewise," said Scott. Some of the congressional records had been moved for safekeeping to a nearby house on North Capitol Street that had once been owned by George Washington, but there was no refuge there from the flames. The townhouse caught fire, apparently from sparks, and the records were destroyed.

As the inferno blazed, troops stood outside watching the Capitol "wrapped in its winding sheet of fire." Some felt chagrin. It was a "pity to burn anything so beautiful," an officer said.

Dr. James Ewell watched the flames mount far into the sky with a thunderous rumble. The forty-one-year-old physician had taken his wife and two daughters from their own home on Capitol Hill to that of an elderly and ill neighbor who had pleaded not to be left alone. Ewell left his own brick home, directly across from the Capitol at the northeast corner of First and A streets, in the care of servants.

As Ewell and his companions contemplated the dismal scene, a loud rapping at the door startled them. A half-dozen British soldiers politely asked for something to eat. Some ham was quickly rustled up and set before the soldiers, along with a loaf of bread, butter, and wine. As they ate, Ewell saw a glow and feared his own home was blazing. Then his servant arrived to report the doctor's house was not on fire; it had, however, been plundered. Ewell hurried to investigate, accompanied by Rev. A. T. McCormick, rector of nearby Christ Church. McCormick had already met Ross and Cockburn, and he assured Ewell they were "perfect gentlemen."

Near the doctor's house, McCormick presented Ewell to a British officer, whom he called "General Ross." The officer coolly corrected them in a quick and piercing tone: "My name is Cockburn, sir." After the proper introductions were made, Ewell complained that his furniture, clothes, and silverware had been plundered. Cockburn was singularly unimpressed. "With whom did you confide your property, sir?" he asked the doctor.

"With my servants," Ewell replied.

"Well, sir, let me tell you it was very ill confidence to repose your property in the care of servants," Cockburn lectured. The doctor had no one to blame but himself.

Fortunately for Ewell, Ross intervened and apologetically asked the doctor to point out his house so a guard could be posted. Ewell showed Ross his home, and to the general's embarrassment, it turned out that Ross's staff had just chosen it as their headquarters. Ross offered to move his baggage out, but stayed at Ewell's insistence; there was no better guarantee that the doctor's home would be safe.

But the British were not done for the evening.

Across town, Louis Sérurier, the French minister, saw the enormous flames at the Capitol and Navy Yard lighting the night. "I have never beheld a spectacle more terrible and at the same time more magnificent," he wrote to Talleyrand. Sérurier's temporary residence at the Octagon, just west of the President's House, was the most elegant private home in Washington and had been built by Colonel John Tayloe, a wealthy Virginia plantation owner. Tayloe was with the Virginia militia and his wife, Ann, had fled the city, but she had encouraged Sérurier to move into the Octagon, hoping that the home would be spared if the French minister occupied it.

A large white sheet, a reasonable facsimile of a Bourbon flag, was flying on a pole from the house, but looking at the flames across the city, Sérurier was unsure that it would be enough protection from the British. "A profound darkness reigned in the part of the city which I live in, and one was delivered up to conjectures and to false reports . . . as to what was occurring in the quarter lighted by this frightful blaze," he wrote. At 11 p.m., Sérurier saw a column, preceded by torches, moving from the Capitol toward the President's House, a mile and a quarter down Pennsylvania Avenue.

The British marched two abreast in two columns, moving quickly but silently down the broad avenue. Ross and Cockburn were taking 150 soldiers and sailors to "Jemmy's Palace," as Cockburn insisted on calling it, leaving about 700 men from the 3rd Brigade camped just east of the Capitol. "[A]s soon as the town was ascertained to be completely, and decidedly in our possession, the troops were kept as much as possible, out of the town, and sufficient guards only were sent with the officers to destroy" the public buildings, according to Cockburn's memoir.

Even at this hour, the avenue was choked with dust, and the troops took care not to fall in the ditches that bordered the road. Still, Lieutenant Scott found himself admiring the grand pretension of the "fine and spacious causeway" laid out by Pierre L'Enfant, the designer of Washington.

From the window of his home on Pennsylvania Avenue, William P. Gardner watched the troops marching by. Ross and Cockburn riding on horseback behind the troops, approached the house. With elaborate courtesy, the officers doffed their *chapeau de bras* and politely greeted him. After some pleasantries, Gardner addressed Cockburn. "I hope, sir, that individuals and private property will be respected," he said. The admiral, joined by Ross, offered a pledge of "sacred honor" that this would be the case.

Cockburn probed for some information. "Where is your president, Mr. Madison?" he asked. Gardner replied that he did not know, "but supposed that by this time he was at a considerable distance." He was similarly noncommittal when Cockburn asked how much American force remained in the city. "Conjectures are various," Gardner replied. "It is impossible for me to say."

By now Cockburn and Ross recognized they would not learn much from Gardner. After some further chat, "they then observed that they were on their way to pay a visit to the President's House, which they were told was but a little distance ahead," Gardner recalled. The officers bowed politely, and with a final suggestion that residents stay in their homes, continued along Pennsylvania Avenue.

The troops paused at the intersection with Fifteenth Street, where the avenue elbowed around the Treasury building before turning back to the President's House. While parched troops drank from the town pump, Ross and several officers stepped into a brick tavern at the corner of F Street to order dinner for the staff. By virtue of its convenient location near the President's House, Mrs. Suter's boardinghouse was a Washington institution, a popular gathering point for locals and government officials. Regular boarders included Postmaster General Return J. Meigs, but he, like the other renters, had vacated town.

Barbara Suter, the elderly widow who ran the establishment, had been out of sorts since the invasion—"hardly sleeping at night, at all the daytime spent in fright," she said. Both her sons were in arms, one as a flotillaman, the other with the militia, and she was alone except for a servant woman.

Ross introduced himself, announcing that they had "come, madam, to sup with you." Mrs. Suter pleaded that she had no food and suggested they try McLeod's Tavern up the street. But Ross insisted he preferred the view at Mrs. Suter's. From there the general and his officers could keep an eye on the troops at the President's House while they conferred on plans. Assured that the British would return soon for their meal, Mrs. Suter and her servant went out to the yard to kill some chickens.

PRESIDENT'S HOUSE, 11 P.M., WEDNESDAY, AUGUST 24

Ross need not have placed the order for food. Moving on to the President's House, the British walked unmolested through the front door and found the mansion deserted, but ready to host visitors. The table in the state dining room was set for dinner for forty. Plate holders by the fireplace were filled with dishes; knives, forks, and spoons were laid out; and fine wine poured into cut-glass decanters was chilling on ice on the sideboard. Unfamiliar with Dolley Madison's hospitality, the British assumed the Americans had prepared a victory banquet.

The sight tickled Ross's Irish fancy. "So unexpected was our entry and capture of Washington, and so confident was Madison (President of the States) of the defeat of our troops, that he had prepared for supper for the expected conquerors; and when our advanced party entered the president's house they found a table laid with 40 covers," he delightedly wrote his brother-in-law, Ned Glascock. "The fare, however, which was intended for *Jonathan* was voraciously devoured by *John Bull*, and the health of the Prince Regent, and success to His Majesty's arms by sea and land, was drunk in the best wines, Madison having taken to his heels and ensured his safety on the opposite bank of the river. . . ."

Exuberant toasts were offered: "Peace with America—war with Madison," proposed Ross. "Nor was Mr. Madison's health forgotten, in his own best claret, for being so good a fellow as to leave us such a capital supper," recalled Major Norman Pringle, commander of the 21st Regiment Grenadier Company.

Lieutenant Scott, exhausted and feverish with heat and thirst, picked up a crystal goblet of Madeira and gulped it down. He pronounced it "super-excellent." The men, including a company of hungry Fusiliers, wolfed down the food.

Cockburn also enjoyed himself thoroughly. The admiral had recruited a local book dealer, Roger Chew Weightman, as a guide. The twenty-seven-year-old businessman had served as a cavalry lieutenant at Bladensburg and "ran as fast as the rest of them," he later said. Weightman was apparently checking on property he owned near the President's House when Cockburn found him. Weightman dutifully complied when Cockburn insisted he take a seat and join in a toast to "Jemmy."

The admiral looked around the magnificently furnished mansion. Beautiful furniture—sofas, writing tables, and cushioned chairs—filled many of the rooms. Thomas Jefferson had collected some of the items in France, and others had belonged to George Washington and John Adams. Most of the Madisons' possessions, including china, wardrobes, clothing, books, wine, letters and papers, and a pianoforte, had been left behind.

"Take something to remember this day," Cockburn magnanimously told Weightman. The book dealer picked something valuable, hoping to save it.

"No, no," cried Cockburn, "*that* I must give to the flames." The admiral had issued strict instructions that nothing valuable be taken, as it might be construed as looting. That had not been the case at Havre de Grace or the other Chesapeake towns, but with Ross on the scene, everyone had to be on their best behavior. The admiral grabbed some ornaments off the mantelpiece. "But here, these will answer as a memento," he said, handing them to Weightman.

"I must take something too," Cockburn muttered. Looking round, he settled on a *chapeau de bras* belonging to Madison. Then he snatched a cushion off Dolley's chair, remarking that it would serve as a lovely reminder of Mrs. Madison's derriere.

Soldiers and sailors roamed through the mansion grabbing souvenirs. Lieutenant Beau Urquhart of the 85th made off with Madison's dress sword. Another soldier grabbed a miniature portrait of the first lady from her parlor. Madison's small medicine chest, made of walnut, brass, and ivory, was taken. (It was presented to President Franklin D. Roosevelt in 1939 by the Canadian grandson of Thomas Kains, who had been purser aboard one of the ships on the expedition. "How time mellows our perspective of events," President Roosevelt wrote in a thank-you note.) Most contented themselves with pictures and books. Someone grabbed a bundle of notes scribbled in pencil sent by the president to Dolley, which she had left in a table drawer.

Scott made his way upstairs and found himself in the president's dressing room. Drawers had been left open and the portmanteaus were half-filled; either the president had packed in a hurry, or someone had already rifled through the place. Coated with dust and grime, Scott eyed Madison's clothing. "The snowy clean linen tempted me to take the liberty of making a very fair exchange," he recalled. The lieutenant stripped off his filthy inner garments and thrust his arms into one of the president's clean shirts.

After an hour of feasting and roaming, it was time to get to the real business of the night. A detail was sent to obtain fire from a small beer-house across from the Treasury. Meanwhile, soldiers and sailors gathered furniture, including three dozen hand-carved, gilded chairs, and piled it in the drawing room. Sailors broke open windows and soaked the bedding with lamp oil. As Ross supervised the men in the salon, a messenger delivered a note from Sérurier requesting a guard be posted at the Octagon. Ross sent word back that the French minister's residence "would be as much respected as if His Majesty found himself there in person."

Under the expert tutelage of Lieutenant Pratt, sailors moved through the mansion, igniting the premises. "I shall never forget the destructive majesty of the flames as the torches were applied to beds, curtains, etc.," wrote Smith. "Our sailors were artists at the work." The glorious house was soon engulfed in flames and smoke.

Troops meanwhile broke into the redbrick Treasury building, just to the east of the President's House, but were disappointed to find the money had already been spirited out of town. The men smashed windows and ignited the building. Then they discovered to their dismay that they had overlooked a ground-floor vault. The soldiers forced in a window and jumped into the burning building, but the "supposed chests of treasure" were found to hold worthless papers.

Ross and Cockburn gathered with their men on the common just north of the President's House and watched as the blaze consumed the house. Not all felt like celebrating. "Although they were the pride of the Americans, I must confess I felt sorrow when witnessing such magnificent buildings demolished," Lieutenant Furlong of the 21st Fusiliers wrote in his diary.

The main body of British troops, having rested several hours in Bladensburg, moved toward Washington after dark, the road illuminated by the dark red light thrown by the flames. "I think this was one of finest, and at the same time, the most awful sights I ever witnessed," Colonel Brooke wrote in his diary. "[T]he columns of fire issuing from the houses, and dock yard, the explosions of magazines at intervals, the sky illuminated from the blazes, the troops all under arms outside the town, struck the mind with a something that can be better conceived than described."

F rancis Scott Key kept watch at his home in Georgetown. Violent explosions shook the city and clouds of thick smoke filled the sky. Key was grateful that his children remained at Terra Rubra and Polly was safely outside the city at the Middlebrook tavern. When the British were finished with the federal city, Key felt "sure they would" continue on to Georgetown. The Foxall Foundry, the leading manufacturer of ordnance for the U.S. government, including the carronades for the USS *Constitution*, was too important a target for the British to ignore.

Nearby, Key's friends William and Anna Maria Thornton had taken refuge at Tudor Place, Martha Peter's neoclassical mansion on the crest of the Georgetown heights. The Thorntons and Peter sat at the dining room window "and there witnessed the conflagration of our poor undefended & devoted city," Anna Thornton wrote in her diary. "[T]he city was light and the heavens redden'd with the blaze!" she told friends. It seemed to her a miracle the whole city was not consumed.

For them, the view was intensely personal. The burning city bore the name of Martha Peter's stepgrandfather; it was a capital he had conceived and created for the new nation. But it was not sadness Peter felt so much as disgust at Madison and his government, so unworthy of George Washington.

Dr. William Thornton, born in the Virgin Islands, had been in Tortola in 1792 when he heard of a competition for the best design of a capitol building. He had no formal architectural study and knew little about structural engineering; moreover, the deadline for entries had already passed, but Thornton was not deterred. Jefferson and Washington were captivated by the grandeur of his design and the practicality of his layout, and Thornton's plan was chosen. Now, watching his creation burn, the normally loquacious Thornton would only say that he "beheld, in deep regret, that night, the tremendous conflagrations of our public buildings."

Mary Hunter watched from her home on Capitol Hill. The fire at the Navy Yard "produced an almost meridian brightness," Hunter wrote her sister. "You never saw a drawing room so brilliantly lighted as the whole city was that night. Few thought of going to bed—they spent the night in gazing on the fires, and lamenting the disgrace of the city."

NORTHERN VIRGINIA COUNTRYSIDE, LATE WEDNESDAY NIGHT, AUGUST 24

President Madison had a clear view of the disgrace as he rode through the Virginia countryside. To the east, columns of fire and smoke climbed through the night. The landmarks of Washington were visible, "some burning slowly, others with bursts of flame and sparks mounting high up in the dark horizon," wrote Attorney General Rush, who, along with General Mason, accompanied Madison in his flight. "This never can be forgotten by me."

Paul Jennings, who had crossed the river with Madison, was left with other servants to follow on foot, but they later caught up with the president and his companions. At one point the group heard a tremendous explosion and saw buildings afire.

Madison and his companions rode west on the Georgetown Road until reaching the Alexandria & Leesburg Road, which they followed to the town of Falls Church, about seven miles from Washington. There they stopped at Wren's Tavern, an unofficial Virginia militia headquarters, where the president apparently sought the latest information on enemy movements. The party rode north about a mile to a home on Minor's Hill, one of the highest points in the area, but the president found it packed with refugees. The group continued another two miles north to the rendezvous location, Salona, the stately Federal-style brick home of Rev. William Maffitt, in present-day McLean. There Madison anxiously awaited his wife.

D olley Madison and her entourage crossed into Virginia at the Little Falls Bridge, where the Potomac narrowed below a series of rapids. They traveled west on the Falls Road, climbing a long hill that ran along Pimmit Run before reaching Rokeby, the farmhouse of Dolley's friend, Matilda Lee Love. The party halted for the night, too tired to continue another mile to Salona.

Dolley did not receive the warmest welcome at Rokeby. When Love instructed her cook to quickly make a cup of coffee for the first lady, the elderly servant grumbled she would not rush, considering the president had "done sold the country to the British." Even Love blamed the "miserable, imbecile government" for the loss of Washington, though tactfully she did not share her opinion with the first lady.

Unable to sleep, Dolley watched the flames from the window at Rokeby.

Tenleytown, midnight, Wednesday, August 24

The sight of the fires imbued General Winder with a new panic. Retreating past Georgetown with what remained of his broken force, he reached Tenleytown, about five miles northwest of the President's House. Perched on the heights, Winder and his men watched the fires across the city.

Hundreds more men abandoned the army at Tenleytown, ignoring Winder's commands to halt. The general blamed the wretched state of his troops on the men themselves; he lectured in his report on "the great defects of all undisciplined and unorganized troops" and made no mention of his own catastrophic leadership.

"[W]hen he might have prepared defenses, he acted as scout; when he might have fought, he still scouted; when he retreated, he retreated in the wrong direction; when he fought, he thought only of retreat; and whether scouting, retreating, or fighting, he never betrayed an idea," Henry Adams wrote.

As the flames below grew, Winder ordered a further retreat—his fourth of the day and "another great error," in the view of Major Peter, the Georgetown Artillery commander. Even in its broken condition, the American force on the heights posed a potential threat to the small British force in the city and would constrain its operations. Lacking cavalry, the British could not have approached the elevated position without plenty of time for the Americans to retreat. Yet the general was not willing to risk even that.

After collecting all the men he could, Winder retreated another five miles northwest up the River Road, in the direction of Montgomery Court House in Maryland. Ensign George Hoffman, whose Maryland militia company had bolted at Bladensburg, could plainly see the Capitol and the President's House burning as they retreated. The sight "made me regret that I survived the disgrace," he wrote his father.

The great fire could be seen in all directions, and for many miles. At Benedict, on the Patuxent River, where the main British fleet was anchored, sailors noticed the sky to the northwest "illuminated with a strong glare of fire during the whole night." To their west, anchored on the Potomac River off Maryland Point, thirty-five miles south of Washington, the men of Captain Gordon's squadron looked with dismay at the red sky. Still fighting contrary tides and winds, they were several days' sail from Alexandria, while Ross had obviously beaten them to the capital. "The reflection of the fire on the heavens was plainly seen from the ships, much to our mortification and disappointment," wrote Captain Napier, second in command. Gordon considered turning back but decided to continue, knowing that his squadron could provide a diversion if Ross's small force was trapped.

Light from the fires was visible in Leesburg, Virginia, thirty-five miles northwest of the capital, and Fredericksburg, Virginia, forty-five miles to the south. Daniel Sheldon, a Treasury employee fleeing to Frederick, Maryland, found "my journey during almost the entire of the night was illumined by the flames of the public buildings, which at the distance of 28 miles, where I stopped at one o'clock in the morn-

ing, were most dismally and most distinctly visible," he wrote his father.

The light was visible in Baltimore, too, forty miles northeast of
Washington. From the ramparts of Fort McHenry, Private Benjamin
Cohen could see an eerie glow on the horizon. "As the moon went
down, the luster became more clear and defined, rising and falling on
the horizon like fitful coruscations of the Aurora Borealis," another
witness wrote. Residents watching from atop Federal Hill wondered if
Baltimore would be next.

Candles were not necessary for dinner at Mrs. Suter's boardinghouse. Admiral Cockburn, by one account, blew them out on the
table, remarking that he preferred to eat by the light of the burning
buildings across the street. Certainly the fires far outshone the pale
moonlight coming through the windows.

The admiral had joined Ross and ten other officers at the boardinghouse, now serving as the general's temporary headquarters. Jaunty
humor aside, Mrs. Suter detected a subdued mood as the officers ate
their chicken dinner. All were disappointed at the escape of Madison,
and they speculated on his whereabouts. Of more immediate concern
to Ross and Cockburn was uncertainty over Captain Gordon's location. The commanders had expected the ships would be available to
evacuate the army if need be; moreover, if the squadron no longer
posed a threat, the Americans might be able to concentrate their forces
and launch a counterattack.

An officer walked in to ask whether the War Department, on the
west side of the President's House, was to be burned. "Certainly,"
Cockburn declared.

But Ross demurred. "It will be time enough in the morning, as it is
now growing late, and the men require rest," he told Cockburn. The
admiral, however, was not ready to quit for the night. He declared the
nearby Bank of Metropolis "ought to be burned," but gave up the idea
when the bank cleaning lady, Sarah Sweeny, persuaded him that the
building was owned by a poor widow.

As the troops marched back along Pennsylvania Avenue to their
camp on Capitol Hill, Cockburn mounted a small gray horse to search

for the offices of the *National Intelligencer*, Washington's premier newspaper. The editor, Joseph Gales, Jr.—Cockburn's nickname for him was "Josey"—was a staunch supporter of Madison and the war, and the admiral had long been annoyed by the newspaper's unflattering coverage of him. The *Intelligencer* was considered an organ for the Madison administration; just that morning, it had assured readers that Washington was safe. Gales, born in Sheffield, England, came to America as a boy with his father, a publisher who had fled Great Britain for fear of being persecuted for selling the works of Thomas Paine. The younger Gales had followed his father into the newspaper business. Cockburn considered Gales a traitor who "had out-heroded Herod in his abuse of his countrymen," in the words of one member of the expedition.

Near the McKeown Hotel on Pennsylvania Avenue, Cockburn encountered Chester Bailey, a U.S. mail stage operator, and asked for directions to the *Intelligencer*, declaring "he must destroy it, as his friend Gales had written some tough stories about him." Bailey claimed he did not know the paper's location, and Cockburn's patience wore thin when two other men similarly pleaded ignorance. The admiral warned them they would be seized unless they showed him. The men promptly pointed out the office just up Pennsylvania Avenue.

Cockburn decreed the building be immediately burned. Before sailors could carry out the order, several women who lived in adjoining houses beseeched him to stop. If he torched the *Intelligencer*, the entire block would burn. Cockburn addressed the crowd of onlookers: "Good people, I do not wish to injure you, but I am really afraid my friend Josey will be affronted with me, if after burning Jemmy's palace, I do not pay him the same compliment."

The admiral turned to his men: "So my lads, take your axes, pull down the house, and burn the papers in the street." Given the late hour, Cockburn agreed the job could wait until morning. Posting a sentry at the newspaper office, Cockburn "bid goodnight" and offered assurances before riding off: "Be tranquil, ladies, you shall be as safely protected under my administration as under that of Mr. Madison."

O say can you see by the dawn's early
light so proudly we hail'd at the twilight's last gleam
Whose broad stripes & bright stars through the perilous fig
O'er the ramparts we watch'd were so gallantly stre
   And the rocket's red glare, the bomb bursting
   Gave proof through the night that our flag was still
O say does that star spangled banner yet wave
O'er the land of the free & the home of the brave

On the shore dimly seen through the mists of t
   Where the foe's haughty host in dread silence
What is that which the breeze, o'er the towering
   As it fitfully blows, half conceals, half discloses
      Now it catches the gleam of the morning's first
      In full glory reflected now shines in the str
Tis the star-spangled banner — O long may it
O'er the land of the free & the home of the br

And where is that band who so vauntingly sw
   That the havoc of war & the battle's confusio
A home & a Country should leave us no more
— [struck through]
      Their blood has wash'd out their foul footste
No refuge could save the hireling & slave
   From the terror of flight or the gloom of the g
And the star-spangled banner in triumph doth w
O'er the land of the free & the home of the br

O thus be it ever when freemen shall stan
   Between their lov'd home & the war's desolation
Blest with vict'ry & peace may the heav'n rescued
   Praise the power that hath made & preserv'd us a
      Then conquer we must when our cause it is
      And this be our motto — In God is our trust
And the star-spangled banner in triumph shall wave
O'er the land of the free & the home of the brave

Cockburn was in high spirits as he made his rounds, chatting
with bystanders and missing no opportunity to blame the
president for the disaster: "You may thank old Madison for
this; it is he who has got you into this scrape."

*After returning to England, George Cockburn posed for this
portrait displayed at the Royal Academy in 1817, which showed
him standing proudly before the burning American capital.*

CHAPTER 9

★

They Feel Strongly the Disgrace

TOWARD DAWN, A brief but violent thunderstorm swept through the captured capital. Flashes of lightning competed for brilliance with the flames, which were dampened by the torrential rain. At 5:30 in the sultry morning, Admiral Cockburn toured the smoldering city on his white mare, accompanied by only three men, a measure of his contempt for any lingering American threat. He rode along Pennsylvania Avenue to the President's House, likely for the satisfaction of seeing Madison's home in ruins. The mansion was a hollow shell, little more than charred sandstone walls. The results at the Treasury building, on the other hand, were disappointing. The rain had doused the flames, and the fire would have to be relit.

Troops from the Light Brigade, who had spent the night at the main British camp on a field one mile northeast of the Capitol, marched into town to rekindle old fires and ignite new ones. The men, wet but rested from the battle, were accompanied by a contingent of thirty African American Colonial Marines carrying rockets and powder. Ross remained at the Capitol Hill headquarters, leaving the troops under the command of Colonel Timothy Jones. The Treasury building was soon burning again, and by 8 a.m., the brick building housing the War, Navy, and State departments went up in flames, fueled by voluminous government records.

Near the Capitol, Lieutenant Scott took a detachment of sailors to burn one of the town's ropewalks, stocked with cordage, hemp, and tar to make the rope crucial for navy ships. The men knocked the heads off dozens of tar barrels and poured it over cords. Once ignited, fire raced through the long building, and a dense, black smoke, with red flames flashing within, rolled over the city, giving "it the appearance of a Tartarus upon earth," Scott wrote.

Cockburn was merry as he made his rounds, chatting with bystanders at the McKeown Hotel and missing no opportunity to blame the president for the disaster: "You may thank old Madison for this; it is he who has got you into this scrape. . . . We want to catch him and carry him to England for a curiosity." He showed off his souvenirs from the President's House and told many "coarse jests" about Madison, whom he likened to an "old woman."

One American told Cockburn that if George Washington were alive "you would not have gotten to this city so easily."

"No, sir," Cockburn was quick to reply. "[I]f General Washington had been president, we should not have thought of coming here." Washington, he added, would never have left his capital defenseless to pursue conquest abroad.

Washingtonians did not quite know what to make of Cockburn. "[S]uch was his manner—that of a common sailor, not of a dignified commander," wrote Margaret Bayard Smith. "He however deserves praise and commendation for his own good conduct and the discipline of his sailors and Marines, for these were the destroying agents."

A delegation led by the mayor of Georgetown approached the admiral and pleaded for the port town to be spared, assuring him the citizens did not intend to resist. "[A]s well they might; for I do not believe there were twenty men in town . . ." Martha Peter scoffed in a letter. "Cockburn replied, that, as our president would not protect us, they would."

The *Intelligencer* would not be as fortunate. Cockburn rode to the paper's office to personally oversee the destruction he had promised the night before. The admiral was ready to have the building pulled down with stout ropes, but neighbors again interceded, this time pointing out that Gales did not actually own the building. Cockburn countermanded his order. Instead his men smashed the presses, destroyed the furniture, and threw all the types and printing materials out the upper windows. "Be sure that all the 'c's are destroyed so the rascals have no further means of abusing my name as they have done," he joked.

Cockburn helped his men dump back issues of the paper, records, and other property on the banks of a canal running behind the building. Gales's reference library of several hundred books was added to the pile, which was then set afire. The editor's nearby home at Ninth and E streets might have met the same fate, but the housekeeper cleverly disguised it by closing the shutters and chalking FOR RENT on the front door.

Gloomily eating breakfast in Georgetown, Dr. William Thornton, designer of the Capitol, learned that the British planned to burn the Patent Office. This was also a matter of direct concern; Thornton, a Renaissance man in the Jeffersonian mold, had been superintendent of patents since Jefferson appointed him to the job in 1802. Thornton had long dabbled in his own interests and inventions, most recently working on a new musical instrument, which was stored at the Patent Office at Blodgett's Hotel. The three-story, government-owned building, which filled much of the block at Eighth and E streets, also housed the Post Office Department. Thornton and his assistants had taken the patent documents to safety before the British arrived, but it had been impossible to remove hundreds of bulky invention models that were stored at the office.

Thornton leapt into action, abandoning his breakfast and gathering a small delegation to rush with him to the city. They approached Colonel Jones, overseeing the destruction of the War, Navy, and State headquarters building. Thornton started with a small request, asking if he could remove his musical instrument from the Patent Office before it was burned. The amiable Jones replied that as the British did not wish to destroy private property, he was "perfectly at liberty to take it."

By the time Thornton reached Blodgett's, British soldiers under the command of Jones's subordinate, Major Waters, were preparing to burn the building. Thornton was inspired to save much more than one instrument. Virtually everything inside was private property, Thornton told Waters. The building contained hundreds of models and it would be impossible to remove them all. Burning them "would be a loss to all the world," Thornton declared. It "would be as barbarous as . . . to burn the Alexandrian Library for which the Turks have been ever since condemned by all enlightened nations."

Flustered by the histrionics, Waters held off, but told Thornton they would need a ruling from Jones. The two men found the colonel a few blocks away at the *Intelligencer*, where his men were helping Cockburn destroy the newspaper's property. Jones readily agreed to spare the patent building; the admiral, busy wreaking vengeance on Gales, was apparently not consulted.

Navy Yard, morning, Thursday, August 25

The British did not seem to mind that the Americans had beaten them to burning the Navy Yard. "Admiral Cockburn said he was glad of it, as it saved him the trouble," according to a witness. Nonetheless, the admiral sent a party under Captain Wainwright to make sure the job was complete.

Arriving at the smoldering yard around 8 a.m., Wainwright found locals roaming the property, scavenging what they could. The neighborhood to the east was home to poor families living in shanties who made meager livings off the Navy Yard and had not bothered to flee the British. Some delinquent youth—"home-nursed ragamuffins," Latrobe called them—tried to follow Wainwright's men into the yard, but the officer ordered them out and shut the gate. Looking about, the British found a surprising amount of material had survived the fire. Down at the wharf, the cooper's shop and timber sheds had escaped the flames, as had stores filled with canvas, lines, and nautical apparatus. These were quickly put to the torch.

The British had hardly left, closing the gate behind them, when a small gig surreptitiously landed at the Navy Yard at 8:45 a.m. A stout man hopped onto the wharf. After spending the night across the Potomac in Alexandria, Captain Thomas Tingey had sailed back to check on his beloved yard.

It was a desolate sight, particularly with the new fires crackling. Tingey found the schooner *Lynx* laying alongside the still-burning wharf, unharmed—Wainwright's men had somehow missed it—and hauled her to a safer position. Tingey was relieved to see that the commandant's home where he lived had been spared; the British had deemed it private property. But to his dismay he saw that "a parcel of wicked boys in the neighborhood" with no such scruples was plundering the home.

Tingey persuaded helpful residents to move his most valuable material and furniture to the homes of reputable neighbors. But a yard supervisor warned Tingey not to stay long, as Cockburn was looking for him—"having expressed an anxious desire to make me captive," Tingey reported. As a native Englishman, Tingey could expect little mercy from the admiral. If Cockburn did not already know of Tingey's return, he would soon, the supervisor warned. Tingey reluctantly sailed off.

A stout man hopped onto the wharf. After spending the night across the Potomac in Alexandria, Captain Thomas Tingey had sailed back to check on his beloved yard.

Captain Thomas Tingey, commandant of the Washington Navy Yard.

Before long, a detachment of Royal Marines arrived at the yard to spike cannons. Entering through the spacious gateway, they were greeted by the Tripoli monument, a column of Italian Carrara marble with allegorical statuary on the base honoring fallen heroes of the Barbary War. As the nation's first military monument, it was a source of great pride to Americans, and a tempting target to the British.

Cheering troops clambered onto the monument, snatching the palm from the hand of *Fame*, breaking the pointed forefinger off the hand of *America*, and grabbing the golden pen from the hand of *History*, a female figure recording the heroics of the Americans at Tripoli. A British officer, seething that the United States had declared war on Britain while she fought Napoleon, later told an American prisoner the act was "a rebuke to the lying Yankee officers, who should have no more deeds of valor to record."

The skies were darkening and it looked as if a storm was coming.

Standing near the monument, Martha Ann Fry, the daughter of a neighborhood widow, saw a red-coated officer with the golden pen in his hand. "[A]fter holding it some time, he threw it down and damn'd himself that they had had trouble enough," she recalled.

The British departed. Fry picked the pen off the ground and gave it to a child.

CAPITOL HILL, MORNING, THURSDAY, AUGUST 25

At his headquarters on Capitol Hill, General Ross showed nothing of Cockburn's good cheer. His face was shrouded with worry, and he seemed to regret some of the night's activities. Ross was particularly chagrined to learn the fires had consumed the Library of Congress. "[H]ad I known it in time the books would most certainly have been saved," he told his host, Dr. Ewell. Moreover, he would not have burned the President's House had Dolley Madison been there, he told the doctor. "I make war neither against letters nor ladies, and I have heard so much in praise of Mrs. Madison that I would rather protect than burn the house which sheltered such an excellent lady," Ross said. Consoling the doctor's frightened wife, Margaret, Ross called the entire affair lamentable and blamed "the necessity" for the British actions on the American rampage in York.

York—modern-day Toronto—had a population of 625, small enough to even make Washington look like a city, and it was the capital of the sparsely populated province of Upper Canada, not a nation. Yet the burning of York provided the British invaders with useful symmetry for justifying their actions in Washington.

Brigadier General Zebulon Pike—the explorer of the Southwest who discovered what became known as Pike's Peak in 1806—led an American landing force on the shores of Ontario near York on April 27, 1813, and routed the British and Canadian defenders. But as the British withdrew, their powder magazine blew, creating a tremendous blast that killed Pike and dozens of American soldiers. Angry and undisciplined American troops went on a rampage through the captured town, looting homes and burning several government buildings, and, acting without orders, were likely responsible for burning the parliament building.

Yet retaliation had not brought the British army to Washington; George Cockburn had. Although the myth would grow that the British had marched to Washington to avenge York, the British were certainly not in arrears for vengeance. How could Cockburn be outraged over American actions in Canada, after Havre de Grace, Georgetown and Fredericktown, and Hampton?

From the start, Cockburn had pressed for the capture of Washington as a strategic blow, the logical continuance of his campaign of terror in the Chesapeake, meant to persuade Americans of the high cost of war, ferment disunity, and punish Madison. Ross had come to share Cockburn's view, seeing the real value of burning Washington as forcing an end to the war. In a letter he wrote to his wife shortly after Washington's capture, Ross made no mention of retaliation, but instead described it as a stroke that would soon end the war.

"They feel strongly the disgrace of having had their capital taken by a handful of men and blame very generally a government which went to war without the means or the abilities to carry it on," Ross wrote. "The injury sustained by the city of Washington in the destruction of the public buildings has been immense and must disgust the country with a government that has left the capital unprotected."

Nonetheless, Ross likely would not have consented to burning Washington's public buildings had he not believed the act to be justified as a response to American actions in Canada. Retaliation was a secondary, but potent, reason. It was not so much York but the more recent burning of Newark and Port Dover that was on British minds. Though the U.S. government later disavowed it, the burning of Newark at the order of an American commander in December 1813 probably fueled more British anger than any other American action during the war and set off a cycle of reprisal along the Niagara frontier. The British soon burned almost every town on the American side of the Niagara, including the village of Buffalo. In retaliation, an American army regiment destroyed Port Dover on the Canadian side of Lake Erie in May. Again the American commander was reprimanded, but Sir Prevost, the British commander in Canada, called for revenge. It was "the disgraceful conduct of the American troops in the wanton destruction of private property on the north shores of Lake Erie" that Prevost cited in his request for retaliation, and which in turn prompted

Cochrane to issue his infamous "lay waste to destroy" order in July.

Before Ross landed at Benedict with his army, Cochrane had re-minded Ross of Newark and York, and shared with him the letter from Prevost, which spoke of "the indispensable necessity of retaliating" to prevent the Americans from repeating such acts.

Ross answered that he "had been accustomed to carry on war in a very different spirit in the Peninsula and France, and that he could not sanction the destruction of private or public property, with the exception of military structures and warlike stores," according to an account written many years later by his aide Captain Duncan MacDougall. "It was not until he was warmly pressed that he consented to destroy the Capitol and President's House, for the purpose of preventing a repetition of the uncivilized proceedings of the troops of the United States," MacDougall added.

"The injury sustained by the city of Washington in the destruction of the public buildings has been immense and must disgust the country with a government that has left the capital unprotected," wrote General Ross.

The U.S. Capitol after burning by the British, sketch by George Munger in 1814.

★

Returning from his tour of the city, Cockburn noticed Margaret Ewell's cheeks were streaked with tears, but he was not as sympathetic as Ross. "Pray, Madam, what could have alarmed you so?" he asked in a sharp voice. "Did you take us for savages?" Introduced to several more Capitol Hill matrons, including Mary Hunter, the admiral laid on the charm as best he could. Cockburn said he "admired the American ladies—they made excellent wives and good mothers; but they were very much prejudiced against him."

Cockburn assured the ladies he would allow no plunder. In that spirit, he and Ross called off troops preparing to burn the Marine barracks and commandant's house after pleas from neighbors that the strong wind would spread fire to their homes. But when an officer reported that the Bank of Washington could not be burned without harming neighboring property, Cockburn was impatient. "Well, then, pull it down," he sternly ordered. Ewell intervened with Cockburn, despite feeling "somewhat of awe in the presence of this son of Neptune," and told the admiral that the bank was private property.

"Well, then, let it alone," the admiral glumly told the officer.

A few isolated incidents shattered the relative calm Thursday morning. A British soldier armed with a musket went on a robbery spree, but after residents reported him, he was apprehended by two British officers, taken back to headquarters, and ordered shot. Ross and Cockburn were about to enter the Ewell house for a midday meal when a drunken and disheveled woman, streaked with blood, ran up screaming. "Oh I am killed, I am killed! A British sailor has killed me!" cried the woman.

An indignant Cockburn ordered his sailors mustered, directing that the man she designated as her assailant be shot. Ewell treated her wounds, which proved to be superficial, and found the delirious woman uncertain whether she had been attacked by an Englishman or an American. Still chagrined, Cockburn dropped the matter, but insisted Ewell take six doubloons to pay for her treatment.

Cockburn's harshest critics acknowledged that the British for the most part had "scrupulously respected" private homes. "Greater respect was certainly paid to private property than has usually been exhibited by the enemy in his marauding parties," the *Intelligencer* conceded when it resumed publication. "No houses were half as much plundered by the enemy, as by the knavish wretches about the town who profited of the general distress."

MONTGOMERY COURT HOUSE, THURSDAY MORNING, AUGUST 25

General Winder had chosen to reconstitute and resupply his army at Montgomery Court House, a small Maryland town now known as Rockville, fifteen miles northwest of Washington. From there, Winder said, "we could best interpose between the enemy and Baltimore," which he and almost everyone else guessed would be the next British target.

After retreating all the way from Bladensburg, Winder now spoke grandiosely of his plans to "intimidate and harass" the enemy. "I shall assemble the largest possible force I can here and make such movements as I think may be necessary to preserve Baltimore," Winder wrote to Brigadier General John Stricker, a militia commander in Baltimore.

Every hour brought reinforcements, some of them stragglers who had fled the field at Bladensburg but sheepishly returned. New volunteers were streaming in from western Maryland and Virginia, many lacking weapons.

The dusty and exhausted men of Captain Jenifer Sprigg's Annapolis regiment reached the town Thursday morning, having marched most of the night with Winder's forces retreating from Tenleytown. Sprigg fell into a trough of muddy water and lapped it up, alongside other parched men. "My horse being very thirsty, himself, pushed in among us and we thus all drank very quietly together," the Maryland militia officer wrote. Since leaving Annapolis three days earlier, Sprigg had taken his sword belt up three notches, and he still had room to fit both his fists inside.

Both the weather outside and the mood in the headquarters were tempestuous, and Winder was soon overwhelmed by the demands of officers clamoring for orders and the complaints of the men camped in the rain.

Jacob Barker and Robert De Peyster, the visiting businessmen who had helped Dolley Madison escape the President's House, arrived at Montgomery Court House to find a chaotic scene. They had left the portrait of George Washington for safekeeping en route at the Maryland farmhouse where they had spent the night. In the morning, they had nearly been arrested as spies by suspicious Americans before making their way to Winder's camp.

Barker was astonished to hear Winder speak of sending some of the reinforcements away. "Troops are pouring in from every direction, we shall have before night more than we can feed," the general complained.

Replied Barker, "Then send them on foraging parties in every direction, but for God's sake do not release a man."

GREENLEAF POINT, WASHINGTON, NOON, THURSDAY, AUGUST 25

The British had nearly completed the destruction of federal Washington, but one more target awaited: the Greenleaf Point Federal Arsenal. Though the retreating Americans had partially destroyed it, the British learned that weapons and a sizable amount of gunpowder were still stored at the site, two miles south of the Capitol at the southernmost tip of the city, where the Eastern Branch flowed into the Potomac River.

Royal Marine Captain Mortimer Timpson, a sturdy and brave veteran of the Napoleonic Wars, was dispatched with a party of Royal Marines early in the afternoon to join another force of 200 men in destroying the arsenal. As the troops marched down a primitive road to Greenleaf Point, a leaden sky portending a storm turned almost midnight black. Low rumbles of distant thunder and faint flashes of lightning were accompanied by fitful gusts of wind.

At the arsenal, the British found a cache of 150 barrels of gunpowder, and a river battery armed with eight cannons. Faced with the problem of destroying so much powder, the men threw barrels into a deep well near the magazine, "fancying there was plenty of water there to wet it," Timpson later recalled. But they rolled so many barrels into the well that casks and loose powder rested above the waterline.

Meanwhile, Timpson's men worked on destroying a cannon. "We wanted to blow off the muzzle of the gun, and for that purpose placed another, loaded, at right angles with it," Timpson said. The gunner stuck a slow-burning fuse in the touch hole of the loaded cannon so the men would have time to escape, but the fire burned down without discharging the cannon. The gunner tossed the fuse on the ground and replaced it with a new one.

Rain was falling hard and the wind blew violently. From what Timpson and others later pieced together, a strong gust picked up the dropped fuse and blew it into the well. At 2:10 p.m., the earth shook and a column of fire shot from the well. Almost instantly, the arsenal's magazine, a dozen yards from the well, blew with a tremendous explosion, tearing men apart and throwing their shredded bodies high in the air.

"I found myself shot up into the air like a rocket," Timpson wrote. "I went up some distance, and then fell on my face, while a quantity of rubbish [fell] on the back of my head at the same moment, I felt a sensation as if my head had been suddenly split open . . . and for some time lay senseless."

Rocks, earth, and body parts rained down through the black smoke, falling on men who had survived the initial blast and burying some of them alive. "The groans of the people almost buried in the earth, or with legs and arms broke, and the sight of pieces of bodies lying about, was a thousand times more distressing than the loss we met in the field the day before," said a second officer.

When he came to, Timpson had a severe contusion on his head and was "pretty well shaken to boot." He found three dead men lying close to him, and two more bodies that had been blown over the trees into the water. In all, at least a dozen were dead and another twenty-five men were terribly wounded, some with limbs blown off.

The survivors picked through the rubble, pulling out those who could be saved. Said Timpson, "We then, those who could work, dug a hasty trench, into which we were forced to throw the dead in the best manner we could; for it was getting late, and we had to retreat."

The sickening concussion of the arsenal explosion was felt across the city, and the smoke, flames, and flying debris were visible for miles. Yet the blast was only part of the fear sweeping the town, as it came in the midst of one of the most powerful storms ever to hit Washington. Strong storms were not unusual in the region, but few people had ever experienced one like this. Some American and British accounts loosely and incorrectly called it a hurricane. But the storm's approach from the west strongly suggests it was a line of severe thunderstorms that spawned one or more destructive tornadoes.

The roaring wind collapsed houses, felled chimneys, and uprooted trees, according to a newspaper account. Roofs were "whisked into the air like sheets of paper," wrote Lieutenant Gleig, and the rain "resembled the rushing of a mighty cataract."

Mary Ingle, then a thirteen-year-old living at her parents' home on Capitol Hill, later recalled "the crash and glare of incessant thunder and lightning, and the wild beating of the rain, mingled with the sound of roofs tearing from their supports, and the whir of heavy bodies flying through the air and falling upon the ground beneath." A flash of lightning illuminated a featherbed flying in the wind.

The storm, by one witness account, seemed "to exert its utmost rage on the Capitol Hill," where the British had their forward camp. The winds knocked down piles of weapons, including two small cannons that were "fairly lifted" from the ground and carried several yards to the rear, according to Gleig.

A few soldiers tried to brave it where they stood, but most flung themselves on the ground or ran for shelter behind walls and buildings. Collapsing houses and chimneys killed several men, by one account. Gleig, on horseback, was nearly carried away by the wind. "It fairly lifted me out of the saddle, and the horse which I had been riding I never saw again," he later wrote. To Captain Harry Smith, the storm seemed of biblical proportions. "I never witnessed such a scene as I saw for a few minutes," he later said. "It resembled the storm in Belshazzar's feast."

In parts of the city, every house was damaged. The Patent Office, spared that morning by the British, lost part of its roof. At the Navy Yard, *Lynx* had its foremast torn off. The winds broke the draws on the Long Bridge, the new mile-long span across the Potomac leading to Alexandria. Militiamen guarding the Virginia side of the bridge, nervous that the British were about to cross, ignited their end of the bridge, causing a British detachment on the Washington side to do the same to prevent any American attack.

Sweeping southeast, the storm hit the British fleet at Benedict at 2:30 p.m., when gale-force winds "lashed the smooth and placid waters of the Patuxent into one vast sheet of foam, which covered both our rigging and the decks with its spray," wrote Midshipman Barrett. The frigates *Hebrus* and *Severn* were driven onto the shore, while *Albion* was knocked off her anchor.

On the Potomac, Gordon's squadron was caught as the ships laboriously beat up the shallow flats of the broad river, still some twenty miles south of Alexandria. The men scarcely had time to take down the sails when the storm hit. "The squall thickened at a short distance, roaring in a most awful manner, and appearing like a tremendous surf," wrote Captain Napier, the second in command. His ship, *Euryalus,* lost her bowsprit and the heads of all three topmasts to the raging wind. *Meteor* was blown over on a bank and all the other ships damaged as well. The damage was so severe, Napier wrote, that "Captain Gordon thought the game up" and made plans to turn back.

In Washington, after the wind subsided, the rain fell in torrents for two hours. Cockburn, who waited out the storm at Dr. Ewell's home, emerged and stood with a group of officers at a well on New Jersey Avenue. Spotting a woman watching from a doorway, Cockburn called to her, "Great God, Madam! Is this the kind of storm to which you are accustomed in this infernal country?"

"No, sir," the woman answered. "This is a special interposition of Providence to drive our enemies from our city."

"Not so, Madam," Cockburn retorted. "It is rather to aid your enemies in the destruction of your city."

NORTHERN VIRGINIA, THURSDAY, AUGUST 25

President Madison had been up since early morning, still searching for his wife. The fresh fires in Washington were visible across the river. He left the Salona mansion, where he had spent the night, and retraced his steps to Wren's Tavern in Falls Church, accompanied by Rush. At the militia headquarters, the president spoke with Captain George Graham, commander of a troop of Fairfax dragoons, hoping for word of Dolley's whereabouts and updates on the location of General Winder and the American army. Graham had little information but assigned two Virginia militia troopers to ride with Madison, the first guard for the president since he left Washington.

Madison left to look again for Dolley at Salona, but upon arriving he discovered that she had come and gone, heading farther west on the Leesburg Pike for Wiley's Tavern. Madison took off in pursuit, but he had only traveled a few miles on the Falls Road when the storm forced him to take shelter at a crossroads tavern five miles from Little Falls bridge. The rains and winds sent trees crashing to the ground and turned the road into a river.

Dolley and her party had left Rokeby well before dawn and had made slow but steady progress to Wiley's, a little tavern in the middle of an apple orchard near an aptly named stream known as Difficult Run. The black sky burst open shortly before they arrived, and the wind dashed apples against the building. The tavern was crowded with angry refugees, few of them happy to see the drenched first lady. Some spoke harshly of the president's "misconduct and pusillanimity." The tavern keeper's wife exploded with anger when she learned the first lady was upstairs. "Miss Madison! If that's you, come down and get out! Your husband has got mine out fighting, and damn you, you shan't stay in my house; so get out!" Others intervened, and Dolley remained, ignoring the hostile glares. After the storm passed, she anxiously awaited the president, saving him a bit of the scant meal that was served.

Madison and his party slogged through the muddy road, covered with debris from the storm. The president finally arrived, weary and anxious, reunited with his wife after one of the most momentous days in the nation's history, and likely the most demeaning for any American president. He ate the food Dolley had saved and slept a few short hours.

CAPITOL HILL, EVENING, THURSDAY, AUGUST 25

A ghastly column of British troops struggled back from the arsenal to the British camp on Capitol Hill. Those who could walk carried mutilated men. "[I]t was with the greatest difficulty that I could manage to march with the men," Major Timpson wrote. The British set up a hospital on Carroll Row, a line of houses across from the Capitol. Dr.

Ewell helped treat the forty-seven wounded, many of them "shockingly mangled," he said.

Ross seemed near tears as he surveyed the men lying burnt, bruised, and torn on the floor. Even Cockburn, legendary for his iron nerves, was shaken. Many of the survivors were "so dreadfully mutilated that instant death would have been a blessing to them," said Lieutenant Scott, Cockburn's aide.

The dual calamities of the explosion and storm had taken a toll on the British and hastened their departure from Washington. The vital Foxall Foundry above Georgetown remained intact, but British scouts had apparently spotted a makeshift American force defending the site. Sending troops across town to destroy it this late in the day would likely mean staying a second night. Ross decided not to delay his departure and expose his small force to counterattack, and the foundry was spared.

"The object of the expedition being accomplished I determined before any greater force of the enemy could be assembled to withdraw the troops," Ross wrote in his official report. Cockburn likewise was satisfied nothing would be gained by staying longer, "the general devastation being completed," he wrote in his report.

Despite all the evidence of Winder's incompetence, it seemed inconceivable that the Americans would not mount a counterattack. The British suspected American troops were still on the heights above Georgetown. Ross had already moved some of the troops farther from the town, "as we could scarce think the Americans . . . would tamely allow a handful of British soldiers to advance through the heart of their country, and burn, and destroy, the Capitol of the United States," Colonel Brooke wrote in his diary.

Ross directed Lieutenant Evans to quietly prepare to retreat but to keep the destination from the men to preserve secrecy. Harry Smith was shocked when Ross informed him of the plan. "Tonight? I hope not, sir," he told the general. Smith urged Ross to wait until early morning, warning that the men were exhausted and a night march would be chaotic. But Ross wanted to take advantage of the confusion wrought by the storm and depart before the Americans regrouped.

The general arranged for Ewell to care for the British soldiers who were too severely wounded to travel. "I am much distressed at leaving these poor fellows behind me," Ross told the doctor, who assured him they would be well cared for by the Americans.

A clever deception disguised the withdrawal. The British set an 8 p.m. curfew to keep residents inside their homes. They broadly hinted they were on their way to Georgetown; Ewell got the impression from Ross that they intended to destroy the foundry. The troops stoked campfires with enough wood to keep them burning for hours.

Shortly after sunset, just twenty-four hours after capturing Washington, the British abandoned the American capital. The 3rd Brigade, positioned at the main British camp a mile from the Capitol, moved in front, followed by the 2nd Brigade, while the Light Brigade, marching from Capitol Hill, covered the withdrawal. The British had gathered "forty miserable looking horses" and seized every wagon, oxcart, and carriage they could find to carry the lightly wounded. Cart wheels and horses' hooves were muffled by cloth, and "they went away so easy that you scarcely could hear them," said Michael Shiner, the young slave.

The troops marched in good order to Bladensburg in ninety minutes, halting to load the wounded and distribute provisions. The moon had risen by the time they reached the village, and the pale light revealed the grim sight of corpses strewn about the battlefield. Although the British rear guard, aided by field slaves from the nearby Riversdale plantation, had already buried more than a hundred bodies, many more remained, grotesquely transformed by the terrible heat and violent rain. "[T]hey appeared to be bleached to a most unnatural degree of whiteness . . . and the smell which arose upon the night air was horrible," recalled Gleig.

The light infantry troops hunted for the haversacks that they had tossed aside in the heat of the battle. Many could not find their own and simply took one belonging to a comrade. In the village, two days of provisions were distributed. Barrels of flour were knocked open, and each soldier loaded some in their packs.

British surgeons who had been tending the wounded at a makeshift hospital in Bladensburg selected those well enough to travel, and they were mounted onto horses or loaded into wagons. Another eighty-three men would have to be left in American hands, among them Colonel Thornton, Lieutenant Colonel Wood, and Major Brown, three of

Ross's best officers. Some of the men were in great pain and distraught at being left in a foreign land. One sergeant, shot through both thighs by a musket ball, cried that he would rather be dead.

Commodore Barney, still recuperating in Bladensburg with Marine Captain Samuel Miller and seventeen other wounded Americans, had been touched by the kind treatment he had received from the British, his lifelong enemy. Captain Wainwright "behaved to me as if I was a brother," the commodore reported. Ross was confident that Barney would ensure that the British wounded would be treated well and exchanged for American prisoners. The general left gold coins to pay for their care.

At midnight, bugles sounded and the British again took up the march. For an army that had scored such a singular victory, the retreat from Bladensburg was oddly panicked. "Such a scene of intolerable and unnecessary confusion I never witnessed," said Smith. Beyond town, the road worsened, covered with trees blown down in the storm. "Exceeding darkness" forced the column to stop frequently.

Exhausted men struggled to keep up and fell off by the dozens. The "fatiguing march through narrow and intricate roads on the night of the 25th August occasioned some men to quit the ranks," Ross reported. Many soldiers tossed out their flour, weary of the extra load, and while a waste of vital provisions, the white powder blazed the trail for lagging troops, who followed like modern-day Hansels and Gretels. "If it had not been for the flour thus marking the track, the whole column would have lost its road," said Smith.

The sun had been up for several hours when Ross finally halted around 8 a.m. The men collapsed under trees, on roadsides, or anywhere they could find, and were asleep in an instant. Said Smith, "Our soldiers were dead done."

O say can you see these by the dawn's early
light so proudly we hail'd at the twilight's last gleaming
Whose broad stripes & bright stars through the perilous fight
O'er the ramparts we watch'd were so gallantly streaming
And the rocket's red glare, the bombs bursting in air,
Gave proof through the night that our flag was still there
O say does that star spangled banner yet wave
O'er the land of the free & the home of the brave

On the shore dimly seen through the mists of the deep
Where the foe's haughty host in dread silence reposes
What is that which the breeze, o'er the towering steep
As it fitfully blows, half conceals, half discloses
Now it catches the gleam of the morning's first beam
In full glory reflected now shines in the stream
'Tis the star spangled banner — O long may it wave
O'er the land of the free & the home of the brave

And where is that band who so vauntingly swore
That the havoc of war & the battle's confusion
A home & a Country should leave us no more
Their blood has wash'd out their foul footsteps pollution
No refuge could save the hireling & slave
From the terror of flight or the gloom of the grave
And the star-spangled banner in triumph doth wave
O'er the land of the free & the home of the brave

O thus be it ever when freemen shall stand
Between their lov'd home & the war's desolation
Blest with vict'ry & peace may the heav'n rescued land
Praise the power that hath made & preserv'd us a nation
Then conquer we must, when our cause it is just
And this be our motto — "In God is our trust,"
And the Star spangled banner in triumph shall wave
O'er the land of the free & the home of the brave

It was perhaps the most destitute moment America had yet experienced.
The country's great landmarks, including the Capitol and the
President's House, were empty, smoldering shells.

*A view of the President's House in the city of Washington after
the conflagration of the 24th August 1814.*

CHAPTER 10

Hide Our Heads

THE BRITISH WERE gone from Washington, residents discovered at first light. But every vestige of American leadership, power, or authority had also vanished. Winder and his army were fifteen miles away at Montgomery Court House. Nobody knew where Madison was. "[H]e fled so swiftly, that he has never been heard of since," Martha Peter wrote on Friday to a friend. "The whole cabinet are off, no one knows where." Even Mayor James H. Blake had fled to Virginia.

It was perhaps the most destitute moment America had yet experienced. The country's great landmarks, including the Capitol and the President's House, were empty, smoldering shells. Every government building save the Patent Office had been destroyed. Many private homes, spared by the British, had been left roofless by the storm, and their contents ruined by rain. "[I]t seems as if the elements were conspiring to make the scene and times truly awful," Anna Thornton recorded in her diary.

Most people were relieved that the damage was not worse. Georgetown was entirely untouched. Francis Scott Key wrote his mother of his astonishment at "how mercifully we have all been spared here, the enemy not even entering our town, which I am sure they would have done, had they not gone off with such unnecessary precipitation."

But no one in town felt safe. Cockburn and Ross would return to burn the foundry above Georgetown, many assumed. Even more worrisome, the British squadron in the Potomac continued its inexorable sail upriver, threatening Alexandria, Washington, and Georgetown. But most of all, residents feared their own slaves. Rumors flew that armed blacks "would take advantage of the absence of the men to insult females, and complete the work of destruction commenced by the enemy."

Adding to the sense of apocalypse, looters were running rampant through the city. Some of the city's dispossessed—poor laborers, blacks and whites alike—helped themselves to whatever they could find.

William Thornton, returning from his country home Friday morning to check on the Patent Office, was surprised to find the British gone, but even more shocked to see looters removing thousands of dollars' worth of property from public buildings and empty homes. Thornton swung into action, claiming authority as a justice of the peace. He organized civilian volunteers to guard the President's House and then rushed to do the same at the Capitol. Hearing of "dreadful" plunder at the Navy Yard, Thornton hurried to the scene, chased off the looters, and was posting guards when Captain Tingey sailed back yet again on his gig. The yard commandant discovered "such a scene of devastation and plunder took place in the houses . . . as is disgraceful to relate—not a movable article from the cellars to the garrets has been left us—and even some of the fixtures, and the locks of the doors, have been shamefully pillaged." Even the yard's bells were stolen.

Thornton spotted four British stragglers roaming near the Navy Yard. With no American troops to be seen, Thornton sought help from Sergeant Robert Sinclair of the 21st Fusiliers, the noncommissioned officer in charge of the wounded British troops left on Capitol Hill. Sinclair, grateful for the care the men were receiving, agreed to supply ambulatory British troops to accompany citizen patrols. The arrangement with the enemy was unusual, but Thornton was acting in a vacuum.

Mayor Blake returned by ferry around 3 p.m. and discovered that 90 percent of the residents had fled, and those who remained were in "great agitation and alarm." He rushed to assert control, though Anna Thornton was dismissive. "Our stupid mayor . . . ran away in the hour of danger," she wrote in her diary. Blake called together all remaining citizens at the McKeown Hotel that evening to set up self-defense patrols. He vetoed Thornton's arrangement with the British troops, saying it reeked of "impropriety." Thornton refused to attend the meeting and retired back to his farm, insulted at the lack of gratitude. The mayor himself patrolled the streets with his musket.

The looting was brought under control, but the damage did not stop. A marine guarding a naval magazine undiscovered by the enemy was spooked by rumors that the British were returning, and dumped four hundred barrels of gunpowder into the river.

At dusk Friday, Captain Elias Caldwell, a Supreme Court clerk serving as a militia commander, entered the city with a troop of Washington Light Horse cavalry. The capital was back in American military hands, and a relative quiet settled on the city.

Captain John Rodgers arrived in Baltimore Thursday night, August 25, on his way to Washington with four hundred marines and sailors, but learned to his shock that he was too late. "Would to God it had been in my power to have reached Washington in time to have aided in its protection," he wrote Navy Secretary Jones.

Now Rodgers's job was to defend Baltimore, but the city seemed ready to raise a white flag. "When we got to Baltimore the citizens had not determined to defend the town," wrote Marine Lieutenant John Harris. "I believe had not

"Would to God it had been in my power to have reached Washington in time to have aided in its protection," Rodgers wrote Navy Secretary Jones.

Captain John Rodgers

Commodore Rodgers and his crew arrived there as soon as they did they would have capitulated."

The news from Bladensburg and Washington had shocked residents and militia alike. "This came upon us like an avalanche causing the spirits of many to sink," recalled Captain James Piper, a company commander with the 6th Maryland Regiment. The militia scattered at Bladensburg returned to Baltimore in a panic. Private Henry Fulford of the 5th Maryland, who had run for his life during the fighting, made his way home to Baltimore and spread word that the city was doomed. "They will be here in a few days and we have no force that can face them," he wrote in a letter on August 26. "I think the only way to save the town and state will be to capitulate."

"We expect every instant to hear that they have taken up the line of march for this place and if they do we are gone," Private David Winchester wrote to his brother in Tennessee.

R esidents of Baltimore had good reason to suspect they would be next. The British had long wished ill to the city, a center of pro-war sentiment and home to many of the privateers who tormented English shipping. Mobtown, as it was sometimes called, was a raucous city of forty-one thousand, teeming with sailors, merchants, ship workers, and laborers from around the world, Germans, Scots-Irish, and French among them. Baltimore was the most pro-war, Republican city in the country, and its ugly mob violence against opponents of the war had given it notoriety both in America and England.

Built around a harbor off the Patapsco River, the port had grown from modest beginnings into the nation's third-largest city, fueled by booming trade that sent flour and tobacco to Europe for manufactured goods, and to the West Indies in exchange for molasses, sugar, and slaves. The British blockade had dried up much of the trade, but ship owners and merchants were still making healthy profits thanks to privateering, and warehouses were filled with captured riches.

Privateering had been a common practice for centuries, but the United States had made particularly good use of the practice over the course of this war. The government issued letters of marque to the owners of hundreds of ships, authorizing them to capture or destroy British vessels and cargo on the high seas. "They will make the merchants of

England feel and squeal and cry out for peace," Jefferson assured Monroe. A veritable private navy had been launched, including fifty-eight privateer ships fitted out from Baltimore alone, more than any other American port. Though the Royal Navy had bottled up the U.S. Navy, they were unable to deal with the swarms of privateers.

Two-masted schooners built at the city's shipyards in Fells Point—Baltimore Clippers, as they were called—were known around the world for their beauty and speed. The ships, with distinctive long raking masts, were ideal for privateering, carrying their weight high and sailing faster and closer to the wind than any in the Royal Navy, making them almost impossible to catch. The privateers inflicted millions of dollars in damages to British commerce, capturing some 1,338 enemy vessels, more than one-third taken by Maryland ships. In the summer of 1814, the British were losing an average of fifty ships a month to American privateers, most of them in British waters.

Two-masted schooners built at the city's shipyards in Fells Point—
Baltimore Clippers, as they were called—were known around
the world for their beauty and speed.

A Baltimore clipper.

The most famous Baltimore privateer—even more successful than Joshua Barney—was Thomas Boyle, the thirty-four-year-old captain of the 14–gun schooner *Chasseur*, which would earn the nickname "Pride of Baltimore." Cruising off the coast of Great Britain in the summer of 1814, Boyle captured or sank seventeen British vessels, causing uproar among English merchants. Even as Washington smoldered, Boyle cheekily delivered a proclamation declaring the entire coasts of Great Britain and Ireland to be "in a state of strict and rigorous blockade." Insurers and merchants petitioned the king, complaining that British waters were infested with American privateers and that their actions had been "injurious to our commerce, humbling to our pride and discreditable" to the Royal Navy.

The Royal Navy—particularly Admirals Cockburn and Cochrane—was eager to make a lesson out of Baltimore.

MONTGOMERY COURT HOUSE, 10 A.M., FRIDAY, AUGUST 26

At his headquarters Friday morning, William Winder received intelligence that the enemy had evacuated Washington and "was in full march for Baltimore." The general sprang into action, ordering his command under arms. At 10 a.m., the army took up the line of march on the road to Baltimore.

In the two days since Bladensburg, Winder had assembled "a force respectable as to numbers and appearance," in the view of Brigadier General Stansbury, the Maryland militia brigade commander. It included the U.S. infantry regiments that had served at Bladensburg, Major Peters's redoubtable Georgetown Artillery, General Smith's District militia, the Annapolis militia under Colonel Beall, riflemen from western Maryland, assorted cavalry, and some of Stansbury's militia from outside Baltimore.

By evening, the army had traveled a dozen miles, about one-third of the way to Baltimore, camping at Snell's Bridge, where the Clarksville Pike crossed the upper Patuxent River. Winder was impatient to get to Baltimore to take command of the defenses, having "concluded his presence there was indispensible," Stansbury recalled.

Winder continued during the night for Baltimore, leaving Stansbury to follow with the troops in the morning. Though he had just presided over one of the greatest military debacles in America's young history, Winder did not yet grasp how tenuous his hold on command was. As he rode obliviously through the evening, Winder was intercepted by a messenger rushing the opposite way, bearing an express from Major General Samuel Smith, the militia commander in Baltimore. Smith informed Winder that he had "assumed the command" in the city.

Winder was astonished. President Madison had appointed Winder commander of the Tenth Military District, which expressly included Baltimore. Moreover, War Department policy held that regular army officers such as Winder were superior to all ranks of militia officers unless the latter had been formally called into federal service. But that had not stopped Smith.

Samuel Smith had never been much for legal formalities, either as a U.S. senator from Maryland or as one of Baltimore's wealthiest merchants. Now sixty-two, with bushy eyebrows, prominent nose, and a stern face, he had commanded the Baltimore militia for three decades. During the Revolutionary War, Smith served as a company commander with Smallwood's Battalion, part of the famed Maryland Line, which helped save the Continental Army with a brave stand at Long Island, and he escaped with George Washington aboard the last boats to evacuate. He served at Brandywine, Fort Mifflin, and Valley Forge, and after the war commanded the Maryland troops sent west to put down the Whiskey Rebellion.

Back in Baltimore, business ventures in shipping, banking, and land speculation made him immensely rich. He launched a political career at age forty, serving first in the House of Representatives and since 1803 as a senator. Once a staunch Jefferson Republican, Smith split with Madison over foreign policy and became a leading member of the "Invisibles," a group of Republicans who opposed the president. His brother and political protégé, Robert, had served as Madison's secretary of state, but the president fired him for disloyalty and incompetence in 1811, replacing him with Monroe. Samuel Smith shared in his brother's political disfavor with the Madison administration, and even fell off Dolley Madison's social list.

When war was declared, Smith, a staunch supporter of the conflict,

Samuel Smith had never been much for legal formalities, either as a U.S. senator from Maryland or as one of Baltimore's wealthiest merchants. Now sixty-two, with bushy eyebrows, prominent nose, and a stern face, he had commanded the Baltimore militia for three decades.

Major General Samuel Smith, commander of American forces in Baltimore.

focused attention on preparing the city's defenses, a job for which he was uniquely qualified. His positions on the Senate naval and military affairs committees gave him powerful perches to ensure Baltimore received its share of military assistance from the government. As champion of the city's merchant and shipping class, he could count on financial backing to build up defenses. Moreover, the militia troops loved him, not least because he regularly supplied them with rum and whisky.

After Bladensburg, city leaders agreed on one thing: They wanted Smith, and not Winder, to take command of the defense of Baltimore. On the morning of August 25, a delegation of senior military commanders in the city, including Major George Armistead, the commander at Fort McHenry; Captain Oliver Perry, the hero of Lake Erie, in town awaiting command of a new ship; and Brigadier General John Stricker, a Maryland militia commander, went to the city's Committee of Vigilance and Safety to make the highly unorthodox request that Smith take command of Baltimore. The committee promptly endorsed the proposal. Smith was eager to do so, but he wanted approval from higher authority. Baltimore Mayor Edward Johnson, chairman of the committee, sent a message by express to Governor Levin Winder in Annapolis asking that Smith be invested with the necessary powers.

Governor Winder seemed no more eager to have his nephew re-main in command than anyone else. "There can be no doubt as to the propriety of . . . Smith's taking command under present circumstances and I conceive it to be his duty to do so," Levin Winder replied after receiving Johnson's letter the night of August 25. The governor sup-plied a nebulous statement implying that Smith's assignment was in "conformity" with a request from the federal government. This was enough for Smith and the committee members, who claimed that Smith had thus been called into service of the United States at the rank of major general and hence could take command from Winder.

General Winder was dumbfounded upon reading Smith's message Friday night. "[T]he manner in which Genl. Smith had placed himself in command in my absence is at least very singular," he wrote to the War Department. Winder rushed on to Baltimore, intending to con-front Smith about "the palpable mistake on his part."

UPPER MARLBORO, FRIDAY, AUGUST 26

Roused from their exhausted sleep at noon Friday, the British troops marched in oppressive heat toward Upper Marlboro, continuing with-out halting until they arrived at dusk. Contrary to American expecta-tions, the British were not en route to Baltimore. As they moved out of Washington, the British had broadly hinted that their destination was Baltimore, asking about the roads to the city, available supplies, and the forces defending the city. The Americans "took the bait," recalled Harry Smith.

Ross had, in fact, seriously considered taking his army overland directly to Baltimore to capitalize on the sensational capture of Wash-ington. "[T]he disorganization of the enemy's public departments, the confusion and dismay of the country seemed to justify the attempt," George De Lacy Evans wrote in his memorandum on the operation.

The distance from Bladensburg to Baltimore by land was little more than thirty miles, no farther than the march back to the ships anchored off Benedict. But attacking Baltimore would take Ross fifty miles from the ships, a dangerous distance for such a small force.

If Cochrane could be persuaded to immediately send at least some of the fleet toward Baltimore, it could be a different matter altogether. "Had there been five or six large vessels, in the upper part of the bay to receive or assist the army in case of disaster this attempt perhaps would have been made," Evans wrote. But given that Cochrane had "decidedly dissented" from attacking Washington, Evans noted, no one on the expedition—not even Cockburn—was willing to further test the vice admiral's ill humor with the suggestion.

Ross decided it best to get his physically spent force back to the ships. Once the army was reunited with the fleet, and his men rested and supplied, an attack on Baltimore could be prepared.

Yet Ross was missing an extraordinary opportunity to fall on the undefended rear of a panicked, demoralized city. Though Baltimore was well defended by water, almost all of its land defenses were oriented for an attack from the east. Baltimore lay wide open to a land attack from the southwest via Washington. Rash as an attack would have been, it may well have succeeded. Baltimore had been given a respite.

BROOKEVILLE, MARYLAND, 9 P.M., FRIDAY, AUGUST 26

Darkness had settled by the time President Madison and his party reached the little town of Brookeville, on the road from Montgomery Court House to Baltimore. The Quaker village, with two mills, a tanning yard, a blacksmith shop, and a private boys' academy, lay in an idyllic valley surrounded by hills and woods. "In this secluded spot one might hope the noise, or rumor of war would never reach," wrote Margaret Bayard Smith, who had taken shelter in the village with her family after fleeing Washington.

But the war came in the shape of an exhausted and homeless president who had been traveling on horseback most of the day without food or rest. Turned down for lodgings at the first house where they stopped, the presidential party continued to a brick Federal-style house that was home to village postmaster and storekeeper Caleb Bentley and his wife, Henrietta. Though as Quakers the Bentleys were staunchly opposed to war, everyone in the household went to work making the president and his party welcome. Beds were placed in the parlor, and supper prepared, and the house overflowed with guests.

Madison had left Dolley at Wiley's Tavern in Virginia at midnight the previous night, just a few hours after joining his wife. Learning that Monroe was on his way to link up with Winder's army at Montgomery Court House, Madison decided to do the same. Rumors circulated that the British had moved into Northern Virginia, and this may have contributed to Madison's decision to leave Wiley's in the middle of the night. Accompanied by a small group that included Rush, Jones, and Mason, and escorted by a growing number of dragoons, the president rode ten miles to Conn's Ferry, above Great Falls. But by the time they arrived, the Potomac was swollen from the storm and impossible to cross.

Jones returned to Wiley's to rejoin his wife and Dolley, while Madison and the rest stayed Thursday night near the ferry landing, likely at the Conn family farmhouse. Even when morning came, it was hours before they could cross the dangerously turbulent river. Once in Maryland, Madison's party traveled ten miles up the Falls Road to Montgomery Court House, where the president hoped to find Winder's army. But when they arrived, Madison learned that the army was already on the march for Baltimore. The exhausted presidential party continued another eight miles to Brookeville.

For one night, the tiny Quaker village served as the de facto capital of the United States. Dragoons pitched tents near the mills along the village stream and lit campfires. Guards trampled Henrietta Bentley's rosebushes and vegetable garden. Villagers came by to pay their respects to the president, who appeared grave but not dispirited by events. Madison "anxiously enquired after Colonel Monroe and Armstrong, saying he did not know where either of them were," a visitor wrote. Madison learned Monroe was with the army, camped five miles up the road at Snell's Bridge, while Armstrong and Campbell were in Frederick. The war and Treasury secretaries were the only ones who had gone to Frederick, as originally instructed by the president.

At the dinner table, fellow refugees did not hold their tongues. "The defense of the city was freely criticized and the situation of the country as freely spoken of," one guest reported. Madison said little other than to express surprise at reports that the British had destroyed the office of the *Intelligencer* but not yet touched the Foxall Foundry.

Around 10 p.m., after finishing dinner, the president sat down in a

Windsor chair with a writing arm in Henrietta Bentley's upstairs bed-room and stayed up late writing and reading dispatches, trying to gather his disparate government. "I will either wait here till you join me, or follow and join you as you may think best," he wrote to Monroe. "If you decide on coming hither, the sooner the better." Secretary of the Navy Jones, still with Dolley in Virginia, would return to Washington "the moment he hears of its evacuation."

Since he had left Washington to inspect the army on the morning of August 22, Madison, sixty-three years old and in poor health, had been in the saddle fifteen to twenty hours a day for four days, through terrible heat and storms. He would be ridiculed as a coward who fled the battlefield, but for all his faults as a commander-in-chief, Madison had shown remarkable courage and determination through the crucible. After writing his final dispatch, Madison slept a few hours in the oasis of the Bentley home.

In the morning, a dispatch arrived in Brookeville from Monroe with the momentous news that the enemy had abandoned the capital and was retreating to their ships. Monroe advised an "immediate return to Washington."

Madison sent messages by express to Armstrong and Campbell in Frederick and to Jones in Virginia urging their quick return. The president also gave the trooper riding to Virginia a note for the first lady. Addressed simply to "my dearest," the president's letter said he was immediately setting out for Washington. "You will all of course take the same resolution," Madison wrote. "I know not where we are in the first instance to hide our heads; but shall look for a place on my arrival."

Monroe showed up in Brookeville soon after his note. At noon, accompanied by Monroe, Rush, and a guard of dragoons, the president set out for the burned capital—"our suffering city," Margaret Bayard Smith called it.

UPPER MARLBORO, AFTERNOON, SATURDAY, AUGUST 27

The departure of the British from Upper Marlboro seemed like cause for celebration to Dr. William Beanes, who had hosted the command-

ers on their way to Washington. After Ross's army left town early in
the morning to march for Nottingham on the Patuxent River, Beanes
invited several local friends and luminaries to join him for a meal at his
home at Academy Hill.

Robert Bowie, the distinguished former governor of Maryland, was
one of the guests invited to join Beanes Saturday afternoon, along with
the doctor's brother, Bradley Beanes; William Hill, another doctor who
lived outside of Marlboro; and two other acquaintances, William
Lansdale of Upper Marlboro and a teenage boy, Philip Weems.

Though the British had left Upper Marlboro, more than a hundred
stragglers were roaming the countryside, pillaging homes, taking
horses, and stealing food. As Beanes and Governor Bowie strolled
around the doctor's property, they encountered a British soldier trying
to "steal the refreshments" from the garden and forced him to surrender. The captive, Thomas Holden, told the men he was a British deserter, and they took him to Dr. Beanes's home.

The guests soon realized that more British were on the loose in
Upper Marlboro. "Whilst at the doctor's we saw several stragglers belonging to the Army of the enemy passing through town to join the
Army," Hill later reported. Bowie, an old warhorse who had commanded a militia company during the revolution, proposed capturing
them. William Beanes readily agreed, perhaps eager to burnish his credentials as a patriot after the friendly welcome he had given the British.
Not everyone thought it a good idea. "[S]everal gentlemen who were
present urged the dangerous consequences might result from it while
the enemy were so near," according to a newspaper account written
several days later. Cockburn had torched towns for less.

Nonetheless, Beanes, Bowie, Hill, and several others set out, armed
with a fowling piece, and caught at least three stragglers. But several
others escaped. Unlike Holden, the stragglers had apparently not deserted but were trying to rejoin their army.

The town was soon in an uproar over fears of British retaliation.
Bowie, concerned that upset residents would release the prisoners,
turned to two reliable local brothers, John and Benjamin Hodges, to
move them to a safer location. The prisoners were taken nine miles
northeast, to the town of Queen Anne, on the upper Patuxent River,
where residents mounted a guard.

Upper Marlboro, it seemed, was safe. The party over, Hill and Weems stayed for the night at Academy Hill, and Dr. Beanes went to bed.

POTOMAC RIVER, EVENING, SATURDAY, AUGUST 27

At 5 p.m., Captain Gordon's Royal Navy squadron came into view of Mount Vernon, George Washington's estate on the Potomac River. The ten-day journey up the Potomac had been arduous, from the endless groundings in the Kettle Bottoms to the contrary winds and the tremendous squall two days earlier. The storm damage had almost compelled Gordon to turn around, but the crews had swiftly repaired the ships, and at last a fair wind brought them up a broad stretch of river leading to Alexandria and Washington. Just beyond Mount Vernon, on the opposite Maryland shore, lay the last obstacle. "Fort Washington appeared to our anxious eyes; and, to our great satisfaction, it was considered assailable," wrote "Black Charlie" Napier, Gordon's second in command.

The squadron stopped just out of the fort's gunshot range while Gordon prepared an attack. The bomb vessels moved within range of the fort, dropping anchor and preparing for an immediate bombardment to weaken the defenses. At first light the next morning, Gordon planned to land forces and storm the fort.

Fort Washington sat on a bluff at the junction of the Potomac River and Piscataway Creek. Its strategic position commanding the river channel had been long recognized, including by George Washington, who in 1794 recommended a fort be built on the promontory. Construction of the fort began in 1808 and was completed a year later. Though formally named Fort Warburton, after a nearby manor home, many people had come to call it after the first president. It was not a particularly grand honor. The fort consisted of little more than a small star-shaped earthwork with a circular gun battery, and was derisively described by a newspaper as "a mere pig pen."

President Madison sent Major Pierre L'Enfant, the engineer who designed the capital, to inspect the fort in 1813; L'Enfant concluded "the whole original design was bad" and recommended it be rebuilt. A few improvements were made, but in the summer of 1814 the guns were in poor condition and there was little ammunition. Yet despite all its problems, Fort Washington remained a formidable obstacle.

Spotting the British sails late Saturday afternoon, U.S. Army Captain Samuel T. Dyson ordered the Fort Washington garrison to their stations. Dyson, an experienced regular army artillery officer recently released from British captivity, had assumed command three weeks earlier, and he was distressed at the condition of the fort and garrison. He had no more than 60 men, only enough to man five of the fort's twenty-seven guns.

Dyson could see smoke still rising from the capital, and to make matters worse, locals reported that the British army was marching on Fort Washington—though no one had actually seen them. Dyson concluded that "my miserable post and little band was all that survived the general wreck." Despite the lack of any hard evidence, the rumors of a British army attack had convinced Dyson the fort was caught in a pincer between land and water.

The panicking captain assembled his four junior officers. He informed them that he had orders from Winder to blow the fort should the enemy threaten capture. The captain asked his lieutenants to vote, and the result was unanimous: Blow the fort.

Dyson gave orders to spike the guns and prepare to destroy and evacuate the fort. The troops were shocked. "We ought at least to give them one shot," a soldier grumbled. Grimly, the men made preparations, setting a gunpowder trail to blow the magazine and leaving it rigged to explode. All the artillery was spiked. The men had barely left Fort Washington when the first British shell landed in a nearby creek.

Aboard *Seahorse*, Captain Gordon was puzzled to see a trail of men apparently abandoning their position. Gordon suspected a ruse and ordered the fire to continue. To his surprise, there was no response from the fort.

JOHNNY BULL and the ALEXANDRIANS.

"The terms of capitulation of the town of Alexandria are so degrading
and humiliating as to excite the indignation of all classes of people,"
Secretary Jones wrote Rodgers.

"Johnny Bull and the Alexandrians," political cartoon
by William Charles published in the U.S. in 1814.

CHAPTER 11

★

The Arrogant Foe

P RESIDENT MADISON RODE back into Washington at 5 p.m. on Saturday, three days after his inglorious departure. It was hardly a triumphant return. The presidential party had scarcely entered the city when they heard thunderous cannon fire coming from down the Potomac. Fort Washington was being battered, Madison and Monroe realized. One invading British force had left the city, but another was arriving.

A report arrived in the traumatized city that six British ships were attacking the fort. If it fell, the British had an open route not only to Alexandria but to Washington and Georgetown as well. The Royal Navy, it seemed, intended to finish the job the British army had begun.

Madison had no time to tour the burned capital. As the President's House was in ruins, the presidential party hurried to Attorney General Rush's home a few blocks away on Pennsylvania Avenue, where Madison conferred with Monroe and Rush. With federal Washington destroyed and a second enemy force on the city's doorstep, the country faced its gravest crisis since independence.

"Such was the state of affairs when the President entered the city on the evening of the 27th," Monroe wrote. "There was no force organized for its defense. . . . The effect of the late disaster on the whole union and the world was anticipated. Prompt measures were indispensable." As Armstrong was still in Frederick and Winder in Balti-

more, Madison directed Monroe to take interim charge of the War
Department as well as military command in Washington.

The cannonading downriver continued until around 8 p.m., when
the entire city shuddered with a severe concussion from that same direction. No one was quite sure what had happened. The city had a
restless night, wondering, as Major McKenney wrote that night from
Georgetown, "whether the explosion was the magazine of the fort, or
a British ship."

UPPER MARLBORO, 1 A.M., SUNDAY, AUGUST 28

During the night, one or more escaped British stragglers made their
way from Upper Marlboro and were picked up by British patrols.
Taken to Ross at the British camp at Nottingham, they reported that
their erstwhile host, Dr. Beanes, had captured some of the men. Ross
was infuriated; Beanes had been "one of those who had met us with a
flag on our entrance into Marlboro," the general observed.

For Ross, it was a question of honor. He had gone to extremes to
respect private property and treat civilians with courtesy, particularly
those he considered gentlemen. Beanes's actions and words when the
British quartered at his home, in Ross's judgment, bound the doctor
not to take up arms until the troops were back on their ships.

He ordered Lieutenant Evans to immediately return to Upper Marlboro, seize Beanes, and deliver an ultimatum to the town: If the prisoners were not returned before noon that day, Upper Marlboro would be
destroyed.

Evans had put together a makeshift cavalry of 85 men mounted on
assorted captured horses—"our Cossacks," the British troops jokingly
called them. At 1 a.m. Sunday the British horsemen thundered into
Upper Marlboro and rode to Academy Hill. Beanes was "taken from
his bed in the midst of his family, and hurried off almost without
clothes," according to an American complaint delivered to the British.
The doctor was handled so roughly and hurriedly that his spectacles
were left behind. Hill and Weems, who had picked the wrong night to
spend at the Beanes home, were taken as well; and the three men were
tossed onto horses without saddles. The British seized the still-loaded
fowling piece the Americans had used to capture the stragglers.

Evans and his men searched other homes, including the nearby residence of the doctor's brother, Bradley Beanes, looking for the British prisoners. When Bradley Beanes opened the door, Evans strode in with troops and scoured the house, but found nothing. Furious at being unable to locate the captives, Evans left town with a warning: "[U]nless they were returned before 12 o'clock the next day, they would lay the town in ashes," a witness reported.

The party rode back to the British camp at Nottingham, with the elderly physician jostling along bareback through the night, clad only in his nightclothes. "To our no small surprise we saw our friend Dr. Bean brought in as a prisoner," Gleig, at the camp, recorded in his diary. The three captives were brought before Ross, and when Beanes attempted to explain their actions, it only further infuriated the general. Beanes had "acted hostilely" toward his soldiers and then "attempted to justify his conduct when I spoke to him on the subject," Ross later wrote. "I conceived myself authorized and called upon to cause his being detained as a prisoner."

Ross, recalled Hill, "ordered us to be sent to the fleet."

QUEEN ANNE, MARYLAND, EARLY MORNING, SUNDAY, AUGUST 28

Upper Marlboro was in a panic after Lieutenant Evans and his horsemen rode off. John Hodges was awoken by neighbors, who told him of the British threat and asked that he bring the prisoners back from Queen Anne. Hodges and his brother took off immediately, fearing their own families would be seized by the British as hostages.

"Never [were] people so universally alarmed on God's earth as the people of Upper Marlboro," former Governor Bowie later testified. "Death and destruction were threatening them every moment if they refused to deliver up these men."

The Hodges arrived in Queen Anne, agitated and exhausted from the hard ride. They immediately met resistance over the idea of returning the prisoners, particularly the deserter, as the British would undoubtedly hang him. William Caton, a Queen Anne resident, told John Hodges "if he surrendered the deserter he was no American—he would stain his hands with human blood." John Randall, in charge of the prisoners, refused to release the men without approval from Bowie,

who was spending the night nearby. Upon arriving, Bowie at first refused to approve their release, but relented after hearing more details
of the British threat.

But the governor insisted that Holden not be turned over. Robert
Bowie, the governor's son, argued emotionally against returning the
deserter. "It would be murder," he wept. Bradley Beanes tried to mediate a compromise, suggesting the "thing could be managed" by allowing the deserter a chance to escape.

Tempers cooled. The governor's son noted "they had enough to do
to fight the enemy." The prisoners were released into the hands of the
Hodges brothers, the younger Bowie, William Lansdale, and several
others. They worked to approach British lines with the captives and
seek to negotiate further.

FORT WASHINGTON, DAWN, SUNDAY, AUGUST 28

Captain Gordon waited until first light Sunday to finish off Fort Washington. The men of the Potomac squadron had been uncertain whether
the tremendous explosion at the fort Saturday night came from a lucky
shot or was an act of self-destruction. Most guessed the latter, but they
were nonetheless amazed when the landing party confirmed the Americans had destroyed the fort. "[W]e were at a loss to account for such
an extraordinary step," wrote Captain Napier, who estimated capturing the fort would have cost the British at least fifty men, given its
commanding location.

During the night, Captain Dyson had retreated with the fort's garrison along a road four miles upriver before taking a ferry across the
Potomac to Virginia. As they marched away in ignominy, Dyson insisted that they had done the right thing.

No one was more dismayed by the destruction of Fort Washington
than the citizens of Alexandria, six miles upriver. The thriving
town remained one of the busier ports in the country, though its days
as a rival to New York and Boston were past. Despite its wealth and
prestige, Alexandria was utterly helpless. There were no fortifications
or natural defenses protecting the city, just deepwater wharves along
an open stretch of the Potomac. Blocks of warehouses and brick homes

stood within easy range of naval gunfire. The city fathers had warned Madison in May 1813 that Alexandria would be defenseless should the enemy ever penetrate the Potomac past Fort Washington, but the president merely observed that it was impossible to defend every assailable point.

After the British landed at Benedict, the Alexandria militia had been called to the defense of Washington, taking all the city's artillery, save two twelve-pounders with no ammunition. The militia had been utterly squandered by General Winder, who left the Alexandrians idling near Fort Washington for several days until after the battle at Bladensburg, and then sent them back across the Potomac and ordered them to march north. When Fort Washington blew, no one in Alexandria knew where the militia was, though it turned out Winder had them sitting nineteen miles from the city. There were perhaps a hundred men left in the city who could hold a musket.

With the enemy squadron in sight, the Alexandria Common Council voted unanimously Sunday morning to seek surrender terms. At 10 a.m., after the British ships sailed past the smoking ruins of Fort Washington, a small boat left Alexandria under a flag of truce, bearing the mayor and two other city delegates. Reaching the squadron, they came aboard *Seahorse* to meet with Gordon. The delegates expressed hope that Gordon would follow the example set by Ross and Cockburn in Washington by respecting private property. The captain curtly replied that he did not need prompting on how to behave.

WASHINGTON, MORNING, SUNDAY, AUGUST 28

Madison, like everyone else in the capital, did not immediately know what had happened to Fort Washington the previous night, though it had not sounded encouraging. As he awaited news Sunday morning, the president wrote to Dolley advising she not return yet to the capital after all. "You may be again compelled to retire from it, which I find would have a disagreeable effect," he wrote. Politically, it would be humiliating to flee the capital a second time. On the other hand, Madison added, "Should the ships have failed in their attack, you cannot return too soon."

Madison and Monroe inspected the city on the warm and windy

day, examining the cracked and blackened walls of the President's House. "Who would have thought that this mass so solid, so magnificent, so grand, which seemed built for generations to come, should by the hands of a few men and in the space of a few hours, be thus irreparably destroyed," wrote Margaret Bayard Smith, also surveying the scene that day. The Madisons' belongings were nothing but ashes.

The presidential party visited the Navy Yard and inspected the federal arsenal, scene of the catastrophic explosion. Most disheartening was the view from Greenleaf Point, where they could see the British ships approaching Alexandria. Fort Washington, obviously, had fallen, and word arrived that Alexandria intended to surrender. It seemed clear that the British would continue upriver to Georgetown, probably to destroy the foundry, Monroe mused.

Madison was determined that Washington and Georgetown not fall again. A fight must be put up. But the idea ran into immediate resistance around the city. "A general alarm in the city as it is expected the fleet will come up, and the sailors be let loose to plunder and destroy," Anna Thornton wrote in her diary. "The people are violently irritated at the thought of our attempting to make any more futile resistance."

Mayor John Peter of Georgetown protested the plans to "give battle again" and reported his town wanted to surrender. Near the still-smoking ruins of the Capitol, panicked citizens accosted Madison. Washington was in a deplorable state and in no condition to mount a defense, they argued.

Dr. Thornton, acting as self-appointed spokesman for the citizens, reported they would send a delegation to the British commander to capitulate. Madison and Monroe angrily forbade any such action. If any delegation moved toward the enemy, Monroe warned, it would "be repelled by the bayonet."

Talk of capitulation quieted. Inspired by the defiance, Thornton rushed home to arm himself, to the dismay of his wife. "Dr. T. came home and distressed us more than ever by taking his sword and going out to call the people and to join them," Anna Thornton wrote in her diary.

Monroe swung into action, ordering batteries thrown up along the city's Potomac shore, including one at Greenleaf Point, another at

Windmill Point south of Georgetown, and a third near the destroyed Long Bridge over the Potomac. He also ordered guns across the river on Mason's Island to be repositioned, but the colonel in charge of the battery refused, disputing Monroe's authority. Monroe told the officer to obey or else retire from the field. "The colonel preferred the latter," Monroe wrote.

Meanwhile, the District militia under General Walter Smith was arriving back in the city. They had been en route to defend Baltimore when General Stansbury learned that the British army was retreating to its ships. Reports also arrived of great alarm in Washington and Georgetown over a rumored slave insurrection. At Smith's urgent plea, Stansbury sent the District troops back to the city and continued with the Maryland troops for Baltimore.

Smith's command camped at Windmill Point, building and manning the Potomac batteries to defend the foundry upriver. Francis Scott Key, who could see the enemy ships from his home in Georgetown, joined in the preparations.

Anna Thornton, for one, was not impressed by all the talk and activity, writing in her diary, "It sounded very bold to say they would not surrender—after we were conquered and the public property lay in ruins."

Dolley Madison returned to Washington Sunday afternoon. "I cannot tell you what I felt on reentering it—such destruction—such confusion!" she later wrote her friend Mary Latrobe. "The fleet full in view and in the act of robbing Alexandria! The citizens expecting another visit . . ." She rode by carriage past the shocking sight of the President's House and continued to the nearby home of her sister, Lucy Cutts, on F Street.

Dolley had not received Madison's letter that morning advising her to stay away, and the president was pleased to find her at the Cutts home when he returned from his tour of the city. The first lady, however, was deeply despondent. "She could scarcely speak without tears," said Margaret Bayard Smith, who along with Anna Thornton paid a call on her that evening. When a few American troops marched by the house, Dolley said she "wished we had 10,000 such men . . . to sink our enemy to the bottomless pit." Monroe, who had joined them, solemnly agreed the British "were all damned rascals from highest to lowest." But Anna Thornton had little sympathy as Dolley railed against the British. "She had better attribute the loss of her palace to the right cause viz want of proper defense in time," Thornton confided to her diary.

The Cutts house had been the Madisons' home for eight years before they had moved into the President's House, and they chose the familiar setting as the new de facto executive mansion. Soldiers and citizens soon surrounded the home, while messengers darted in and out. Dragoons camped outside the house to guard the president, not so much against the British as against threats of violence from angry citizens. Madison conferred with his cabinet about whether he should issue a proclamation from Washington responding to the burning of the capital's public buildings.

That evening, back at his home, Rush wrote a memorandum urging the president to do so. It was critical that the administration shape the narrative of "an event . . . destined to be always prominent in our national history," Rush wrote. "We should be prompt to tell of the act ourselves and in our own way, without holding back as if from shame and suffering our enemies alone to embarrass it with nothing but their own malicious comments."

If issued quickly, the proclamation would reach Europe on the same ships bearing the news of Washington's fall, offering immediate reassurance that the union still held. "The very dating of it so soon again from Washington" would squelch the inevitable talk of moving the capital, Rush wrote.

To this point, Madison's wartime leadership had been largely disastrous, hemmed in by his constitutional principles against a powerful executive. Moreover, Secretary Jones observed, Madison's accommodating nature was not well suited to "the vicious nature of the times." Yet now, at the lowest point of his presidency, Madison recognized that the moment demanded a show of strength.

BRITISH LINES, SOUTHERN MARYLAND, MIDDAY, SUNDAY, AUGUST 28

The American party seeking to save Upper Marlboro hurried toward enemy lines with their captives, as the deadline for returning the prisoners to the British was fast approaching. "There was no time to spare, it being then near 12 o'clock," recalled Gustav Hay, one of the Americans. Hoping to clarify the British demands, Robert Bowie and William Lansdale rode ahead. They soon encountered the British party led by Lieutenant Evans, who told them the conditions were simple: Deliver the men, or Upper Marlboro would be "utterly destroyed."

The remainder of the American party had traveled about eight miles when they decided it was too risky to bring the deserter any closer to British lines. Holden and a second prisoner who had just confessed that he, too, was a deserter, were left at a brick house on the road, under the guard of Benjamin Oden, Jr. Continuing with the remaining prisoners, the Americans almost immediately ran headlong into the British force. Evans exploded with rage upon finding two of the British missing. "By God, gentlemen, you'll all be ruined; you are keeping them prisoners yet," Evans told the Americans.

When Hodges protested they could not give up a deserter, the threats grew more dire. "Gentlemen, do you mean to cheat us?" another British officer interjected. "If you treat us this way, we shall do as we did in Spain—put you all to death, and destroy everything."

"Where are the other two?" Evans demanded. "You wanted to sneak off with two, did you?" Terrified, Hodges and Lansdale denied it. "No we don't—they are up at that house," one of the Americans replied, pointing to the location.

Inside the house, the two deserters saw the British detachment approaching, and with Oden's assent, they took off running. Within minutes Evans reached the house and knocked Oden to the ground. When Oden denied knowing the whereabouts of the two men, Evans threatened to set the house afire. Then a woman in the house—unidentified in later court testimony—pointed in the direction the men had fled. Evans and his men chased after them. Both deserters were captured, though Holden later managed to escape.

Evans returned to the British camp at Nottingham with the rest of the prisoners. Upper Marlboro had been spared.

ALEXANDRIA, 10 A.M., MONDAY, AUGUST 29

Alexandria faced its own ultimatum. By early Monday morning, Captain Gordon's squadron, including the 38–gun *Seahorse*, the 36–gun *Euryalus*, two rocket ships, two bomb ships, and a schooner, was arrayed several hundred yards offshore from the city. Their menacing guns covered the waterfront from north to south, with enough firepower for the entire town to be "laid in ashes in a few minutes," by Mayor Charles Simms's estimation.

At 10 a.m., an officer from *Seahorse* delivered Gordon's terms of surrender: Every ship in the city would be taken by the British, as well as all the merchandise and naval supplies in the warehouses. Ships that had been sunk to avoid capture would be raised, and all merchandise taken from the city for safekeeping must be retrieved and turned over to the British. Alexandria was given one hour to reply.

When city officials pointed out that they had no way to retrieve merchandise already sent from the city, the officer waived the requirement. He also said the British sailors would take care of raising the scuttled vessels. Beyond that, there was little to discuss. The Alexandria council deliberated only a short time before agreeing. The city had been "abandoned to its fate," Mayor Simms said.

"One hardly knows which to admire most," marveled the British naval historian William James: Gordon's delay in delivering his surrender terms until the ships were set up, "or the peremptory and humiliating conditions which he did enforce." Gordon himself later told his wife he had given the city "pretty hard terms."

The news soon reached Washington, fueling outrage at "the arrogant foe," as Secretary Jones called the British. "The terms of capitulation of the town of Alexandria are so degrading and humiliating as to excite the indignation of all classes of people," he wrote Rodgers on Monday.

There was as much, if not more, indignation at Alexandria as at the British, particularly over its unseemly eagerness to surrender. Dolley Madison derided the citizens of Alexandria as "slaves" to the British and declared they "ought to have suffered their town to be burnt rather than submit to such terms," according to Anna Thornton's diary entry that Monday. "But they had no defense," Thornton added. She understood what the first lady and others forgot, or chose to ignore: Alexandria had been left defenseless by the federal government.

The Alexandria warehouses were filled with tobacco, flour, cotton, and other goods—"immense booty," Jones called it. The British had their work cut out for them, and began loading ships on the wharf at the foot of King Street.

WASHINGTON, 1 P.M., MONDAY, AUGUST 29

At the bustling American camp at Windmill Point early Monday afternoon, General Walter Smith heard a sudden commotion. Secretary of War John Armstrong had just returned to the city, and when he appeared at the camp, troops erupted in indignation. Charles Carroll of Bellevue, one of the city's most prominent citizens, made a show of refusing to shake Armstrong's proffered hand. In a loud voice, Carroll denounced the secretary. He declared that Armstrong's conduct demanded a "full investigation and explanation before he would meet him as a gentleman, or as an honorable man."

Since the day of the battle, the city had seethed with rage at Armstrong. The citizens and militia blamed Armstrong more than Madison or Winder for the disaster. "All confidence in him was gone," Monroe later told Jefferson. There were reports American soldiers had hung Armstrong in Frederick. That was untrue, but he was hung in effigy at the burned-out Capitol, with a sign reading ARMSTRONG THE TRAITOR.

One rumor held that Armstrong had been in treasonous correspondence with a British army officer at Bladensburg; another claimed he had issued orders for Captain Dyson to blow Fort Washington. The story was told that Armstrong had been unconcerned when he learned of the destruction in Washington, remarking "that the city would make as good a sheep walk as before, and was never fit for anything else."

Upon Armstrong's appearance at Windmill Point, officers laid down their swords in protest, and troops digging ditches threw down their shovels. The brigade officers unanimously agreed they would no longer serve under Armstrong, whom they blamed as "the willing cause of the destruction of the city of Washington."

Smith sent his aides, Major John Williams and Major Thomas

McKenney, to report the uprising to the president, who had left the camp a short time earlier. Catching up with Madison as he approached the Cutts house, they reported that "every officer would tear off his epaulettes" rather than have anything to do with Armstrong. But the men would cheerfully serve under any other cabinet officer, they added.

The militia's declaration amounted to mutiny, but the president was sympathetic. Madison sent the officers back to Smith with word that he would give the matter immediate consideration and that in the meantime he would ensure that Armstrong issued no orders conflicting with his own.

Early in the evening, Madison rode to Armstrong's boardinghouse on Pennsylvania Avenue. The president gingerly noted that a matter of "much delicacy" had arisen, he recalled in a memorandum a few days after the meeting. "Violent prejudices" were being directed against the administration for its failure to protect the capital, Madison noted, and "threats of personal violence had, it was said, been thrown out against us both, but more especially against him."

No officer in the city was willing to serve under him any longer, Madison told Armstrong. "Any convulsion at so critical a moment could not but have the worst consequences," the president added. He suggested Armstrong relinquish his duties related to the defense of Washington.

Armstrong haughtily replied that he had no intention to bow "to the humors of a village mob" and insisted he must be secretary of war "wholly or not at all." If the president insisted on stripping him of any authority, he would resign.

Even now, Madison preferred to preserve the façade of harmony in his cabinet. He declined the offer, telling Armstrong that a resignation might be misconstrued. Armstrong then suggested he might temporarily "retire from the scene" by visiting family in New York, an idea Madison latched on to.

But as Armstrong defended his actions, the meeting turned angrier. Madison noted that "it would not be easy to satisfy the nation that the event was without blame somewhere and I could not in candor say that all that ought to have been done had been done and in proper time." When Armstrong insisted that he had spared nothing to protect

Washington, Madison finally lost his patience. Armstrong had failed in a number of respects, the president told him. He had never appreciated the danger to the city, nor taken "a single precaution" for its safety. Moreover, Armstrong had failed to implement the preparations ordered by the president.

The icy conversation came to a close when Madison told the secretary he would have no objection if Armstrong departed in the morning. At sunrise Tuesday, Armstrong left town.

BENEDICT, MORNING, TUESDAY, AUGUST 30

The shore of the Patuxent River at Benedict was crowded with sailors heartily cheering Ross's army on their return. News of Washington's capture had arrived three days earlier in a note from Cockburn, and the sailors basked in the army's reflected glory. One by one, the regiments marched down to the beach, and the exhausted soldiers responded with their own hoarse shouts.

"Ross and Cockburn have immortalized themselves," Captain Robert Rowley, commander of the troopship *Melpomene*, wrote to a friend on Tuesday. All were stunned to hear the extent of the American incompetence. Ross reported that "three thousand men well posted would have obliged them to retreat," Rear Admiral Malcolm wrote his daughter. "The truth is they could not bring themselves to believe that with so small a force we should undertake such an enterprise."

Ross was no less shocked that he had succeeded. "It was never expected that an Army of 4,000 men could march with little or no difficulties, take and have at its mercy the capital of the United States," he wrote his sister-in-law.

Everyone took particular delight in Madison's flight; in the British telling, the president scampered off the battlefield in terror and then personally ordered the Potomac River bridge burned to protect his retreat. Madison "must be rather annoyed at finding himself obliged to fly with his whole force from the seat of government," Rear Admiral Codrington wrote his wife. Most popular of all were stories of the sumptuous meal waiting at the President's House.

It seemed as if the capture of the capital might force a quick end to the war, as Cockburn had predicted. "We are all well content with what has been done and consider that it will have the most beneficial effect," Malcolm wrote. "The inhabitants appeared to be lost in amazement that our army of 5000 men should have burned their capital. . . . [T]hey are certainly more desirous of peace. . . ."

Vice Admiral Cochrane likewise relished Madison's "humiliating" experience. Forgotten, at least publicly, was Cochrane's opposition to attacking Washington; he made no mention of it in his subsequent report to London. He sent a letter to the Duke of Gloucester, the king's nephew, boasting of the accomplishments and omitting any reference to Cockburn.

Ross had no compunctions about acknowledging Cockburn's central role when he sat down that day aboard *Tonnant* to write his official dispatch to London. "To Rear Admiral Cockburn who suggested the attack upon Washington and who accompanied the Army I confess the greatest obligation," the general wrote.

Cockburn, however, did not want to rest on his laurels. As soon as he returned to the fleet, the admiral proposed that they take advantage of American panic and immediately sail for Baltimore. There was "every reason to expect" the city could be captured without difficulty, the admiral argued at a planning conference.

But Cochrane had already decided otherwise. "Baltimore may be destroyed or laid under severe contribution, but our present force is not adequate to the attempt without incurring more risk than it would be prudent to do," he wrote to Bathurst on August 28, requesting an additional 4,000 troops. In the meantime, Cochrane informed London, he would soon sail to Rhode Island to escape the Chesapeake's feared "sickly season."

BALTIMORE, TUESDAY, AUGUST 30

As the British rested, militia flocked to Baltimore from every direction. The capture of Washington spawned a surge of fear, anger, and patriotism that swept the coast. "Every American heart is bursting with shame and indignation at the catastrophe," Private George Douglass, a Baltimore merchant who volunteered with an artillery company at

Fort McHenry, wrote Tuesday to his friend Henry Wheaton, editor of the *National Advocate* in New York.

> The people of Baltimore were at first surprised and confounded and expected at any moment to be attacked . . . but the agony is past, the panic dissipated. . . . All hearts and hands have cordially united in the common cause. Every day, almost every hour, bodies of troops are marching in to our assistance. At this moment we cannot have less than 10,000 men under arms.

Across the region, new companies of volunteers sprang up within hours of hearing the news. Travelers found the roads packed with militia heading to Baltimore. More than 3,000 men marched for Baltimore from western Maryland, and militia from Virginia and Pennsylvania had begun arriving.

All of Baltimore, it seemed, was under arms. "[I]t is a perfect military camp—no business is done," Sailing Master William Taylor, who had arrived from the Washington Navy Yard to assist in the defense of Baltimore, wrote his wife. "[E]very man is a soldier. . . . [T]hey swear to die in the trench before they will give up the city." From dawn to dusk, the hills east of the port were covered with troops training with artillery and practicing infantry skills. Tents, baggage wagons, and cannon stretched in every direction.

Those not in arms were summoned to report with wheelbarrows, pickaxes, and shovels to dig earthworks. On Sunday morning, August 28, as martial music played, the citizens brigade broke ground on Hampstead Hill, a large promontory that commanded the east side of town. The Baltimore Committee of Vigilance and Safety divided the city into four quarters, and all citizens free from militia duty were requested to report every fourth day at 6 a.m. and work until dusk. Free blacks were "most earnestly invited" to join, and owners were requested to send their slaves.

By the end of the first day, wrote Private Douglass, "at least a mile of entrenchments with suitable batteries were raised as if by magic, at which are now working all sorts of people, old and young, white and black. . . ." Each day, the works grew more elaborate, and soon included two long lines of breastworks interspersed with semicircular batteries stretching northwest from the harbor mouth to Perry Hall Road—today Bel Air Road—protecting the city from attack from the east, where the British would likely land.

More than anything, there was a determination not to repeat the mistakes that had lost the capital. Said Douglass, "The horrible mismanagement at Washington has taught us a useful lesson, and we must be worse than stupid if we do not make proper use of it."

That determination did not bode well for William Winder. The general had arrived in Baltimore at 3 a.m. on August 27, soaked by a heavy rain and irate at Major General Samuel Smith for usurping power. When Smith finally made time to see him, Winder received no satisfaction. Smith "to my astonishment still conceives himself in command and persists to exercise it," Winder complained to the War Department. Winder suggested he be promoted, thereby ending Smith's claim to higher rank. But no assistance was forthcoming from Washington; Madison thought it "advisable" that Smith stay in command, and Winder was ordered to report to the capital. Governor Winder was likewise of no help to his nephew, disingenuously disavowing any responsibility for Smith's appointment.

Just as important for Baltimore's new spirit was the remarkable trio of navy officers defending the city. Captain John Rodgers formally took command of all naval forces in Baltimore on August 28 and established a brigade with two regiments, one commanded by Captain David Porter, the other by Captain Oliver Haz-

His audacity cheered the nation, as did his terse dispatch after the battle: "We have met the enemy and they are ours."

Commodore Oliver Hazard Perry

ard Perry. It was Baltimore's good fortune that the three commodores, each waiting for new ships to be completed, happened to be available. The very presence of such illustrious officers serving under Smith's overall command lent credibility to the general's plans. "[Y]our name is worth a thousand men to us, and the animating influence of your presence a thousand more," Captain Robert T. Spence, chief of the Baltimore naval station, told Rodgers.

The twenty-eight-year-old Perry, from a distinguished family of Rhode Island mariners, had been catapulted to fame by his signal victory a year earlier at Lake Erie, fighting under a battle flag bearing the words DON'T GIVE UP THE SHIP. His audacity cheered the nation, as did his terse dispatch after the battle: "We have met the enemy and they are ours." Perry was a natural leader long on pluck and courage, though his streaks of petulance sometimes marred his performance as an officer. Perry's performance at Lake Erie had earned him command of the new 44-gun *Java*, a beautiful frigate of hand-hewn timber built at Fells Point and nearly ready to sail, but bottled up in Baltimore by the British threat. The men who had followed Perry to Baltimore to serve aboard *Java* would instead defend the city. The handsome and vigorous Perry appeared "tranquil as an unruffled lake" at the change in plans, a witness recalled.

Porter, a Bostonian who had grown up in Baltimore, was likewise a celebrated figure, having just returned from one of the most daring cruises in the history of the U.S. Navy. On his own initiative, Porter in February 1813 sailed the

The thirty-four-year-old Porter, a Bostonian who had grown up in Baltimore, was likewise a celebrated figure, having just returned from one of the most daring cruises in the history of the U.S. Navy.

Captain David Porter

frigate *Essex* around the treacherous Cape Horn and into the Pacific Ocean, where he harassed British whalers around the Galapagos, nearly shutting down the industry single-handedly. The British finally destroyed *Essex* off Valparaiso, Chile, in March 1814. Released with his men on a prisoner exchange, Porter returned as a hero to the United States in July after a year-and-a-half absence. After traveling to the capital and meeting the president, the thirty-four-year-old Porter had been given command of a new 44–gun frigate *Essex* under construction at the Washington Navy Yard. Porter had been in New York when Jones called him and his crew to the capital, but he had arrived too late to save his new ship, destroyed in the Navy Yard fire.

Despite the fame of Perry and Porter, it was Rodgers, the senior naval officer in the war, who was the most powerful and influential. The veteran Rodgers had fought the French in the Caribbean in 1799 during the Quasi-War and the Barbary pirates off Tripoli. An hour after learning that war had been declared with Britain in 1812, he took to sea from New York in the frigate *President* and was credited with firing the first shot of the war. The war had become personal for Rodgers, the son of a tavern keeper from near Havre de Grace. He was at sea when Cockburn struck the town in May 1813, and his wife, sons, and sisters had been forced to flee to safety. The Rodgers family home, Sion Hill, was among those looted and damaged.

Rodgers had been awaiting the completion of his new frigate, *Guerriere*, in Philadelphia when he, too, was summoned south. Though he had no experience commanding land forces, Rodgers gamely oversaw the preparations of fortifications and the training of his sailors for ground combat. "If you were to see what a figure I cut with spurs on, accompanied by my aides and gig-men on horseback, you'd split your sides a laughing," he confessed to his wife, Minerva.

The sea-loving sailors were instructed on the fine points of ground combat. "To charge" meant the same as "to board," an officer explained. "Here they were at home," a witness reported. "Their eyes glistened."

The key redoubt in the center of the line on Hampstead Hill was soon known as Rodgers Bastion, and it was a formidable position, fortified with 16 guns, including twelve-pounders from the sloop-of-war *Erie*. The 450 sailors in Baltimore were reinforced by 220 marines and some 500 flotillamen, spoiling for another fight with the British even without Barney at their side. The addition of these battle-hardened men to the city's defenses was electric, giving courage and confidence to the raw militiamen, as Rodgers proudly noted in a letter to Minerva on August 29: "I have the satisfaction to tell you that our little band of seamen coming here at the moment they did has changed the complexion of things very much."

EASTERN SHORE OF MARYLAND, 11 P.M., TUESDAY, AUGUST 30

Across the Chesapeake Bay from Baltimore, on Maryland's Eastern Shore, Sir Peter Parker was eager for "one more frolic with the Yankees." Boats carrying Royal Marines and sailors left HMS *Menelaus* at 9 p.m., the men rowing in silence with muffled oars until the keels grated on the sandy shore.

Dashing and reckless, Captain Parker was descended from three generations of British admirals. With his bouffant hair, winning smile, and aristocratic bearing, Parker was "the handsomest man in the navy," by one estimate. He had inherited his good looks from his mother, the celebrated beauty Augusta Byron, aunt to the poet Lord Byron. Parker had gone to sea with the Royal Navy at the age of thirteen, and propelled by family connections and his own affinity to command, made captain at age twenty, and now, at age twenty-eight, had fifteen years of service through two wars with France. Inspired by Cockburn's exploits, Parker was eager to lay claim to his own glory in the Chesapeake.

Parker had done well with his assignment to create a diversion in the upper Chesapeake while the rest of the force attacked up the Patuxent and Potomac. With only a frigate and two schooners, Parker kept the Americans off balance with a foray up the bay that stoked fears of a British strike on Annapolis or Baltimore. After probing Baltimore Harbor on August 27, Parker crossed the bay to the Eastern Shore, where he learned that a large body of militia was camped in the woods near Fairlee Creek. Parker decided to seize the opportunity for a surprise attack.

Yet the captain was melancholic in the hours before the landing. When his gold-lace cocked hat fell overboard, Midshipman Frederick

Chamier heard him mutter, "My head will follow this evening." Just before departing the ship, Parker dashed off a note to his wife, Marianne. "If any thing befalls me, I have made a sort of will," he wrote. "My country will be good to you and our adored children."

Parker recovered his customary vim when the barges landed around 11 p.m. with a force of 260 sailors and marines. The British had been told the Americans were camped only a half mile from the beach, but after landing they learned from a slave that the militia had moved another mile inland. One mile turned into two, but at Parker's insistence they kept marching. Soon they had moved four or five miles from the boats. "It was the height of madness to advance into the interior of a country we knew nothing about," Chamier later said.

The British believed their landing had gone undetected, but the Americans had spotted their barges even before they reached shore. At 11:30 p.m., Lieutenant Colonel Philip Reed, commander of the 21st Maryland Regiment, received a report that the British were landing and immediately ordered his 200 militiamen to break camp. The fifty-four-year-old Reed, an Eastern Shore native, was a tough, battle-tested Revolutionary War veteran and former U.S. senator. Once he learned the British were marching in his direction, Reed set up at the nearby Caulk farm, placing his men and five artillery pieces in a field in front of a line of woods.

A moon shone brilliantly on the rising ground occupied by the Americans. In the early morning hours of Wednesday, the British marched through a narrow path leading to the field. As they reached the clearing, the militia guns opened up with devastating fire. Parker led the Royal Marines in a charge. "[H]is Turkish sabre sparkled in the moonlight as he waved it over his head, and his continual cry of 'Forward! Forward!' resounded amidst the firing," Chamier recalled. But then Parker's voice failed, and he fell. Buckshot had cut his femoral artery, and he was bleeding profusely. "I fear they have done for me," he gasped to his men before passing out. "[Y]ou had better retreat, for the boats are a long way off."

Parker bled to death as his men carried him back. The Maryland militia, meanwhile, had run out of ammunition and was likewise retreating. But while American casualties were light, the British had lost

14 dead and 27 wounded. The Battle of Caulk's Field had proven costly and foolhardy for the British.

The next morning, during a truce, the Americans brought the British a fine leather shoe, marked with Parker's name, that had been found on the battlefield. "We guess that your captain was not a man to run away without his shoes," a militiaman remarked. The loss of Parker, beloved by his crew and the English public alike, was anguishing for the British. Byron would write a poem saluting the valor of the "gallant Parker."

The reaction was much different among the Americans. "Huzza for the militia!" declared a Washington newspaper. Following the humiliation of Bladensburg, it was an impressive performance by the Maryland militia. And it was the first sign that British fortunes in the Chesapeake were changing.

"I have to make a journey to the fleet to try to
get Dr. Beanes released from the enemy—
I hope I may succeed but I think it
very doubtful."

Francis Scott Key

CHAPTER 12

The Mission of Francis Scott Key

THE BRITISH FLEET slowly sailed out from the Patuxent River, the men savoring the triumph of Washington. Officers planned dinner parties and balls aboard the ships. Landing parties held picnics on the shores, serenaded by band music, while sailors and soldiers happily foraged for pigs and chickens.

But aboard *Tonnant*, the man who conquered Washington was not celebrating. Instead, General Robert Ross sat at a table and composed a painful letter to his wife. "It is my best loved Ly with feelings of the most acute misery that I take my pen to write to you," Ross began. Two letters from Elizabeth Ross had arrived while he was gone. Written from Bordeaux, they made clear that his wife was deeply depressed at his absence and perhaps on the verge of a breakdown.

Reading the letters "has completely overwhelmed me," Ross told his wife. "I declare to you that were it in my power to leave the Army I would without hesitation fly to you," he wrote. "This war cannot last long, we then meet my Ly *never* again to separate."

Almost as an aside, Ross mentioned that he had captured the capital of the United States. The news offered hope that he would soon return, he told her. "I trust all our differences with the Yankees will be shortly settled," Ross wrote. "That wish is, I believe, very prevalent with them."

That wish was doubtless on Ross's mind when he met with Vice

Admiral Cochrane that same day and urged him to attack Baltimore "without delay." Echoing Cockburn's sentiments, the general argued that "the paramount consideration" was to strike before the Americans could fortify the town. Cockburn, too, continued to press for an attack, believing it could be a decisive stroke, possibly ending the war.

Cochrane conceded an attack on Baltimore would doubtless succeed, but he still refused to give his assent, insisting that it was imperative to sail for Rhode Island to escape the "fatal" Chesapeake weather.

After some "ineffectual solicitations" by the general failed to sway Cochrane, according to Evans, Ross decided it advisable to bow to the vice admiral's plans. But other officers saw that Ross was miserable.

Ross attended to other business as well. On Wednesday, before the fleet departed Benedict, an American emissary, Richard West, arrived to plead for the release of Dr. Beanes and the other two American prisoners. West, a close friend of Beanes, lived near Upper Marlboro at the Woodyard plantation with his wife, an older sister of Francis Scott Key's wife. West carried "necessaries" for the three prisoners and a letter from Governor Winder complaining of the "great rudeness and indignity" by which Beanes had been carried off from his home, and requesting he be freed.

Ross not only refused, he declined to let West even see the doctor. But he sent for Dr. William Hill and young Philip Weems, the other two Americans. Hill used his audience with the general to make the case that he, unlike Beanes, had not surrendered to Ross upon his entry to town. After hearing Hill out, Ross concluded that his imprisonment was "an injustice" and ordered him freed.

"I thought you and Doctor Beanes were alike in trouble, nor was I undeceived until a few minutes ago," Ross told Hill. "It is my wish to alleviate as much as possible the horrors of war, therefore I shall let you return to your friends and family. . . ." Pointing to Weems, Ross said he "could return with me, as he was under age and not found in arms," Hill recalled. Ross invited Hill into the cabin for some refreshments before he and Weems were put ashore at Benedict.

Beanes was another matter altogether. As the fleet moved down the Chesapeake, the doctor languished in harsh conditions aboard *Tonnant*.

ALEXANDRIA, THURSDAY MORNING, SEPTEMBER I

After four days of methodically stripping Alexandria of its merchandise, Captain Gordon's Potomac squadron was almost done. Nearly 16,000 barrels of flour, 1,000 hogsheads of tobacco, and 150 bales of cotton, as well as quite a bit of wine and sugar, had been loaded from warehouses along the river. Plenty more remained, but there was no more room on the twenty-one prize vessels they had captured, even including the sunken ships that had been raised, caulked, and rigged by the sailors.

Through it all, the British had been terribly polite. After emptying one merchant's cellar, they invited the man on board for some wine. "They dismissed him with many smooth words and good-natured recommendations to think no more about the flour," a witness recalled. Alexandria Mayor Charles Simms was delighted at the good manners. "It is impossible that men could behave better than the British," Simms wrote approvingly to his wife.

U.S. Navy Captain David Porter watched the proceedings with disgust. With Baltimore safe for the moment, Navy Secretary Jones had summoned the three commodores—Rodgers, Perry, and Porter—to defend Washington from a second attack and to lay a trap for the British along the Potomac when they left Alexandria. Porter had arrived in Washington with sailors and marines on the evening of August 30, and was ordered to set up a battery on the Virginia shore of the Potomac above Mount Vernon to batter the British.

Reaching Alexandria on his way south, Porter rode into town on the hot and calm Thursday morning to get a firsthand look at the strength of the British force. He was accompanied by Captain John Creighton. Both officers had a score to settle with the British; *Argus*, the sloop-of-war Creighton was supposed to command, had been destroyed in the Washington Navy Yard fire, as had Porter's new frigate, *Essex*.

Near the river, they watched sailors rolling barrels of flour from a warehouse. The city had proven so cooperative that the British walked around without any precautions. A young British officer, Midshipman John Went Fraser of *Euryalus*, had wandered off from the rest of his party. On impulse, Porter and Creighton made a dash for him, likely looking for a prisoner they could interrogate.

The powerful Creighton grabbed Fraser by his cravat and tried to throw him onto his horse. "The youngster, quite astonished, kicked and squalled most lustily," recalled Captain Napier, the British second in command. Creighton dragged the bawling midshipman a hundred yards until the kerchief tore. Free from Creighton's grasp, Fraser ran to the wharf, where the alarmed British landing parties retreated to their boats and prepared the carronades, expecting a cavalry attack. *Seahorse*, anchored in the Potomac, hoisted its battle signal, and all the warships prepared for action, ready to "put the town in a blaze," Napier said. Women and children ran screaming through the streets, seeking shelter.

A distressed Mayor Simms hastily sent an apologetic delegation to Captain Gordon disavowing any responsibility for the action. Gordon seemed more amused than angry. He called off the attack but warned that a repetition "might lead to the destruction of the town." Gordon remained wary, having heard rumors that the Americans were setting up a trap downriver.

Thursday evening, the 18–gun British brig *Fairy* arrived in Alexandria bearing a dispatch from Admiral Cochrane ordering Gordon's immediate return to the bay. Moreover, the *Fairy* commander reported coming under heavy American fire that afternoon below Mount Vernon. Gordon and his Potomac squadron would have to fight their way out.

WASHINGTON, THURSDAY, SEPTEMBER 1

Even while seething at the enemy's "cupidity," Navy Secretary Jones had not been blind to the opportunity presented while the British loaded their ships with loot in Alexandria. The three commodores had responded quickly to his plan "to annoy or destroy the enemy on his return down the river."

Jones believed it critical that the government take the offensive in the wake of the humiliation of Washington and the capitulation of Alexandria. Around the country, there were calls for Madison to be impeached and his cabinet to resign. "Poor, contemptible pitiful, dastardly wretches!" declared the Virginia *Gazette*. "Their heads would be but a poor price for the degradation into which they have plunged our bleeding country."

"Is it possible that after being two years at war, our capital, the seat of our general government, should have been left so defenseless? . . . Can men who manage in this way be fit to govern a great and free people?" asked the New York *Evening Post*.

"The President and the whole administration are damned men in Baltimore—neither of them I believe could get one vote in the city," Sailing Master William Taylor wrote his wife.

Upon hearing of Alexandria's capitulation, half the residents of Salem, Massachusetts, removed their furniture and belongings from town, fearing the British would sail north. "How much has Mr. Madison to answer for!" Salem resident Leverett Saltonstall wrote to his father. "All these evils are occasioned by his rushing into war unjustly, to assist Bonaparte in his nefarious project of conquering the world. No wonder the British are irritated and impelled to carry on war harshly against us."

Newspapers were filled with doggerel such as these lines published in New York:

> *Fly, Monroe, fly! Run, Armstrong, run!*
> *Were the last words of Madison*

To Jones, a show of defiance would be the best way to stop the mockery and rally the war effort. Echoing advice from Rush, Jones presented Madison with a memo on September 1 urging the president to immediately issue a proclamation from Washington responding to the burning of the capital.

"The effect will not be confined to this nation, but will be felt with surprise and admiration in Europe, where the conquest of the capital is generally equivalent to the subjugation of the nation," Jones told Madison. "The enemy, moreover, will be thus robbed of the fruit, of his enterprise, and will have acquired nothing, but the shame of his vandalism."

The previous day, Monroe had received a letter from Cochrane publicly revealing his orders in July to "destroy and lay waste" towns along the coast in retaliation for American actions in Canada. At the risk of furthering panic, Madison and his cabinet decided to make Cochrane's threat public, hoping to continue rallying public support by painting the British as vandals.

On September 1, Madison issued a presidential proclamation. In forceful, contemptuous language, drafted by Rush but altered by the president, Madison condemned the British for "wantonly" destroying public buildings and archives that had no military value but were "precious to the nation as the memorials of its origins." He accused the British of "a deliberate disregard of the principles of humanity and the rules of civilized warfare."

Madison dismissed Cochrane's claim that the British actions were in retaliation for Canada, as an "insulting pretext," given the "multiplied outrages" already committed by Admiral Cockburn.

Madison concluded with an appeal to the American people to "unite their hearts and hands" to expel the invaders, harkening to the spirit of an earlier generation: "On an occasion which appeals so forcibly to the proud feelings and patriotic devotion of the American people none will forget what they owe to themselves, what they owe to their country and the high destinies which await it, what to the glory acquired by their fathers in establishing the independence which is now to be maintained by their sons."

Georgetown, evening, Thursday, September 1

Roger Brooke Taney, Francis Scott Key's brother-in-law, was making no progress in persuading Polly Key to leave Georgetown. Taney had traveled from Frederick to the Key home on Bridge Street, hoping to bring Key's wife back to the safety of Maryland, but she had refused.

For several days, Frank Key had been assisting with the defenses to protect Georgetown against the British squadron, still within sight at Alexandria. "He would not, and indeed could not, with honor, leave the place while it was threatened by the enemy," Taney later wrote. For her part, Polly Key would not leave if her husband stayed.

Though the six Key children had been sent to their grandparents' home at Terra Rubra, the family was worried that Polly remained in harm's way. "Believing, as we did, that an attack would probably be made on Georgetown, we became very anxious about the situation of his family," Taney recalled.

But the talk of Polly's departure was put on hold on Thursday evening, when another family member showed up at Key's home: Polly's brother-in-law, Richard West. Key and West, each married to Lloyd sisters, had grown close over the years, and West had participated in many of the salon debates at the Georgetown home with John Randolph and other members of Key's circle.

West shared the latest alarming news about their mutual friend, Dr. Beanes, whom Key knew primarily through West. Reports of Beanes's seizure had already reached Georgetown, and West described the disheartening British response to his attempt the previous day to free the doctor. Given Beanes's advanced age and frail condition, and the depth of the British rancor toward the doctor, friends were deeply worried. Unless Beanes was released before the enemy ships departed the Chesapeake, the doctor would be taken to the British prison in Halifax, likely never to return to Maryland.

Beanes's friends wanted Key to put together a mission sanctioned by the Madison administration seeking the doctor's release. Key's connections with the government, his tact, and his ability as an attorney made him a natural choice. Key immediately agreed to help.

That evening, Key called on President Madison, who promptly approved the mission. The president consulted with General John Mason, the commissary general of prisoners, and they agreed that Key should be accompanied by the American prisoner of war agent, a veteran of many dealings with the British: John S. Skinner.

ALEXANDRIA, 5 A.M., FRIDAY, SEPTEMBER 2

It was still dark when *Seahorse* left her moorings and the British began departing Alexandria. The Potomac squadron was considerably more weighed down than on its way upriver, the eight warships and twenty-one prize vessels loaded to the brim with loot.

The visit to Alexandria had been quite profitable for the British and humiliating for the Americans, but now the tables might be turned.

Gordon had been entrusted with three of Admiral Cochrane's five vital bomb ships. Losing the squadron would be a devastating blow to British plans along the east coast and Gulf of Mexico.

Once again, the weather conspired against Gordon. Contrary winds forced the squadron to laboriously warp down the channel, dashing hopes for a quick escape. With reports that the Americans were constructing a battery just downriver, Gordon sent ahead some lighter vessels, including the bomb ship *Meteor* and several barges, with orders to attack the battery and prevent its further fortification.

The American battery, on the Belvoir Neck below Mount Vernon, commanded the Potomac channel from atop a hundred-foot-high bluff at White House Landing. Porter and his crew from the *Essex,* along with a contingent of marines, had reached the location Thursday, joining Virginia militia who had been clearing the site for cannon. By Friday morning, two eighteen-pounders and smaller pieces were in place, making a formidable obstacle. A large flag carrying the slogan FREE TRADE AND SAILORS RIGHTS—which Porter had flown from *Essex* on her Pacific cruise—was planted defiantly atop the bluff.

Porter's fellow commodores, Oliver Perry and John Rodgers, remained at the smoldering Washington Navy Yard, hurrying preparations to join the attack. At the urging of James Monroe, Perry would bring artillery and men to a point on Maryland's Potomac shore downriver from Porter's position. With the naval heroes manning batteries on both sides of the river, Monroe told Rodgers, "I think we might demolish them." Rodgers, for his part, was forming a squadron of three "fire vessels" loaded with incendiary materials. These would be set ablaze and directed at the British ships as they tried to escape.

At daylight Friday, Porter saw the lead enemy ships approach the American battery and anchor out of range of the American guns. *Meteor* opened fire at 9 a.m., dropping shells around the battery, and a British barge moved close to rake the shore with grape and canister. Porter moved an eighteen-pounder up the shore to fire back. To the navy captain's pleasant surprise the Virginia militiamen protecting the battery proved unflinchingly brave through the fire.

Heavy fire rumbled back and forth all day Friday and well into the night. It was obvious to Gordon that without a fair wind, it would be suicidal to push past the strongpoint. The battle on the Potomac was just beginning.

WASHINGTON, FRIDAY, SEPTEMBER 2

For the Madison administration, Key's mission had implications well beyond the fate of Dr. Beanes, prominent though he was. Conferring with Key, General John Mason told the attorney that allowing the British to claim the noncombatant Beanes as a prisoner of war would establish a dangerous precedent. "[I]t is impossible that the government can yield a point of so much national importance involved in this case, as to admit that he is an exchangeable prisoner of war, since it would at once induce the enemy to seize and carry off every unarmed citizen of whatever age they may have in their power," Mason said.

The forty-eight-year-old Mason, who had accompanied Madison on much of his sojourn after the capture of Washington, was a close confidant of the president. Madison had been a friend of his father, the great Virginia patriot George Mason, a prime force in the creation of the Bill of Rights. John Mason was a prominent merchant, banker, and landholder in Washington—he owned Mason's Island along the Virginia shore of the Potomac, where he and Madison stopped briefly during the flight from Washington. Mason had proven effective as commissary general of prisoners, navigating intricate rules governing the exchange of prisoners with the British.

Mason wrote a letter Friday formally authorizing Key and Skinner to launch the mission and instructing them on the negotiations. He was brief, telling Key that Skinner was already "well possessed of all the general arguments on our side."

The Americans, Mason instructed, would argue that Beanes "was absolved" from any truce agreement he made with the British because when the doctor captured the stragglers, the British had already withdrawn from Upper Marlboro. Should the British still refuse to release Beanes as a noncombatant, Mason authorized Key and Skinner to issue as a "last resort" a receipt that the British could use in a future prisoner exchange, but to be accompanied by a statement of the American position.

Mason also wrote letters for the Americans to deliver to Cochrane and Ross describing Key as "a citizen of the highest respectability" who had been authorized along with Skinner to seek Beanes's release. "I confidently trust, sir, that when you shall have been made acquainted with the facts in the case, you will order the immediate release and restoration to his family of that gentleman," Mason wrote Ross. "[H]e is far advanced in life, infirmed; and unaccustomed to privations by which he must now suffer severely."

Mason took time to scribble one more note, the most important he would write. It was addressed to Colonel William Thornton, the British officer who had led the charge across the bridge at Bladensburg, and who was now the senior officer among the wounded left behind. In the week since the battle, the British wounded had been treated quite humanely by the Americans, in keeping with instructions from Mason.

In his note, Mason told Colonel Thornton that a truce party would leave shortly and would take any open letters the wounded men wished to send back to the fleet. Several prisoners, among them Sergeant Hutchinson of the Royal Sappers and Miners and Alexander Gunn of the 21st Fusiliers, wrote letters to Ross expressing gratitude for the humane American treatment. Thornton, who had received what he considered "the most marked kindness," also picked up pen and paper.

At his home on Bridge Street, Key on Friday made final preparations for his mission. With Georgetown now safe, Polly would travel with Taney to join the family in Maryland. Key wrote notes for her to carry to his parents. They show Key to be deeply pessimistic as he undertook his mission, not only about winning Beanes's freedom, but also the prospects for peace, and his own personal finances. While relieved that Georgetown was spared, Key could not shake his belief that the British assault in the Chesapeake represented divine retribution for an unjust American war.

"Polly goes up in the morning with Mr. Taney," he wrote his father. "I cannot go yet, as I have to make a journey to the fleet to try to get Dr. Beanes released from the enemy—I hope I may succeed but I think it very doubtful."

To his mother, he apologized for his silence since the battle. "You have made allowances, I hope for our confusion & anxiety here, & have therefore excused my not writing sooner," he wrote. "Indeed for two or three days after our disgrace I had neither time or mind to do anything. And since then I have been much engaged." The British, he reported, "have today left Alexandria, & I trust we shall see no more of them. I hope we shall be grateful to God for this deliverance, & remember how much more light our chastisement has been that we expected or deserved."

In the morning, he would depart for Baltimore to try to help "Old Dr. Beanes," he told her. "I hope to return in about 8 or 10 days, though [it] is uncertain, as I do not know where to find the fleet," he wrote. Upon his return, Key promised, he would join the family. "The children will be delighted to see their mother.—Give my love to them & to Papa."

Early the next morning, after parting with Polly and Taney, Key stopped at Mason's office to pick up papers for the mission. He traveled past the smoldering Capitol to pick up letters written by the British prisoners recuperating at Dr. Ewell's makeshift hospital. Then he continued to Bladensburg, which remained a grim landscape more than a week after the battle, with bodies found daily under bushes and in gullies. Key picked up more letters from prisoners recuperating in the village, including one addressed to Ross from Colonel Thornton. From Bladensburg, likely traveling by stagecoach, Key continued up the turnpike to Baltimore.

His mind was heavy with worry. "In these distressing times I really know not what I shall do to provide for the necessities of my family," he had told his father "There is no hope of peace."

POTOMAC RIVER, MORNING, SATURDAY, SEPTEMBER 3

By Saturday morning Captain John Rodgers was set to attack the departing British squadron. The three fire vessels, ready to burn, launched from the Washington Navy Yard, accompanied by sixty seamen armed with muskets in four small cutters and a boat.

Moving down the Potomac ahead of the rest of the vessels, Rodgers sailed his gig by the Alexandria waterfront and was shocked to see that the city was still not flying the American flag, twenty-four hours after the British departed. Alexandria's Mayor Simms, worried that the British would return upon finding the river blocked, did not consider the town safe yet. The outraged navy commander maneuvered near the city wharf. "I hailed and ordered the American flag to be hoisted," he reported to Jones, "otherwise, that I would set fire to the town." Rodgers crossed out the last words before sending his report, but he made the threat, and meant it. The Alexandrians feared Rodgers more than the British; an American flag was hastily raised, and the captain continued downriver.

Below Alexandria, a perfect target awaited Rodgers. The bomb ship *Devastation* had grounded two miles south of the city. Rodgers and his men bore down on the stranded ship, and reaching musket range, the captain ordered his lead fire vessel set ablaze. But the British responded quickly, putting their own boats into the water. The blazing vessel was nearly upon *Devastation*, but the wind died. A midshipman in one of the British barges coolly caught the burning boat with a grappling hook and towed it harmlessly to shore. British crews similarly warded off the two other fire vessels. By now the British had twenty barges in the water, firing guns and chasing the Americans. Rodgers and his outnumbered men retreated to Alexandria, with the enemy on their tail the whole way. The British fired a few parting shots into the city and returned to their ships.

Rodgers found Alexandria still in a state of capitulation, with 1,500 pounds of fresh beef on the wharves ready to be delivered to the enemy. "I mention this to show the state, that place was in at the time," a disgusted Rodgers reported to Jones. With Rodgers in town, there would be no meat delivery to the British. Instead, the captain mounted two twelve-pound carronades on the wharves and placed his sailors along the shore, reinforced by 200 Virginia militia. Alexandria was finally ready to mount a defense.

CHESAPEAKE BAY, SATURDAY, SEPTEMBER 3

Iphigenia, one of the fastest frigates in the British Chesapeake fleet, had been selected to speedily carry the news of Washington's capture to London. As the ship prepared for its voyage, Vice Admiral Alexander Cochrane put the finishing touches on a letter to the Admiralty reiterating his refusal to attack Baltimore—just yet, anyway—and instead attack Rhode Island. Cochrane intended to return to the Chesapeake by early November, after the weather cooled, and with the hope that more troops would have been sent from Europe. "[I]f the reinforcements arrive I propose an attack upon Baltimore the most democratic town & I believe the richest in the country," Cochrane wrote.

After torching Baltimore, Cochrane planned to continue south on a path of destruction, along the Carolinas and Georgia, and ending at New Orleans. His main worry was that the peace negotiations in Ghent might bear fruit before he had a chance to completely crush the Americans. "[I]f peace makers will only stay their proceedings until Jonathan is brought to the feet of G. Britain further wars will be prevented," he wrote.

Cochrane had a second concern. He believed General Ross had been far too easy on Washington, and should be told not to show any such mercy to Baltimore. "As this town ought to be laid in ashes, . . . some hints ought to be given to Genl. Ross as he does not seem inclined to visit the sins committed upon H. Maj's Canadian subjects upon inhabitants of this state," Cochrane wrote.

This he blamed on a certain naïveté on the part of Ross. "When he is better acquainted with the American character he will possibly see as I do that like spaniels they must be treated with great severity before you make them tractable," Cochrane wrote.

Ross, for his part, appeared to have accepted Cochrane's decision to delay the attack on Baltimore, to the relief of his aide, Captain Harry Smith, who argued that it would be too risky. Ross had chosen Smith to carry the army's dispatches back to Lord Bathurst, the war secretary. Apart from the honor, the selection afforded the young officer a chance to visit his Spanish bride, Juana, whom he had been forced to leave behind when he joined the expedition to America.

Iphigenia's departure Saturday from the mouth of Patuxent was delayed a few minutes when a dispatch boat arrived from the Eastern Shore with the shocking news of Sir Peter Parker's death. Cochrane hastily added a dispatch to London reporting that the headstrong Parker had apparently been "drawn into an attack upon a force which proved to be greatly his superior." The news seemed to underscore the need for caution before taking on Baltimore.

Ross accompanied Smith to the gangway of *Iphigenia*, giving him a bundle of letters to carry to England, including one for his wife. Ross asked Smith to personally deliver that letter to her at the home of the general's brother, where it had been arranged for Elizabeth to stay after she left Bordeaux.

"A pleasant voyage, dear Smith . . . I can ill spare you," Ross told the young officer. Smith seized the moment to get one last promise from the general.

"May I assure Lord Bathurst you will not attempt Baltimore?" Smith asked.

"You may," said Ross.

BALTIMORE, MORNING, SUNDAY, SEPTEMBER 4

Francis Scott Key arrived in Baltimore Sunday morning, locating Skinner and sharing with him the instructions and dispatches from Mason. Skinner could not have been particularly happy to learn Key was to accompany him, having just written a letter to Secretary of State Monroe suggesting that only the authorized government agent—and no amateur diplomats—go on such missions.

"Under existing circumstances when our city is threatened by a powerful force it seems highly impolitic, in my humble judgment, to suffer any intercourse with the enemy except through the most trustworthy agents," Skinner wrote. The request was in reference to "several French gentlemen" who wanted to go on the next truce mission, but Skinner suggested Monroe issue general instructions that "no person will be allowed . . . with me on board."

Nonetheless, the government clearly wanted Key to accompany him, and Skinner dutifully made final preparations for the mission. Skinner leased a sloop-rigged packet ship belonging to John and Benjamin Ferguson, brothers who had operated a cargo and passenger service between Baltimore and Norfolk until forced to cease by the British blockade. The Fergusons owned about a dozen packets, and which one Skinner leased is uncertain, but it may have been *President,* a sixty-foot sloop that Skinner had used on other missions. Departure was set for Monday morning.

Key found Baltimore more of a garrison than a city, filled with troops, cavalry, work details, artillery trains, and supply wagons. Women rolled bandages in makeshift hospitals. Gangs of boys and old men built barracks for the troops, while carpenters hammered together gun platforms.

Yet Samuel Smith was ever more nervous. Despite the strong defenses on Hampstead Hill protecting the city's eastern flank, Baltimore remained exposed in other directions, and an attack on an undefended flank would be disastrous. Troops were pouring into the city, but many were arriving without weapons, ammunition, food, or blankets. Moreover, to Smith's great irritation, most of Rodgers's naval brigade was still fighting along the Potomac.

Smith also had to fight the War Department to keep five of the big eighteen-pounder cannons defending Baltimore. The guns belonged to the War Department, which wanted to use them along the Potomac. But Smith cleverly noted that the carriages needed to move the heavy guns belonged to Baltimore. These the city refused to give to the federal government. The guns stayed.

The War Department did offer Smith assistance he would have preferred to do without. Monroe had sent General Winder back to Baltimore, not wanting him to interfere with military command in Washington. Smith was supposed to assign him duties but had thus far simply ignored him. "I have no order and consequently have no command," Winder complained to Monroe on Sunday.

John Armstrong was also in Baltimore, as delusional as Winder about reassuming command. Rather than travel to New York as expected after leaving Washington, Armstrong lingered in Baltimore, expecting to be recalled to the capital at any moment. Gradually, it dawned on him that the president intended to keep Monroe in charge, and on September 3, Armstrong announced his resignation in an angry letter to the *Baltimore Patriot* exonerating himself and blaming the militia for the capture of Washington. "[I]f all the troops assembled at Bladensburg had been faithful to themselves and to their country, the enemy would have been beaten and the capital saved," Armstrong wrote.

His departure was a relief to the rest of the cabinet. "He is gone and has told his story, which is as destitute of candor as of truth," Jones wrote.

★

Monroe was now serving in two cabinet positions, in addition to his military command overseeing Washington's defense. In the storm of criticism of Armstrong, Winder, and Madison, Monroe's role in the disastrous repositioning of troops at Bladensburg had been largely overlooked, to his relief. "I wish nothing to be said about me in the affair," Monroe wrote his son-in-law George Hay.

At the moment, most were glad to have Monroe fill the power vacuum. He was a constant, reassuring presence in and around Washington. Monroe visited Porter's battery on Belvoir Neck to watch the ongoing battle on the Potomac. He slept on a camp bed in his office so he could receive reports arriving at all hours. Monroe called out more militia, assembled supplies, and tried to get better intelligence on British intentions.

Baltimore was only one of his concerns. The British had assembled a large army in Canada, ready to invade New York State. Monroe was also worried about the threat to the Mississippi and sent a letter to General Andrew Jackson, the commander of American forces in the Southeast, urging him to leave Mobile, Alabama, for New Orleans. As for the British fleet hovering at the mouth of the Patuxent, Monroe believed Philadelphia, Norfolk, and Richmond, as well as Baltimore, were likely targets. "[T]hat it will soon move against some one of those places, cannot well be doubted," he wrote Sunday. "Desolation is its object. . . ."

Yet Monroe, perhaps wary after his tactical disaster at Bladensburg, left command in Baltimore to Smith, who in any event was paying little attention to Washington.

CHESAPEAKE BAY, SUNDAY, SEPTEMBER 4

Aboard *Tonnant*, Ross and Cochrane set sail Sunday evening with most of the fleet from the mouth of the Patuxent, preparing to depart the Chesapeake. They would stop first at Tangier to shuffle troops and supplies for the sail north.

Cochrane had distributed a dispatch to be read Sunday aboard all the ships. "The commander in chief cannot permit the fleet to separate without congratulating the flag officers, captains, commanders, officers, seamen and marines upon the brilliant success which has attended the combined exertions of the Army and Navy employed within the Chesapeake," Cochrane declared. The Capitol, the "Palace of the President," and other public buildings "have all been either destroyed or rendered useless," he added.

But the days of glory in the bay were passing, it seemed. Cockburn was ordered to sail *Albion*, filled with prize tobacco, to Bermuda, and then rendezvous with Cochrane off Rhode Island. "Further operations in this quarter appeared to be abandoned," wrote Lieutenant Scott. Rear Admiral Malcolm would sail separately with the army aboard the troop transports.

A smaller force of thirteen ships would stay in the Chesapeake. Those staying behind could not help but feel disappointed. "We shall feel the dull monotony of a tedious winter in the Chesapeake," wrote Captain Robert Rowley. "The Army gone, God knows where."

PATAPSCO RIVER, MONDAY, SEPTEMBER 5

If Francis Scott Key was pessimistic about the prospects of the mission to rescue Dr. Beanes, John Skinner was downright dubious. At least they would be done with it quickly. Skinner dashed off a letter to General Mason as he and Key sailed Monday morning from Baltimore down the Patapsco River in search of the British. "We are now on our way to and expect to find them in the Patuxent and hope to be back on Wednesday night," Skinner wrote.

He added a postscript: "To get Doctor Beanes upon giving a receipt under the circumstances is as much as I expect—if not more—making allowance for the opinion and feelings of enemy," Skinner wrote. From long experience, Skinner knew Cockburn was unforgiving in matters of honor. It was obvious Ross felt the same way.

After the letter was posted from the shore, they continued into the Chesapeake Bay, passing a landscape familiar to Key from his days at Annapolis. The ship and its crew of nine seamen was captained by John Ferguson, the packet's co-owner. But as the government's agent, Skinner was in overall command of the mission.

Skinner was "a man of mingled character of daring and pernicious

Skinner was as "a man of mingled character of daring and pernicious principles, or restless and rash, and yet of useful and honorable enterprise," John Quincy Adams would later write. "Ruffian, patriot and philanthropist are so blended in him that I cannot appreciate him without a mingled sentiment of detestation and esteem."

John Stuart Skinner in 1825.

principles, or restless and rash, and yet of useful and honorable enterprise," John Quincy Adams would later write. "Ruffian, patriot and philanthropist are so blended in him that I cannot appreciate him without a mingled sentiment of detestation and esteem."

The twenty-six-year-old Skinner, from an old, well-to-do family, had been raised on a plantation in southern Maryland's Calvert County. His upbringing left him with a lifelong fascination with agriculture and field sports—the science of plowing and fox hunting were two particular passions—but like Key, he studied law in Annapolis. After the war started, Madison appointed him inspector of mail from Europe, which arrived in Annapolis on British ships under a truce agreement. The sensitive job involved keeping America's transatlantic communications secure, and Skinner's skill soon led to his appointment to a second job as agent for prisoners of war.

This even more delicate position required regular contact with the British fleet. The good relations Skinner had cultivated with Cockburn and other British officers had paid off. In Annapolis, he would often climb the steps of the State House to the cupola, where he could scan a long stretch of the Chesapeake for enemy maneuvering. Together with odd scraps of conversations with British officers about sailing dates and destinations, and newspaper accounts regarding the location of ships, Skinner sent regular reports to the State Department filled with useful military intelligence. The government moved him from Annapolis to Baltimore in the fall of 1813, when he was assigned the additional job of purser for Barney's flotilla.

Despite Skinner's reservations, he and Key were well matched for the mission. Key brought "tact and persuasive manners" to the mission, Skinner later noted. For his part, Skinner knew how to deal with the British.

WHITE HOUSE LANDING, NOON, MONDAY, SEPTEMBER 5

After three days of backbreaking work, *Devastation* was finally freed from the Potomac River mud Monday morning. Just as propitiously for the British, a cool front swept in and the wind turned fair. Gordon finally had his opportunity to escape past Captain Porter's battery.

The battle on the Potomac was now in its fourth day. *Meteor* had been joined by *Aetna* and rocket ship *Erebus* to continue a fierce bombardment of the battery. The British "rain[ed] down rockets, bomb shells and cannon balls on us as if heaven and earth were coming together," recalled Thomas Brown, an aide to General John Hungerford, the commander of Virginia militia troops at the battery. Porter had nonetheless built up the position to include thirteen guns, entrenchments, and a furnace for heating shot.

Neither side had been able to gain an advantage. The British attempted a landing to storm the guns, but pickets repulsed them. Rodgers's men had launched another fireship attack Sunday night on *Devastation* while the bomb ship still lay aground, but retreated after a sharp fight with the British barges in the bright moonlight. A final attempt Monday morning likewise failed.

Making good use of the wind, Gordon gave the signal to weigh anchor shortly after noon Monday. On the bluffs above White House Landing, the waiting Americans saw the British sails unfurl and a line of warships approaching. The 38–gun *Seahorse* and 36–gun *Euryalus* led the way, sailing through heavy but ill-directed fire from the American guns. Gordon had modified his frigates so his guns could reach the high bluff, weighting the port side with ballast to raise the guns on the starboard side. Taking position broadside to the battery, the frigates dropped anchor and opened a devastating fire. The first two shots fired

The British "rain[ed] down rockets, bomb shells and cannon balls on us as if heaven and earth were coming together," recalled Thomas Brown.

The American battery on the Belvoir Neck, commanding the Potomac channel from atop a bluff at White House Landing.

from *Seahorse* took out American guns, splitting one to the touchhole and knocking the other off its carriage.

Broadsides rained in on the outgunned Americans, and the bluffs were enveloped in smoke. Each of the frigates carried vastly more firepower than the entire battery. Behind them came the bomb ships, firing lethal shells loaded with musket balls. After more than an hour of heavy fire, American casualties were mounting, and it was clear they could no longer hold back the squadron. "I determined not to make a useless sacrifice," Porter reported. By 3 p.m. the battery had fallen silent.

But the British still had to contend with militia sharpshooters from the mountains of western Virginia. Hiding in the trees along the shore, they took a deadly toll on sailors on the decks and in the rigging. Napier was hit in the neck by a musket ball, but the wound was slight.

The British fired immense quantities of round shot, grape, and rockets on the Virginians, who held up "notwithstanding the dreadful cross fire of every species of missive," Hungerford said. While the British bombardment continued, the brig *Fairy* escorted the convoy of prize ships past the American position unharmed, aided by a strong wind. "[W]e calculated all was over for that day," recalled Napier. "We were mistaken."

Across the river, on the Maryland shore about six miles downstream, Captain Oliver Perry was waiting. Joined by the Georgetown and Washington light artillery companies, Perry had taken position at Indian Head, which like the battery at White House Landing commanded the Potomac passage from cliffs overlooking the river channel.

The encounter began disastrously for the British. *Erebus,* trying to slip past Indian Head early in the evening, grounded within range of the battery, and the Americans poured fire on the rocket ship. The bomb ships came to her rescue, unleashing a furious fusillade at Perry's position, and finally silencing the battery at around 8 p.m. Gordon anchored for the night, prepared to resume the battle in the morning.

But appearances aside, Perry's battery at Indian Head was weak. Baltimore's refusal to part with its guns had made it impossible to collect the heavy artillery needed. Perry only had one eighteen-pounder, which arrived thirty minutes before the firing began. The Georgetown and Washington artilleries kept up a spirited fire with their six-pound cannons, but the small shot did little damage.

At daylight Tuesday, Gordon weighed anchor, expecting a heavy fight. But to the surprise of the British, they passed beneath Indian Head unmolested. Perry had run out of ammunition and retreated during the night.

Over the course of five days, the battle along the Potomac had cost the British 7 dead and 35 wounded, while the Americans had lost 12 dead and some 20 wounded, most of them Virginia militia who bravely held their ground at Porter's battery. The Americans "behaved remarkably well—but their efforts were useless," Napier wrote. The British squadron now had clear sailing down the Potomac. Gordon had sprung the trap.

Samuel Smith would keep more than 10,000 men, representing the bulk of his force, in the trenches on Hampstead Hill.

Assembly of the Troops Before the Battle of Baltimore

CHAPTER 13

— ★ —

The Town Must Be Burned

CHESAPEAKE BAY, MORNING, WEDNESDAY, SEPTEMBER 7

GEORGE COCKBURN HAD resigned himself to leaving the Chesapeake, swallowing his disappointment over the failure to attack Baltimore. Aboard *Albion,* he parted from Cochrane and the fleet Wednesday morning and sailed south from Tangier toward the Atlantic Ocean, destination Bermuda. But *Albion* had not gained more than eight or ten miles when the ship received a signal from Vice Admiral Cochrane: Turn back.

It took the convergence of the sun, earth, and moon—and the fateful arrival of intriguing news—for the British to reverse course.

Cochrane had learned that the approaching equinoctial new moon made "it unsafe to proceed immediately out of the Chesapeake," he later informed the Admiralty. The new moon was less than a week away, on September 13, while the autumnal equinox would take place September 22. A new moon coinciding at or near the date of the equinox, when the sun crosses the equator, creates the year's highest tides and strongest tidal currents. In the confines of the Chesapeake Bay, the currents presented a threat to the large British ships. If the British tried to depart the Chesapeake now, the fleet would face dangerous conditions at the mouth of the bay, where the tides would be strongest. The ships would have to wait a week or two before they tried to sail out, Cochrane decided.

Expedition commanders suddenly had time on their hands. At the urging of Lieutenant Evans, Ross again pressed for an attack.

The timely receipt of new intelligence may have tipped the balance. *Menelaus* arrived Tuesday with a dispatch the late Captain Peter Parker wrote the day before he died. In it, Parker described reconnoitering Baltimore Harbor in a tender a few days earlier, sailing unmolested close to Fort McHenry and sounding the passage. Parker included the tantalizing news that a brand-new American frigate—Oliver Perry's *Java,* rigged and nearly ready to go—was sitting in the harbor, as well as two sloops-of-war.

That same day, the fleet received several American newspapers with the latest news from Baltimore. The papers "depict in such strong colours the general alarm, and defenceless state of Baltimore, as to have induced the Vice Admiral (contrary to his previous intention) to resolve on the attack of that place," Evans wrote in his operations memo.

Cochrane relented. "General Ross and myself resolved to occupy the intermediate time to advantage, by making a demonstration upon the city of Baltimore; which might be converted into a real attack should circumstances appear to justify it," Cochrane later informed the Admiralty. In a private letter appended to his official report, Cochrane reported that an attack on Baltimore was "extremely urged by the General to which I reluctantly consented, but to preserve unanimity between the two services."

Rear Admiral Codrington, the fleet captain, had misgivings. He was astonished at the sway that Evans, a mere lieutenant, held over Ross. Codrington tried to talk the general out of it, arguing that the attack would be too risky given the lack of intelligence about Baltimore's defenses. "I pointed out to him all the difficulties I saw in the attack, into which he was persuaded by Cockburn and a Mr. Evans, who acts as quarter-master general in this army," Codrington told his wife. "I was surprised that so sensible a man as General Ross should be led away by the opposite opinions."

Aboard *Albion*, Cockburn was more than a little surprised himself that his arguments had finally taken hold. It had been nearly two weeks since the capture of Washington, and more than a week since Cockburn had pressed for an immediate attack on Baltimore upon the army's return to the ships. The delay "had of course materially altered the case . . . as ample time, had now been afforded to the Americans to call in their troops, from all around," Cockburn later noted in his memoir of service.

But Cockburn raised no objections, readily and enthusiastically endorsing the plan.

MOUTH OF THE POTOMAC, AFTERNOON, WEDNESDAY, SEPTEMBER 7

As the American sloop sailed down the Chesapeake Bay Wednesday morning under a white flag of truce, John Skinner and Francis Scott Key were not expecting to find the main British fleet for many hours yet.

The previous day, the Americans had rendezvoused with *Royal Oak* and the British troopships near the mouth of the Patuxent, and learned that Dr. Beanes was aboard *Tonnant,* presumed to be with the rest of the fleet near Tangier, thirty-five miles to the southeast. Rear Admiral Pulteney Malcolm, the troopship commander, courteously assisted the Americans, sending the letters they carried ahead to *Tonnant* in a swift dispatch boat and assigning the frigate *Hebrus* to escort the American sloop to Tangier.

But around noon Wednesday, the Americans spotted *Tonnant*'s sails near the mouth of the Potomac, moving up the Chesapeake in their direction. At 2:10 p.m., the flagship anchored and sent a boat to bring Key and Skinner aboard.

The Americans arrived in the midst of a swirl of activity throughout the fleet. It could not have been a more inopportune time, but Cochrane welcomed Key and Skinner aboard. The Americans quickly realized that an attack on Baltimore was in the works. Admiral Cockburn, rejoining the fleet, came on board *Tonnant* soon after the Americans to confer with Cochrane. But Cockburn had little time for his usual banter with Skinner, who observed that the rear admiral "was the prime mover of the expedition going on and his mind much taken up." When Key mentioned their mission to free Beanes, it "was received so coldly, that he feared it would fail," according to the account Key gave Taney. Cockburn spoke of Beanes "in very harsh terms," and none of the British seemed disposed to release him.

The Americans were soon summoned for a mid-afternoon meal

with the commanding officers. Skinner sat on the right of Cochrane, and Key to the right of Codrington. Wine flowed "in free circulation," Skinner recalled, and tongues were loosened. Codrington made a cutting remark about Captain David Porter, who was much disliked by the British admirals—Cockburn considered him a "vagabond." Cochrane erroneously believed that Porter had violated the parole governing his release from captivity in the Pacific, and was sending a warning to the American government that if he encountered the captain or his *Essex* crew, the result would be "most painful." Skinner heatedly defended Porter.

One man remained quiet during the meal. Skinner had barely noticed the plainly dressed army officer on his right, who had not been introduced to the Americans and was "the most reserved gentleman at the table." From an offhand comment, Skinner was startled to learn he was General Ross. Whatever the opinions of the Royal Navy officers, Beanes was Ross's prisoner, and it was the general who would decide his fate. Studying him more closely, Skinner saw the unhealed neck wound Ross had received in France in February.

During a pause in the discussion, Ross politely invited Skinner to meet with him privately while the others continued their talk at the dinner table. Settling with the American agent in the admiral's cabin, Ross immediately turned to the matter at hand: Dr. Beanes. Ross had seen General Mason's appeal and was not persuaded by any of the American legal arguments. But he had also read the letters the Americans brought from the British prisoners of war, and these had a profound effect on the general.

The American promise to treat British prisoners well "has been more than confirmed by their own letters," Ross told Skinner. Colonel Thornton's letter reported that the wounded were doing well and that "the Americans behaved very kindly to them." For that reason, Ross told Skinner, Beanes would be released.

Speaking with Key later, Ross brushed off the attorney's "strong representations" as to Beanes's character. Ross told Key that Beanes "deserved much more punishment than he had received; but that he felt himself bound to make a return for the kindness which have been shown to his wounded officers . . . and upon that ground, and that only, he would release him," Key reported.

Key visited Beanes, whom he found in the forward part of the ship, among the sailors and soldiers; the doctor had not had a change of clothes from the time he was seized and "was constantly treated with indignity by those around him," according to Key. Beanes had been treated as a criminal, not as a prisoner of war, and had feared he might be tossed overboard.

Securing Beanes's freedom had been surprisingly easy. Ross wrote a letter for the Americans to take back to Mason, explaining that Beanes was being released "purely in proof of the obligation which I feel for the attention with which the wounded have been treated."

Key's famed eloquence "was not put to the test in this instance," Skinner later said. Nor had it been necessary for Skinner to negotiate any terms for exchange. But the journey for the Americans was far from over.

E arly the next morning, Thursday, September 8, Key was informed "that neither he, nor anyone else, would be permitted to leave the fleet for some days," until after the attack on Baltimore. Cochrane also informed the Americans that they could no longer stay aboard *Tonnant*, as the flagship was too crowded with officers preparing for the attack.

Key, Skinner, and Beanes were transferred to HMS *Surprize*, the frigate commanded by Sir Thomas Cochrane, the admiral's son, who the elder Cochrane promised would make the Americans comfortable. At 7 a.m., a party of Royal Marines from *Surprize* took charge of the truce ship and placed her under tow. The ten-man American crew also came aboard the British frigate.

Baltimore, however, was not the first destination for the British. Captain Gordon's squadron had not returned from the Potomac, and learning of the American effort to destroy the ships, Cochrane sailed his entire force into the river on Thursday. If necessary, he would land troops to relieve the pressure on the squadron. "We were bent on other plans; but hearing reports of vessels being sunk & batteries formed to prevent their return, we decided on making the safety of these ships our first consideration," Codrington wrote. In any event, the bomb ships with Gordon were needed for any assault on Fort McHenry, which guarded Baltimore Harbor.

Before dawn Friday, Cockburn continued upriver ahead of the troopships. Twenty miles from the mouth of the Potomac, *Albion* spotted a procession of sails approaching. At 6:45 a.m., Cockburn sent the signal Cochrane was awaiting: "All our ships standing down."

Gordon's return from his squadron's epic twenty-three-day journey into the Potomac electrified the rest of the fleet. The squadron had overcome treacherous shoals and a powerful squall, forced the destruction of Fort Washington, captured Alexandria, and fought its way back down the river with twenty-one prize ships stuffed with booty. For the British, the expedition was a grand triumph in the finest traditions of Royal Navy seamanship. "In short it is nothing less brilliant than the capture of Washington, and those employed deserve laurel crowns," Codrington wrote his wife. Theodore Roosevelt agreed in his famous history, *The Naval War of 1812*, calling Gordon's expedition "a most venturesome feat, reflecting great honor on the captains and crews."

But all the glory and loot had come with a price: Baltimore had gained precious time to prepare. At least two days had been lost because the fleet had been forced to sail into the Potomac looking for Gordon.

At 11 a.m. Friday, *Albion* led the reunited fleet back down the Potomac. The ships raced downriver with a good wind, rounded Point Lookout late that afternoon, and began to beat their way up the Chesapeake Bay. Gleig wrote in his diary of the men's delight: "We now put about again all in a body and took the direction of Baltimore which is confidently stated to be the next point of attack."

T he Potomac battle over, Captain John Rodgers and his men rushed back to Baltimore, soon followed by Porter's and Perry's detachments. Fourteen wagonloads of Porter's men paraded out of Washington Tuesday evening, September 6, with their captain at the head of the procession, accompanied by the sounds of a boatswain whistle and the famed "Free Trade and Sailors Rights" banner flying from the first wagon.

Arriving in Baltimore on Wednesday evening, Rodgers found more than 15,000 troops in the city, not including the thousand seamen and marines in his naval brigade. Rodgers threw himself back into the city's defenses, positioning his men at gun batteries along the water and at Hampstead Hill, conferring with Samuel Smith, and making plans to sink boats to protect the harbor. Porter, however, was ordered north to aid in the defense of New York City, and Perry was ill after his exertions at Indian Head. Rodgers was unconcerned about losing the assistance of his fellow captains, believing the situation well in hand.

"Forts, redoubts and entrenchments are thrown up all around the town and the place now has nothing to fear, even should the enemy make his appearance tomorrow," Rodgers wrote on Friday, September 9, to Commodore Alexander Murray in Philadelphia. The British would not attack Baltimore, Rodgers added. "It is understood however that he has descended the Bay and whatever might have been his intentions that he will not now attempt an attack on this place with any such force as he can command at present," he wrote. "I hope to leave here in two or three days for Phila., as I begin to feel tired of playing soldier, and more particularly as there will not be any occasion for our services."

BALTIMORE, MORNING, SATURDAY, SEPTEMBER 10

At Fort McHenry, the garrison commander, Major George Armistead, also believed that the crisis was ending. He finished a letter Saturday morning to his wife, Louisa, who was expecting the birth of their second child at any moment. The British threat to Baltimore had forced her to flee to Gettysburg, Pennsylvania. It now seemed as if the upsetting evacuation had been unnecessary. "I wish to God you had not been compelled to leave Baltimore but you now must be contented as it is impossible from your present situation to attempt a return," Armistead wrote.

Armistead, the coolheaded and courageous thirty-four-year-old son of a Virginia planter, had served fifteen years in the army at posts around the nation. He had a special connection to Fort McHenry and Baltimore, where he had served before the war and had met and married Louisa, the daughter of a prominent Baltimore merchant. After hostilities broke out, Armistead was sent to the Niagara frontier. His role in the seizure of Fort George on the Canadian border in early 1813 earned him promotion to major and the honor of bringing the captured British flags to President Madison. While in Washington in June 1813, he was given command of Fort McHenry, replacing a lackluster officer who had balked at cooperating with Samuel Smith.

The latest intelligence had the British at the mouth of the Potomac, moving down the Chesapeake. Armistead hoped to reunite soon with his family. "[S]hould they depart from the Bay I will be with you immediately so be not alarmed if I should pop in on you," he wrote Louisa.

"I dreamt last night you presented me with a fine son," he added. "God grant it be so and all well."

With Armistead's blessing, Captain Joseph Nicholson, commander of Fort McHenry's Baltimore Fencibles, a volunteer artillery company, marched his 80 men to town at noon. The British were reported to be departing, and "we were led to hope we should have a little rest from our incessant labors, in preparing to resist them," wrote Private Isaac Munroe, an editor of the *Baltimore Patriot* and one of the "gentleman volunteers" serving with the Fencibles.

The handsome and dashing Nicholson, forty-four, was a judge on Maryland's highest court. He had raised the fencibles, as the home guard units were called, drawing volunteers from many of Baltimore's finest families, among them merchants, tradesmen, and bankers who were defending not only homes but also considerable wealth. Nicholson, from a prominent family on Maryland's Eastern Shore, was a born leader—passionate, impatient, and bursting with energy.

Nicholson, from a prominent family on Maryland's Eastern Shore, was a born leader—passionate, impatient, and bursting with energy.

Joseph Hopper Nicholson, in an 1810 engraving.

Like Francis Scott Key and Richard West, Nicholson was married to one of the high-society Lloyd girls of Annapolis—Rebecca, the eldest of the sisters. He was close to Key, serving as something of an avuncular figure to the younger attorney.

Elected to the House of Representatives in 1799, Nicholson proved to be a loyal supporter of Jefferson, never more so than when the disputed 1800 presidential contest against Aaron Burr came to the House for resolution. Nicholson, though severely ill, stayed in the chamber nursed by his wife through seven days of balloting, and cast a crucial vote helping Jefferson to victory. But Nicholson left Congress in 1806 for a seat on the Maryland Court of Appeals after he and fellow Maryland representative Samuel Smith had a bitter falling-out vying for House leadership positions.

Nicholson had been a staunch war supporter from the start, but was also a realist, and after Napoleon's fall, he recognized that the United States was fighting for survival. "We should have to fight hereafter not for 'free trade and sailors rights,' not for the conquest of the Canadas, but for our national existence," he wrote Navy Secretary Jones, a friend from their days in Congress.

Nicholson, visiting New York City when he learned that the British had sailed in force into the Chesapeake, made it back to Baltimore one day after the capture of Washington. "Good God! How have we been disgraced," Nicholson wrote Jones. "Our cursed militia have been coming in one, two, and three at a time, and all speak highly of their gallantry."

Despite a high fever, Nicholson reported to Fort McHenry to take command of his Baltimore Fencibles. He was appalled to see his despised rival, Samuel Smith, with unfettered command of Baltimore, and he began a one-man campaign to get him replaced, convinced that Smith would surrender at the first chance. "[I]f general Ross had marched to this place instead of to Patuxent he could've been master of our city, with even less trouble than he had at Washington," Nicholson groused to Jones.

Nicholson was ambivalent about whether Winder should resume command, but he was sure Smith must go, telling Jones, "for God's sake let us have a commander who has nerve and judgment."

Chesapeake Bay, Saturday afternoon, September 10

Along the coast, a column of more than 50 British ships raced up the Chesapeake Bay on a fine breeze, triggering the greatest alarm on the shore. Sailors and soldiers on the decks watched delightedly as warning guns fired, beacons lit up, horsemen galloped about, and carts headed to the hinterlands loaded with furniture. Annapolis, the picturesque state capital, was particularly panicked. "We could plainly perceive the inhabitants flying in all directions," exulted Midshipman Robert Barrett, aboard *Hebrus*.

Watching from the cupola of the State House in Annapolis, Major William Barney, Samuel Smith's chief intelligence officer, sent reports to Smith that the British fleet was sailing north toward Baltimore. Barney, the son of Commodore Joshua Barney, had set up an elaborate network of observation stations along the coast all the way to Baltimore, with horse relays at ten-mile intervals. But Smith was receiving contradictory information and delayed taking action.

Around dusk, lookouts near Baltimore saw the first distant ships coming up the bay under a press of sail and a fair wind. At Fort McHenry Saturday night, Armistead learned that some 30 British vessels—ships-of-the-line, heavy frigates, and bomb vessels—had been spotted near the mouth of the Patapsco, "with every indication of an attempt on the City of Baltimore."

Armistead ordered the garrison to man their stations. In town, Captain Nicholson received orders at 9:30 p.m. to gather the Baltimore Fencibles from their homes and march them back to the fort. Noncommissioned officers knocked on doors, telling the volunteers to muster at once at the corner of Howard and Market streets. The men marched in a torrential rain and reached the fort by midnight. "On our arrival," Private Munroe wrote, "we found the matches burning, the furnaces heated and vomiting red shot, and every thing ready for a gallant defense."

Baltimore, morning, Sunday, September 11

An odd calm prevailed in Baltimore on Sunday morning. Unlike Armistead, Major General Smith was uncertain whether the reported sightings of British ships meant an attack was pending. He sounded no general alarm, and many residents attended church. Militia troops joined the services at the Wilkes Street Methodist Church, leaving their arms stacked peacefully out front.

Around noon, the quiet dissolved. Messengers arrived from observation posts at North Point reporting that British warships escorting troop transports were plainly visible through the haze at the mouth of the Patapsco. The speed of the British fleet caught Smith by surprise. He ordered three alarm guns fired from the courthouse green, signaling the troops to muster.

Church bells rang, drums beat, and couriers hurried about with messages. At the Methodist church, the preacher abruptly slammed his Bible shut. "My brethren and friends, the alarm guns have just fired," he announced. "The British are approaching, and commending you to God and the word of His Grace, I pronounce the benediction, and may the God of battles accompany you." The troops rushed out, grabbed their weapons, and took off running.

Samuel Smith's plan for defending Baltimore was predicated on one premise: A British attack would come via the Patapsco Neck, the ten-mile-long peninsula leading northwest from the Chesapeake Bay to the city. Unlike Winder at Bladensburg, Smith had carefully thought out a scheme of defense.

The commander would keep more than 10,000 men, representing the bulk of his force, in the trenches on Hampstead Hill. The vast majority were militia, mostly from Maryland, including the ill-trained 1st Brigade from Cecil and Harford counties, along the upper Chesapeake Bay, and General Stansbury's 11th Brigade, from Baltimore County outside the city, which had performed so poorly at Bladensburg. Another 2,600 Virginia and 1,000 Pennsylvania militia were inexperienced and of unknown quality. Rounding out the force were about 900 U.S. Army regulars from the 36th and 38th regiments, some of them veterans of Bladensburg. Smith hoped that this time, protected in their formidable position on Hampstead Hill and supported by the naval brigade, the troops would hold and fight.

Smith had chosen his best militia brigade—the 3rd, or City Brigade—to march out on the neck Sunday afternoon to block the ex-

John Stricker

Stricker had served under Samuel Smith for years, accompanying him as second in command of the Maryland troops sent to put down the Whiskey Rebellion.

Sketch of Brigadier General John Stricker, commander of the City Brigade.

pected invasion. The 3,200 men in the brigade were virtually all from Baltimore—clerks, blacksmiths, laborers, sail makers, carpenters, merchants, and apprentices, most of them volunteers. They served in companies of Hussars, Chasseurs, Dragoons, Yagers, and Blues, among others, names that bespoke their notion of war as a noble pursuit. The heart of the brigade were the 5th Maryland Regiment and the Baltimore Rifle Battalion, both quite familiar with the British from Bladensburg—"not entirely a recommendation," author Walter Lord noted. Humiliating as it was, the experience had taught the men what to expect from the Invincibles, and it had left them eager to restore their reputations. And this time, they would be fighting for their homes.

Brigadier General John Stricker, a taciturn descendant of Swiss pioneers, commanded the City Brigade. He was an experienced officer, quick to take offense at perceived insults. During the American Revolution, Sticker had fought at Princeton, Brandywine, and Monmouth, and he had stood a few paces from the gallows when Major John André, the British spy, was executed for assisting Benedict Arnold in his treason. Stricker had served under Samuel Smith for years, accompanying him as second in command of the Maryland troops sent to put down the Whiskey Rebellion. But Stricker's reputation had been tarnished by his failure as commander of the city militia to curb the Baltimore mob during the infamous 1812 riot.

By 3 p.m., Stricker and the City Brigade moved out. The men marched east on Baltimore Street, behind fife and drums and flags, but with less swagger than three weeks earlier, when the 5th Maryland paraded to Bladensburg. The regiment's blue uniforms were not as splendid now, after the dust, toil, and blood of battle; some of the other units lacked uniforms altogether, and the men wore civilian clothes, ranging from work togs to silk top hats. The brigade took the Philadelphia Road through the defensive lines at Hampstead Hill, then followed the North Point Road out to the Patapsco Neck, which was framed by the Patapsco and Back rivers. The day remained intensely hot, and some men sank to the road in the suffocating dust.

Around 8 p.m., Stricker reached the spot he wanted, just beyond the Methodist Meeting House, a plain, wooden one-room church about halfway to North Point. Stricker had scouted the site a year earlier with Major Barney, the intelligence officer, and they had chosen the ground as the most defensible position. It was at one of the narrowest points of Patapsco Neck, where Bear Creek, an inlet of the Patapsco River, cut far up into the peninsula. The neck was further pinched from the north by the marshy black mud around Bread and Cheese Creek, which narrowed the land to little more than a half-mile-wide stretch of solid ground.

Smith did not want to challenge the British at their likely beachhead at North Point, where the American defenders could easily be cut off and destroyed by an amphibious landing. Still, the American commander was taking a risk positioning his troops even halfway out the neck. Though the Patapsco was shallow, the British had many small craft that could bypass the American position, sail closer to Baltimore, and cut off Stricker's force.

Stricker pushed the Baltimore Rifle Battalion with some cavalry several miles forward to watch for the British. The remainder of the force camped around the Methodist Meeting House, near a grove of trees known as Godley Wood. "We lay that night without tents on the bare ground at the distance of about 7 miles from Baltimore," wrote Corporal John McHenry of the 5th Maryland. The fort defending Baltimore harbor was named after his uncle, James McHenry, the Irish-born secretary of war under George Washington and John Adams who had pushed to bolster coastal defenses. But on this night, Corporal McHenry was just another cold and sleepless militiaman, anxiously awaiting the British.

WASHINGTON, SUNDAY, SEPTEMBER 11

In the capital, President Madison and James Monroe—the one-man secretary of war, secretary of state, and military district commander— were doing their best to show the government back in control. On Saturday, Madison and Monroe toured the ruins of Fort Washington, stepping over the mounds of sandstone block, bricks, and timber turned to rubble when the 3,300 pounds of gunpowder in the magazine had exploded.

Monroe ordered Major Pierre L'Enfant, the French engineer, to oversee the immediate construction of a new, stronger fort on the site. The *Intelligencer* lauded the decision. "The early and vigilant attention of the government to this object is a pledge of their determination that hostile tread shall never again pollute the soil of this district," the paper declared, too loyal to point out that it would have been wiser to strengthen the fort before the British arrived, as L'Enfant had recommended the previous year.

On Sunday afternoon, the quiet in the capital was interrupted by alarming reports arriving from the north via express messenger and stagecoach: An attack on Baltimore appeared imminent. The British fleet was working its way into the Patapsco. Madison and Monroe could only wait with everyone else for more news. The fate of Baltimore was out of their hands.

PATAPSCO RIVER, EVENING, SUNDAY, SEPTEMBER 11

Cockburn and Ross were not long in deciding North Point was the best place to launch their attack on Baltimore. From his earlier probes, Cockburn knew the Patapsco was not deep enough to allow the line-of-battle ships and the heavy frigates to approach the harbor. This was confirmed Sunday afternoon when Captain Gordon, probing the channel, sank *Seahorse*'s keel in several feet of mud. The water at North Point, however, was deep enough to allow troop transports close to shore.

The commanders planned a dual land and sea assault as simple as it was brutal. Ross and his army, accompanied by Cockburn and a brigade of seamen and Royal Marines, would land at North Point before dawn Monday. They would march up the Patapsco Neck, destroy any militia in the way, and move on the city. There would be no flotilla to chase or elaborate feints to fool the enemy. Compared to the sixty-mile route the British had taken from Benedict to Washington, the fifteen-mile march to the outskirts of Baltimore would be easy, probably taking no more than a day.

Meanwhile, Admiral Cochrane would take the lighter frigates, sloops, bomb vessels, and rocket ship up the Patapsco closer to Baltimore to bombard Fort McHenry, the linchpin of the harbor's defense. "With an uncommonly favorable coincidence of fair wind with a high tide, which then existed, . . . the Admiral expected to silence the fort . . . and then, turning his guns upon the entrenchments, drive away its defenses . . . , and so let the army in, or up to a position from which the town might be laid under contribution or burnt," John Skinner later wrote.

All day, British ships arrived in the mouth of the Patapsco, gathering "like birds to a rookery." The ships-of-the-line—*Tonnant, Albion*, and *Royal Oak*—anchored in deep water at the mouth of Patapsco about twelve miles from Baltimore, while the landing vessels under Cockburn's command moved to deep anchorage in Old Roads Bay off North Point. At 7 p.m., Cockburn and Ross transferred from *Albion* to the brig *Fairy* off North Point, where they finalized plans. Each of the troops stuffed three days' provisions, a spare shirt, and a blanket in his haversack. Every man was to be packed by sunset and ready to land anytime during the night.

Francis Scott Key watched the preparations for invasion with growing dread. Since boarding *Surprize* more than three days earlier, Key had listened in disquietude as officers openly discussed plans for the "plunder and desolation" of Baltimore. Admiral Cochrane was determined that Baltimore see nothing of the kid gloves Ross had shown Washington, and the attitude permeated down the ranks. The city would either be destroyed or pay a healthy ransom to be spared.

For Key, who had expected that British officers would conduct themselves as gentlemen, it was a disillusioning experience. "Never was man more disappointed in his expectations than I have been as to the character of British officers," Key wrote soon afterward to John

Randolph. "With some exceptions they appeared to be illiberal, ignorant & vulgar, seemed filled with a malignity against everything American." Ever charitable, Key hastened to add, "Perhaps however, I saw
them in unfavorable circumstances."

Now that they were in sight of the city, Skinner pressed for the release of the American delegation. Cochrane turned him down with a
chilling smile. "Ah, Mr. Skinner, after discussing so freely as we have
done in your presence our purposes and plans, you could hardly expect
us to let you go on shore now in advance of us," the admiral said. As
soon as the business at hand was ended, the Americans would be freed,
Cochrane promised.

But the Americans would at least be returned to their own vessel, as
Skinner demanded, and not be forced to witness the attack from a British ship. It was more convenient for the British as well; Admiral Cochrane was planning to move with his retinue to *Surprize* the following
morning in order to supervise the attack by water.

Key, Skinner, and Beanes, along with the American crew, were
transferred back to their sloop on Sunday, accompanied by guards to
prevent their escape. They anchored with Cockburn's ships in Old
Roads Bay, below Sparrow Point.

The return to an American ship was small consolation to Key. Cochrane's plans for Baltimore were perfectly clear, Key wrote Randolph:
"To make my feelings still more acute the Admiral had intimated his
fears that the town must be burned; and I was sure that if taken, it
would have been given up to plunder. I have reason to believe that such
a promise was given to their soldiers. It was filled with women & children!"

O say can you see, ~~through the~~ by the dawn's early
light so proudly we hail'd at the twilight's last gleaming
whose broad stripes & bright stars through the perilous fight
O'er the ramparts we watch'd were so gallantly streaming
    And the rocket's red glare the bomb bursting in
    air, gave proof through the night that our flag was still
O say does that star spangled banner yet wave
O'er the land of the free & the home of the brave

On the shore dimly seen through the mists of the deep
    Where the foe's haughty host in dread silence reposes
What is that which the breeze, o'er the towering steep
As it fitfully blows, half conceals half discloses
    Now it catches the gleam of the morning's first
    In full glory reflected now shines in the stream
Tis the star-spangled banner — O long may it wave
O'er the land of the free & the home of the brave

And where is that band who so vauntingly swore
    That the havoc of war & the battle's confusion
A home & a Country should leave us no more
    ~~Their blood~~
    Their blood has wash'd out their foul footstep's
    pollution
No refuge could save the hireling & slave
    From the terror of flight or the gloom of the grave
And the star-spangled banner in triumph doth wave
O'er the land of the free & the home of the brave

O thus be it ever when freemen shall stand
Between their lov'd home & the war's desolation
Blest with vict'ry & peace may the heav'n rescued land
Praise the power that hath made & preserv'd us a nation!
    Then conquer we must, when our cause it is just,
    And this be our motto — "In God is our trust,"
And the star-spangled banner in triumph shall wave
O'er the land of the free & the home of the brave

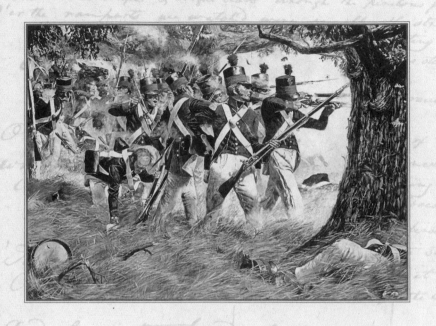

Stricker wanted a fight, and now he had one.

The 5th Maryland at the Battle of North Point

CHAPTER 14

★

The Battle for Baltimore

AN UNWORLDLY CALM settled over the waters of Old Roads Bay during the overnight hours. The heat of the day had passed, and the night felt delightfully balmy. No moon shone, giving the stars an unrivaled brilliance. The decks of the British troopships and brigs were covered with soldiers who had escaped the suffocating berths below to sleep in the refreshing air. Every man in the invasion force was fully dressed and ready for immediate action.

Few sounds disturbed the night, but those that did carried far over the water: the splash of an oar as a solitary boat picked up orders from the admiral, the small waves lapping on the side of a ship, or the sentinels' voices calling "all's well" every half hour. Lieutenant Gleig, unable to sleep after the solemn preparations for battle, was mesmerized by the tranquillity as he restlessly paced the deck of the troopship *Golden Fleece*. "I do not recollect to have seen a more heavenly night than the present," he wrote.

But around 3 a.m., the stillness of the night passed. Boats were lowered from every ship, and the men were roused by thumping and splashing as the landing craft came alongside the frigates and transports. In the darkness, the gun brigs moved to within 250 yards of the shore and anchored broadside to cover the landing, ready to shred any defenses with grape and shot. "Though no enemy appeared the *Madagascar* sent a shot into the wood which must have given a terrible shock to some innocent tree," wrote Major Peter Bowlby of the 4th Foot, aboard the British frigate.

Waves of boats rowed toward the dark shore. As soon as the keels struck sand, the soldiers ran up a low ridge, spread out, and set up a perimeter. Within thirty minutes, a thousand men had landed. Scouts fanned out but found no resistance.

Ross and Cockburn landed before daylight. The admiral, at Ross's request, would stay at the general's side to oversee the naval piece of the attack and "render him every assistance within my power." With a minimum of confusion despite the darkness, Ross and Cockburn expertly assembled an invasion force from scores of ships.

All told, some 4,700 British troops would land, about two hundred more than at Benedict. Despite the loss of hundreds of men to battle, illness, and desertion, the British had more than made up for the deficiency by scraping together a 600-man naval brigade including every seaman and Royal Marine who could be spared from the ships. The Colonial Marines, the escaped slaves who had impressed commanders with their discipline at Washington, were again part of the invasion force. Even Royal Marine Major Mortimer Timpson, nearly killed by the arsenal explosion in Washington, took himself off the sick list to join the landing, "finding myself rather better."

With the beach secure, the landing troops assembled into assault units. Three companies of light infantry would lead the way, followed by the Light Brigade. The naval brigade would be next, followed by horses pulling six field pieces and two howitzers, and then the remainder of the infantry.

Ross did not wait for all the troops to land before beginning the march. He left Colonel Brooke, his second in command, to supervise the rest of the landing, with orders to advance once the 21st Fusiliers and artillery were ashore. Ross and Cockburn, the confident and cheerful conquerors of Washington, moved toward Baltimore.

As the army advanced on land, Cochrane, aboard *Surprize,* pushed up the Patapsco with the remainder of the frigates, brigs, and bomb ships. Three frigates grounded on the mud shoals off Sparrow Point, but the ships' crews competed to free them, and all were soon afloat, defiantly continuing upriver. Again and again they grounded, but each time sailors pulled the ships through the shoals with kedge anchors, chanting in unison as they heaved. Midshipman Barrett, accompanying *Hebrus,* was covered head to toe with mud, but was nonetheless cheered at the progress. "As we proceeded up the river, doubtless the Americans were struck with panic and amazement," he wrote.

Aboard *Tonnant*, anchored at the mouth of the Patapsco, Codrington scribbled a note to his wife. "The work of destruction is now about to begin, and there will probably be many broken heads tonight," he wrote. Despite his misgivings about the attack, Codrington managed to drum up some enthusiasm: "I do not like to contemplate scenes of blood and destruction; but my heart is deeply interested in the coercion of these Baltimore heroes, who are perhaps the most inveterate against us of all the Yankees."

METHODIST MEETING HOUSE, 7 A.M., MONDAY, SEPTEMBER 12

Cavalry scouts raced to bring word to Brigadier General Stricker at his headquarters at Cook's Tavern: The enemy was landing in full force at North Point. The City Brigade hurriedly broke camp. Stricker formed a battle line stretching across the narrow neck along woods facing the open fields of the Boulden farm.

The 5th Maryland anchored the right flank at the head of a branch of Bear Creek. In the center, the Union Artillery set up six field guns across North Point Road. The 27th Regiment was positioned on the left, with its flank on the marsh around Bread and Cheese Creek. Stricker established a second line three hundred yards back, with the 51st Regiment on the right and the 39th Regiment on the left. One mile back, the 6th Maryland waited in reserve.

The Baltimore Rifle Battalion, under Captain William Dyer's command since William Pinkney's wounding at Bladensburg, was two miles ahead, where it had camped the previous night. Stricker ordered Dyer to take cover in a nearby patch of pine trees and surprise the lead elements of the British when they appeared. Stricker settled back to await the British advance, annoyed only that some of the regiments had been "thoughtless enough" to march out without pans for making bread. He sent a dispatch to Sam Smith alerting him of the landing, and a message asking for cooking ware.

At a cavalry outpost at the Todd plantation house, about three miles from the landing point, scouts hoisted a signal flag from the cupola. Ten miles away, atop Federal Hill overlooking Baltimore Harbor,

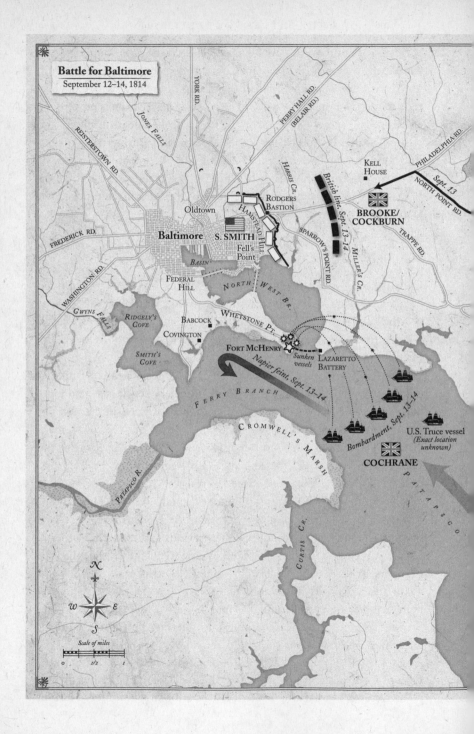

Battle for Baltimore
September 12–14, 1814

YORK RD.

JONES FALLS

PERRY HALL RD.
(BELAIR RD.)

KELL
HOUSE

PHILADELPHIA RD.

NORTH POINT RD.

Sept. 13

REISTERSTOWN RD.

HARRIS CR.

British line, Sept. 13–14

BROOKE/
COCKBURN

Oldtown

RODGERS
BASTION

HAMSTEAD HILL

Baltimore   S. SMITH

Fell's
Point

SPARROW'S POINT RD.

MILLER'S CR.

TRAPPE RD.

FREDERICK RD.

WASHINGTON RD.

BASIN

FEDERAL
HILL

NORTH WEST BR.

GWYNS FALLS

RIDGELY'S
COVE

BABCOCK

WHETSTONE PT.

COVINGTON

WHETSTONE PT.

SMITH'S
COVE

FORT McHENRY

Sunken
vessels

LAZARETTO
BATTERY

Napier feint, Sept. 13–14

FERRY BRANCH

CROMWELL'S MARSH

Bombardment, Sept. 13–14

U.S. Truce vessel
(Exact location
unknown)

PATAPSCO R.

COCHRANE

PATAPSCO

CURTIS CR.

N
W   E
S

Scale of miles

0   1/2   1

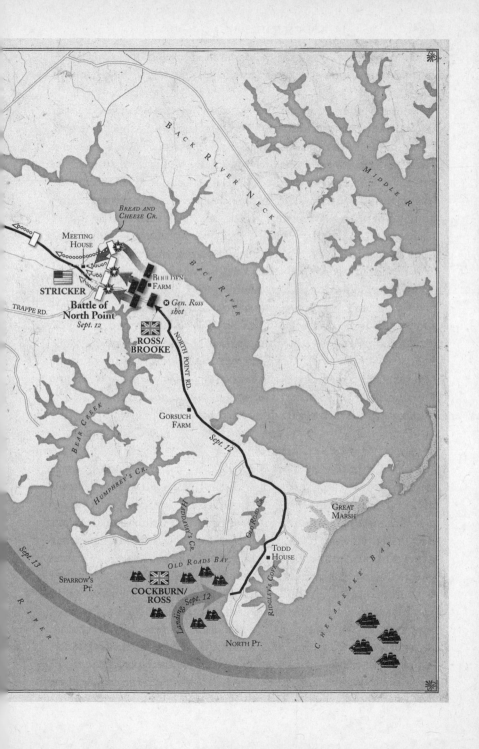

BACK RIVER NECK

MIDDLE R.

BREAD AND
CHEESE CR.

MEETING
HOUSE

BACK RIVER

STRICKER

BODLEY
FARM

⊗ *Gen. Ross
shot*

Battle of
North Point
Sept. 12

TRAPPE RD.

ROSS/
BROOKE

NORTH POINT RD.

BEAR CREEK

GORSUCH
FARM

Sept. 12

HUMPHREY'S CR.

HADDAWAY'S CR.

OLD ROAD RD.

GREAT
MARSH

Sept. 13

SPARROW'S
PT.

OLD ROADS BAY

TODD
HOUSE

RIDGLEY'S COVE

COCKBURN/
ROSS

Landing Sept. 12

CHESAPEAKE BAY

RIVER

NORTH PT.

a sailing master who spotted the signal fired three shots in quick succession from his one-gun battery, alerting the town that the British had landed.

Sailing Master George La Roche, watching from the deck of the sloop-of-war *Erie,* anchored off Fort McHenry, was shocked to see that three British frigates had passed the Sparrow Point shoals and "were coming up with a fine breeze, contrary to our expectations," he wrote in his diary. The Royal Navy had once more confounded the Americans with its sea skills and determination, dashing hopes that warships of that size would be unable to sail inside the Patapsco shoals. By prearranged plan, La Roche began to sink two dozen merchant ships in the Northwest Branch channel, obstructing the British fleet's path to the harbor.

At noon, John Hewes, a Baltimore printer and a onetime newspaperman, wrote to his father, cautioning him not to believe all the "hideous" rumors in circulation. "The truth is, however, bad enough," Hewes continued. "The British fleet, say about 40 sail of all sizes, are in full view of this city. . . . They are actually landing men at and about North Point. . . . 3 frigates are now at Sparrow's Point. . . . [T]hus vanishes the hope that frigates of 40 guns could not pass our bar! . . . I have some doubts of being in town tomorrow."

GORSUCH FARM, 8 A.M., MONDAY, SEPTEMBER 12

Moving swiftly from North Point, the British encountered no sign of the Americans until reaching an unfinished entrenchment about three miles up the road, at a narrow neck between Humphrey Creek and Back River. The freshly overturned dirt was a sign that the Americans might not be far off. It "became evident that the enemy were in a state of activity, and alarm," according to Cockburn.

One mile farther along the road, the column halted around 8 a.m. at the Gorsuch farmhouse, where Ross and Cockburn enjoyed a country breakfast while waiting for the rest of the army to catch up. Ross's men kept good order, but the blue-jacketed sailors, not used to discipline ashore, chased pigs and chickens in every direction, ignoring orders from officers to stop. Even Ross laughed at the ridiculous sight.

Ross assumed a stern visage when a British patrol brought in three

American cavalry scouts captured nearby. The "young gentlemen" volunteers, from the 1st Baltimore Hussars, had blundered too close to the enemy. Ross interrogated them. The three dragoons painted a vivid, if exaggerated, portrait of the defenses waiting in Baltimore. Every man in the city capable of bearing arms was waiting in the trenches, they reported, some 20,000 troops in all, along with one hundred cannon. Ross listened, expressionless. "But they are mainly militia I presume," Ross noted, and the prisoners confirmed this. Ross responded that he would take Baltimore "if it rained militia," according to a newspaper account published twelve days later.

The wait at the Gorsuch farm dragged on. At the landing beach, officers struggled to move the entire army ashore. All the guns had landed by 8 a.m., but the 21st Fusiliers troops were still aboard the ships. Meanwhile, the heat was building fast—"one of the hottest days I ever remember," Royal Marine Captain John Robyns recorded in his journal.

Colonel Brooke, in command of the landing beach, did not want to leave the troops waiting on the open ground at North Point, "as the men were falling in twentys, from the heat of the sun," he wrote in his diary. Brooke advanced with the second column toward the cover of woods, leaving behind those still landing. The colonel rode forward to report the delay to the general, and he found Ross and Cockburn sitting on the steps of the farmhouse. The commanders agreed Brooke should wait for the remainder of the force while Ross and Cockburn resumed the advance; Ross was anxious to keep moving.

As Ross prepared to leave, Robert Gorsuch asked if he should expect them for supper—perhaps a sarcastic jibe, implying that the British would soon be retreating. "No," Ross is said to have replied. "I shall sup in Baltimore tonight, or in hell."

The infamous comment, together with the remark about raining militia, has been cited ever since as evidence of the general's hubris. Yet the comments are out of character for Ross, who in any event was not planning on attacking Baltimore until the following morning. If Ross spoke those words, they are better understood not as boasting, but as an ironic Irish fatalism, joshing retorts to the American prisoners and farmer. Given his cautious nature, Ross would have harbored doubts about whether his small force could capture Baltimore.

AMERICAN CAMP, METHODIST MEETING HOUSE, 11 A.M., MONDAY,
   SEPTEMBER 12

Stricker, learning that the British were rapidly advancing, expected any minute to hear the crackling of rifle fire announcing that the Baltimore Rifle Battalion had found the enemy. Instead, around 11 a.m., the riflemen trickled back to the American line. Captain Dyer had retreated, spooked by a rumor that the British had landed behind them on Back River. Stricker was apoplectic. The needless retreat had, it seemed, ruined his plan to strike the first blow.

Stricker settled back once more to await the British, but there was still no sign of them. Instead, around noon, cavalry scouts reported that the enemy "was enjoying himself at Gorsuch's farm." Stricker was again furious, this time at the British; he proclaimed himself "insulted at the idea of a small marauding party thus daringly provoking chastisement." He also worried that the British were waiting for nightfall to launch a bayonet charge, which could terrify and scatter his men. Stricker decided to again try to provoke an immediate fight.

Officers vied for the assignment. In short order, Stricker assembled a task force of about 250 men under Major Richard Heath, an officer well regarded for his bravery. The force included two of the 5th Maryland's best companies: the Mechanical Volunteers, commanded by Captain Benjamin Chew Howard, and the Independent Blues, under the command of Captain Aaron Levering.

About 70 riflemen were also chosen, most of them from Captain Edward Aisquith's rifle company. In contrast to the vivid uniforms of the 5th Maryland, the sharpshooters wore drab green jackets and trousers, which blended well with the leaves and tall grass, and they had no ornaments to catch the eye save a silver bugle embroidered on the cap band. The riflemen were drawn from the city's merchant class, and among the youngest were two apprentice saddlers: Henry McComas, a polite and sociable eighteen-year-old described by a fellow soldier as "tall, slender of emaciated form," and his friend Daniel Wells, a nineteen-year-old from an old Annapolis family.

At 1 p.m., the task force moved forward in arrowhead formation, centered on North Point Road. Armed with long-barreled rifles and carrying powder horns on their right hips and bullet pouches on the left, the riflemen marched with a flag showing a coiled snake with the words DON'T TREAD ON ME.

GODLEY WOOD, EARLY AFTERNOON, MONDAY, SEPTEMBER 12

General Ross was no less impatient than Stricker. It was the middle of the day, and if the British did not hurry, they would not be in position to assault Baltimore in the morning. Around 12:30 p.m., he ordered the advance to continue.

Beyond the Gorsuch farm, a canopy of heavy woods shaded the road, with occasional clearings for cornfields. Lieutenant George De Lacy Evans accompanied the scouts as they moved through the woods, covering the front and flanks and watching for an ambush.

Ross and Cockburn, near the front as usual, moved forward with the advance party, accompanied by a few officers. Among them was Ross's aide, Captain Duncan MacDougall and Captain Edward Crofton, commander of the naval brigade.

After they had ridden about two miles, Cockburn, by his later account, grew concerned that the advance guard was moving too far ahead, the "main force being at this time a very long way in the rear." He recalled raising the matter with Ross, who assured Cockburn he would not advance much farther before halting to allow the column to close. Soon afterward, the scouts at the front were surprised to run into an American skirmish line. The three American prisoners who had described the extensive defenses at Baltimore had said nothing about a militia brigade positioned just ahead.

The Americans opened up with sharp and unexpected fire. Cockburn and Ross saw the enemy posted at a turn of the road, extending into woods to their left. "[T]here was nothing left for it, but to dash forward against them, returning their fire, as quickly as possible," according to Cockburn's memoir. Two aides rode back to hurry on the main column.

Ross grew concerned as the fire continued and rode farther up to investigate. "He was upon all occasions the most forward, and upon the present occasion particularly so," Major Richard Gubbins, the acting commander of the 85th Light Infantry, wrote.

Reaching the crest of a knoll, Ross examined the American positions with a spyglass. The enemy seemed stronger than expected, and he was eager to bring up the column. Some four hundred yards to their front, Sergeant William Sannford, a courier accompanying Ross, spotted three Americans, one of them in a tree. Then Sannford saw the three men fire simultaneously in their direction.

Major Heath's skirmishers were no less surprised than the British to run into the enemy. After departing the American line, they had moved through a tangle of scrub pine, honeysuckle, and blackberry so thick that a small detachment of cavalry accompanying the task force quickly fell behind. The men had advanced a half mile ahead of Stricker's line when they discovered the British were no longer breakfasting at the Gorsuch farm. The enemy advance guard rose from the woods and poured fire onto the Americans.

Heath ordered Howard's Mechanical Volunteers at the front of the skirmish line to fire a volley. The Independent Blues followed with a second volley a few seconds later. Captain Levering had ordered his men to drop three buckshot down their barrels atop a musket ball; "buck and ball," as it was known, combined the lethality of a large-caliber ball with the spreading pattern of buckshot. "Take good aim, there's an officer," Levering said, by one account.

Aisquith's riflemen were also firing, arrayed in the tall grass and behind trees. An officer instructed several men to climb trees so they could see farther. Others braced their rifles on the boughs of trees looking for targets. By later accounts, the riflemen spotted one or more British officers on a knoll. "I see a mark," McComas is said to have called to Wells. "So do I," Wells replied.

The shot that hit Ross passed through his right arm and buried itself in his chest, likely breaking ribs and puncturing at least one lung. "My arm is broken," the general exclaimed. He collapsed from his horse, his fall broken by Captain Crofton, who gently lowered Ross to the ground with help from Captain MacDougall and other nearby officers.

A soldier ran to Cockburn, nearby on his horse, and asked if he knew the general had been shot. "No, it is impossible," the admiral replied. "I parted with him this moment." Cockburn rushed to Ross's side.

As Cockburn later described it, Ross had been "cantering to the rear to hurry up the column" when he was hit by one of the "last straggling shots" from the retreating Americans. Evans, however, recalled that Ross "was at the moment stationary and fronting the enemy" when shot.

From the start, accounts likewise varied about what had hit Ross. Cockburn and others called it a musket ball. Cochrane called it a "musket ball" in one official report and a "rifle ball" in another. Other British accounts called it a rifle shot, but an army officer with Ross later insisted the general's wound bore evidence of being from buck and ball.

There was no doubt, however, that the wound was devastating. Ross recognized this right away. "Send immediately for Colonel Brooke," he gasped. Evans took off at a gallop for the rear.

The shot that hit Ross passed through his right arm and buried itself in his chest, likely breaking ribs and puncturing at least one lung. "My arm is broken," the general exclaimed.

Death of Genl. Ross at Baltimore

The Light Brigade was nearing the front when Captain MacDougall galloped back, calling for a surgeon. Then the general's horse plunged through the woods riderless, its saddle stained with blood. "We all dreaded something was wrong, and our fears were too soon realized," Gleig wrote in his diary.

Private Aquila Randall, a twenty-four-year-old with the Mechanical Volunteers, might have been the first American to die in the defense of Baltimore. The British had recovered from their initial surprise and poured fire on the Americans, aiming at telltale puffs of smoke. Randall was killed near the spot where Ross had been hit. Another shot felled Lieutenant Gregorius Andre from the fence where he had been firing. His third sergeant, Alexander MacKensie, was hit and wounded, but Dr. Sam Martin managed to throw him on a horse and get him out.

With the arrival of the Light Brigade, Major Heath was completely outnumbered. "The greater part of one company fled immediately in great confusion," McHenry wrote. The rest kept up their fire, but Heath, whose own horse was shot dead from underneath him, was soon forced to order a retreat. The Americans "took to their heels in all directions," by Cockburn's account.

McComas, the rifleman with Aisquith's company, was still by the tree where he had fired and was reloading his rifle with the ramrod halfway down the barrel when he was shot through the chest. His friend Wells, close behind, was shot in the back of the head. Heath's men stumbled back to Stricker's line, exhausted from their brief but sharp engagement. Stricker wanted a fight, and now he had one.

Ross lay underneath an old oak tree on the side of the road, sheltered by a canopy of blankets. He had asked to be covered so the arriving troops would not recognize him and be disheartened, but none were fooled. "All eyes were turned upon him as we passed, and a sort of involuntary groan ran from rank to rank, from the front to the rear of the column," recalled Gleig.

Cockburn stayed at Ross's side while a surgeon bound his wound. As he was placed on a stretcher, Ross spoke to the admiral. "He assured me the wounds he had received in the performance of his duty to his country caused him not a pang, but he felt a lone anxiety for a wife and family dearer to him than his life," Cockburn reported. Ross handed the admiral a locket. "Give that to my dear wife, and tell her I commend her to my king and my country," he told Cockburn.

In the month since the general arrived in the Chesapeake, Ross and Cockburn had forged a close bond—"the friendship and confidence which existed between us to the last, having been most unreserved and complete," Cockburn would later write. He must have felt some responsibility for Ross's fate. The admiral's early and insistent advocacy for an attack on Baltimore had undoubtedly influenced the general, and Cockburn confessed to "heartfelt sorrow."

Two miles back, Evans found Brooke advancing with the main body. Evans "came galloping up to me, and told me, General Ross was wounded, and he feared mortally," Brooke recorded in his journal. The colonel rode as fast as he could to the front. When he arrived at Ross's side, the general was unable to give him any details on his plan of attack, but requested the colonel consult with Cockburn.

Recognizing his wound was mortal, Ross asked to be taken to the ships. A rocket wagon, the only vehicle available, was brought up, but the general waved it off. "Go on, you are more wanting in front," he told the artillery drivers. "He positively refused [transport] in a rocket wagon, declaring he would rather die on the spot than deprive his brave troops," according to an army report.

The columns of troops streaming forward parted to allow the stretcher-bearers through. "Genl. Ross was beloved by the whole army, most of whom shed tears as they saw him carried through the ranks," Royal Marine Lieutenant Benjamin Beynon wrote in his diary. An attendant followed, leading the general's horse.

The party transferred Ross into a horse and cart borrowed from a farmhouse en route, but the jolting ride down the road did the general no good. Ross lingered for two hours after his wounding. Before he died, he was taken from the cart and placed under the shade of a large poplar tree near the Gorsuch farm. Ross let out a final sigh. "Oh! My dear wife."

GODLEY WOOD, 2 P.M., MONDAY, SEPTEMBER 12

The fight was not going to wait. Arthur Brooke had been thrust into command at the start of battle. Like Ross, he was Anglo-Irish, the third son of a prominent Northern Ireland family with a long military tradition—it would later produce Alan Brooke, chief of the Imperial General Staff during World War II. The new commander was "perhaps, better calculated to lead a battalion, than to guide an army," George Gleig, an eighteen-year-old lieutenant at the time of the Battle of North Point, would later write, and the characterization has followed Brooke ever since. In fact, Brooke was a veteran, ambitious officer with more than twenty years' experience in the army, from Egypt to Sicily to Flanders, and he had commanded a brigade in the Peninsula under Wellington. Ross had entrusted him with independence at Bladensburg and at North Point. And Brooke did not hesitate now.

The Light Brigade, pursuing the routed militia skirmishers across open fields, soon ran headlong into a much larger American force—the City Brigade. Brooke, riding ahead of Cockburn, could see the Americans "drawn up in a very dense order" just inside thick woods at the edge of the fields, behind a sturdy wooden fence. "In this situation, [I] had but little time for thought, knowing nothing of the intentions of the General, and without a single person to consult with, I determined on an instant attack," Brooke wrote in his diary.

Brooke ordered his rockets and two six-pounder cannons to move forward and open fire, hoping to distract the Americans while he reconnoitered farther and waited for his remaining troops to arrive. The first British rockets flew over the militiamen's heads around 2:30 p.m., followed by cannon fire directed at the American artillery in the center. Major Heath's foray had stirred quite a hornet's nest, the Americans realized. "This advance seems to have awakened the whole British Army which immediately advanced, and attacked our line," Corporal McHenry wrote. Stricker responded with his own cannon fire, and a sharp artillery duel developed.

Meanwhile the Light Brigade wheeled expertly to the right across the American line, covering the front. "We lost no time in pushing the Light Brigade as close to them as possible," said Major Gubbins. Lying amid the grass and trees safely out of firearms range, the troops took what refreshment they could from their haversacks and canteens while the rest of the British force moved up.

Brooke, soon joined by Cockburn, surveyed the American line. It was a strong position, its flanks defended by creeks and marsh. The woods protecting the Americans were so thick that the British could see nothing beyond the double line of militia strung along the front. The British would have to cross the open fields of the Boulden farm to reach the Americans.

Brooke quickly grasped that his best prospects lay to his right. The Americans had left a gap of several hundred yards between their left flank and the bank of the Back River. Brooke ordered the 4th Foot to move through the swampy ground on the right, and try to turn the American left flank. The King's Own, as it was known, was one of the most ancient regiments in the British army, the badges on their shakos emblazoned with lions that denoted their royal status. Undetected at first, the men scurried through a hollow in the woods toward the enemy's left. The deep thunder of artillery fire shook the ground to their front, as the British poured barrages on the American left to cover the flanking movement.

The 44th Foot, bolstered by the Royal Marines and a contingent of seamen, took position behind the Light Brigade. The 21st Fusiliers remained in column on the road with orders to attack the American right, but were peppered by destructive grape shot as they waited. A British rocket fell short and landed on a haystack, igniting a fire that spread to surrounding stacks and farm buildings and produced billowing smoke between the opposing forces.

At 2:45 p.m., Brooke and Cockburn inspected the positions. Brooke and his staff galloped down the line, ensuring that all was ready. The admiral rode at a more leisurely pace along the line from left to right, a tempting target atop a white horse. The fire of the enemy guns seemed to follow him every step of the way.

"Look out, my lads, here is the Admiral coming, you'll have it directly," troops called sardonically. But Cockburn's show of defiance in the wake of Ross's death boosted spirits, "cheering the army on and showing himself in every place where danger was, even at the very muzzle of the enemy's guns," Corporal Brown wrote in his diary.

Across the front, Stricker rode behind the American line. Seeing the concentration of British fire on his left flank, he ordered the two regiments on his second line to shore up the line. The 39th Regiment took position to the far left, extending the American line, while the 51st Regiment was ordered to form a right angle at the end of the line, creating a square corner to protect the flank. The maneuver confused the untested 51st, and neither its commander, Lieutenant Colonel Henry Amey, nor his men understood what to do. Stricker's aides rushed to properly position the men, but the 925 men of Stricker's largest regiment were teetering before the real fighting had even started.

The King's Own was in place by 2:50 p.m., hiding in a thicket on the American left flank. The whole British force was ready. Brooke ordered a charge, and the call was relayed down the line by bugle and drum. "As soon as everything was ready, we sounded the advance and made a grand dash at them," Major Gubbins recalled. Lieutenant Evans took off his hat and cheered the troops forward. Across the front, thousands of red-coated troops sprang to their feet and moved forward in unison.

From the center of the American line, the guns of the Union Artillery let loose with a murderous barrage. Some fired grapeshot, while others were loaded with an equally deadly mix of scrap metal.

The British advanced through the shower of iron. As Gleig moved forward, his stuffed haversack swung low and caught a shot that would otherwise have hit his groin. "[I]t pounded the biscuit to powder but did not hurt me in the least," he wrote his mother. Even as fellow soldiers went down, the British troops did not break pace, moving within 150 yards of the American line. Until then, neither side had fired a musket, but upon orders the American militiamen leveled their firearms. A volley of fire rippled down the line from right to left, tearing into the British.

For the Americans, it was a heady experience. "The men took deliberate aim, and the carnage was great—the 'invincibles' dodging to the ground, and crawling in a bending posture, to avoid the militia," according to an account in *Niles' Weekly Register*. But while the British were ducking and diving, they were not stopping.

The King's Own moved through muck and swamp grass and suddenly appeared on the far left of the American flank. A creek stymied the advance, but the mere approach of the redcoats was enough to panic the wavering 51st Regiment. The men "fired one round at they knew not what, and they immediately fled," McHenry wrote his cousin. The fear spread to one of the battalions of the neighboring 39th Regiment, which also bolted. By the time the King's Own found a shallow point to cross, the entire 51st and half the 39th had disappeared into the thick woods.

Yet despite the collapse of the left flank, the rest of the American line held. On the American right, the battle-tested men of the 5th Maryland stood their ground against the column of Fusiliers, who suffered terribly from American artillery and musket fire. Lieutenant Furlong was the only Fusilier officer in his company to escape injury, and even so found a bullet in his black silk neck cloth. In the center, the 44th Foot met stiff resistance from the 27th Maryland. "Of the 5th, much was expected, but the 27th behaved at least as gallantly," *Niles'* reported.

Brooke could see terrible holes opening up in his line. The American fire "was so destructive, and thinning our ranks so much," he wrote in his diary.

Once again, the British rose to the occasion. "[W]e returned a hearty cheer, and giving them back a volley rushed on at double quick," Gleig wrote in his diary. Some did not make it far. Captain Robyns, leading the Royal Marines forward, tumbled to the ground, hit by a musket ball that passed through his left thigh. All around him men were falling.

Hoping to destroy the American force before it could escape, Brooke ordered the men to fire as they charged forward. This time, however, the American line held determinedly as the British advanced within twenty yards, only wavering as the gleaming steel bayonets drew near. Even Cockburn credited the Americans with a dogged stand. "[T]he enemy kept up without flinching till our army reached the palings and began to break over, and through them," the admiral recalled in his memoir of service.

Without its left wing, the 1,400 militia troops holding the front were outnumbered and in grave danger of being cut off. The British Light Brigade moved in on the abandoned ground, turning the American left and throwing them "into great confusion," Major Gubbins recalled. The King's Own, which had completed its flanking maneuver, was close behind.

As the British swarmed forward, Stricker at 3:45 p.m. ordered the line to retreat to the rear position held by the 6th Regiment at Cook's Tavern. The troops had held the British off for an hour, but now wasted no time falling back.

Cavalry, infantry, and artillery were jumbled together, looking for the best way out. Within fifteen minutes of the British charge, the Americans had been "utterly broken & dispersed," Brooke said. The militia abandoned two cannons, and left behind its dead and at least two dozen wounded. The British gave no quarter to several sharpshooters discovered hiding in trees, who "were shot from their perches at leisure," wrote Major Bowlby, with the King's Own.

The 5th Maryland brought up the American rear. Corporal McHenry carried out the regimental colors, and not a moment too soon, in his view. "Had not our company retreated at the time it did, we should have been cut off in two minutes," he wrote. As it was, nearly a third of his company had been killed, wounded, or taken prisoner. Every field officer in the regiment "received a touch," but all escaped serious harm; Lieutenant Colonel Sterett, the 5th Maryland commander, was hit in the arm by a spent musket ball. Major Heath had a second horse shot from under him and was briefly stunned by a ball that passed through his hat and bruised his head.

To the British, it looked like a rout; the Americans insisted it was an orderly retreat. Though bordering on panic, the American withdrawal possessed an order that had been entirely absent at Bladensburg. The City Brigade remained intact as a fighting unit, moving one mile to the rear and taking up a new position behind the 6th Regiment, nervously waiting at Cook's Tavern. The men "mostly rallied well," Stricker reported. *Niles'* was measured in its judgment: "They retired in better order than could have been expected under a galling fire."

PATAPSCO RIVER, AFTERNOON, MONDAY, SEPTEMBER 12

Admiral Cochrane anchored *Surprize* at 3:30 p.m. near the mouth of Bear Creek, four miles from Fort McHenry. All day, the fleet had continued its steady but laborious progress through the Patapsco mud shoals. The five bomb ships, key to the attack, were expected to reach Cochrane's position by evening; for safety reasons, they had been kept separate from the troopships and frigates while crews loaded them with munitions from tenders. The "bombs," as they were called, would be anchored for the evening out of range from the fort.

Cochrane trained a spyglass on the defensive line protecting Baltimore and could see the Americans hard at work throwing up earthworks. But from Cochrane's vantage point, the earthworks did not appear to extend any great distance, and in a note intended for General Ross he suggested that rather than launch a frontal assault, the army might be able to simply skirt the defenses. Cochrane worried over one development. "The enemy have been sinking ships across their harbor all day, and in front of the fort," he wrote. That meant the British ships would not be able to reach the inner harbor to bombard the town's defenses. They would first have to capture or destroy Fort McHenry.

Cochrane added a final message before sealing the note and sending it via boat up Bear Creek for delivery to Ross: "[A]t daylight we shall place the bombs and begin to bombard the fort."

METHODIST MEETING HOUSE, EVENING, MONDAY, SEPTEMBER 12

Though the Americans had only moved back one mile, Colonel Brooke soon gave up the chase. Rather than press his advantage against the retreating militia and move closer to Baltimore, still seven miles away, the British army commander stopped. Hungry, thirsty, and exhausted, the men were in no shape to continue the march, Brooke and Cockburn agreed.

But halting with hours of sunlight remaining meant the army would not be in position to attack Baltimore first thing the following morning. The caution reflected the fact that the British had been bloodied. As at Bladensburg, the attacking British had suffered more dearly than the Americans at North Point, with at least 46 dead and 295 wounded. The British grossly exaggerated American casualties, reporting hundreds dead or wounded and a thousand men taken prisoner. The 5th Maryland had been "nearly annihilated," Brooke claimed in his report to London. But in reality, the American toll was relatively light: 24 dead, 139 wounded, and 50 taken prisoner.

The British established their headquarters around the Methodist Meeting House, which had been abandoned by the Americans. The church was converted into a hospital treating wounded from both sides. "The temple of God—of peace and goodwill towards men—vibrated with the groans of the wounded and the dying," Scott wrote. A Methodist minister visiting the meeting house soon afterward described it as looking more like a slaughterhouse than a place of worship.

James H. McCulloh, Jr., a U.S. Army garrison surgeon who had received his medical degree two months earlier, ministered side by side with the British surgeons, who showed great "humanity" to the wounded Americans, he reported. McCulloh helped treat twenty-eight wounded Americans, two of whom died. The dead were consigned to hastily dug graves.

As Cockburn watered his horse at a pool below a wooded rise, a party of retreating Americans fired a volley, hitting several men and wounding the admiral's horse. "Oh you damned Yankee, I'll give it to you," Cockburn yelled, shaking his fist, but the men escaped.

PATAPSCO RIVER, EVENING, MONDAY, SEPTEMBER 12

General Ross's body arrived by the waterside early in the evening, wrapped in the Union Jack. Commander William Stanhope Badcock, captain of the frigate *Brune*, carried the general's body by boat to the warships anchored in the Chesapeake. The general was placed in a hogshead of Jamaican rum to preserve his remains for burial.

For Admiral Codrington aboard *Tonnant*, the "distressing tidings" about Ross rekindled his doubts about the wisdom of the attack on Baltimore. "He is a most severe loss to his country and to us at this most important juncture," Codrington wrote his wife. He added, "Heroism will do wonders certainly, and there is that still to look to; but, I believe there is too much on hand even for that, and I wish the job were well over."

Aboard *Surprize*, anchored upriver four miles from Baltimore, Cochrane received word of Ross's death at 7:30 p.m.; shortly afterward the letter he had sent to the general was returned unopened. Cochrane readdressed it to Colonel Brooke and penned a cover note. "The sad accounts of the death of General Ross has just reached me," Cochrane wrote Brooke.

With Ross gone, Cochrane's main concern was to make sure that Brooke understood Baltimore was to be destroyed. "It is proper for me to mention to you, that a system of retaliation was to be proceeded upon—in consequence of the barbarities committed in Canada," Cochrane wrote. The admiral had received a new letter from Sir Prevost, the British commander in Canada, reporting that American troops had burned and looted the village of St. David's in Ontario, and asking that Cochrane take "severe retribution" for the act.

"[I]f Genl. Ross had seen the second letter from Sir George Prevost he would have destroyed Washington and Georgetown," Cochrane informed Brooke. The plan to retaliate against Baltimore was "perfectly known to Rear Adl Cockburn and I believe Mr. Evans," Cochrane added. Brooke had some leeway to demand ransom instead of burning homes and other private property, though all public property should be destroyed.

Added Cochrane: "You will best be able to judge what can be attempted—but let me know your determination as soon as possible that I may act accordingly."

COOK'S TAVERN, EVENING, MONDAY, SEPTEMBER 12

General Stricker was relieved to find the British were not giving chase, and he was not inclined to wait for them to change their mind. The American commander feared his weary men could be turned by another enemy attack. Before sunset, Stricker ordered a further retreat, back to the defensive line protecting the city.

Samuel Smith had ordered Stricker to delay as long as feasible, not to hold at all cost. The City Brigade had accomplished its goals, and then some. They had slowed the British advance and inflicted significant casualties on the enemy. And most important, though the Americans did not yet know it, General Ross had been killed.

Still, the retreat had the taste of defeat—it carried a sickening similarity to the disaster at Bladensburg three weeks earlier. The fall of Baltimore, like Washington, appeared inevitable to many.

John Moore, a civilian riding into town in his two-wheel cart, encountered retreating 5th Maryland soldiers who told him the American army had been defeated. Moore took two wounded men in his gig, including one who had been shot through the thigh and another who looked close to death. Reaching the city, Moore found pandemonium. "Heavens, what a scene was exhibited here last evening!" Moore wrote the next morning to his pregnant wife, Elizabeth, who had fled town. "As I rode along with my wounded up the street, I was surrounded with crowds, clasping their hands together, writhing with agony, and uttering in loud exclamations their despair and grief." A nervous militia commander had ordered a ropewalk burned to prevent it from falling into British hands, and the black smoke drifting across the city only added to the despair.

At Fort McHenry, Major Armistead studied the approaching Royal Navy flotilla and feared an amphibious attack was imminent. "From the number of barges and the known situation of the enemy, I have not a doubt but that an assault will be made this night upon the fort," he wrote Smith at 4:30 p.m.

All day, booming cannon fire had reverberated from the Patapsco Neck, carrying to Baltimore and to the ships on the river, including the American truce ship, where Francis Scott Key heard "the sound of battle," he later said.

By midnight, the City Brigade had reached Worthington's Mill, just ahead of the defensive line at Hampstead Hill. The men spent a sleepless night, expecting a British attack at any time. Captain James Piper, a militia company commander, later recalled the wait: "Our guns were charged, our ammunition boxes replenished and our matches lighted & our eyes anxiously directed to the eastern hills & the main road leading from North Point, for hours expecting to see the enemy in full force to commence the onslaught."

METHODIST MEETING HOUSE, 12:30 A.M., TUESDAY, SEPTEMBER 13

Just after midnight, a torrential downpour began. At the British camp, the rain fell with such violence that the sodden troops, most lying in the open, spent much of the night trying to keep the firelocks of their muskets dry under their elbows. Some found sleep impossible, as agonizing cries from the wounded carried through the dark night.

At the Meeting House headquarters, Brooke reviewed plans with Lieutenant Evans and other officers. At 12:30 a.m., a messenger delivered Cochrane's note promising naval support. "[Y]our fire I should think on the town would be of infinite service to us," Brooke wrote in a hastily scribbled reply to the admiral.

Brooke also made clear in his note that he had no intention of sparing Baltimore. The army, he assured Cochrane, would move in the morning "to work our destruction."

"The hissing rockets and the fiery shells glittered in the air, threatening destruction as they fell," wrote Midshipman Barrett, aboard *Hebrus*.

Bombardment of Fort McHenry *by Alfred Jacob Miller.*

CHAPTER 15

★

The Rockets' Red Glare

A T DAWN, THE bomb ships *Devastation, Terror, Volcano, Aetna,* and *Meteor* maneuvered into place in the water off Fort McHenry, casting an appearance as ominous as their names. Another dozen ships, including the rocket ship *Erebus,* took their stations in close support, awaiting orders to begin the bombardment. Although the morning was hazy, soldiers at the fort had no trouble seeing the threatening warships, anchored in a half circle two miles out.

The low and squat bomb ships had none of the grace and grandeur of the ships-of-the-line and frigates. Yet the bombs were the most devastating siege artillery afloat. They carried a mix of enormous 10- and 13–inch mortars, capable of firing 200-pound explosive shells as far as two and a half miles. *Volcano* was armed with a particularly insidious bomb known as a carcass, a hollow shell filled with flammable ingredients—pitch, powder, sulfur, and saltpeter—perfectly designed to incinerate a city.

Cockburn was convinced Fort McHenry could not hold up to the punishment they would deliver. "[T]here is not a fort, from Norfolk to Baltimore that has a bombproof casement in it," he had assured Cochrane. Still, it had been a struggle to get the bomb ships. Cockburn had been asking for them since arriving in the Chesapeake in March 1813, and a year later, the Admiralty had only sent rocket ships, which he complained were "of no more to throw against a fort than a toasted biscuit would be."

But Cockburn's persistence had finally paid off, and the Admiralty sent the bomb ships. The last one, *Terror*, the newest and most advanced of its kind, had arrived in the Chesapeake just days earlier. Her addition meant that most of England's capability—five of the eight bomb ships in the Royal Navy—was anchored in the Patapsco. The fall of Fort McHenry seemed just a matter of time—probably no more than two hours, Cochrane boasted.

Fort McHenry guarded the water approach to Baltimore from the tip of Whetstone Point, where the Ferry Branch led to the west of the city, and the Northwest Branch led to the harbor.

Five bastions protruding from each corner of the pentagon-shaped structure gave the fortress its nickname: the Star Fort. The bastions, the fort's most recognizable feature, were designed to protect the all-important shoreline batteries, which served as its first line of defense against a land assault. The fort's brick walls surrounded a powder magazine, guardhouse, two enlisted men's barracks, and officers' quarters.

But by 1812, the fort had fallen into disrepair. The river had washed away the ground from beneath the lower battery, and the gun platform was gone. As the British threat grew in 1813, Samuel Smith rushed to make repairs, organizing gangs of militia and civilians to rebuild the batteries. The most important improvement came courtesy of onetime enemy France, which loaned the city fifty-six big naval guns from *L'Eole*, a man-of-war that had wrecked off the Virginia Capes in a storm a few years earlier.

Cockburn scouted the fort and harbor during a foray into the Patapsco in April 1813, learning much about Baltimore's defenses, including the French guns. But Smith made good use of Cockburn's visit to drum up support to improve the fort, using his clout in Washington and Baltimore to get the needed manpower and materials. He built two shore batteries and furnaces for heating shot, acquired gun barges, and set up river lookouts.

A three-gun battery was also constructed across the water from the fort at Lazaretto Point, home to a quarantine hospital for contagious fevers. Lazaretto gave the Americans the ability to lay a deadly cross-fire on any ships trying to approach the harbor. To protect against a landing via the Ferry Branch, two earthworks were thrown up along the shore west of Fort McHenry: Fort Babcock, which despite its name was little more than a four-foot-high earthwork, and Fort Covington, a more substantial fortification with ten-foot brick walls and a gun platform.

Major Armistead, taking command at Fort McHenry in the summer of 1813, found the undersized garrison consisted of less than half a company. Armistead bolstered its size, placing newspaper ads offering enlistment bounties of forty dollars and 160 acres of land in the western territories.

Armistead insisted on one other improvement soon after taking command. "We, Sir, are ready at Fort McHenry to defend Baltimore against invading by the enemy," Armistead, by one account, wrote Samuel Smith in June 1813. "That is to say, we are ready except that we have no suitable ensign to display over the Star Fort, and it is my desire to have a flag so large that the British will have no difficulty in seeing it from a distance."

The popular but unfounded story is that a delegation of officers including Armistead, Joshua Barney, and General Stricker called on Mary Pickersgill, a Baltimore flag maker, to request she sew two flags: a large garrison flag, measuring 30 feet high and 42 feet long, and a storm flag, smaller but respectably sized at 17 feet by 25 feet. The more prosaic truth is that they were likely requisitioned from Pickersgill by James Calhoun, the deputy quartermaster officer for the War Department in Baltimore.

However she came by her assignment, the thirty-eight-year-old Pickersgill had quite a job on her hands. Born in 1776 in Philadelphia, she

However she came by her assignment, the thirty-eight-year-old Pickersgill had quite a job on her hands. Born in 1776 in Philadelphia, she had flag making in her blood.

Photograph of Mary Pickersgill later in life.

had flag making in her blood. Mary's mother, Rebecca Young, had supported her family as a young widow by making flags, uniforms, and blankets for the Continental Army in Philadelphia, where her competitors included Betsy Ross. After her own husband died in 1805, Mary Pickersgill moved her family to the booming port of Baltimore, where she could expect steady business supplying the navy, merchants, and privateers with the colors and signal flags needed for communication on the water. Pickersgill ran the business from her brick home on Queen Street (now East Pratt Street), where she lived in the summer of 1813 with her mother, thirteen-year-old daughter Caroline, and three nieces.

Given the size of the flags and the speed with which the army wanted them, everyone in the household would have to work on it. Rebecca Young, who was seventy-three years old and ill at the time, may not have done much sewing, but she doubtless chimed in with advice. Two other women lived at the home: a female slave and a young African American indentured servant named Grace Wisher. They, too, would almost certainly have had a hand in creating what would become the nation's most enduring icon.

The garrison flag's size was not unusual for the time. Forts and ships often flew big flags to project power, and to make perfectly clear to both friend and foe who was in control. Armistead had a particular penchant for them, having ordered one measuring 36 feet by 48 feet a decade earlier while posted at Fort Niagara.

The flag was to have fifteen stars and fifteen stripes, as dictated by the regulations governing the second official version of the American flag. Two stars and two stripes for Kentucky and Vermont had been added to the thirteen representing the original states, and though three more states had since joined the union, they were not included, as Congress had not authorized further additions.

Pickersgill used some four hundred yards of top-quality bunting—worsted wool manufactured, ironically, in England. Each stripe had to be twenty-three inches wide, and as the bunting was woven in strips no wider than eighteen inches, two had to be painstakingly sewn together for each stripe. The blue for the union came from dye made of indigo; while red for the stripes came from madder with tin mordant. The fifteen white cotton stars, each measuring two feet from point to point, were cut from cotton cloth. Rather than sew stars on both sides, Pickersgill employed a reverse appliqué method, cutting holes through the blue bunting so they showed through, saving on fabric and weight.

The women worked in the upstairs bedroom, but when it was time to sew the stripes and the field together, the flag was too big for the house. Pickersgill received permission to use a nearby brewery, spreading the flag on the malt house floor, where the women sewed by sunlight during the day and candlelight by night. "I remember seeing my mother down on the floor, placing the stars," Caroline wrote many years later. "My mother worked many nights until 12 o'clock to complete it in the given time." Some six weeks and 350,000 hand-sewn stitches later, the flag was finished.

Pickersgill delivered the flags to Fort McHenry on August 19, 1813. For her labors, Pickersgill was paid $405.90 for the garrison flag and another $168.54 for the storm flag. Two seven-foot-long, hand-hewn oak timbers had been sunk in the fort's parade ground as supporting cross braces for the flagstaff that would carry the flag, which weighed at least fifty pounds. Pickersgill supervised the flag's placement, Caroline recalled, "having it fastened in the most secure manner to prevent it being torn away by [cannon] balls."

All along the shore around Fort McHenry, the final dispositions had been made, and the troops manning the garrison and batteries awaited the bombardment. Seasoned sailors were positioned at every critical point along the water. At Lazaretto, across from Fort McHenry, the three-gun battery of eighteen-pounders was manned by 45 flotillamen commanded by the veteran Lieutenant Solomon Frazier, who had led the escape of Barney's men from Pig Point after scuttling the flotilla. Along the Ferry Branch, six French eighteen-pounders were manned by 50 flotillamen led by Sailing Master John Webster, Barney's right-hand man at Bladensburg. Farther west, at Fort Covington, 50 of the best sailors from Rodgers's ship *Guerriere* waited with ten eighteen-pounders under the command of Lieutenant Henry Newcomb, one of Rodgers's most trusted officers.

A thousand troops were ready to defend Fort McHenry, including

300 men to service the thirty-six guns. The garrison included a company of army regulars from the U.S. Artillery Corps, and two companies of U.S. Sea Fencibles, federal units that manned coastal fortifications. Nicholson's Baltimore Fencibles and two companies of volunteer artillery from Baltimore augmented the garrison. Sixty flotillamen helped man the big guns on the river battery. Not least were four musicians from the U.S. Corps of Artillery, stationed behind the parapets of the water batteries, holding the critical role of sounding orders and keeping up morale. All four were young; the youngest, George Schellenberg, was just fifteen years old.

Some 600 infantrymen from four U.S. Army regiments were positioned in a dry moat that circled the fort, ready to meet the enemy should they land. Among them was Frederick Hall, a twenty-one-year-old slave who had escaped five months earlier from a tobacco plantation in Prince George's County. Hall signed up with the 38th U.S. Infantry in April under the alias of William Williams, receiving an enlistment bounty of fifty dollars and a private's wage of eight dollars a month. Though slaves were prohibited from enlisting, the officer who signed him up asked no questions, possibly because Hall's skin was "so fair as to show freckles," according to a notice published in May offering forty dollars for his return. In the anonymity of the army, Hall hoped to save his freedom by fighting for the preservation of the country that had allowed him to be enslaved.

A final boost to morale came in the form of Captain Oliver Hazard Perry, who pulled himself out of a sickbed to report for duty. Perry had been near collapse after the disappointing British escape past his guns at Indian Head. His physical constitution had been weakened from his service on Lake Erie a year earlier. "Perry, I am sorry to say, was so indisposed and worn out with the fatigue he had experienced on the Potomac" that he had been unable to take an active role in the defense of Baltimore, Rodgers reported to Jones.

But at the last minute Perry arrived "ready to render every assistance in his power," Rodgers added. Perry was determined to prevent the British from capturing USS *Java*, his nearly completed frigate, which presented a tempting target at Fells Point, its masts readily visible to the enemy. "I shall stay by my ship and take no part in the militia fight," Perry wrote a friend. "I expect to have to burn her."

PATAPSCO RIVER, 6:30 A.M., TUESDAY, SEPTEMBER 13

Volcano began the bombardment of Fort McHenry at 6:30 in the morning, lofting several shells to test the range. Each time the enormous four-ton mortars fired, the hull of the bomb ship was pushed two feet into the water. When the first shots fell short, the squadron moved to within a mile and a half of the fort. Cochrane, aboard *Surprize*, ordered all the ships to open fire.

A broadside from the small frigate *Cockchafer* shook the city and brought residents to their rooftops. "The firing at the fort has just commenced," John Moore wrote to his wife. "Don't wonder if my writing looks as if my hand trembles, for the house begins to shake."

Fort McHenry came under what Armistead called "an incessant and well directed bombardment." Private Severn Teakle, a volunteer with the Baltimore Independent Artillerists, was astonished at the firepower. "[F]rom such a rattling and whistle Good Lord forever deliver me," he wrote to his brother-in law.

Major Armistead mounted the parapet at the water battery and ordered the guns to return fire. "Then the whole fort let drive at them," reported Private Isaac Munroe, the newspaper editor serving with Nicholson's Fencibles. "We could see the shot strike the frigates in several instances, when every heart was gladden[ed], and we gave three cheers, the music playing Yankee Doodle."

Cochrane ordered the bombardment squadron moved back to a more circumspect distance of two miles, out of American range. But the bomb ships were still able to loft one shot after another into the fort. Private Schellenberg and the other musicians soon broke off the celebratory music.

The American guns kept firing, but now their shots did nothing but kick

"Four or five bombs were frequently in the air at a time, and, making a double explosion, with the noise of the *foolish* rockets and the firings of the fort, Lazaretto and our barges, created a horrible clatter," *Niles'* reported.

Bomb fired at Fort McHenry.

up spouts of water, falling well short of the British ships. The range of
the biggest guns at Fort McHenry was a mile and a half, no match for
the British mortars. This was no surprise to Armistead. Months earlier,
he had asked for larger mortars that could match the British range, but
Secretary of War Armstrong had turned him down on the grounds that
the French guns were sufficient.

To gain further distance, the fort's gun crews raised their barrels to
the maximum elevation and increased the powder to dangerous levels,
risking bursting a barrel, but it was to no avail. "[T]his was to me a
most distressing circumstance as it left us exposed to a constant and
tremendous shower of shells without the most remote possibility of
our doing him the slightest injury," Armistead reported.

Once the futility of fire became obvious, Armistead ordered his
crews to cease fire. Skeleton crews manned the guns, firing occasionally to show the fort was not giving up, but at Armistead's order, most
of the men took cover in the dry moat. There were no bomb shelters in
the fort, and soldiers resorted to digging slit trenches with their bayonets for extra cover.

Hundreds of shells and rockets had been fired by noon, landing at
the rate of more than one a minute. "Four or five bombs were frequently in the air at a time, and, making a double explosion, with the
noise of the *foolish* rockets and the firings of the fort, Lazaretto and
our barges, created a horrible clatter," *Niles'* reported.

Erebus fired incendiary rockets, which trailed smoke as they flew
wildly in the sky, but did little damage to the fort. "Harmless indeed,"
said Munroe. But the iron mortar shells, packed with up to twenty
pounds of powder, flew in high arcs that easily carried over the fort's
walls. Their wooden fuses, timed to explode immediately before or
upon landing, worked erratically, but many set off tremendous explosions. One shell crashed on the arched roof of the fort's magazine, a
brick vault packed with as many as three hundred powder barrels
stacked three tiers high. If it had exploded, the fort would likely have
been destroyed and the garrison decimated, but somehow, the shell did
not go off.

To lessen the chances of a catastrophic hit, Armistead ordered men
to remove the barrels from the magazine and place them behind the
fort's rear wall. Private Teakle survived a minor explosion as he rolled

out a barrel, receiving "no other damage than getting my pantaloons torn nearly off me," he wrote.

Most of the garrison kept relatively safe, but some were unlucky. Private Williams—the escaped slave, Frederick Hall—had his leg blown off by shrapnel. Another soldier, shaking uncontrollably after three mortars crashed into the fort in quick succession, took shelter under a gun carriage but was killed by a direct hit. The wife of a soldier, talking to her husband near the tents pitched outside the fort, "was cut in two pieces," a witness wrote.

Captain Joseph Nicholson's men stayed in place manning the guns at the bastions. Nicholson bluntly described the garrison's helplessness in a letter to James Monroe: "We were like pigeons tied by the legs to be shot at."

The lack of fire from Fort McHenry alarmed Francis Scott Key. But the stirring sight of the American flag streaming above the ramparts offered reassurance. As Key later told Roger Taney, the Americans aboard the truce ship "thought themselves fortunate in being anchored in a position which enabled them to see distinctly the flag of Fort McHenry from the deck of the vessel." The exact location of the truce ship has never been determined, and it is possible the vessel was moved over the course of the bombardment. One likely spot is near the mouth of Bear Creek, about two miles behind the bombardment squadron and four miles from the fort. From that distance, the flag would have been visible, particularly with a spyglass, which the sloop almost certainly would have carried.

For at least part of the attack, the truce ship may have been up front with the bombardment squadron, near Cochrane aboard *Surprize*. The vice admiral apparently wanted the American emissaries close at hand, believing they could help negotiate the fort's surrender. "[P]revious to the attack he asked Mr. Key, a lawyer from Georgetown who was on board the flag whether there was any person in the fort authorized to surrender," Private Teakle, who spoke to Skinner after the attack, wrote to his brother-in-law. A contemporary sketch of the bombardment by a Maryland militia officer watching from Hampstead Hill shows what appears to be the American truce ship positioned on the left edge of the bombardment squadron.

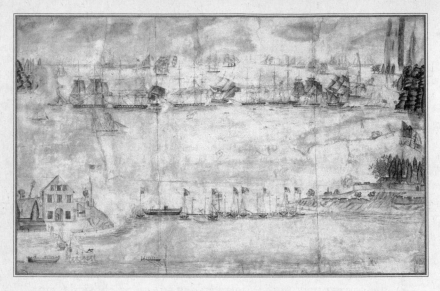

A sketch of the bombardment by a Maryland militia officer
watching from Hampstead Hill shows what appears to be the American
truce ship positioned on the left edge of the bombardment squadron.

Battle of Baltimore *by Lt. Henry Fisher of the*
27th Maryland Regiment.

Key's mood swung from despair to hope as the bombardment continued. His revulsion at Baltimore's pro-war riots in 1812 had left him
with the sinking fear that the city had earned a horrible fate. Yet many
people Key admired and loved were in the city—not least Nicholson,
married to Polly's eldest sister. "[Y]ou may imagine what a state of
anxiety I endured," Key wrote to John Randolph. "Sometimes when I
remembered it was there the declaration of this abominable war was
received with public rejoicings, I could not feel a hope that they would
escape, and again when I thought of the many faithful, whose piety
lessens that lump of wickedness, I could hardly feel a fear."

The thousands of troops nervously waiting in their rain-sopped
trenches along Hampstead Hill had a clear view of the punishment being inflicted upon Fort McHenry, about a mile and a half to

their southeast. General Smith and Captain Rodgers, who each had established headquarters on the hill to better coordinate the naval and land forces, watched anxiously through field glasses, in contact with the fort and shore batteries via messengers dashing back and forth through the shower of bombs and rockets.

Rodgers Bastion, at the top of the hill, had a mix of sixteen field and naval guns manned by 200 seamen. The Corps of Seamen, a hearty band of privateers under command of Captain George Stiles, anchored the Philadelphia Road with five eighteen-pounder field guns. Four smaller batteries running south to the harbor were under the command of navy officers from *Guerriere* and *Erie*. The 1st Regiment of Maryland Artillery was positioned to the north. At Gambles Redoubt, a convergence of roads where the brunt of the attack was expected, 170 marines were positioned.

The American firepower was heartening to the troops of the City Brigade, recuperating from their fight at Godley Wood. Private Levi Hollingsworth of the 5th Maryland had been painfully wounded in the left arm by a musket ball that passed between his elbow and hand, yet the battle left him encouraged. "I believe we handled them in a manner they little expected and I think they will be cautious in advancing on this place," Hollingsworth wrote Tuesday morning to his wife, Ann. "Today we look for them here, and I now for the first time entertain a hope that we shall be able to avert so awful a calamity as that of this city falling into their possession—an hour or two may determine."

KELL HOUSE, TUESDAY MORNING, SEPTEMBER 13

The British army moved at the first glimmer of dawn, with the light infantry leading the way as they advanced toward Baltimore along the North Point Road. Flanking parties, alert for ambush, were soaked moving through long grass and bushes wet with the night's rain, their progress was slowed by trees cut across the road by the retreating Americans. But by 9 a.m., the light troops spotted the American lines and halted.

An hour later, Brooke and Cockburn rode ahead to scout the position. From the upstairs windows of Judge Thomas Kell's house on a hill off the Philadelphia Road, the British commanders had a fine view of the entrenchments on Hampstead Hill, two miles away. The sight was both breathtaking and sobering. Hampstead Hill, which commanded the town, was covered with earthworks, artillery, and men—some 15,000 to 20,000 troops and 110 guns, the British estimated. The chain of redoubts, interspersed with bastions for crossfire, stretched for more than a mile. The British would have to charge up the hill across muddy ground that had been cleared of any building or trees that might provide cover.

Cockburn could not help regretting that the attack had not been made sooner. It was obvious that the Americans had put to good use the two weeks that had passed since the British returned to their ships on the Patuxent. Brooke was of the same mind. "[I]n short saw it was impossible to attack them," the colonel wrote in his diary.

But the commanders were hardly ready to give up. While the Light Brigade pushed out to form a line, Brooke and Cockburn reconnoitered the American line more closely, looking for a weak spot. Cochrane had suggested in his note that the defenses to the northwest were less formidable, and upon examination Brooke concluded they indeed "were in a very unfinished state." Around noon, he led his troops on a probe to the northwest, looking for a way around the earthworks.

But Samuel Smith, watching from the command post atop Hampstead Hill, countered by sending his reserve, including Stricker's City Brigade, to shadow the British. The American force took position between the Perry Hall and York roads defending the left flank. Seeing that Smith had forcefully countered the British move, Brooke broke off his probe.

The chess match continued. Early in the afternoon, Brooke massed his force before the center of the American line, forming a battlefront more than a mile long and two ranks deep. He advanced to within a mile of the entrenchments, driving back the American scouts. Though Brooke had no intention of assaulting the American lines in the daylight, he showed every sign of an immediate attack, hoping to throw Smith off balance. The American commander promptly prepared a counterattack, maneuvering his reserve into position to fall on the British right and rear should they advance.

Brooke had no choice but to hold his position and await dark. By now the British commanders had concluded that their best—and perhaps only—opportunity lay with a night attack. The American artillery would be of little use in the dark, and the militia would likely panic in the face of a bayonet by Wellington's Invincibles. The British column would penetrate the defenses and sweep down the American line, clearing the redoubts. But to do it, the army needed supporting fire from the Royal Navy on the southern end of the American line, to keep the big guns from turning their fire on the British infantry and to divert attention from the point of attack. Cockburn sent his aide, Lieutenant Scott, to request Admiral Cochrane's help for a 2 a.m. attack.

Settling down for the wait, some troops from the Light Brigade established an outpost at Surrey Farm, a fine mansion on the Philadelphia Road, a mile and a half from the American lines. The home, which had been left in the care of the butler and the cook, seemed disappointingly bare, with scarcely any provisions. Then a suspicious soldier, using the butt end of his musket to force aside some odd-looking bricks, let out a cry of joy, discovering a hastily disguised wine cellar filled with a magnificent array of bottles of every size and description.

Within five minutes the cellar was packed with men quaffing wine, filling haversacks, and handing out flasks of cognac and magnums of Bordeaux. Upstairs, the men helped themselves to bedding, candles, and whatever valuables they could find. To their great delight, they learned that the mansion belonged to the 5th Maryland commander, Lieutenant Colonel Joseph Sterett. Before departing, several officers left a cheeky thank-you note on the sideboard:

"Captains Brown Wilcocks and McNamara of the Light Brigade [and] Royal Marines met with everything they could wish for at this house. They return their thanks—notwithstanding this was received from the hands of the butler and in the *absence* of the colonel."

FORT MCHENRY, 2 P.M., TUESDAY, SEPTEMBER 13

By early afternoon, a nor'easter was bringing heavy showers and wind. At the southwest bastion, the men in Private Isaac Munroe's gun crew were soaked but at least relatively protected from British fire by the sunken rampart wall. The crew, from Captain Nicholson's company,

was under the command of Lieutenant Levi Claggett, a prosperous
flour merchant and investor in Baltimore's privateer trade. Thus far,
the gentlemen volunteers had held up with the same composure as the
regulars.

In the pouring rain, none of the men saw the bomb that slammed
directly into the southwest bastion at 2 p.m. Claggett was killed instantly, four other men were severely wounded, and a twenty-four-
pounder gun was knocked off its carriage. Before the stunned men
could respond, a second bomb burst over the bastion, directly over
Munroe's head. A piece of shrapnel the size of a silver dollar tore
through Sergeant John Clemm, who was next to Munroe, and plowed
two feet deep in the ground. Clemm, a flour merchant like Claggett
and "a young man of most amiable character, gentlemanly manners
and real courage," in Munroe's estimation, died on the spot. The survivors rushed to remove the wounded and remount the gun. The bustle
of activity "probably induced the enemy to suspect that we were in a
state of confusion," Armistead later surmised.

Cochrane sent pennants up the halyards of *Surprize* around 3 p.m.,
signaling the bomb ships and rocket ship to move closer. *Erebus* moved
especially close, within a mile. Armistead, recognizing that several ships
were now within striking distance, ordered his crews to resume firing.
"We immediately opened all the batterys on them," Teakle wrote.

For thirty minutes, a furious cannonade erupted back and forth.
"The balls now flew like hailstones," *Niles'* reported. *Volcano* was hit
five times, suffering one casualty, and *Devastation* took on water when
an American shot crashed into her port bow. Cochrane signaled his
ships to withdraw beyond reach of the American guns. The bomb ships
promptly retreated, but *Erebus*'s Captain David Bartholomew was
slow to respond, apparently eager to keep up the fight. Cochrane impatiently sent boats to tow the rocket ship out of range.

"We gave three cheers and again ceased firing," Armistead reported.
The bomb ships retreated to a safe distance and then petulantly resumed their fire, "more furiously than before," another officer reported.

★

The bombardment had been thus far decidedly disappointing, in Cochrane's view. The vice admiral had hoped for a repeat of Fort Washington, where the defenders immediately gave up. But it was clear that Fort McHenry would not capitulate easily.

Despite the vaunted power of the bomb ships and the huge volume of fire, the long-range shelling seemed to have had little effect. The pitch of the swells on the water, churning from the force of the bombardment and whipped up by the wind, made it difficult to aim the shells. The rain was becoming heavier and dousing the fuses, and many bombs failed to explode. Few buildings had suffered direct hits, and the garrison, scattered behind the sunken walls, held firm.

Mercurial as always and separated from the fleet's firebrands, Cochrane was now in favor of aborting the operation. Cockburn was ashore, and the more experienced captains were on other ships. If Cochrane had been with Gordon on *Seahorse* or Nourse on *Severn,* their spirit might have instilled vigor. But aboard *Surprize,* captained by his pampered son Thomas, Cochrane was quick to revert to his usual pessimism and indecision. The commanders of several small frigates volunteered to lighten their ships, sail within close range of the fort, and pulverize it with cannon fire. But Cochrane refused, fearing the fort's batteries would pound the frigates.

Cochrane had closely inspected the American defenses after the bombardment started. "I had now an opportunity of observing the strength and the preparations of the enemy," Cochrane later reported to his superiors. Even if the British could get past the heavy guns of Fort McHenry and Lazaretto guarding the mouth of the Northwest Branch, the entrance to the harbor was entirely obstructed by the merchant ships the Americans had sunk in the channel, as well as chains stretching from shore to shore, positioned along the water. As a final line of defense, eleven gun barges lurked behind the sunken hulks, manned by 340 sailors. Any attempt to push past the fort could be catastrophic for the squadron.

Cochrane's thoughts had already turned to the Gulf of Mexico. He had learned that another 7,000 troops were on their way to Jamaica to bolster his force in preparation for an attack on New Orleans, the key to the Mississippi. Keeping in mind the "ulterior operations of this force," Cochrane did not want to squander the force in a hopeless assault on Hampstead Hill.

At 9:30 a.m., just three hours after the bombardment started, Cochrane wrote a note to Cockburn warning that the fleet would be unable to directly support any attack by the army, and recommending that Brooke withdraw. But communication between the ships and the British army headquarters was dreadfully slow, involving miles of travel on the river, through woods and along back roads to the Kell House. By mid-afternoon, Cochrane's note had not been delivered, and it would be hours more before it arrived.

Likewise, it was not until 3:30 p.m. that an army officer delivered the note that Brooke had written to Cochrane some fifteen hours earlier. Reading it, Cochrane learned that the army commander was eagerly expecting naval fire in support of an attack. Moreover, Lieutenant Scott, Cockburn's aide, arrived in the afternoon with an update from the army headquarters. Scott, who delivered his message in good time thanks to a fortuitous boat ride, reported "the determination" of Cockburn and Brooke to attack the American lines at 2 a.m.

Cochrane faced a dilemma. He could not simply order Brooke to retreat. His instructions from London explicitly left command of land operations to the army. Moreover, given the hours it would take for his note to reach Cockburn and Brooke, and the hours more for a reply, Cochrane had no way of knowing whether Brooke would continue the attack. Cockburn, after all, had persuaded Ross to continue the attack on Washington against Cochrane's wishes. The same could happen at Baltimore. "[T]here was not sufficient time remaining for him to learn whether his advice would be followed, [so] he was obliged to proceed with his part of the plan," Skinner later wrote.

Cochrane was convinced a landing into the guns at Fort McHenry or Lazaretto was out of the question, meaning he was unable to reach the harbor for a direct assault on the American redoubts on Hampstead Hill.

But as an alternative, Cochrane decided to create a diversion. An attack on the more vulnerable Ferry Branch, which offered a back door to both the city and the fort, would perhaps give the army the distraction needed to attack the American line.

Early in the evening, Cockburn and Brooke returned to their headquarters at the Kell House, having reconnoitered the American lines
and positioned the British troops in preparation for their assault. The
commanders' spirits were buoyed by the discovery of a weak spot in
the American defenses. Brooke planned to follow the Philadelphia
Road toward the city and attack the American line at a bend where the
Hampstead Hill ridge fell back sharply. The curve of the land would
protect the British from the murderous crossfire they could expect if
they attacked head-on.

The rain fell in torrents, and what little visibility remained soon
faded almost entirely. Using the dark as cover, the British troops massed
into an assault column, waiting for the order to attack. The 85th Light
Infantry and the seamen would launch a bayonet assault, backed by
the 4th and 44th Foot. Once they penetrated, they would consolidate
and hold their position at the summit for the night. At first light, with
the hoped-for support of naval fire on the big American guns at the
southern end of the line, the troops would wheel down the inside of the
line, capturing the redoubts one by one. Cockburn was confident the
operation could be done "with a loss not exceeding five hundred men."

Cockburn pointed to Hampstead Hill. Before dawn, he boasted,
"all that you now see will be ours." But around 8 p.m., a messenger
arrived with the note Cochrane had written at 9:30 that morning.
Cockburn's face fell as he read.

"My dear Admiral," Cochrane began. "It is impossible for the ships
to render you any assistance—the town is so far retired within the
forts. It is for Colonel Brook [sic] to consider under such circumstances
whether he has force sufficient to defeat so large a number as it [is] said
the enemy has collected. . . . [I]t will be only throwing the men's lives
away and prevent us from going upon other services."

Cockburn handed Brooke the message. "This was a blow not easy
to explain," the stunned colonel wrote in his journal.

The army commander summoned his officers for a council of war
to consider whether to continue with the planned attack. The colonel
agonized over the choice. "If I took the place, I should have been the

greatest man in England," he wrote in his journal. "If I lost, my military character was gone for ever."

Neither Brooke nor Cockburn knew that subsequent to writing the note, Cochrane had devised a diversion as a substitute for a direct attack, and that it would soon be under way.

PATAPSCO RIVER, 10 P.M., TUESDAY, SEPTEMBER 13

"Black Charlie" Napier came aboard *Surprize* at 10 p.m. to receive his orders from Cochrane. Napier was known as a fighter—"his fire-eating qualities were even then fully understood," Chesterton later wrote. Napier's exploits from the West Indies to the Mediterranean had established him as an energetic and brave mariner, and a man quick to speak his mind regardless of the offense it might cause.

Black Charlie—the name came from his swarthy appearance and dark side-whiskers—had assembled a collection of twenty vessels, including barges, launches, gigs, a rocket boat, and a long schooner. A select force of several hundred seasoned seamen and Royal Marines were loaded on the boats.

Cochrane ordered Napier to take the force up the Ferry Branch. "This is intended to take off the attention of the enemy opposite to where our army [is], as an attack is to be made upon their lines directly at two o'clock," the admiral informed Napier. They were to row with muffled oars past Fort McHenry and continue a mile into the Ferry Branch, where they would anchor and "remain perfectly quiet." At exactly 1 a.m., Cochrane told the captain, the bomb ships would open up the fort and skyrockets would be fired. That would be the signal for Napier to open fire with a mix of regular ammunition and blank cartridges, trying to draw as much attention as possible until the army launched its surprise attack at 2 a.m. Once the army was seriously engaged, Napier and his men were to rejoin the bombardment squadron.

Their assignment was daunting. Napier's force would have to get past a line of sunken hulls that stretched across the Ferry Branch, all the while exposed to fire from Fort McHenry and Lazaretto. Beyond that, the British knew, at least one battery awaited in the Ferry Branch.

If they succeeded in making it through and launching the diversion, they might not make it out; every American gun in range would likely target them. Despite the steep odds, Napier was confident enough to bring scaling ladders, ready to exploit any breakthrough if they landed.

The barges took off around midnight. The black sky and heavy rain might work in Napier's favor. If the barges kept to the far side of the Ferry Branch, they might slip undetected past Fort McHenry and the batteries. But the night presented its own problems to the British. Napier soon discovered more than half his force had vanished in the inky darkness. A string of eleven boats became disoriented, rowing toward Lazaretto; by the time they realized their mistake it was too late, and they rowed back to the bombardment squadron.

Napier waited a while to see if the boats would turn up, but then continued without them. The nine remaining boats, with just 128 men, found a gap in the line of sunken hulks and slipped undetected past Fort McHenry.

BRITISH ARMY HEADQUARTERS, MIDNIGHT, WEDNESDAY, SEPTEMBER 14

At the Kell House, Colonel Brooke's deliberations continued for hours. Every officer in his council of war agreed the assault would succeed, according to George De Lacy Evans, but three senior officers thought it improper to attack in the face of Cochrane's opposition.

Brooke's confidence had been shattered by the withdrawal of Cochrane's support, and he was now plagued with doubts about the wisdom of the operation. He wrote in his journal that he had perhaps been "presumptuous" to say he could capture the hill "without great loss," given he only had 4,000 men. The humiliated Brooke viewed Cochrane's message as a stinging vote of no confidence.

Cockburn's initial impulse was to attack. He strongly urged Brooke to continue and offered to take full responsibility. The admiral reminded Brooke that Cochrane had no authority over the land forces, and he assured the colonel that his seamen were eager to charge the lines. But even Cockburn had second thoughts as he digested the full implications of Cochrane's message.

Cochrane's language made clear that Brooke—and by extension

Cockburn—would be held responsible if the plan to attack New Orleans was harmed. "[T]he onus . . . was to be thrown upon" him and Brooke, Cockburn observed in his memoir of service. Given the state of defenses of Hampstead Hill, it was impossible to argue convincingly that the Americans were unprepared, as had been the case in Washington. Brooke and Cockburn had hoped for naval fire on the big American guns nearest the harbor. But Cochrane had made clear no such help was coming. The two commanders felt "obliged to abandon this attempt," Cockburn noted.

At midnight, Brooke addressed a curt note to Cochrane: "[T]hough I had made all my arrangements for attacking the enemy," he and his staff agreed Cochrane's decision had placed him in a "situation" where it was best he should retire. "I have therefore ordered the retreat to take place tomorrow morning."

FERRY BRANCH, EARLY MORNING, WEDNESDAY, SEPTEMBER 14

Miserable in the cold, driving rain, the flotillamen manning the six guns at Fort Babcock drew their clothes closer around their chilled bodies. They were, at least, safely out of range of the shells. But around 1 a.m., Sailing Master John Adams Webster noticed that the British bombardment squadron was firing "with redoubled energy" at Fort McHenry. "[T]he lurid glare from the bursting bombs revealed momentary glimpses of the enemy's fleet, standing in bold relief against the dark, somber background," Webster recalled years later.

Around that time, troops on both sides watched a bright blue flare ascend into the sky, briefly illuminating the dark river below. It was a Royal Navy signal rocket, meant to alert the army that a diversion was under way.

Webster sensed something might be in the works. He ordered the guns double-shotted with eighteen-pound balls and grapeshot. Then he took a blanket and lay down atop the earth breastwork, trying to rest. Though only twenty-seven, Webster knew how to stay calm in such situations. The young, powerfully built Marylander had served aboard *Rossie* on Barney's legendary privateering run in 1812, and had fought alongside the commodore at Bladensburg, barely escaping after his hat was shot off.

Webster was half asleep when he heard splashing. It sounded like oars. Peering out in the water, Webster could make out several gleaming lights, perhaps two hundred yards offshore. He felt sure it was the British barges. Webster rushed to the guns and examined the priming mechanisms, making sure the powder had stayed dry in the pouring rain. "All being well I trained the guns and then opened on them," he said. The battery thundered with a torrent of well-directed fire at the barges. At nearby Fort Covington, Lieutenant Newcomb also spotted the lights on the water and opened fire at about the same time.

Napier's raiders ceased rowing and, with hearty cheers, opened fire with their bow guns, rockets, and eighteen-pounder cannon, aiming at the red glare of the American guns. A fierce firefight was soon under way. Cannon shots slammed into Fort Covington, but most of the British shells and rockets went high, thudding into the hill and doing little damage.

Webster likewise guided his fire by the flashes of light from the British guns. Soon his men could hear the shrieks of wounded men in the barges.

As the diversion continued, the bomb ships opened up on Fort McHenry with unmatched fury. "The hissing rockets and the fiery shells glittered in the air, threatening destruction as they fell," wrote Midshipman Barrett, aboard *Hebrus*.

From the roofs of houses and atop Federal Hill in Baltimore, residents watched "the whole awful spectacle of shot and shells and rockets, shooting and bursting through the air," wrote a correspondent for the *Salem Gazette*. A man climbed to the roof of the Holliday Street Theater, one of the tallest buildings in town, and reported on the fight to anxious crowds below.

The ground was shaking at Fells Point, where terrifying rumors swept through the streets that the British had taken the fort and were on the way to the city. Rev. John Baxley, the Methodist minister, was awakened by the furor at 1 a.m. "Such a terrible roar of cannon and mortars I never heard before, and never wish to hear again," he wrote in his diary. Fearing the British had landed, Baxley woke his entire family and had them ready to flee.

The night "will never be erased from my memory," John Moore, watching from his roof, wrote to his wife. "The portals of hell appeared to have been thrown open—the earth and air, nay all the elements, seem to have been combined for the destruction of man."

PATAPSCO RIVER, EARLY MORNING, WEDNESDAY, SEPTEMBER 14

From the deck of the truce ship, Key and Skinner watched each shell and rocket from the moment it was fired, following the red trace of fire high through the sky until it fell, and then listening anxiously for its explosion. The Americans saw the blue signal rocket, so memorable and ominous, but were uncertain as to its meaning. The bursting shells and flaring rockets illuminated the air above. Sheets of rain were accompanied by terrific flashes of lightning and rumbles of thunder.

Earlier, in the twilight, Key had seen an American flag still flying over Fort McHenry. In keeping with military practice given the tempestuous weather, the storm flag would likely have been flying. The garrison flag was too big to fly in such a raging storm; the weight of such a large, sopping-wet wool flag might snap the flagpole.

Once night fell, Key could no longer see the flag. He paced the deck, surrounded by a hostile fleet and held against his will, as the assault on Fort McHenry reached ever-higher levels of ferocity. Yet, he recalled many years later, his step was firm and his heart strong. The bombardment was proof enough that the fort had not surrendered.

BRITISH ARMY HEADQUARTERS, EARLY MORNING, WEDNESDAY,
    SEPTEMBER 14

The British troops facing Hampstead Hill remained in assault position for hours, expecting the order to attack at any moment, unaware they would soon be retreating. The tremendous cannonading was at once thrilling and terrifying to Corporal David Brown with the 21st Fusiliers. "It was the most wonderful night I ever spent in my life," he wrote in his memoir. "The rain fell in torrents. The roaring of the thunder and the tremendous flashing of lightning was truly awful; at the same time, being within musket shot of the enemy, made it such as I never had experienced before—it was most dreadful."

Brooke, like everyone else, watched and listened to the sound and fury of Napier's valiant diversion. Whether the colonel was tempted to change his mind and order an attack, he never said. Yet it must have been agonizing.

At 3 a.m., the men were ordered to fall in; Corporal Brown, like many others, expected the order to attack had at last arrived. Instead, the men soon realized to their shock that they were marching away from Baltimore. "I cannot express the discontent and murmuring that every soldier felt when he found they were to retreat, though every man knew it was to be a great saving of their lives," he wrote.

Some blamed the Royal Navy, others Brooke. "It was the universal belief throughout our little army, that had General Ross survived, Baltimore would have been in our possession within two hours of our arrival at the foot of [the] Hill," one man wrote.

But others made little secret of their relief.

FERRY BRANCH, EARLY MORNING, WEDNESDAY, SEPTEMBER 14

Black Charlie was still fighting, determined to give the army its chance. Napier's diversion had succeeded in at least drawing American fire. Armistead and Rodgers were convinced the British were trying to land troops and storm the fort. But Samuel Smith was not budging, showing no intention of abandoning the trenches of Hampstead Hill to defend the Ferry Branch.

Napier looked toward the hill, but he could see no sign of the expected army attack on the American line. After several hours, he finally ordered the barges to retreat. To get to the ships, they had to run a gauntlet of fire past Fort McHenry.

The Fort McHenry crews spotted the barges and were delighted to finally have a target. "We once more had an opportunity of opening our batteries and kept up a continued blaze for nearly two hours," reported Armistead. The gun barges and battery at Lazaretto joined in for good measure, catching the barges in a crescent of American fire. One barge flipped over and bodies were strewn in the river. Teakle heard cries for help. "By God, they'll blow us out of the water," a man called.

Finally, the barges pulled out of range, and the American guns fell silent. The British bomb ships had likewise ceased fire, allowing Napier's men to pass back in safety.

"All was for sometime still," *Niles'* reported, "and the silence was awful."

O say can you see ~~through the~~ by the dawn's early
what so proudly we hail'd at the twilight's last gleaming,
whose broad stripes & bright stars through the perilous fight
O'er the ramparts we watch'd, were so gallantly streaming
    And the rocket's red glare, the bomb bursting
    Gave proof through the night that our flag was still
O say does that star spangled banner yet wave
    O'er the land of the free & the home of the brave?

On the shore dimly seen through the mists of the
    where the foe's haughty host in dread silence
what is that which the breeze, o'er the towering
Its so fitfully blows, half conceals, half discloses
        Now it catches the gleam of the morning's first
        In full glory reflected now shines on the stre
Tis the star-spangled ~~banner~~ O long may it
    O'er the land of the free & the home of the bra

And where is that band who so vauntingly swo
    That the havoc of war & the battle's confusion
A home & a Country should leave us no more
~~_____~~
        Their blood has wash'd out their foul footste
No refuge could save the hireling & slave
    From the terror of flight or the gloom of the g
And the star-spangled banner in triumph doth w
    O'er the land of the free & the home of the bra

O thus be it ever when freemen shall stand
    Between their lov'd home & the war's desolation
Blest with vict'ry & peace may the heav'n rescued
    Praise the power that hath made & preserv'd us a
        Then conquer we must, when our cause it is
        And this be our motto—"In God is our trust"
And the star-spangled banner in triumph shall wave
    O'er the land of the free & the home of the brave

"I hope I shall never cease to feel the warmest gratitude when I think of this most merciful deliverance," Key wrote.

Dawn's Early Light, *by Edward Percy Moran, circa 1912.*
Francis Scott Key, aboard truce ship, gestures toward the
American flag flying above Fort McHenry.

CHAPTER 16

★

Does That Star-Spangled
Banner Yet Wave?

THE QUIET WAS terrible for Francis Scott Key and the other Americans watching and listening from the deck of the truce ship. Had the attack been abandoned, or had Fort McHenry surrendered?

In the predawn blackness, the bomb ships resumed a sporadic fire, but with none of the fury of the night, and the Americans were unsure what to make of it. They had no communication during the night with the enemy ships surrounding them, and the Royal Marine guards aboard the truce ship knew no more than they did. The storm had finally passed, but it remained cloudy and misty.

Key and Skinner paced the deck in painful suspense, anxiously awaiting the return of day, looking every few minutes at their watches. Finally, the first pale signs of dawn brightened the sky. Even before there was light enough to see distant objects, they trained their glasses on the fort, as Key later told Taney, "uncertain whether they should see there the stars and stripes, or the flag of the enemy."

Through the morning mist, "on the shore dimly seen," Key would write, the Americans finally could make out a flag, towering over the grassy knoll of the ramparts. But the banner hung limply from the flagpole, and it was impossible to tell if it was American or British.

As the morning lightened, a slight breeze blew fitfully from the northeast, scattering the mist. The flag stirred with a tantalizing hint, but Key and Skinner remained unsure. Finally a beam of sun illuminated the flag, revealing it to be American. "Through the clouds of war, the stars of that banner still shone," Key later said.

He was overcome with relief. "I hope I shall never cease to feel the warmest gratitude when I think of this most merciful deliverance," Key wrote soon afterward to John Randolph. "It seems to have given me a higher idea of the 'forbearance, long-suffering and tender mercy' of God than I had ever before conceived."

FORT McHENRY, MORNING, WEDNESDAY, SEPTEMBER 14

Soon after sunrise, the bombardment of Fort McHenry halted. Aboard *Surprize*, Cochrane at 7 a.m. signaled the bombardment squadron to withdraw. There was no point in further fire. Captain Napier had returned with the remaining barges, and the fort clearly was not surrendering. The bomb ships and rocket ship set sail by 9 a.m., and the rest of the squadron followed soon afterward.

From Baltimore, the drained residents watched the ships depart. "The work of destruction, intended by the enemy, they have failed to carry into execution, and they are now all standing under sail and appear to be going down the river," John Moore wrote his wife. Fort McHenry was reported not to have suffered "any great injury." Some residents hurried to the fort to see for themselves. Rev. Baxley arrived at 8 a.m. with warm coffee and refreshments—"greatly reviving to the men, who had been standing in the mud and wet for a number of hours," he recalled.

The bombardment had lasted twenty-five hours with two brief intermissions. Armistead calculated—and ships logs verify—that some 1,500 to 1,800 shells had been fired at the fort. The five bomb ships alone fired some 133 tons of shells during the bombardment. "[A] few of these fell short, a large proportion burst over us, throwing their fragments among us and threatening destruction, many passed over, and about four hundred fell within the works," Armistead reported. The British had also fired 700 to 800 rockets. Yet the casualties had been astonishingly light. Only 4 of the fort's garrison had been killed, and 24 wounded. Some of the wounds were severe; Frederick Hall, the escaped slave who lost a leg, died two months later in a Baltimore hospital.

At 9 a.m., the Fort McHenry garrison stood at attention as the storm flag was lowered, and the great banner was raised in its place. The ceremony was performed every morning at that time, in keeping with regulations, but there was no denying the special resonance it held this day.

An "ear-piercing fife and spirit-stirring drum" carried through the air, courtesy of George Schellenberg and the other U.S. Corps of Artillery musicians. "At this time our morning gun was fired, the flag hoisted, Yankee Doodle played, and we all appeared in full view of a formidable and mortified enemy," Private Munroe wrote.

The sailors of the retreating British fleet were mortified indeed. "In truth it was a galling spectacle for British seamen to behold," wrote Midshipman Robert Barrett, aboard *Hebrus*. "And as the last vessel spread her canvas to the wind, the Americans hoisted a most superb and splendid ensign on their battery, and fired at the same time a gun of defiance."

Hampstead Hill, morning, Wednesday, September 14

Only as morning dawned did the American forces entrenched on Hampstead Hill realize that the British army was no longer perched on their doorstep. American scouts moved forward to find empty British camps with untended fires still burning, as well as abandoned cartridges, powder, slaughtered cattle, and even some swords, evidence of a hurried departure in the dark.

Some of Smith's subordinates urged an attack on the retreating enemy. But Smith refused, fearing the British withdrawal was a trick to lure him out of the trenches. Though the bombardment squadron was pulling back from Fort McHenry, the British fleet remained in the Patapsco. The fight in the Ferry Branch was over, but perhaps the British were preparing to test the city's defenses elsewhere.

Smith would only consent to sending General Winder with a brigade of Virginia militia accompanied by cavalry to follow the British. Stricker and the City Brigade were eager for the assignment, but Smith wanted them close at hand. Some grumbled that Smith was allowing the British to escape unmolested, and the pursuit was indeed lackluster. "All the troops were however so worn out with . . . being under arms during three days & nights exposed the greater part of the time to very inclement weather that it was found impracticable to do any thing more than pick up a few stragglers," Smith said.

British prisoners reported that Ross had been mortally wounded. Captain Rodgers was confident the day had been won, and the enemy "severely drubbed." But Smith remained cautious, ordering his commanders to keep the men ready to march at a moment's warning. "The enemy have retired not departed," Smith wrote in his general orders. "Their retiring may be a stratagem to throw us off our guard."

MEETING HOUSE, MORNING, WEDNESDAY, SEPTEMBER 14

Colonel Brooke fervently wished the Americans would attack. With forlorn visions of glory, the British commander halted his army at 7 a.m. at the Methodist Meeting House, hoping the enemy would pursue and give him a last chance at victory.

Cockburn was under no such illusions and used the time to arrange a prisoner exchange. Many of the British wounded who had been left at the Meeting House after the battle were in no shape to be carried to the ships. James McCulloh, the young U.S. Army surgeon helping treat the wounded at the makeshift hospital, was the senior American present and agreed to exchange the wounded British for American prisoners captured at Bladensburg.

Cockburn candidly told the surgeon that the British were departing. At the nearby headwaters of Bear Creek, McCulloh soon saw the British loading those wounded able to travel onto small boats, to bring them to the ships ahead of the retreating army.

AMERICAN TRUCE SHIP, PATAPSCO RIVER, MORNING, WEDNESDAY, SEPTEMBER 14

Key and Skinner watched from the truce ship's deck as the morning lightened, their hopes soaring at every sign of British retreat. The bombardment squadron sullenly sailed downriver. A stream of small boats came down Bear Creek, carrying wounded British soldiers and Royal Marines. From their numbers and condition, Key concluded they had been "roughly handled." Looking toward Baltimore, Key could see the big garrison flag flying defiantly over the ramparts at Fort McHenry.

Inspiration, Key told Roger Taney, came "in the fervor of the moment, when he saw the enemy hastily retreating to their ships." For a man who had spent his life scribbling poems and verse for every occasion, it was a natural impulse. "[I]n that hour of deliverance, and joyful triumph, the heart spoke," Key recalled many years later. "Does not such a country, and such defenders of their country, deserve a song?"

Key pulled a letter from his pocket and wrote some notes on the back. "With it came an inspiration not to be resisted," he said, "and if it had been a hanging matter to make a song [I] must have made it."

GODLEY WOOD, LATE MORNING, WEDNESDAY, SEPTEMBER 14

After waiting in vain for three hours to see if the Americans would follow, the British army continued its grim retreat to North Point. Brooke sent word to Cochrane that the army would reach the landing beach by the following morning, and he requested the boats be ready to load the men.

Passing through the Godley Wood battlefield, the troops were greeted by the ghastly sight of Americans hanging lifeless in tree branches. Other corpses lay on the ground "bleached as white as snow" after two days of rain and heat. British soldiers who had died from their wounds lay along the roadside. "Putting all together it was a shocking sight to see," recalled Corporal Brown, with the 21st Fusiliers. The melancholy only grew around noon, when they passed the spot where Ross had been shot.

As the rear guard moved from the thick woods into a clearing, the troops heard a crackle of musket fire from behind. The Americans were reportedly on their heels. Bugles sounded and the troops expertly wheeled into line, but it was only a few American horsemen, reconnoitering the British departure.

The frustrated British resorted to name-calling: "What! You are not satisfied, Jonathan, aren't you! You want another dose! . . . Come along then, you beggars! We are all ready for you." One sailor, "burning to meet the enemy," jumped a fence "and rushed singly towards the enemy, uttering nautical defiance," recalled Chesterton. An officer dragged him back to British lines with a "few well-applied strokes" from his scabbard.

Two straggling seamen from *Tonnant* had their chance at revenge when an American hiding in a tree fired a rifle shot through the hat of one of the sailors, grazing his ear. When the sailors drew their pistols on the American, he begged for mercy. "Devil burn me if I do," replied one of the seamen. "It was just such a [fellow] as you, killed our general."

The sailors each took a shot at the American. "They both misfired, and then agreed that as they had their turn, it would not be fair play to kill the fellow," Midshipman John Bluett wrote in his diary. "They therefore made him come down, and drawing their cutlasses placed him between them and marched him arm to arm into the camp."

GODLEY WOOD, AFTERNOON, WEDNESDAY, SEPTEMBER 14

As the British withdrew, parties of Americans moved through the battlefield, collecting the dead. Farmers brought two wagonloads of corpses to a camp, where the bodies, grotesquely swollen from the heat, were laid in a ring. Families came from town searching for husbands, sons, and brothers. A woman gazed at a disemboweled corpse. "My God, there is the body of my dear husband," she cried. Militia Captain Sam Dewees stayed only a short while. "I cleared myself, for I could not endure the heart-rending cries of the women," he recalled.

Sometime after midday, Private Henri Dukehart of the 5th Maryland found the bodies of Daniel Wells and Henry McComas where they had fallen, a few paces apart. William McComas, Henry's brother, never forgot the terrible walk along the North Point road back to Baltimore, following the two-wheeled cart carrying the bodies. Henry's long legs hung over the edge, swinging in a macabre dance all the way home.

Over time, the story grew that Wells and McComas were the ones who felled Ross with their rifles. In 1851, their bodies would be exhumed, laid in state for three days, and taken in a procession to Ashland Square in Baltimore, where they were reburied and a twenty-one-foot-tall obelisk monument eventually constructed. Wells and McComas were in the right spot and may indeed have shot Ross. But it is also plausible that the general was killed by a musket shot fired by an unknown militiaman with the Mechanical Volunteers or the Independent Blues.

The debate would never end. What could not be disputed was that Wells and McComas died at the start of their lives, defending their city from an enemy invasion. They would remain, as Baltimore native H. L. Mencken wrote more than a century after their deaths, "two imperishable heroes in the shape of a pair of Baltimore boys."

WASHINGTON, AFTERNOON, WEDNESDAY, SEPTEMBER 14

News from Baltimore had been slow to arrive in the capital. Reports were received that militia had marched from the city to meet the invading army, but little more was known. "The moment of suspense is awful," the *Intelligencer* wrote Wednesday.

But late in the day, a messenger arrived with a brief note for Secretary of War Monroe from Major General Samuel Smith at his Hampstead Hill headquarters, written at 10 a.m. "Sir," Smith began, "I have the honor of informing you, that the enemy, after an unsuccessful attempt both by land and water on this place, appear to be retiring." Smith added that all the British vessels in the Patapsco could be seen going down the river. "I have good reason to believe that General Ross is mortally wounded," Smith concluded.

The *Intelligencer* rushed the letter into print under an exultant headline: HUZZA FOR BALTIMORE!

NORTH POINT, THURSDAY, SEPTEMBER 15

There were no cheers when the British army arrived at the North Point beach. The brigades moved down one by one to the water's edge, boarding boats to carry them out to the ships.

The ships crews were shocked by the condition of the injured troops. "Sad, sad wounds, some of them," wrote Captain Robert Rowley, commander of the troopship *Melpomene*. "I have 18 poor creatures on board—doing as well as can be expected."

Cots were slung for the wounded aboard *Hebrus*, and the whole half deck of the man-of-war was transformed into a hospital. Midshipman Barrett, serving as mate of the main deck, was haunted by the "piteous groans" of the blanched-faced soldiers. Two or three died and their bodies were slipped into the water.

Still anchored off North Point, every ship crackled with heated debate about the decision to retreat from Baltimore. The story of Admiral Cochrane's message, which effectively forced retreat, had spread through the fleet.

"The failure of our attempt upon Baltimore has caused much talk amongst us," Major Gubbins, the commander of the 85th Light Infantry, wrote to a friend from aboard HMS *Diadem*. "[M]any think that the Navy should, even with the heavy loss they might have sustained, have stormed the Fort—others think the troops should have gone on notwithstanding the Admiral's advice and want of assistance." Gubbins believed the army could have broken through anywhere it attacked, "but whether we could have maintained ourselves with an inferior force, or attempted the destruction of the town without the assistance of our men-of-war I cannot pretend to say."

Aboard *Severn*, Cockburn wrote his official report to Cochrane. It had been the vice admiral's message, Cockburn pointedly noted, that "induced" Brooke to break off the army's attack. As for Cochrane's failed attack on Fort McHenry, Cockburn wrote coolly, "As you Sir were in person with the advanced frigates, sloops, and bomb ships, and as from the road the Army took I did not see them after quitting the beach, it would be superfluous for me to make any report to you respecting them."

As the fleet prepared to withdraw from the Patapsco on Friday, a wet, tempestuous day, a message from Cochrane was read congratulating the men for "the decisive victory" over a larger enemy force. The admiral's words seemed directed at the intense discontent that prevailed aboard the ships: "[T]he best proofs of steady and cool bravery are a scrupulous obedience of orders & a strict attention to discipline." Few were mollified, and spirits were low as they sailed toward the bay.

"I regret we ever returned up the Chesapeake again," Rowley wrote in a letter Thursday, "but it was so fated."

PATAPSCO RIVER, FRIDAY, SEPTEMBER 16

The American truce ship remained in British custody, anchored with the fleet off North Point. The American delegation and crew would be set free when all "the troopers were on board, and the fleet ready to sail," Key was informed.

Skinner sought fruitlessly to get a list of American prisoners who had been taken to the ships. "After the attack here, as Mr. Key can explain, there was such a state of hurry and bustle that we could scarcely obtain decent attention to any application," Skinner reported to General Mason in Washington. After repeated requests, Skinner was given an incomplete list of eighty-nine prisoners along with a promise to send the rest of the names later.

Dispensing with the usual salutations when he saw Skinner, Cockburn readily acknowledged the attack had failed: "Ah, Mr. Skinner, if it had not been for the sinking of those ships across the channel, with the wind and tide we had in our favor, we should have taken the town; as it was, we flurried you, any how."

By late Friday afternoon, the British had finished loading their ships, and Key, Skinner, Beanes, and the American crew were told they were free. As the truce ship sailed toward Baltimore that evening, Key worked on his composition. He was writing a song, not a poem. Later, the myth would take hold that Key's words were adapted to song by an alert singer who noticed that the words coincidentally matched "To Anacreon in Heaven," a well-known tune of the day. Yet the evidence is clear that Key had that tune in mind from the start.

Written in London around the time of the American Revolution, "Anacreon" was an old American standard by 1814. It is often referred to dismissively as "a drinking song," a misleading label. The Anacreontic Society was a popular and convivial gentleman's club in London named after the sixth-century B.C. Greek poet Anacreon, whose verse celebrated the joys of wine and women.

The society's meetings, usually at the Crown and Anchor Tavern in the Strand, often featured a concert with some of the best performers in London. After the music, an elegant supper was served, and then all members would join in singing lighthearted songs. The first song was always the club's constitutional song, "To Anacreon in Heaven," whose words had been written by the club president, Ralph Tomlinson, a London attorney.

> To Anacreon in Heav'n, where he sat if full glee
> A few sons of harmony sent a petition,
> That he their inspirer and patron would be;
> When this answer arrived from the Jolly Old Grecian
> "Voice, Fiddle and Flute, no longer be mute,
> I'll lend you my Name and inspire you to boot,
> And, besides, I'll instruct you like me to entwine
> The Myrtle of Venus with Bacchus's Vine."

Music to accompany the four verses was written around 1775 by another member of the society, John Stafford Smith, an accomplished organist, tenor singer, and composer from Gloucester, England, who composed a great deal of secular and sacred music. The society members, many of them proud of their musical abilities, wanted a song that would both challenge and show off their vocal range, and "Anacreon" fit the bill.

The song's popularity soon spread across the Atlantic, where various Anacreontic societies were established—including one in Baltimore. Songwriters continually adapted new words to the melody, and by 1814, no fewer than eighty-five versions had been published in the United States. The most famous was Robert Treat Paine, Jr.'s "Adams and Liberty," a rousing patriotic number written in 1798 that became the most popular political song of the era, sung around the country.

There is no doubt Key was quite familiar with the melody. He had used the tune for a song he had written nine years earlier saluting Navy Lieutenant Stephen Decatur for his heroism during the first Barbary War. At Tripoli harbor in February 1804, Decatur boarded the captured USS *Philadelphia* with U.S. Marines, set fire to the ship, and escaped under a hail of fire. Lord Nelson called the raid "the most bold and daring act of the age," and Decatur was celebrated across America.

Key viewed it as not only a triumph against pirates, but also a victory of Christianity over Islam. When a dinner party was thrown in Georgetown on November 30, 1805, in honor of Decatur, Key wrote a song for the occasion. Titled "When the Warrior Returns from the Battle Afar," it was sung to the tune of "Anacreon."

> When the warrior returns, from the battle afar
> To the home and the country he has nobly defended
> Oh, warm be the welcome to gladden his ear
> And loud be the joys that his peril has ended!
> In the full tide of song, let his fame roll along
> To the feast flowing board let us gratefully throng
> Where mixed with the olive the laurel shall wave
> And form a bright wreath for the brow of the brave

The third verse included this couplet:

> And pale beamed the Crescent, its splendor obscured,
> By the light of the star-spangled flag of our nation.

The song was printed in several newspapers, including the Boston *Independent Chronicle*. Though inferior to the song that would follow nine years later, *Warrior* contains the unmistakable genesis of "The Star-Spangled Banner," showing metric agreement and similar phrasing. It guided Key as he composed his new song.

FELLS POINT, 9 P.M., FRIDAY, SEPTEMBER 16

Darkness was approaching as the American truce ship sailed past Fort McHenry and carefully maneuvered through the obstacles blocking the mouth of the channel. Sometime between 8 and 9 p.m., the ship glided into Hughes Wharf at Fells Point. Word of the ship's arrival quickly spread in Baltimore, eager for any news from the British fleet.

At 9 p.m., a correspondent for the *True American and Commercial Advertiser* sent a hasty dispatch via stagecoach to the newspaper's office in Philadelphia: "A flag of truce has just arrived from the enemy's fleet, which had gone down before the late bombardment, bringing a list of the prisoners taken at the battle of the meeting-house," he wrote.

"The flag officer states that they intend to send them to Halifax—many of them are the most respectable citizens of this place. All is now quiet in this city, though no one doubts but that we shall have another bout with the enemy."

Reporters gathered around Skinner, Key, and Beanes. Skinner told one correspondent that the British had lost at least five hundred men, as well as a barge sunk in the Ferry Branch attack. Beanes reported that the British were "much disappointed in not being able to carry Baltimore." Key told a correspondent with the Philadelphia *Political and Commercial Register* that British officers spoke of repairing their ships at their island base in the Chesapeake and then sailing to Halifax. "But he believed this to be far from their intention," the paper added ominously.

Once the excitement died, Key took lodging a few blocks away at the Indian Queen Tavern, at the corner of Market and Hanover streets. That night in his room, he picked up a pen and paper to write his song longhand. The notes written on the back of the letter served as the basis for much of his composition. But for some of the lines, as he told Taney, "he was obliged to rely altogether on his memory."

"O say can you see through"—Key paused here, scratched out "through" and substituted "by," and then continued: "the dawn's early light." The verse, when completed, asked one long question:

> O say can you see by the dawn's early light
> What so proudly we hail'd at the twilight's last gleaming
> Whose broad stripes & bright stars through the perilous
> fight
> O'er the ramparts we watched were so gallantly streaming
> And the rocket's red glare, the bombs bursting in air
> Gave proof through the night that our flag was still there
> O say does that star spangled banner yet wave
> O'er the land of the free & the home of the brave?

The question mark at the end of the verse, Mencken later noted, is essential to understanding Key's meaning, revealing "the poet is not at all sure that the Republic will survive." The second verse carries the answer, describing the tension at dawn as Key and his companions tried to make out what flag was flying:

> On the shore dimly seen through the mists of the deep,
> Where the foe's haughty host in dread silence reposes,
> What is that which the breeze, o'er the towering steep
> As it fitfully blows, half conceal, half discloses?
> Now it catches the gleam of the morning's first beam
> In full glory reflected now shines in the stream,
> Tis the star-spangled banner, O! long may it wave
> O'er the land of the free and the home of the brave

In the third verse, Key's disgust with the British spilled out, and his language took on uncharacteristically angry and vengeful tones, reflecting the emotion of the moment.

> And where is that band who so vauntingly swore
> That the havoc of war and the battle's confusion,
> A home and a country, shall leave us no more?
> Their blood has washed out their foul footsteps pollution
> No refuge could save their hireling and slave,
> From the terror of flight or the gloom of the grave
> And the star-spangled banner in triumph doth wave
> O'er the land of the free & the home of the brave

"Hireling" apparently refers to professional British soldiers fighting for money, unlike the American volunteers. Key's use of "slave" may be a reference to the Colonial Marines; an ironic choice of words if so, as the escaped slaves were fighting for their freedom.

Key took a more pious tone with his fourth verse. His song was ultimately a hymn, a prayer of thanks to God for saving the city, and this is most evident in the final verse.

> O thus be it ever when freemen shall stand
> Between their lov'd home & the war's desolation;
> Blest with vict'ry and peace, may they heav'n rescued land
> Praise the power that hath made and preserved us a nation!

Then conquer we must, when our cause it is just,
And this be our motto—"In God is our trust."
And the star-spangled banner in triumph shall wave
O'er the land of the free & the home of the brave.

The four verses filled a single piece of paper, though Key had to write compactly to make the last one fit. He may have thrown out his notes from the truce ship, as they have never been located.

Key had no way of knowing that in a single night, he had written what would become the United States' national anthem, as well as coined a motto for the nation: "In God We Trust." Yet before he fell asleep, he must have felt satisfied.

BALTIMORE, MORNING, SATURDAY, SEPTEMBER 17

When Skinner called on Key the following morning at the Indian Queen, the attorney showed him the composition. Skinner was impressed—it captured the long night and the coming of dawn perfectly. The song, he later said, "was but a versified and almost literal transcript of our expressed hopes and apprehensions, through that ever memorable period of anxiety to all, but never of despair."

Key was anxious to see how Nicholson had weathered the bombardment. The judge had only returned home from the fort the night before. It had been a chaotic several days at the fort, still on the alert for another British attack. Major Armistead was exhausted after days of stress. His wife had given birth to a daughter on Thursday, September 15, one day after the bombardment ended. That evening, Armistead collapsed with fever brought on by fatigue and exposure. Nicholson sent word Friday warning that Armistead was "in a high state of delirium," and Samuel Smith placed Captain Rodgers in charge of Fort McHenry.

After arriving at the Nicholson home on Saturday, Key presented his composition to the judge. Two of the volunteers Nicholson had enlisted to fight with his company—Lieutenant Claggett and Sergeant Clemm—were dead, and several more were severely wounded. The emotional Nicholson was anguished at the loss, and reading Key's words, profoundly moved. "[Y]ou may easily imagine the feelings with which, at such a moment, he read it," Tancy later wrote. Nicholson wanted the song shared with the public.

Key apparently gave permission, but did not stay long. "I . . . was obliged to leave Baltimore immediately," he would soon write to John Randolph, apologizing that he did not have time to visit Randolph's brother, who lived in the city. Anxious to reunite with his family, Key made arrangements to travel to Frederick.

Either Nicholson or Skinner—or possibly the two working together—took the composition to the office of *Baltimore American and Commercial Daily Advertiser* that day to be set as a handbill. The *American*, like other newspapers in Baltimore, had shut down during the attack. Thomas Murphy, the *American*'s master printer, served with Aisquith's sharpshooters, but he had been granted leave to reopen the *American*'s office, and the shorthanded paper had resumed sporadic publication.

When Key's composition was brought in, apprentice Samuel Sands was minding the office. "I was the only one . . . who was on hand," Sands recalled many years later. The fourteen-year-old Sands, too young to serve with the militia, had divided his time during the invasion between watching the shop and visiting friends in the trenches on Hampstead Hill.

Sands, possibly with the help of Murphy, set up the print for the handbill, painstakingly fishing out the letters, a task that likely would have taken several hours. Once it was finished, one or more galley proofs were struck, and then at least one thousand handbills printed.

The song carried the title "Defence of Fort M'Henry"—a bit unimaginative, perhaps, but entirely appropriate from the perspective of Nicholson, who apparently gave it the name. The judge likely also wrote the introduction that appeared above the song, which described the circumstances that placed an unnamed "gentleman" on a mission to gain the release of a friend held captive by the British. "He watched the flag at the Fort through the whole day with an anxiety that can be better felt than described, until the night prevented him from seeing it," the introduction read. "In the night he watched the bomb shells, and at early dawn his eye was again greeted by the proudly waving flag of his country."

Key's name did not appear on the handbill. Given Nicholson's affection for Key, the omission would likely have been at Key's request, perhaps out of modesty or embarrassment.

Hundreds of copies of "Defence of Fort M'Henry" were delivered to the fort, probably at the behest of Nicholson, and it was quite popular with the garrison. Private Teakle, with the Baltimore Independent Artillerists, wrote to his brother-in-law, "We have a song composed by Mr. Key of G. Town which was presented to every individual in the fort in a separate sheet. . . ."

The song, by Taney's account, was soon "all over town, and hailed with enthusiasm."

At least one printed copy made it into Key's hands before he left town Saturday. He likely rode the mail coach to Frederick, forty-five miles to the west, on a road that took him past fields where farmers sowed their fall wheat and rye, and through a familiar rolling landscape as he approached the hills of home.

Once in Frederick, Key hurried to the small brick house where his sister Anne lived with Roger Taney. "We had heard nothing from him . . . and we were becoming uneasy about him, when, to our great joy, he made his appearance at my house, on his way to join his family," Taney recalled.

After a happy reunion, Key told his sister and brother-in-law of the momentous events he had witnessed—the sail to find the enemy fleet, and gaining the release of Dr. Beanes, only to be detained by the British. "He proceeded then with much animation to describe the scene on the night of the bombardment," Taney recalled. "He then told me that, under the excitement of the time, he had written a song, and handed me a printed copy."

Taney read the handbill and was astonished at the composition's elegance. "I asked him how he found time, in the scenes he had been passing through, to compose such a song?" Taney recalled. Key described the song's creation and modestly mentioned that he "believed it to have been favorably received by the Baltimore public."

Before long, Key borrowed a horse for the last twenty miles of his journey, riding up the old road leading to Terra Rubra and then up the driveway to the grand columned home, where his parents, wife, and six children waited. Overjoyed to be back with his family, Key apparently gave the song little more thought.

FORT McHENRY, SUNDAY, SEPTEMBER 18

At noon Sunday, the guns of Fort McHenry fired once more. News had arrived in Baltimore the previous day from Captain Thomas Macdonough of his "signal victory" over a British fleet on Lake Champlain, and the concurrent defeat of Sir Prevost's army at Plattsburgh, New York. The powerful British force, invading New York from Quebec, had been repulsed. The American triumph, one of the most decisive of the war, had been fought September 11—coincidentally, just as the British prepared to land at North Point.

Together with the British reversal at Baltimore, the American victories represented a stunning turnaround for British fortunes in North America. "The invincibles of Wellington are found to be vincible, and are melting away by repeated defeats," William Wirt, a prominent Virginia legislator and attorney, wrote to his wife. "A few more such repulses as they met at Baltimore . . . and we shall have a peace on terms honorable to us."

General Samuel Smith ordered the defenders of Baltimore to fire a federal salute in honor of the victory in the north. Atop Hampstead Hill, gunners at Rodgers Bastion set off their cannons in answer to the guns of Fort McHenry, and the guns at Forts Covington and Babcock followed last.

Despite the good news from near and far, Baltimore was a nervous town. Many expected another British attack at any time. "Some say the enemy has gone down the bay—others, that he has received a reinforcement—but the most correct opinion, I believe, is that he still lays round North Point, and is preparing for the fatal blow he means to give this place," John Moore wrote to his wife Saturday.

In taking command of Fort McHenry, Captain Rodgers had extracted a promise from Smith that he would only stay as long as the enemy was in sight. Despite the fears of others, the eternally optimistic Rodgers felt sure it would not be long, and he was soon proven right.

Even before the thunderous salute had ended Sunday, scarcely any

British ships remained in sight. "The last of the enemy's ships are passing the mouth of the river standing down the bay with a fresh wind from the NW," Rodgers promptly reported to Navy Secretary Jones.

"I have now the pleasure to inform you that the last ships got under way this morning and are sailing down the Bay—never I hope to return," Private David Winchester wrote to his brother James. "Where they will next make their appearance God knows—This is a day of great exultation to Baltimore."

Chesapeake Bay, Sunday, September 18

The British doubtless could hear the thunderous salute from Fort McHenry as they sailed away from Baltimore and moved down the Chesapeake. Aboard *Tonnant*, Vice Admiral Alexander Cochrane put the finishing touches on dispatches for London. In his official report, the admiral painted as positive a picture as he could of the Baltimore operation, terming it "a demonstration" that had "fully accomplished" its goals. The British threat had forced the city to sink ships and destroy a ropewalk, sent civilians fleeing, and diverted forces from across the region to Baltimore.

But in a private letter to the Admiralty, Cochrane emphasized that the attack was made "contrary to my opinion," and he admitted the whole affair was a mistake. "I now exceedingly regret my deviation from my original plan," Cochrane wrote. With a few thousand more troops, Cochrane lamented, Baltimore would have been "either laid in ashes or under a heavy contribution."

Aboard *Albion*, Cockburn wrote a regretful letter for Captain MacDougall, Ross's aide, to carry to the general's older brother, Rev. Thomas Ross, at Clifton in Bristol, England, where Elizabeth Ross was waiting. "Having had the honor of accompanying your gallant brother General Ross in all his late active and brilliant achievements against our insidious enemy in this country . . . I consider myself particularly called upon to trouble you with this letter to inform you of the melancholy and unfortunate event which has deprived me of a friend and our country of one of its best and bravest soldiers," Cockburn wrote. He asked that Elizabeth Ross be told "how anxious I shall always be to prove the real friendship I bore her husband. . . ."

★

Late in the afternoon, the fleet anchored in familiar waters off the mouth of the Patuxent. From here, the fleet would split up. Cochrane would sail aboard *Tonnant* to Halifax and hurry the construction of flat-bottomed boats needed to attack New Orleans via the shallow bayous and lakes protecting the city. Cockburn would sail to Bermuda with *Albion*, which badly needed repairs before any further operations. Rear Admiral Malcolm, aboard *Royal Oak*, would sail in the morning toward the Potomac with several frigates, bomb ships, and troopships, keeping a reduced British presence in the Chesapeake.

A final piece of business demanded attention before the ships sailed. Two seamen held in chains—James Crosby of *Tonnant* and Michael Welch of *Weser*—were found guilty by court-martial on Sunday of attempting to desert to the enemy. "[T]wo wretches . . . have been condemned and will suffer tomorrow," Cochrane noted in his report.

At daylight Monday, with the fleet anchored below Drum Point, work ceased on the ships and every sailor in the fleet witnessed "the awful execution," recalled Midshipman Barrett. While the bodies dangled in the air from the yardarm of *Weser*, officers aboard each ship read an admonition from Cochrane warning of "the necessity of a strict attention to discipline."

With that, the mighty British fleet in the Chesapeake dissipated.

WASHINGTON, MONDAY, SEPTEMBER 19

Congress reconvened in Washington on the morning of September 19, assembling in the Patent Office, the only government building left untouched by the British. Though the three-story building at 8th and E streets filled nearly a block, "every spot up to the fireplace and windows" was filled by legislators and spectators. "[T]he galleries (if they deserve that title) were so crowded, that it was utterly impossible for me to get even a view of the hall," wrote one visitor, J. Stith.

Tempers flared in the hot and cramped quarters. Representative Willis Alston of North Carolina pushed Alexander Contee Hanson, the *Federalist* newspaper publisher, who responded by giving Alston "a pretty severe whipping," according to Stith.

Many of the arriving congressmen had passed along the turnpike through Bladensburg, where they were horrified by the sights and stench from the battle three weeks earlier. Along the road where the British had charged Barney's guns, the ditches were filled with corpses, their forms still visible, hardly covered with earth. "The hogs root them up, and the waters wash them up, they are covering them up daily again," Senator Robert Henry Goldsborough of Maryland wrote to his wife.

The sight of Washington was no less mortifying. "The City of Washington once very beautiful to my eye is now an odious miserable object," wrote Goldsborough, a Federalist. "It is the dreadful monument of an unfortunate and illy timed war, and the unerring evidence of a weak, incompetent and disgraced administration."

The President's House remained an empty shell, its white exterior walls scarred by "great licks of soot" rising from the windows. "The rooms which you saw so richly furnished, exhibited nothing but un-roofed naked walls, cracked, defaced and blackened with fire," William Wirt wrote his wife. "I cannot tell you what I felt as I walked amongst them." Laborers under the guidance of "French John" Sioussat had shoveled through the thick bed of ashes and rubble in the basement, salvaging some iron pots and the iron range from the kitchen, but finding little else of value.

The Capitol was "a most magnificent ruin," architect Benjamin Latrobe later wrote. A story circulating among the arriving legislators held that Cockburn had mounted the Speaker's chair in the grand House chamber and addressed the gathered soldiers and sailors. "Shall this harbor of Yankee democracy be burned?" Cockburn had supposedly asked. "All for it will say aye." Pronouncing that the measure had carried unanimously, the tale went, the admiral had ordered the Capitol burned. Such was Cockburn's reputation that many believed it.

Congress was meeting in Washington at the insistence of Madison, who had called the session before the capture of Washington. Fears ran high of another attack, with the British still lurking in the Chesapeake, and there was little confidence in the administration's ability to defend the capital. Some had suggested that Congress meet in a less precarious location. But Madison had refused. He had ordered the Patent Office prepared to house Congress.

The Madisons, at least, had nice accommodations. They had moved from the Cutts home into the Octagon, after French minister Louis Sérurier offered to vacate the mansion. The president "excused himself at first, but in such a fashion as to make me insist, and he finally accepted it," Sérurier reported to Talleyrand, the French minister of foreign affairs. It was "the best house in the city," by Sérurier's estimation, and the rent was accordingly high—more than $110 a month.

The Treasury occupied the former home of the British minister; the War Department took space in a building next to the Bank of Metropolis; the Navy Department was in a Mr. Mechlin's house near the West Market; and the General Post Office occupied yet another private home. Few were happy with the arrangements, and many legislators were ready to abandon the city altogether.

Several cities had offered to host the capital. Philadelphia wanted to lure the government back and promised comfortable accommodations for the president. Georgetown, eager to gain an edge on its neighbor Washington, offered the use of Georgetown College as well as board for congressman at ten dollars per week, instead of the sixteen dollars charged in Washington. Baltimore, New York, and Lancaster, Pennsylvania, were suggested, and even Cincinnati and Baton Rouge mentioned. The House soon appointed a committee to study the temporary removal of the government from Washington. While all of New England supported the move, Virginia, Maryland, and all the southern states protested vehemently, fearing it would lead to a permanent move of the capital north.

Regardless of where they met, Congress and the Madison administration faced a financial and political crisis unprecedented in the country's history. After Washington's fall, banks from New York and the South were refusing to redeem paper money for coins. The refusal to raise taxes to pay for the conflict had left the Treasury without enough money to fund the war, or even to meet interest payments on the national debt. The government had only half the money needed to pay war costs in 1814, and none on hand to pay for 1815, reported Treasury Secretary Campbell, who was in such feeble health and so "humbled" by the crisis that he promptly resigned.

Another blow came from Navy Secretary Jones, who had served the president more ably and loyally than any other member of the cabinet.

Disastrous business dealings in Europe had left Jones deeply in debt, and he had warned the president in April that he might have to resign. Now, hounded by creditors, Jones could wait no longer. On September 11, he tendered his resignation, though he agreed to serve until December. Jones was ashamed at abandoning the president during this moment of crisis, but believed he had no choice. "My own afflictions are rendered still more poignant by the contemplation of the savage warfare now waging against our beloved country," Jones told Madison. To his wife, Eleanor, Jones expressed sympathy for his successor, whoever that would be: "Instead of a wreath of laurels he has a much greater chance of acquiring a crown of thorns."

Everyone was eager to assign blame for the loss of Washington. "Each one now knows how the memorable battle of Bladensburg ought to have been conducted and had he commanded things would not be as they are at this day," government surveyor Seth Pease wrote to a friend.

"Every ignorant booby is sporting his opinion on the combat at Washington," Colonel Allen McLane, an aide to Winder, wrote to the general, who was a particular object of derision. Winder "ought to be hung & would b[e in] any other country," Captain Bacon, the U.S. Marine quartermaster, wrote another officer. James Monroe wrote a "private and confidential" letter to Winder advising him to immediately report to Washington. "The tempest of dissatisfaction at the late events here, rages with great fever, and among others against you," Monroe wrote. "An enquiry into the causes of the disaster will probably be set on foot." The House established a committee of inquiry—comprised of members supportive of the administration—to investigate the fall of Washington.

On Tuesday, September 20, the president addressed Congress. It was no moment of glory for Madison. Yet the very act of meeting in Washington served as notice that the British attack on Washington had failed in its most important goal of forcing the collapse of the American government. Moreover, the news from Baltimore and Lake Champlain allowed Madison to take a victorious tone that would have been unimaginable even a week earlier.

The enemy, the president warned, "is aiming, with his undivided force, a deadly blow at our growing prosperity, perhaps at our national existence." But the capture of Washington, Madison predicted, would unite the nation in a new way against the British. "The American people will face it with the undaunted spirit which, in their revolutionary struggle, defeated his unrighteous projects," Madison declared. "His threats and his barbarities, instead of dismay, will kindle in every bosom an indignation not to be extinguished, but in the disaster and expulsion of such cruel invaders."

BALTIMORE, EVENING, TUESDAY, SEPTEMBER 20

The *Baltimore Patriot* was exultant when it resumed publication on Tuesday evening for the first time since the British fleet appeared before the city ten days earlier. "[H]ow nobly is the fame of our country rescued!" the paper declared. "How is the flame which was bust forth at *Lexington*, and blazed in perfect brightness at *Yorktown*, rekindled!"

The *Patriot* used the occasion to print "Defence of Fort M'Henry" at the top left of the first column on page 2. "The following beautiful and animating effusion, which is destined long to outlast the occasion, and outlive the impulse, which produced it, has already been extensively circulated," the *Patriot* editor informed readers in an unusually prescient introduction. "In our first renewal of publication, we rejoice in an opportunity to enliven the sketch of an exploit, so illustrious, with strains, which so fitly celebrate it."

John Skinner later took responsibility for the song's appearance in the newspaper, writing that he "passed it on to the Baltimore *Patriot* and through it to immortality." Skinner may have done so, though as the newspaper noted, the song was already all over town, and the *Patriot* might have acquired it from any number of sources.

The *Baltimore American*, though it had printed the handbill on September 17 and had published a newspaper edition on the morning of September 20, had missed the chance to scoop the *Patriot,* its great rival. After the *Patriot* appeared, the *American* apparently changed its mind about the song's worth and published it the next morning, though without an effusive introduction. Both the *American* and the *Patriot* circulated widely along the Atlantic seaboard, and the song soon appeared in many eastern cities.

The *Mercantile Advertiser* in New York was the first to publish it outside of Maryland, on September 22. In Washington, the *Intelligencer* printed the song on September 26. "Whoever is the author of those lines, they do equal honor to his principles and his talents," the newspaper remarked. The *Federal Republican* in Georgetown was quick to follow, printing the composition the next day with its own high praise: "A friend has obligingly favored us with a copy of the following stanzas, which we offer to our readers as a specimen of native poetry, which will proudly rank among the best efforts of our national muse." The *Boston Patriot* and the *Richmond Enquirer* printed the song on September 28, and papers as far away as Georgia and New Hampshire followed within days.

The hometown *Frederick-Town Herald*, perhaps tipped off by Taney or someone else close to Key, was the first to identify the heretofore-unidentified gentleman who wrote the song, naming him as "F.S. Key Esq. formerly of this place" when it published the song on September 24. Within a week, many in Washington knew Key to be the song's author. On September 30, Navy Secretary Jones sent a copy to his wife. Jones assumed, incorrectly, that Key was a Federalist, though in truth Key remained disgusted with both political parties. In any event, Jones was willing to overlook any supposed party affiliation: "He is a Federalist, but with such Federalists I can have but a common feeling."

O say can you see by the dawn's early
light so proudly we hail'd at the twilight's last gleaming
those broad stripes & bright stars through the perilous fight
O'er the ramparts we watch'd, were so gallantly streaming
And the rocket's red glare, the bomb bursting in air
Gave proof through the night that our flag was still there
O say does that star spangled banner yet wave
O'er the land of the free & the home of the brave

On the shore dimly seen through the mists of the deep
Where the foe's haughty host in dread silence reposes
What is that which the breeze, o'er the towering steep
As it fitfully blows, half conceals, half discloses
Now it catches the gleam of the morning's first beam
In full glory reflected now shines on the stream
Tis the star-spangled banner — O long may it wave
O'er the land of the free & the home of the brave

And where is that band who so vauntingly swore
That the havoc of war & the battle's confusion
A home & a Country should leave us no more
Their blood has wash'd out their foul footsteps pollution
No refuge could save the hireling & slave
From the terror of flight or the gloom of the grave
And the star-spangled banner in triumph doth wave
O'er the land of the free & the home of the brave

O thus be it ever when freemen shall stand
Between their lov'd home & the war's desolation
Blest with vict'ry & peace may the heav'n rescued land
Praise the power that hath made & preserv'd us a nation
Then conquer we must, when our cause it is just
And this be our motto — "In God is our trust"
And the Star-spangled banner in triumph shall wave
O'er the land of the free & the home of the brave

"I hear Uncle Key's song is sung every night . . . to a crowded audience and with great applause."

The first sheet music for "The Star Spangled Banner," printed in 1814 by Thomas Carr of Baltimore.

CHAPTER 17

✦

Our Glorious Peace

T HE ROYAL NAVY frigate *Iphigenia* made swift passage across the Atlantic, landing at Spithead on the south coast of England just three weeks after Captain Harry Smith had parted from General Ross in the Chesapeake. Smith immediately rode by carriage to London, arriving at midnight, on Monday, September 26. Under his arm, the young army officer carried a wooden box with dispatches bearing the momentous news of Washington's capture.

Smith went straight to the War Office on Downing Street, filed his dispatches, and then found lodging in an overcrowded coffeehouse to get a few hours sleep. In the morning, he was brought before Lord Bathurst, the war secretary, who told him the intelligence he brought was so important that the prince regent, the de facto king of England, insisted on seeing him. They hurried to Carlton House, the royal mansion on Pall Mall in central London, where Smith waited in a large anteroom for thirty minutes while the secretary briefed the regent. Then the door opened. "The prince will see you," Bathurst announced.

Brash and ambitious though he was, Smith felt momentary qualms. "I know nothing of the etiquette of a court," Smith warned the minister as they walked down a corridor. "Oh, just behave as you would to any gentleman," Bathurst assured him. "Call him 'Sir' and do not turn your back on him."

They entered the dressing room, filled with every manner of clothing, perfume, snuff boxes, and wigs, all befitting the prince regent's extravagant lifestyle. George Augustus Frederick had assumed the regency in 1811, when his father, King George III, had relapsed into insanity, and whatever restraint the prince had ever shown quickly disappeared.

The prince regent rose to greet the visitors. General Ross had spoken highly of Smith in his report, he told the captain. Studying a map of Washington brought by Smith, the regent peppered him with questions about the operation. All the burned buildings were marked in red: the Capitol, and with it the Supreme Court and the Library of Congress; the President's House; the Navy Yard; the Treasury; and the State, War, and Navy headquarters building. "He asked the name of each, and in his heart I fancied I saw he thought it a barbarian act," said Smith.

If so, the regent kept those thoughts to himself. His audience over,

"The reign of Madison, like that of Bonaparte,
may be considered as at an end,"
wrote the *Evening Star*.

"*The Fall of Washington—or Maddy in full flight*,"
a cartoon published in London in 1814.

Smith backed out of the room with the secretary. "Bathurst," the regent called as they left, "don't forget this officer's promotion."

Outside, at the prince regent's order, the guns of Parliament and the Tower of London thundered in salute of the news. As bells rang and word spread, a raucous celebration erupted in Hyde Park and spread across the city.

"We stop the press to announce the receipt of the following most important intelligence from America," the London *Times* declared in its September 27 edition: "the CAPTURE and DESTRUCTION, by his Majesty's Forces, of the CITY OF WASHINGTON, on the 24th ult., after a severe, but brilliant action, in which the enemy was defeated with great loss."

The war, it seemed, was all but over. The United States had been given its just comeuppance. The newspapers were filled with righteous celebration of the victory over the treacherous Americans. "The reign of Madison, like that of Bonaparte, may be considered as at an end," wrote the *Evening Star*. A satirical cartoon showed "Maddy in full flight," off to Elba to join "his bosom friend" Napoleon.

The *Times*, which dubbed Madison "the fugitive of Bladensburg," was particularly triumphant. "Washington,—the proud seat of that nest of traitors, whose accursed arts involved us in war with our brethren beyond the Atlantic,—Washington captured, its dock, its arsenal, and all its public buildings destroyed, the heads of the faction beaten, disgraced and flying for their lives;—these are indeed impressive lessons, which we fervently hope and trust will produce their proper effect on the people of the United States."

"Admiral COCKBURN, it is said, will have the red ribband," the *Times* reported. "The merits of this gallant officer are spoken of in the highest possible terms by great authorities, who admire his conduct, particularly in the exploit at Washington, which was his plan; and look, if an opportunity offers, to his becoming a second NELSON."

A brilliant future was likewise predicted for Ross. The prince regent sent word to the general of his admiration for the Washington affair, "so well calculated to humble the presumptuousness of the American government."

*

Eager to deliver the coup de grace on the reeling Americans, the government agreed to send Ross more troops, adding two battalions to the reinforcements already sailing to attack New Orleans. "The superior talents which you have displayed in your first battle prize are a sufficient pledge of the ability with which you would conduct operations on a larger scale," Bathurst wrote Ross. The minister noted the general's refusal to allow Washington to be plundered "will be remembered by the enemy, if not with gratitude, at least with admiration."

That said, Bathurst urged the general to show no such mercy to Baltimore, suggesting that if Ross were to "make its inhabitants *feel* a little more the effects of your visit than what has been experienced at Washington, you would make that portion of the American people experience the consequences of the war, who have most contributed to its existence."

Keeping his promise to General Ross, Captain Harry Smith traveled by stagecoach to Clifton, in Bristol, on England's southwest coast, to deliver the general's letter to Elizabeth Ross. "We found . . . Mrs. Ross in the highest spirits at the achievements of our arms under her husband," Smith later wrote.

A family friend wrote to Elizabeth that Ross would be delighted with the sensation caused by his feat. "I cannot imagine any addition *he even* could wish to the fame he has so well earned, to be the wonder of the day," he wrote. In Ross's home village of Rostrevor, at the foot of the Mourne Mountains on the coast of northern Ireland, the streets were illuminated by bonfires and the leading citizens threw a joyous banquet toasting the general's accomplishment.

Unknown to anyone in England or Ireland, *Surprize* arrived from the Chesapeake in Halifax Harbor in Nova Scotia on September 28, one day after Smith's arrival in London. The next day, salute guns on land and sea were fired while Ross's coffin was carried to the burial ground at St. Paul's Church, where his remains were interred in the churchyard.

The latest American rejection of the British demands at the peace talks in Ghent reached London just after the news of Washing-

The carillon at St. Bavon Cathedral was ringing for Christmas by the time the delegates sat at a long table at 6 p.m. to sign, seal, and exchange the treaty.

The Signing of the Treaty of Ghent, Christmas Eve, 1814

ton's capture. The British prime minister, Lord Liverpool, told Bathurst there was no rush to reply to the Americans: "Let them feast in the meantime upon Washington."

Bathurst immediately dispatched the news to the British delegation in Ghent. "I hope you'll be able to put on a face of compress'd joy at least, in communicating this news to the American ministers," the war secretary wrote to Henry Goulburn, leader of the delegation. The Americans were to be reminded of Washington at every opportunity, Bathurst added, and told "that considering the force now directed against them their affairs are more likely to become worse than better."

GHENT, SATURDAY, OCTOBER 1

John Quincy Adams had read newspaper accounts that described the large British fleet threatening the Chesapeake, and he had a premonition of ill tidings. "The next news will be the taking of Washington or Baltimore," Adams wrote in his diary on September 30.

Adams and Albert Gallatin were the only members of the American delegation in Ghent at the moment. The rest of the American commissioners had made use of another interminable delay in the talks to make a field trip to Brussels, as much to get away from the tediousness of Ghent as to escape Adams. Strong personalities all, the commissioners had spent much of their time squabbling and were thoroughly sick of one another's company in the three-story house they shared on the Rue des Champs. The pious Adams took many solitary walks, seeking to avoid the endless card games, bad wine, and cigars of which Henry Clay was so fond. More than once, Adams had risen in the predawn blackness just in time to hear the party winding down in Clay's room.

Returning from his walk on the evening of October 1, Adams found Gallatin waiting. The Swiss-born diplomat spoke quietly and matter-of-factly. Washington had been captured and its public buildings destroyed, he reported. Gallatin feared the news would shake continental Europe's confidence in America's prospects. Adams spent a restless night, too distressed to sleep. Though awake when the morning finally came, he stayed in bed an hour longer than normal, unable to face the cold day. The burning of Washington was a "catastrophe," he said, and would prove a "trial of the national spirit." But reflecting further, he concluded it disgraced Britain more than the United States.

Henry Clay, Jonathan Russell, and Christopher Hughes, the secretary to the legation, were attending the theater in Brussels when Hughes overheard a British officer boasting in the lobby: "Have you heard the news? We have taken and burned the Yankee capital and thrown those American rebels back half a century." Hughes gathered Clay and Russell and told them they must leave immediately. The mortified Americans returned to Ghent, where they found a packet of the most recent London newspapers sent by Goulburn, along with a sarcastic note suggesting that the news would relieve the Americans' boredom.

It was the insult of it all that bothered Clay. The loss of the buildings "gives me comparatively no pain," Clay wrote in a letter. "What does wound me to the very soul is that a set of pirates and incendiaries should have been permitted to pollute our soil, conflagrate our Capital, and return unpunished to their ships."

On October 8, the British delivered new terms to the Americans. Coming as it did after the fall of Washington, the note was dressed in moderation. The British had quietly dropped their earlier demand for military control of the Great Lakes. Liverpool had also concluded that the Americans would never accept the British demand to create a buffer state for the Indian tribes in the Northwest. The British replaced it with a new ultimatum: Restore to the Indians all rights, possessions, and privileges they held before the war. This would afford some protection to Canada. If the Americans did not agree, the peace conference would end.

The Americans felt they had no choice but to accept, though they worried it would set a dangerous precedent. On October 14, the delegation sent a mildly worded reply raising no objection, with the stipulation that it not set a precedent. The language they used was so nimble that Goulburn was not even convinced the Americans had accepted the demand. But London seemed satisfied, and negotiations continued.

The American position was precarious, Adams knew. In his diary, he wrote, "May it please God to forgive our enemies, and to turn their hearts."

TERRA RUBRA, MARYLAND, WEDNESDAY, OCTOBER 5

After months of disruption from the war, Francis Scott Key was eager to return his family to Georgetown and try to resume some semblance of normal life, though he had grave doubts this would be possible. By October 5, Key, Polly, and their six children had all gathered at Terra Rubra for the journey to the capital.

Key had already been back in Georgetown briefly to attend to business, and found two letters from John Randolph waiting. Key learned that even Randolph, the most inveterate of war opponents, had taken up arms and volunteered to Virginia's defense when the British attacked up the Potomac. Back at his home, Randolph had grown alarmed at the lack of any word from Key since the eve of Bladensburg. "Thank God! Georgetown is safe," Randolph wrote. "Pray, let me hear from you."

Before leaving Terra Rubra, Key composed a long letter of reply to Randolph, apologizing for not writing since the battle. "From that day to this I have hardly been a day at home & could write you such an account of my adventures as would tire us both," he wrote. "You will be surprised to hear that I have since then spent eleven days in the British fleet."

Describing the bombardment he had witnessed, Key called Baltimore's escape providential. But he worried the country had not learned its lesson. "Whether this gentle paternal chastisement we have been suffering will be sufficient for us is yet to be seen—I have my fears," he wrote.

Key made no mention to Randolph of the song lyrics he had written, which seemed to have fallen from his mind. Indeed, Key offered no soaring rhetoric about the land of the free and the home of the brave. Instead his feelings of helplessness with the war, disgust with the government, and humiliation over Bladensburg spilled out.

"There is great alarm in the city and Georgetown about the removal of the seat of government," Key wrote. "I am so uncertain about my own movements that I care but little about those of the government. If the war lasts (as I think it will) I cannot see how I can live in Georgetown; & perhaps if the great folks move off little people can live cheaper. As to the disgrace of abandoning the seat of government & acknowledging that the Conquerors of Canada cannot defend their own Capital, it would be a serious thing to a people not already in the very dust & mire of ignominy."

WASHINGTON, SATURDAY, OCTOBER 8

That ignominy was plainly evident at the new presidential quarters at the Octagon. No one used to turn down invitations to Dolley Madison's gatherings; now people sent regrets, or did not bother turning up. The *Washington City Gazette* was disappointed the Madisons even bothered; it had hoped that burning the President's House would have "put an end to drawing-rooms and levees; the resort of the idle, and the encouragers of spies and traitors."

The Madisons did their best to ignore the disgust directed their way. "The administration are severely and almost universally condemned for their misconduct on that occasion," Senator Jeremiah Mason of New Hampshire, a Federalist, wrote on October 6 to his wife, Mary. "They seem to be falling into general contempt. Poor Mrs. Madison, it is said, shows the most sensibility on the subject. . . . The disgraceful and distressing stories told are innumerable." Virginia attorney William Wirt called on Madison a few days later and found the president in poor condition. "He looks miserably shattered and woebegone," Wirt wrote his wife. "In short, he looks heart-broken."

George M. Dallas, Gallatin's secretary, arrived from Ghent Saturday afternoon, October 8, with ominous news from the American delegation. The British were sending up to 15,000 reinforcements for an attack on New Orleans. Dallas also brought dispatches from the conference, written in late August, that described the British demands for the creation of an Indian buffer state and control of the Great Lakes. The private diplomatic correspondence was now out of date. But Madison shrewdly made the British demands and American responses public, thereby showing the Americans willing to negotiate but the British demanding fantastic concessions.

Wirt found Madison's "heart and mind were painfully full" of developments in New England, where unhappiness with the war had reached new heights and a regional conference was planned to consider action, possibly including secession. Some governors had refused to put their state militias under federal control and were discouraging enlistment in the U.S. Army. Unknown to Washington, Massachusetts Governor Caleb Strong was about to enter into secret talks with the British commander in Halifax to make a separate peace with Great Britain.

Meanwhile, the movement to relocate the capital appeared to gain ground. On October 6, the House narrowly approved a nonbinding resolution to leave Washington. Almost imperceptibly at first, but then with increasing fervor, the mood changed, fueled by the victories in Baltimore and Plattsburgh: The nation should rally around Washington. Remaining in place showed defiance to British power. If the capital were put on wheels, it was said, it would never stop rolling.

Supporters were bolstered by reports from engineers that the walls of the President's House and both wings of the Capitol were in good enough shape to rebuild. At a mass meeting, citizens of Washington pledged to loan money to the government. While the bill to move the capital narrowly passed the House on its first reading, supporters of the city mustered their forces, and on October 17, a resolution to remain in Washington passed the House, 83 to 74.

Dr. William Thornton took no small measure of the credit for himself. Had he not persuaded the British to save the Patent Office, Congress would have had no place to meet. Without it, the opponents of Washington would have carried the day, Thornton later claimed in a letter to the identically named British Colonel William Thornton, whom he considered a bosom friend by this point. "I believe they would now have succeeded if I had not prevailed on Major Waters & Colonel Jones to spare the Patent Office, containing the Museum of the Arts, which temporarily accommodates the Congress," Dr. Thornton wrote. "Thus it was observed that *one* William Thornton took the city, & another preserved it by that single act."

Another ray of hope arrived in Washington in the form of a letter from Monticello. "I learn from the newspapers that the vandalism of our enemy has triumphed at Washington over science as well as the arts, by the destruction of the public library with the noble edifice in which it was deposited," Thomas Jefferson wrote to his friend Samuel H. Smith, founder of the *Intelligencer*.

Jefferson's library at Monticello held more than six thousand books and was the largest personal collection in the United States, including many volumes acquired during the revolution and others while he was U.S. minister to France. The subjects were as wide-ranging as Jefferson's mind: politics, law, history, science, Greek and Latin classics, rhetoric, and poetry were just a few.

The seventy-one-year-old Jefferson had planned to offer the library to Congress upon his death, but Washington's misfortune coincided with the fact that the former president was short on cash. Congress could name the price, but Jefferson insisted the collection be taken in its entirety or not at all, save for a few books he would keep for his personal use. He sent Smith a copy of his catalog for Congress to peruse.

Debating the offer in October, some members of Congress welcomed it as an unmatched opportunity. But others raised objections to the size and potential cost of the library, and they criticized Jefferson's book selection as "embracing too many works in foreign languages, some of too philosophical a character, and some otherwise objectionable." The works of Voltaire were cited as a prime example.

Madison sent a note to Jefferson as the debate continued in Congress: "It will prove a gain to them, if they have the wisdom to replace it by such a collection as yours."

Chesapeake Bay, early October

The British remaining in the Chesapeake under Rear Admiral Malcolm followed the debate over Washington's fate in the newspapers with great interest. When John Skinner visited the fleet, several British officers confided to the American agent that abandoning Washington would be a craven act. "No, I would sooner build a barn to meet in than remove under existing circumstances," Captain Sir Thomas Hardy told Skinner.

Malcolm had secret orders to join the attack on New Orleans with most of the frigates, bomb ships, and troops. Privately, Malcolm was much disheartened by the death of Ross and wanted the war over. "[I]f any inquire of you my opinion, . . . say—he is decidedly of opinion that we should make peace," he wrote his wife, Clementina. "Just now we have an advantage and the Americans suffer severely, but soon they will be driven to become soldiers."

The British were preparing to depart the bay when they received a visit from an old nemesis: Commodore Joshua Barney. The flotilla commander, after several weeks of recuperation at his home in Elkridge, remained in great pain from the musket ball lodged in his hip. Nonetheless, in order to gain his own release from parole and reassume command of the flotilla, Barney sailed from the Washington Navy Yard on October 5 aboard a truce ship with eighty British prisoners to exchange for Americans captured at Bladensburg and Baltimore.

Barney found Malcolm's fleet two days later near the mouth of the Piankatank River in Virginia. Among the prisoners Barney brought with him was the redoubtable Colonel William Thornton. Bladensburg's gentry had grown attached to the charming man who had led the charge across the bridge six weeks earlier, and they were sorry to see him go. "If a bullet is not an obstacle, I am sure that Colonel Thornton will become one of the most important generals, and he is a very pleasant man," Rosalie Stier Calvert wrote her sister.

The British were delighted to have Thornton back before they sailed for the Gulf of Mexico. Though walking with a limp, Thornton was in good spirits, telling stories he had learned while in captivity, including one that President Madison had fled the battlefield "at about nine miles an hour, whipping his horse with all his might."

"I rejoice," Cockburn wrote upon hearing of Thornton's release. "[T]here are in my opinion very few like him to be met with."

With the departure of Malcolm and most of the ships on October 14 for the Gulf of Mexico, the remaining British force in the Chesapeake no longer posed a serious threat.

BERMUDA, FRIDAY, OCTOBER 14

That same day, the British garrison guns overlooking the blue waters of St. George's Harbor in Bermuda fired in salute as the remains of Captain Sir Peter Parker were laid to rest. Rear Admiral George Cockburn, joined by every officer in his squadron, stood at attention as the mournful sound carried far over the water.

With the sad business of Parker completed, Cockburn settled down to wait while *Albion*, in wretched shape after a year at sea, was refitted. Bermuda was a homecoming of sorts for Cockburn. His elder brother James had been appointed governor of Bermuda a year earlier, and the admiral stayed with him at a house on Mount Wyndham. Cockburn learned for the first time of "the sensation" the capture of Washington had created in England. He grandly presented his brother with the presidential book he had taken from the Capitol. (A rare books dealer would return it to the Library of Congress 126 years later, during the early days of the Anglo-American alliance in World War II, to the delight of President Franklin D. Roosevelt.)

Cockburn was eager to set sail again, but he would not be joining the expedition to New Orleans. Instead, he was to return to the Chesapeake, collect the little force that remained, and then sail south to create a diversion along the coasts of South Carolina and Georgia.

Cochrane, perhaps tired of being outshone by his dashing subordinate, would keep the glory of New Orleans to himself.

Cockburn was philosophical about being left out. He wrote Colonel Brooke on October 25 that he would "most happily" join with "my Chesapeake friends" on the attack. "It has however been decreed that I am not to take part in your present expedition and it is perhaps for the best, for the longer I live the more I am convinced of the old adage that 'too many cooks spoil the broth,' and by my being kept away, you will at all events have one the less who, if present, could not possibly resist having his finger in the pie."

LONDON, MONDAY, OCTOBER 17

Still heady from the capture of Washington, London expected more good news any day from America. Rumors spread that Baltimore had already fallen, and that Philadelphia, New York, and Boston were at risk.

On October 17, Captain Duncan MacDougall arrived from the Chesapeake, carrying dispatches for the War Office. The news was stunning, but it was not what the British expected. The American forces defending Baltimore had repulsed the British army and Royal Navy, and General Ross was dead. "The death of this brave and accomplished officer will throw a gloom over the public feeling throughout the Empire," a newspaper wrote. In Rostrevor, which had barely finished celebrating Ross's capture of Washington, the news brought "grief indescribable."

Concurrently, reports arrived of the shocking American victory over British forces in Lake Champlain and Plattsburgh. Together with the report from Baltimore, the news "materially counteracted" the coup of Washington's capture, said Lord Castlereagh, the foreign minister.

Harry Smith was visiting his father at Whittlesea in Cambridgeshire when a letter arrived with the news from London. He was ordered to report back to duty immediately to serve as assistant adjutant general for the reinforcements being sent under Sir Edward Pakenham, Wellington's brother-in-law, who had been appointed to succeed Ross and lead the attack on New Orleans.

All around the nation, the mood toward the American war turned abruptly pessimistic, from the highest levels of government to the man in the street. The public's war weariness was acute after two decades of war with France. Citizens had tired of high taxes, a strained economy, and the loss of lucrative trade with America.

Further, the news fueled a growing debate in London on the propriety of burning the public buildings of Washington. After the initial rush of excitement, the country was chagrined to be condemned around the continent for an act "more suitable to the times of barbarism." France reveled in the proof that Napoleon was not alone in wartime excesses; the Washington episode was "unworthy of civilized nations," the *Journal de Paris* declared.

In Parliament, Samuel Whitbread, the reformer and Whig leader, condemned the act as "abhorrent to every principal of legitimate warfare." On the defensive, the government sent orders to Cochrane November 2 to suspend his policy of retaliation.

"Willingly, would we throw a veil of oblivion over our transactions at Washington," wrote the London *Statesman*. "The Cossacks spared Paris, but we spared not the capital of America."

BALTIMORE, EVENING, WEDNESDAY, OCTOBER 19

The war years had not been good for the Holliday Street Theater in Baltimore. After a dismal season in 1811 on the eve of the conflict, the theater had not even bothered to open in 1812. Owner William Wood used the time to rebuild the original wooden structure with a "fine brick edifice" seating two thousand, but the ongoing war prevented it from opening in 1813. The theater finally reopened on October 12, 1814, a few weeks after the British departed. *Count Benyowski*, a five-act tragicomedy translated from German, was on the bill for October 19. Trying to spice up the program, Wood placed an advertisement in the newspapers promising additional entertainment:

After the play, Mr. Hardinge will sing a much admired NEW SONG, written by a gentleman of Maryland, in commemoration of the GALLANT DEFENCE OF FORT M'HENRY, called THE STAR-SPANGLED BANNER

Almost certainly, there had already been many informal perfor-
mances of the song, whether by a handful gathered around a piano or
by larger gatherings of citizens and soldiers at taverns and squares. But
the performance at the Holliday Street Theater was the first known
public rendition of Key's song, and the first known use of its new title,
"The Star-Spangled Banner." As advertised, the song was "sung with
great applause" on Wednesday night by J. Hardinge, an Irishman with
the Warren & Wood Chestnut Street Company who was said to have
a rich brogue.

The song's popularity in Baltimore continued to grow, one of Key's
nieces proudly noted. "I hear Uncle Key's song is sung every night . . .
to a crowded audience and with great applause," she wrote in October.
Judge Nicholson had done his best to spread the song, sending copies
to relatives near and far. "We are delighted with Mr. Key's little piece
and can readily imagine what the feelings of so grand a man must have
been on such an occasion," Nicholson's sister-in-law wrote in reply.

"I do not know when I have been so charmed with any thing as
with the sweet little piece he enclosed," a cousin wrote from Greenwich, Connecticut. 'O say, does that star spangled banner still wave,
O'er the land of the free and the home of the brave."

GHENT, FRIDAY, OCTOBER 21

Henry Goulburn could not conceal his dismay when the reports of
Baltimore and Plattsburgh were delivered to the British delegation in
Ghent, along with new instructions from London: The British would
settle for keeping the American ground already held, and not insist on
any further territorial gains.

"The news is very far from satisfactory," Goulburn petulantly
wrote Bathurst on October 21. "We owed the acceptance of our article
respecting the Indians to the capture of Washington; and if we had either burnt Baltimore or held Plattsburg, I believe we should have had
peace on the terms which you have sent us in a month at least. As
things appear to be going on in America, the result of our negotiation
may be very different."

The British delegation dutifully followed instructions, delivering a
note to the Americans later that day: If there were to be peace, it would

have to be made on the basis of *uti possidetis*—the retention of territories actually held. This at least allowed territorial gains and guarantees for the Indians that would allow the British to protect Canada and claim victory. The United States would have to cede all territory occupied by the British, including Fort Niagara, and give up a slice of northern Maine, providing the British a direct route between Halifax and Quebec. The Americans would doubtless "appreciate the moderation of His Majesty's Government," the British note stated.

The Americans did not. Acting in rare unison, the delegation refused to even consider *uti possidetis*. In Adams's room on Monday morning, October 24, they signed a note proposing that each side revert to the status quo ante bellum. Reading the American response that afternoon, Goulburn thought the American stance warranted breaking off the talks. The British delegates sent a message to London that night asking for further instructions.

The news from America had altered the balance in Ghent, deflating the British as much as it invigorated the U.S. delegation. "The Capture of Washington was a source of great triumph and exultation and inspired a belief that their troops could not be resisted," American delegate James Bayard wrote to his cousin on October 26. "This error has been sadly corrected by the repulse in the attack upon Baltimore, by the destruction of their fleet on Lake Champlain, and by the retreat of Prevost from Plattsburg."

ENGLAND, NOVEMBER 1814

Lord Liverpool, the prime minister, concluded that the Americans were delusional upon reading their note. Yet the British government could not be seen as breaking off peace negotiations over a demand for territory. The war "will probably now be of some duration," he lamented in a note to Castlereagh, the foreign minister.

An extended war was a most unwelcome development, both agreed. It already had cost the government 10 million pounds. Castlereagh was eager to be rid of "the millstone of an American war" so he could concentrate on European affairs at the Congress of Vienna, which had begun in September. Liverpool wanted to demobilize the military, reduce the country's enormous debt, and end wartime taxation.

Some change was needed to bring the war to a quick and satisfactory end. After a cabinet discussion on November 4, Liverpool informed the Duke of Wellington that the government was considering appointing him chief of command in America. "The more we contemplate the character of the American war, the more satisfied we are of the many inconveniences which may grow out of the continuance of it," Liverpool wrote Wellington at his headquarters in Paris. He would be sent with full powers to bring the war to "an honorable conclusion," either by making peace or prosecuting it "with renewed vigor."

Wellington held military stature unmatched in the British Empire— his name alone might be enough to end the war. "[T]he knowledge that he is to have the command in America, if the war continues, may be expected to produce the most favorable effects," Liverpool told Castlereagh.

Wellington's lack of enthusiasm for the scheme was obvious, though his sense of duty made it impossible for him to simply turn it down. "Does it not occur to you that by appointing me to go to America at this moment, you give ground for belief all over Europe that your affairs there are in a much worse situation than they really are?" he asked the prime minister. Without British control of the Great Lakes, Wellington noted, "I shall do you but little good in America. . . ."

More sobering for Liverpool than Wellington's reluctance was his pointed advice that Britain drop its demands for territory. "I confess that I think you have no right from the state of the war to demand any concession of territory from America," Wellington wrote. "You can get no territory, indeed the state of your military operations, however creditable, does not entitle you to demand any."

Wellington's views could not be ignored. On November 13, Liverpool assured the duke that Britain would give up its territorial demands. That being the case, the prime minister concluded it made little sense to extend the war in the hope of taking more territory.

Following instructions from London, the British delegation informed the Americans that Great Britain was dropping its insistence on *uti possidetis*. Only a few minor issues remained to be settled. When the note was delivered to the Americans in Ghent on Sunday, November 27, even Adams, the most pessimistic of the ministers, thought peace was now "probable."

WASHINGTON, CHRISTMAS EVE, 1814

A gloomy holiday was settling at Francis Scott Key's home in Georgetown. His parents, tending to business at Terra Rubra, had been unable to join the family for the holiday as expected. On Christmas Eve, Key anxiously awaited the arrival of his uncle, Philip Barton Key, from Annapolis, where it was rumored British ships might attack to drive away the state legislature.

As he waited, Key wrote a letter to his mother. Three months after Fort McHenry, Key was even more pessimistic about the war than usual. "There is nothing new here—some people think we shall have peace but I have not the least expectation of it," he wrote. "As things are going on we shall be wretchedly prepared to meet any of the evils which threaten us and I fear the next year will be one of great suffering."

Key was not alone in this view. "The prospect of peace appears to get darker and darker," Hannah Gallatin wrote to Dolley Madison on December 26. In Connecticut, Federalists had convened the Hartford Convention to air grievances against the war. The twenty-six delegates, mostly from Massachusetts, Connecticut, and Rhode Island, were discussing the nullification of federal laws and taxes that supported the war. Some extremists called for secession. "The bond of Union is already broken," a Boston newspaper declared. The delegates did not seriously consider secession, but as they met behind closed doors, rumors of treason spread. James Madison complained to a friend that the northern movement "certainly is the greatest, if not the sole, inducement" for the British to continue prosecuting the war.

Despite his opposition to the war, Key was nonetheless dismayed by the developments in New England. "These Yankees are sad fellows," he told John Randolph. He was considering founding a national, nonpartisan newspaper to fight the threat of disunion. "I have thought something might be done by an impartial anti-party paper to prevent this & other evils to which we are exposed," Key said.

Late on Christmas Eve, Philip Barton Key showed up safely from Annapolis. Relieved, Frank Key added a postscript to the letter to his mother: There was "no danger" to report from the British.

GHENT, CHRISTMAS EVE, 1814

At 4 p.m., the five American ministers arrived by carriage at the British residence at the Chartreux Convent, stepping out into a crisp Christmas Eve that carried the hint of snow in the air. After weeks of final bargaining, the American and British delegations had agreed to terms.

Much of the bickering in the last weeks had not been with the British, but among the members of the American delegation, with Gallatin forced to broker shouting matches between Adams and Clay. The Americans and British were able to reach agreement on the final disputed issues by leaving them out of the treaty altogether, including the fate of disputed islands off the coast of Maine, questions of British navigation on the Mississippi, and the rights of American fishermen in Newfoundland.

For two hours, both delegations painstakingly examined and corrected copies of the peace treaty, which were read aloud to make sure each was precisely the same. The carillon at St. Bavon Cathedral was ringing for Christmas by the time the delegates sat at a long table at 6 p.m. to sign, seal, and exchange the treaty.

The problem now was to get three copies to Washington as fast and safely as possible. Usually, signing a peace treaty ended a war. But at the insistence of the British, the nations would remain at war until both ratified the treaty. Three times previously, to Britain's great annoyance, the United States had insisted on changes to signed treaties. "Even if peace is signed I shall not be surprised if Madison endeavours to play us some trick in the ratification of it," Liverpool had warned. Bathurst told General Pakenham before he departed for New Orleans that "hostilities should not be suspended until you shall have official information that the President has actually ratified the treaty."

One of three American copies of the treaty would be sent with Charles Hughes, who would sail from France. Henry Carroll, Clay's private secretary, would leave for England to seek passage across the ocean with the second copy. A third would be sent via ship from Amsterdam. Anthony St. John Baker, the British secretary, rushed to London with the three British copies. After the prince regent ratified the treaty December 27, Baker set sail for America a few days later aboard the British sloop-of-war *Favourite*, which also carried Carroll.

John Quincy Adams thought the American commissioners would be "censured and reproached" at home for the terms of the treaty. Nonetheless, before going to bed on Christmas Eve, Adams offered a prayer of thanks in his diary. "I cannot close the record of the day," he wrote, "without a humble offering of gratitude to God for the conclusion to which it has pleased him to bring the negotiations for peace at this place."

WASHINGTON, JANUARY AND FEBRUARY 1815

In the New Year, Washington anxiously awaited news of the British assault in the Gulf of Mexico. "The fate of N. Orleans will be known to day—on which so much depends," Dolley wrote on January 14 to Hannah Gallatin.

But no word arrived that day, and a week later, when the young visiting scholar George Ticknor attended a dinner at the Octagon hosted by the Madisons, the city was still in the dark. The twenty guests, including some congressmen and army officers, among them William Winder, stood about awkwardly before dinner was served, despite Dolley's efforts at polite talk. A servant whispered in the ear of Madison, who immediately left the room, followed by his secretary, Edward Coles. The southern mail had arrived, perhaps with word from New Orleans.

"The President soon returned, with added gravity, and said that there was no news! Silence ensued," Ticknor wrote to his father. "No man seemed to know what to say at such a crisis, and, I suppose, from the fear of saying what might not be acceptable."

Finally, on February 4, news arrived of a tremendous victory at New Orleans. Major General Andrew Jackson's army had repulsed a British attack, inflicting enormous casualties on the enemy and forcing their retreat. A happy crowd gathered that night on Pennsylvania Avenue, which was illuminated by torches and candles in windows. At Fort McHenry the next day, Armistead ordered the guns fired once again from the ramparts in salute.

The celebration paled in comparison to the one ten days later. On February 13, rumors of peace swirled into Washington like a fresh breeze. The city waited in suspense until late afternoon on February

14, when a coach pulled by four foaming steeds thundered down Pennsylvania Avenue. Inside, Henry Carroll held a copy of the treaty he had brought by ship to New York and then by stagecoach to Washington. Cheering crowds followed the carriage as it picked up Secretary of State Monroe at his residence on I Street and continued to the Octagon. There the rest of the cabinet joined Madison and Monroe to carefully review the document. Soon after nightfall, members of Congress and citizens gathered at the house. When Joseph Gales, the editor of the *Intelligencer*, showed up around 8 p.m., he found the drawing room filled with people anticipating an announcement of peace.

While Madison was tucked away with the cabinet in the round study on the second floor, Dolley presided over the festivities below, exchanging congratulations with well-wishers. "[T]he most conspicuous object in the room, the observed of all observers, was Mrs. Madison herself, then in the meridian of life and queenly beauty," wrote Gales. He was invited to the study, where the cabinet members sat with "subdued joy" written on their faces. Even the prim Madison had a "sportive tone" as he announced the results of their deliberations: The treaty had been received and would in all likelihood be accepted.

Dolley's cousin, Sally Coles, came to the head of the stairs, crying "Peace! Peace!" and instructed John Freeman, the butler, to dole out wine liberally to all. "I played the President's March on the violin, [Jean-Pierre Sioussat] and some others were drunk for two days, and such another joyful time was never seen in Washington," Paul Jennings, the president's servant, later wrote. Madison and his cabinet, Jennings hastened to add, "were as pleased as any, but did not show their joy in this manner."

The next morning, the Senate convened at the Patent Office to consider the treaty, and on February 16 voted 35–0 in favor of ratification. Madison sat at a circular mahogany table in the Octagon's round study that day and signed the treaty. At 11 p.m., Monroe exchanged ratified copies of the treaty with St. John Baker, the British secretary, who had arrived from New York. The treaty was binding.

On February 18, Madison sent a message to Congress calling the conclusion of the war "highly honorable to the nation" and marked by "the most brilliant successes."

"The late war," Madison continued, "although reluctantly declared by Congress, had become a necessary resort to assert the rights and independence of the nation." In that, the president said, it had succeeded. Now that peace had come, Madison added with a tone of hopefulness, "the nation can review its conduct without regret and without reproach."

GULF OF MEXICO, FEBRUARY 1815

Word of Ghent arrived in the Gulf of Mexico a month after the disastrous Battle of New Orleans, carrying with it the air of defeat for what was left of the British expeditionary force. "I cannot help viewing the terms of this peace as discreditable to the country, and I feel it the more since our failure at New Orleans," Codrington wrote. The scale of the defeat was unimaginable for the British. "There never was a more complete failure," he told his wife.

The New Orleans campaign, with more than two thousand British casualties, had taken a heavy toll on the men who had captured Washington. Navy Lieutenant George Pratt, who had directed the firing of President's House, was riddled with musket balls and killed during a gunboat battle on December 14 for control of Lake Borgne, east of New Orleans.

The British army paid an especially heavy price during the Battle of New Orleans on January 8, and the battalions that had fought in the Chesapeake, which by dint of their experience were chosen to lead the attack, suffered many of the casualties. The 44th Foot had been assigned to carry bundles of cane stalks and ladders to enable the follow-on troops to cross a ditch and scale the ramparts protecting the American line at the Rodriguez Canal. But Lieutenant Colonel Thomas Mullins, leading the 44th, botched the job and the materials were left behind, throwing the entire attack into confusion and leaving the troops to be mowed down by the American line. The 4th Foot and 21st Fusiliers were "exposed to a sweeping fire which cut them down by whole companies," recalled Lieutenant Gleig. "They fell by the hands of men whom they absolutely did not see."

Captain Harry Smith, who had arrived from England with Pakenham and the reinforcements on Christmas Day, watched the general gallop forward into "the most murderous and destructive fire." Within minutes, Pakenham was cut down and lay dying. Trying to rally the attack, Major General Sir Samuel Gibbs was killed, and Major General Sir John Keane seriously wounded.

Colonel William Thornton nearly turned the tide of the battle by capturing an American battery on the opposite side of the Mississippi. Jackson feared his victory might be lost if the British were able to turn the guns on the American line across the river. But with Pakenham's force decimated, Major General John Lambert, the senior British commander still on the field, ordered Thornton to retreat.

Including Ross, the British had lost three generals and a fourth incapacitated since the attack on Baltimore. "It is certainly a fault in these Peninsular Generals—their exposing themselves as they do," Codrington chided in the letter to his wife.

Following the British army's defeat at New Orleans, Vice Admiral Alexander Cochrane attempted to attack the city by sailing up the Mississippi, but the Royal Navy could not get past Fort St. Philip, thirty miles downriver from the city. British forces withdrew nine days after the battle. Sailing east along the Gulf Coast, the British captured Fort Bowyer on February 11 and were threatening nearby Mobile when news of the treaty arrived.

Cochrane "seems most amazingly cast down by this peace," Rear Admiral Codrington wrote his wife. Cochrane anxiously sailed for the Chesapeake, hoping to attack Baltimore or other eastern cities if Madison rejected the peace. But on March 7, as the fleet approached Georgia to rendezvous with Admiral Cockburn, Cochrane learned from a passing American schooner that the treaty had been ratified.

Codrington, for one, was ready to go home. "I would give all my share in the harvest of prize-money to be now making sail for dear old England," he told his wife.

CUMBERLAND ISLAND, GEORGIA, MARCH 1815

Rather than sulk at being left out of the New Orleans expedition, George Cockburn had seized the opportunity to operate free from Cochrane's fickle decisions. After departing Bermuda and collecting the remaining British force from the Chesapeake in December, he had sailed south. In January, his forces seized Cumberland Island, Georgia, which Cockburn intended to use as a base to terrorize the southeast coast, including Charleston and Savannah. But a note arrived from Cochrane about January 20 with the stunning news of New Orleans—"a reverse so little expected," Cockburn called it.

Nonetheless, he seemed little discouraged. From his headquarters in Dungeness House, the grandest home on the island, he pursued an ambitious scheme to form an alliance with the Creek Indian confederation and encourage them to rise up against the Americans. Cockburn relished the thought of the fright such an alliance would create. "I think the *savage* Cockburn, as I am termed among my Yankee neighbors, when joined by the Indians will create no small consternation in the country," he wrote to the Admiralty on January 28.

Cockburn fortified the island and launched work on an immense wharf. He recruited more escaped slaves for the Colonial Marines from plantations along the coast, and as many as 1,700 slaves descended on the British. Cockburn contented himself with raids on St. Simons and Jekyll islands while he prepared to attack Savannah and Charleston. But on February 25, an American officer under a flag of truce brought word that a peace treaty had been signed.

Cockburn was incredulous. "That Jonathan should have been so easily let out of the cloven stick in which I thought we so securely had him I sincerely lament," he wrote to Captain Edmund Palmer, the captain of *Hebrus*.

The senior American commander in the region proposed suspending hostilities. Cockburn declined, awaiting word of the treaty's ratification, but he took no more offensive action. He made good use of the time, sending ships loaded with prize goods to Bermuda and taking in more escaped slaves. Then a Swedish cruiser arrived from England with the deflating news that the British prince regent had ratified the treaty. "This peace . . . has knocked all my schemes on the head and I suppose I shall soon have official notification on this subject from Washington," Cockburn wrote.

/The Americans sent official word of Washington's ratification on March 2. Cockburn agreed to end hostilities, but he did not stop loading booty. When a delegation of Americans arrived March 5 seeking the return of property as stipulated by the treaty, the admiral was not helpful. The Americans produced as evidence a copy of the treaty as printed in the *National Intelligencer*, but Cockburn was disdainful, insisting that the newspaper was not an authoritative document.

The Americans also demanded the return of their slaves, as specified by the treaty. But Cockburn refused to turn over slaves unless they wanted to leave, and few did. Consulting Blackstone's legal reference, Cockburn argued that slaves became free the moment they arrived on British soil, and that a British ship of war qualified as such. But five escaped slaves who had enlisted in the Colonial Marines after the treaty was ratified were handed back, as Cockburn concluded they should not have been taken.

Cockburn evacuated Cumberland Island on March 18, quitting American soil. When he arrived in Bermuda on March 28, he learned he had been nominated in England as a knight commander of the military order of the Bath.

On April 8, Cockburn issued his last orders to the fleet, saluting his men for their "invariably cheerful, gallant and steady behavior." With that, the admiral abandoned the waters of North America and, after a two-and-a-half-year absence, set sail aboard *Albion* for England.

WASHINGTON, MARCH 1815

Cockburn and the British had done Washington a great service, some residents had come to believe. "The burning of the public buildings in Washington is the best thing that has happened in a long time, as far as we are concerned, since this has finally settled the question of whether the seat of government would stay here," Rosalie Stier Calvert wrote to her sister. "In the future they will no longer keep trying to change it, and as long as the union of states stands, the government will remain in Washington, despite the jealousy of Philadelphia, New York and Baltimore."

Before word of peace arrived, Congress had debated whether Washington should be rebuilt on a smaller, less grandiose scale. Laws "need not be enacted in a palace," argued Senator Eligius Fromentin of Louisiana, who proposed a plain, functional building to replace the Capitol. But the Senate voted 20–13 to restore the federal city as it was. On

February 13, Madison signed legislation authorizing the government to borrow a half million dollars to rebuild the President's House, the Capitol, and other public buildings.

"We are under great obligation to the British who burnt our buildings, for the Congress determined to repair them, & have given perfect confidence now by having voted half a million of dollars for this end," Dr. Thornton wrote to Colonel Thornton.

With the ratification of the treaty, the reconstruction of Washington began in earnest. James Hoban, the Irish-born designer and builder of the President's House, was hired to rebuild the mansion, as well as the nearby War and Treasury buildings. Hoban, the foremost builder in Washington, soon had artisans and mechanics hired in good numbers and stonecutters ready to work. Architect Benjamin Latrobe was brought back to oversee the Capitol's reconstruction, and after inspecting the building, he was relieved to see how much had survived. "The mischief is much more easily repaired than would appear at first sight," he wrote. Rebuilding was well under way at the Navy Yard, including a new ten-foot-high wall to protect against looters.

Gilbert Stuart's portrait of George Washington was back in the city. Six weeks after the burning of Washington, businessman Jacob Barker had picked it up at the Maryland farmhouse where he had left it for safekeeping and turned it over to Monroe, who, by Barker's account, promised to have it varnished and placed in a new frame.

Ten wagonloads of books were on their way to Washington from Monticello, as Congress had purchased Jefferson's library for $23,950. They would not regret the decision, Jefferson said, calling it "unquestionably the choicest collection of books in the U.S.; and I hope it will not be without some general effect on the literature of our country."

With the arrival of "our glorious peace," as Dolley Madison termed it, the rancor toward the president had dissipated and the crowds had returned to the first lady's social gatherings. Though Congress adjourned March 4, "still our house is crowded with company," she wrote to Hannah Gallatin the following day. "[I]n truth ever since the peace my brain has been turn'd with noise & bustle. Such over flowing rooms I never saw before—I sigh for repose. . . ."

O say can you see by the dawn's early light
what so proudly we hail'd at the twilight's last gleaming,
Whose broad stripes & bright stars through the perilous fight
O'er the ramparts we watch'd were so gallantly streaming
And the rocket's red glare, the bomb bursting in air
Gave proof through the night that our flag was still there
O say does that star spangled banner yet wave
O'er the land of the free & the home of the brave —

On the shore dimly seen through the mists of the deep
Where the foe's haughty host in dread silence reposes
What is that which the breeze, o'er the towering steep,
As it fitfully blows, half conceals, half discloses?
Now it catches the gleam of the morning's first beam,
In full glory reflected now shines in the stream,
'Tis the star-spangled banner — O long may it wave
O'er the land of the free & the home of the brave.

And where is that band who so vauntingly swore,
That the havoc of war & the battle's confusion
A home & a Country should leave us no more?
Their blood has wash'd out their foul footstep's pollution
No refuge could save the hireling & slave
From the terror of flight or the gloom of the grave,
And the star-spangled banner in triumph doth wave
O'er the land of the free & the home of the brave.

O thus be it ever when freemen shall stand
Between their lov'd home & the war's desolation.
Blest with vict'ry & peace may the heav'n rescued land
Praise the power that hath made & preserv'd us a nation!
Then conquer we must, when our cause it is just,
And this be our motto — "In God is our trust,"
And the star-spangled banner in triumph shall wave
O'er the land of the free & the home of the brave.

O say can you see ~~through~~ by the dawn's early light,
What so proudly we hail'd at the twilight's last gleaming,
Whose broad stripes & bright stars through the perilous fight
O'er the ramparts we watch'd, were so gallantly streaming?
  And the rocket's red glare, the bomb bursting in air,
  Gave proof through the night that our flag was still there,
O say does that star-spangled banner yet wave
O'er the land of the free & the home of the brave?

On the shore dimly seen through the mists of the deep,
Where the foe's haughty host in dread silence reposes,
What is that which the breeze, o'er the towering steep,
As it fitfully blows, half conceals, half discloses?
  Now it catches the gleam of the morning's first beam,
  In full glory reflected now shines in the stream,
'Tis the star-spangled banner — O long may it wave
O'er the land of the free & the home of the brave!

And where is that band who so vauntingly swore,
That the havoc of war & the battle's confusion
A home & a Country should leave us no more?
~~Their blood has~~
  Their blood has wash'd out their foul footstep's pollution.
No refuge could save the hireling & slave
From the terror of flight or the gloom of the grave,
And the star-spangled banner in triumph doth wave
O'er the land of the free & the home of the brave.

O thus be it ever when freemen shall stand
Between their lov'd home & the war's desolation!
Blest with vict'ry & peace may the heav'n rescued land
Praise the power that hath made & preserv'd us a nation!
  Then conquer we must, when our cause it is just,
  And this be our motto — "In God is our trust,"
And the star-spangled banner in triumph shall wave
O'er the land of the free & the home of the brave. —

Key did not disguise his pride in the song,
paraphrasing an old saying that "if he could be
allowed to make a nation's songs, he cared not who made its laws."

Francis Scott Key's original handwritten manuscript
of "The Star-Spangled Banner"

EPILOGUE

══════ ★ ══════

A T NOON ON August 7, 1815, a small British cutter came alongside the 74–gun HMS *Northumberland,* anchored away from public view off Berry Head on the Devonshire coast of England. The short but somewhat heavyset Corsican captive aboard the cutter was instantly recognizable, even had he not been wearing the Grand Croix of the Legion d'Honneur on his left breast. Coming aboard the warship, Napoleon Bonaparte grandly greeted the British officer who was to carry him to his final exile.

"Here I am, Admiral, at your orders!" If there was any mockery in Napoleon's tone, Rear Admiral George Cockburn ignored it. Still, Cockburn could hardly disguise his annoyance later that day when Napoleon condescendingly pinched his ear, a habit of Bonaparte's when he spoke to subordinates. But Napoleon would soon learn who was in charge.

Returning from America, Cockburn had landed at Spithead on the south coast of England on May 5, 1815. But instead of the peace he had expected, Cockburn found Europe in convulsion. Napoleon had escaped from exile in Elba, reclaimed power in France, and raised a great army. Then on June 18, 1815, an allied force under Wellington defeated Napoleon at Waterloo, and a month later, the emperor surrendered to the British.

Cockburn barely had time to reacquaint himself with his wife, Mary, and their now four-year-old daughter, Augusta, at their home in Cavendish Square, London, before he was called back to duty for a special assignment: "the perfectly secure detention of the person of general Bonaparte," and his removal to one of remotest places on the planet, the windswept island of St. Helena in the South Atlantic, 4,600 miles from England. There could be no repeat of Elba. The prince regent had personally approved Cockburn's selection, depending "on the well known zeal and resolute character of sir Geo. Cockburn, that he will not suffer himself to be misled imprudently to deviate from the performance of his duty," wrote Lord Bathurst, the war secretary.

Cockburn was unruffled by the task. "You may depend on my taking care of the common disturber," he assured London.

Meeting with Cockburn, Napoleon bitterly protested his exile, having expected to live "in tranquility" in England, but Cockburn had none of it. "We did not think it necessary to enter into the merits of the question with him," wrote Cockburn. Napoleon was likewise "extremely indignant" to have his entourage's baggage examined before it was allowed on board *Northumberland*, but Cockburn ignored the protests, confiscating weapons, as well as four thousand gold napoleons to be held by the British government.

The admiral and the former emperor were soon locked in psychological battle. "It is clear he is still inclined to act the sovereign occasionally; but I cannot allow it and the sooner therefore he becomes convinced it is not to be admitted, the better," Cockburn wrote in his diary of the voyage.

Napoleon walked the deck of the ship bareheaded, expecting the English officers to remove their hats. "Observing this, I made a point of putting my hat on immediately," Cockburn wrote. His officers followed suit, and Napoleon "seemed considerably piqued," Cockburn noted with satisfaction. Every night, Cockburn sat next to Napoleon for dinner and listened bemusedly to Napoleon's extravagant accounts of his wars, from the failed Russian campaign to his foiled hopes to conquer India. Cockburn was particularly interested when Napoleon mentioned he would have lent the United States "any number" of ships-of-the-line to fight Britain, but Madison had never asked for help. Cockburn and Napoleon followed their dinners with long walks on the deck, their conversations sometimes "free and pleasant" and other times under "a frank strain."

Cockburn was not overly impressed with Napoleon, considering him to be hypocritical and often irrational, as well as an accomplished liar. "[O]n the score of talent, he was an ordinary character," he later said. Still, the admiral took care to make sure Napoleon was comfortable, in keeping with the prince regent's instructions. They had not sailed far before Cockburn realized he was short one critical supply. "I find General Bonaparte and all his suite drink great quantities of claret which my present stock will perhaps not be adequate to maintain," Cockburn wrote. He sent one of the ships escorting the expedition to fetch sixty cases.

After seventy-two days at sea, *Northumberland* sighted St. Helena on October 15. Cockburn alerted Napoleon, who took a spyglass and dourly scanned the brown and gray wall of volcanic rock rising 2,500 feet from the sea. Once on the island, an aide to Napoleon complained that the temporary accommodations in Jamestown were not adequate for the emperor. "I have no cognizance of any Emperor being actually upon this island," Cockburn replied.

Cockburn set up the strictest security across the island. Boats patrolled the coast, sentries manned checkpoints, troops enforced curfews, and the admiral received reports twice a day of Napoleon's exact whereabouts. The former emperor was not going to escape on Cockburn's watch.

After turning charge of Napoleon over to Lieutenant General Sir Hudson Lowe, Cockburn sailed for England in June 1816. Napoleon was relieved to see the admiral leave, describing Cockburn in terms not unlike those Cockburn used to describe him: "He is not a man of a bad heart; on the contrary I believe him to be capable of a generous action; but he is rough, overbearing, vain, choleric, and capricious; never consulting anybody; jealous of his authority; caring little of the manner in which he exercises it, and sometimes violent without dignity."

Still, Napoleon compared him favorably to Lowe, who would remain in charge until Napoleon's death in 1821. "Cockburn was at least straightforward and sincere," said Napoleon. "He was a man—an Englishman."

Returning to England, Cockburn found his fame assured, both as the man who burned Washington and the man who escorted Napoleon to exile. He would soon reach the highest levels of the Royal Navy.

As first lord of the Admiralty and a Tory member in the House of

Commons, Cockburn enjoyed holding other government officials in fear and awe. Cockburn was unconcerned by the notoriety of the Chesapeake campaign—to the contrary, his portrait displayed at the Royal Academy showed him standing proudly before the burning American capital, shrouded by black smoke, one hand resting on his hip, the other on his sword.

Nearly two decades after the war ended, Cockburn sailed once again for American waters, assigned in 1833 as commander-in-chief of the North American Station. In the face of rising American power in the Western Hemisphere, Cockburn's return was a not-so-subtle reminder of the continued reach of Great Britain. Nor was the ship Cockburn chose for his flag without irony: the 52–gun *President*. "My Friend Jonathan," Cockburn wrote, unable to resist the old derisive nickname for the Americans, was "very quietly and friendly disposed toward us."

Cockburn served a second stint as first naval lord in the 1840s, overseeing the Royal Navy's transition from sailing ships to steam and screw technology. After retiring as first naval lord in 1846, he was promoted in 1851 to admiral of the fleet by Queen Victoria.

Two years later, while visiting the Royal Leamington Spa with Lady Cockburn and their daughter, Augusta, to take the waters, Cockburn suffered a major heart attack on August 19, 1853. The "Wellington of the Navy," as the local journal called him, died at age eighty-two.

Cockburn was "one of the ablest and most distinguished officers that ever wore the Royal naval uniform," wrote *The Nautical Standard* in London. "He became a scourge, as his name became a terror, to the United States," the *United Services Magazine*, an English military journal, wrote admiringly. "Here, he carried everything before him."

The admiral was remembered with less affection in the United States, where the *Star and Banner* of Gettysburg reported his death with some satisfaction. "No biography is needed [to] tell Americans of the character of a man, who, whatever may be the estimate of his valor in England, has secured an immortality of infamy by his cruelties in Chesapeake Bay during the last war between this country and Great Britain."

*

Elizabeth Ross's terrible premonitions had come true, and upon her husband's death, she left England and returned to the family estate in Rostrevor to raise their two young sons and daughter. Despite her grief, Ross had the presence of mind to request an unusual honor. Writing to Lord Bathurst in 1815, she suggested it would be "most gratifying" if the prince regent granted the family permission to add the title "of Bladensburg" to her children's names. The prince regent agreed, and the title Ross of Bladensburg, "unique among official distinctions of commoner families," was bestowed.

In Rostrevor, the local nobility and gentry joined with Ross's former officers in 1826 to raise a hundred-foot-high granite obelisk on a hill with a majestic view overlooking the waters of Carlingford Lough, an arm of the Irish Sea. By the mid-twentieth century, the memorial had fallen into neglect. During the years of sectarian violence in Northern Ireland, some feared the memorial to a British army officer might be blown up by Irish Republicans, as happened in 1966 to Nelson's Pillar in Dublin. But the local government council refurbished and reopened the monument in 2009, preparing for the two-hundredth anniversary of Ross's death in 2014.

Ross himself remains in a tomb in the old burying ground of St. Paul's Church in Halifax, Nova Scotia, an ocean from home.

Elizabeth Ross's terrible premonitions had come true.

Memorial to Robert Ross erected by his officers and citizens of his hometown of Rostrevor.

Sir Alexander Cochrane escaped any official sanction for the disaster at New Orleans, though he "should have been tried by court-martial and shot," in the view of British army historian John Fortescue, who accused the admiral of callously sacrificing troops for the purpose of "filling his own pockets" with the loot he hoped to capture. Wellington blamed Cochrane for the death of his brother-in-law, General Pakenham. "I cannot but regret that he was ever employed on such a service or with such a colleague," Wellington lamented.

As predicted by his American friends, the unstoppable Colonel William Thornton eventually won promotion to major general in 1825 and was knighted in 1836. But Thornton never fully recovered from the multiple wounds he had received at Bladensburg and New Orleans, and becoming "subject to delusions," he shot himself in 1840.

Two of Ross's officers—Harry Smith and George De Lacy Evans—"were to grow into the most accomplished British generals of the coming half century," in the view of one British historian. In India, Smith won a decisive victory over the Sikhs at the Battle of Aliwal in 1846, and in South Africa, he served as governor of the Cape Colony, where his much-beloved Spanish bride, Juana, gave her name to the town of Ladysmith.

Evans, though seriously wounded at New Orleans, returned to Europe in time to fight at Waterloo. His army career would span nearly a half century, including as a field commander in the Crimean War. Evans reacted sharply to the publication of the *Historical Memoirs of Sir George Cockburn* in 1828, with its insinuation that the admiral, not Ross, had directed the capture of Washington; most blamed the editor for the slights to the general, though the account is clearly based on Cockburn's handwritten "Memoir of Service." Evans wrote a response maintaining that the admiral had accompanied Ross's army to Washington "only as a volunteer." Cockburn and Evans, the two men most responsible for Ross's decision to capture Washington and attack Baltimore, are buried within a stone's throw of each other at the atmospheric Kensal Green Cemetery in west London.

Lieutenant George Gleig, after finishing his studies at Oxford, served thirty years as chaplain-general of the army. The publication of his memoirs about the campaign for Washington, Baltimore, and New Orleans launched a prolific literary career. Gleig died in 1888 at age ninety-two, possibly the last surviving member of the remarkable little army that captured Washington.

⋆

The estimated 3,000 to 5,000 former slaves from the Chesapeake who fled to the British seeking their freedom met mixed fates. The majority of the slaves who did not enlist to fight were sent to Nova Scotia. More than 2,000 were left standing on the docks in Halifax in the early months of 1815, with no money and little clothing, and they shivered through their first winter in deplorable condition. Hundreds died of disease or poverty. Some scratched out lives as farmers or servants, eventually establishing themselves in communities where their descendants still live. Other former slaves went to the West Indies, where, it was alleged, some were sold back into slavery.

The Colonial Marines had better control over their destinies. After the war ended, the six companies of former slaves were garrisoned in Bermuda for fourteen months, helping build a new Royal Navy dockyard. The British, eager to keep the services of the reliable Colonials, wanted to transfer them into the army's West India regiments. But the Colonials refused; they had done their service and wanted to live as free men. The British offered to send them to settle as independent farmers on Trinidad, the British colony off the coast of South America.

About seven hundred Colonial Marines arrived in Trinidad in August 1816, and though they formally disbanded, they organized villages based by military company, each supervised by a former sergeant. They proudly identified themselves as Americans and were soon known colloquially as "the Merikens."

Among them was Sergeant Ezekiel Loney, the young slave who had escaped from Virginia's Northern Neck in the summer of 1814 and fought at Washington and Baltimore. Loney married, had children, and remained part of the thriving community of company villages that still exist. Nearly two hundred years later, in 2009, some of Loney's descendants traveled from Trinidad to Tangier Island in the Chesapeake, where the Colonials had trained. The waters of the bay had long since claimed Fort Albion, which lay submerged off the southern coast of the island. The family members said prayers and poured libations, and the children cast origami boats made of rice paper into the water.

The community of Colonial Marine descendants, said Tina Dunkley, one of the Loney family members who made the journey, is an "extraordinary testament to the intrepidness of thousands of enslaved Africans who vied for their liberation under the most daunting conditions."

The capture of Washington by the British took its place as one of the boldest military feats of the age. "The world was astonished to see a handful of seven or eight thousand Englishmen making their appearance in the midst of a state embracing ten millions of people, taking possession of its capital, and destroying all the public buildings, results unparalleled in history," the Baron de Jomini wrote in his classsic, *The Art of War.*

Cockburn, for his part, displayed no false modesty about the operation, later describing it as a "hostile tour in the heart of the enemy's country which for the extent of ground passed over, the importance of its objects, and the mischief done the enemy, ashore, and afloat, in so short a space of time, is scarcely perhaps to be paralleled."

But what, in the end, had the Chesapeake campaign accomplished for the British? American troops were not diverted from Canada, as London had expected. Cockburn's raids did leave Americans disgusted with their government's failure to defend the homeland, but they sparked an even greater fury at the British. Beyond that, Cockburn and Ross had hoped the capture of Washington would bring down Madison's government and force the United States to sue for peace on British terms. Had Baltimore fallen, their remarkable venture may well have succeeded. Instead, the reversal turned the tables, as the British faced growing pressure to make peace.

"We should have been saved from that success, a thousand times more disgraceful and disastrous than the worst defeat," Sir James Mackintosh, the Scottish historian and Whig parliamentarian, said during the debate on the Treaty of Ghent. "It was a success which made our naval power hateful and alarming to all Europe; which gave the hearts of the American people to every enemy who might rise against England; an enterprise which most exasperated a people, and least weakened a government of any recorded in the annals of war."

New Year's Day dawned sunny and pleasant in Washington, ideal weather for the public debut of the rebuilt President's House. The mansion's black burns and cracked stone were now covered by coats of white lead paint, better suited to hide the scars of war than the whitewash used prior to the British attack. Though the building was far from finished, some three thousand guests tromped through the house over raw yellow pine floorboards covered with carpets.

President James Monroe graciously greeted the visitors who packed the house for three hours. "It was gratifying to be able once more to salute the President of the United States with the compliments of the season in his appropriate residence," the *Intelligencer* wrote. Monroe had been so eager to move in after taking office in 1817 that he took up residency long before the mansion was ready, living for months amid hammering, sawing, painting, and varnishing.

Monroe wanted to restore the presidency as a symbol of unity, with a rebuilt President's House at its center. He and his regal wife, Elizabeth, shared a taste for elegance acquired from his diplomatic days in Paris in the late 1790s, and they brought French decorative arts and furniture to the mansion.

Monroe's eight-year presidency would be regarded as a great success, a period of peace, prosperity, and nonpartisanship that became known as the "Era of Good Feelings." Monroe was able to point to the war as a triumph. "It has been said that our Union, and system of government, would not bear such a trial," Monroe said. "The result has proved the imputation to be entirely destitute of foundation. . . . [O]ur Union has gained strength, our troops honor, and the nation character, by the contest."

James Madison, so reviled and ridiculed after the fall of Washington, left office riding a wave of goodwill and nationalism when he passed the torch of the Virginia dynasty to Monroe. "Not withstanding a thousand faults and blunders, his administration has acquired more glory, and established more Union, than all his three predecessors, Washington, Adams and Jefferson, put together," John Adams wrote to Thomas Jefferson.

The year 1814 had been a turning point in American history. It began with the United States facing great peril in its war with one of the world's great powers. The country's coasts were blockaded, its treasury was depleted, and some in New England were in favor of dissolving the union. When Washington fell in late August, the outlook could not have been bleaker.

But just a few months later, by the war's conclusion in February 1815, the outlook was very different. By many measures, the United States had lost the war. The invasions of Canada had ended in disgrace, and from a military standpoint, the U.S. Army's history concedes, the war "at best . . . was a draw."

Yet the circumstances of the war's end created a different sense in America. The chain of victories in the final months of the war, including Baltimore and Plattsburgh, proved the United States capable of stopping mighty Great Britain, and allowed the American delegation at Ghent to escape with far better terms than what could have been expected when negotiations commenced in August. The final triumph at New Orleans was so one-sided that it created a lasting belief in America that the United States had won the war .

Nonetheless, most Americans, including Madison, realized it had been a narrow escape from a national collapse. The public—especially those living in the Chesapeake region or along the frontier with Canada—was well aware of the failures, but saw survival as victory. That the nation suffered from partisan strife, economic chaos, and poor military leadership, and was led by a president who refused to seize additional executive authority, made it all the more remarkable.

The Constitution had survived its first great test. American independence and sovereignty had been validated and the Founders' grand revolutionary experiment preserved. Madison's refusal to abandon the republican concept of government had been vindicated. "The ultimate good flowing from the disaster which at one moment clouded its prospects . . . is among the proofs of that spirit in the American people, as a free people, which, rising above adverse events, and even converting them into sources of advantage, is the true safeguard against dangers of every sort," Madison noted upon leaving office.

Ghent did not, on paper, address a single goal laid out by the United

States in declaring war. Henry Clay considered the agreement "a damned bad treaty" because it ignored free trade and sailors' rights. Yet in practice, British restrictions on the trading rights of neutral nations and impressments of sailors at sea into the Royal Navy declined dramatically with the end of the Napoleonic Wars. "Although the treaty seemed to have settled none of the issues that had caused the War of 1812, it actually had settled everything," historian Gordon Wood has observed.

This Second War of Independence, as many Americans of the day considered it, severed ties with America's colonial past and represented a definitive end to the American Revolution.

"I think it will be a long time before we are disturbed again by any of the powers of Europe," James Bayard wrote to his son on Christmas Day 1814 from Ghent. Within a decade, the Monroe Doctrine warned European nations against any further colonization in America. A grudging respect had been established between the United States and Britain, neither of which would ever again go to war against the other.

"The war has renewed and reinstated the national feelings and character which the Revolution had given, and which were daily lessening," Albert Gallatin wrote a year after the treaty was ratified. "The people have now more general objects of attachment, with which their pride and political opinions are connected. They are more American; they feel and act more as a nation; and I hope that the permanency of the Union is thereby better secured."

America turned its attention west. Ghent called for an end to all hostilities with Indians and restoring pre-war boundaries, but this proved to be an empty promise. The ambiguous and unenforceable terms of the treaty did not impede the drive west. The Northwest Territory, rather than becoming the buffer envisioned by Britain, was soon carved up into the states of Indiana and Illinois, and later Michigan and Wisconsin.

What the United States had learned was as important as what it gained. The war's many failures demonstrated the need for a stronger regular army, including better officers and a superior military academy. The U.S. Navy was launched on a path toward becoming a global force, with steady congressional funding for ships. One troubling lesson was put aside: The war—the Chesapeake campaign in particular—had exposed the military, social, and economic vulnerability of a nation dependent on slavery.

Three years after Ghent, Madison offered this wishful benediction: "[I]f our first struggle was a war of our infancy, this last was that of our youth, and the issue of both, wisely improved, may long postpone if not forever prevent, a necessity for exerting the strength of our manhood."

James Madison would never return to Washington and spent his nineteen remaining years in happy retirement at Montpelier, overseeing the five-thousand-acre plantation, experimenting with agricultural techniques, and consulting with his friend Thomas Jefferson on weather observations. With the aid of Dolley, he spent years creating an enormous record of the Constitutional Convention, believing it would serve "the cause of liberty throughout the world," and that its publication would provide Dolley a source of income.

His manservant Paul Jennings, who had accompanied Madison on his flight from Washington, was at his side throughout, particularly as the former president's health began to fail. On a June morning in 1836, Madison was unable to swallow his breakfast. His niece asked what was wrong. "Nothing more than a change of mind, my dear," Madison replied.

"His head dropped and he stopped breathing as quietly as the snuff of a candle goes out," Jennings recalled.

After his death, Dolley moved to Washington, scene of her glory days. She reveled in her role as grande dame of the capital, a familiar presence in her black velvet gown and white satin turban. A stream of callers visited her home across Lafayette Square from the President's House, which served "like the residence of the Queen dowager."

She was careful to ensure that she received credit for saving the portrait of George Washington. Her famous letter dated August 23–24, 1814, often quoted as a contemporaneous account of the capture of Washington, appears to have been written around 1834, when her friend Margaret Bayard Smith asked her to furnish letters and recollections for a book. In 1848, when a controversy erupted over the circumstances of removing the portrait, Dolley wrote to a newspaper explaining why she ordered the servants to save the portrait: "I acted thus because of my respect for General Washington, not that I felt a desire to gain laurels; but, should there be a merit in remaining an hour in danger of life and liberty to save the likeness of anything, the merit in this case belongs to me."

In her later years, an economic downturn and crop failures at Montpelier left Dolley in a precarious financial situation, exacerbated by the spending sprees of her wastrel son, Payne Todd. In debt, she was forced to sell Montpelier in 1844. Dolley had promised to free Jennings in her will but instead sold him in 1846. In the last years of Dolley's life, Jennings would often bring by baskets of goods sent by Senator Daniel Webster, who bought Jennings his freedom. Despite her hard last years, her death in 1849 brought the largest state funeral Washington had ever seen.

Jennings flourished in freedom, raising a family and working for the Department of the Interior. He owned a home in Washington when he died in 1874, and his descendants still live in the area. In 2009, on the 195th anniversary of the burning of the President's House, family members visited the White House of President Barack Obama and viewed the portrait of George Washington that Paul Jennings helped save.

Blame for Bladensburg was assiduously avoided. Madison and Monroe, riding the triumphs of the war's last months and its happy conclusion at Ghent, escaped with their reputations intact. Secretary of War John Armstrong fought against any responsibility from his exile in New York, where he wrote a bitter memoir blaming Monroe, "this busy and blundering tactician," for his disastrous movement of the troops before the battle.

A sympathetic military court of inquiry concluded in 1815 that William Winder warranted no censure for the Bladensburg disgrace, taking "into consideration the complicated difficulties & embarrassments under which he laboured." Winder resumed his law practice, was elected to the Maryland State Senate, and was nearly elected to the U.S. House of Representatives. Though everyone seemed to think more highly of Winder when he was out of uniform, there was no escaping the cloud of Bladensburg, which hung about him until his death in 1824.

★

Joshua Barney's last battle was with Congress. Returning to Baltimore during the final months of the war to take command of the flotilla, Barney learned that not only was Congress refusing to compensate his men for their belongings lost when the flotilla was scuttled, but the government had no money for their back pay. "[T]he conduct of Congress to those under my command has been infamous," Barney fumed. He resigned in disgust but soon returned to duty with a pledge not to "lay down my sword, until death, or a peace such as our country ought to obtain; external enemies or internal traitors, notwithstanding." Once peace was ratified, Barney presided over the disestablishment of the Chesapeake flotilla.

Doctors had been unable to remove the musket ball lodged in his hip at Bladensburg, and he never fully recovered. Nonetheless, Barney

Two centuries after its demise in a noble but futile attempt to defend the nation's capital, Barney's flotilla was returning to light.

Wood trim from boat recovered at the Scorpion *excavation on the Patuxent River in 2012.*

was ready for new adventures, and in 1818 he pulled up stakes in Maryland, packed up his family, and headed west to start a new life in Kentucky. But he died en route in Pittsburgh in December 1818 at age fifty-nine, from lingering effects of the wound, possibly including lead poisoning.

For more than a century, the hulks of some of Barney's flotilla boats remained visible in the mud of the Patuxent River, visited by fishermen, relic hunters, and adventuresome children. But gradually the remains receded, whittled by salvage hunters and buried in silt. By the 1950s, they had disappeared entirely.

In 1979, a team of marine

researchers, led by Donald Shomette and Ralph Eshelman, explored the waters near Pig Point and located a seventy-five-foot-long shipwreck, which they tentatively identified as *Scorpion*, the flagship of Barney's flotilla. After a limited, monthlong excavation, the wreck was reburied under four feet of mud to protect it from decay. Three decades later, divers from the U.S. Navy and the state of Maryland began exploring the site, with hopes to one day excavate it. Two centuries after its demise in a noble but futile attempt to defend the nation's capital, Barney's flotilla was returning to light.

Unlike Bladensburg, the commanders at Baltimore were lionized after the war. The city of Baltimore commissioned portraits by the artist Rembrandt Peale of its heroes, among them George Armistead, Samuel Smith, John Stricker, and Joshua Barney. Armistead, recovering from his exhaustion after the battle, soon won promotion to lieutenant colonel and wide acclaim as the hero of Fort McHenry. "So you see my Dear Wife all is well, at least your husband has got a name and standing that nothing but divine providence could have given him, and I pray to our Heavenly Father that we may live long to enjoy," he wrote Louisa.

But Armistead lived only four years after the bombardment, remaining in command at Fort McHenry until his death in 1818. "The procession of military and citizens was the most numerous ever witnessed in Baltimore," *Niles'* reported.

Smith resigned his commission when General Winfield Scott was given authority over the Baltimore militia in 1815. But Smith was not finished with public life, winning election to the House in 1816 and later returning to the Senate. When a bank failure led to riots in the streets of Baltimore, Smith, then eighty-three, was called back to take command of the militia and promptly restored order. Citizens turned to him one last time to serve as mayor until shortly before his death in 1839.

The three navy captains who rallied Baltimore would never return to the glory they achieved during the war. John Rodgers, who feared he would "nearly go crazy" with the coming of peace, had to content himself with largely administrative chores for much of the next twenty years as president of the Board of Navy Commissioners, until his death in 1837. Oliver Hazard Perry, whose remaining career was marred by a bitter dispute over a subordinate's performance at Lake Erie, was sent by President Monroe to combat piracy in South America in 1819. He contracted yellow fever and died at age thirty-four. David Porter, court-martialed for insubordination after attacking a Spanish town in Puerto Rico without orders in 1825, served three years as commander-in-chief of the Mexican navy and twelve years as U.S. chargé d'affaires in Constantinople, where he died in 1843.

John Skinner, who accompanied Francis Scott Key on his journey to lasting fame, was rewarded for his energetic wartime service with a job as Baltimore's postmaster, but left his most enduring mark as founder of two pioneering periodicals: *The American Farmer*, the first successful publication covering agriculture in the United States, and *American Turf Register and Sporting Magazine*, the nation's first sports magazine. Bustling until the end, he died in 1851 at age sixty-three, after he fell down a cellar door at the Baltimore post office while hurrying to pick up some papers. Joseph Nicholson, who ensured Key's song would be heard, suffered from faltering health and lived for only three years after the defense of Fort McHenry.

Within days of his release from captivity, William Beanes was back in Upper Marlboro seeing patients. For the rest of his life, he remained close to Key, who witnessed Beanes's will in 1827. Any time Beanes showed signs of temper, according to the tale later told by his grand-niece, his wife, Sarah, silenced him by threatening to "to send for Admiral Cockburn." True or not, Beanes lived quietly at Academy Hill until his death at age eighty in 1828, and was buried next to his wife in the garden.

Three thousand citizens assembled on the lawn of the old courthouse in Frederick, Maryland, on August 6, 1834, for a great public dinner thrown by supporters of President Andrew Jackson to celebrate the town's most famous resident, Roger Brooke Taney, who had just resigned after three years as Jackson's attorney general. Rows of tables were covered with hams, beef, jellies, wines, and vegetables. Among the guests at the head table was the man Jackson had selected as U.S. attorney for the District of Columbia, the capital's chief prosecutor: Francis Scott Key.

A speaker toasted Key as "an incorruptible patriot, worthy of being honored, wherever genius is admired or liberty cherished, as the author of the Star-Spangled Banner." After glasses were raised and applause subsided, Key rose to make his own remarks. Modest and self-effacing, he had said little publicly about the song, but now, for one of the few recorded times in his life, he described the emotions that led to its creation. Key did not disguise his pride in the song, paraphrasing an old saying that "if he could be allowed to make a nation's songs, he cared not who made its laws." But Key was careful to note that "the honor was due, not to him who made the song, but to the heroism of those who made him make it."

Key by then was one of the most prominent citizens of Washington, not just as author of the song, but also as an attorney and in his new capacity as prosecutor. The years after the war had seen his law practice busier than ever. Key was capable of arguing both sides of the slavery issue. He once successfully represented a slave owner in opposing freedom for the children of a free mulatto woman, but he also provided legal advice to those seeking emancipation, and represented on a pro bono basis free blacks who were being sold back into slavery, "ready to brave odium or even personal danger on their behalf," according to his friend, Rev. John T. Brooke. In 1825, after the Spanish slave-trade vessel *Antelope* was captured by a Baltimore privateer, Key unsuccessfully tried to persuade the Supreme Court that the slaves aboard the ship should not be returned to Spain, closing his argument with "a thrilling and even an electrifying picture of the horrors connected with the African slave trade," a witness wrote.

Fearing that mass emancipation would bring dire social and economic unrest, Key championed the American colonization movement, an odd venture that envisioned a gradual end to slavery by creating a colony in Africa for free blacks willing to leave America. Key helped write the American Colonization Society's constitution, and traveled to churches, schools, and town halls to raise money. In 1820, the first free American blacks settled in what would become Liberia, whose capital, Monrovia, was named after President Monroe, a supporter of the effort. Colonization was met with scorn from southerners and bitter opposition from abolitionists, who saw it as a palliative that would perpetuate slavery. The idea never amounted to much, but Key, with utopian fervor, never abandoned it.

There were happy days at the Key home in Georgetown, with its terraced garden leading down to the Potomac. Key had the gardener plant tiny round gardens for each child, with their names spelled by seedlings. But the idyllic times were shattered on July 8, 1822, when his eight-year-old son, Edward—the second-youngest of their nine children—went swimming in the river after school and drowned. Edward, the heartbroken Key wrote, was "a beautiful boy, and his gentle and pleasing countenance was a true index of his disposition."

Key had been away on business in Annapolis, and he berated himself for his "unfaithfulness as a parent." But in his absence, Key saw "the tenderness and compassion of the Heavenly Father who saw it necessary thus to chasten me. . . . I was spared all that stormy tumult of feeling endured by my poor wife and children who were at the scene of suffering, all that agony (which I know not how I could have borne) of hearing he was in the water, that they were searching for him, that he was found, that they were attempting to revive him, that it was in vain."

Key and Polly had two more children, and they were grandparents by the time their eleventh child, Charles Henry Key, was born in the summer of 1827. But after three decades in their Georgetown home, the Keys moved around 1833 to a smaller house on C Street in Washington. By then, only four children were still living at home. Beyond that, the character of the once-serene Georgetown home had been irreparably altered by "turbulence" from the construction of the Chesapeake & Ohio Canal, directly behind the house along the Potomac shore.

After years of eschewing party politics, Key had embraced the new Democratic Party, which had emerged from the ruins of the old party system. In particular, Key supported its leader, Jackson, the hero of the common man. Though many of the Washington elite were leery of the backwoods war hero, Key found Jackson's brand of populism refreshing, and he enthusiastically campaigned for his election in the bitter 1828 race against President John Quincy Adams. When a crowd of twenty thousand gathered in front of the Capitol to celebrate Jackson's inauguration in 1829, Key was exhilarated. "It is beautiful!" he exclaimed to Margaret Bayard Smith, who nervously clutched his arm as they navigated the masses. "It is sublime!"

Key became a confidant and legal adviser to Jackson; the general reportedly told Key that the "Star-Spangled Banner" helped inspire the troops at New Orleans. When Jackson's friend, the rising legend Sam Houston, caned a congressman in 1832 and was put on trial before the House of Representatives, it was Key who got him off with a reprimand. After appointing Key U.S. attorney for the District of Columbia in 1833, Jackson sent the lawyer on a delicate mission to Alabama to mediate a dispute with the state government over federal promises to move settlers from Creek Indian reservations. Passions against the federal government were running high, with talk of secession, but Key was welcomed in Alabama, and serenaded by a band playing "The Star-Spangled Banner" upon his arrival in Tuscaloosa. ("That is a pretty air," Key, who some claimed was tone-deaf, reportedly asked. "What is it?") Key mediated a settlement to the crisis through a mixture of political savvy and personal charm that included penning poems for the governor's wife and daughter.

Key had a hand in the rise of Roger Taney, who would make decisions with far-reaching consequences for the country. When Jackson considered appointing Taney attorney general in 1831, he called Key to the White House, wanting assurances Taney would accept. Key persuaded his hesitant brother-in-law to take the job, telling Taney "you will find yourself . . . acting with men who know and value you & with whom you will have the influence you ought to have." Key later worked behind the scenes for Taney's confirmation as chief justice of the Supreme Court in 1836, to replace John Marshall. More than two decades later, Taney—by then cynical and suffering a "broken spirit" following the death of his wife, Anne, and their youngest daughter from yellow fever—authored the notorious *Dred Scott* decision, an assault on free black citizenship and one of the final steps leading to the Civil War.

The post as federal prosecutor in Washington thrust Key into the midst of dramatic and unsettling events. On January 30, 1835, a demented house painter named David Lawrence tried to shoot Jackson at point-blank range on the steps of the Capitol, but his pistol misfired. An enraged Jackson was convinced the assassination attempt was part of a political plot, but after interrogating Lawrence at the city jail, Key believed the man was insane and had acted alone. Despite political pressure, Key saw that the law protected Lawrence when he was tried in April. Key "did not lose his calmness, allowing only a sense of justice and a desire for the truth to influence him in the matter," a newspaper wrote. Lawrence was found not guilty by reason of insanity and sent to an asylum.

The sorriest episode in Key's career erupted later that year and centered around Anna Maria Thornton, the widow of Key's longtime friend, patent supervisor William Thornton, who had died in 1828. In August 1835, Anna Thornton woke up one night to find her eighteen-year-old slave, Arthur Bowen, hovering in her bedroom door with an axe. She fled unharmed, and Bowen was arrested. For some Washingtonians, the incident evoked terrifying memories of Nat Turner's bloody slave rebellion in Virginia four years earlier. Angry whites threatened to tear down the jail and lynch Bowen, and at Key's request, marines were called out to restore order. The nights that followed saw some of the most violent riots in Washington's history, as lower-class whites rampaged against free blacks. In this highly charged atmosphere, Key won the death penalty against Bowen for attempted murder. But a distraught Anna Thornton pleaded for clemency from the president, insisting that Bowen had simply been drunk. Jackson pardoned the slave.

Key had meanwhile brought charges against abolitionist Reuben Crandall, claiming that Bowen's actions had been instigated by anti-slavery pamphlets and accusing Crandall of a "base and demonical" effort to incite slaves. Key's aggressive prosecution brought condemnation from many critics, including abolitionist editor William Lloyd Garrison, who accused Key of a "deep malignity of purpose." During the trial, Crandall's attorney, Joseph Bradley, read an eloquent statement decrying the evils of slavery, and then revealed its author: Francis Scott Key. After deliberating for three hours, the jury found Crandall not guilty, a stinging rebuke for the prosecutor.

Days later came tragedy. Key's nineteen-year-old son, Daniel, serving a tour of duty with the navy, had quarreled at sea with a fellow midshipman. Encountering each other back in Washington, they agreed to a duel, in which Daniel was fatally shot. When his lifeless body was brought back to the Key house on C Street, the family was utterly devastated. Less than a year later, Key's son John, a tall and promising twenty-seven-year-old lawyer and himself the father of two young boys, died after a brief illness, bringing "fresh and heavy affliction" to the household. Key would be spared the death of a fourth son, Philip Barton Key II, his youngest and most brilliant child, who had followed in his father's footsteps to become U.S. Attorney for the District of Columbia. He was shot and killed in 1859 by Representative Daniel Sickles for having an affair with Sickles's wife, one of the most sensational crimes in Washington's history.

The tragedies and tumult sapped Key of some of his vitality. He retired after two terms as U.S. attorney in 1841 but continued his private practice, living most of the year at Terra Rubra and returning to Washington only when his presence was required in court.

Key had emancipated seven of his slaves by 1838, although, he fretted, "when age and infirmity come upon them, they will probably suffer." The rest of his slaves he left to Polly with the request that she free them before she died. Key remained deeply opposed to abolition, telling a minister in 1838 that the Bible gave "neither an express sanction nor an express prohibition" to slavery and calling blacks "a distinct and inferior race." But in the same letter, Key said that for his entire life, "I have had the greatest desire to see Maryland become a free state, and the strongest conviction that she could become so . . . I feel sure that it will be so."

By then the lyrics of "The Star-Spangled Banner" were being used in parodies by abolitionists condemning the hypocrisy of slaveholders. Whether he was aware of this or not, Key was clearly troubled by the juxtaposition of slavery in the land of the free. "Where else, except in slavery, was ever such a bed of torture prepared by man for man?" he asked in 1842, in one of his last speeches.

In early January 1843, Key traveled to Washington to appear before Taney's Supreme Court and then continued to Baltimore on legal business. Along the way, he wrote a long poem he called "The Nobleman's Son," about the prayers of a mother saving her dying child. By the time Key arrived in the city and walked to the home on Mount Vernon Place where his daughter Elizabeth lived with her husband, he was feverish with a cold.

"So long as patriotism dwells upon us, so long will this song be the theme of our nation."

Sculpture of Francis Scott Key atop his grave at Mount Olivet Cemetery in Frederick, Maryland.

The next morning, a Sunday, Key stayed in bed at the insistence of his daughter rather than go to church. "Lizzie, I have a feeling I never had before," he told her. Key seemed better Tuesday after his wife arrived. But by Wednesday morning, Polly was alarmed at his deteriorating condition. Key was soon in a state of delirium. Occasionally he recited passages from the Bible or favorite hymns. "I cannot agree to that proposition," he said at one point. "Tell them not to bother me."

Key asked someone to read the Ninety-First Psalm, and he listened through the end of the second verse—*I will say of the Lord, He is my refuge and my fortress: my God; in him will I trust*—and then his mind drifted off. Around 8 p.m. on Wednesday, January 11, 1843, at age sixty-three, Key died of pleurisy complicated by pneumonia, just a few miles from Fort McHenry.

"Francis S. Key, the author of the Star-Spangled Banner, is no more," reported the *Baltimore American*. "So long as patriotism dwells upon us, so long will this song be the theme of our nation." Flags in Washington and Baltimore were lowered to half-mast, and the Supreme Court promptly adjourned in his memory.

Key was buried in the family vault of his son-in-law, Charles Howard, at St. Paul's Church in Baltimore, and when Polly died in 1859, she was placed next to him. But in 1866, their remains were moved to Frederick and buried beneath a small headstone at Mount Olivet Cemetery, in keeping with the wish Key once expressed to rest "'neath the shadows of the everlasting hills" of Frederick County. The Keys were reinterred at Mount Olivet in 1898 underneath a graceful monument with a sculpture of Key atop a granite pedestal, doffing his hat in joy upon spotting the flag. By resolution of Congress, the American flag flies over Key's grave twenty-four hours a day.

On October 8, 1824, the Marquis de Lafayette visited Baltimore, part of a triumphant tour of America by the French aristocrat who had served at George Washington's side during the Revolutionary War. As Lafayette sailed into Baltimore Harbor, the garrison at Fort McHenry fired its guns in salute and hoisted a great banner on the flagpole.

It was the last time that the Star-Spangled Banner would fly at Fort McHenry. The flag by then was in the possession of George Armistead's widow, Louisa, who had loaned it for the occasion. The family later said the flag was presented to George Armistead after the battle, but more likely, he felt a proprietary interest and simply kept it. Had he not, the banner would probably have been discarded or destroyed. Such was the apparent fate of the storm flag, which likely flew during the bombardment and has long since disappeared. But the great banner, raised on the morning of September 14, 1814, at the end of the bombardment, was the one Armistead saved. After her husband's death, the flag took on enormous sentimental value to Louisa Armistead, and it was likely she who sewed a red chevron on one of the stripes, the beginning of the letter A.

The family loaned the flag to be displayed at appropriate events. For a time, the flag occasionally appeared at Baltimore's annual celebration of Defenders' Day, the state holiday on September 12, marking the successful defense of Baltimore. "On the staff we saw the old flag of Fort McHenry . . . amidst the joyous shouts of those who recognized its tattered folds," a correspondent wrote following a celebration at Hampstead Hill in 1828. "A holy relic never disgraced, and receiving now the homage of friends, as in 1814, it commanded the respect of foes." The Armistead family offered the flag for Key's funeral procession, but it was not used.

When Louisa Armistead died in 1861, a few months after the outbreak of the Civil War, her youngest daughter, Georgiana Armistead Appleton, who was born at Fort McHenry and named after her father, inherited the flag. In the terrible conflict that followed, some of George

Armistead's descendants would fight against the flag he had defended. His nephew, Confederate Brigadier General Lewis Addison Armistead, died of his wounds from leading an assault on Cemetery Ridge at Gettysburg. His grandson, George Armistead Appleton, was arrested for possessing a Confederate flag on Defenders' Day in 1861 and was held as a prisoner at Fort McHenry, which was used by Union forces during the war as a prison for Confederate soldiers and southern sympathizers. On that same anniversary of the British attack, Frank Key Howard, editor of the pro-South *Baltimore Exchange*, was also arrested and imprisoned at Fort McHenry. The irony was inescapable for Howard, the grandson of Francis Scott Key. "As I stood upon the very scene of that conflict, I could not but contrast my position with his, forty-seven years before," Howard later wrote. "The flag which he had then so proudly hailed, I saw waving at the same place, over the victims of as vulgar and brutal a despotism as modern times have witnessed."

Though a southern sympathizer herself, Georgiana Appleton and her family safeguarded the Star-Spangled Banner through the war. "[W]ith me it has remained ever since, loved and venerated," she wrote in 1873. But the flag by then was deteriorating badly, "just fading away, being among our earthly treasures where moth and rust must corrupt," she said. It did not help that the Armistead family occasionally allowed those deemed worthy of the honor to cut out pieces of the flag, a common custom at the time.

The flag had remained through this time a family keepsake, largely unknown to the American public outside of Baltimore. But in 1873, Georgiana Appleton lent the flag to Commodore George Henry Preble, a naval officer and historian. Preble had a canvas sail stitched to the flag to give it support, put it on display in New England, and had it photographed for the first time. His lectures and articles brought great attention to the flag at a time when the public, in the years after the Civil War, was hungry for symbols of national unity.

By the time Eben Appleton, a New York stockbroker, inherited the flag upon his mother's death in 1878, it was an America icon. Appleton, the grandson of George Armistead, was a private and proper man greatly concerned with keeping the flag's dignity. He refused to lend the flag for events that lacked proper decorum, keeping it locked much of the time in a Manhattan safe-deposit vault. The flag made a last visit

"A holy relic never disgraced, and receiving now the homage of friends,
as in 1814, it commanded the respect of foes."

*The first known photograph of the Star Spangled Banner, taken at the
Boston Naval yard in 1873.*

to Baltimore in 1880, when it was carried in a great procession celebrating the city's sesquicentennial. But Appleton was dissatisfied with
the arrangements for the seventy-fifth anniversary of the bombardment in 1889, and refused to lend the flag, sparking outrage in Baltimore. Appleton was vilified amid suggestions that the flag was public
property.

Gravely insulted, Appleton refused to discuss the flag for the next eighteen years. By then he was looking for a public institution to take on the burden of caring for what had become a national symbol. A cousin directed Appleton's attention to the Smithsonian Institution in Washington, which, since its founding in 1846, had taken an increased role as the national museum.

In 1907, Appleton loaned the flag to the Smithsonian, and, pleased with its handling, he made it a permanent gift five years later. Even so, a Baltimore committee preparing for the centennial of the Star-Spangled Banner in 1914 pressed Appleton to have the flag brought to Baltimore, even printing programs announcing it would be carried on parade. An irritated Appleton sent a condition to the Smithsonian: The flag was to "remain there forever" and never moved.

The disintegrating flag was in any event in no condition for further public tours. By the time the flag was turned over to the Smithsonian, it was eight feet shorter than the one sewn by Mary Pickersgill, and more than two hundred square feet of fabric were missing, including one star. In 1914, a team led by noted flag restorer Amelia Fowler stitched a linen backing to the flag, allowing it to be displayed in the Smithsonian's Arts and Industries Building on the National Mall.

The flag remained there for the next quarter century, folded over inside a glass case. But the outbreak of World War II and the destruction of public buildings in the London blitz raised concerns about the Star-Spangled Banner's safety in the event of an enemy air raid. Soon after Pearl Harbor, despite Eben Appleton's admonition, the flag was placed in a fifteen-foot-long crate and taken in secrecy to Shenandoah National Park in Virginia. It was stored in a park warehouse, along with other priceless artifacts—including George Washington's uniform and the desk on which Thomas Jefferson drafted the Declaration of Independence—until late 1944, when Washington was deemed safe.

In 1964, the flag was freed from the growing clutter of glass cases in its old home and made the dramatic centerpiece of a new building now known as the National Museum of American History. For thirty-four years, the stirring sight of the Star-Spangled Banner suspended from fifty feet high greeted visitors to the flag hall.

But the flag suffered from exposure to light and pollution, even after a screen was added to protect it. In 1998, the Star-Spangled Banner was lowered and a new restoration begun. Examining the material, conservators concluded that the linen sewn to the back in 1914 had to go, as it forced the flag into a uniform rectangle that distorted its true, irregular shape. Working with scissors and tweezers and often lying prone on a movable bridge suspended above the flag, conservators painstakingly removed the 1.7 million stitches that held the backing.

The results were spectacular, revealing a side of the flag unseen by the public since 1873, with vivid colors that had been protected from light and dirt. The preservation team cleaned the flag with more than ten thousand common cosmetic sponges, and then brushed a solvent mixture of water and acetone on the surface to remove dirt, further revealing the flag's original colors. Cotton fibers on the stars bore traces of exposure to battle conditions, but there was no evidence any where on the flag of damage caused by shot or shrapnel—supporting the notion that the storm flag flew during the bombardment. The holes were not from battle, as was often assumed, but rather from time, including insect damage and snippets cut out as relics. The largest hole, which entirely removed the fifteenth star, was apparently cut out by Louisa Armistead to give as a memento to an unknown distinguished recipient.

The flag was far too fragile to ever be again hung vertically, it was clear. A strong, lightweight, and almost sheer backing was attached to give the flag support. The conservation, expected to last three years, ended up taking eight years and costing $8.5 million, but the flag was not yet ready for display. As part of a major renovation of the museum begun in 2006, a special $19 million chamber was constructed on the second floor to protect the banner from light, air, and water. The flag was placed on a display platform, raised to an angle of 10 degrees for viewing. In November 2008, the flag was restored to public view in the new gallery, and the effect was mesmerizing.

The banner hovers in the dimly lit chamber like a ghostly apparition, thin as a wisp, but its vibrant colors startlingly alive. The holes and tears previously disguised by a painted background are now plainly visible. Two hundred years after the battle, tattered and frail, the Star-Spangled Banner seemed more powerful than ever.

★

The transformation of the American flag into the preeminent symbol of American identity and ideals had begun with Francis Scott Key's song. The flag had not been a major national symbol before the War of 1812. It served a more functional role during and after the American Revolution, marking U.S. military installations, while other symbols, including the eagle and Lady Liberty, represented national identity. Key's description of the American flag flying over Fort McHenry after the tremendous British bombardment created an indelible image for the nation. It would be followed over the years by flags raised during other defining moments in American history: "Old Glory," the flag flown over Nashville, Tennessee, after it was taken by Union troops during the Civil War; the flag raised by U.S. Marines during the battle on Iwo Jima; and the flags displayed by firefighters at the World Trade Center and the Pentagon after the terrorist attacks of September 11, 2001.

The rise of "The Star-Spangled Banner" to become America's national anthem was similarly gradual. In the years after the war, the song became a standard at patriotic gatherings, including Independence Day and Washington's Birthday, and was especially popular around Washington and Baltimore. It was often called a national anthem, though there was no sense until decades later that the country needed a single anthem. "The Star-Spangled Banner" was one of several songs that served informally as a national anthem, along with "Hail Columbia" and "Yankee Doodle," and until the Civil War, it probably ranked behind the other two.

But with the war, Key's anthem "rushed to the front of our national songs," wrote anthem scholar Oscar Sonneck. "Yankee Doodle" seemed too frivolous and "Hail Columbia" too dull, while the lyrics of "The Star-Spangled Banner" resonated at a time when the American flag was under attack at Fort Sumter. Federal armies embraced the song, playing it as they entered Savannah, Richmond, and New Orleans.

Beginning in 1889, the U.S. Navy and the U.S. Army gave "The Star-Spangled Banner" a more formal status as a national anthem through a series of orders directing that it be played at the ceremonial raising and lowering of the flag. In 1903, the navy ordered sailors to stand at attention during its playing, and the army quickly followed suit. Civilians soon adopted the custom at theaters and baseball games. As the nation entered World War I, the army and navy designated "The Star-Spangled Banner" as the national anthem to be played at ceremonies.

But the song still lacked the imperator of Congress. The first bill to designate the song as the national anthem was introduced in 1912, but legislation languished for almost two decades, in part because of persistent opposition from people who disliked the song.

A common complaint was that the song glorified war. It was ironic, given that Key hated the war with a passion that he himself noted could have been labeled "treason" in the divided and partisan America of 1814. Others objected that "Anacreon's" English origins somehow made the song un-American. (Sonneck gave this reply in 1914: "We took the air and we kept it. Transplanted on American soil, it thrived.") Prohibitionists and some religious leaders seized on the "drinking song" label as proof of the tune's unsavory origins; the doughty Augusta Stetson took out ads in national newspapers denouncing it as a "barroom ballad composed by a foreigner." And some said the song was simply too hard to sing—"words that nobody can remember to a tune that nobody can sing," the *New York Herald Tribune* complained. "America the Beautiful" was proposed by many as a lovely and inoffensive anthem easy for all to sing.

Nonetheless, Representative J. Charles Linthicum of Maryland doggedly pushed for the song by his state's native son, and a bill designating "The Star-Spangled Banner" as the national anthem was finally passed by the House and Senate and signed into law by President Herbert Hoover on March 3, 1931.

Critics have never stopped demanding a new national anthem, often dredging up the same complaints. One writer summed them up succinctly in 1965: "Our National Anthem is about as patriotic as 'The Stein Song,' as singable as *Die Walkure*, and as American as 'God Save the Queen.'"

The song "bristles with a blood-and-thunder spirit we neither feel nor want," a *Washington Post* music critic wrote in 1977. The song's lyrics are "empty bravado," and "mindless nonsense about rockets and bombs," syndicated columnist Michael Kinsley informed readers in 2009.

Among those who felt differently about "The Star-Spangled Banner" was·the great American composer and bandleader John Philip Sousa, who considered it a "soul-stirring song" that made for "a very satisfactory anthem."

"The only possible chance that we might have a new National anthem would be when the eyes of all Americans are directed toward some particular cause and another genius captures the spirit of the moment in a thrilling song of patriotism," Sousa wrote late in his life. "Until that time I do not believe the veneration for Francis Scott Key's anthem will ever be displaced."

As director of the U.S. Marine Band from 1880 to 1892, before "The Star-Spangled Banner's" official designation, Sousa recalled, he was encouraged to enter a contest to establish a national anthem. He did so, but halfheartedly, and was not disappointed at losing, nor surprised that the winning song disappeared without a trace.

"Nations will seldom obtain good national anthems by offering prizes for them," Sousa observed. "The man and the occasion must meet."

UNITED STATES CAPITOL, WASHINGTON, MONDAY, JULY 4, 1831

The American flag waved from the dome of the U.S. Capitol, and inside, the Rotunda echoed with the "heroic" airs of "The Star-Spangled Banner," played as a prelude by the United States Marine Band for the large crowd of Jacksonian Democrats gathered to celebrate Independence Day, 1831. The copper-covered wooden dome—not the one familiar to later generations—had been built atop a new center section, giving the Capitol a finished look it had lacked in 1814, when a wooden gangway had connected the north and south wings.

All shops in the city had closed, and the day was marked by the "universal suspension of all labors but those of the culinary kind," the *Intelligencer* reported. At noon, Mayor John P. Van Ness called the audience to order for the reading of the Declaration of Independence. Then he introduced the orator of the day: Francis Scott Key. It had been seventeen years since Key had written "The Star-Spangled Banner," but at age fifty-two, the slender and energetic lawyer seemed at the prime of his life. Not yet U.S. attorney for the District of Columbia, he had many personal and public tribulations ahead of him.

Key took the podium, surrounded by paintings on the Rotunda walls depicting great moments in American history: the presentation of the Declaration of Independence to the Continental Congress; the surrender of the British at Yorktown; George Washington resigning his commission. Key's gift for words was well-known, and expectations for the occasion ran high. His speech on July 4, 1831, resonated with a power and grace he had perhaps only surpassed with the four verses he wrote in Baltimore. "Mr. Key's oration was eloquent, and seemed to have been inspired by the grand memorials with which he was surrounded," commented the *Richmond Enquirer*.

Fifty-five years had passed since the Declaration of Independence, Key noted, and all but one of the signers, Charles Carroll of Maryland, had died. The Founding Fathers were slipping away. No one in Washington yet knew it, but James Monroe had died that day in New York City, the third consecutive president to die on the Fourth of July, following John Adams and Monroe's great friend and mentor, Thomas Jefferson, who had each passed away on Independence Day 1826.

We are here, in the rich possession of what valor has won, and wisdom has preserved for us.

Key spoke loudly, in clear and precise language, but his voice reverberated through the Rotunda, making it difficult for some to hear. Others, depending on where they sat, could understand every word, and listened intently as Key described the dangers facing the United States in 1831. In the South, especially South Carolina, there was a growing clamor for nullification—the demand that states be given the right to disallow federal laws they did not like. The threat to the union was clear, and Key asked the question on the minds of many: *There are . . . loud complaints of oppression in some of our states. But do they portend a dissolution of our Union?*

The Constitution, Key said, would surely remedy unjustness in America, and in the end, he predicted, the union would hold. *The tree of liberty may be shaken by these blasts, but its roots are in all our hearts, and it will stand.*

The greatest danger lay in apathy. *We who inherit freedom may learn to value it less than the men who won it.*

Nearing the end of his speech, Key described the stakes for the nation. He reframed the question he had asked on the perilous night so many years earlier, when the fate of the country was very uncertain. Would the American experiment of government by the people survive? It was a question every future generation of Americans would bear the responsibility to answer.

My countrymen, we hold a rich deposit in trust for ourselves and for all our brethren of mankind. It is the fire of liberty. If it becomes extinguished, our darkened land will cast a mournful shadow over the nations. If it lives, its blaze will enlighten and gladden the whole earth.

ACKNOWLEDGMENTS

★

MY JOURNEY INTO the War of 1812 in the Chesapeake brought me in touch with many friends, old and new, as well as family members. These encounters, on both sides of the ocean, made this exploration of history a joy for me, and were of infinite help in writing this book.

Early in my research, I crossed paths with John McCavitt, an Irish scholar preparing a biography of Robert Ross. John encouraged me to visit Northern Ireland to examine the general's papers. Along with his wife, Siobhann, and sons, Mark and Niall, John welcomed me to his home in Rostrevor, and he graciously shared his knowledge. In turn, over the course of several visits by the McCavitts to the Washington area, we explored a number of 1812 sites by land and water.

I was also very fortunate early on to encounter Ralph Eshelman, one of the leading scholars of the war in the Chesapeake, who generously shared his unmatched knowledge during numerous tours across Maryland, greatly improved the book by his careful reading of the draft, and in the process became a friend. Ralph, John, and our families came together for a memorable War of 1812 Potomac River boat cruise during which, among other accomplishments, we avoided sinking.

Joe Balkoski, a scholar of the Maryland National Guard and a friend since our days traipsing over the battlefields of Normandy for a *Washington Post* story, pointed me to holdings at Maryland Military Museum, and gave the manuscript a valuable read. Ron Jensen, old friend and good journalist, went through the draft with a red pen.

Thanks to Bill Pencek, Kate Marks, and the Maryland War of 1812

Bicentennial Commission, which sponsored a series of informative, on-the-ground and on-the-water conferences about the war in the Chesapeake that took us from the site of the British invasion in Benedict on the Patuxent River to the upper reaches of the bay at Havre de Grace. I am also grateful to Burt Kummerow and the staff at the Maryland Historical Society, a tremendous repository of documents, books, and artifacts related to the war.

Special thanks are due to the historians at the Naval History and Heritage Command at the Washington Navy Yard, who have produced the Naval War of 1812 documentary histories, an invaluable resource for scholars. Christine Hughes, Charles Brodine, and Michael Crawford very kindly gave me access to their historical files and offered guidance in my research.

A number of veterans of scholarship into the War of 1812 in the Chesapeake—a very welcoming community—generously shared their deep knowledge, among them Don Shomette, Scott Sheads, Vince Vaise, Chris George, David Hildebrand, and Patrick O'Neill.

I am also indebted to previous work done in this area by generations of writers and historians, among them John Williams, William Marine, Neil Swanson, Anthony Pitch, Joesph Whitehorne, and most especially Walter Lord.

Deep thanks also to White House curator Bill Allman, U.S. Capitol historian Bill Allen, Mark Dimunation at the Library of Congress, and Ed Marolda at the Washington Navy Yard, for the tours they provided and knowledge they shared of their respective institutions.

Many other librarians and researchers, from regimental history offices in Scotland to local historical societies in Virginia, Maryland, and the District of Columbia, aided my research, and I am grateful to them all. Thanks also to the captain and crew of the Coast Guard cutter *James Rankin* for allowing me to see Fort McHenry from the vantage point Francis Scott Key might have had, and to the captain and crew of the Coast Guard tallship *Eagle* for taking me along on a Norfolk-to-Baltimore journey that allowed me to see much of the water route taken by the British during their invasion.

Thanks to old friends Dennis Sheehan, who put me up in his flat during my research in London and accompanied me on a quest on a foggy Sunday to find Admiral Cockburn's final resting spot at Kensal

Greens, and to John Simonson and family, for hosting me during a visit to Oxford.

I am indebted to *The Washington Post*, including company president Don Graham, publisher Katharine Weymouth, and many other colleagues, for their support of this project. Bobbye Pratt, an indefatigable researcher, tracked down several hard-to-find documents. Gene Thorp, a superb *Post* cartographer and a student of history, made the excellent maps.

At Random House, it was a pleasure to team up again with Will Murphy, my editor for *The Pentagon,* and many others who helped with the book, including Ben Steinberg, Jennifer Rodriguez, Tom Pitoniak, Carole Lowenstein, Katie Donelan, and Mika Kasuga. Also thanks to my agent, Rafe Sagalyn, and his assistants Shannon O'Neill and Lauren Clark, who believed in this project and helped every step of the way.

Special thanks to my uncle, John B. Fiery, a great student of early American history, who embraced my project and brought me on a memorable and informative tour of James Madison's Montpelier and James Monroe's Ash Lawn–Highland. Jock, my aunt Diann, and the Fiery family were a great source of encouragement. My mother, Joan Vogel, was once again an enthusiastic supporter, as were my siblings, Stuart, Peter, and Jenny, and our dear family friends Ben and Perky Pepper.

Most of all, I thank my wife, Tiffany, and our children, Donald, Charlotte, and Thomas, for their love, support, and good cheer during the many long hours of work that took me away from my family. Tiffany picked up that burden, even while managing to edit the manuscript, for which I will always be grateful. She also put up with our family's many 1812 expeditions in recent years. From joining in an archaeological excavation in search of Joshua Barney's position at Bladensburg, to Defenders Day visits to Baltimore, to exploring Tangier Island on a golf cart, we have memories that will last a lifetime.

NOTES

All dates are 1814, unless otherwise noted. References for one or more paragraphs are often grouped in a single note. The order of the citations in each note generally corresponds to the information or quotation referenced. The following abbreviations are used in the endnotes and bibliography:

ADM—Admiralty Records, National Archives of the United Kingdom
AOC—Architect of the Capitol
ASP—American State Papers
CCW—*Capture of the City of Washington,* American State Papers
CMS—George Cockburn Memoir of Service, National Maritime Museum
CRG—*The War of 1812 in the Chesapeake: A Reference Guide*
DMDE—Dolley Madison Digital Edition, University of Virginia Press
GWU—Gelman Library, Special Collections, George Washington University
HSF—Historical Society of Frederick
HSP—Historical Society of Pennsylvania
NWR—Niles' Weekly Register
LOC—Library of Congress
MdHS—Maryland Historical Society
MdHM—Maryland Historical Magazine
NARA—National Archives and Records Administration
NAUK—National Archives of the United Kingdom
NHHC—Naval History and Heritage Command, Naval War of 1812 papers
NI—National Intelligencer
NLS—National Library of Scotland
NMM—National Maritime Museum, Greenwich, England
NW II—The Naval War of 1812: A Documentary History, vol. 2
NW III—The Naval War of 1812: A Documentary History, vol. 3
PRONI—Public Records Office of Northern Ireland
RCHS—Records of the Columbia Historical Society
RG—record group
RMM—Royal Marine Museum, Portsmouth, England
RNM—Royal Navy Museum, Portsmouth, England

UM—William L. Clements Library, University of Michigan
USJ—*The United Service Journal and Naval and Military Magazine*
UVa—Papers of James Madison, Alderman Library, University of Virginia
WO—War Office records, National Archives of the United Kingdom
WP—*Washington Post*

PRELUDE: *I See Nothing Left*

3 **Sailing under a white flag** New York *Evening Post,* Aug. 15; Journal kept during the years 1813–1814 by Lieut. Beynon, Royal Marines, serving on board HMS *Menelaus* on the American Station during the War of 1812, Western Reserve Historical Society, Cleveland, transcript of original courtesy of NHHC (hereafter Beynon journal), 127.

3 **The Great Bandit** Ralph Eshelman and Burt Kummerow, *In Full Glory Reflected,* 28; Walter Lord, *The Dawn's Early Light,* 52.

4 **"[T]here breathes not"** William M. Marine, *The British Invasion of Maryland 1812–1815,* 23.

4 **man in person** Oswald Tilghman, *History of Talbot County,* 407

4 **prisoner of war agent** Anthony G. Dietz, "The Use of Cartel Vessels during the War of 1812," *American Neptune,* July 1968, 193.

4 **burned the Maryland plantation** Ralph E. Eshelman, Scott S. Sheads, and Donald R. Hickey, *The War of 1812 in the Chesapeake: A Reference Guide to Historic Sites in Maryland, Virginia, and the District of Columbia,* 178 (hereafter *CRG*); author visit Jefferson-Patterson Park & Museum, St. Leonard, Md., Sept. 19, 2009.

4 **As usual, Skinner** Skinner letter, *Essex Register* [Salem, Mass.], June 20, 1821; James Scott, *Recollections of a Naval Life,* vol. 3, 239.

4 **At 2 a.m** Cockburn to Cochrane, Aug. 8, NW III, 169.

5 **Pemberton Claughton** Myron (Mike) E. Lyman and William W. Hankins, *Encounters with the British in Virginia During the War of 1812,* 29.

5 **"What! Englishmen"** Scott, *Recollections,* 261.

5 **village was burned** Peter Rowley, ed., "Captain Robert Rowley Helps to Burn Washington, D.C., Part 1," *MdHM,* Fall 1987; Lord, *Dawn's Early Light,* 53; Journal of John Robyns, RMLI, 1796–1834, 143, RMM (hereafter Robyns journal).

5 **"I suppose some"** Rowley, "Captain Robert Rowley," 246.

6 **"Within forty-eight"** Cockburn to Cochrane, secret letter, July 17, NW III, 137.

6 **"It is quite impossible"** Cockburn to Cochrane, July 17, NW III, 136.

6 **For many Americans** J. C. A. Stagg, *The War of 1812: Conflict for a Continent,* 2.

7 **"not an independent"** Ralph Ketcham, *James Madison: A Biography,* 533.

7 competing visions Alan Taylor, *The Civil War of 1812: American Citizens, British Subjects, Irish Rebels and Indian Allies*, 5–6.

7 Walking the deck New York *Evening Post*, Aug. 15; Skinner to Graham, July 17, Misc. Letters of the Department of State, NARA RG 59, M179, Roll 30.

7 "severe" fighting Beynon journal, 127.

8 "I believe, Mr. Skinner" Skinner to Madison, Aug. 13, UVa.

CHAPTER 1: *How Do You Like the War Now?*

TERRA RUBRA, MARYLAND, WEDNESDAY, AUGUST 10, 1814

11 "The government seem" Key to Randolph, Aug. 10, Francis Scott Key papers in Howard Papers, MS 469, MdHS.

12 Slender and of medium Harold R. Manakee, "Anthem Born in Battle," in P. W. Filby and Edward G. Howard, comps., *Star-Spangled Books*, 29.

12 "almost bordering on sadness" Henry S. Foote, *Casket of Reminiscences*, 12.

12 "like lightning" Edward S. Delaplaine, *Francis Scott Key: Life and Times*, 44–45.

12 Key was a child Victor Weybright, *Spangled Banner: The Story of Francis Scott Key*, 1, 4, 8, 11.

12 Terra Rubra, named Ibid., 4–7; Carroll County Historical Society.

13 He and his younger Weybright, *Spangled Banner*, 25.

13 Most unforgettable: Ibid., 15; John T. Silkett, *Francis Scott Key and the History of the Star-Spangled Banner*, 4.

13 Philip Barton Key Delaplaine, *Francis Scott Key*, 9–23.

14 "Polly Lloyd is" Margaret L. Calcott, ed., *Mistress of Riverdale: The Plantation Letters of Rosalie Stier Calvert, 1795–1821*, 31.

14 Key established a law Delaplaine, *Francis Scott Key*, 33–36; Weybright, *Spangled Banner*, 47.

14 After two years Weybright, *Spangled Banner*, 42–44; Delaplaine, *Francis Scott Key*, 43–46.

15 The Keys made Anna Key Bartow, "Recollections of Francis Scott Key, by his Granddaughter," *Modern Culture*, Nov. 12, 1900, 7; Francis Scott Key-Smith, *Francis Scott Key, Author of the Star-Spangled Banner, What Else He Was and Who*, 89.

16 He was an indulgent Weybright, *Spangled Banner*, 65, 227.

16 The home served Ibid., 45, 64; Delaplaine, *Francis Scott Key*, 79.

16 Randolph's small head Delaplaine, *Francis Scott Key*, 77–78; Walter Edgar McCann, "Francis Scott Key," *Popular Monthly*, 1888.

16 Key, a devout Weybright, *Spangled Banner*, 61, 66.

17 Some seven thousand American citizens Donald R. Hickey, *Don't Give Up the Ship! Myths of the War of 1812*, 21.

17 **Kentucky's militia alone** Walter Borneman, *1812: The War That Forged a Nation*, 57.

17 **Randolph led the opposition** Ketcham, *James Madison*, 525, 554; Paul Woehrmann, "National Response to the Sack of Washington," *MdHM*, 1971, 231.

17 **Clay even ordered** Ketcham, *James Madison*, 509.

18 **With a measure** Ibid., 529–33.

18 **"[T]housands of American"** President's Message, June 1, 1812, in Brannan, *Official Letters*, 10.

18 **"a state of war"** President's Message, June 1, 1812, in John Brannan, ed., *Official Letters of the Military and Naval Officers of the United States During the War with Great Britain in the Years 1812, 13, 14, & 15*, 14.

18 **Nonetheless, on June 16** Hickey, *Don't Give Up the Ship!*, 44.

19 **Congress's vote** Ibid., 42.

19 **"Gentlemen, you have"** *Federal Republican*, Sept. 9.

19 **No less than Randolph** Weybright, *Spangled Banner* 77; Delaplaine, *Francis Scott Key*, 83.

19 **Randolph considered** Ibid., 86–87.

20 **"The state of society"** Weybright, *Spangled Banner* 79, 213, 59. Key was echoing Randolph's own words to him.

20 **"I begin to fancy"** Key to Randolph, May 14, 1813, Howard Papers, MdHS.

20 **"I did feel"** Weybright, *Spangled Banner*, 71.

20 **He was given** Key to Randolph, Feb. 26, 1814, Howard Papers, MdHS; Clarence Wroth, "Francis Scott Key as a Churchman," *MdHM*, 1909, 156–58; Weybright, *Spangled Banner*, 65, 74.

20 **"[D]oes it not appear"** Delaplaine, *Francis Scott Key*, 94–95.

21 **"The people of Montreal"** Ibid., 100.

21 **Most of the U.S. Army** J. C. A. Stagg, *Mr. Madison's War: Politics, Diplomacy and Warfare in the Early American Republic, 1783–1830*, 388.

21 **"We see what"** Key to Randolph, Aug. 10, Howard Papers, MdHS.

HMS ALBION, POTOMAC RIVER, WEDNESDAY, AUGUST 10, 1814

21 **So much loot** Cockburn to Edward Griffiths, Aug. 10, NHHC.

21 **"Cockburn's confidence"** William Napier, *The Life and Opinions of General Sir Charles James Napier, G.C.B.*, vol. 1, 229.

22 **The Cockburn family** James Pack, *The Man Who Burned the White House: Admiral Sir George Cockburn, 1772–1853*, 21–25; Roger Morriss, *Cockburn and the British Navy in Transition: Admiral Sir George Cockburn 1772–1853*, 7–9.

23 **"zeal, ability"** Pack, *Man Who Burned the White House*, 45.

23 **"we so exactly"** Morriss, *Cockburn and the British Navy*, 28.

23 **Nelson and Hood** Ibid., 54–61; Pack, *Man Who Burned the White House*, 115, 123.

23 **In 1812, at** Ibid., 137, 140.

24 **"would scarcely have known"** William James, *The Naval History of Great Britain from the Declaration of War by France in 1793, to the Accession of George IV*, 32.

24 **"I have no hesitation"** Cockburn to Warren, March 13, 1813, NW II, 320.

24 **Cockburn believed Warren too passive** Morriss, *Cockburn and the British Navy*, 89; J. Ralfe, *The Naval Biography of Great Britain: Consisting of Those Officers of the British Navy Who Distinguished Themselves During the Reign of His Majesty George III*, vol. 3, 285.

24 **Chesapeake Bay** Charles G. Muller, *The Darkest Day: The Washington-Baltimore Campaign During the War of 1812*; Donald G. Shomette, *Flotilla: The Patuxent Naval Campaign in the War of 1812*, ix.

24 **Cockburn's instructions** Pack, *Man Who Burned the White House*, 145.

25 **"I am sorry to say"** Wybourn to Joseph Shipton, April 4, 1813, in Anne Petrides and Jonathan Downs, eds., *Sea Soldier: An Officer of Marines with Duncan, Nelson, Collingwood and Cockburn: The Letters and Journals of T. Marmaduke Wybourn RM, 1797–1813*, 175–76.

25 **"This of course"** NW II, 341–42.

25 **"Exhausted with"** Marine, *British Invasion*, 38.

25 **"leaving not a single"** Wybourn journal, May 5, 1813, in Petrides and Downs, eds., *Sea Soldier*, 183.

26 **"He was unmoved"** Marine, *British Invasion*, 38.

26 **"what they were liable"** NW II, 242.

26 **"what had happened"** CMS, 109.

26 **"a droll character"** Wybourn journal, May 7, 1813, in Petrides and Downs, eds., *Sea Soldier*, 185.

26 **"Had you not fired"** James J. Wilmer, *A Narrative Respecting the Conduct of the British from Their First Landing on Spesutia Island Till Their Progress to Havre de Grace*, 28; CRG, 126.

27 **This will do** Wilmer, *Narrative Respecting the Conduct of the British*, 28.

27 **"On my way from"** Charles J. Ingersoll, *Historical Sketch of the Second War Between the United States of America and Great Britain*, vol. 1, 198.

27 **"terror and reproach"** Dolley Madison to Edward Coles, May 13, 1813, DMDE.

28 **"These examples had"** CMS, 110.

28 **"guilty of the unnatural"** Captain Frederick Chamier, R.N., *The Life of a Sailor*, 176, 181.

28 **"the price of"** CMS, 128.

28 **"my ideas"** Cockburn to Cochrane May 10, NW III, 63.

28 **Cockburn had a firm** CMS, 103.

29 **"Apparently affected"** William H. Love, "Two Maryland Heroines," *MdHM*, 1908, 134–35.

29 **In mid-June, Vice Admiral Warren** NW II, 310, 361–64; CRG, 237.

29 "When our boats" *The Naval Chronicle*, 1813, 182–83.

30 "for which England" Napier, *Life and Opinions of General Sir Charles James Napier*, 371.

30 "no mischief" Cockburn to Warren, July 12, 1813, NW II, 185; Pack, *Man Who Burned the White House*, 159.

30 Around the country Ingersoll, *Historical Sketch*, vol. 1, 202.

30 "The affair of Hampton" Margaret Bayard Smith, *The First Forty Years of Washington Society*, 90.

30 The panic grew NW II, 369.

30 "Alarm guns" Claude G. Bowers, ed., *The Diary of Elbridge Gerry, Jr.*, 188.

30 Major George Peter Grace Dunlop Ecker, *A Portrait of Old Georgetown*, 150; Weybright, *Spangled Banner*, 69.

31 "Each new-made" Martha Peter to Mrs. Josiah Quincy, July 13, 1813, in Harold Donaldson Eberlein and Cortlandt Van Dyke Hubbard, *Historic Houses of George-town and Washington City*, 128.

31 The militia marched Joseph A. Whitehorne, *The Battle of Baltimore 1814*, 77.

31 Aboard his flagship Warren to Croker, NW II, 369.

31 Cockburn and most Donald G. Shomette, *Flotilla*, 19.

CHAPTER 2: *Laid in Ashes*

33 "You are at perfect" Cochrane to Cockburn, April 28, NW III, 51.

33 Moreover, eight months before Robert Malcolmson, *Capital in Flames*, 289.

34 Cochrane was eager Cochrane to Prevost, March 11, NW III, 38.

34 "The Rear-admiral" Scott, *Recollections*, 239.

34 Parson Joshua Thomas Adam Wallace, *The Parson of the Islands. A Biography of Rev. Joshua Thomas*, 129–30.

35 By late spring Tangier Museum visit, July 10, 2010; CMS, 124; "The British fortifying an Island in Chesapeake Bay," Essex *Register* [Salem, Mass.], July 16; Lieutenant Colonel Thos. Bayly to Gov. James Barbour, June 23, in H. W. Flournoy, ed., *Calendar of Virginia State Papers and other Manuscripts*, vol. 10, 348.

35 "myriads of mosquitoes" Robyns journal, RMM, 132; CRG, 262.

35 Cockburn distributed NW III, 60.

35 The Union Jack Shomette, *Flotilla*, 72; Frank Cassell, "Slaves of the Chesapeake Bay Area and the War of 1812," *Journal of Negro History*, April 1972, 150.

35 Ezekiel Loney Transcription of notice, John Richeson to W. Tucker, April 20, 1814, Tangier History Museum, from the archives of the University of Virginia Library.

36 Fort Albion witnessed Christopher T. George, "Mirage of Freedom: African

Americans in the War of 1812," *MdHM*, Winter 1996; 435–36; Cassell, "Slaves of the Chesapeake," 151; Robyns journal, RMM, 134.

36 **"are really very fine"** Cockburn to Cochrane, May 10; NW III, 65.

36 **At their first test** Cockburn to Cochrane, June 25, NW III, 115; Robyns Journal, RMM, 135–36.

36 **The only time Cockburn** Cockburn to Barrie, July 8, George Cockburn Papers, Manuscript Division, LOC.

36 **While freeing the slaves** Scott, *Recollections*, 118–20.

37 **"[T]he country is"** Cockburn to Cochrane, June 25, NW III, 115.

37 **"Not a militia man"** Cockburn to Barrie, July 16, NW III, 152.

37 **Red-nosed** Mary Barney, ed., *Biographical Memoir of the Late Commodore Joshua Barney: From Autobiographical Notes and Journals in Possession of His Family, and Other Authentic Sources*, 299.

37 **The Maryland native** Shomette, *Flotilla*, 34.

37 **Raised on a farm** *Ibid.*, 23; Charles E. Brodine, Jr., Michael J. Crawford, and Christine F. Hughes, *Against All Odds: U.S. Sailors in the War of 1812*, 27; Glenn Tucker, *Poltroons and Patriots: A Popular Account of the War of 1812*, vol. 2, 512; M. I. Weller, "The Life of Commodore Joshua Barney," *RCHS*, 1911, 98, 160.

38 **"To content himself"** Barney, *Biographical Memoir*, 250–51.

38 **Barney packed** Brodine et al., *Against All Odds*, 31.

39 **On Independence Day** Shomette, *Flotilla*, 33–35; 39, 43.

39 **"[Y]our force"** Jones to Barney, Feb. 18, NW III, 33.

39 **Barney sailed** Cockburn to Barrie, May 30, NW III, 76; Brodine et al., *Against All Odds*, 41–42.

39 **"[H]ere we passed"** Barrie to Cockburn, June 19, NW III, 111.

39 **Early on June 18** *Richmond Enquirer*, June 22; Key to Randolph, Aug. 10, Howard Papers, MdHS; Weybright, *Spangled Banner*, 84.

40 **Peter marched** Frederick Todd, "The Militia and Volunteers of the District of Columbia, 1783–1820," *RCHS*, 1948, 429; Josephine Seaton, *William Winston Seaton of the "National Intelligencer": A Biographical Sketch*, 115; Shomette, *Flotilla*, 129–32; *Hartford Courant*, July 5.

40 **By the time Key** Key to Randolph, July 3, Howard Papers, MdHS.

40 **Key wrote a reassuring** Delaplaine, *Life and Times*, 130.

40 **I fear that** Key to Randolph, July 3, Howard Papers, MdHS.

41 **Cockburn was certainly** Cockburn to Barrie, July 3, NHHC.

41 **On the night of June** Ralph E. Eshelman, *Maryland's Largest Naval Engagement: The Battles of St. Leonard Creek, 1814*; Shomette, *Flotilla*, 154–55.

41 **"How sharply"** Cockburn to Cochrane, June 25, NW III, 115.

41 **"I had the mortification"** Brown to Cockburn, June 27, NW III, 127.

42 **"two heroes on horseback"** Cockburn to Barrie, July 11, NW III, 151; Shomette, *Flotilla*, 171.

43 **Cockburn did not want to linger** Cockburn to Barrie, July 16, NW III, 152; Shomette, *Flotilla,* 177.

43 **"Jonathan I believe"** Nourse to Cockburn, July 23, NW III, 159.

43 **"Mr. Maddison must"** Cockburn to Barrie, July 16, NW III, 152.

BERMUDA, AUGUST 1, 1814

43 **"[W]ith them properly"** Cochrane to Cockburn, July 1, NW III, 130.

43 **Certainly Washington** Cochrane to Bathurst, July 14, NW III, 131; NW III, 189.

44 **A discouraged Cochrane** Cochrane to Melville, July 17, NW III, 132, 135.

44 **Then on July 25** NW III, 189; Ross to Elizabeth, July 30, 1814, PRONI, D 2004/A/3/4; Lady Bourchier, ed., *Memoir of the Life of Admiral Sir Edward Codrington, with Selections from His Public and Private Correspondence,* vol. 1, 312; Shomette, *Flotilla,* 234.

BALTIMORE, THURSDAY, AUGUST 11

44 **On the morning of August** New York *Evening Post,* Aug. 15; Scott, *Recollections,* 239; Skinner to Madison, Aug. 13, UVa.

WASHINGTON, SATURDAY, AUGUST 13

45 **The war had kept** Madison to mother, Aug. 8, UVa; Ketcham, *James Madison,* 573.

45 **Certainly, conditions were better** William Seale, *The White House: The History of an American Idea,* 34; William Seale, *The President's House: A History,* vol. 1, 88.

45 **Jefferson, a widower** "Dolley Madison," n.d., James Madison's Montpelier; William Seale, "The White House Before the Fire," *White House History,* Fall 1998, 21–23.

46 **Though the roof** Author tour with White House curator Bill Allman, Feb. 23, 2010; Anthony S. Pitch, *The Burning of Washington: The British Invasion of 1814,* 28; CRG, 291.

46 **"I can not yet say"** Madison to mother, Aug. 8, UVa.

46 **It was becoming increasingly** J. C. A. Stagg, *Mr. Madison's War,* 407.

46 **"At Sea, July 27"** July 27, Winder Papers, MdHS.

46 **At least as worrisome** Irving Brant, *James Madison, Commander in Chief, 1812–1836,* 288; Stagg, *Mr. Madison's War,* 396.

47 **Even with the British** Ibid., 397, 407.

47 **Dressed head to toe** Paul Jennings, *A Colored Man's Reminiscences of James Madison,* 17.

47 **"the air of a country schoolmaster"** Pitch, *Burning of Washington,* 28; Ketcham, *James Madison,* 476.

47 **Madison's selection in 1776** "James Madison," n.d., James Madison's Mont-

pelier; Gordon S. Wood, *Revolutionary Characters: What Made the Founders Different,* 170.

48 **When war had been declared** Richard Stewart, ed., *American Military History,* vol. 1, *The United States Army and the Forging of a Nation, 1775–1917,* 132.

48 **"swaggerers, dependents, decayed"** Whitehorne, *Battle for Baltimore,* 22.

48 **"so Lilliputian"** Mark Collins Jenkins and David A. Taylor, *The War of 1812 and the Rise of the U.S. Navy,* 25.

48 **With this feeble force** Stewart, *American Military History, vol. 1,* 134.

48 **Madison put out peace** Hickey, *Don't Give Up the Ship!,* 43.

49 **"[T]he acquisition of Canada"** Ibid., 37; Borneman, *1812,* 57–58.

49 **"in a manner worthy"** Ketcham, *James Madison,* 534.

49 **in the northwest** Hickey, *Don't Give Up the Ship!,* 8–10.

50 **Almost every ship** John Williams, *History of the Invasion and Capture of Washington, and of the Events which Preceded and Followed,* 27; Ingersoll, *Historical Sketch,* vol. 1, 162; Edward D. Ingraham, *A Sketch of the Events Which Preceded the Capture of the City of Washington by the British,* 6.

50 **Wellington was ordered** Lord, *Dawn's Early Light,* 36–37.

50 **The Madison administration** Monroe to American delegation, June 27, in James Monroe, *The Writings of James Monroe,* vol. 5, 371; Stagg, *Mr. Madison's War,* 395.

51 **Madison warned "unequivocally"** Rush narrative, Oct. 15, CCW, 541.

51 **Yet no one else** Jones, NW III, 311.

51 **Still, the cabinet** CCW, 524.

51 **"The administration are beginning"** Key to Randolph, July 3, Howard Papers, MdHS.

51 **"In the discharge"** C. Edward Skeen, *John Armstrong, Jr., 1758–1843: A Biography,* 205.

51 **Madison had chosen** Harry Ammon, *James Monroe: The Quest for National Identity,* 316–17.

52 **Armstrong, a former senator** Skeen, *John Armstrong,* ix. Armstrong had shown a dubious allegiance to democratic principles during the Revolutionary War as the anonymous author of the infamous Newburgh Addresses, which raised the specter of mutiny during a pay dispute near the end of the war.

52 **"presumptuous, obstinate"** Jefferson to John Eppes, Sept. 9, Paul Leicester Ford, ed., *The Writings of Thomas Jefferson,* vol. 9, 484.

52 **In one area** John C. Fredriksen, *The United States Army in the War of 1812,* 19–20; Ketcham, *James Madison,* 574; Borneman, *1812,* 223.

52 **"[T]his man if continued"** Monroe to Madison, December 1813, Monroe, *Writings,* 275; Ammon, *James Monroe,* 324.

52 **Most disastrous** John Van Ness, Nov. 23, 1814, CCW 580; Stagg, *Mr. Madison's War,* 411.

53 **Armstrong considered Madison** John Armstrong, *Notices of the War of 1812*, vol. 2, 140; Stagg, *Mr. Madison's War*, 397; Williams, *History of the Invasion*, 72.

53 **"the spur of the occasion"** Winder narrative, CCW, 552.

53 **"disorderly crowd,"** Winder to Armstrong, July 9, CCW, 542.

53 **Preoccupied by events** Ketcham, *James Madison*, 585; Wood, *Revolutionary Characters*, 171.

53 **"the defenseless state"** Mayor Blake to Captain Caldwell, July 19, Winder Papers, MdHS; Pontius Stelle to Jonathan Rhea, July 22, Ross Papers, Gelman Library, GWU.

53 **"For some weeks"** Peter to Quincy, Aug. 26, in Eberlein and Hubbard, *Historic Houses*, 128.

54 **"[O]ur preparations for defence"** Dolley Madison to Hannah Gallatin, July 28, DMDE.

CHAPTER 3: *The British Invasion*

CHESAPEAKE BAY, SUNDAY, AUGUST 14, 1814

57 **The British squadron** Beynon journal, Aug. 14; Diary kept by Midshipman J. C. Bluett, 1995.48, RNM Manuscript Collection, 27; Shomette, *Flotilla*, 214.

57 **Cochrane's hatred** Alfred Mahan, *Sea Power in Its Relation to the War of 1812*, 330.

57 **"They are a whining"** Shomette, *Flotilla*, 232; Pack, *Man Who Burned the White House*, 198; Lord, *Dawn's Early Light*, 52.

57 **Cochrane's grudge** Alexander Cochrane, *The Fighting Cochranes*, 162.

57 **"all mad, money-getting"** Ibid., 267.

58 **"[H]is first resolves"** Malcolm to Clementina, Oct. 3, Pulteny Malcolm Papers, UM, transcript at NHHC.

58 **While in Bermuda** Cochrane to Melville, July 17, NW III, 132.

58 **"I have it much"** Cochrane to Bathurst, July 14, NW III, 131.

58 **Before departing** Prevost to Cochrane, June 2, Records of the Admiralty, Letters from Commanders-in-Chief, North America: 1814, ADM 1/506, NAUK.

58 **"You are hereby required"** Cochrane, July 18, NW III, 140.

58 **"I cannot at present"** Cochrane to Croker, Aug. 11, NW III, 190.

58 *Tonnant,* **a magnificent** Tucker, *Poltroons*, 506; Shomette, *Flotilla*, 236.

59 **"appeared rather inclined"** CMS, 132.

59 **Cockburn had served** Morriss, *Cockburn and the British Navy*, 60–61.

59 **Cockburn emphasized** [Sir George De Lacy Evans], *Facts Relating to the Capture of Washington, in Reply to Some Statements Contained in the Memoirs of Admiral Sir George Cockburn, G.C.B.,* 5–6.

60 **Retaliation for Canada** Robin F. A. Fabel, "The Laws of War in the 1812 Conflict," *Journal of American Studies,* August 1980, 211.

60 **Beyond the strategic goals** Taylor Peck, *Roundshots to Rockets: A History of the Washington Navy Yard and U.S. Naval Gun Factory,* 48; Edward J. Marolda, *The Washington Navy Yard: An Illustrated History,* 9.

60 **The reports of disease** Ross had seen his regiment decimated by fever during the disastrous 1809 Walcheren expedition in the Netherlands, where two-thirds of his regiment's strength was lost to disease. W. A. Maguire, "Major General Ross and the Burning of Washington," *Irish Sword,* Winter 1980, 118.

60 **Ross's instructions from London** Bathurst to Barnes, May 20, NW III, 72; Bathurst to Ross, Aug. 10, WO 6/2, 5156–5220, NAUK.

60 **Based on his instructions** Evans, *Facts,* 6, 14; George De Lacy Evans, "Memorandum of Operations on the Shores of the Chesapeake in 1814," NLS, Adv.MS.46.6.6 ff 1–28 (hereafter Evans memorandum; I am grateful to Ross scholar John McCavitt for providing me a transcript).

60 **sea general** Chamier, *Life,* 176.

61 **Cockburn proposed** Cockburn to Cochrane, Aug. 15, NW III, 190.

61 **Major General Robert Ross** Description based on Robert Ross portrait owned by descendant Stephen Campbell, Rostrevor, Northern Ireland; "Memoir of Maj.-Gen. Robert Ross," *USJ,* Part 1, 1829, 412; MaGuire, "Major General Ross and the Burning of Washington," 117–19; Christopher T. George, "The Family Papers of Maj. Gen. Robert Ross, the Diary of Col. Arthur Brooke, and the British Attacks of Washington and Baltimore of 1814," *MdHM,* Fall 1993, 307. London had asked Wellington to select the officer he thought "best calculated" to lead an independent command against the coast of America. Wellington considered sending Major General Edward Barnes, an able officer on his staff, but instead chose Ross.

61 **Wellington was fond** "Ross of Bladensburg," *National Review,* 1929, 443–44; research by John McCavitt.

61 **"the hit I got in the chops"** Benjamin Smyth, comp., *History of the XX Regiment, 1688–1888,* 323.

62 **"Be therefore my Ly"** Ross to Elizabeth, n.d., D 2004/1A/3/1, PRONI.

POTOMAC RIVER, MONDAY, AUGUST 15

62 **At 2 a.m.** Beynon journal, Aug. 15, NHHC; Robyns Journal, Aug. 15, 145, RMM; Chamier, *Life,* 176; Pack, *Man Who Burned the White House,* 180.

62 **That evening** Cockburn to Cochrane, Aug. 15, NW III, 190; Codrington, Aug. 15, in Bourchier, ed., *Codrington.*

CHESAPEAKE BAY, TUESDAY, AUGUST 16

63 **Early Tuesday morning** Jones, Oct. 31, CCW, 540; Lord, *Dawn's Early Light*, 19.

63 **Rear Admiral Pulteney Malcolm** Pack, *Man Who Burned the White House*, 181; "Recollections of the Expedition to the Chesapeake, and Against New Orleans, in the Years 1814–15. By an old Sub," Part 2, *USJ*, May 1840.

63 **"The sight is glorious"** Diary of George Gleig, Aug. 15, 131, in C. R. B. Barrett, ed., *The 85th King's Light Infantry*, (hereafter Gleig diary).

63 **Aboard the ships** John R. Grodzinski, "The Duke of Wellington, the Peninsular War and the War of 1812. Part II: Reinforcements, Views of the War and Command in North America," *War of 1812 Magazine*, April 2007.

63 **"I could have done"** Tucker, *Poltroons*, 503.

63 **The 44th** Howard Green, *The Kings Own Royal Regiment*, i; Neil H. Swanson, *The Perilous Fight*, 405; Tucker, *Poltroons*, 503.

65 **Crammed aboard** Gleig diary, July 2, 124; Green, *Kings Own*, 61; Lord, *Dawn's Early Light*, 20; Shomette, *Flotilla*, 215.

POINT LOOKOUT, MARYLAND, DAWN, WEDNESDAY, AUGUST 17

65 **The morning light** CCW, 527; Shomette, *Flotilla*, 239; Pack, *Man Who Burned the White House*, 181.

CHESAPEAKE BAY, 8 A.M., WEDNESDAY, AUGUST 17

66 **The paneled great cabin** Harry Smith, *The Autobiography of Lieutenant-General Sir Harry Smith*, 197; Evans, *Facts*, 7–8.

66 **The briefing was** Diary of Col Arthur Brooke, D 3004/D/2, PRONI; see also Christopher T. George, "The Family Papers of Maj. Gen. Robert Ross, the Diary of. Col. Arthur Brooke, and the British Attacks on Washington and Baltimore of 1814," *MdHM*, Fall 1993 (hereafter Brooke diary); Edward H. D. E. Napier, *The Life and Correspondence of Admiral Sir Charles Napier*, 41; Lord, *Dawn's Early Light*, 55; [George R. Gleig,] *A Narrative of the Campaigns of the British Army at Washington and New Orleans in the years 1814–15*, 86.

WASHINGTON, 8 A.M., THURSDAY, AUGUST 18

67 **"a solitude"** John Clagett Proctor, ed., *Washington Past and Present*, 86; H. Paul Caemmerer, *A Manual on the Origin and Development of Washington*, 40; Stilson Hutchins and Joseph West Moore, *The National Capital Past and Present*, 51.

67 **Washington's population** Constance McLaughlin Green, *Washington: A History of the Capital, 1800–1950*, 21.

68 **The capital's elite** Gibb Myers, "Pioneers in the Federal Area," *RCHS*, 1942–43, 137, 147, 151–53.

68 Washington was a curious Whitehorne, *Battle for Baltimore*, 136; Scott Berg, "The Beginning of the Road," *WP Magazine*, Aug. 31, 2008, 22.

68 "It was no trophy" Rush to Williams, July 10, 1855, in Williams, *History of the Invasion*, 277.

68 The village awoke CCW, 527.

68 Secretary of State Monroe Monroe letter, Nov. 13, CCW 536.

69 Working from his makeshift CCW 527; Lord, *Dawn's Early Light*, 29.

69 Nothing close Winder narrative, CCW 554.

69 "The Creator has not thought" Albert Ellery Bergh, *The Writings of Thomas Jefferson*, vols. 13–14, 216.

69 Any marks of greatness William Frick to William Winder, Jr., May 1847, Winder Papers, MdHS; Fredriksen, *The United States Army in the War of 1812*, 149; Winder, *American National Biography*; Ralph J. Robinson, "Controversy over the Command at Baltimore in the War of 1812," *MdHM*, 1944.

70 "Be careful of" Ralph J. Robinson, "Retaliation for the Treatment of Prisoners in the War of 1812," *American Historical Review*, vol. 49, October 1943.

70 "It is a misfortune" Tucker, *Poltroons*, 496.

70 Madison and Monroe Ibid., 497–98, 724.

71 Winder's inexperience Winder narrative, CCW, 553; Rush to Williams, July 10, 1855, in Williams, *History of the Invasion*, 277.

71 Moreover, no states Winder correspondence, CCW, 543–46; CCW, 526, 550.

71 As for the District Van Ness, Washington, Nov. 23, CCW, 580; Whitehorne, *Battle for Baltimore*, 117.

PATUXENT RIVER, THURSDAY, AUGUST 18

71 The mighty British fleet George Laval Chesterton, *Peace, War, and Adventure: An Autobiographical Memoir of George Laval Chesterton*, vol. 1, 113–15; Gleig, *Narrative of the Campaigns*, 86–87; Shomette, *Flotilla*, 245.

72 The big ships Codrington, Aug. 15, 1814, in Bourchier, ed., *Codrington*, 314.

72 Finally, in late afternoon "War of 1812—Logs of British Ships in the Patuxent—1814," *Chronicle's of St. Mary's*, August 1966.

72 "The air literally resounded" Chesterton, *Peace, War, and Adventure*,114–15.

72 "comparatively extraordinary" Codrington, Aug. 15, in Bourchier, ed., *Codrington*, 315.

CHAPTER 4: *What the Devil Will They Do Here?*

BENEDICT, FRIDAY MORNING, AUGUST 19

75 The first landing boats Gleig diary, Aug. 19, 131.

75 At Benedict, the gun *Benedict, Maryland, Cultural Resources Survey and*

Context Study, Charles County Department of Planning and Growth Management, July 2009, David Brown, *Diary of a Soldier, 1805–1827,* 23–24; Evans memorandum, NLS, 3.

76 **As waves of troops** Gleig diary, Aug. 19, 1814, 132–33; Shomette, *Flotilla,* 250–51; Eshelman and Kummerow, *Full Glory Reflected,* 40.

NOTTINGHAM, MIDDAY FRIDAY, AUGUST 19

76 **Ten miles upriver** Barney to Jones, Aug. 19, 1814, Winder Papers, MdHS.

77 **"[W]e have again beat"** Shomette, *Flotilla,* 156; Hulbert Footner, *Sailor of Fortune: The Life and Adventures of Commodore Barney, USN,* 277.

WASHINGTON, 2 P.M., FRIDAY, AUGUST 19

77 **"Appearances indicate"** Jones to Barney, Aug. 19, NW III, 187.

77 **Nevertheless, Jones ordered** NW III, 198–200.

77 **Another report arrived** Winder to Stricker and Stansbury, Aug. 19, Winder Papers. MdHS.

77 **Winder hurried to** Winder to Armstrong, Aug. 19, CCW, 547; Lord, *Dawn's Early Light,* 59–61.

78 **"By God, they would"** Van Ness, Nov. 23, CCW, 581.

78 **Secretary of State Monroe** Monroe letter, Nov. 13, CCW; Winder narrative, CCW, 554.

78 **Tall and slim** Seale, *The President's House,* 145; Bryan Hockensmith, "James Monroe," *Army History,* Summer 2008.

79 **Monroe had gone on** Author visit, Ash Lawn-Highland, April 27, 2010.

79 **But Monroe's three-decade-old** Ammon, *James Monroe,* 273.

79 **But from the day** Ketcham, *James Madison,* 584.

79 **"I had a horror"** Skeen, *John Armstrong,* 203.

GHENT, FRIDAY, AUGUST 19

80 **At 3 p.m.** Fred L. Engelman, "The Peace of Christmas Eve," *American Heritage,* December 1960.

80 **The very makeup** Borneman, *1812,* 264–66; Ketcham, *James Madison,* 557.

80 **As soon as the Americans** John Quincy Adams, Aug. 19, in Charles Francis Adams, ed., *Memoirs of John Quincy Adams, Comprising Portions of His Diary from 1795 to 1848,* vol. 3, 20; Engelman, "The Peace of Christmas Eve"; Robert V. Remini, *Henry Clay: Statesman for the Union,* 111–12.

81 **"We need hardly say"** "From Our Ministers at Ghent," Niles *Weekly Register,* Oct. 15.

WASHINGTON, 9 A.M., SATURDAY, AUGUST 20

81 **The ragtag troops** Walter Smith, Oct. 6, CCW, 563; [Colonel Allen McLane], Nov. 14, 1853, Winder Papers, MdHS.

81 **Captain John J. Stull's** Stull letter, Jan. 16, 1847, in appendix to Thomas L.

McKenney, *Reply to Kosciusko Armstrong's Assault Upon Col. McKenney's Narrative,* 24–26; Muller, *The Darkest Day,* 74.

82 **Adding to the chaos** Van Ness, CCW, 581–82; Van Ness to Armstrong, Aug. 20, CCW 583.

82 **As the forces mustered** Allen McLane, "Col. McLane's Visit to Washington, 1814," *Bulletin of the Historical Society of Pennsylvania,* 17.

82 **But at 11:30 a.m.** Barney to Jones, Aug. 20, NW III, 187; Jones to Johnson, Oct. 3, NW III, 312.

82 **A landing at Benedict** Williams, *History of the Invasion,* 128.

82 **While the men milled** McLane, "Col. McLane's Visit," 17.

83 **"teach our haughty"** NI, Aug. 22, 1814.

83 **At 2 p.m.** CCW, 527; Tucker, *Poltroons,* 521; Lord, *Dawn's Early Light,* 62.

AQUASCO, MARYLAND, MIDDAY SATURDAY, AUGUST 20

83 **From his hilltop position** Monroe to Madison, Aug. 20, CCW, 537; Winder narrative, CCW, 554; Henry Adams, *The War of 1812,* 228.

BENEDICT, LATE AFTERNOON, SATURDAY, AUGUST 20

84 **With the sounding** [George R. Gleig], *A Subaltern in America: Comprising His Narratives of the Campaigns of the British Army at Baltimore, Washington, &c. &c. During the Late War,* 22.

84 **On the river below** Robyns journal, Aug. 22, RMM, 145.

84 **Ross was obliged** Shomette, *Flotilla,* 251; Brown, *Diary of a Soldier,* 24; Smith, *Autobiography,* 198.

84 **A party of twenty skirmishers** L. I. Cowper, *The King's Own: The Story of a Royal Regiment,* 4.

84 **Even by late afternoon** Gleig, *Narrative of the Campaigns,* 99.

85 **Cockburn's fleet** Cockburn to Cochrane, Aug. 22, NW III, 195; author tour of British path of invasion, with Ralph Eshelman, Sept. 5, 2009; Robyns Journal, Aug. 22, RMM, 146.

85 **After six miles** *Royal Oak* log, Aug. 20, copy in NHHC; Brown, *Diary of a Soldier,* 24; Gleig, *Narrative of the Campaigns,* 100.

85 **Four miles outside** Smith, CCW 563; Lord, *Dawn's Early Light,* 62.

BALTIMORE, SUNDAY MORNING, AUGUST 21

85 **The 5th Maryland Militia** Joseph Sterett, Nov. 22, CCW, 568; Henry T. Tuckerman, *The Life of John Pendleton Kennedy,* 65; Glenn Williams, "The Rock of North Point," in *The Todd House,* Friends of Todd's Inheritance, 2001.

85 **Spectators crowded** Tuckerman, *Life of John Pendleton Kennedy,* 65, 74.

86 **The column left** Tobias Stansbury, Nov. 5, CCW, 560; Sterett, Nov. 22, CCW, 568; Winder to Stansbury and Sterett, Aug. 21, Winder Papers, MdHS.

86 **His fear was "they"** Van Ness, CCW, 582.

THE ROAD TO NOTTINGHAM, SUNDAY, AUGUST 21

86 **At daylight** Samuel Davies letter, Aug. 31, in T. A. J. Burnett, *The Rise and Fall of a Regency Dandy: The Life and Times of Scrope Berdmore Davies,* 223; Pitch, *Burning of Washington,* 34.

86 **The open fields** Gleig, *Narrative of the Campaigns,* 102.

87 **Cockburn's naval force** Cockburn to Cochrane, Aug. 22, NW III, 195; Codrington, Aug. 21, in Bourchier, ed., *Codrington,* 315.

NOTTINGHAM, EARLY EVENING, SUNDAY, AUGUST 21

87 **Colonel Monroe** Monroe to Winder, Aug. 21, CCW 537; Barney to Jones, Aug. 21, NW III, 195; Thomas Carter, *Historical Record of the Forty-Fourth, or the East Essex Regiment,* 44; Shomette, *Flotilla,* 267.

88 **Monroe's dragoons** Brown, *Diary of a Soldier,* 24; Horatio King, "The Battle of Bladensburg," *Magazine of American History,* July–December 1885, 440.

88 **Ross and Cockburn** Evans memorandum, Aug. 22, NLS, 4; Cockburn to Cochrane, Aug. 22, NW III, 195–96.

THE WOODYARD, SUNDAY NIGHT, AUGUST 21

88 **Colonel Monroe raced** Monroe, Nov. 13, *CCW;* Smith, Oct. 6, *CCW;* Winder narrative, *CCW,* 555; Shomette, *Flotilla,* 270.

WASHINGTON, PREDAWN, MONDAY, AUGUST 22

89 **At the President's House** Monroe to Madison, [Aug. 21], UVa; Madison to Monroe, Aug. 22, James Madison, *The Writings of James Madison,* vol. 8, 291.

NOTTINGHAM, DAWN, MONDAY, AUGUST 22

89 **Admiral Cockburn's barges** Scott, *Recollections,* 276.

89 **The little army marched** Gleig diary, Aug. 22, 137; Shomette, *Flotilla,* 275.

ODEN'S FARM, 8:30 A.M., MONDAY, AUGUST 22

89 **Peering out** Winder narrative, *CCW,* 555; Shomette, *Flotilla,* 27; Williams, *History of the Invasion,* 170.

PIG POINT, MARYLAND, 11 A.M., MONDAY, AUGUST 22

90 **Cockburn pushed upriver** Cockburn to Cochrane, Aug. 22, NW III, 196.

90 **high-quality pig iron** Prince George's County Star-Spangled 200 Conference, Sept. 24, 2009; Robyns journal, Aug. 22, RMM, 146.

90 **Approaching Pig Point** Scott, *Recollections,* 277–78.

91 **"[A] look of blank dismay"** [Robert J. Barrett], "Naval Recollections of the Late American War," *USJ,* part 1, April 1841, 459; Codrington, Aug. 22,

1814, in Bourchier, ed., *Codrington*; Cockburn to Cochrane, Aug. 22, NW III, 196.

CHAPTER 5: *Be It So, We Will Proceed*

THE WOODYARD, MONDAY, AUGUST 22

95 **By noon Monday** Charles Ball, *Slavery in the United States: A Narrative of the Life and Adventures of Charles Ball*, 403; Barney, *Biographical Memoir*, 323; Barney to Jones, Aug. 21, NW III, 194; Smith, Oct. 6, CCW, 563.

95 **At the American camp** Jones, Oct. 3, NW III, 313.

96 **But Barney was astonished** Barney, *Biographical Memoir*, 263; Williams, *History of the Invasion*, 359–60.

96 **"Our officers said"** "Battle at Bladensburg," Aug. 29, *Baltimore Patriot*; Monroe to Madison, [Aug. 22], CCW, 538.

UPPER MARLBORO, MARYLAND, 2 P.M., MONDAY, AUGUST 22

96 **Ross, too, had turned** Evans memorandum, NLS, 5; Gleig, *Narrative of the Campaigns*, 107; CCW, 527.

96 **The homesick soldiers** Chesterton, *Peace, War, and Adventure*, 122; Evans memorandum, NLS, 6.

97 **Dr. William Beanes** John Mason to Skinner and Key, Sept. 2, Zack Spratt collection, book manuscript, box 1, part 1, MdHS; Eugene Conner, "William Beanes, M.D. (1749–1829) and the 'Star-Spangled Banner,'" *Journal of the History of Medicine*, April 1979; Caleb Clarke Magruder, Jr., "Dr. William Beanes, the Incidental Cause of the Authorship of the Star-Spangled Banner," *RCHS*, 1919; Sam Meyer, *Paradoxes of Fame: The Francis Scott Key Story*, 35–36.

97 **Beanes by nature** Anna H. Dorsey, "Origin of the Star-Spangled Banner," *The Historical Magazine, and Notes and Queries Concerning the Antiquities, History and Biography of America*, 1861; Weybright, *Spangled Banner*, 94; Gleig diary, Aug. 23, 137; Gleig, *Subaltern*, 46.

WASHINGTON, MONDAY AFTERNOON, AUGUST 22

97 **"The enemy are in full"** Monroe to Madison, Aug. 22, CCW, 538. This letter was written Monday, and not Tuesday, as Armstrong mistakenly reported, CCW, 539. See Williams, *History of the Invasion*, 170, and Carole L. Herrick, *August 24, 1814: Washington in Flames*, 213.

97 **Monroe's message** Benson J. Lossing, *The Pictorial Field-book of the War of 1812*, 923; Williams, *History of the Invasion*, 158.

98 **A visiting New York** "Extract of a Letter from a Gentleman at Washington," *Spectator*, Aug. 27.

98 **At the President's House** Madison to Monroe, Aug. 22, *Writings of James Madison*, 292; King, *Battle of Bladensburg*, 438.

98 **Secretary of Navy Jones** Jones, Oct. 3, NW III, 313; Benjamin Homans, Nov. 5, 13th Congress, 3d Sess., Misc., Books, &c, Destroyed by the Conflagration in 1814, 255, ASP; Booth to Tingey, Aug. 22, NW III, 204.

98 **At the Senate, Lewis Machen** Machen, Sept. 12, 1836, Papers of William Rives, LOC; Pitch, *Burning of Washington*, 45–46.

99 **The House of Representatives** "Explanation of the Clerk of the House of Representatives," Dec. 17, 1814, 13th Congress, 3rd Sess., Misc., 245, 258–60, ASP.

99 **One man in Washington** Brant, *James Madison*, 283.

99 **Armstrong "observed to me"** Pleasonton to Winder, Aug. 7, 1848, Winder Papers, MdHS; also in Ingraham, *Sketch of the Events*, 48.

MIDDLEBROOK MILLS, MARYLAND, EVENING, MONDAY, AUGUST 22

100 **Accompanied by his wife** F. S. Key to Ann Key, Aug. 22, misc. letters, Howard Papers, MdHS.

POTOMAC RIVER, EVENING, MONDAY, AUGUST 22

100 **No ships with heavy guns** Shomette, *Flotilla*, 201; Cockburn to Cochrane, Aug. 4, NW III, 168.

101 **He had joined** Bryan Perrett, *The Real Hornblower: The Life of Admiral of the Fleet Sir James Alexander Gordon, GCB*, i.

101 **Gordon's Potomac squadron** Gordon to Cochrane, Sept. 9, NW III, 238.

101 **"No one could tell"** Napier, *Admiral Sir Charles Napier*, 76; Patrick O'Neill, "The Potomac Squadron," Fairfax County History Conference, Nov. 7, 2009; *CRG*, 143.

OLD FIELDS, EVENING, MONDAY, AUGUST 22

102 **Late Monday afternoon** Dolley Madison to Lucy Payne Washington Todd, Aug. 23, 1814, DMDE.

102 **"Our chief, thinking"** Peter to Quincy, Aug. 26, in Eberlein and Hubbard, *Historic Houses*, 130; Rush to Williams, July 10, 1855, in Williams, *History of the Invasion*, 277.

102 **Old Fields, a hamlet** *CRG*, 147. Old Fields today is the site of Forestville, Maryland.

102 **the presidential party** Winder narrative, *CCW*, 555.

103 **The scene at Old Fields** McLane, "Col. McLane's Visit," 19; Ingersoll, *Historical Sketch*; Williams, *History of the Invasion*, 175–76.

103 **"[H]e informed me"** Peter to Williams, May 24, 1854, in Williams, *History of the Invasion*, 360.

103 **Winder offered a variety** Winder to Armstrong, Sept. 1, NARA RG 107, Letters Received by the Secretary of War M-221, Roll 67, transcript in NHHC.

103 **Armstrong, for his part** Colonel Allen McLane journal, in Armstrong, *Notices,* 232.

104 **Madison and his entourage** *CCW,* 527; McLane, "Col. McLane's Visit," 19; Shomette, *Flotilla,* 285; Tucker, *Poltroons,* 732.

104 **"appearance and preparation"** Jones, NW III, 314; Ball, *Slavery in the United States,* 403.

104 **Madison asked Barney** Jennings, *A Colored Man's Reminiscences,* 7.

104 **Madison spoke briefly** Barney, *Biographical Memoir,* 264.

104 **"I have passed"** James Madison to Dolley Madison, Aug. 23, 1814, DMDE.

104 **As the president** Thomas L. M'Kenney, *Memoirs, Official and Personal,* vol. 1, 44–45.

ACADEMY HILL, UPPER MARLBORO, MORNING, TUESDAY, AUGUST 23

105 **General Ross** Evans memorandum, NLS, 6–7; Evans, *Facts,* 10–11.

106 **"leaders devoid of talent"** Evans memorandum, NLS, 7.

106 **"completely overstepped"** Evans, *Facts,* 11.

106 **The hard-knit and sinewy Irishman** Edward M. Spiers, *Radical General: Sir George de Lacy Evans 1787–1870,* 1–4, 17; Evans, *Facts,* 15.

106 **As the council of war** Evans, *Facts,* 11.

107 **"Let us now push on"** J. S. Skinner, "Incidents of the War of 1812, From the *Baltimore Patriot,*" [May 23, 1849], in *MdHM,* December 1937, 341 (hereafter Skinner, "Incidents").

107 **"would go himself"** Davies letter, *Rise and Fall of a Regency Dandy,* 223.

107 **Ross was soon persuaded** Cockburn to Cochrane, Aug. 27, NW III, 220.

107 **"I congratulate you"** Cochrane to Cockburn, Aug. 22, CMS, 134.

107 **Cockburn sent a note** Cockburn to Cochrane, Aug. 23, NW III, 197.

107 **The failure of the Americans** Ross to Bathurst, Aug. 30, NW III, 223.

108 **One road from Upper** Ralph J. Robinson, "New Light on Three Episodes of the British Invasion of Maryland in 1814," *MdHM,* 1942, 283; Whitehorne, *Battle for Baltimore,* 124.

108 **At 2 p.m., bugles** Gleig, *Narrative of the Campaigns,* 107–108.

OLD FIELDS, MORNING, TUESDAY, AUGUST 23

108 **General Winder** Winder narrative, *CCW,* 555–56; Beall to Winder, Aug. 23, Winder Papers, MdHS; Christopher T. George, *Terror on the Chesapeake: The War of 1812 on the Bay,* 92.

109 **Winder wanted to unite** Winder to Armstrong, Sept. 1, NARA RG 107, Letters Received by the Secretary of War M-221, Roll 67, transcript in NHHC; Smith, Oct. 6, *CCW,* 563; Stansbury, Nov. 5, *CCW,* 560; Williams, *History of the Invasion,* 177.

109 **After a quick meal** Ketcham, *James Madison,* 576.

GEORGETOWN, TUESDAY, AUGUST 23

109 **Arriving at his home** Key to Randolph, Aug. 10, with addendum dated Aug. 23, Howard Papers, MdHS.

ROAD TO UPPER MARLBORO, EARLY AFTERNOON, TUESDAY, AUGUST 23

109 **But the British** Gleig diary, Aug. 23, 137; Gleig, *Narrative of the Campaigns*, 107–108.

109 **Major Peter** Peter to Williams, May 24, 1854, in Williams, *History of the Invasion*, 360.

110 **At the American camp** Smith, *CCW*, 564; Barney to Jones, Aug. 29, *CCW*, 207.

110 **Winder was still** Winder narrative, *CCW*, 556; M'Kenney, *Memoirs*, 46; Smith, *CCW*, 564; Winder to Armstrong, Sept. 1, 1814, NARA RG 107.

110 **a night attack was exactly** Evans memorandum, Aug. 23, NLS, 6; Winder narrative, *CCW*, 556. According to Winder, Barney "concurred" in the decision, though the commodore left no record of his opinion. But Major Peter, Winder's most accomplished officer, considered it another serious error, noting the Americans had "nothing" to fear of an attack on the Eastern Branch Bridge. Peter to Williams, May 24, 1854, in Williams, *History of the Invasion*, 360.

111 **A half hour before sunset** [Thomas L. McKenney], *A Narrative of the Battle of Bladensburg in a Letter to Henry Banning, esq.*, 4; Hanson Catlett, *CCW*, 584.

PRESIDENT'S HOUSE, LATE AFTERNOON, TUESDAY, AUGUST 23

111 **At the President's House** Dolley Madison to Lucy Todd, Aug. 23, DMDE.

111 **"In the present state of alarm"** Jones to Dolley Madison, Aug. 23, DMDE.

111 **Canceling a party** Seale, *The President's House*, 127–28.

112 **"fat and forty"** Ketcham, *James Madison*, 496; Seaton, *William Winston Seaton*, 115.

112 **Dolley was bemused** A. J. Langguth, *Union 1812: The Americans Who Fought the Second War of Independence*, 64–67.

112 **Dolley proved to be** J. Madison Cutts, "Dolly Madison," *RCHS*, 1900, 53; Thomas Fleming, "Dolley Saves the Day," *Smithsonian Magazine*, March 2010, 51; "Dolley Madison," James Madison's Montpelier; Calcott, ed., *Mistress of Riverdale*, 224; Seale, *The President's House*, 130; Jennings, *A Colored Man's Reminiscences*, 14.

112 **"Disaffection stalks"** Dolley Madison to Lucy Todd, Aug. 23, DMDE.

WASHINGTON, EVENING, TUESDAY, AUGUST 23

112 **James Madison arrived** Jones, NW III, 314; Ketcham, *James Madison*, 576; Minor, *CCW*, 568–69; Minor to McKenney, April 10, 1847, in Ingraham,

Sketch of the Events, 57; Walter Smith, Jan. 14, 1847, letter, in appendix to Thomas L. McKenny, *Reply to Kosciusko Armstrong's Assault,* 23.

113 **As far as Armstrong** Kosciuszko Armstrong, review of *T. L. McKenney's Narrative of the Causes Which, in 1814, led to General Armstrong's Resignation of the War Office,* 20; Campbell, CCW, 598.

113 **Winder, riding ahead** Winder narrative, CCW, 557; Winder to Armstrong, Sept. 1, NARA RG 107.

113 **News of the retreat** King, "The Battle of Bladensburg," 438.

113 **"Go, for Gods sake go"** Smith, *The First Forty Years,* 99.

113 **That night** Ketcham, *James Madison,* 577.

BLADENSBURG, TUESDAY NIGHT, AUGUST 23

114 **Six miles northeast** Stansbury, CCW, 560; Swanson, *Perilous Fight,* 146.

114 **Private John Pendleton** Tuckerman, *John Pendleton Kennedy,* 77–78.

114 **Around midnight** Stansbury, CCW, 560.

114 **The secretary advised** Monroe, CCW 536; McLane, "Col. McLane's Visit," 20.

115 **Monroe dashed off** Tuckerman, *John Pendleton Kennedy,* 78.

115 **Stansbury, a prominent** Franklin R. Mullaly, "The Battle of Baltimore," *MdHM,* 1959; David S. Heidler and Jeanne T. Heidler, eds., *Encyclopedia of the War of 1812;* Pinkney, CCW, 572; Stansbury, CCW, 560–61.

116 **"Nothing could keep"** Tuckerman, *John Pendleton Kennedy,* 78.

WASHINGTON, EARLY WEDNESDAY MORNING, AUGUST 24

116 **The march of General Winder's** John Law, CCW, 585; McKenney, *Narrative of the Battle of Bladensburg,* 4; Smith, CCW, 564.

116 **Leaving the President's House** Winder narrative, CCW, 557; Burch testimony, CCW, 574.

116 **Winder arrived at camp** Barney to Jones, Aug. 29, NW III, 207; Peter to Williams, May 24, 1854, in Williams, *History of the Invasion,* 362.

BRITISH HEADQUARTERS, MELWOOD PLANTATION, PREDAWN, WEDNESDAY, AUGUST 24

117 **Lieutenant James Scott** Scott, *Recollections,* 280–84; Evans memorandum, Aug. 23, NLS, 6. Scott's account describes Ross as saying they must retreat; Evans's contemporaneous and more reliable account says Ross "did not hesitate to disregard" Cochrane's recommendation. Evans memorandum, Aug. 25, NLS, 8–9; Walter L. Kraus, "Belle Chance at Andrews Air Force Base: A Piece of Maryland's Past," *MdHM,* Fall 1988.

118 **In contradicting** Cochrane Pack, *Man Who Burned the White House,* 14.

118 **"I felt an apprehension"** Ross to Elizabeth Ross, Sept. 1, D 2004/1A/3/5, PRONI.

CHAPTER 6: *The Enemy in Bladensburg!*

AMERICAN HEADQUARTERS, WASHINGTON, WEDNESDAY, AUGUST 24

121 **Early Wednesday morning** Madison memorandum, Aug. 24, *Writings of James Madison*, 294; Winder to Armstrong, Aug. 24, CCW, 548; Winder narrative, CCW, 557. They met at the home of Griffith Combs.

121 **The war council** James Wilkinson, *Memoirs of My Own Times*, vol. 1, 774–75.

121 **Winder learned** Winder narrative, CCW, 557; Monroe, CCW, 536.

122 **With Monroe gone** Winder to Armstrong, Aug. 24, CCW, 548; Rush narrative, CCW, 542.

122 **Then a messenger** Winder narrative, CCW, 557; Jones report, NW III, 314.

OLD FIELDS, EARLY MORNING, WEDNESDAY, AUGUST 24

122 **The British army** Cockburn to Cochrane, Aug. 27, NW III, 221; Gleig, *Narrative of the Campaigns*, 112.

122 **General Ross took** Evans memorandum, Aug. 25, NLS, 9; Rush to Williams, July 10, 1855, in Williams, *History of the Invasion*, 278.

AMERICAN HEADQUARTERS, WASHINGTON, MID-MORNING, WEDNESDAY, AUGUST 24

123 **At 10 a.m. a messenger** Williams, *History of the Invasion*, 202–203; George Campbell, CCW, 598; Winder narrative, CCW, 557.

123 **As Winder prepared** Armstrong, CCW, 539; Skeen, *John Armstrong*, 195; Rush narrative, CCW, 542.

123 **"seemed to be in a high"** George Biscoe to Winder, Jr., March 18, 1849, Winder Papers, MdHS.

123 **Barney, livid, confronted** Armstrong, CCW, 540; Ingersoll, *Historical Sketch*, vol. 2, 173; Barney, *Biographical Memoir*, 264; Barney to Jones, Aug. 29, NW III, 207; Jones to Creighton, Aug. 24, NW III, 206.

124 **Madison and the cabinet** Campbell, CCW, 598–99; Jones memorandum, [Aug. 24], NW III, 214.

124 **Madison was shocked** Madison memorandum, Aug. 24, *Writings of James Madison*, 294; Armstrong, CCW, 539.

125 **Madison prepared to ride** Adams, *War of 1812*, 229; "An Important Incident in the Last War with Great Britain," Jan. 31, 1848, *New York Herald;* [Jacob Barker], *Incidents in the Life of Jacob Barker of New Orleans, Louisiana*, 113, 121.

BLADENSBURG, MORNING, WEDNESDAY, AUGUST 24

125 **The town of Bladensburg** James Riehl Arnold, "The Battle of Bladensburg," 1937, *RCHS*, 145; John Biddle, "Bladensburg: An Early Trade Center," 1953–54, *RCHS*.

125 **People come from all** Calcott, ed., *Mistress of Riverdale*, 57.

125 **favor as a dueling ground** Milton Adkins, "The Bladensburg Dueling Ground," *Magazine of American History*, January 1886.

126 **Just the previous year** Shomette, *Flotilla*, 42.

126 **After abandoning Bladensburg** Stansbury, *CCW*, 561; Pinkney, *CCW*, 572; Sterett, *CCW*, 568.

126 **The roads from Washington** Stansbury, *CCW*, 561; Williams, *History of the Invasion*, 205–207; Pinkney, *CCW*, 572.

127 **Word spread that** Ibid.; Swanson, *Perilous Fight*, 64–65.

EN ROUTE TO BLADENSBURG, MORNING, WEDNESDAY, AUGUST 24

127 **Maryland militia Captain Jenifer** Jenifer Sprigg to J. Hughes, Aug. 25, LOC Manuscript Division, copy in Spratt Collection, Box 1, Part 2, MdHS; Pinkney, *CCW*, 572.

128 **Forces were converging** McKenney, *Narrative of the Battle of Bladensburg*, 4.

128 **Commodore Barney led** Barney to Jones, Aug. 29, NW III, 207.

128 **Last of all** Minor, *CCW*, 568; James Ewell, "Unwelcome Visitors to Early Washington," *RCHS*, 1895, 4–5.

ADDISON CHAPEL, LATE MORNING, WEDNESDAY, AUGUST 24

128 **Ross wanted** Perrett, *The Real Hornblower*, 108; Gleig, *Narrative of the Campaigns*, 111; Ross to sister-in-law, D 2004/1A/3/9, PRONI; Codrington, Aug. 31, Letters from Codrington, May 21, 1814–March 26, 1815, COD/7/1, NMM.

129 **Ross halted at Addison** Gleig, *Subaltern*, 65; *CRG*, 24; Scott, *Recollections*, 285.

BLADENSBURG, LATE MORNING, WEDNESDAY, AUGUST 24

129 **Francis Scott Key** Winder narrative, *CCW*, 557.

129 **accompanying his neighbor** Irvin Molotsky, *The Flag, the Poet and the Song: The Story of the Star-Spangled Banner*, 56; Delaplaine, *Francis Scott Key*, 137.

129 **Key "informed me"** Winder narrative, *CCW*, 557; Smith, *CCW*, 567.

130 **Up front, another cloud** Law, *CCW*, 586; Pinkney, *CCW*, 573; Stansbury, *CCW*, 561.

130 **The plan belonged** Sterett, *CCW*, 568; Monroe, *CCW*, 537; Lavall, *CCW*, 570.

130 **Monroe would later** Monroe, *CCW*, 536–37; Monroe to Charles Everett, Sept. 16, "Letters of James Monroe," *Tyler's Quarterly Historical and Genealogical Magazine*, April 1923.

131 **Stansbury rode back** Stansbury, *CCW*, 561; Winder narrative, *CCW*, 557.

131 **Winder appeared to** Williams, *History of the Invasion*, 215; Albert J. Hadel, "The Battle of Bladensburg," *MdHM*, 1906, 163.

131 **Winder made a few** Winder narrative, *CCW*, 558; Law, *CCW*, 586.

BLADENSBURG, NOON, WEDNESDAY, AUGUST 24

131 **A cheer rose** Madison memorandum, Aug. 24, *Writings of James Madison*, 294; Rush, *CCW*, 542; George, *Terror*, 95.

131 **Madison's party** "William Simmons," July 7, *NI*.

132 **Not only was Madison** Ingersoll, *Historical Sketch*, vol. 2, 175; Borneman, *1812*, 227.

132 **Madison found Winder** Madison memorandum, Aug. 24, *Writings of James Madison*, 294; Rush narrative, *CCW*, 542.

132 **Winder rode forward** Winder narrative, *CCW*, 557.

132 **Rush, the son** Heidler, *Encyclopedia of the War of 1812*, 455; Ingersoll, *Historical Sketch*, vol. 2, 175.

BLADENSBURG, 12:30 P.M., WEDNESDAY, AUGUST 24

133 **The final push** King, "Battle of Bladensburg," 446; Catlett, *CCW*, 585.

133 **"Our poor fellows"** Brooke diary, 303; Barker, *Incidents*, 103; Delaware *Gazette*, 1 September 1814.

133 **Ross paused outside** Gleig, *Narrative of the Campaigns*, 115–17; Lord, *Dawn's Early Light*, 119; Brown, *Diary of a Soldier*, 25; Catlett, *CCW*, 584.

133 **The American forces** Ross to Bathurst, Sept. 30, NW III, 223; Muller, *Darkest Day*, 121–22; Swanson, *Perilous Fight*, 109; Prince George's County Star-Spangled 200 Conference, Sept. 24, 2009.

134 **The Irish-born Thornton** Barrett, *85th King's Light Infantry*, 531; Heidler, *Encyclopedia of the War of 1812*, 511; Cockburn to Cochrane, Aug. 27, NW III, 221.

134 **But some of Ross's** Smith, *Autobiography*, 198–99.

134 **"What will be said"** Ingersoll, *Historical Sketch*, vol. 2, 175; Lord, *Dawn's Early Light*, 120.

134 **Bypassing Bladensburg** Adams, *War of 1812*, 222.

CHAPTER 7: *The Battle for Washington*

BLADENSBURG, 12:30 P.M., WEDNESDAY, AUGUST 24

137 **Two columns of British** Pinkney, *CCW*, 573.

137 **No one could explain** Stansbury, *CCW*, 562.

137 **When the British** George Hoffman to John Hoffman, Sept. 9, War of 1812 Collection, MS 1846, MdHS; Gleig, *Narrative of the Campaigns,* 117.

137 **The Americans whooped** John Buchan, *The History of the Royal Scots Fusiliers, 1678–1918,* 170; Scott, *Recollections,* 286.

138 **The sounds** Ingersoll, *Historical Sketch,* vol. 2, 173; McKenney, *Narrative of the Battle of Bladensburg,* 5.

138 **The District troops** Lossing, *Pictorial Field-book,* 928; Pinkney, CCW, 573.

138 **Francis Scott Key rode** Peter to Williams, May 24, 1854, in Williams, *History of the Invasion,* 363.

138 **The 1st District Regiment** CCW, 529; Smith, CCW, 565; Barney to Jones, Aug. 29, NW III, 207.

139 **President Madison, accompanied** Barker, *Incidents,* 113; Catlett, CCW, 584.

139 **The rockets were a portable** Brodine et al., *Against All Odds,* 46–47; Ralph Robinson, "The Use of Rockets by the British in the War of 1812," *MdHM,* March 1945.

140 **The first rockets flew high** Rush to Williams, July 10, 1855, in Williams, *History of the Invasion,* 279; Barker, *Incidents,* 113.

140 **"The enemy had saluted"** Monroe, *CCW,* 537.

140 **"a more respectful distance"** Winder narrative, CCW, 584; Madison memorandum, Aug. 24, *Writings of James Madison,* 294.

140 **Armstrong fumed** Armstrong, CCW, 539.

BLADENSBURG BRIDGE, EARLY AFTERNOON, WEDNESDAY, AUGUST 24

140 **The British in the village** Gleig, *Subaltern,* 70–71; Brown, *Diary of a Soldier,* 25.

140 **Galloping ahead, Thornton** *Federal Republican,* Sept. 2; Gleig to Horatio King, Nov. 11, 1885, *Magazine of American History,* January 1886; Gleig, *Narrative of the Campaigns,* 118–19.

141 **The Washington Artillery gun** Burch, CCW, 574; Gleig diary, Aug. 24, 138; Buchan, *History of the Royal Scots Fusiliers,* 170.

141 **Thornton emerged unharmed** Scott, *Recollections,* 286.

141 **"Come on my boys"** Smith, *Autobiography,* 199.

141 **A stream of troops** Winder narrative, CCW, 558.

141 **"The fire I think"** Marine, *British Invasion,* 114.

141 **The numbers of British** Gleig, *Narrative of the Campaigns,* 118; Scott, *Recollections,* 286; Ingersoll, *Historical Sketch,* vol. 2, 192–93.

142 **To Major Pinkney's right** Pinkney, CCW, 573–74; McKenney, *Narrative of the Battle of Bladensburg,* 8; Swanson, *Perilous Fight,* 101; Ingersoll, *Historical Sketch,* vol. 2, 176.

142 **Winder, on the hill** Winder to Armstrong, Sept. 1, 1814, NARA RG 107; Lord, *Dawn's Early Light,* 127; Winder narrative, CCW, 558; Glenn F. Williams, "The Bladensburg Races," *MHQ,* Autumn 1999, 64; Swanson, *Perilous Fight,* 111; Gleig diary, Aug. 24, 138.

143 **But a new barrage** Winder narrative, *CCW*, 558; Swanson, *Perilous Fight*, 127; Hoffman, Sept. 9, War of 1812 Collection, MdHS; Ewell, "Unwelcome Visitors," 10; Winder narrative, *CCW*, 558.

143 **Ragan, a cool-headed** Whitehorne, *Battle for Baltimore*, 26.

143 **By now, though, more** Ibid., 132; Ross to Bathurst, Aug. 30, NW III, 224; Brooke diary, 303.

143 **For the militiamen** Winder to Armstrong, Aug. 27, *CCW*, 548.

143 **"cut down those"** Stansbury, *CCW*, 562; Swanson, *Perilous Fight*, 126–28; Shomette, *Flotilla*, 317–19; Winder narrative, *CCW*, 558; Burch, *CCW*, 574; Williams, "The Bladensburg Races," 65.

144 **"I shaped my course"** Marine, *British Invasion*, 114.

144 **"All of a sudden"** Laval, *CCW*, 570–71.

145 **"We made a fine"** Tuckerman, *John Pendleton Kennedy*, 79–80.

145 **The collapse** Swanson, *Perilous Fight*, 105–106; Stansbury, *CCW*, 562; Williams, *History of the Invasion*, 232.

145 **"Each individual"** Law, *CCW*, 586.

145 **Madison sent his servant** Barker, *Incidents*, 113; *Writings of James Madison*, 297 fn.; Monroe, *CCW*, 537; Rush, *CCW*, 543.

THIRD AMERICAN LINE, MID-AFTERNOON, WEDNESDAY, AUGUST 24

145 **Barney saw the American militia** Barney to Jones, Aug. 29, NW III, 207; Peter to Williams, *History of the Invasion*, 364; Barney, *Biographical Memoir*, 265; Ockerbloom, "The Discovery of a U.S. Marine Officer's Account of Life, Honor, and the Battle of Bladensburg, Washington and Maryland, 1814," 260.

146 **Thornton had no taste** McKenney, *Narrative of the Battle of Bladensburg*, 9.

146 **Barney saw his opening** Barney to Jones, Aug. 29, NW III, 207; Shomette, *Flotilla*, 322–23.

146 **"Board them!"** Barney letter to *NI* in Barney, *Biographical Memoir*, appendix, 321.

146 **Thornton lay** Barney, *Biographical Memoir*, 266.

146 **The British tried** Gleig, *Subaltern*, 73; Peter to Williams, *History of the Invasion*, 364.

147 **But General Winder** Winder narrative, *CCW*, 558.

147 **Ross and Cockburn** Brooke diary, 303; Codrington, Aug. 31, in Bourchier, ed., *Codrington*;

147 **one hundred feet** "Sight Lines From Lowndes Hill," Ralph Eshelman monograph, 27 Sept. 2012.

147 **The tall Irish general** Ball, *Slavery in the United States*, 404; *Federal Republican*, Sept. 2; Barney 1815 letter to *NI* in Barney, *Biographical Memoir*, appendix, 321; Ingersoll, *Historical Sketch*, vol. 2, 179–80; Shomette, *Flotilla*, 323.

148 **As Ross directed** Torrens to Vansittart, Nov. 11, WO 3/608, NAUK; Smith, *Autobiography*, 199–200.

148 **Cockburn directed rocket** Scott, *Recollections*, 288–89; Cockburn to Cochrane, Aug. 27, NW III, 221.

148 **Ross had no interest** Barney letter to NI in Barney, *Biographical Memoir*, appendix, 321; Sprigg, Aug. 25, Spratt Collection, MdHS.

148 **"Does General Winder order"** Williams, *History of the Invasion*, 244; Ingersoll, *Historical Sketch*, vol. 2, 193; Scott, *Recollections*, 287; Beall, CCW, 571.

149 **"[T]he militia ran"** Ball, *Slavery in the United States*, 404.

149 **On Barney's left, the District** Smith, CCW, 565; Lord, *Dawn's Early Light*, 136.

149 **"Victory was doubtful"** "Extract of a letter to the Editors of the American, dated Washington, Aug, 29," *Baltimore Patriot*, Sept. 1.

149 **The U.S. regulars** Ingersoll, *Historical Sketch*, vol. 2, 194; Williams, *History of the Invasion*, 242–43.

149 **With the British** Ibid.; Winder narrative, CCW, 558; Smith, CCW, 565; Williams, "The Bladensburg Races," 65.

149 **The commodore was infuriated** Barney to Jones, Aug. 29, NW III, 207.

150 **Loss of blood** Ibid.; Barney, *Biographical Memoir*, 266.

150 **The British swarmed** Davies letter, *Rise and Fall of a Regency Dandy*, 223.

150 **Bullets flew** Marine, *British Invasion*, 178.

150 **A British corporal** Barney, *Biographical Memoir*, 267. Scott, *Recollections*, 290–92; Lord, *Dawn's Early Light*, 138.

151 **"Those officers behaved"** Barney to Jones, Aug. 29, NW III, 208.

151 **"Well, Admiral"** Scott, *Recollections*, 291.

151 **"I told you it was"** Barney, *Biographical Memoir*, 267.

151 **As the surgeon dressed** Barney to Jones, Aug. 29, NW III, 208; Tucker, *Poltroons*, 548.

151 **Barney winced** Barney, *Biographical Memoir*, 267; Weller, "The Life of Commodore Joshua Barney," 148.

151 **"Well, damn my eyes!"** Barney, *Biographical Memoir*, 268.

PRESIDENT'S HOUSE, 3 P.M., WEDNESDAY, AUGUST 24

152 **Dolley Madison** Dolley Madison to Lucy Todd, Aug. 23, DMDE; Ingersoll, *Historical Sketch*, vol. 2, 187.

152 **"She was so confident"** Smith, Aug. 30, *First Forty Years*, 110.

152 **In the dining room, Paul** Jennings, *A Colored Man's Reminiscences*, 8; Beth Taylor, "Paul Jennings: Enamoured with Freedom," James Madison's Montpelier, 2009.

152 **In the kitchen below** Seale, *The President's House*, 122, 134; Ingersoll, *Historical Sketch*, vol. 2, 206.

153 "To the last proposition" Dolley Madison to Lucy Todd, Aug. 23, DMDE.

153 Shortly before 3 p.m. Anna Thornton, "Diary of Mrs. William Thornton. Capture of Washington by the British," in W. B. Bryan, ed., *RCHS*, 1916 (hereafter Anna Thornton diary); Jennings, *A Colored Man's Reminiscences*, 8–10; Dolley Madison to Lucy Todd, Aug. 23, DMDE.

153 The president wanted "his lady" Herrick, *August 24, 1814*, 80.

153 The wagon was hastily loaded Dolley Madison to Mrs. Latrobe, Dec. 3, in Allen C. Clark, ed., *Life and Letters of Dolley Madison*, 166; Conover Hunt-Jones, *Dolley and the "Great Little Madison,"* 48.

153 A small crowd Dolley Madison to Lucy Todd, Aug. 23, DMDE; Anna Payne Cutts to Dolley Madison, [ca. Aug. 23], DMDE.

154 Passing through the dining Jennings, *A Colored Man's Reminiscences*, 10.

154 Barker and others Lucia B. Cutts, ed., *Memoirs and Letters of Dolly Madison*, 106–107; Hunt-Jones, *Dolley and the "Great Little Madison,"* 46–47.

154 Dolley ordered the servants Ingersoll, *Historical Sketch*, vol. 2, 206; Seale, *The President's House*, 133–34; Dolley Madison to Lucy Todd, Aug. 23, 1814, DMDE.

154 Finally, Dolley ordered the frame Barker, *Incidents*, 118.

154 "I directed my servants" Dolley Madison to New York *Express*, Feb. 11, 1848, in Barker, *Incidents*, 110–11; Ingersoll, *Historical Sketch*, vol. 2, 206.

154 "It has often been stated" Jennings, *A Colored Man's Reminiscences*, 12–13.

155 at nearly eight feet Pitch, *Burning of Washington*, 87.

155 Dolley agreed to depart Cutts, ed., *Memoirs and Letters of Dolly Madison*, 58–59; Hunt-Jones, *Dolley and the "Great Little Madison,"* 46.

155 By 3:30, Dolley Jennings, *A Colored Man's Reminiscences*, 9–10.

155 "I lived a lifetime" Cutts, ed., *Memoirs and Letters of Dolly Madison*, 107; Catherine Allgor, *A Perfect Union: Dolley Madison and the Creation of the American Nation*, 314.

155 "I confess" Madison to Mary Latrobe, Dec. 3, in Allen C. Clark, ed., *Life and Letters of Dolley Madison*, 166.

U.S. CAPITOL, LATE AFTERNOON, WEDNESDAY, AUGUST 24

155 "[L]ooking round" McKenney, *Narrative of the Battle of Bladensburg*, 9.

155 Winder ordered a further Winder narrative, CCW, 558; Whitehorne, *Battle for Baltimore*, 134.

156 Winder was conferring Winder narrative, CCW, 559; Peter to Williams, *History of the Invasion*, 364.

156 "[W]e united" Armstrong letter to Baltimore *Patriot*, Sept. 3, in Williams, *History of the Invasion*, 96; Monroe, CCW, 237.

156 For the District militia Smith, CCW, 565.

156 "in pursuit of refreshments," CCW, 530.

156 "Some shed tears" Williams, *History of the Invasion*, 238.

156 From the third Ewell, "Unwelcome Visitors," 6–7.

157 Francis Scott Key Weybright, *Spangled Banner*, 101–102.

157 "memorable flight" Key to Randolph, Oct. 5, Howard Papers, MdHS.

PRESIDENT'S HOUSE, WASHINGTON, 4 P.M., WEDNESDAY, AUGUST 24

157 Weary after sixteen miles Herrick, *August 24, 1814*, 84; *Writings of James Madison*, 297 fn.; Hadel, "The Battle of Bladensburg"; Ingersoll, *Historical Sketch*, vol. 2, 207.

157 Barker and De Peyster Jennings, *A Colored Man's Reminiscences*, 13; Hunt-Jones, *Dolley and the "Great Little Madison,"* 46; Herrick, *August 24, 1814*, 81.

157 Madison took a seat Seale, *The President's House*, 134.

157 "I could never" Barker, *Incidents*, 121; Lord, *Dawn's Early Light*, 151.

158 Outside, exhausted troops Ingersoll, *Historical Sketch*, vol. 2, 207.

158 Madison lingered Herrick, *August 24, 1814*, 84–85; Ketcham, *James Madison*, 578; Brant, *James Madison*, 303–304.

158 After the president's departure Barker, *Incidents*, 114; Anna Thornton diary, Aug. 24, 175.

159 "[A] rabble" Jennings, *A Colored Man's Reminiscences*, 10; Ingersoll, *Historical Sketch*, vol. 2, 207; Seale, *The President's House*, 134; George E. Pettengill, "The Octagon and the War of 1812," *AIA Journal*, February 1965.

WASHINGTON NAVY YARD, WEDNESDAY, AUGUST 24

159 Around 4 p.m., smoke Booth to Tingey, NW III, 210; Tingey to Jones, Aug. 27, NW III, 215; Armstrong letter to *Baltimore Patriot*, Sept. 3, in Williams, *History of the Invasion*, 100; Jones, [Aug. 24], NW III, 214.

159 Short, stout, and temperamental, Tingey Marolda, *The Washington Navy Yard*, 1–2.

160 "any farther importunities" Tingey to Jones, Aug. 27, NW III, 217.

BLADENSBURG, 5 P.M., WEDNESDAY, AUGUST 24

160 "owing to the swiftness" Cockburn to Cochrane, Aug. 27, NW III, 221; Brooke diary, 302; Barrett, *85th King's Light Infantry*, 156.

160 Ross decided Ross to Bathurst, Aug. 30, NW III, 224; Scott, *Recollections*, 297; Cowper, *The King's Own: The Story of a Royal Regiment*, 8.

161 The Americans, by and large Winder to Armstrong, Aug. 27, CCW, 548; Shomette, *Flotilla*, 323.

161 As the British rested CMS, 135; George, *Terror*, 105.

GHENT, MIDNIGHT (6 P.M., WASHINGTON), WEDNESDAY, AUGUST 24

161 For five days, the American delegation Adams, ed., *Memoirs of John Quincy Adams*, 22–23; Fred L. Engelman, *The Peace of Christmas Eve*, 156.

Washington, evening, Wednesday, August 24

162 **The sun was setting** Madison memorandum, Aug. 24, *Writings of James Madison*, 294; Jennings, *A Colored Man's Reminiscences*, 10; Brant, *James Madison*, 306; Herrick, *August 24, 1814*, 103.

162 **Meanwhile, Dolley Madison** Jones, [Aug. 24], NW III, 214; Jones, NW III, 314; Robert Ames Alden, "Madison's Desperate Ride," May 2, 1972, *WP*.

162 **Those left in the city** "Destruction of the American Capital," Sept. 6, *Hartford Courant*.

162 **"[T]he poor creatures"** Anna Thornton diary, Aug. 26, 177.

162 **"saw no army"** Laval, CCW, 571.

163 **"But all was silent"** Booth to Tingey, NW III, 212.

CHAPTER 8: *A Spectacle Terrible and Magnificent*

165 **Moving at a fast clip** Scott, *Recollections*, 297–98; Evans memorandum, Aug. 25, NLS, 12; Norman Pringle, *Letters by Major Norman Pringle, Late of the 21st Royal Scots Fusiliers*, 2; Tucker, *Poltroons*, 552.

165 **On Capitol Hill, Michael Shiner** John G. Sharp, ed., *The Diary of Michael Shiner Relating to the History of the Washington Navy Yard 1813–1869* (hereafter Shiner diary), 6–7.

167 **Approaching the Capitol** J. S. Skinner, "To the Editors of the National Intelligencer," *Essex Register* [Salem, Mass.], June 20, 1821; James, *Naval History of Great Britain*, 178.

167 **An officer sent forward** 28th Congress, 1st Sess., Report No. 254, Feb. 28, 1844, in "The Sewall-Belmont House Historic Structure Report," 2001, courtesy of Sewall-Belmont Home.

167 **drums for a parley** Gleig, *Narrative of the Campaigns*, 125; Lord, *Dawn's Early Light*, 160.

167 **The general's instructions** Bathurst, May 20, NW III, 72.

167 **"Such of the inhabitants"** Brooke diary, 303; A. P. W. Malcolmson, Introduction to Ross of Bladensburg Papers, D. 2004, PRONI; Ingraham, *Sketch of the Events*, 36.

167 **President Madison later said** Lossing, *Pictorial Field-Book*, 932.

167 **"intention to enter the city"** 28th Congress, 1st Sess., Report No. 254, Feb. 28, 1844, in "The Sewall-Belmont House Historic Structure Report."

167 **a volley of musket fire** Memoir of Major Mortimer Timpson, RMM, 32 (hereafter Timpson memoir).

167 **"the English buggers"** Davies letter, *Rise and Fall of a Regency Dandy*, 223; William Thornton to Benjamin Russell, April 30, 1817, American Antiquarian Society Records, Correspondence 1812–1899, box 2, posted on "Past Is Present," AAS online forum, Oct. 2, 2009; Rene Chartrand, "An Account of the Capture of Washington, 1814," *Military Collector & Historian*, Winter

1985; Buchan, *History of the Royal Scots Fusiliers*, 171; Brown, *Diary of a Soldier*, 26.

167 **Ross ordered the house** James, *Naval History of Great Britain*, 178.

167 **"in a twinkle"** Shiner diary, 7.

168 **Over the years** Tucker, *Poltroons*, 553; Eberlein and Hubbard, *Historic Houses*, 428.

168 **Yet the evidence** S. Rep. to accompany bill S. 115, S. Doc No. 89, 29th Congress, 2nd Sess. (1847), in "The Sewall-Belmont House Historic Structure Report."

168 **"the only brave Yankees"** Thornton to Russell, April 30, 1817, AAS.

168 **The captured flotillamen** S. Rep. to accompany bill S. 115, S. Doc No. 89, 29th Congress, 2nd Sess. (1847).

168 **"I was informed"** Ewell, "Unwelcome Visitors," 8.

168 **Ross ordered the Sewall** H. Rep. No. 254, 28th Cong., 1st Sess. (1844), in "The Sewall-Belmont House Historic Structure Report."

168 **"they made the rafters fly"** Shiner diary, 7.

WASHINGTON NAVY YARD, 8:20 P.M., WEDNESDAY, AUGUST 24

169 **Captain Tingey was beside** Tingey to Jones, Aug. 27, NW III, 217; "Officers in the Battle of Lake Erie," *New England Historical and Genealogical Register*, 1863, 18; William Taylor to Abby Taylor, Aug. 30, transcript in NHHC.

169 **"incontestable proof"** Tingey to Jones, Aug. 27, NW III, 217; Booth to Tingey, NW III, 213.

170 **Almost everything else** Ibid.; Thomas Beall account book, Aug. 24, MS 112, MdHS; William Taylor to Abby, Aug. 30, NHHC.

U.S. CAPITOL, 9 P.M., WEDNESDAY, AUGUST 24

170 **That sight lit the night** Ewell, "Unwelcome Visitors," 8; Charles O. Paullin, "Washington City and the Old Navy," *RCHS*, 1932, 169; Mary Hunter, "The Burning of Washington, D.C.," *New-York Historical Society Quarterly Bulletin*, 1924, 81.

171 **The Capitol—or the "palace"** Caemmerer, *A Manual on the Origin and Development of Washington*, 40; "History of the U.S. Capitol Building," AOC, http://www.aoc.gov/history/us-capitol-building; William C. Allen, *History of the United States Capitol*, 97.

171 **to immediately "burn"** Gleig, *Narrative of the Campaigns*, 125–26.

171 **"the conduct adopted"** Scott, *Recollections*, 301.

171 **But in the report** Ross to Bathurst, Aug. 30, NW III, 224.

172 **Captain Harry Smith** Smith, *Autobiography*, 200.

172 **Wary of another ambush** King, "Battle of Bladensburg," 446; Ingersoll, *Historical Sketch*, 185; Tucker, *Poltroons*, 554; Spiers, *Radical General*, 9.

172 **grandeur of the building** Scott, *Recollections*, 301.

172 **Cockburn poked into** "The Library of Congress Recovers a Book Lost for 126 Years," Library of Congress press release, Jan. 13, 1940, LOC Rare Book and Special Collections Division; Pack, *Man Who Burned the White House*, 17; author tour with Mark Dimunation, chief of the Rare Book and Special Collections Division, LOC, Oct. 19, 2009.

172 **The British considered blowing it** Hunter, "The Burning of Washington, D.C.," 82; Ingersoll, *Historical Sketch*, 185.

173 **The British started** Seale, "The White House Before the Fire," 18; Allen, *History of the United States Capitol*, 98; Muller, *Darkest Day*, 140; Latrobe to Jefferson, July 12, 1815, in Van Horn, *Papers of Benjamin Henry Latrobe*, vol. 3, 670.

174 **Driven from the south** Tour of Capitol with William Allen, chief historian, AOC, Oct. 19, 2009; Allen, *History of the United States Capitol*, 98.

175 **"The flames floated away"** Scott, *Recollections*, 302; *CRG*, 295.

175 **As the inferno blazed** Ingersoll, *Historical Sketch*, 185; Glenn Brown and William Bushong, *Glenn Brown's History of the U.S. Capitol*, 119.

175 **Dr. James Ewell watched** Ewell, "Unwelcome Visitors," 11–16, 33–34; Lord, *Dawn's Early Light*, 165.

176 **Across town, Louis Sérurier** Brant, *James Madison*, 305; Benjamin Ogle Tayloe, *Our Neighbors on Lafayette Square*, 14.

176 **A large white sheet** Ingersoll, *Historical Sketch*, 201.

176 **The British marched** Arnold, "The Battle of Bladensburg," 157; CMS, 136; Scott, *Recollections*, 303.

177 **From the window of his** William Gardner, "To the Editor of the Federal Republican," Sept. 27, *Hartford Courant*.

177 **The troops paused** Ingersoll, *Historical Sketch*, vol. 2, 186–87.

PRESIDENT'S HOUSE, 11 P.M., WEDNESDAY, AUGUST 24

178 **Moving on to the President's** Gleig, *Narrative of the Campaigns*, 130.

178 **"So unexpected was our entry"** Smyth, *History of the XX Regiment*, 325.

178 **"Peace with America"** King, "Battle of Bladensburg," 455.

178 **"Nor was Mr. Madison's health"** Pringle, *Letters*, 2.

179 **"super-excellent"** Scott, *Recollections*, 303; Buchan, *History of the Royal Scots Fusiliers*, 171.

179 **Cockburn also enjoyed** Allen C. Clark, "Roger Chew Weightman, A Mayor of the City of Washington," *RCHS*, 1919; Hunt-Jones, *Dolley and the "Great Little Madison,"* 46; Cutts, ed., *Memoirs and Letters of Dolly Madison*, 112.

179 **"Take something"** Smith, Aug. 30, *First Forty Years*, 111–12; Seale, *The President's House*, 135.

179 **Soldiers and sailors roamed** Barrett, *85th King's Light Infantry*, 156.

180 **miniature portrait of the first** Hunt-Jones, *Dolley and the "Great Little Mad-*

ison," 47. The portrait was turned over to an American in Europe by a British soldier in 1827.

180 **Madison's small medicine chest** Franklin Delano Roosevelt to Archibald MacLeish, Jan. 24, 1940, LOC Rare Book and Special Collections Division; Betty Monkman, "Reminders of 1814," *White House History,* Fall 1998, 34; Ingersoll, *Historical Sketch,* vol. 2, 187.

180 **Scott made his way** Scott, *Recollections,* 304.

180 **After an hour** Ingersoll, *Historical Sketch,* vol. 2, 187; Seale, "The White House Before the Fire," 18; Brant, *James Madison,* 305.

180 **"I shall never forget"** Smith, *Autobiography,* 200; Smith, Aug. 30, *First Forty Years,* 111.

180 **Treasury building** Ibid.; Scott, *Recollections,* 305.

181 **Ross and Cockburn gathered** Seale, *The President's House,* 136.

181 **"Although they were"** Buchan, *History of the Royal Scots Fusiliers,* 171.

181 **The main body of British** Gleig, *Narrative of the Campaigns,* 128; Brooke diary, 303.

181 **Key felt "sure they would"** Franklin R. Mullaly, "A Forgotten Letter of Francis Scott Key," *MdHM,* December 1960, 359–60; "To Arms! To Arms!," *Richmond Enquirer,* Aug. 27; Delaplaine, *Francis Scott Key,* 145.

181 **The Foxall Foundry** Louis F. Gorr, "The Foxall-Columbia Foundry: An Early Defense Contractor in Georgetown," *RCHS,* 1971; *CRG,* 275.

181 **The Thorntons and Peter** Anna Thornton diary, Aug. 24; Smith, *First Forty Years,* 111; Eberlein and Hubbard, *Historic Houses,* 128.

182 **Dr. William Thornton** Glenn Brown, "The U.S. Capitol in 1800," *RCHS,* 1901; Seale, *The President's House,* 110.

182 **"beheld, in deep regret"** William Thornton, "To the Public," *NI,* Sept. 7.

182 **"almost meridian brightness"** Hunter, "The Burning of Washington, D.C.," 82.

NORTHERN VIRGINIA COUNTRYSIDE, LATE NIGHT, WEDNESDAY, AUGUST 24

182 **President Madison had a clear** Rush to Williams, July 10, 1855, in Williams, *History of the Invasion,* 274; Jennings, *A Colored Man's Reminiscences,* 11.

182 **Madison and his companions** Herrick, *August 24, 1814,* 104.

183 **Dolley Madison and her** Ibid., 107; Anne Hollingsworth Wharton, *Social Life in the Early Republic,* 172; Cutts, ed., *Memoirs and Letters of Dolly Madison,* 108.

TENLEYTOWN, MIDNIGHT, WEDNESDAY, AUGUST 24

183 **Retreating past Georgetown** Winder narrative, *CCW,* 559.

183 **"[W]hen he might"** Adams, *The War of 1812,* 229.

184 **Winder ordered a further retreat** Peter to Williams, *History of the Invasion,* 367; Van Ness, *CCW,* 583.

184 "made me regret" Hoffman, Sept. 9, War of 1812 Collection, MdHS.

184 At Benedict [Barrett], "Naval Recollections of the Late American War," part 1, 460.

184 Captain Gordon's squadron Napier, *Admiral Sir Charles Napier*, 78; Perrett, *The Real Hornblower*, 111.

184 Light from the fires Ingraham, *Sketch of the Events*, 48; Martha S. Jones, "Letter of Martha Selden Jones," *William and Mary Quarterly*, July 1938, 292.

184 "my journey during" [Daniel Sheldon], "An Unpublished Letter, August 26, 1814: The Burning of Washington," *Magazine of American History*, 1892, 467.

185 visible in Baltimore Scott S. Sheads, *The Rockets' Red Glare: The Maritime Defense of Baltimore in 1814*, 57.

185 "As the moon" London *Times*, Sept. 29.

185 Admiral Cockburn, by one account Ingersoll, *Historical Sketch*, vol. 2, 186.

185 Bank of Metropolis CRG, 274.

186 the *National Intelligencer* Williams, *History of the Invasion*, 265; Allen C. Clark, "Joseph Gales, Junior, Editor and Mayor," RCHS, 1920; "Old Sub," part 2, 25.

187 Near the McKeown Hotel "Fall of Washington. Phil. True American Extra," in *Long Island Star*, Aug. 31; Scott, *Recollections*, 306.

187 "Good people" Smith, *First Forty Years*, 111–12; Chester Bailey to *Poulson's Advertiser*, Philadelphia, Aug. 29, reprinted in Boston *Repertory*, 1 Sept.; Lord, *Dawn's Early Light*, 170.

CHAPTER 9: *They Feel Strongly the Disgrace*

189 Toward dawn Gleig, *Narrative of the Campaigns*, 211; Chester Bailey to *Poulson's Advertiser*, Tucker, *Poltroons*, 576; Seale, *The President's House*, 135; Ingersoll, *Historical Sketch*, vol. 2, 189, 205; CRG, 277.

189 Near the Capitol, Lieutenant Scott Scott, *Recollections*, 311–12; Cockburn to Cochrane, Aug. 27, NW III, 222.

190 "coarse jests" Williams, *History of the Invasion*, 270.

190 One American told Cockburn *Nantucket Gazette*, July 1816; *Connecticut Journal*, Sept. 5; "Cheers for the British," WP, Aug. 23, 1993.

190 "[S]uch was his Smith, *First Forty Years*, 112; Peter to Quincy, Aug. 26, *in* Eberlein and Hubbard, *Historic Houses*, 131.

190 The *Intelligencer* would Scott, *Recollections*, 306; Williams, *History of the Invasion*, 265.

190 "Be sure that all the 'c's" Ingersoll, *Historical Sketch*, vol. 2, 188.

191 Cockburn helped his men Seaton, *William Winston Seaton*, 116; Clark, "Joseph Gales," 100.

191 Dr. William Thornton Thomas B. Brumbaugh, ed., "A Letter of Dr. William

Thornton to Colonel William Thornton," *MdHM,* March 1978, 64; Lord, *Dawn's Early Light,* 175; Tucker, *Poltroons,* 577.

191 **Thornton leapt** Thornton, "To the Public," *NI,* Sept. 7; Anna Thornton diary, Aug. 25, 175.

NAVY YARD, MORNING, THURSDAY, AUGUST 25

192 **"Admiral Cockburn said he was glad"** "Fall of Washington Phil. True American Extra," in *Long Island Star,* Aug. 31.

192 **Some delinquent youth** Thomas Ap Catesby Jones and Martha Fry, "Mutilation of the Monument," *Army and Navy Chronicle,* vol. 8, 1839, 261; "History of the Washington Navy Yard, 1799–1921," part 2, Special Collections, Washington Navy Yard Library, 258, 275; Tingey to Jones, Oct. 18, NW III, 319.

192 **"parcel of wicked boys"** "Mutilation of the Monument," 259–61.

193 **Cheering troops clambered** "Mutilation of the Monument," 260–61.

CAPITOL HILL, MORNING, THURSDAY, AUGUST 25

194 **At his headquarters** Ewell, "Unwelcome Visitors," 16.

194 **York—modern-day Toronto** Fabel, "The Laws of War in the 1812 Conflict," 211.

194 **Brigadier General Zebulon** Ibid., 216; Hickey, *Don't Give Up the Ship!,* 216.

195 **"They feel strongly"** Ross to Elizabeth Ross, Sept. 1, D 2004/1A/3/5, PRONI.

195 **It was not so much York** Fabel, "The Laws of War in the 1812 Conflict," 216; Mahan, *Sea Power,* 333. Malcolmson, *Capital in Flames,* 390; Prevost to Cochrane, June 2, ADM 1/506, NAUK.

196 **Before Ross landed** Handwritten copy of MacDougall letter to London *Times,* May 1861, GWU.

197 **Returning from his tour** Ewell, *Unwelcome Visitors,* 16; Hunter, "The Burning of Washington, D.C.," 82.

197 **In that spirit, he and Ross** Evans memorandum, Aug. 31, NLS, 16; Smith, *First Forty Years,* 113. The oft-told story that the British spared the barracks as a gesture of respect to the U.S. Marines is a myth.

197 **A few isolated** Ewell, *Unwelcome Visitors,* 19–22; Gardner, "To the Editor of the Federal Republican."

197 **Cockburn's harshest critics** Scott, *Recollections,* 323.

MONTGOMERY COURT HOUSE, THURSDAY MORNING, AUGUST 25

198 **General Winder** Winder narrative, CCW, 551.

198 **"I shall assemble"** Winder to Stricker, Aug. 25, Winder Papers, MdHS.

198 **Every hour brought** Stansbury, CCW, 262; Sheldon, "Unpublished Letter."

198 **The dusty and exhausted** Sprigg, Aug. 25, Spratt Collection, MdHS.

198 **Both the weather** Winder narrative, CCW, 557.

199 **Jacob Barker** Barker, *Incidents,* 110.

GREENLEAF POINT, WASHINGTON, NOON, THURSDAY, AUGUST 25

199 **The British had nearly** Williams, *History of the Invasion,* 268.

199 **Royal Marine Captain Mortimer Timpson** Timpson memoir, RMM, i, 32; Virginia Campbell Moore, "Reminiscences of Washington as Recalled by a Descendant of the Ingle Family," *RCHS,* 1900, 103.

199 **At the arsenal** *CCW,* 587; Timpson memoir, RMM, 32; Scott, *Recollections,* 312; Williams, *History of the Invasion,* 268.

200 **"I found myself shot"** Timpson memoir, RMM, 33.

200 **Rocks, earth** Arnold, "The Battle of Bladensburg," 160–61; Williams, *History of the Invasion,* 268.

200 **When he came to** Timpson memoir, RMM, 33–35.

200 **The sickening concussion** Ingersoll, *Historical Sketch,* vol. 2, 189; Shiner diary, 8; Gleig, *Narrative of the Campaigns,* 136; Smith, *Autobiography,* 203; Kevin Ambrose, Dan Henry, and Andy Weiss, *Washington Weather: The Weather Sourcebook for the D.C. Area,* 31.

201 **The roaring wind** *Baltimore Patriot and Evening Advertiser,* Aug. 31; Gleig, *Narrative of the Campaigns,* 136–37.

201 **Mary Ingle** Moore, "Reminiscences of Washington."

201 **The storm, by one** Ingersoll, *Historical Sketch,* vol. 2, 294; Gleig, *Narrative of the Campaigns,* 137.

201 **"It fairly lifted me"** King, "Battle of Bladensburg," 456.

201 **"I never witnessed"** Smith, *Autobiography,* 203.

201 **In parts of the city** "Destructive Hurricane," Sept. 1, *NI;* Seth Pease letter, Sept. 1, Individual Manuscripts Collections, GWU; Ingersoll, *Historical Sketch,* vol. 2, 191; Lord, *Dawn's Early Light,* 182; *CCW,* 586; Pringle, *Letters,* 8.

202 **Sweeping southeast** [Barrett], "Naval Recollections of the Late American War," part 1, 460; logbook of *Royal Oak,* ADM 50/87, NAUK; Shomette, *Flotilla,* 328.

202 **On the Potomac** Napier, *Admiral Sir Charles Napier,* 79, 87.

202 **In Washington, after** Ambrose, et. al., *Washington Weather,* 32; Moore, "Reminiscences of Washington."

NORTHERN VIRGINIA, THURSDAY, AUGUST 25

202 **President Madison** Alden, "Madison's Desperate Ride"; Herrick, *August 24, 1814,* 113; Booth to Tingey, Sept. 10, transcript at UVa.

203 **Dolley and her party** Cutts, ed., *Memoirs and Letters of Dolly Madison,* 114–15; Jeremiah Mason to Mary Means Mason, Oct. 6, DMDE; Ingersoll, *Historical Sketch,* vol. 2, 208; Jennings, *A Colored Man's Reminiscences,* 11.

CAPITOL HILL, EVENING, THURSDAY, AUGUST 25

203 **A ghastly column** Timpson journal, 37, RMM; Ewell, "Unwelcome Visitors," 23; Ingersoll, *Historical Sketch*, vol. 2, 189; Scott, *Recollections*, 312.

204 **The vital Foxall Foundry** [McLane], Nov. 14, 1853, Winder Papers, MdHS; Gorr, "The Foxall-Columbia Foundry." Owner Henry Foxall, a devout Methodist, later built a church in Washington in thanks. *CRG*, 275; *Baltimore Patriot*, Aug. 31.

204 **"The object of the expedition"** Ross to Bathurst, Aug. 30, NW III, 223.

204 **"the general devastation"** Cockburn to Cochrane, Aug. 27, NW III, 222.

204 **Despite all the evidence** Catlett, *CCW*, 584; Brooke diary, 303–304.

204 **Ross directed Lieutenant Evans** Smith, *Autobiography*, 201; King, "Battle of Bladensburg," 454; Cowper, *The King's Own: The Story of a Royal Regiment*, 9.

204 **The general arranged for Ewell** Ewell, "Unwelcome Visitors," 24; Scott, *Recollections*, 324.

205 **Shortly after sunset** Beall account book, Aug. 24, MS 112, MdHS; Gleig, *Narrative of the Campaigns*, 141.

205 **"forty miserable"** Catlett, *CCW*, 584; Smith, *Autobiography*, 201; Shiner diary, 9; Calcott, ed., *Mistress of Riverdale*, 272.

205 **The light infantry troops** Scott, *Recollections*, 325; Cowper, *The King's Own*, 9; Gleig, *Subaltern*, 89.

206 **Commodore Barney** Barney to Jones, Aug. 29, NW III, 207; Gleig, *Narrative of the Campaigns*, 139; Barney, *Biographical Memoir*, 268–69.

206 **At midnight, bugles** Catlett, *CCW*, 584; *CCW*, 531; Smith, *Autobiography*, 202.

206 **"Exceeding darkness"** Scott, *Recollections*, 325.

206 **The "fatiguing march"** Ross to Bathurst, Sept. 1, WO 1/141, NAUK.

206 **Many soldiers tossed** Smith, *Autobiography*, 202; Gleig diary, Aug. 27.

CHAPTER 10: *Hide Our Heads*

WASHINGTON, MORNING, FRIDAY, AUGUST 26

209 **The British were gone** Peter to Quincy, Aug. 26, in Eberlein and Hubbard, *Historic Houses*, 128.

209 **"[I]t seems as"** Anna Thornton diary, Aug. 27, 177.

209 **Francis Scott Key wrote** Mullaly, "A Forgotten Letter of Francis Scott Key."

210 **Rumors flew that armed blacks** Stansbury, *CCW*, 562.

210 **Adding to the sense** Arnold, "The Battle of Bladensburg," 166; Lord, *Dawn's Early Light*, 194.

210 **William Thornton, returning** Thornton, "To the Public," *NI*, Sept. 7.

210 **The yard commandant discovered** Tingey to Jones, Aug. 27, NW III, 217.

210 **Mayor Blake returned** Blake to Monroe, Aug. 27, Misc. Letters of the Department of State, NARA RG 59, M179, Roll 30; M. I. Weller, "Four Mayors of the City of Washington," *RCHS*, 1899.

210 **"Our stupid mayor"** Anna Thornton diary, Aug. 28, 177.

211 **A marine guarding** Tingey to Jones, Oct. 7, NARA RG 45, M125, roll 40, copy at NHHC; Peck, *Roundshots to Rockets*, 68.

211 **At dusk** James H. Blake, "To The Editors," *NI*, Sept. 9.

211 **Captain John Rodgers arrived** Rodgers to Winder, Aug. 26, NHHC; Rodgers to Jones, Aug. 27, NW III, 259.

211 **"Would to God"** Rodgers to Jones, Aug. 29, NW III, 244.

211 **"When we got to Baltimore"** John Harris to William Harris, Sept. 27, War of 1812 Collection, MdHS; Porter to Jones, Aug. 27, NARA RG 45, subject file, Box 151, copy at NHHC.

212 **"This came upon us"** James Piper, "Defence of Baltimore, 1814," *MdHM*, 1912.

212 **Private Henry Fulford** Marine, *British Invasion*, 114.

212 **"We expect every"** Annie L. Sioussat, *Old Baltimore*, 192.

212 **Residents of Baltimore** Don Hickey, "The Pro-War Riots in Baltimore in the Summer of 1812," lecture at National War of 1812 Symposium, Baltimore, Oct. 2, 2010; Lord, *Dawn's Early Light*, 227; Fells Point tour with Jack Trautwein, Nov. 14, 2009.

212 **"They will make"** Marine, *British Invasion*, 16, 18.

213 **A veritable private navy** Scott S. Sheads, *Fort McHenry*, 17.

213 **Two-masted schooners** John V. Trautwein and Ellen von Karajan, "Fell Point's Untold Story," Trautwein, "Sudden End to the War of 1812: A Chronology (1813–1815),"and *Pride of Baltimore II* tour, Baltimore City Star-Spangled 200 Conference, Nov. 10, 2010; Marine, *British Invasion*, 14–15.

MONTGOMERY COURT HOUSE, 10 A.M., FRIDAY, AUGUST 26

214 **At his headquarters** Winder narrative, *CCW*, 559.

214 **"a force respectable"** Stansbury, *CCW*, 562.

214 **Winder continued during** Ralph J. Robinson, "Controversy over the Command at Baltimore in the War of 1812," *MdHM*, 1944; Swanson, *Perilous Fight*, 199–200.

215 **Samuel Smith had never** Frank A. Cassell, *Merchant Congressman in the Young Republic: Samuel Smith of Maryland, 1752–1839,* 18, 175, 181–83, 201; Lossing, *Pictorial Field-book,* 947; Ketcham, *James Madison,* 488.

215 **When war was declared** Frank A. Cassell, "Baltimore in 1813: A Study of Urban Defense in the War of 1812," *Military Affairs*, December 1969, 350, 358–60.

216 **After Bladensburg, city leaders** Marine, *British Invasion,*135.

217 **"There can be no doubt"** Governor Winder to Edward Johnson, Aug. 26,

Baltimore City Archives, RG 22, War of 1812 Records; George, *Terror*, 127; Robinson, "Controversy over the Command."

217 **"[T]he manner in which"** Winder to Secretary of War, Aug. 28, Winder Papers, MdHS.

Upper Marlboro, Friday, August 26

217 **The Americans "took the bait"** Smith, *Autobiography*, 203–204.

217 **Ross had, in fact** Evans memorandum, 13–14, NLS; Ross to Bathurst, Aug. 30, NW III, 223.

218 **Yet Ross was missing,** Mullaly, "Battle of Baltimore," 67, 82; James, *Naval History of Great Britain*, 187.

Brookeville, Maryland, 9 p.m., Friday, August 26

218 **The Quaker village** CRG, 92; Smith, *First Forty Years*, 100.

218 **But the war came** "Destruction of the American Capital," Sept. 6, *Hartford Courant;* Smith, *First Forty Years*, 107. Bentley was also a silversmith, and had made the cornerstone plate placed in 1793 by George Washington for the groundbreaking of the now-destroyed Capitol.

219 **Madison had left Dolley** Booth to Tingey, Sept. 10, UVa; Madison to Monroe, Aug. 26, *Writings of James Madison*, 298; Brant, *James Madison*, 307; Madison to Jones, Aug. 27, Historical Society of Pennsylvania, copy at UVa; Herrick, *August 24, 1814*, 116–17.

219 **Madison "anxiously enquired"** "Extract of a letter, dated Brookville, Augt. 27," Sept. 6, Hudson, N.Y., *Northern Whig.*

219 **Around 10 p.m.** White House Historical Association, *The White House: An Historic Guide*, 118; author tour, Bentley home, March 10, 2012.

220 **"I will either wait"** Madison to Monroe, Aug. 26, *Writings of James Madison*, 298.

220 **Since he had left** Brant, *James Madison*, 308; Ketcham, *James Madison*, 580.

220 **In the morning** Madison to Jones, Aug. 27, UVa; Madison to Dolley Madison, Aug. 27, DMDE; Smith, *First Forty Years*, 108; Lord, *Dawn's Early Light*, 193.

Upper Marlboro, afternoon, Saturday, August 27

220 **The departure of the British** Gleig diary, Aug. 27, 153; *Report of the Trial of John Hodges, Esq. on a Charge of High Treason. Tried in the Circuit Court of the United States for the Maryland District, at the May Term, 1815*, 13, 17 (hereafter Hodges trial).

221 **more than a hundred stragglers** Anna Thornton diary, Sept. 3, 180; John Godrey affidavit, [Sept. 3], RG 45, Naval Records Collection of the Office of Naval Records and Library; Shomette, *Flotilla*, 332; Hodges trial, 11, 14–15.

221 **The guests soon realized** Ibid., 15, 18; Shomette, *Flotilla*, 332.

221 **"[S]everal gentlemen"** "From the Baltimore Federal Gazette of August 30," Sept. 1, *Delaware Gazette.*

221 **Nonetheless, Beanes, Bowie** Hodges trial, 5, 9–10, 15–16.

POTOMAC RIVER, EVENING, SATURDAY, AUGUST 27

222 **At 5 p.m., Captain Gordon's** Napier, *Admiral Sir Charles Napier,* 79–80; Gordon to Cochrane, Sept. 9, NW III, 238; Perrett, *The Real Hornblower,* 112.

222 **Fort Washington** James Morgan, "Historic Fort Washington on the Potomac," *RCHS,* 1904, 1, 4, 9; *CRG,* 122; Kyle Jillson, "Fort Washington, Maryland," *On Point,* Summer 2009; Scott Berg, *Grand Avenues: The Story of the French Visionary Who Designed Washington, D.C.,* 122.

223 **Spotting the British sails** Dyson to Armstrong, Aug. 29, CCW, 588; Ingraham, *Sketch of the Events,* 53.

223 **"my miserable post"** Pitch, *Burning of Washington,* 156–57.

223 **orders from Winder** CCW, 530.

223 **Dyson gave orders** Pitch, *Burning of Washington,* 157; Gordon to Cochrane, Sept. 9, NW III, 238; Napier, *Admiral Sir Charles Napier,* 80.

CHAPTER 11: *The Arrogant Foe*

WASHINGTON, EVENING, SATURDAY, AUGUST 27

225 **President Madison rode** Monroe to Winder, Aug. 28, in John C. Hildt, "Letters Relating to the Capture of Washington," *South Atlantic Quarterly,* 1907, 62; Anna Thornton diary, Aug. 27, 177; McKenney to Winder, Aug. 27, Winder Papers, MdHS; Brant, *James Madison,* 310.

225 **"Such was the state"** "J.M's Notes Respecting the Burning City in 1814," *Writings of James Monroe,* 373–74; Ketcham, *James Madison,* 581.

UPPER MARLBORO, 1 A.M., SUNDAY, AUGUST 28

226 **During the night** Roger B. Taney letter, 1856, in [Francis Scott Key], *Poems of the Late Francis Scott Key, Esq., Author of "The Star Spangled Banner." With an Introductory Letter by Chief Justice Taney* (hereafter Taney narrative), 18–19, 22; Anna Thornton diary, Sept. 3, 180.

226 **He ordered Lieutenant Evans** Hodges trial, 17; Gleig diary, Aug. 28, 154.

226 **"taken from his bed"** John Mason to Ross, Sept. 2, NARA RG 45; "From the Baltimore Federal Gazette of August 30," Sept. 1, *Delaware Gazette.*

227 **"[U]nless they were returned"** Hodges trial, 22.

227 **The party rode back** Gleig diary, Aug. 28, 154.

227 **Beanes had "acted hostilely"** Ross to Mason, Sept. 7, NARA RG 45.

227 **Ross, recalled Hill** William Hill letter to General Heath, Aug. 27, in "Visit of the British in 1812," *Baltimore Sun,* July 25, 1890.

QUEEN ANNE, MARYLAND, EARLY MORNING, SUNDAY, AUGUST 28

227 **Upper Marlboro** Hodges trial, 5, 11, 17.

227 **"Never [were] people"** Bowie, in ibid., 16.

227 **The Hodges arrived in Queen** Ibid., 10–11, 16.

227 **"if he surrendered"** Caton, in ibid., 10.

228 **But the governor insisted** Ibid., 12, 16–17.

228 **The governor's son noted "they had"** Ibid., 12, 15; Shomette, *Flotilla*, 334–35.

FORT WASHINGTON, DAWN, SUNDAY, AUGUST 28

228 **Captain Gordon waited** Napier, *Admiral Sir Charles Napier*, 80.

228 **During the night, Captain Dyson** Pitch, *Burning of Washington*, 158; CCW, 589. The army disagreed; nine weeks later, a court-martial found that Dyson did "shamefully abandon the fort" and convicted him of conduct unbecoming an officer, but acquitted him on a charge of being drunk on duty. He was dismissed from service.

228 **No one was more dismayed** Report of Alexandria Council, Sept. 7, CCW, 590; letter from the citizens of Alexandria, CCW, 593; Williams, *History of the Invasion*, 284. The city claimed as its own George Washington, who by tradition was said to have helped lay out the town as a seventeen-year-old surveyor, and who had worshipped, socialized, and joined the volunteer fire department in Alexandria. Alexandria was also home to seven-year-old Robert E. Lee, who lived with his mother and siblings in a modest brick house on Oronoco Street. His father, the Revolutionary War hero Henry "Light-Horse Harry" Lee, crippled by the pro-war mob in the 1812 Baltimore riot, sailed to the West Indies in 1813 in a futile attempt to recover his health and never saw his son again.

229 **With the enemy squadron** Report of Alexandria Council, Sept. 7, CCW, 591; Lord, *Dawn's Early Light*, 198.

WASHINGTON, MORNING, SUNDAY, AUGUST 28

229 **"You may be again"** Madison to Dolley, Aug. 28, DMDE; Brant, *James Madison*, 310.

230 **"Who would have"** Smith, *First Forty Years*, 109–10.

230 **The presidential party** Jones to Rodgers, Aug. 28, Series 3B, Vol. 8, Rodgers Family Papers, LOC,, copy in NHHC; Monroe to Winder, Aug. 28, in Hildt, "Letters Relating to the Capture of Washington."

230 **"A general alarm"** Anna Thornton diary, Aug. 28, 177.

230 **Mayor John Peter** Peter to Winder, ca. Aug. 27, Winder Papers, MdHS; Smith, *First Forty Years*, 114.

230 **Dr. Thornton, acting** Thornton, "To the Public"; "J.M's Notes," *Writings of James Monroe*, 373–74.

230 **"Dr. T. came home"** Anna Thornton diary, Aug. 28, 178.

230 **Monroe swung** Monroe to Jefferson, Dec. 21; *Writings of James Monroe,* 304; "J.M's Notes," *Writings of James Monroe,* 375.

231 **Meanwhile, the District** Stansbury to Winder, Aug. 26, Winder Papers, MdHS; M'Kenney, *Memoirs, Official and Personal,* 46; Stansbury, *CCW,* 562; Peter Hansell, "Francis Scott Key," *Maryland Online Encyclopedia.*

231 **Anna Thornton, for one** Anna Thornton diary, Aug. 28, 178.

231 **Dolley Madison returned** Madison to Mrs. Latrobe, Dec. 3, in Allen C. Clark, ed., *Life and Letters of Dolley Madison,* 16; Lord, *Dawn's Early Light,* 204.

231 **"She could scarcely speak"** Smith, *First Forty Years,* 110; Anna Thornton diary, Aug. 28, 178.

232 **Dragoons camped outside** Ibid.,179; Madison memorandum about Armstrong, [Aug. 29], *Writings of James Madison,* 300 (hereafter Madison memo on Armstrong).

232 **That evening, back** Rush to Madison, Aug. 28, HSP, copy at UVa.

232 **To this point, Madison's wartime** Hickey, *Don't Give Up the Ship!,* 138; Gordon S. Wood, *Empire of Liberty: A History of the Early Republic, 1789–1815,* 698.

232 **"the vicious nature"** Brant, *James Madison,* 329; Garry Wills, *James Madison,* 139.

BRITISH LINES, SOUTHERN MARYLAND, MIDDAY, SUNDAY, AUGUST 28

232 **The American party** Hodges trial, 13–15.

233 **"By God, gentlemen"** Ibid., 14.

233 **"Gentlemen, do you"** Ibid., 14.

233 **"Where are the other two?"** Ibid., 13.

233 **Inside the house** Ibid., 14, 16; Shomette, *Flotilla,* 335.

ALEXANDRIA, 10 A.M., MONDAY, AUGUST 29

234 **Alexandria faced** Report of Alexandria Council, Sept. 7, CCW, 591–92.

234 **"One hardly knows"** James, *Naval History of Great Britain,* 182.

234 **"pretty hard terms"** Perrett, *The Real Hornblower,* 115.

234 **"the arrogant foe"** Jones to Rodgers, Aug. 29, NW III, 243.

234 **There was as much** *Baltimore Patriot,* Sept. 1.

234 **Dolley Madison derided** Anna Thornton diary, Aug. 29, 178; letter from the citizens of Alexandria, CCW, 593.

235 **The Alexandria warehouses** Jones to Rodgers, Aug. 29, NW III, 243.

WASHINGTON, 1 P.M., MONDAY, AUGUST 29

235 **At the bustling American** Madison memo on Armstrong, 301; Smith letter, Jan. 14, 1847, Stull letter, Jan. 16, 1847, and Daniel Mallory letter, Jan. 25, 1847, in appendix to McKenney, *Reply to Kosciusko Armstrong's Assault,* 24–26.

235 **"All confidence"** Monroe to Jefferson, Dec. 21, *Writings of James Monroe,* 304; Herrick, *August 24, 1814,* 160.

235 **One rumor** Smith, *First Forty Years,* 115; Barker, *Incidents,* 117.

235 **"that the city would make"** McKenney letter, Jan. 15, 1847, in appendix to McKenney, *Reply to Kosciusko Armstrong's Assault,* 28.

235 **Upon Armstrong's appearance** M'Kenney, *Memoirs, Official and Personal,* 46–47; Williams, *History of the Invasion,* 105; Madison memo on Armstrong, 301; Barker, *Incidents,* 115; Smith, appendix to McKenney, *Reply to Kosciusko Armstrong's Assault,* 24.

236 **Early in the evening, Madison** Madison memo on Armstrong, 301–302; Armstrong letter to *Baltimore Patriot,* Sept. 3, in Williams, *History of the Invasion,* 96–98.

236 **Even now, Madison** Stagg, *Mr. Madison's War,* 421.

236 **But as Armstrong defended** Madison memo on Armstrong, 303; Barker, *Incidents,* 114.

BENEDICT, MORNING, TUESDAY, AUGUST 30

237 **The shore of the Patuxent** Gleig diary, Aug. 30, 155; [Barrett], "Naval Recollections of the Late American War," part 1, 461; Codrington, Aug. 28, in Bourchier, ed., *Codrington,* 316.

237 **"Ross and Cockburn"** Rowley, "Captain Robert Rowley," 249.

237 **Ross reported that** Malcolm to Nancy Malcolm, Sept. 1, Pulteny Malcolm Papers, UM, transcript at NHHC.

237 **"It was never expected"** Ross to Maria Ross, Sept. 2, D 2004/1A/3/1/6, PRONI.

237 **Madison "must be rather"** Codrington, Aug. 28, in Bourchier, ed., *Codrington,* 316.

238 **"We are all well"** Malcolm to Nancy Malcolm, Sept. 1, NHHC.

238 **Vice Admiral Cochrane** Cochrane to Bathurst, Aug. 28, WO 1/141, NAUK; "British Embassy Gives Library Letter on Washington Capture," *Washington Evening Star,* Nov. 14, 1934.

238 **Ross had no compunctions** Ross to Bathurst, Aug. 30, NW III, 225.

238 **Cockburn, however** CMS 137–38; Scott, *Recollections,* 326–27; Cochrane to Bathurst, Aug. 28, WO 1/141, NAUK; Cochrane to Melville, NW III, 269.

BALTIMORE, TUESDAY, AUGUST 30

238 **As the British rested** Woehrmann, "National Response to the Sack of Washington," 240.

238 **"Every American heart"** Sheads, *Rockets' Red Glare,* 60.

239 **Across the region** Whitehorne, *Battle for Baltimore,* 142; Marine, *British Invasion,* 147; Lord, *Dawn's Early Light,* 233.

239 **"[I]t is a perfect military"** Taylor to Abby, Aug. 30, NHHC.

239 **Those not in arms** Swanson, *Perilous Fight,* 235; William D. Hoyt, Jr., "Ci-

vilian Defense in Baltimore, 1814–1815: Minutes of the Committee of Vigilance and Safety," *MdHM*, September 1944.

239 **"at least a mile"** Sheads, *Rockets' Red Glare*, 60.

240 **The general had arrived** Winder to Secretary of War, Aug. 28, Winder Papers, MdHS; Swanson, *Perilous Fight*, 205; Governor Winder to General Winder, Aug. 27, Winder Papers, MdHS.

240 **Captain John Rodgers** Rodgers General Orders, Aug. 28, NW III, 260; John H. Schroeder, *Commodore John Rodgers: Paragon of the Early American Navy*, 138–40.

241 **The twenty-eight-year-old Perry** Charles Brodine, "Commodore Oliver Hazard Perry and the Battle of Lake Erie," lecture at National War of 1812 Symposium, Baltimore, Oct. 2, 2010.

241 **Perry's performance** Swanson, *Perilous Fight*, 208; Sheads, *Rockets' Red Glare*, 40.

241 **"tranquil as an unruffled"** Lewis P. Balch, "Reminisces of the War of 1812," *Historical Magazine*, September 1863, 284.

242 **The thirty-four-year-old Porter** Linda M. Maloney, "Porter, David" American National Biography Online, http://www.anb.org/articles/03/03–00394. html; Brodine et al., *Against All Odds*, 1, 24. Porter ranged as far west as the Marquesas Islands, some four thousand miles off the coast of South America, laying claim to Nuku Hiva, which he renamed Madison's Island. The president declined to recognize the annexation.

242 **Despite the fame** Charles Oscar Paullin, "Services of Commodore John Rodgers in the War of 1812," *Proceedings*, 1909, 474; Hickey, *Don't Give Up the Ship!*, 104; Schroeder, *Commodore John Rodgers*, 130.

242 **Rodgers had been awaiting** Ibid., 128.

242 **"If you were to see"** Paullin, "Services of Commodore John Rodgers," 502.

242 **"To charge"** Ibid., 505–506.

242 **The key redoubt** George, *Terror*, 128; Sheads, *Fort McHenry*, 34; John Rodgers to Minerva Rodgers, [Aug. 29], John Rodgers Papers, UM, transcript at NHHC.

EASTERN SHORE OF MARYLAND, 11 P.M., TUESDAY, AUGUST 30

243 **"one more frolic"** Marine, *British Invasion*, 126; Chamier, *Life*, 184.

243 **Dashing and reckless** Ibid., 178; [Sir George Dallas], *A Biographical Memoir of the Late Sir Peter Parker, Baronet*, 57; Parker to Cochrane, Aug. 30, NW III, 233.

244 **"My head will follow"** Chamier, *Life*, 183.

244 **"If any thing befalls"** Dallas, *Sir Peter Parker*, 69.

244 **Parker recovered** Marine, *British Invasion*, 118–20.

244 **"It was the height"** Chamier, *Life*, 185.

244 **The British believed** Marine, *British Invasion*, 117–19, 125; George, *Terror*, 118, 122; Beynon journal, Aug. 28, NHHC.

244 **"[H]is Turkish sabre"** Chamier, *Life*, 188.

245 **"We guess that your captain** Ibid., 193.

245 **Byron would write** Dallas, *Sir Peter Parker*, 70.

CHAPTER 12: *The Mission of Francis Scott Key*

TONNANT, CHESAPEAKE BAY, THURSDAY, SEPTEMBER 1

247 **The British fleet** Rowley, "Captain Robert Rowley," 250; Chesterton, *Peace, War and Adventure*, 135.

247 **But aboard** *Tonnant* Ross to Elizabeth Ross, Sept. 1, D 2004/1A/3/6, PRONI.

247 **That wish was doubtless** Evans memorandum, 18, NLS; Cochrane to Bathurst, Sept. 2, WO 1/141, NAUK; Codrington, Aug. 31, Letters from Codrington, May 21, 1814–March 26, 1815, COD/7/1, NMM.

248 **On Wednesday, before the fleet** Lev Winder to Ross, Aug. 31, in Marine, *British Invasion*, 189–90.

248 **Ross not only refused** Taney narrative, 17, 22.

248 **"I thought you and Doctor Beanes"** Hill, "Visit of the British in 1812,"; Captain George Graham to Monroe, Aug. 31, Series 3B, vol. 8, Rodgers Family Papers, LOC, copy in NHHC.

ALEXANDRIA, MORNING, THURSDAY, SEPTEMBER 1

249 **After four days** Napier, *Admiral Sir Charles Napier*, 80; CCW, 533; James, *Naval History of Great Britain*, 184.

249 **"They dismissed him"** Muller, *Darkest Day*, 162.

249 **"It is impossible"** Charles Simms to Nancy Simms, Sept. 3, NW III, 246.

249 **U.S. Navy Captain David Porter** Jones to Porter, Aug. 31, NW III, 245; Porter to Jones, Sept. 7, NW III 251.

249 **Reaching Alexandria** Admiral David Porter, *Memoir of Commodore David Porter of the United States Navy*, 256; James, *Naval History of Great Britain*, 182.

250 **The powerful Creighton** Porter, *Memoir of Commodore David Porter*, 257.

250 **"The youngster, quite"** Napier, *Admiral Sir Charles Napier*, 83.

250 **A distressed Mayor** Simms to Nancy Simms, Sept. 3, NW III, 246; Napier, *Admiral Sir Charles Napier*, 83–84; Codrington to Adm. Durham, Sept. 4, Tonnant Letter Book, Codrington papers, 6/3, NMM.

WASHINGTON, THURSDAY, SEPTEMBER 1

250 **Even while seething** Jones to Rodgers, Aug. 28, NW III, 242.

250 **"Poor, contemptible pitiful"** Lord, *Dawn's Early Light*, 215.

251 **"Is it possible"** Tucker, *Poltroons*, 595.

251 **"The President and the whole"** Taylor to Abby, Aug. 30, NHHC.

251 **"How much has Mr. Madison"** Lev Saltonstall to Nathaniel Saltonstall, Sept. 9, Leverett Saltonstall, *The Saltonstall Papers, 1602–1815,* vol. 2.

251 *Fly, Monroe, fly!* Lossing, *Pictorial Field-book,* 935.

251 **"The effect will not"** Jones to Madison, Sept. 1, William Jones Papers, Reel 2, HSP, copy at NHHC.

251 **The previous day, Monroe** John Mason, *CCW,* 595; Stagg, *Mr. Madison's War,* 424.

252 **On September 1,** Madison Sept. 1, Madison proclamation, in Hunt, ed., *Writings of James Madison,* 304.

GEORGETOWN, EVENING, THURSDAY, SEPTEMBER 1

252 **Roger Brooke Taney** Taney narrative, 14–16. Taney wrote in his narrative that the Key children were still in Georgetown, but Key's letter to his mother makes it clear they had already been sent to Terra Rubra. Mullaly, "A Forgotten Letter of Francis Scott Key."

253 **Key and West, each** Weybright, *Spangled Banner,* 66; Rebecca Lloyd Shippen, "The Star-Spangled Banner," *Pennsylvania Magazine of History and Biography,* 1901, 321.

253 **Reports of Beanes's seizure** Anna Thornton diary, Aug. 30, 179.

253 **That evening, Key** Taney narrative, 19; Mason to Skinner and Key, Sept. 2, NARA RG 45.

ALEXANDRIA, 5 A.M., FRIDAY, SEPTEMBER 2

253 **It was still dark** Simms to Nancy Simms, Sept. 3, NW III, 246; letter from the citizens of Alexandria, *CCW,* 593; Lord, *Dawn's Early Light,* 207; Napier, *Admiral Sir Charles Napier,* 82.

254 **Once again, the weather** Ibid., 84.

254 **The American battery** Porter to Jones, Sept. 7, NW III, 251; A. G. Monroe to Jones, Sept. 5, RG 45, Letters Received by the Secretary of Navy, vol. 6, copy at NHHC.

254 **A large flag** Napier, *Admiral Sir Charles Napier,* 85.

254 **Porter's fellow commodores** Monroe to Rodgers, Sept. 2, NW III, 245.

254 **At daylight Friday** Porter to Jones, Sept. 7, NW III, 253; A. G. Monroe to Jones, Sept. 5, NHHC; Perrett, *The Real Hornblower,* 117.

WASHINGTON, FRIDAY, SEPTEMBER 2

255 **For the Madison administration** Mason to Skinner and Key, Sept. 2, NARA RG 45.

255 **The forty-eight-year-old Mason** Frederick P Todd, "The Militia and Volunteers of the District of Columbia," *RCHS,* 1948, 387–88, 398.

255 **Mason wrote a letter** Mason to Skinner, Sept. 2, NARA RG 45.

256 **"a citizen of the highest respectability"** Mason to Ross, Sept. 2, NARA RG 45.

256 **Mason took time to scribble** Mason to Charles Worthington, Aug. 28, copy

in Spratt Collection, Box 1, Part 2, MdHS; Mason to Colonel Thornton, Sept. 2, Ibid.

256 **Several prisoners** Arnold, "The Battle of Bladensburg," 161; Ingersoll, *Historical Sketch*, vol. 2, 214; John T. Silkett, *Francis Scott Key and the History of the Star-Spangled Banner*, 24; Taney narrative, 20.

256 **"the most marked kindness,"** Codrington, Aug. 28, in Bourchier, ed., *Codrington*, 328.

256 **At his home on Bridge Street** Taney narrative, 19.

256 **"Polly goes up"** Key to John Ross Key, copy in FSK vertical file, HSF, original at Rare Book and Manuscript Library of Columbia University.

256 **To his mother** Mullaly, "A Forgotten Letter of Francis Scott Key."

257 **Early the next morning** Lord, *Dawn's Early Light*, 242; Weybright, *Spangled Banner*, 2; Smith, *First Forty Years*, 118; Eleanor Jones to William Jones, Sept. 1, William Jones Papers, HSP, copy at NHHC; Sam Meyer, "Religion, Patriotism and Poetry in the Life of Francis Scott Key," *MdHM*, 1989, 274.

POTOMAC RIVER, MORNING, SATURDAY, SEPTEMBER 3

257 **By Saturday morning** Rodgers to Jones, Sept. 3, NW III, 247; Rodgers to Jones, NW III, Sept. 9, NW III, 257; Herrick, *August 24, 1814*, 172.

258 **Below Alexandria** Napier, *Admiral Sir Charles Napier*, 84; Gordon to Cochrane, Sept. 9, NW III 240.

258 **Rodgers found Alexandria** Rodgers to Jones, Sept. 9, NW III, 258; Rodgers to Jones, Sept. 3, NW III, 247.

CHESAPEAKE BAY, SATURDAY, SEPTEMBER 3

259 **Cochrane intended to return** Cochrane to Melville, Sept. 3, NW III, 269.

259 **Ross, for his part** Smith, *Autobiography*, 204–206.

259 *Iphigenia's* **departure** Cochrane to Croker, Sept. 3, London *Gazette, Extraordinary*, Sept. 27.

260 **Ross accompanied** Smith Maguire, "Major General Ross and the Burning of Washington," 120; Smith, *Autobiography*, 207.

BALTIMORE, MORNING, SUNDAY, SEPTEMBER 4

260 **Francis Scott Key arrived** Skinner to Mason, Sept. 2, 5, NARA RG 45.

260 **"Under existing circumstances"** Skinner to Monroe, Sept. 2, Misc. Letters of the Department of State, NARA RG 59, M179, Roll 30.

260 **Skinner leased a sloop-rigged** Ralph J. Robinson, "The Men with Key: New Facts in the National Anthem Story," *Baltimore,* September 1956, 35; Ralph J. Robinson, "Mystery of Key's Vessel Nears Solution," *Baltimore,* January 1955, 35; Skinner account, Dec. 8, 1813, Spratt Collection, Box 1, Part 2, MdHS; Manakee, "Anthem Born in Battle," in Filby and Howard, comps., *Star-Spangled Books*, 31. Contrary to many accounts repeating an old error, the ship was not *Minden*.

261 **Women rolled bandages** Frank A. Cassell, "A Response to Crisis: Baltimore in 1814," *MdHM*, 1971.

261 **Yet Samuel Smith** Mullaly "The Battle of Baltimore," 74; Swanson, *Perilous Fight*, 278–80; Marine, *British Invasion*, 145.

261 **The War Department did** Monroe to Madison, Sept. 3, Monroe, *Writings of James Monroe*, vol. 5, 291.

261 **"I have no order"** Winder to Monroe, Sept. 4, Winder Papers, MS 919, MdHS.

261 **John Armstrong was also** Stagg, *Mr. Madison's War*, 421–22; Armstrong letter to *Baltimore Patriot*, Sept. 3, in Williams, *History of the Invasion*, 102.

261 **"He is gone"** Brant, *James Madison*, 315; Skeen, *John Armstrong*, 201–203.

262 **Monroe was now** Lord, *Dawn's Early Light*, 203; CRG, 265; Ammon, *James Monroe*, 337, 342.

262 **"[T]hat it will soon"** Monroe to Joseph Bloomfield, Sept. 4, RG 107; Letters Sent by the Secretary of War, vol. 7, pp. 294–95, copy at NHHC; Stagg, *Mr. Madison's War*, 428.

CHESAPEAKE BAY, SUNDAY, SEPTEMBER 4

262 **Aboard** *Tonnant* Brooke diary, Sept. 4, 305.

262 **"The commander in chief** Tonnant Memo Book, Codrington papers, 6/3, NMM.

263 **"Further operations"** Scott, *Recollections*, 330–31; Rowley, "Captain Robert Rowley," 250.

PATAPSCO RIVER, MONDAY, SEPTEMBER 5

263 **"We are now on our"** Skinner to Mason, Sept. 5, NARA RG 45.

263 **After the letter was posted** Robinson, "The Men with Key," 37.

263 **Skinner was "a man"** Weybright, *Spangled Banner*, 114.

264 **The twenty-six-year-old Skinner** Benjamin Perley Poore, "Biographical Notice of John S. Skinner," *The Plough, the Loom and the Anvil*, vol. 7, 2–3; Dietz, *"The Use of Cartel Vessels*, 193.

265 **"tact and persuasive manners"** Skinner, "Incidents," 341.

WHITE HOUSE LANDING, NOON, MONDAY, SEPTEMBER 5

265 **After three days** Gordon to Cochrane, Sept. 9, NW III, 241; Napier, *Admiral Sir Charles Napier*, 85; Anna Thornton diary, Sept. 5, 180.

265 **The battle on the Potomac** Porter to Jones, Sept. 9, NW III, 256; Thomas Brown, "An Account of the Lineage of the Brown Family," Ambler-Brown Family Papers, Manuscript Department, William R. Perkins Library, Duke University, copy at NHHC, 12; CRG, 265.

265 **The British attempted a landing** Henry Newcomb to Rodgers, Sept. 5, Series 3B, vol. 8, Rodgers Family Papers, LOC, copy in NHHC; Herrick, *August 24, 1814*, 167.

265 On the bluffs above Brown, "An Account of the Lineage of the Brown Family," 16–17.

266 "I determined not" Porter to Jones, Sept. 9, NW III, 254.

266 But the British still had to contend John S. Gallaher, Sept. 5, 1856, in Williams, *History of the Invasion*, 370; Napier, *Admiral Sir Charles Napier*, 85–86.

266 "notwithstanding the dreadful" *CRG*, 266.

267 Across the river Napier, *Admiral Sir Charles Napier*, 85; Gordon to Cochrane, Sept. 9, NW III, 241.

267 But appearances aside Monroe to Barbour, Sept. 6, in H. W. Flournoy, ed., *Calendar of Virginia State Papers and Other Manuscripts*, vol. 10, 385; Perry to Jones, Sept. 9, NW III, 256.

267 Over the course of five Porter to Jones, Sept. 9, NW III, 256.

267 "behaved remarkably" Napier, *Admiral Sir Charles Napier*, 85.

CHAPTER 13: *The Town Must Be Burned*

CHESAPEAKE BAY, MORNING, WEDNESDAY, SEPTEMBER 7

269 George Cockburn had resigned CMS, 138; Scott, *Recollections*, 331.

269 Cochrane had learned Cochrane to Croker, Sept. 17, NW III, 286; Scott Sheads, "Equinoctial Storms over the Chesapeake, Summer 1814," Maryland in the War of 1812 blog, http://maryland1812.wordpress.com/2011/03/29/equinoctial-storms-over-the-chesapeake-summer-1814/trackback/.

270 *Menelaus* arrived Tuesday Journal of Pulteney Malcolm, Sept. 7, ADM 51/87, NAUK, copy in NHHC; Parker to Cochrane, Aug. 30, NW III, 233.

270 That same day, the fleet Evans memorandum, Sept. 7, NLS, 19.

270 Cochrane relented Cochrane to Croker, Sept. 17, NW III, 286.

270 "extremely urged" Cochrane to Melville, Sept. 17, NW III, 289.

270 Rear Admiral Codrington Codrington, Sept. 13, in Bourchier, ed., *Codrington*, 320.

270 Aboard *Albion*, CMS, 138–39.

MOUTH OF THE POTOMAC, AFTERNOON, WEDNESDAY, SEPTEMBER 7

271 As the American sloop Malcolm to Mason, Sept. 6, 138, and Malcolm to Cochrane, Sept. 6, 139, Malcolm Letter Book, Sir Pulteney Malcolm Papers, MAL/106, NMM.

271 But around noon Taney narrative, 20; Lord, *Dawn's Early Light*, 242, 245.

271 At 2:10 p.m. Log of *Tonnant*, Sept. 7, War of 1812 Collection, MdHS.

271 The Americans arrived James, *Naval History of Great Britain*, 188.

271 "was the prime mover" Skinner to Mason, Oct. 7, Spratt Collection, Box 1, Part 1, MdHS.

271 When Key mentioned Taney narrative, 20.

271　**The Americans were soon summoned** Skinner, "Incidents," 342–43.

272　**a "vagabond"** Cockburn to Cochrane, July 17, NW III, 136.

272　**"most painful"** Cochrane to Mason, Sept. 7, Mason to Cochrane, Sept. 27, and Cochrane to Mason, March 1815, David Porter and David Dixon Porter Papers, UM, transcripts at NHHC.

272　**One man remained quiet** Skinner, "Incidents," 343.

272　**"the Americans behaved"** Gleig diary, Sept. 10, 168.

272　**Speaking with Key** Taney narrative, 21–22; Delaplaine, *Francis Scott Key*, 158.

273　**"purely in proof"** Ross to Mason, Sept. 7, NARA RG 45.

273　**"was not put to the test"** Skinner, "Incidents," 343.

273　**Early the next morning** Ibid., 346; Taney narrative, 21; Skinner to Mason, Oct. 7, Spratt Collection, Box 1, Part 1, MdHS.

273　**The ten-man American crew** 1929 review "re Messrs Key and Skinner," War of 1812 Collection, MdHS.

273　**Captain Gordon's squadron** Codrington to Jane Codrington, Sept. 10, NW III, 271; Log of *Tonnant*, Sept. 8 and 9, War of 1812 Collection, MdHS.

274　**"All our ships"** Log of *Albion*, Sept. 9, copy in Tangier History Museum.

274　**"In short it is nothing"** Codrington to Jane Codrington, Sept. 10, NW III, 271.

274　**"a most venturesome"** Theodore Roosevelt, *The Naval War of 1812*, 292.

274　**At least two days** NW III, 238; O'Neill, "The Potomac Squadron."

274　**At 11 a.m. Friday** Log of *Albion*, Sept. 9, Tangier; Journal of Pulteney Malcolm, Sept. 7, ADM 51/87, NAUK, copy in NHHC; Lossing, *Pictorial Fieldbook*, 941.

274　**The Potomac battle over** Paullin, "Services of Commodore John Rodgers," 505; Whitehorne, *Battle for Baltimore*, 167; Schroeder, *Commodore John Rodgers*, 138.

275　**"Forts, redoubts"** Rodgers to Murray, Sept. 9, NW III, 263.

BALTIMORE, MORNING, SATURDAY, SEPTEMBER 10

275　**At Fort McHenry** George Armistead to Louisa Armistead, Sept. 10, War of 1812 Collection, MdHS.

275　**Armistead, the coolheaded** Scott Sumpter Sheads, *Guardian of the Star-Spangled Banner: Lt. Colonel George Armistead and the Fort McHenry Flag*, vii, 4, 6–8, 49.

276　**With Armistead's blessing** Scott Sheads, " 'Yankee Doodle Played': A Letter from Baltimore, 1814," *MdHM*, Winter 1981, 380–82.

276　**The handsome and dashing Nicholson** Scott S. Sheads, "Joseph Hopper Nicholson: Citizen-Soldier of Maryland," *MdHM*, Summer 2003, 141,145; Filby, and Howard, *Star-Spangled Books*, 18.

277　**Elected to the House** Sheads, "Joseph Hopper Nicholson," 137–38.

277　**"We should have to fight"** Ibid., 144.

277 **"Good God!"** Nicholson to Jones, Aug. 28, William Jones Papers, HSP, copy at NHHC; Sheads, "Joseph Hopper Nicholson," 146.

CHESAPEAKE BAY, AFTERNOON, SATURDAY, SEPTEMBER 10

278 **Along the coast** Gleig, *Narrative of the Campaigns,* 165; [Barrett], "Naval Recollections of the Late American War," part 1, 461.

278 **Watching from the cupola** Nathaniel Hickman, *The Citizen Soldiers at North Point and Fort McHenry, September 12 & 13, 1814,* 72; Newcomb to Rodgers, Sept. 18, NW III, 292; Cassell, "A Response to Crisis," 279–80.

278 **Around dusk, lookouts** Sheads, "Yankee Doodle," 380.

278 **At Fort McHenry Saturday** Armistead to Monroe, Sept. 24, NW III 302.

278 **In town, Captain Nicholson** Sheads, "Yankee Doodle," 380–81.

BALTIMORE, MORNING, SUNDAY, SEPTEMBER 11

278 **An odd calm** Lord, *Dawn's Early Light,* 251; Marine, *British Invasion,* 147; Sheads, *Rockets' Red Glare,* 81.

279 **The speed** Swanson, *Perilous Fight,* 288, 292.

279 **Church bells** Whitehorne, *Battle for Baltimore,* 175.

279 **"My brethren"** Marine, *British Invasion,* 147.

279 **Samuel Smith's plan** Mullaly, "The Battle of Baltimore," 70; Cassell, "A Response to Crisis," 279–81.

279 **Smith had chosen his best** Ibid., 281; Smith to Monroe, Sept. 9, NW III, 294; Williams, "The Rock of North Point," 13; Lord, *Dawn's Early Light,* 253.

280 **Brigadier General John Stricker** "Battle of North Point, 1814," Defenders Day booklet, 1990, Maryland Museum of Military History, Archives and Research Center; John Stricker, Jr., "General John Stricker," *MdHM,* September 1914; Swanson, *Perilous Fight,* 297; George, *Terror,* 16; Frederick M. Colston, "The Battle of North Point," *MdHM,* 1907.

280 **By 3 p.m., Stricker** Whitehorne, *Battle for Baltimore,* 176; Colston, "The Battle of North Point," 113; Swanson, *Perilous Fight,* 300–302.

281 **Around 8 p.m., Stricker reached** Cassell, *Merchant Congressman,* 196, 205–206; Cassell, "A Response to Crisis," 281; Swanson, *Perilous Fight,* 317–18.

281 **Stricker pushed the Baltimore** Stricker to Smith, Sept. 15, Brannan, *Official Letters,* 420; George, *Terror,* 136.

281 **"We lay that night"** John McHenry to John McHenry, Sept. 20, War of 1812 Collection, MdHS (hereafter McHenry letter); Sheads, *Fort McHenry,* 6–7.

WASHINGTON, SUNDAY, SEPTEMBER 11

282 **On Saturday, Madison and Monroe** "Protection of the District," *NI,* Sept. 12; CCW, 587; Berg, *Grand Avenues,* 230.

282 **An attack on Baltimore** "The Enemy at Baltimore!," *NI,* Sept. 12.

PATAPSCO RIVER, EVENING, SUNDAY, SEPTEMBER 11

282 **Cockburn and Ross were not long** Gleig, *Subaltern*, 108–10; Morriss, *Cockburn and the British Navy*, 110; Cassell, "A Response to Crisis," 279; Swanson, *Perilous Fight*, 320.

283 **"With an uncommonly favorable"** Skinner, "Incidents," 344.

283 **All day, British ships** Swanson, *Perilous Fight*, 320; Malcolm journal, Sept. 11, ADM 51/87, NAUK, copy in NHHC; CSM, 139.

283 **At 7 p.m., Cockburn and Ross** Log of *Albion*, Sept. 11, Tangier; Battalion Order Book, 1814, 3rd Battalion Royal Marines, B1/208, RMM.

283 **Francis Scott Key watched** "At a Political Meeting," in [Key], *Poems of the Late Francis Scott Key* (hereafter Key Frederick speech), 197; Cochrane to Brooke, Sept. 12, NW III, 276.

283 **"Never was man"** Key to Randolph, Oct. 5, Howard Papers, MdHS.

284 **"Ah, Mr. Skinner"** Skinner, "Incidents," 347; Taney narrative, 24.

284 **Key, Skinner, and Beanes** 1929 review "re Messrs Key and Skinner," War of 1812 Collection, MdHS; Robinson, "The Men with Key."

284 **"To make my feelings"** Key to Randolph, Oct. 5, Howard Papers, MdHS.

CHAPTER 14: THE BATTLE FOR BALTIMORE

287 **An unworldly calm** Gleig, *Narrative of the Campaigns*, 168–69; Lossing, *Pictorial Field-book,* 950.

287 **But around 3 a.m.** Gleig diary, 168; Mullaly "The Battle of Baltimore," 82.

287 **"Though no enemy"** Major Peter Bowlby memoir, 2002-02-729, National Army Museum, 18.

288 **Ross and Cockburn landed** CMS, 140; Swanson, *Perilous Fight*, 327.

288 **All told, some 4,700 British** Lord, *Dawn's Early Light*, 256–57; John McNish Weiss, "The Corps of Colonial Marines: Black freedom fighters of the War of 1812," http://www.mcnishandweiss.co.uk/history/colonialmarines.html.

288 **Even Royal Marine Major Mortimer Timpson** Timpson journal, 36, RMM.

288 **With the beach secure** Mullaly, "Battle of Baltimore," 83; Brooke diary, 310.

288 **As the army advanced** Cochrane to Croker, Sept. 17, NW III, 286.

289 **"As we proceeded"** [Barrett], "Naval Recollections of the Late American War," part 1, 462.

289 **Aboard** *Tonnant* Codrington, in Bourchier, ed., *Codrington*, 319–20.

METHODIST MEETING HOUSE, 7 A.M., MONDAY, SEPTEMBER 12

289 **Cavalry scouts** Stricker to Smith, Sept. 15, Brannan, *Official Letters,* 420; Mullaly, "Battle of Baltimore," 84; Whitehorne, *Battle for Baltimore*, 179.

289 **The Baltimore Rifle** Stricker to Smith, Sept. 15, Brannan, *Official Letters,* 420; Baltimore City Archives, RG 22, War of 1812 Records.

289 **At a cavalry outpost** Author visit, Todd House, Oct. 3, 2009; Scott S. Sheads,

"Defending Baltimore in the War of 1812: Two Sidelights," *MdHM*, Fall 1989, 256.

292 **Sailing Master George La Roche** Sheads, *Rockets' Red Glare*, 84–85; Lord, *Dawn's Early Light*, 272.

292 **At noon, John Hewes** John Hewes to Edward Hewes, Sept. 12, War of 1812 Collection, MdHS; Richard J. Cox, " 'The Truth Is, However, Bad Enough': A Rediscovered Letter Relating to the Origins of Our National Anthem," *Manuscripts*, Spring 1975.

GORSUCH FARM, 8 A.M., MONDAY, SEPTEMBER 12

292 **Moving swiftly from North** Gleig, *Narrative of the Campaigns*, 171; Gleig, *Subaltern*, 119–20; Whitehorne, *Battle for Baltimore*, 179; Scott, *Recollections*, 333.

293 **"But they are mainly militia"** Marine, *British Invasion*, 150; "Attack Upon Baltimore," *NWR*.

293 **At the landing beach** Brooke diary, Sept. 12, 310.

293 **"one of the hottest"** Robyns journal, Sept. 12, 150, RMM.

293 **"No,"** Ross is said William George Hawkins, *The Life of John H. W. Hawkins*, 9. Samuel Martin, a surgeon with the City Brigade, reported hearing Gorsuch tell the story a few days later. Hickey, *Don't Give Up the Ship!* 85.

AMERICAN CAMP, METHODIST MEETING HOUSE, 11 A.M., MONDAY, SEPTEMBER 12

294 **Stricker, learning that** Stricker to Smith, Sept. 15, Brannan, *Official Letters*, 420; Swanson, *Perilous Fight*, 365, 367–68.

294 **About 70 riflemen** Hickman, *The Citizen Soldiers at North Point and Fort McHenry, September 12 & 13, 1814*, 72.

294 **In contrast to the vivid** [Spencer H. Cone], *Some Account of the Life of Spencer H. Cone*, 124.

294 **"tall, slender of emaciated"** Henry Clay McComas, *The McComas Saga: A Family History Down to the Year 1950*, Maryland Museum of Military History.

294 **At 1 p.m., the task force** Ibid.

GODLEY WOOD, EARLY AFTERNOON, MONDAY, SEPTEMBER 12

295 **General Ross was no** Evans, *Facts*, 16; Mullaly "The Battle of Baltimore," 85.

295 **The Americans opened up** CMS, 141; Cockburn to Cochrane, Sept. 15; Gleig diary, 12 Sept., 168.

295 **Ross grew concerned** Gleig, *Subaltern*, 121; Barrett, *85th King's Light Infantry*, 179.

295 **Reaching the crest** CSM, 192; Lossing, *Pictorial Field-book*, 964; Scott, *Recollections*, 334; Marine, *British Invasion*, 192.

296 **Major Heath's skirmishers** Buzz Chriest, *Defenders Trail,* 7; Stricker to Smith, Sept. 15, Brannan, *Official Letters,* 421; McHenry letter, MdHS.

296 **Heath ordered Marine,** *British Invasion,* 193; Curtis Carroll Davis, *Defenders Dozen,* 19.

296 **Aisquith's riflemen** [Cone,] *Some Account of the Life of Spencer H. Cone,* 125; McComas, *The McComas Saga;* Lossing, *Pictorial Field-book ,* 951.

296 **The shot that hit Ross** Cockburn to Rev. Thomas Ross, Sept. 17, D/2004/1A/4, PRONI; George, *Terror,* 138.

296 **"My arm is broken"** Ross papers, misc. newspaper clippings, 1:19, 1:14, GWU; Crofton letter, Aug. 7, 1815, D/2004/1A/4/16, PRONI; Marine, *British Invasion,* 192.

296 **A soldier ran to Cockburn** Skinner, "Incidents," 344.

297 **As Cockburn later** CMS, 142.

297 **Evans, however** Evans, *Facts,* 12.

297 **From the start, accounts** Cochrane to Croker, Sept. 17, NW III, 286; Cochrane to Melville, Sept. 17, NW III, 289; Cockburn to Cochrane, Sept. 15, NW III, 279; Lord, *Dawn's Early Light,* 363.

297 **an army officer with Ross** Davis, *Defenders' Dozen,* 20.

297 **Ross recognized this right** London *Evening Star,* Oct. 18; Ross papers, misc. newspaper clippings, 1:15, GWU.

298 **The Light Brigade** Gleig, *Narrative of the Campaigns,* 173; Gleig diary, Sept. 12, 168.

298 **Private Aquila Randall** Sioussat, *Old Baltimore,* 188; Davis, *Defenders' Dozen,* 6–7.

298 **"The greater part of one"** McHenry letter, MdHS.

298 **The Americans "took to their heels"** CMS, 142; McComas, *The McComas Saga.*

298 **Ross lay underneath** Lossing, *Pictorial Field-book,* 951; Scott, *Recollections,* 336; Robyns journal, Sept. 12, 150, RMM.

298 **"All eyes were turned"** Gleig, *Narrative of the Campaigns,* 175.

298 **Cockburn stayed** CMS, 142.

298 **"He assured me"** Cockburn to Cochrane, Sept. 15, NW III, 280.

299 **"Give that to my dear"** Skinner, "Incidents," 344.

299 **"the friendship and confidence"** Cockburn to Rev. Ross, Sept. 17, D 2004/1A/4/7, PRONI.

299 **Two miles back,** Evans Brooke diary, 310.

299 **When he arrived** Beynon journal, Sept. 12, NHHC.

299 **Recognizing his wound** Ross papers, misc. newspaper clippings, 1:15, 1:19, GWU.

299 **"He positively refused"** Torrens to Vansittart, Nov. 11, Office of the Commander-in-Chief: Out-letters, WO 3/608, NAUK.

299 **The columns of troops** Scott, *Recollections,* 336.

299 **"Genl. Ross was beloved"** Beynon journal, Sept. 12, NHHC; Robert Lingel,

ed., "The Manuscript Autobiography of Gordon Gallie Macdonald," *New York Public Library Bulletin*, March 1930, 144.

299   The party transferred Ross Skinner, "Incidents," 344; *CRG*, 161, 168; Ross papers, misc. newspaper clippings, 1:14, 1:19, GWU; C. H. Echols, *Defenders' Day Remembered: The Battle of North Point and the Defense of Baltimore*, 10.

299   "Oh! My dear wife" London *Evening Star*, Oct. 18; Crofton letter, Aug. 7, 1815, D/2004/1A/4/16, PRONI.

GODLEY WOOD, 2 P.M., MONDAY, SEPTEMBER 12

300   Like Ross, he was Anglo-Irish George, "The Family Papers of Maj. Gen. Robert Ross, the Diary of. Col. Arthur Brooke, and the British Attacks on Washington and Baltimore of 1814," 300, 313.

300   "perhaps, better calculated" Gleig, *Narrative of the Campaigns,* 175; George, *Terror,* 138; "Brooke, Arthur," *Oxford Dictionary of National Biography,* vol. 7, 869; Colston, "The Battle of North Point," 116; Chriest, *Defenders Trail,* addendum.

300   The Light Brigade, pursuing Brooke to Bathurst, Sept. 17, NW III, 283.

300   "In this situation" Brooke diary, 310.

300   Brooke ordered his rockets Mullaly, "The Battle of Baltimore," 87.

300   "This advance seems" McHenry letter, MdHS; Gleig, *Narrative of the Campaigns,* 178.

300   Meanwhile the Light Brigade Ibid., 175–76; Barrett, *85th King's Light Infantry,* 180; Gleig diary, Sept. 12, 16.

301   Brooke quickly grasped Brooke diary, 310; Mullaly, "Battle of Baltimore," 86; Brooke to Bathurst, Sept. 17, NW III, 283; Carter, *Historical Record of the Forty-Fourth,* 48; Gleig, *Narrative of the Campaigns,* 177.

301   At 2:45 p.m., Brooke Ibid., 179; Lord, *Dawn's Early Light,* 266.

301   "Look out, my lads" Scott, *Recollections,* 337.

301   "cheering the army" Brown, *Diary of a Soldier,* 31.

301   Across the front, Stricker Stricker to Smith, Sept. 15, Brannan, *Official Letters,* 421; Colston, "The Battle of North Point," 114.

302   The King's Own Mullaly, "Battle of Baltimore," 86; Cowper, *The King's Own,* 11; Gleig, *Narrative of the Campaigns,* 177.

302   "As soon as everything" Barrett, *85th King's Light Infantry,* 178.

302   Lieutenant Evans London *Evening Star,* Oct. 18.

302   Across the front Robyns journal, Sept. 12, 151.

302   From the center George, *Terror,* 142.

302   "[I]t pounded the biscuit" Ibid., 140; Gleig, *Narrative of the Campaigns,* 179.

302   "The men took deliberate" "Attack Upon Baltimore," NWR.

303   "fired one round" McHenry letter, MdHS; Cowper, *The King's Own,* 11.

303   On the American right Gleig, *Narrative of the Campaigns,* 180; Buchan, *History of the Royal Scots Fusiliers,* 172; "Attack Upon Baltimore," NWR.

303 The American fire "was so" Brooke diary, 311.

303 "[W]e returned a hearty" Gleig diary, Sept. 12, 169; Robyns journal, Sept. 12, 151.

303 Brooke ordered the men Gleig, *Narrative of the Campaigns,* 180.

303 "[T]he enemy kept CSM, 143.

303 "into great confusion" Barrett, *85th King's Light Infantry,* 181.

304 As the British swarmed Stricker to Smith, Sept. 15, Brannan, *Official Letters,* 422; Mullaly, "Battle of Baltimore," 88.

304 Cavalry, infantry, and artillery Gleig diary, Sept. 12, 169.

304 "utterly broken" Brooke to Bathurst, Sept. 17, NW III, 283; Carter, *Historical Record of the Forty-Fourth,* 48.

304 The British gave no quarter Bowlby memoir, National Army Museum, 18.

304 The 5th Maryland brought McHenry letter, MdHS; Robert H. Goldsborough, "Report of the Battle of Baltimore," *MdHM,* September 1945, 231.

304 The City Brigade remained George, *Terror,* 145; Stricker to Smith, Sept. 15, Brannan, *Official Letters,* 422; "Attack Upon Baltimore," *NWR.*

PATAPSCO RIVER, AFTERNOON, MONDAY, SEPTEMBER 12

304 Admiral Cochrane anchored Lord, *Dawn's Early Light,* 270; Scott S. Sheads, "HM Bomb Ship Terror and the Bombardment of Fort McHenry," *MdHM,* Fall 2008; Codrington to Nourse, Sept. 12, Codrington papers, COD/6/4, NMM, copy at NHHC; Cochrane to Ross, Sept. 12, NW III, 273.

METHODIST MEETING HOUSE, EVENING, MONDAY, SEPTEMBER 12

304 Though the Americans Brooke to Bathurst, Sept. 17, NW III, 283; CSM, 143–44; Mullaly, "The Battle of Baltimore," 91; Swanson, *Perilous Fight,* 428; George, *Terror,* 145.

306 "The temple of God" Scott, *Recollections,* 342; CRG, 162–63; James H. McCulloh report, *NWR,* Sept. 24, 1814.

306 As Cockburn watered Scott, *Recollections,* 340; Gleig, *Narrative of the Campaigns,* 182.

PATAPSCO RIVER, EVENING, MONDAY, SEPTEMBER 12

306 General Ross's body William Stanhope Lovell, *Personal Narrative of Events, From 1799 to 1815,* 163; Beynon journal, Sept. 12; Marine, *British Invasion,* 126.

306 For Admiral Codrington Codrington, Sept. 13, in Bourchier, ed., *Codrington,* 320.

306 "The sad accounts" Cochrane to Brooke, Sept. 17, NW III, 276; Prevost to Cochrane, Aug. 3, Cockburn Papers, Reel 10, Manuscript Division, LOC.

COOK'S TAVERN, EVENING, MONDAY, SEPTEMBER 12

307 **General Stricker** Stricker to Smith, Sept. 15, Brannan, *Official Letters*, 422.

307 **Samuel Smith** Cassell, *Merchant Congressman*, 206.

308 **John Moore** John Moore to Elizabeth Moore, [Sept. 13], John Moore Papers, Manuscript Department, William R. Perkins Library, Duke University, 3742, copy at NHHC (hereafter John Moore Papers).

308 **At Fort McHenry** Sheads, *Rockets' Red Glare*, 90.

308 **"the sound of battle"** Key Frederick speech, 196.

308 **By midnight, the City Brigade** Swanson, *Perilous Fight*, 429.

308 **"Our guns were charged"** Piper, "Defence of Baltimore, 1814."

METHODIST MEETING HOUSE, 12:30 A.M., TUESDAY, SEPTEMBER 13

308 **Just after midnight, a torrential** Gleig, *Narrative of the Campaigns*, 185; Chesterton, *Peace, War, and Adventure*, 147.

309 **"[Y]our fire I should"** Brooke to Cochrane, Sept. 13, NW III 277.

CHAPTER 15: *The Rockets' Red Glare*

311 **At dawn, the bomb ships** Newcomb to Rodgers, Sept. 18, NW III, 292; Sheads, "Yankee Doodle," 381.

311 **The low and squat bomb** Swanson, *Perilous Fight*, 460–64; author tour of Fort McHenry with Scott Sheads, Oct. 19, 2009.

311 **Cockburn was convinced** Cockburn to Cochrane, April 2, NW III, 45; Swanson, *Perilous Fight*, 464; Sheads, "HM Bomb Ship Terror," 257; "Attack Upon Baltimore," *NWR*.

312 **Fort McHenry guarded** Sheads, *Fort McHenry*, 5–8, 19, 23–24; Sidney Bradford, "Fort McHenry: The Outworks in 1814," *MdHM*, June 1959, 199; Sheads, *Rockets' Red Glare*, 13–14.

312 **But by 1812** William P. Craighill, "Baltimore and Its Defences, Past and Present," *MdHM*, 1906, 30.

312 **A three-gun battery** *CRG*, 67; Swanson, *Perilous Fight*, 480.

313 **Armistead insisted on one** Lord, *Dawn's Early Light*, 274. The existence of this oft-quoted letter cannot be verified; National Park Service historian Scott Sheads has not been able to find documentation for the letter in Lord's papers at Fort McHenry.

313 **The popular but unfounded** Lonn Taylor, Kathleen M. Kendrick, and Jeffrey L. Brodie, *The Star-Spangled Banner: The Making of an American Icon*, 63–64; Sheads, *Guardian of the Star-Spangled Banner*, 8–9. Barney and Stricker may have been involved; they were related by marriage to Pickersgill's uncle, and Pickersgill's daughter Caroline later said that "family connections" played a role in her mother's selection.

313 **Born in 1776** Author tour of Star-Spangled Banner Flag House, April 17, 2010.

314 **Grace Wisher** Ibid.; Molotsky, *The Flag, the Poet, and the Song*, 73.

314 **The garrison flag's size** Hickey, *Don't Give Up the Ship!*, 87; Taylor et al., *The Star-Spangled Banner*, 64.

314 **The flag was to have fifteen** Ibid., 65, 72–74; Molotsky, *The Flag, the Poet, and the Song*, 81–82.

315 **The women worked** Manakee, "Anthem Born in Battle," 33.

315 **"I remember seeing"** Taylor et al., *The Star-Spangled Banner*, 66.

315 **Pickersgill delivered** Ibid.; Sheads, *Guardian of the Star-Spangled Banner*, 9, 41.

315 **All along the shore** Rodgers to Jones, Sept. 23, NW III, 300; Shomette, *Flotilla*, 339; *CRG*, 67; Marine, *British Invasion*, 178–79; Gamble to Rodgers, Sept. 10, Series 3B, vol. 8, Rodgers Family Papers, LOC, copy in NHHC.

315 **A thousand troops** Rodgers to Jones, Sept. 23, NW III, 300; Sheads, *Rockets' Red Glare*, 80–82; author tour, Fort McHenry.

316 **Among them was Frederick Hall** *CRG*, 76; George, "Mirage of Freedom," 442–43. Hall was from Benjamin Oden's tobacco plantation in Prince George's County, where General Winder and Monroe had watched the advance of the British army toward Washington.

316 **A final boost** Rodgers to Jones, Sept. 23, NW III; David Curtis Skaggs, *Oliver Hazard Perry: Honor, Courage and Patriotism in the Early U.S. Navy*, 161–62; Sheads, *Rockets' Red Glare*, 82.

PATAPSCO RIVER, 6:30 A.M., TUESDAY, SEPTEMBER 13

317 *Volcano* **began** Cochrane to Croker, Sept. 17, NW III, 287; Sheads, *Fort McHenry*, 37; Swanson, *Perilous Fight*, 462.

317 **When the first shots** Newcomb to Rodgers, Sept. 18, NW III, 292; Armistead to Monroe, Sept. 24, NW III, 302; Sheads, *Rockets' Red Glare*, 92.

317 **A broadside** Whitehorne, *Battle for Baltimore*, 187.

317 **"The firing at the fort"** Moore, Sept. 13, John Moore Papers.

317 **"an incessant"** Armistead to Monroe, Sept. 24, NW III, 302.

317 **"[F]rom such a rattling"** Severn Teakle to Philip Wallis, Sept. 23, War of 1812 Collection, MdHS (hereafter Teakle letter).

317 **"Then the whole fort"** Sheads, "Yankee Doodle," 381.

317 **Cochrane ordered** Lord, *Dawn's Early Light*, 278.

317 **The American guns** Mullaly, "Battle of Baltimore," 93–95. Finally one ten-inch mortar was sent, but it lacked a base or fuses. Among the ordnance captured by the British at the Washington arsenal were three unused 13-inch mortars.

318 **To gain further distance** Sheads, "Yankee Doodle"; Swanson, *Perilous Fight*, 440.

318 **"[T]his was to me** Armistead to Monroe, Sept. 24, NW III, 302; "Attack Upon Baltimore," *NWR.*

318 **Once the futility** M. I. Cohen, "Reminiscences of the Bombardment of Fort McHenry," War of 1812 Collection, MdHS; Mullaly, "Battle of Baltimore," 94.

318 **Hundreds of shells** Sheads, *Rockets' Red Glare,* 93; "Attack Upon Baltimore," *NWR.*

318 *Erebus* **fired** Sheads, "Yankee Doodle," 381.

318 **One shell crashed** Author tour, Fort McHenry; Cohen, "Reminiscences of the Bombardment of Fort McHenry"; Teakle letter, MdHS.

319 **Private Williams** George, "Mirage of Freedom," 443; "Description of Battle," War of 1812 Collection, MdHS.

319 **"We were like pigeons"** Sheads, "Joseph Hopper Nicholson," 148.

319 **The lack of fire** Taney narrative, 24.

319 **The exact location** Scott Sheads, MdHS/National Park Service "Battle for Baltimore" tour, Oct. 3, 2009; Vince Vaise, "The Battle of Baltimore," Baltimore City Star-Spangled 200 Conference, Nov. 10, 2010.

319 **"[P]revious to the attack"** Teakle letter, MdHS; Lieutenant Henry Fisher, "An Eyewitness Sketch of the Bombardment of Fort McHenry," Baltimore City Life Museum Collection, MdHS; Eshelman and Kummerow, *Full Glory Reflected,* 141.

320 **Key's mood swung** Key to Randolph, Oct. 5, Howard Papers, MdHS.

320 **The thousands of troops** Piper, "Defence of Baltimore, 1814," 383–84; Schroeder, *Commodore John Rodgers,* 138–41.

321 **Rodgers Bastion** George, *Terror,* 128; Lossing, *Pictorial Field-book,* 949; Sheads, *Rockets' Red Glare,* 72; CRG, 72.

321 **"I believe we handled"** Levi Hollingsworth to Ann Hollingsworth, [Sept. 13], War of 1812 Collection, MdHS.

KELL HOUSE, MORNING, TUESDAY, SEPTEMBER 13

321 **The British army moved** Gleig, *Narrative of the Campaigns,* 185–87; Evans memorandum, NLS, 23; Brooke to Bathurst, Sept. 17, NW III, 283.

321 **An hour later, Brooke and Cockburn** Colston, "The Battle of North Point," 119; Cockburn to Cochrane, Sept. 15, NW III, 281; Mullaly, "Battle of Baltimore," 66; Gleig *Narrative of the Campaigns,* 187–88.

322 **Cockburn could not** CMS, 144.

322 **"[I]n short saw"** Brooke diary, 311.

322 **But the commanders** Ibid.; Barrett, *85th King's Light Infantry,* 180; Scott, *Recollections,* 344.

322 **"were in a very"** Brooke to Bathurst, Sept. 17, NW III, 283.

322 **But Samuel Smith** Smith to Monroe, Sept. 19, NW III, 296–97; Swanson, *Perilous Fight,* 448–52; Brown, *Diary of a Soldier,* 29.

323 **Brooke had no choice** Brooke to Bathurst, Sept. 17, NW III, 284; Brooke diary, 311; Lord, *Dawn's Early Light*, 284–85; Gleig, *Subaltern*, 140; Evans memorandum, NLS, 25; Scott, *Recollections*, 344.

323 **Settling down for the wait** Gleig, *Subaltern*, 152–54; Lossing, *Pictorial Fieldbook*, 958, 964; note from Captains Brown, Wilcocks and McNamara, Sept. 13, War of 1812 Collection, MdHS.

FORT MCHENRY, 2 P.M., TUESDAY, SEPTEMBER 13

323 **By early afternoon, a nor'easter** Newcomb to Rodgers, Sept. 18, NW III, 292; Fort McHenry tour.

323 **The crew** Sheads, "Joseph Hopper Nicholson."

324 **In the pouring rain** Sheads, "Yankee Doodle," 383.

324 **The bustle of activity** Armistead to Monroe, Sept. 24, NW III, 303.

324 **Cochrane sent pennants** Sheads, *Rockets' Red Glare*, 95; James, *Naval History of Great Britain*, 190; Teakle letter, MdHS.

324 **For thirty minutes, a furious** Log of *Surprize*, Sept. 13, War of 1812 Collection, MdHS; "Attack Upon Baltimore," *NWR*; Whitehorne, *Battle for Baltimore*, 188.

324 **Cochrane signaled** James, *Naval History of Great Britain*, 191; Swanson, *Perilous Fight*, 455.

324 **"We gave three cheers"** Armistead to Monroe, Sept. 24, NW III, 303; Newcomb to Rodgers, Sept. 18, NW III, 292.

325 **The bombardment** NW III, 291; Ed Seufert, "The British Perspective During the War of 1812," North Point Star-Spangled 200 Conference, June 22, 2010.

325 **Mercurial as always** Pack, *Man Who Burned the White House*, 206.

325 **The commanders of several** James, *Naval History of Great Britain*, 192; Swanson, *Perilous Fight*, 466.

325 **Cochrane had closely inspected** Cochrane to Croker, Sept. 17, NW III, 287; George, *Terror*, 133.

325 **He had learned that another 7,000** Whitehorne, *Battle for Baltimore*, 195.

325 **"ulterior operations"** Cochrane to Croker, Sept. 17, NW III, 287.

326 **At 9:30 a.m.** Cochrane to Cockburn, Sept. 13, NW III, 277.

326 **But communication** Swanson, *Perilous Fight*, 470.

326 **Likewise, it was not** Brooke to Cochrane, Sept. 13, NW III 277; Scott, *Recollections*, 344.

326 **"[T]here was not sufficient"** Skinner, "Incidents," 345.

326 **But as an alternative** James, *Naval History of Great Britain*, 191; Swanson, *Perilous Fight*, 470.

BRITISH ARMY HEADQUARTERS, EVENING, TUESDAY, SEPTEMBER 13

327 **Early in the evening** Scott, *Recollections,* 344; CMS, 145; Swanson, *Perilous Fight,* 467; Evans memorandum, NLS, 25.

327 **The 85th Light Infantry** Gleig, *Subaltern,* 156.

327 **"with a loss"** Skinner, "Incidents," 345.

327 **Cockburn pointed** Scott, *Recollections,* 345; CMS, 145.

327 **"My dear Admiral"** Cochrane to Cockburn, Sept. 13, NW III, 277.

327 **"This was a blow"** Brooke diary, 311.

PATAPSCO RIVER, 10 P.M., TUESDAY, SEPTEMBER 13

328 **"Black Charlie"** Napier Lord, *Dawn's Early Light,* 287; Chesterton, *Peace, War, and Adventure,* 144; James, *Naval History of Great Britain,* 191.

328 **Cochrane ordered Napier** Cochrane to Napier, NW III, 278. Parts of Cochrane's instructions are crossed out but still legible.

328 **Their assignment was daunting** Swanson, *Perilous Fight,* 479; Armistead to Monroe, Sept. 24, NW III, 303.

329 **The barges took off** James, *Naval History of Great Britain,*191; Lord, *Dawn's Early Light,* 287; Swanson, *Perilous Fight,* 481.

BRITISH ARMY HEADQUARTERS, MIDNIGHT, WEDNESDAY, SEPTEMBER 14

329 **At the Kell House** Evans memorandum, NLS, 25.

329 **Brooke's confidence** Brooke diary, 311; Skinner, "Incidents," 346.

329 **Cockburn's initial impulse** John Moore to Elizabeth Moore, Sept. 15, John Moore Papers.

329 **The admiral reminded** Sheads, *Rockets' Red Glare,* 97; George, *Terror,* 150.

330 **"[T]he onus"** CMS, 146; Gleig, *Subaltern,* 156.

330 **"[T]hough I had made"** Brooke to Cochrane, Sept. 14, NW III, 279.

FERRY BRANCH, EARLY MORNING, WEDNESDAY, SEPTEMBER 14

330 **Miserable in the cold** John Webster account, July 1853, in Marine, *British Invasion,* 179.

330 **Around that time, troops** Piper, "Defence of Baltimore, 1814," 383; Sheads, *Rockets' Red Glare,* 99.

330 **The young, powerfully** Muller, *Darkest Day,* 201.

331 **Webster was half asleep** Webster account, Marine, *British Invasion,* 179–80; Piper, "Defence of Baltimore, 1814," 384; Newcomb to Rodgers, Sept. 18, NW III, 292.

331 **Napier's raiders** "Attack Upon Baltimore," *NWR*; Swanson, *Perilous Fight,* 482; Newcomb to Rodgers, Sept. 14, Rodgers Family Papers, container 26, LOC, copy in NHHC.

331 **"The hissing rockets"** [Barrett], "Naval Recollections of the Late American War," part 1, 463.

331 "the whole awful spectacle" Sheads, *Rockets' Red Glare*, 101; Eleanor Callahan, "Ear-Witness to History: James McConkey and the Star Spangled Banner," *Journal of Erie Studies*, 1980.

331 The ground was shaking Fells Point tour with Jack Trautwein.

331 "Such a terrible" Hawkins, *The Life of John H. W. Hawkins*, 13.

332 The night "will never" John Moore to Elizabeth Moore, Sept. 14, John Moore Papers.

PATAPSCO RIVER, EARLY MORNING, WEDNESDAY, SEPTEMBER 14

332 From the deck Taney narrative, 24; Skinner, "Incidents," 346–47; Thomas Forman to Martha Brown Forman, Sept. 14, War of 1812 Collection, MdHS. Beanes, also aboard the ship, apparently spent much of his time belowdecks. Key, Taney, and Skinner do not mention the doctor watching the bombardment.

332 Earlier, in the twilight Key, "The Star-Spangled Banner."

332 In keeping with military Taylor et al., *The Star-Spangled Banner*, 70.

332 Once night fell Key Frederick speech, 197; Taney narrative, 24.

BRITISH ARMY HEADQUARTERS, EARLY MORNING, WEDNESDAY, SEPTEMBER 14

332 The British troops Mullaly, "Battle of Baltimore," 99.

332 "It was the most wonderful Brown, *Diary of a Soldier*, 29.

333 Brooke, like everyone Swanson, *Perilous Fight*, 484.

333 At 3 a.m., the men Gleig, *Narrative of the Campaigns*, 193; Brown, *Diary of a Soldier*, 29; "Old Sub," part 2, 32; Lingel, ed., "The Manuscript Autobiography of Gordon Gallie Macdonald," 145.

FERRY BRANCH, EARLY MORNING, WEDNESDAY, SEPTEMBER 14

333 Black Charlie was still Armistead to Monroe, Sept. 24, NW III, 302; Swanson, *Perilous Fight*, 484; Lord, *Dawn's Early Light*, 291.

333 The Fort McHenry crews James, *Naval History of Great Britain*, 191; Smith to Monroe, Sept. 19, NW III, 297; Teakle letter, MdHS.

334 "All was for sometime" "Attack Upon Baltimore," *NWR*.

CHAPTER 16: Does That Star-Spangled Banner Yet Wave?

337 The quiet was terrible Taney narrative, 25.

337 In the predawn [Barrett], "Naval Recollections of the Late American War," part 1, 463; Sheads, *Fort McHenry*, 41.

337 Key and Skinner paced Taney narrative, 25; Key, "The Star-Spangled Banner."

337 As the morning lightened Log of *Tonnant*, Sept. 14, War of 1812 Collection, MdHS.

338 "Through the clouds" Key Frederick speech, 197.

338 "I hope I shall never" Key to Randolph, Oct. 5, Howard Papers, MdHS.

FORT MCHENRY, MORNING, WEDNESDAY, SEPTEMBER 14

338 **Soon after sunrise** Armistead to Monroe, Sept. 24, NW III, 303; Beynon journal, Sept. 14.

338 **Aboard** *Surprize* Lord, *Dawn's Early Light*, 292.

338 **The bomb ships** Sheads, "HM Bomb Ship Terror," 257.

338 **From Baltimore** John Moore to Elizabeth Moore, Sept. 14, John Moore Papers.

338 **Rev. Baxley** Hawkins, *The Life of John H. W. Hawkins*, 14.

338 **The bombardment had lasted** Armistead to Monroe, Sept. 24, NW III, 303; Sheads, "HM Bomb Ship Terror," 257.

338 **The British had also fired** Rodgers to Jones, Sept. 14, NW III, 293.

338 **Yet the casualties** Marine, *British Invasion*, 172–73; George, "Mirage of Freedom," 443.

339 **At 9 a.m., the Fort** Sheads, *Rockets' Red Glare*, 104; Fort McHenry tour.

339 **"At this time"** Sheads, "Yankee Doodle," 382.

339 **"In truth it was"** [Barrett], "Naval Recollections of the Late American War," part 1, 464.

HAMPSTEAD HILL, MORNING, WEDNESDAY, SEPTEMBER 14

339 **Only as morning** Smith to Monroe, Sept. 19, NW III, 297; Goldsborough, "Report of the Battle of Baltimore"; Swanson, *Perilous Fight*, 486–88.

340 **Captain Rodgers was confident** Rodgers to Jones, Sept. 14, NW III, 293.

340 **"The enemy"** Smith order, Sept. 14, Winder Papers, MdHS.

MEETING HOUSE, MORNING, WEDNESDAY, SEPTEMBER 14

340 **Colonel Brooke** Brooke diary, 311.

340 **Cockburn candidly** McCulloh, n.d., Winder Papers, MdHS.

AMERICAN TRUCE SHIP, PATAPSCO RIVER, MORNING, WEDNESDAY, SEPTEMBER 14

340 **Key and Skinner watched** Taney narrative, 25, 28; Lord, *Dawn's Early Light*, 293.

341 **"[I]n that hour"** Key Frederick speech, 198.

GODLEY WOOD, LATE MORNING, WEDNESDAY, SEPTEMBER 14

341 **After waiting in vain** Brooke diary, 311.

341 **Passing through** Gleig, *Narrative of the Campaigns*, 194.

341 **"bleached as white"** Gleig diary, Sept. 14.

341 **"Putting all together"** Brown, *Diary of a Soldier*, 29–30.

341 **The frustrated British** Scott, *Recollections*, 346; Gleig diary, 171; Chesterton, *Peace, War, and Adventure*, 154.

342 **Two straggling seamen** Bluett diary, RMM, 36.

GODLEY WOOD, AFTERNOON, WEDNESDAY, SEPTEMBER 14

342 **As the British withdrew** John Smith Hanna, ed., *A History of the Life and Services of Captain Samuel Dewees,* 345.

342 **Sometime after midday** McComas, *The McComas Saga.*

342 **In 1851, their bodies** *CRG,* 71.

343 **"two imperishable heroes"** Dora Jean Ashe, *A Maryland Anthology, 1608–1986,* 71.

WASHINGTON, AFTERNOON, WEDNESDAY, SEPTEMBER 14

343 **News from Baltimore** "From Baltimore," *NI,* Sept. 14; "Huzza For Baltimore!" *NI,* Sept. 14.

NORTH POINT, THURSDAY, SEPTEMBER 15

343 **There were no cheers** Log of *Surprize,* Sept. 14, War of 1812 Collection, MdHS.

343 **"Sad, sad"** Peter Rowley, ed., "Captain Rowley Visits Maryland; Part II of a Series," *MdHM,* Fall 1988, 249.

344 **Cots were slung** [Barrett], "Naval Recollections of the Late American War," part 1, 465–66.

344 **Still anchored** Pulteney Malcolm to Clementina, Oct. 3, Pulteny Malcolm Papers, UM, transcript at NHHC.

344 **"The failure of our attempt"** Barrett, *85th King's Light Infantry,* 180–81.

344 **Aboard *Severn,* Cockburn** Cockburn to Cochrane, Sept. 15, NW III, 281; Pack, *Man Who Burned the White House,* 206.

344 **As the fleet prepared** Log of *Tonnant,* Sept. 16, War of 1812 Collection, MdHS; Tonnant Memo Book, Sept. 16, Codrington papers, 6/3, NMM; Rowley, ed., "Captain Rowley Visits Maryland; Part II," 249.

PATAPSCO RIVER, FRIDAY, SEPTEMBER 16

345 **The American truce ship** Taney narrative, 25.

345 **Skinner sought** Skinner to Mason, Oct. 7, Spratt Collection, Box 1, Part 1, MdHS; "Late from Baltimore," *Philadelphia Political and Commercial Register,* Sept. 19, in Filby and Howard, *Star-Spangled Books,* 44.

345 **Dispensing with** Skinner, "Incidents," 346–47. Skinner said he used the occasion to condemn the burning of the Capitol and the President's House. By Skinner's unconfirmed recollection, Cockburn did not defend the action. "He said not one word about any *'flag of truce'* nor did he attempt to justify the act," Skinner wrote in 1821.

345 **Later, the myth** Oscar George Theodore Sonneck, *The Star Spangled Banner,* 79–81.

345 **Written in London** William Lichtenwanger, "The Music of 'The Star-Spangled Banner': From Ludgate Hill to Capitol Hill," *Library of Congress*

Quarterly Journal, July 1977; Joseph Muller, *The Star Spangled Banner: Words and Music Issued Between 1814–1864,* 13–15; Weybright, *Spangled Banner,* 36, 145, 148.

346 **There is no doubt Key** Otto Ortmann, "Notes on 'The Star Spangled Banner,'" *Peabody Bulletin,* May 1939.

346 **Key viewed it** Delaplaine, *Francis Scott Key,* 40; Taney to Howard, April 9, 1856, Howard Papers, MdHS.

347 **The song was printed** Filby and Howard, *Star-Spangled Books,* 115; Ortmann, "Notes on the Star Spangled Banner"; Weybright, *Spangled Banner,* 148.

FELLS POINT, 9 P.M., FRIDAY, SEPTEMBER 16

347 **Darkness was approaching** Filby and Howard, *Star-Spangled Books,* 46.

347 **"A flag of truce"** Ibid., 51.

348 **Reporters gathered** Ibid., 44, 47; Herrick, *August 24, 1811,* 194.

348 **Once the excitement died** Skinner, "Incidents," 347; Robinson, "The Men with Key," 58; Taney narrative, 26; Manakee, "Anthem Born in Battle," 37.

348 **"O say can you see through"** Original manuscript of "The Star-Spangled Banner," MdHS.

348 **The verse, when completed** Manakee, "Anthem Born in Battle," 37.

348 **"the poet is not"** H. L. Mencken and George Jean Nathan, "The National Hymn," 1924, Mencken Society, http://www.mencken.org/text/txt003/Mencken.H_L.1924.The_National_Hymn.html.

349 **In the third verse** Manakee, "Anthem Born in Battle," 37; Francis Scott Key-Smith, "The Story of the Star-Spangled Banner," *Current History,* May 1930.

349 **Key took a more pious** Meyer, "Religion, Patriotism and Poetry in the Life of Francis Scott Key," 267; Sonneck, *The Star Spangled Banner,* 89.

350 **Key had no way** Manakee, "Anthem Born in Battle," 37; Proclamation by the President of the United States of America, "50th Anniversary of Our National Motto, 'In God We Trust,'" 2006, http://georgewbush-whitehouse.archives.gov/news/releases/2006/07/20060727–12.html.

BALTIMORE, MORNING, SATURDAY, SEPTEMBER 17

350 **When Skinner** Skinner, "Incidents," 347.

350 **Major Armistead was** Sheads, *Guardian of the Star-Spangled Banner,* 2, 17; Smith to Rodgers, Sept. 17, John Rodgers Papers, UM, copy at NHHC.

350 **After arriving at the Nicholson** Taney narrative, 26–27.

350 **The emotional Nicholson** Family letter to Rebecca Nicholson, Sept. 24, Shippen Family Papers, MSS 39859, container 21, reel 12, Manuscript Division, LOC; Sheads, "Joseph Hopper Nicholson," 147.

351 **"I . . . was obliged"** Key to Randolph, Oct. 5, Howard Papers, MdHS.

351 **Either Nicholson or Skinner** Taney narrative, 26; Taylor et al., *The Star-Spangled Banner,* 42; Filby and Howard, *Star-Spangled Books,* 52, 55.

351 **When Key's composition** Sonneck, *The Star Spangled Banner*, 82. "I always had the impression that Mr. John S. Skinner brought it," Sands recalled in 1877. But Sands, with what Sonneck called "engaging naiveté," concluded he must have been mistaken after reading Taney's account, which asserted that Nicholson delivered the song.

351 **The song carried the title** Filby and Howard, *Star-Spangled Books*, 59; Shippen, "The Star-Spangled Banner," 325; "Defence of Fort McHenry" broadside, MdHS.

352 **"We have a song"** Teakle letter, MdHS.

352 **"all over town"** Taney narrative, 28.

352 **At least one printed** Weybright, *Spangled Banner*, 150–53.

352 **Once in Frederick** Taney narrative, 19–20, 24–27.

FORT MCHENRY, SUNDAY, SEPTEMBER 18

353 **At noon Sunday** Sheads, *Rockets' Red Glare*, 108; Borneman, *1812*, 213; John Pendleton Kennedy, *Memoirs of the Life of William Wirt, Attorney General of the United States*, 336.

353 **"Some say the enemy"** John Moore to Elizabeth Moore, Sept. 17, John Moore Papers.

353 **In taking command** Rodgers to Jones, Sept. 18, NHHC.

354 **"I have now the pleasure"** Sioussat, *Old Baltimore*, 194.

CHESAPEAKE BAY, SUNDAY, SEPTEMBER 18

354 **The British doubtless** Sheads, *Rockets' Red Glare*, 108; Cochrane to Croker, Sept. 17, NW III, 287; Cochrane to Melville, Sept. 17, NW III 289.

354 **Aboard *Albion*** Cockburn to Rev. Ross, Sept. 17, D 2004/1A/4/7, PRONI.

355 **Late in the afternoon** Gleig, *Narrative of the Campaigns*, 199; Shomette, *Flotilla*, 343; NW III, 329; Morriss, *Cockburn and the British Navy*, 114; Cockburn to Cochrane, Oct. 24, NW III, 333.

355 **A final piece** Cochrane to Melville, Sept. 17, NW III 290; [Barrett], "Naval Recollections of the Late American War," part 1, 466; Tonnant Memo Book, Sept. 16 and 18, Codrington papers, 6/3, NMM; Shomette, *Flotilla*, 344.

WASHINGTON, MONDAY, SEPTEMBER 19

355 **Congress reconvened** William B. Bushong, "Ruin and Regeneration," *White House History*, Fall 1998; J.Stith to Winder, Sept. 17, Winder Papers, MdHS; Pitch, *Burning of Washington*, 223.

356 **Many of the arriving** Ingersoll, *Historical Sketch*, vol. 2, 178; Goldsborough, "Report of the Battle of Baltimore," 231.

356 **The President's House** Seale, *The President's House*, 134.

356 **"The rooms which"** Kennedy, *Memoirs of the Life of William Wirt*, 334.

356 **The Capitol was "a most"** "History of the U.S. Capitol Building," AOC.

356 **"Shall this harbor"** Ingersoll, *Historical Sketch,* vol. 2, 185.

356 **Congress was meeting** Stagg, *Mr. Madison's War,* 428; Ketcham, *James Madison,* 587; Reginald Horsman, *The War of 1812;* Weller, "Four Mayors of the City of Washington"; Pettengill, "The Octagon and the War of 1812."

357 **Several cities had offered** Tucker, *Poltroons,* 592; Proctor, ed., *Washington Past and Present,* 91; Herrick, *August 24, 1814,* 201; Horsman, *The War of 1812,* 210; Ketcham, *James Madison,* 588; Jeremy Black, *The War of 1812 in the Age of Napoleon,* 188, 213; Brant, *James Madison,* 327; Stagg, *Mr. Madison's War,* 422.

357 **Another blow** Ibid.; Brant, *James Madison,* 329; Jones to Madison, Sept. 11, William Jones Papers, HSP, copy at NHHC.

358 **"Instead of a wreath"** Jones to Eleanor, Sept. 20, Ibid.; Seth Pease letter, Sept. 12, Individual Manuscripts Collections, GWU.

358 **"Every ignorant booby"** McLane to Winder, Sept. 6, Winder Papers, MdHS; Ockerbloom, "The Discovery of a U.S. Marine Officer's Account of Life, Honor, and the Battle of Bladensburg, Washington and Maryland, 1814," 260. Monroe to Winder, Sept. 21, in Hildt, "Letters Relating to the Capture of Washington," 63; CCW, 524; Brant, *James Madison,* 328.

358 **On Tuesday, September** Ketcham, *James Madison,* 587.

358 **The enemy, the president** Madison message to Congress, Sept. 15, in Brannan, *Official Letters,* 434–35.

BALTIMORE, EVENING, TUESDAY, SEPTEMBER 20

359 **The *Baltimore Patriot*** Muller, *Darkest Day,* 208; Filby and Howard, *Star-Spangled Books,* 66.

359 **John Skinner later** Skinner, "Incidents," 341.

359 **The *Baltimore American*** Filby and Howard, *Star-Spangled Books,* 65, 68, 119.

359 **The *Mercantile Advertiser*** Ibid., 119–20; George J. Svejda, *History of the Star Spangled Banner from 1814 to the Present,* 87–89.

360 **The hometown** *Frederick-Town* Filby and Howard, *Star-Spangled Books,* 50, 113.

360 **"He is a Federalist"** Pitch, *Burning of Washington,* 221.

CHAPTER 17: *Our Glorious Peace*

363 **The Royal Navy frigate** Smith, *Autobiography,* 214–15.

365 **"We stop the press"** "Capture of the City of Washington," London *Times,* Sept. 27.

365 **"The reign of Madison"** Lord, *Dawn's Early Light,* 301–302; CRG, 273.

365 **The *Times,* which dubbed** London *Times,* Sept. 28 and 29.

365 **"Admiral COCKBURN"** London *Times,* Oct. 10.

365 **The prince regent sent** Bathurst to Ross, Sept. 28 and two dispatches Sept. 29, Secretary of State for War and Secretary of State for War and the Colonies, Out-letters, America and West Indies, WO 6/2, 5156–5220, NAUK.

366 **Keeping his promise** Torrens to Ross, Sept. 30, Office of the Commander-in-Chief: Out-letters, WO 3/608, NAUK; Smith, *Autobiography,* 217.

366 **A family friend** Maguire, "Major General Ross and the Burning of Washington," 125; Ross papers, misc. newspaper clippings, 1:14, GWU.

366 **Unknown to anyone** Robyns journal, Sept. 29, 153.

367 **The latest American** Engelman, *The Peace of Christmas Eve,* 206–207.

GHENT, SATURDAY, OCTOBER 1

367 **John Quincy Adams** Adams, ed., *Memoirs of John Quincy Adams,* vol. 3, 45; Engelman, "The Peace of Christmas Eve."

368 **Returning from his walk** Engelman, *The Peace of Christmas Eve,* 197; Woehrmann, "National Response to the Sack of Washington," 247–48.

368 **Henry Clay, Jonathan Russell** Ingersoll, *Historical Sketch,* vol. 2, 215; Lord, *Dawn's Early Light,* 304.

368 **It was the insult** Woehrmann, "National Response to the Sack of Washington," 248.

369 **On October 8, the British** Engelman, *The Peace of Christmas Eve,* 200, 203, 206.

369 **"May it please God"** Ibid., 206.

TERRA RUBRA, MARYLAND, WEDNESDAY, OCTOBER 5

369 **After months of disruption** Key to Randolph, Oct. 5, Howard Papers, MdHS.

369 **"Thank God!"** Weybright, *Spangled Banner,* 171.

WASHINGTON, SATURDAY, OCTOBER 8

370 **No one used to turn** Seale, *The President's House,* 137.

370 **The** *Washington City Gazette* Allgor, *A Perfect Union,* 328.

370 **"The administration are severely"** Mason to Mary Mason, Oct. 6, DMDE.

371 **"He looks miserably"** Kennedy, *Memoirs of the Life of William Wirt,* 339.

371 **George M. Dallas** Madison to Jefferson, Oct. 10, Brant, *James Madison,* 334–35; Monroe to Willie Blount, Oct. 10, RG 107, Letters Sent by the Secretary of War, vol. 7, pp. 342–43, copy at NHHC.

371 **Wirt found Madison's** Kennedy, *Memoirs of the Life of William Wirt,* 339; Wood, *Empire of Liberty,* 693; Troy Bickham, *The Weight of Vengeance: The United States, the British Empire and the War of 1812,* 201.

371 **On October 6** Pitch, *Burning of Washington,* 221; Tucker, *Poltroons,* 593; Woehrmann, "National Response to the Sack of Washington," 246.

371 **Supporters were bolstered** CCW, 596; Green, *Washington: A History of the Capital,* 65; Pitch, *Burning of Washington,* 224–25.

372 **Dr. William Thornton took** Brumbaugh, ed., "A Letter of Dr. William Thornton to Colonel William Thornton," 68.

372 **Another ray of hope** Jefferson to Samuel H. Smith, Sept. 21, in Ford, ed., *The Writings of Thomas Jefferson,* vol. 9, 485; "Thomas Jefferson's Library," LOC, http://myloc.gov/Exhibitions/jeffersonslibrary/Pages/Overview.aspx; Herrick, *August 24, 1814,* 203.

373 **Madison sent** Madison to Jefferson, Oct. 10, in Hunt, ed., *Writings of James Madison,* 314.

CHESAPEAKE BAY, EARLY OCTOBER

373 **"No, I would sooner"** Skinner to Monroe, Oct. 4, Misc. Letters of the Department of State, NARA RG 59, M179; Roll 30.

373 **Malcolm had secret** Malcolm to Clementina, Oct. 3, Poulteny Malcolm Papers, UM, transcript at NHHC.

373 **The British were preparing** Barney to Jones, Oct. 10, RG 45, Miscellaneous Letters Received by the Secretary of the Navy, Roll 66, vol. 7, NARA, copy at NHHC.

373 **Barney found Malcolm's** Barney, *Biographical Memoir,* 271, 322; Mason to Brooke, Oct. 3, WO 1/141, NAUK; Barney to Mason, Oct. 10, RG 45; Barney to Jones, Oct. 26, NW III, 351.

374 **"If a bullet"** Calcott, ed., *Mistress of Riverdale,* 82.

374 **"at about nine miles"** Codrington, Dec. 3, in Bourchier, ed., *Codrington,* 328.

374 **"I rejoice"** Cockburn to Malcolm, Oct. 25, Cockburn Papers, reel 10, Manuscript Division, LOC.

374 **With the departure** Mullaly, "Battle of Baltimore," 103.

BERMUDA, FRIDAY, OCTOBER 14

374 **That same day** Scott, *Recollections,* 349.

374 **With the sad business** Cockburn to Cochrane, Oct. 24, NW III, 332–34; Pack, *Man Who Burned the White House,* 208; Morriss, *Cockburn and the British Navy,* 114; author tour with Dimunation, LOC; Franklin Delano Roosevelt to Archibald MacLeish, Jan. 24, 1940, LOC, Rare Book and Special Collections Division.

375 **Cockburn was philosophical** Cockburn to Brooke, Oct. 25, Cockburn Papers, reel 10, Manuscript Division, LOC.

LONDON, MONDAY, OCTOBER 17

375 **On October 17, Captain Duncan** Bathurst to Brooke, Nov. 3, WO 6/2, 5156–5220, NAUK; Ross papers, misc. newspaper clippings, 1:15, GWU.

375 **Concurrently, reports** Whitehorne, *Battle for Baltimore,* 201.

375 **Harry Smith,** Smith, *Autobiography,* 221.

376 **Further, the news** *The Annual Register; or a View of the History, Politics and Literature For the Year 1814,* 1815; "French Papers," London *Times,* Oct. 11.

376 **"unworthy of civilized"** Ingersoll, *Historical Sketch,* vol. 2, 215.

376 **In Parliament** Maguire, "Major General Ross and the Burning of Washington," 126; John Barrow to Cochrane, Nov. 2, NHHC.

376 **"Willingly, would we"** Williams, *History of the Invasion,* 255.

BALTIMORE, EVENING, WEDNESDAY, OCTOBER 19

376 **The war years** Callahan, "Ear-Witness to History," 42; Filby and Howard, *Star-Spangled Books,* 58–59, 61.

377 **The song's popularity** Elizabeth Lloyd to Mrs. Nicholson, Oct. 29, Rebecca Lloyd to Mrs. Nicholson, Sept. 28, and letter from Greenwich, Conn., Sept. 24 to Mrs. Nicholson, Shippen Family Papers, MSS 39859, container 21, reel 12, Manuscript Division, LOC.

GHENT, FRIDAY, OCTOBER 21

377 **Henry Goulburn** Lord, *The Dawn's Early Light,* 309; Engelman *The Peace of Christmas Eve,* 233.

377 **The British delegation** Ibid., 231–34; Woehrmann, "National Response to the Sack of Washington," 247.

378 **The Americans did** Engelman *The Peace of Christmas Eve,* 235; Wood, *Empire of Liberty,* 695.

378 **The news from America** Woehrmann, "National Response to the Sack of Washington," 248.

378 **"The Capture of"** Bayard to Andrew Bayard, Oct. 26, in Elizabeth Domman, ed., "Papers of James A. Bayard, 1796–1815," in *Annual Report of the American Historical Association for the Year 1913,* vol. 2.

ENGLAND, NOVEMBER 1814

378 **Lord Liverpool** Engelman *The Peace of Christmas Eve,* 236.

378 **An extended war** Langguth, *Union 1812,* 339.

378 **"the millstone"** Whitehorne, *Battle for Baltimore,* 201; Black, *The War of 1812 in the Age of Napoleon,* 207–209.

379 **After a cabinet discussion** Colston, "The Battle of North Point," 121–22.

379 **"The more we contemplate"** Lord, *Dawn's Early Light,* 313–14.

379 **"Does it not occur"** J. W. Fortescue, *A History of the British Army,* vol. 10, 136.

379 **"I confess that"** Lord, *Dawn's Early Light,* 313–14.

379 **Wellington's views** Black, *The War of 1812 in the Age of Napoleon,* 211.

379 **Following its instructions** Lord, *Dawn's Early Light,* 316; Engelman, "The Peace of Christmas Eve."

WASHINGTON, CHRISTMAS EVE, 1814

380 **A gloomy holiday** Key to Ann Key, Dec. 24, "Letters of Francis Scott Key," *MdHM*, December 1949, 286.

380 **"The prospect of peace"** Hannah Gallatin to Dolley Madison, DMDE, Dec. 26; Donald R. Hickey, *The War of 1812: A Forgotten Conflict,* 259; Wood, *Empire of Liberty,* 693.

380 **"The bond of Union"** Ketcham, *James Madison,* 595; Borneman, *1812,* 254.

380 **"certainly is the greatest"** Madison to William Cary Nicholas, Nov. 26; *Writings of James Madison,* 319.

380 **"These Yankees"** Key to Randolph, Nov. 3, Howard Papers, MdHS.

380 **"I have thought"** Key to Randolph, Nov. 17, ibid.

380 **There was "no danger"** Key to Ann Phoebe Key, Dec. 24, "Letters of Francis Scott Key."

GHENT, CHRISTMAS EVE, 1814

381 **At 4 p.m.** Engelman *The Peace of Christmas Eve,* 285; Lord, *Dawn's Early Light,* 316; Engelman, "The Peace of Christmas Eve," *American Heritage.*

381 **For two hours** Ibid.; Chester G. Dunham, "Christopher Hughes, Jr. at Ghent, 1814," *MdHM,* Fall 1971; Pitch, *Burning of Washington,* 225.

381 **The problem now** Hickey, *Don't Give Up the Ship!* 295.

381 **"Even if peace"** Lord, *Dawn's Early Light,* 317.

381 **"hostilities should not"** Bathurst to Pakenham, Oct. 24, WO 6/2, 5156–5220, NAUK.

381 **One of three American copies** Dunham, "Christopher Hughes, Jr. at Ghent, 1814"; Hickey, *Don't Give Up the Ship!* 295.

382 **John Quincy Adams thought** Engelman, "The Peace of Christmas Eve," *American Heritage.*

382 **"I cannot close"** Borneman, *1812,* 270.

WASHINGTON, JANUARY AND FEBRUARY 1815

382 **"The fate of N. Orleans"** Dolley Madison to Hannah Gallatin, Jan. 14, 1815, DMDE.

382 **But no word** Eberlein and Hubbard, *Historic Houses,* 311.

382 **Finally, on February 4** Ketcham, *James Madison,* 596; Jennings, *A Colored Man's Reminiscences,* 16; Sheads, *Rockets' Red Glare,* 110.

382 **The celebration paled** Clark, "Joseph Gales," 123–26; Dunham, "Christopher Hughes, Jr. at Ghent, 1814"; Jennings, *A Colored Man's Reminiscences,* 14.

383 **The next morning** Pitch, *Burning of Washington,* 226; Engelman, *The Peace of Christmas Eve,* 287; Hickey, *The War of 1812,* 298.

383 **On February 18, Madison** Madison message to Congress, Feb. 18, 1815, *Writings of James Madison,* 324.

GULF OF MEXICO, FEBRUARY, 1815

384 **Word of Ghent** Codrington, Feb. 13, 1815, and Jan. 8, 1815, in Bourchier, ed., *Codrington*, 336, 340.

384 **Navy Lieutenant George Pratt** Lossing, *Pictorial Field-book*, 933.

384 **The British army paid** Gleig, *Narrative of the Campaigns*, 328–30.

384 **Captain Harry Smith** Smith, *Autobiography*, 237.

385 **Colonel William Thornton nearly** Borneman, *1812*, 290–91.

385 **"It is certainly a fault"** Codrington, Jan. 9, in Bourchier, ed., *Codrington*, 335.

385 **Following the British army's defeat** Borneman, *1812*, 292.

385 **Cochrane "seems most"** Codrington, Feb. 14, 1815, in Bourchier, ed., *Codrington*, 340.

385 **"I would give"** Codrington, March 7, in ibid., 342.

CUMBERLAND ISLAND, GEORGIA, MARCH 1815

385 **Rather than sulk** Scott, *Recollections*, 356; Pack, *Man Who Burned the White House*, 207; Morriss, *Cockburn and the British Navy*, 114–17.

386 **"I think the *savage*"** Ibid., 117.

386 **Cockburn fortified** CMS, 152; Scott, *Recollections*, 361; James, *Naval History of Great Britain*, 236.

386 **"That Jonathan should"** Pack, *Man Who Burned the White House*, 211.

386 **The Americans sent** CMS, 153; Morriss, *Cockburn and the British Navy*, 119.

387 **The Americans also demanded** Bathurst, Oct. 19, 1817, WO 1/144, NAUK; Weiss, "The Corps of Colonial Marines"; Pack, *Man Who Burned the White House*, 212.

387 **Cockburn evacuated** Ibid., 213, NW III, 349; CMS, 153.

WASHINGTON, MARCH 1815

387 **"The burning"** Calcott, *Mistress of Riverdale*, 82.

387 **Before word** Allen, *History of the United States Capitol*, 100; Green, *Washington: A History of the Capital*, 65.

388 **"We are under great"** Brumbaugh, "A Letter of Dr. William Thornton to Colonel William Thornton," 67.

388 **James Hoban** Seale, *The President's House*, 139.

388 **"The mischief"** Allen, *History of the United States Capitol*, 102; Marolda, *The Washington Navy Yard*, 10.

388 **Gilbert Stuart's portrait** A. K. Hadel, "A Review of the Battle of Bladensburg," *MdHM*, September 1906, 209–10.

388 **Ten wagonloads of books** Herrick, *August 24, 1814*, 204.

388 **With the arrival** Dolley Madison to Hannah Gallatin, 5 March, 1815, DMDE.

EPILOGUE

391 **At noon on August 7** Pack, *Man Who Burned the White House*, 218.

391 **"Here I am"** [George Cockburn], "Extract from a Diary of Rear-Admiral Sir George Cockburn, with Particular Reference to Gen. Napoleon Buonaparte, on Passage from England to St. Helena, in 1815," 6 [hereafter Cockburn diary]; Morriss, *Cockburn and the British Navy*, 127.

392 **"You may depend"** Ibid., 127.

392 **Meeting with Cockburn** Cockburn diary, 4.

392 **"It is clear"** Ibid., 13.

392 **Napoleon walked the deck** Ibid., 11–12; Morris, *Cockburn and the British Navy*, 130.

392 **"[O]n the score of talent"** Williams, *History of the Invasion*, 125.

393 **"I find General Bonaparte"** Pack, *Man Who Burned the White House*, 219.

393 **After seventy-two days** Ibid., 223, 229.

393 **Cockburn set up** Morriss, *Cockburn and the British Navy*, 132.

393 **"He is not a man"** Williams, *History of the Invasion*, 125.

393 **As first lord** Morriss, *Cockburn and the British Navy*, 2; Chamier, *Life*, x; Sidney Hart and Rachael L. Penman, *1812: A Nation Emerges*, 159. When Midshipman Frederick Chamier wrote a memoir in 1833 renouncing the burning and plundering of homes during the expedition, Cockburn considered his accuser "so unimportant" that he did not even bother reading the allegations.

394 **Nearly two decades** Morriss, *Cockburn and the British Navy*, 6, 220.

394 **Cockburn served a second** Ibid., 5; Pack, *Man Who Burned the White House*, 273.

394 **Cockburn was "one"** *United Services Magazine, and Naval and Military Journal*, 1853, part 3, 157; *Nautical Standard*, Aug. 27, 1853.

394 **"No biography is needed"** Gettysburg *Star and Banner*, September 1853.

395 **Elizabeth Ross's terrible** "Capture of Washington by the British in 1814," *Genealogical Magazine*, 1897, 178; Maguire, "Major General Ross and the Burning of Washington," 128.

395 **In Rostrevor, the local** Ibid., 127; author visit to Rostrevor with John McCavitt, March 13, 2010.

395 **Sir Alexander Cochrane** Fortescue, *A History of the British Army*, vol. 10, 177; Richard Holmes, *Wellington: The Iron Duke*, 206.

396 **As predicted** Heidler, *Encyclopedia of the War of 1812*, 511; Brumbaugh, ed., "A Letter of Dr. William Thornton to Colonel William Thornton," 69.

396 **Two of Ross's officers** G. N. Wood, "Burning Washington: The Lighter Side of Warfare," *Army Quarterly Defense Journal*, 1974, 352; Smith, *Autobiography*, xv.

396 **Evans, though seriously** Spiers, *Radical General*, 12; "Old Sub," part 2, 35; Morriss, *Cockburn and the British Navy*, 2.

396 "only as a volunteer" Evans, *Facts*, 2.

396 Cockburn and Evans Author's visit, Kensal Green Cemetery, Feb. 28, 2010.

396 Lieutenant George Gleig J. R. B. Moulsdale, *The King's Shropshire Light Infantry*, 23; "Gleig, George Robert," *Oxford Dictionary of National Biography*, vol. 7, 460.

397 The estimated 3,000 Cassell, "Slaves of the Chesapeake," 153; George, "Mirage of Freedom," 444–46.

397 The Colonial Marines Ibid.; Weiss, "The Corps of Colonial Marines"; John McNish Weiss, *The Merikens: Free Black American Settlers in Trinidad*, excerpt at http://www.mcnishandweiss.co.uk/history/merikensp2.html; Tina Dunkley email to author, July 16, 2010.

398 "The world was astonished" Antoine-Henri Jomini, *The Art of War*, 349.

398 Cockburn, for his part CMS, 137.

398 "We should have been saved" Ingersoll, *Historical Sketch*, vol. 2, 199–200.

WASHINGTON, JANUARY 1, 1818

399 New Year's Day Bushong, "Ruin and Regeneration," 31–32.

399 Though the building Seale, *The President's House*, 149.

399 "It was gratifying" Ibid.

399 Monroe had been so eager Ibid., 148–50.

399 Monroe wanted to restore Seale, *The White House*, 63; Seale, *The President's House*, 145, 152; author visit, Ash Lawn–Highland.

399 "It has been said" Ammon, *James Monroe*, 344.

399 "Not withstanding a thousand" Hunt-Jones, *Dolley and the "Great Little Madison,"* 57.

400 The year 1814 Harry L. Coles, "1814: A Dark Hour Before the Dawn," *MdHM*, 1971, 220.

400 The invasions Stewart, ed., *American Military History*, 134.

400 Yet the circumstances Ketcham, *James Madison*, 598; Hickey, *Don't Give Up the Ship!*

400 allowed the American delegation Hickey, *Don't Give Up the Ship!*, 305.

400 The final triumph Wood, *Empire of Liberty*, 696.

400 Nonetheless, most Americans Coles, "1814: A Dark Hour Before the Dawn"; Lord, *Dawn's Early Light*, 343.

400 The Constitution had survived Wood, *Empire of Liberty*, 698; Ketcham, *James Madison*, 598–99.

400 "The ultimate good" Allen C. Clark, "James Heighe Blake, The Third Mayor of the Corporation of Washington [1813–17]," *RCHS*, 1922, 157.

400 Ghent did not Black, *The War of 1812 in the Age of Napoleon*, 217; Wills, *James Madison*, 151.

401 Henry Clay considered Hickey, *Don't Give Up the Ship!*, 305.

401 "Although the treaty" Wood, *Empire of Liberty*, 697–98.

401 **This Second War** Joseph Whitehorne, *While Washington Burned: The Battle for Fort Erie 1814*, preface; Taylor et al., *The Star-Spangled Banner*, 32.

401 **"I think it will"** Lord, *Dawn's Early Light*, 342; Whitehorne, *Battle for Baltimore*, 202.

401 **"The war has renewed"** Gallatin to Matthew Lyon, May 7, 1816, in Henry Adams, ed., *The Writings of Albert Gallatin*, vol. 1.

401 **Ghent called for an end** Hickey, *Don't Give Up the Ship!*, 304; Borneman, *1812*, 269.

401 **The war's many failures** Jenkins and Taylor, *The War of 1812 and the Rise of the U.S. Navy*, 242; National Park Service, "Star Spangled Banner National Historic Trail Feasibility Study and Environmental Impact Statement," 2004, 14–15.

402 **"[I]f our first struggle"** Ketcham, *James Madison*, 598.

402 **James Madison would never** "Dolley Madison" and "James Madison," James Madison's Montpelier.

402 **His manservant Paul Jennings** Jennings, *A Colored Man's Reminiscences*, 18–19.

402 **After his death, Dolley** Cutts, "Dolly Madison," 67.

402 **Her famous letter** David B. Mattern, "Dolley Madison Has the Last Word: The Famous Letter," *White House History*, Fall 1998.

403 **"I acted thus"** Barker, *Incidents*, 111.

403 **In her later years** "Dolley Madison," James Madison's Montpelier; Taylor, "Paul Jennings: Enamoured with Freedom."

403 **Jennings flourished** Ibid.; David Montgomery, "Heritage's House," *WP*, Aug. 25, 2009.

403 **Secretary of War John Armstrong** Armstrong, *Notices*, 148.

403 **A sympathetic military court** Ingraham, *Sketch of the Events*, 38–39, 63–64.

404 **Joshua Barney's last battle** Barney to Homans, Jan. 3, 1815, NW III, 354; Shomette, *Flotilla*, 348; Brodine et al., *Against All Odds*, 50–52.

404 **In 1979** Shomette, *Flotilla*, 355.

405 **Armistead, recovering** Sheads, *Guardian of the Star-Spangled Banner*, 23, 25, 34.

405 **"So you see"** George Armistead to Louisa Armistead, War of 1812 Collection, MdHS.

405 **Smith resigned** Cassell, *Merchant Congressman*, 211; John C Fredriksen, "Smith, Samuel," *American National Biography Online*, http://www.anb.org/articles/03/03–00455.html.

405 **John Rodgers** Schroeder, *Commodore John Rodgers*, 143; Linda M. Maloney, "Rodgers, John," *American National Biography Online*, http://www.anb.org/articles/03/03–00428.html.

406 **Oliver Hazard Perry** Robert G. Baker, "Perry, Oliver Hazard," *American National Biography Online*, http://www.anb.org/articles/03/03–00378.

406 **David Porter** Linda M. Maloney, "Porter David," *American National Biography Online*, http://www.anb.org/articles/03/03-00394.

406 **John Skinner** Charles W. Turner, "Some Newly Discovered John Stuart Skinner Correspondence," *MdHM*, Summer 1981; Parrish, ed., *The Plough, the Loom, and the Anvil*, vol. 7, 20; W. Farrell O'Gorman, "Skinner, John Stuart," American National Biography Online, http://www.anb.org/articles/16/16-01516.html.

406 **Joseph Nicholson** Sheads, "Joseph Hopper Nicholson," 148.

406 **Within days** Meyer, *Paradoxes of Fame*, 42; Magruder, Jr., "Dr. William Beanes," 222; Dorsey, "Origin of the Star-Spangled Banner."

406 **Three thousand citizens** Weybright, *Spangled Banner*, 261; Key Frederick speech, 195-203.

407 **Key was capable of arguing** Meyer, *Paradoxes of Fame*, 30-32; Rev. John Brooke, "Discourse on the Character of the late Francis Scott Key," Jan. 29, 1843, copy in Spratt Collection, Book Manuscript Box 2, MdHS; Hansell, "Francis Scott Key."

407 **"a thrilling and even"** Weybright, *Spangled Banner*, 194.

407 **Fearing that mass emancipation** Ibid., 181, 184-87, 202.

408 **There were happy** Delaplaine, *Francis Scott Key*, 219.

408 **Edward, the heartbroken** "Drowning of Edward Key," excerpt from Francis Scott Key diary, 8 July 8, 1822, F. S. Key vertical file, HSF.

408 **Key and Polly had two** Delaplaine, *Francis Scott Key*, 244, 427; "Francis Scott Key Park," http://www.nps.gov/olst/planyourvisit/keypark.htm; Douglas Zevely, "Old Houses on C Street and Those Who Lived There," *RCHS*, 1902, 154; Mike High, *The C&O Canal Companion*, 107.

408 **After years of eschewing** Weybright, *Spangled Banner*, 232.

408 **"It is beautiful!"** Smith, *The First Forty Years*, 293-94.

409 **Key became a confidant** Eugene L. Didier, "Francis Scott Key as a Lawyer," *Green Bag*, May 1904; Delaplaine, *Francis Scott Key*, 277.

409 **When Jackson's friend** Ibid., 328-31.

409 **Jackson sent the lawyer** Weybright, *Spangled Banner*, 246-51.

409 **Key had a hand** Ibid., 237, 267; Jefferson Morley, *Snow-Storm in August*, 208-209.

409 **"you will find yourself"** Delaplaine, *Francis Scott Key*, 294.

409 **More than two decades** Sandra F. VanBurkleo and Bonnie Speck, "Taney, Roger Brooke," *American National Biography Online*, http://www.anb.org/articles/11/11-00834.html.

409 **The post as federal** Weybright, *Spangled Banner*, 268; Didier, "Francis Scott Key as a Lawyer."

410 **Key "did not lose"** Delaplaine, *Francis Scott Key*, 399.

410 **The sorriest episode** Jefferson Morley, "The Snow Riot," *WP Magazine*, Feb. 6, 2005.

410 **Key had meanwhile** Ibid.; Weybright, *Spangled Banner*, 268.

410 **"deep malignity"** Morley, *Snow-Storm in August*, 222.

410 **Key's nineeen-year-old son** Ibid., 227–31.

411 **Less than a year later** Delaplaine, *Francis Scott Key*, 428–29; Weybright, *Spangled Banner*, 226.

411 **He retired after two** Ibid., 271–73.

411 **Key had emancipated** Ibid., 188; Delaplaine, *Francis Scott Key*, 430, 447–49.

411 **By then the lyrics** Taylor et al., *The Star-Spangled Banner*, 51.

411 **"Where else, except"** Weybright, *Spangled Banner*, 188.

411 **In early January 1843** Ibid., 286–87.

412 **"Lizzie, I have a feeling"** McHenry Howard to K. Mackenzie Brevitt, May 8, 1912, Key vertical file, HSF.

412 **Key asked someone** Delaplaine, *Francis Scott Key*, 476–77.

412 **just a few miles** Key-Smith, *Francis Scott Key*, 96.

412 **"Francis S. Key, the author"** Taylor et al., *The Star-Spangled Banner*, 39–40.

412 **Key was buried** Delaplaine, *Francis Scott Key*, 478; author visit to Mount Olivet, Frederick/Montgomery Star-Spangled 200 Conference, Dec. 14, 2011.

413 **On October 8, 1824** Taylor et al., *The Star-Spangled Banner*, 83.

413 **It was the last** Ibid., 81; Sheads, *Guardian of the Star-Spangled Banner*, 35; "History of the Star-Spangled Banner," National Museum of American History, November 2008.

413 **The family loaned** Taylor et al., *The Star-Spangled Banner*, 84.

413 **When Louisa Armistead died** Ibid., 86–87.

413 **In the terrible conflict** Sheads, *Guardian of the Star-Spangled Banner*, 29, 38.

414 **"As I stood"** Molotsky, *The Flag, the Poet, and the Song*, 147.

414 **"[W]ith me it has remained"** Taylor et al., *The Star-Spangled Banner*, 86, 89.

414 **The flag had remained** Ibid., 4.

414 **By the time Eben Appleton** Ibid., 98–101; Sheads, *Guardian of the Star-Spangled Banner*, 39.

416 **Gravely insulted** Taylor et al., *The Star-Spangled Banner* 103, 107–108.

416 **The disintegrating flag** Ibid., 5, 89, 109–10.

416 **The flag remained there** Ibid., 112–14.

416 **In 1964, the flag** Ibid., 127–28.

416 **But the flag suffered** Ibid., 135–36, 140, 146–48.

417 **The results were spectacular** Ibid., 148–54.

417 **The largest hole** Ibid., 71.

417 **The flag was far too fragile** Ibid., 155.

417 **The conservation, expected** Jacqueline Trescott, "Museum Is Going Dark to Add Light," *WP*, April 13, 2006; Jacqueline Trescott, "America's Attic Is Ready for Its Public," *WP*, Nov. 20, 2008; Taylor et al., *The Star-Spangled Banner*, 162–63.

417 **The banner hovers** Author tour with James Gardner, senior scholar, National Museum of American History, June 8, 2011.

418   **The transformation** Taylor et al., *The Star-Spangled Banner*, 2.

418   **The rise of** "The Star-Spangled" Ibid., 46–47; Lichtenwanger, "The Music of 'The Star-Spangled Banner.' "

418   **But with the war** Ibid.; Sonneck, *The Star Spangled Banner*, 83; Taylor et al., *The Star-Spangled Banner*, 52.

418   **Beginning in 1889** Ibid., 53.

419   **Key hated the war** Delaplaine, *Francis Scott Key*, 100; Sonneck, *The Star Spangled Banner*, 12; Meyer, *Paradoxes of Fame*, 56.

419   **"barroom ballad"** "Hats On," *Time*, Aug. 17, 1925; Norman Gelb, "Reluctant Patriot," *Smithsonian*, September 2004.

419   **Nonetheless, Representative** Edward T. Folliard, "Capital Echoes," *WP*, March 8, 1931; "Star-Spangled Banner Is Now Official Anthem," *WP*, March 5, 1931.

419   **Critics have never** Lichtenwanger, "The Music of 'The Star-Spangled Banner.' "

419   **The song "bristles"** Paul Hume, "Blood, Thunder and a Recycled National Anthem," *WP*, July 3, 1977.

419   **The song's lyrics are "empty"** Michael Kinsley, "Oh, Say Can You Sing It?," *WP*, June 12, 2009.

420   **Among those** "The Opinion of John Philip Sousa Concerning 'The Star-Spangled Banner' as the National Anthem of the United States, Written for the Home of Chief Justice Taney, Frederick, Maryland," n.d., F. S. Key vertical file, HSF.

420   **"Nations will seldom"** Hollister Noble, "Many National Anthems of Doubtful Standing," *New York Times*, March 9, 1930.

UNITED STATES CAPITOL, WASHINGTON, MONDAY, JULY 4, 1831

420   **The American flag waved** Richmond *Enquirer*, July 8, 1831; Delaplaine, *Francis Scott Key*, 300; "History of the U.S. Capitol Building," AOC.

420   **All shops** "From the National Intelligencer of Wednesday," Philadelphia *National Gazette*, July 9, 1831; Delaplaine, *Francis Scott Key*, 300.

421   **Key took the podium** *Richmond Enquirer*, July 8, 1831.

421   **Fifty-five years had passed** Delaplaine, *Francis Scott Key*, 301; Hockensmith, "James Monroe."

421   **"We are here, in the rich"** Delaplaine, *Francis Scott Key*, 301.

421   **Key spoke loudly** *Richmond Enquirer*, July 8, 1831; Delaplaine, *Francis Scott Key*, 299, 309.

421   **The Constitution** Ibid., 309.

421   **We who inherit freedom** Weybright, *Spangled Banner*, 239.

422   **"My countrymen"** Muller, *Darkest Day*, 212; Delaplaine, *Francis Scott Key*, 311–12.

SELECTED BIBLIOGRAPHY

★

BOOKS

Adams, Charles Francis, ed. *Memoirs of John Quincy Adams, Comprising Portions of His Diary from 1795 to 1848.* Vol. 3. Philadelphia: J. B. Lippincott, 1874.

Adams, Henry. *The War of 1812.* Edited by H. A. DeWeerd. Introd. John R. Elting. 1944; reprint, New York: Cooper Square Press, 1999.

——, ed. *The Writings of Albert Gallatin,* Vol. 1. Philadelphia: J. B. Lippincott, 1879.

Allen, William C. *History of the United States Capitol.* Washington, D.C.: U.S. Government Printing Office, 2001.

Allgor, Catherine. *A Perfect Union: Dolley Madison and the Creation of the American Nation.* New York: Henry Holt, 2006.

Ammon, Harry. *James Monroe: The Quest for National Identity.* 1971; reprint, Charlottesville: University Press of Virginia, 1990.

Armstrong, John. *Notices of the War of 1812.* Vol. 2. New York: Wiley & Putnam, 1840.

Armstrong, Kosciuszko. *Review of T. L. McKenny's Narrative of the Causes Which, in 1814, Led to General Armstrong's Resignation of the War Office.* New York: R. Craighead, 1846.

Ashe, Dora Jean, ed. *A Maryland Anthology, 1608–1986.* Lanham, Md.: University Press of America, 1987.

Ball, Charles. *Slavery in the United States: A Narrative of the Life and Adventures of Charles Ball, A Black Man.* 1836; reprint, Pittsburgh: Western, 1854.

[Barker, Jacob]. *Incidents in the Life of Jacob Barker of New Orleans, Louisiana.* Washington, D.C.: n.p., 1855.

Barney, Mary, ed. *Biographical Memoir of the Late Commodore Joshua Barney: From Autobiographical Notes and Journals in Possession of His Family, and Other Authentic Sources.* Boston: Gray & Bowen, 1832.

Barrett, C. R. B., ed. *The 85th King's Light Infantry.* London: Spottiswoode, 1913.

Berg, Scott. *Grand Avenues: The Story of the French Visionary Who Designed Washington, D.C.* New York: Pantheon, 2007.

Bergh, Albert Ellery. *The Writings of Thomas Jefferson,* Vols. 13–14. Washington, D.C.: Thomas Jefferson Memorial Association, 1907.

Bickham, Troy. *The Weight of Vengeance: The United States, the British Empire, and the War of 1812.* New York: Oxford University Press, 2012.

Black, Jeremy. *The War of 1812 in the Age of Napoleon.* Norman: University of Oklahoma Press, 2009.

Borneman, Walter R. *1812—The War That Forged a Nation.* New York: Harper Perennial, 2005.

Bourchier, Lady, ed. *Memoir of the Life of Admiral Sir Edward Codrington, with Selections from His Public and Private Correspondence.* Vol. 1. London: Longmans, Green, 1873.

Bowers, Claude G., ed. *The Diary of Elbridge Gerry, Jr.* New York: Brentano's, 1927.

Brant, Irving. *James Madison, Commander in Chief, 1812–1836.* New York: Bobbs-Merrill, 1961.

Brodine, Charles E., Jr., Michael J. Crawford, and Christine F. Hughes. *Against All Odds: U.S. Sailors in the War of 1812.* Washington, D.C.: U.S. Government Printing Office, 2004.

Brown, David. *Diary of a Soldier, 1805–1827.* Ardrossan, Scotland: Arthur Guthrie & Sons, n.d.

Brown, Glenn. *Glenn Brown's History of the U.S. Capitol.* William Bushong, ed. 1900, 1903; reprint, Washington, D.C.: U.S. Government Printing Office, 2007.

Brown, Gordon S. *The Captain Who Burned His Ships: Captain Thomas Tingey, USN, 1750–1829.* Annapolis, Md.: Naval Institute Press, 2011.

———. *Incidental Architect: William Thornton and the Cultural Life of Early Washington, D.C., 1794–1828.* Athens: Ohio University Press, 2009.

Buchan, John. *The History of the Royal Scots Fusiliers, 1678–1918.* London: Thomas Nelson, 1925.

Burnett, T. A. J. *The Rise and Fall of a Regency Dandy: The Life and Times of Scrope Berdmore Davies.* London: Murray, 1981.

Caemmerer, H. Paul. *A Manual on the Origin and Development of Washington.* Washington, D.C.: U.S. Government Printing Office, 1939.

Calcott, Margaret L., ed. *Mistress of Riverdale: The Plantation Letters of Rosalie Stier Calvert, 1795–1821.* Baltimore: Johns Hopkins University Press, 1991.

Carter, Thomas, ed. *Historical Record of the Forty-Fourth, or the East Essex Regiment.* Chatham, England: Gale & Polden, 1887.

Cassell, Frank A. *Merchant Congressman in the Young Republic: Samuel Smith of Maryland, 1752–1839.* Madison: University of Wisconsin Press, 1971.

Chamier, Frederick. *The Life of a Sailor*. London: Richard Bentley, 1850.

Chesterton, George Laval. *Peace, War, and Adventure: An Autobiographical Memoir of George Laval Chesterton*. Vol. 1. London: Longman, Brown, Green, & Longmans, 1853.

Chriest, Buzz. *Defenders Trail*. Dundalk, Md.: Dundalk–Patapsco Neck Historical Society, 2003.

Clark, Allen C., ed. *Life and Letters of Dolley Madison*. Washington, D.C.: W. F. Roberts, 1914.

Cochrane, Alexander. *The Fighting Cochranes: A Scottish Clan over Six Hundred Years of Naval and Military History*. London: Quiller Press, 1983.

[Cockburn, George]. *Extract from a Diary of Rear-Admiral Sir George Cockburn, with Particular Reference to Gen. Napoleon Buonaparte, on Passage from England to St. Helena, in 1815*. London: Simpkin, Marshall, 1888.

[Cone, Spencer H.]. *Some Account of the Life of Spencer Houghton Cone*. New York: Livermore & Rudd, 1856.

Cowper, L. I. *The King's Own: The Story of a Royal Regiment*. Vol. 2. Oxford: University Press, 1939.

[Cutts, Lucia B., ed.]. *Memoirs and Letters of Dolly Madison: Wife of James Madison, President of the United States*. Boston and New York: Houghton, Mifflin, 1887.

[Dallas, Sir George]. *A Biographical Memoir of the Late Sir Peter Parker, Baronet*. London: Longman, Hurst, Rees, Orme & Brown, 1815.

Davis, Curtis Carroll. *Defenders' Dozen: Some Comments Along the Way at the Halts During the Cavalcade of the Society of the War of 1812 (Maryland)*. Baltimore: Society of the War of 1812 in the State of Maryland, 1974.

Delaplaine, Edward S. *Francis Scott Key: Life and Times*. 1937; reprint, Westminster, Md.: Willow Bend Books, 2001.

Eberlein, Harold Donaldson, and Cortlandt Van Dyke Hubbard. *Historic Houses of George-town and Washington City*. Richmond, Va.: Dietz Press, 1958.

Echols, C. H. *Defenders' Day Remembered: The Battle of North Point and the Defense of Baltimore*. Dundalk, Md.: Dundalk–Patapsco Neck Historical Society, 2000.

Ecker, Grace Dunlop. *A Portrait of Old Georgetown*. Richmond, Va.: Dietz Press, 1951.

Elting, John R. *Amateurs to Arms! A Military History of the War of 1812*. New York: Da Capo Press, 1995.

Engelman, Fred L. *The Peace of Christmas Eve*. New York: Harcourt, Brace, 1962.

Eshelman, Ralph E. *Maryland's Largest Naval Engagement: The Battles of St. Leonard Creek, 1814*. St. Leonard, Md.: Jefferson Patterson Park & Museum, 2005.

Eshelman, Ralph E., and Burt Kummerow. *In Full Glory Reflected: Discovering the War of 1812 in the Chesapeake.* Marceline, Mo.: Walsworth, 2012.

Eshelman, Ralph E., Scott S. Sheads, and Donald R. Hickey. *The War of 1812 in the Chesapeake: A Reference Guide to Historic Sites in Maryland, Virginia, and the District of Columbia.* Baltimore: Johns Hopkins University Press, 2010.

[Evans, Sir George de Lacy]. *Facts Relating to the Capture of Washington, in Reply to Some Statements Contained in the Memoirs of Admiral Sir George Cockburn, G.C.B.* London: Henry Colburn, 1829.

Filby, P. W. and Edward G. Howard, comps. *Star-Spangled Books.* Baltimore: Maryland Historical Society, 1972.

Foote, Henry S. *Casket of Reminiscences.* Washington, D.C.: Chronicle, 1874.

Footner, Hulbert. *Sailor of Fortune: The Life and Adventures of Commodore Barney, USN.* Introd. Geoffrey M. Footner. 1940; reprint, Annapolis, MD: Naval Institute Press, 1998.

Ford, Paul Leicester, ed. *The Writings of Thomas Jefferson.* Vol. 9. New York: G. P. Putnam's Sons, 1898.

Fortescue, J. W. *A History of the British Army.* Vols. 9 and 10. London: Macmillan, 1920.

Fredriksen, John C., comp. *Free Trade and Sailors' Rights: A Bibliography of the War of 1812.* Westport, Conn.: Greenwood Press, 1985.

———. *The United States Army in the War of 1812.* Jefferson, N.C.: McFarland, 2009.

———, comp. *War of 1812 Eyewitness Accounts: An Annotated Bibliography.* Westport, Conn.: Greenwood Press, 1997.

Garland, Hugh A. *The Life of John Randolph of Roanoke.* New York: D. Appleton, 1874.

George, Christopher T. *Terror on the Chesapeake: The War of 1812 on the Bay.* Shippensburg, Pa.: White Mane Books, 2000.

[Gleig, George R.]. *A Narrative of the Campaigns of the British Army at Washington and New Orleans in the Years 1814–15.* London: John Murray, 1821.

———. *A Subaltern in America: Comprising His Narratives of the Campaigns of the British Army at Baltimore, Washington, &c. &c. During the Late War.* Philadelphia: E. L. Carey & A. Hart, 1833.

Green, Constance McLaughlin. *Washington: A History of the Capital, 1800–1950.* Princeton, N.J.: Princeton University Press, 1962.

Green, Howard. *The Kings Own Royal Regiment, (Lancaster) (The 4th Regiment of Foot).* London: Leo Cooper, 1972.

Grodzinski, John R. *The War of 1812: An Annotated Bibliography.* New York: Routledge, 2008.

Hanna, John Smith, comp. *A History of the Life and Services of Captain Samuel Dewees.* Baltimore: Robert Neilson, 1844.

Hart, Sidney, and Rachael L. Penman. *1812: A Nation Emerges*. Washington, D.C.: Smithsonian Institution Scholarly Press, 2012.

Hawkins, William George, comp. *The Life of John H. W. Hawkins*. Boston: Briggs & Richards, 1862.

Heidler, David S., and Jeanne T. Heidler, eds. *Encyclopedia of the War of 1812*. Annapolis, Md.: Naval Institute Press, 1997.

Herrick, Carole L. *August 24, 1814: Washington in Flames*. Falls Church, Va.: Higher Education Publications, 2005.

Hickey, Donald R. *Don't Give Up the Ship! Myths of the War of 1812*. Urbana: University of Illinois Press, 2006.

———. *The War of 1812: A Forgotten Conflict*. Urbana: University of Illinois Press, 1989.

Hickman, Nathaniel. *The Citizen Soldiers at North Point and Fort McHenry, September 12 &13, 1814*. Baltimore: N. Hickman, 1858.

High, Mike. *The C&O Canal Companion*. Baltimore: Johns Hopkins University Press, 2000.

Holmes, Richard. *Wellington: The Iron Duke*. London: HarperCollins, 2003.

Hopkins, James F., and Mary W. Hargreaves, eds. *The Papers of Henry Clay*. Vol. 1. Lexington: University Press of Kentucky, 1959.

Horsman, Reginald. *The War of 1812*. London: Eyre & Spottiswoode, 1969.

Hunt-Jones, Conover. *Dolley and the "Great Little Madison."* Washington, D.C.: American Institute of Architects Foundation, 1977.

Hutchins, Stilson, and Joseph West Moore. *The National Capital Past and Present*. Washington, D.C.: Gedney & Roberts, 1892.

Ingersoll, Charles J. *Historical Sketch of the Second War Between the United States of America and Great Britain*. Vols. 1 and 2. Philadelphia: Lea & Blanchard, 1845, 1849.

Ingraham, Edward D. *A Sketch of the Events Which Preceded the Capture of the City of Washington by the British*. Philadelphia: Carey & Hart, 1849.

James, William. *The Naval History of Great Britain from the Declaration of War by France in 1793, to the Accession of George IV*. 1847; reprint, London: Macmillan, 1902.

———. *Naval Occurrences of the War of 1812: A Full and Correct Account of the Naval War Between Great Britain and the United States of America, 1812–1815*. Introd. Andrew Lambert. 1817; reprint, London: Conway Maritime Press, 2004.

Jenkins, Mark Collins, and David A. Taylor, *The War of 1812 and the Rise of the U.S. Navy*. Washington, D.C.: National Geographic Society, 2012.

Jennings, Paul. *A Colored Man's Reminiscences of James Madison*. Brooklyn: George C. Beadle, 1865.

Jomini, Antoine-Henri. *The Art of War*. 1862; reprint, Mineola, N.Y.: Dover, 2007.

Kennedy, John Pendleton. *Memoirs of the Life of William Wirt, Attorney General of the United States.* Vol. 1. Philadelphia: J. B. Lippincott, 1860.

Ketcham, Ralph. *James Madison: A Biography.* Charlottesville: University Press of Virginia, 1990.

[Key, Francis Scott]. *Poems of the Late Francis Scott Key, Esq., Author of "The Star Spangled Banner."* With an Introductory Letter by Chief Justice Taney. New York: Robert Carter & Bros., 1857.

Key-Smith, Francis Scott. *Francis Scott Key, Author of the Star-Spangled Banner, What Else He Was and Who.* Washington, D.C.: Key-Smith, 1911.

Langguth, A. J. *Union 1812: The Americans Who Fought the Second War of Independence.* New York: Simon & Schuster, 2006.

Lehmann, Joseph H. *Remember You Are an Englishman: A Biography of Sir Harry Smith, 1787–1860.* London: Jonathan Cape, 1977.

Lichtenwanger, William. *The Music of "The Star-Spangled Banner": From Ludgate Hill to Capitol Hill.* Washington, D.C.: Library of Congress, 1977.

Lord, Walter. *The Dawn's Early Light.* New York: Norton, 1972.

Lossing, Benson J. *The Pictorial Field-book of the War of 1812.* New York: Harper & Bros., 1869.

Lovell, William Stanhope. *Personal Narrative of Events, from 1799 to 1815.* London: William Allen, 1879.

Lyman, Myron (Mike) E., and William W. Hankins. *Encounters with the British in Virginia During the War of 1812.* Virginia: Society of the War of 1812 in the Commonwealth of Virginia, 2008–2009.

Madison, James. *The Writings of James Madison.* Vol. 8, 1808–1819. Ed. Gaillard Hunt. New York: G. P. Putnam's Sons, 1908.

Mahan, Alfred T. *Sea Power in its Relation to the War of 1812.* 1903; reprint, New York: Greenwood Press, 1968.

Malcolmson, Robert. *Capital in Flames: The American Attack on York, 1813.* Montreal: Robin Brass Studio, 2008.

Marine, William M. *The British Invasion of Maryland 1812–1815.* Baltimore: Society of the War of 1812 in Maryland, 1913.

Marolda, Edward J. *The Washington Navy Yard: An Illustrated History.* Washington, D.C.: Naval Historical Center, 1999.

McComas, Henry Clay, comp. *The McComas Saga: A Family History Down to the Year 1950.* Typescript, Maryland Museum of Military History, 1950.

[McKenney, Thomas L.]. *A Narrative of the Battle of Bladensburg; In a Letter to Henry Banning, Esq.* Washington, D.C.: n.p., [1814].

M'Kenney, Thomas L. *Memoirs, Official and Personal, with Sketches of Travels Among Northern and Southern Indians; Embracing a War Excursion, and Descriptions of Scenes Along the Western Borders.* Vol. 1. New York: Paine & Burgess, 1846.

———. *Reply to Kosciusko [sic] Armstrong's Assault Upon Col. McKenney's*

Narrative of the Causes That Led to General Armstrong's Resignation of the Office of Secretary of War in 1814. New York: William H. Graham, 1847.

Meyer, Sam. *Paradoxes of Fame: The Francis Scott Key Story.* Annapolis, Md.: Eastwind, 1995.

Molotsky, Irvin. *The Flag, the Poet, and the Song: The Story of the Star-Spangled Banner.* New York: Plume, 2001.

Monroe, James. *The Writings of James Monroe.* Vol. 5. Ed. Stanislaus Murray Hamilton. New York: G. P. Putnam's Sons, 1901.

Moody, Robert, ed. *The Saltonstall Papers, 1602–1815.* Vol. 2. Boston: Massachusetts Historical Society, 1974.

Morley, Jefferson. *Snow-Storm in August: Washington City, Francis Scott Key, and the Forgotten Race Riot of 1835.* New York: Doubleday, 2012.

Morriss, Roger. *Cockburn and the British Navy in Transition: Admiral Sir George Cockburn 1772–1853.* Columbia: University of South Carolina Press, 1997.

Moulsdale, J. R. B. *The King's Shropshire Light Infantry.* London: Leo Cooper, 1972.

Muller, Charles G. *The Darkest Day: The Washington-Baltimore Campaign During the War of 1812.* 1963; reprint, Philadelphia: University of Pennsylvania Press, 2003.

Muller, Joseph, comp. *The Star Spangled Banner: Words and Music Issued Between 1814–1864.* New York: Da Capo Press, 1973.

Napier, Edward D. H. E. *The Life and Correspondence of Admiral Sir Charles Napier, K.C.B.* London: Hurst & Blackett, 1862.

Napier, William. *The Life and Opinions of General Sir Charles James Napier, G.C.B.* Vol. 1. London: John Murray, 1857.

Pack, James. *The Man Who Burned the White House: Admiral Sir George Cockburn, 1772–1853.* Westbourne, Hampshire, England: Kenneth Mason, 1987.

Paullin, Charles Oscar. *Commodore John Rodgers: Captain, Commodore, and Senior Officer of the American Navy, 1773–1838: A Biography.* Cleveland: Clark, 1910.

Peck, Taylor. *Roundshots to Rockets: A History of the Washington Navy Yard and U.S. Naval Gun Factory.* Annapolis, Md.: Naval Institute Press, 1949.

Perrett, Bryan. *The Real Hornblower: The Life of Admiral of the Fleet Sir James Alexander Gordon, GCB.* Annapolis, Md.: Naval Institute Press, 1997.

Petrides, Anne, and Jonathan Downs, eds. *Sea Soldier: An Officer of Marines with Duncan, Nelson, Collingwood and Cockburn: The Letters and Journals of T. Marmaduke Wybourn RM, 1797–1813.* Kent, England: Parapress, 2000.

Pitch, Anthony S. *The Burning of Washington: The British Invasion of 1814.* Annapolis, Md.: Naval Institute Press, 1998.

Porter, David. *Memoir of Commodore David Porter of the United States Navy.* Albany, N.Y.: J. Munsell, 1875.

Pringle, Norman. *Letters by Major Norman Pringle, Late of the 21st Royal Scots*

Fusiliers, Vindicating the Character of the British Army Employed in North America in the Years 1814–15, From Aspersions Cast Upon It in Stuart's Three Years in North America. Edinburgh: Blackwood, 1834.

Proctor, John Clagett, ed. *Washington Past and Present,* Vol. 1. New York: Lewis, 1930.

Ralfe, James. *The Naval Biography of Great Britain: Consisting of Those Officers of the British Navy Who Distinguished Themselves During the Reign of His Majesty George III.* Vol. 3. London: Whitmore & Fenn, 1828.

Remini, Robert V. *Henry Clay: Statesman for the Union.* New York: Norton, 1991.

Roosevelt, Theodore. *The Naval War of 1812.* Introd. Edward K. Eckert. 1882; reprint, Annapolis, Md.: Naval Institute Press, 1987.

Schroeder, John H. *Commodore John Rodgers: Paragon of the Early American Navy.* Gainesville: University Press of Florida, 2006.

Scott, James. *Recollections of a Naval Life.* Vol. 3. London: Richard Bentley, 1834.

Seale, William. *The President's House: A History.* Vol. 1. Washington, D.C.: White House Historical Association, 1986.

———. *The White House: The History of an American Idea.* Washington, D.C.: White House Historical Association, 2001.

Seaton, Josephine. *William Winston Seaton of the "National Intelligencer": A Biographical Sketch.* Boston: James R. Osgood, 1871.

Sharp, John G., ed. *The Diary of Michael Shiner Relating to the History of the Washington Navy Yard, 1813–1869.* Washington, D.C.: Navy Department Library, 2007.

Sheads, Scott S. *Fort McHenry.* Baltimore: Nautical & Aviation Publishing Company of America, 1995.

———. *Guardian of the Star-Spangled Banner: Lt. Colonel George Armistead and the Fort McHenry Flag.* Baltimore: Toomey Press, 1999.

———. *The Rockets' Red Glare: The Maritime Defense of Baltimore in 1814.* Centreville, Md.: Tidewater, 1986.

Shomette, Donald G. *Flotilla: The Patuxent Naval Campaign in the War of 1812.* Baltimore: Johns Hopkins University Press, 2009.

Silkett, John T. *Francis Scott Key and the History of the Star-Spangled Banner.* Washington, D.C.: Vintage America, 1978.

Sioussat, Annie L. *Old Baltimore.* New York: Macmillan, 1931.

Skaggs, David Curtis. *Oliver Hazard Perry: Honor, Courage and Patriotism in the Early U.S. Navy.* Annapolis, Md.: Naval Institute Press. 2006.

Skeen, C. Edward. *Citizen Soldiers in the War of 1812.* Lexington: University Press of Kentucky, 1999.

———. *John Armstrong, Jr., 1758–1843: A Biography.* Syracuse, N.Y.: Syracuse University Press, 1981.

Smith, Harry. *The Autobiography of Lieutenant-General Sir Harry Smith*. London: John Murray, 1903.

Smith, Margaret Bayard. *The First Forty Years of Washington Society*. Gaillard Hunt, ed., New York: Charles Scribner's Sons, 1906.

Smyth, Benjamin, ed. *History of the XX Regiment, 1688–1888*. London: Simpkin, Marshall, 1889.

Sonneck, Oscar George Theodore. *The Star-Spangled Banner*. 1914; reprint, New York: Da Capo Press, 1969.

Spiers, Edward M. *Radical General: Sir George de Lacy Evans 1787–1870*. Manchester, England: Manchester University Press, 1983.

Stagg, J. C. A. *Mr. Madison's War: Politics, Diplomacy and Warfare in the Early American Republic, 1783–1830*. Princeton, N.J.: Princeton University Press, 1983.

———. *The War of 1812: Conflict for a Continent*. New York: Cambridge University Press, 2012.

Stewart, Richard, ed. *American Military History*. Vol. 1, *The United States Army and the Forging of a Nation, 1775–1917*. Washington, D.C.: Center of Military History, U.S. Army, 2005.

Svejda, George J. *History of the Star Spangled Banner from 1814 to the Present*. Washington, D.C.: National Park Service, U.S. Department of the Interior, 1969.

Swanson, Neil H. *The Perilous Fight*. New York: Farrar & Rinehart, 1945.

Tayloe, Benjamin Ogle. *Our Neighbors on Lafayette Square*. 1872; reprint, Washington, D.C.: Junior League of Washington, 1982.

Taylor, Alan. *The Civil War of 1812: American Citizens, British Subjects, Irish Rebels and Indian Allies*. New York: Knopf, 2010.

Taylor, Elizabeth Dowling. *A Slave in the White House: Paul Jennings and the Madisons*. New York: Palgrave Macmillan, 2012.

Taylor, Lonn, Kathleen M. Kendrick, and Jeffrey L. Brodie. *The Star-Spangled Banner: The Making of an American Icon*. New York: HarperCollins, 2008.

Tilghman, Oswald, comp. *History of Talbot County Maryland 1661–1861*. Vol. 2. Baltimore: Williams & Wilkins, 1915.

Tucker, Glenn. *Poltroons and Patriots: A Popular Account of the War of 1812*. Vol. 2. Indianapolis: Bobbs-Merrill, 1954.

Tuckerman, Henry T. *The Life of John Pendleton Kennedy*. New York: G. P. Putnam & Sons, 1871.

Wallace, Adam. *The Parson of the Islands; A Biography of the Rev. Joshua Thomas*. 1861; reprint, Cambridge, Md.: Tidewater, 1978.

Weybright, Victor. *Spangled Banner: The Story of Francis Scott Key*. New York: Farrar & Rinehart, 1935.

Wharton, Anne Hollingsworth. *Social Life in the Early Republic*. Philadelphia: Lippincott, 1902.

Whitehorne, Joseph A. *The Battle of Baltimore 1814.* Baltimore: Nautical & Aviation Publishing Company of America, 1997.

———. *While Washington Burned: The Battle for Fort Erie 1814.* Baltimore: Nautical & Aviation Publishing Company of America, 1992.

White House Historical Association. *The White House: An Historic Guide.* Washington, D.C.: National Geographic Society, 1973.

Wilkinson, James. *Memoirs of My Own Times.* Vol. 1. Philadelphia: Abraham Small, 1816.

Williams, John. *History of the Invasion and Capture of Washington, and of the Events Which Preceded and Followed.* New York: Harper & Bros., 1857.

Wills, Garry. *James Madison.* New York: Times Books, 2002.

[Wilmer, James J.]. *A Narrative Respecting the Conduct of the British from Their First Landing on Specutia Island, Till Their Progress to Havre de Grace.* Baltimore: P. Mauro, 1813.

Wood, Gordon S. *Empire of Liberty: A History of the Early Republic, 1789–1815.* New York: Oxford University Press, 2009.

———. *Revolutionary Characters: What Made the Founders Different.* New York: Penguin Press, 2006.

ARTICLES

(The list includes only those cited multiple times in the text; all others are listed in the notes.)

Arnold, James Riehl. "The Battle of Bladensburg." *RCHS,* 1937.

[Barrett, Robert J.]. "Naval Recollections of the Late American War," part 1. *USJ,* April 1841.

Brumbaugh, Thomas B., ed. "A Letter of Dr. William Thornton to Colonel William Thornton." *MdHM,* Mar. 1978.

Bushong, William B. "Ruin and Regeneration." *White House History,* Fall 1998.

Callahan, Eleanor. "Ear-Witness to History: James McConkey and the Star Spangled Banner." *Journal of Erie Studies,* 1980.

Cassell, Frank A. "A Response to Crisis: Baltimore in 1814." *MdHM,* 1971.

———. "Slaves of the Chesapeake Bay Area and the War of 1812." *Journal of Negro History,* April 1972.

Clark, Allen C. "Joseph Gales, Junior, Editor and Mayor." *RCHS,* 1920.

Coles, Harry L. "1814: A Dark Hour Before the Dawn." *MdHM,* 1971.

Colston, Frederick M. "The Battle of North Point." *MdHM,* 1907.

Cutts, J. Madison. "Dolley Madison." *RCHS,* 1900.

Dietz, Anthony G. "The Use of Cartel Vessels During the War of 1812." *American Neptune,* July 1968.

Dorsey, Anna H. "Origin of the Star-Spangled Banner." *The Historical Magazine, and Notes and Queries Concerning the Antiquities, History and Biography of America,* 1861.

Dunham, Chester G. "Christopher Hughes, Jr. at Ghent, 1814." *MdHM*, Fall 1971.

Engelman, Fred L. "The Peace of Christmas Eve." *American Heritage,* December 1960.

Ewell, James. "Unwelcome Visitors to Early Washington." *RCHS*, 1895.

Fabel, Robin F. A. "The Laws of War in the 1812 Conflict." *Journal of American Studies,* August 1980.

Gardner, William. "To the Editor of the Federal Republican." *Hartford Courant,* September 17, 1814.

George, Christopher T. "The Family Papers of Maj. Gen. Robert Ross, the Diary of Col. Arthur Brooke, and the British Attacks of Washington and Baltimore of 1814." *MdHM,* Fall 1993.

———. "Mirage of Freedom: African Americans in the War of 1812." *MdHM,* Winter 1996.

Goldsborough, Robert H. "Report of the Battle of Baltimore." *MdHM,* September 1945.

Hadel, Albert J. "The Battle of Bladensburg." *MdHM,* 1906.

Hildt, John C. "Letters Relating to the Capture of Washington." *South Atlantic Quarterly,* 1907.

Hockensmith, Bryan. "James Monroe," *Army History,* Summer 2008.

Hunter, Mary. "The Burning of Washington, D.C." *New-York Historical Society Quarterly Bulletin,* 1924.

King, Horatio. "The Battle of Bladensburg." *Magazine of American History,* July–December 1885.

Lingel, Robert, ed. "The Manuscript Autobiography of Gordon Gallie Macdonald." *New York Public Library Bulletin,* March 1930.

Magruder, Caleb Clarke, Jr. "Dr. William Beanes, the Incidental Cause of the Authorship of the Star-Spangled Banner." *RCHS,* 1919.

Maguire, W. A. "Major General Ross and the Burning of Washington." *Irish Sword,* Winter 1980.

McLane, Allen. "Col. McLane's Visit to Washington, 1814." *Bulletin of the Historical Society of Pennsylvania,* 1845.

Meyer, Sam. "Religion, Patriotism and Poetry in the Life of Francis Scott Key." MdHS, 1989.

Mullaly, Franklin R. "The Battle of Baltimore." *MdHM,* March 1959.

———. "A Forgotten Letter of Francis Scott Key." *MdHM,* Dec. 1960.

Ockerbloom, John N. "The Discovery of a U.S. Marine Officer's Account of Life, Honor, and the Battle of Bladensburg, Washington and Maryland, 1814," Military Collector & Historian, Winter 2009.

Ortmann, Otto. "Notes on 'The Star Spangled Banner.'" *Peabody Bulletin,* May 1939.

Paullin, Charles Oscar. "Services of Commodore John Rodgers in the War of 1812." *Proceedings,* 1909.

Pettengill, George E. "The Octagon and the War of 1812." *AIA Journal*, February 1965.

Piper, James. "Defense of Baltimore, 1814." *MdHM*, December 1912.

Poore, Benjamin Perley. "Biographical Notice of John S. Skinner." *The Plough, the Loom, and the Anvil*, July 1854.

"Recollections of the Expedition to the Chesapeake, and Against New Orleans, in the Years 1814–15. By an old Sub," part 2. *USJ*, May 1840.

Robinson, Ralph J. "Controversy over the Command at Baltimore in the War of 1812." *MdHM*, 1944.

———. "The Men with Key: New Facts in the National Anthem Story." *Baltimore*, September 1956.

Rowley, Peter, ed. "Captain Robert Rowley Helps to Burn Washington, D.C., Part 1." *MdHM*, Fall 1987.

———. "Captain Rowley Visits Maryland; Part II of a Series." *MdHM*, Fall 1988.

Seale, William. "The White House Before the Fire." *White House History*, Fall 1998.

Sheads, Scott S. "HM Bomb Ship Terror and the Bombardment of Fort McHenry." *MdHM*, Fall, 2008.

———. "Joseph Hopper Nicholson: Citizen-Soldier of Maryland." *MdHM*, Summer 2003.

———. " 'Yankee Doodle Played': A Letter from Baltimore, 1814." *MdHM*, Winter 1981.

[Sheldon, Daniel]. "An Unpublished Letter, August 26, 1814: The Burning of Washington." *Magazine of American History*, 1892.

Shippen, Rebecca Lloyd. "The Star-Spangled Banner." *Pennsylvania Magazine of History and Biography*, 1901.

Skinner, J. S. "Incidents of the War of 1812: From the *Baltimore Patriot* [23 May 1849]." *MdHM*, December 1937.

Thornton, Anna. "Diary of Mrs. William Thornton. Capture of Washington by the British." W. B. Bryan, ed. *RCHS*, 1916.

Weiss, John McNish. "The Corps of Colonial Marines: Black Freedom Fighters of the War of 1812." http://www.mcnishandweiss.co.uk/history/colonialmarines.html (accessed September 15, 2009).

Weller, M. I. "The Life of Commodore Joshua Barney." *RCHS*, 1911.

Williams, Glenn F. "The Bladensburg Races." *MHQ*, Autumn 1999.

———. "The Rock of North Point." *The Todd House*. Friends of Todd's Inheritance, 2001.

Woehrmann, Paul. "National Response to the Sack of Washington." *MdHM*, Fall 1971.

DOCUMENTS, REPORTS, AND MISCELLANY

American State Papers: Documents, Legislative and Executive, of the Congress of the United States. Class V. Military Affairs. Vol. 1. No. 137. "Capture of the City of Washington." Washington, D.C.: Gales & Seaton, 1832.

Brannan, John, ed. *Official Letters of the Military and Naval Officers of the United States During the War with Great Britain in the Years 1812, 13, 14, & 15.* Washington, D.C.: Way & Gideon, 1823.

"Dolley Madison" and "James Madison." James Madison's Montpelier, n.d.

Dudley, William S., and Michael J. Crawford, et al., eds. *The Naval War of 1812: A Documentary History.* Vols. 2 and 3. Washington, D.C.: Naval Historical Center, 1992, 2002.

Flournoy, H. W., ed. *Calendar of Virginia State Papers and Other Manuscripts.* Vol. 10. 1892; reprint, New York: Kraus Reprint, 1968.

[Hall, John E., ed.]. *Report of the Trial of John Hodges, Esq. on a Charge of High Treason. Tried in the Circuit Court of the United States for the Maryland District, at the May Term, 1815.* [Baltimore: n.p., 1815?], Darnall's Chance Manuscript Collection, Upper Marlboro, Md.

O'Neill, Patrick. "The Potomac Squadron." Fairfax County History Conference, November 7, 2009.

"The Sewall-Belmont House Historic Structure Report." Prepared for the National Woman's Party, Sewall-Belmont House and Museum, June 1, 2001.

"Star Spangled Banner National Historic Trail Feasibility Study and Environmental Impact Statement." Philadelphia: National Park Service, 2004.

COLLECTIONS

Bodleian Library, Oxford University, Oxford, England. Journal of the Royal Highland Fusiliers.

Fort McHenry National Monument and Historic Shrine, Baltimore. War of 1812 collection.

George Washington University Gelman Library, Special Collections. Ross papers; Individual Manuscripts Collection.

Historical Society of Frederick, Frederick, Md. Francis Scott Key vertical file.

Institute of Historical Research, London. Reference library.

Library of Congress, Washington, D.C. Manuscript Division. Papers of James Madison, George Cockburn, Alexander Cochrane, Lewis Machen, William Rives, and Shippen family; Rare Book and Special Collections Division; Music Division.

Maryland Historical Society. Papers of John Eager Howard, William Henry Winder, General John Stricker, and Zaccheus Spratt; Matthias E. Bartgis Collection; Samuel Smith Collection; Thomas Beall account book; Winder Letter Book; War of 1812 Collection.

Maryland Museum of Military History, Archives and Research Center, Baltimore. War of 1812 files.

National Archives and Records Administration. General Records of the Department of State; Records of the Office of the Secretary of War; Records of the Office of the Secretary of the Navy; Records of the Adjutant General's Office.

National Archives of the United Kingdom, Kew, Richmond, Surrey, England: Admiralty Records; War Office Records.

National Army Museum, Templer Study Centre, London. Major Peter Bowlby memoir.

National Maritime Museum, Caird Library, Greenwich, England. Papers of George Cockburn; Edward Codrington; Pulteney Malcolm.

Naval History and Heritage Command, Washington Navy Yard, Washington, D.C. Naval War of 1812 papers.

Navy Library, Washington Navy Yard, Washington, D.C. Washington Navy Yard history files.

Public Records Office of Northern Ireland, Belfast. Papers of Major General Robert Ross; Diary of Colonel Arthur Brooke.

Royal Marine Museum, Portsmouth, England. Captain Mortimer Timpson Memoir; Journal of John Robyns; Battalion Order Book 1814.

Royal Naval Museum, Portsmouth, England, Manuscript Collection. Diary of Midshipman J. C. Bluett.

Sewall-Belmont House and Museum, Washington, D.C. Sewall-Belmont House Historic Structure Report.

Tangier History Museum, Tangier, Va. War of 1812 files.

Tudor Place Archives, Washington, D.C. George Peter Papers.

INDEX

——— ★ ———

STEVE VOGEL is the author of *The Pentagon* and a veteran national reporter for *The Washington Post*. He has written exclusively about military affairs and the treatment of veterans from the wars in Afghanistan and Iraq. His reporting on the war in Afghanistan was part of a package of *Washington Post* stories selected as a finalist for the 2002 Pulitzer Prize. Vogel covered the September 11 terrorist attack on the Pentagon, and the building's subsequent reconstruction. He covered the war in Iraq and the first Gulf War, as well as U.S. military operations in Rwanda, Somalia, and the Balkans. A graduate of the College of William and Mary, Vogel received a master's degree in international public policy from the Johns Hopkins School of Advanced International Studies.